VBScript Programmer's Reference

Susanne Clark, Antonio De Donatis,
Adrian Kingsley-Hughes, Kathie Kingsley-Hughes,
Brian Matsik, Erick Nelson, Piotr Prussak
Daniel Read, Carsten Thomsen, Stuart Updegrave,
Paul Wilton

Wrox Press Ltd. ®

VBScript Programmer's Reference

Latest Reprint   November 2000

Published by Wrox Press Ltd
Arden House, 1102 Warwick Road, Acock's Green, Birmingham B27 6BH, UK
Printed in USA
ISBN 1-861002-71-8

Trademark Acknowledgements

Credits

Authors
Daniel Read
Susanne Clark
Antonio De Donatis
Adrian Kingsley-Hughes
Kathie Kingsley-Hughes
Brian Matsik
Erick Nelson
Piotr Prussak
Carsten Thomsen
Stuart Updegrave
Paul Wilton

Additional Material
Jerry Ablan
Jeff Hart
Alex Homer
David Sussman
Chris Ullman

Editors
Gregory Beekman
Lums Thevathasan
Robert Shaw
Devin Lunsford

Managing Editor
Victoria Hudgson

Development Editor
Peter Morgan

Technical Reviewers
Chris Behrens
Steve Danielson
John Granade
Michael Harris
Richard Harrison
Dan Pfeffer
Nic Roche

Design / Layout
Tom Bartlett
Mark Burdett
William Fallon
Jonathan Jones
John McNulty

Illustrations
William Fallon
Jonathan Jones

Cover Design
Chris Morris

Project Manager
Chandima Nethisinghe

Index
Martin Brooks

About the Authors

Daniel Read

Daniel Read is Senior Developer at Compass, Inc. in Atlanta, GA, where he and fellow team members build IIS/ASP/VB/MTS e-commerce web sites, as well as client/server and distributed systems. Daniel sometimes longs for his simpler, statically linked days as an X-Base developer and DOS command line junkie, but today enjoys the power afforded by the arsenal of Microsoft's Windows DNA tools and technologies. His other interests include camping, crime fiction, listening to music of all sorts, and going to as many concerts as he can. He's not sure if co-authoring a programming book will help him meet the woman of his dreams, but it sure would be nice.

Carsten Thomsen

Carsten Thomsen is a Microsoft Certified Systems Engineer, who started programming in Visual Basic back in 1993, when it was version 3.0. Presently he is pursuing Microsoft Certified Systems Developer certification and was recently awarded the MVP title for his contributions to the Microsoft Visual Basic newgroups. For the last 4 years he has been developing 2-tier and 3-tier client/server solutions based on MS SQL Server, MTS and MSMQ, but has more recently been moving towards browser-based development, based on MS IIS, using ASP/VBScript, COM/ActiveX components and Visual Basic WebClasses.

In whatever spare time he has, he enjoys traveling and spending time with his two daughters, Nicole and Caroline, and his girlfriend Mia. He works out at a local gym and (at spectator-level) enjoys ice hockey and soccer. He is generally considered a computer freak, and spends too much time at the computer.

Piotr Prussak

Piotr Prussak works for ACEN in Buffalo, NY as a developer (although he is originally from Poland). He creates ASP, VB and Java Applications for the company and its clients. He also spends some time working with the SQL server and ColdFusion, probably more than he should. When he's not programming and mentoring, he either writes stuff, or edits stuff written by others. Sometimes he sleeps, eats and relaxes like any other human being. In a past life he used to be a photographer, but that was just too relaxing.

Piotr (or Peter, as some might call him) is married to lovely Joanne, who is an MIS student at a local University. Sometimes they travel all over the world and are disconnected from the world of computers and 24 hour news.

Brian Matsik

Brian Matsik is the President and Senior Consultant at OOCS in Charlotte, NC. He is MCSD certified and has been working with Visual Basic, VBScript, and VBA for over six years. He currently specializes in ASP, SQL Server, and VB COM. Brian can be reached at `brianmat@oocs.com`.

Brian would like to thank Tracy for her support, Mike Dunner for keeping him on his toes when it comes to ADO and MTS, and Mark Harris for taking care of the books while he stays glued to the PC.

Paul Wilton

After an initial start as a Visual Basic applications programmer, Paul found himself pulled into the net and has spent the last 18 months helping create internet and intranet solutions.

Currently he is developing web-based systems, primarily using Visual Basic 6 and SQL Server 7, along with numerous other technologies.

Paul would like to wish lots of love to his fiancée Catherine, who ensures his sanity chip remains plugged in.

Antonio De Donatis

Antonio De Donatis (`adedonatis@yahoo.com`) began programming in 1984, using a mixture of Basic and assembler on a Commodore 64. Since then, he has designed software the object-oriented way, employing more programming languages and technologies than he can count. He finds programming to be one of the best activities to exercise creativity and to be intellectually active. He has worked for many of the major firms in IT either as employee or as freelance. His current interests include all the technologies involved in the design and implementation of e-commerce solutions. Antonio holds a BS degree in Computer Science from Pisa University (Italy) and he is a Microsoft Certified Professional.

Susanne Clark

Susanne has worked with the latest internet technologies, including DHTML, XML, XSL, IE5 programming and scripting, and has contributed chapters on these subjects to the recently published *Professional Visual InterDev 6 Programming* from Wrox Press. She is currently working as a user interfaces developer in Seattle, USA. When not dealing with computers, she enjoys spending time with her cats, and reading mystery books. Susanne would like to thank Luca for all of his patience and help. Ti amo.

Adrian Kingsley-Hughes

Adrian Kingsley-Hughes is Technical Director of Kingsley-Hughes Development Ltd., a UK-based training and development firm, where he is a consultant in Internet Development and Windows platform programming. He has co-authored 8 books for Active Path and Wrox Press. His abiding passion is the Search for Extra Terrestrial Intelligence and he is the Welsh Regional Coordinator for SETILeague Inc. In his spare time he writes horror novels, plays the didgeridoo and is currently building a radio telescope in his back yard.

Kathie Kingsley-Hughes

In addition to writing web development books for Active Path and Wrox Press, Kathie Kingsley-Hughes is the Managing Director of UK-based Kingsley-Hughes Development Ltd., where she specializes primarily in the development and delivery of training courses in web development skills. She began teaching in 1985 and has lectured at several UK colleges and other training establishments and she is currently teaching at ZDU. Any spare time is taken up with astronomy, photography and hiking in the mountains.

Eric Nelson

Erick Nelson is an 18 year old Internet developer and programmer, and creator of the award winning website cues.com. about which he spoke at both the 1998 and 1999 Professional ASP Developer's Conference. Erick began his programming career at age 16, and now has experience using ASP, VBScript and Visual Basic to design sites.

Erick enjoys playing computer games and working on his online RPG system. His outdoor activities include mountain biking, swimming, cliff jumping, playing tennis and snow skiing. He can be reached at erick@ericknelson.com.

Erick would like to thank his Mom, Cindy Cashman, for helping him start his business, and his Dad, Mark Nelson, for teaching him how to build things and raising him better than anyone could under the circumstances. Thanks must also go to Bill Stroud and Charlie Bass.

Table of Contents

Chapter 4: Error Handling, Prevention and Debugging   111

Chapter 6: Using COM Components with MTS   179

Chapter 7: The Built-In and Scripting Runtime Objects   199

Chapter 8: Classes in VBScript (Writing Your Own COM Objects)   227

Chapter 9: Windows Script Components   253

Chapter 10: The Windows Script Host 283

Chapter 11: General Client-Side Web Scripting 325

Chapter 12: High-Powered Client Scripting 345

Chapter 13: HTML Applications (HTAs)   381

Chapter 15: Talking to Databases: ActiveX Data Objects 439

Chapter 16: Microsoft Script Control   459

Part 3: The Reference

Appendix A: Visual Basic Functions and Keywords   499

Appendix B: Differences between VB/VBA and VBScript5   579

Appendix G: Windows Script Host 2.0   625

Appendix H: IE4 Browser Object Model   641

Appendix I: The Browser Object Model – IE5   673

Appendix J: The Integral ASP Objects   693

Introduction

The aim of this book is to provide an introduction to, overview of, and reference for:

❏ The VBScript 5 language

❏ The many 'contexts' in which the VBScript language can exist and be useful

Our first goal probably seems pretty straightforward: we're going to cover what you need to know to write VBScript code. We'll go over general syntax, functions, keywords, style, error handling, and similar **language-specific** topics. However, VBScript the language is of limited use without something to *do*. That's where the scripting **contexts** (or **hosts**) come in.

Microsoft has done an excellent job over the last couple of years in building robust support for scripting into the Windows operating systems (Windows 95/98, Windows NT, and now, Windows 2000). Support for scripting is an important aspect of a mature operating system environment. 'support for scripting' simply means that the operating system provides a mechanism through which users can write programs in a scripting language, such as VBScript. A scripting language differs from 'normal' programming languages in some key ways, which we will discuss in this introduction. Scripting allows you to extend the capabilities of an existing computer environment. This book will provide you with the knowledge you need to leverage all of this dormant power.

Who is this Book For?

VBScript, and this Programmer's Reference book, can be extremely useful to all sorts of information technology professionals, and even for the casual user who wants to automate some common tasks or learn a little bit about the art and science of programming. For example:

❏ Network administrators can use VBScript with the **Windows Script Host** to write powerful login scripts and automate formerly time-consuming and error-prone tasks – all without using clumsy DOS batch files

❏ Application developers can use VBScript to extend their Windows applications with powerful macro and customization features

❑ Web developers and designers can use VBScript with **DHTML** to create amazing browser-based and stand-alone **HTML Applications**

❑ Web application developers can use VBScript to create dynamic, high-performance web sites with **Internet Information Server** and **Active Server Pages**

These are just examples – the full range of people and tasks for which VBScript can be useful cannot be expressed in a single paragraph. If you're not sure if this book is for you, or if VBScript can help you, please read on because VBScript can do a lot more than you might think.

How to Use this Book

This book is divided up into three parts. Part 1 covers the VBScript language – the keywords, functions, syntax, etc. For those who are new to writing code, Part 1 also includes a *very* short introduction to programming. Advanced readers might not need to read Part 1 straight through, but should probably read the chapters on VBScript's new support for classes and **Windows Script Components**, a very exciting new technology.

Part 2 covers what we call 'VBScript in Context.' Although powerful in its own right, the VBScript language derives its real power from:

❑ The hosts that support it – such as the Windows Script Host (formerly known as the Windows Scripting Host) and Active Server Pages

❑ The objects that are made available to it, such as the **Scripting Runtime Objects** and **Active Data Objects**

You'll learn, among lots of other things, how to create an HTML Application and how to write a **scriptlet** and attach it to a DHTML **behavior**.

At the end of the book there is a large set of appendices, which cover things such as naming conventions, the syntactic differences between Visual Basic and VBScript, and the object models that are important to VBScript developers. Although the chapters will cover these object collections in detail, the object diagrams provide a very helpful high level view of the objects and their properties and methods. Appendix A also contains a complete reference to the functions, keywords, and operators of the VBScript 5 language.

Finally, don't forget that we, at Wrox, offer comprehensive on-line support and references. www.webdev.wrox.co.uk has an HTML listing and www.asptoday.com is a dedicated ASP resource center.

> Advanced readers who are already familiar with VBScript and the concept of a scripting language might want to skip these introductory sections. However, if you are not yet familiar with all of the new features of VBScript 5 and with the new types of solutions supported by Microsoft's latest scripting hosts, you might want to take a look at the *What Can You Do With VBScript?* and *What's New in VBScript 5* sections of this Introduction.

What is VBScript?

As its name suggests, VBScript is what's known as a **scripting language**. How is a scripting language different from other types of programming languages? One big difference is the point at which the code you have written is 'compiled'.

A Little Background

All programming languages are compiled at some point – otherwise the computer would not be able to respond to their commands. As you undoubtedly know, at the lowest level, the language of a computer is broken down into a series of 1's and 0's. This ones-and-zeroes language is also known as **binary** or **machine** language. Different combinations of 1's and 0's mean different things to the low-level hardware of the computer. One binary arrangement of 1's and 0's might mean "add these two numbers together." Another might mean, "store this value in such-and-such a memory address." This is an oversimplification, but hopefully you get the idea. It's pretty amazing, but all of the different things you can ask a computer to do are ultimately broken down into a fairly small set of machine language commands.

There was once a time when programmers had to write computer programs in binary – as you might imagine, this is pretty difficult. Over time, more advanced programming languages were developed, each of which added ever-higher levels of **abstraction**, so that programmers could use syntax that was a little closer to the English language. However, even as programming languages have become increasingly abstract, the computer hardware has continued to understand only machine language.

Scripting Languages are Compiled Later than Other Languages

Compilation is the process of turning the higher-level language into the binary that the computer understands. The difference with 'normal' languages and scripting languages is not *whether* they are compiled but *when*. Languages like C and C++ are commonly known as **compiled languages**. This may seem a bit confusing since we just said that all languages are ultimately compiled, but they are called this because they are compiled down to machine code at **design time**. That is, the programmer writes the code, then issues a command to a special program called a **compiler** to compile the code down to machine language.

A scripting language, on the other hand, is 'compiled' (or more precisely, 'interpreted') at **runtime**, which means that until it is executed, the script remains a plain text file. If you looked at a compiled C program, it would not make any sense, because it's been broken down into machine language. However, a script is always stored as a plain text file. You can write and read the script in plain text, change it at will, and just tell a script engine to run it. You do not have to go through a separate design-time step to compile the program. Certainly, there are special formatting conventions that you must follow when you write a script, but the code itself always remains plain text that you can read and edit in any text editor (such as the Notepad application that is included with all Windows versions).

A script is compiled at runtime by a **scripting engine**, which is a special program that knows how to interpret the text you type into the script and turn it into commands that the computer can understand. In this respect, it is not unlike the C programmer's design-time compiler.

Compiling a program at design time affords three major advantages, which, conversely, translate into disadvantages for a scripting language such as VBScript:

❑ A compiled program will run *much* faster when executed. This is because it has already been translated into machine language. Since the translation step does not need to take place every time the program is executed, it will run faster than a script that must be compiled at runtime, *every single time it is run*.

❑ Once translated into machine language, a compiled program cannot be changed. This protects the intellectual property of the developer or company that owns the program because it is compiled into a form that is unreadable. A curious user or malicious hacker cannot read the code and see how the developer achieved their results, or 'borrow' parts of the code for their own. Since a script is plain text, anyone who can gain access to the text file can read it. Some scripts, such as those embedded in Active Server Pages (which are a combination of HTML and script), are not normally available to the user to see because they reside on the server, and the web server prevents them from being downloaded directly. However, other kinds of scripts, such as those embedded in a client-side web page or a Windows Script Host file that a network administrator places on everyone's machine, can be opened, read, and easily copied.

> **Ironically, this apparent transparency disadvantage has helped scripting achieve huge gains in popularity in recent years. Since you can find script code all over the web, it's relatively easy for people to find it, read it, copy it, and learn from it. Microsoft has developed a new technology for Internet Explorer 5, called script encoding, that helps web script developers protect their intellectual property.**

❑ A compiler catches syntax errors at design time but syntax errors in a script cannot be caught until runtime. Even expert programmers make syntax mistakes when they write code. Both a design-time compiler and a runtime script engine expect the code you write to follow certain rules of syntax. For example, if you call a function that displays a message to the user, you must use the proper name for the function, and pass the parameters that the function expects in the proper order. If you don't do this, the compiler or script engine will complain at you. With a compiled language, such inevitable mistakes are caught at design time, and the compiler won't compile the program until the programmer fixes them. However, since a scripting language is not compiled until runtime, syntax errors might slip through for your users to see.

Script languages have the following advantages over compiled languages:

❑ Script code can be embedded as plain text with other types of code, such as HTML, XML, and scripts written in different languages. The classic example of this is web scripting, in which you can mix scripts in different languages (which provide functionality) with HTML (a 'markup' language which handles presentation) and XML (another markup languages that handles data structure) all in the same file. This mixture of plain-text script code, HTML, and XML can be downloaded very quickly into a web browser, at which time it is executed. While you can do this with a compiled language, such solutions are usually proprietary in nature and don't work in different brands of browsers.

❑ Script code is very good for quick, ad-hoc solutions. You can whip out a simple script to solve a simple problem in no time. For example, if you wanted to backup several groups of files stored in different directories on different drives, you could write a simple script that would find these files and compress them into an archive file. You could, of course, also do this by hand. However, if this were a task that you needed to repeat on a regular basis, writing a script to perform the task for you would probably make repetitions of the task faster and more reliable.

❑ Since scripting does not require a complicated **Integrated Development Environment** (IDE), such as those used by Visual Basic and C++ programmers, a scripting language is generally easier to learn. For a person new to software construction, scripting can be a great entryway into the vast world of programming. Scripting languages are generally more forgiving than compiled languages, and, as we've mentioned, they're ideal for automating simple tasks. VBScript, with its roots in the BASIC programming language, is especially easy for a non-programmer to learn.

VBScript, Visual Basic, and Visual Basic for Applications

Microsoft is famous for unleashing myriad acronyms and often confusing terms and phrases onto the world, and you'll encounter plenty of these in this book. This includes the alphabet soup of **VBScript** (VBS), **Visual Basic** (VB), and **Visual Basic for Applications** (VBA). The distinction between these three can be somewhat confusing. Hopefully, we can make things a little clearer.

We'll start with Visual Basic of which both VBA and VBScript are subsets. Visual Basic is a stand-alone, compiled language, with its own Integrated Development Environment (IDE), which includes a language editor, debugger, form designer, project manager, source code control integration, wizards, and other features that facilitate application development. Visual Basic is typically used to develop stand-alone, compiled applications and components. VB provides a full set of language features, including the ability to access the Windows API, which is a set of low-level functions that allow an application to directly access the functionality of the Windows operating system.

> It is not exactly correct to call Visual Basic a 'compiled' language. It is more like a hybrid between a compiled language and an interpreted language. VB applications are compiled, but rely on a large 'runtime library', which is a set of DLLs that must be installed in order for the compiled VB application to run. VB applications can also be compiled to interpreted 'P-Code', which is a kind of intermediate compilation step that still requires some compilation at runtime (and is therefore slower). However, since version 5 of Visual Basic brought 'real' compilation to VB, few VB developers compile to P-Code any longer.
>
> Finally, to add to the confusion, although VBA is, in terms of functionality, considered a sub-set of Visual Basic, VB actually uses VBA as its core. The VBA library defines the Visual Basic language itself and allows other applications (such as Word and Excel) to add (or host) Visual Basic capabilities. In a sense, the VB IDE is simply another one of these hosting applications.

Visual Basic for Applications is an 'embedded' version of Visual Basic. VBA can be integrated with an existing application to provide a facility for customization and extension of the application that hosts VBA. The best example of this is the Microsoft Office family of applications. Microsoft Word, Excel, and Access (among others) all support VBA, and even provide a full-blown VBA Integrated Development Environment similar to VB's stand-alone IDE. Using the VBA IDE, you can write Visual Basic code to provide rich functionality that goes well beyond the basic word processing, spreadsheet, and database features provided by these applications. Many of the same powerful language features of VB are available in VBA, the difference being that VBA code can only live in the context of the hosting application. VBA can be compiled to 'P-Code' within the hosting application, which makes it faster than VBScript, but not as fast as fully compiled VB applications and components.

Although VBScript is similar syntactically to VB and VBA, it is quite a different animal. Like VBA, VBScript is also an embedded language and cannot be compiled into a stand-alone application or executable. However, VBScript depends on a scripting host, which is a special application that knows how to compile and execute plain-text VBScript code at runtime. Originally, Microsoft created VBScript as an alternative to Netscape's JavaScript. Besides a simple desire to beat Netscape at their own game, Microsoft wanted to provide a way for Visual Basic developers to embed script code in plain-text HTML pages, which can't be done with design-time-compiled VB and VBA. Over time, Microsoft expanded support for VBScript beyond simple client-side HTML scripting in Microsoft's Internet Explorer web browser. VBScript still requires a 'host', however, and we're going to learn about these hosts in this book.

Is VBScript a 'Real' Programming Language?

Professional software developers who are masters of full-blown, stand-alone, compiled languages such as C++, Visual Basic, and Delphi often look down their noses at VBScript, and at scripting languages in general. 'Scripting is not *real* programming,' they'll say. This point of view is understandable, and in a sense correct, since a scripting language generally does not provide the kind of flexibility, control, power, and speed that a 'real' programming language does. However, this point of view fails to account for the fact that a scripting language like VBScript exists in order to solve a different set of problems. Microsoft did not create VBScript to *compete* with languages such as VB and C++, but rather to *supplement* them, to solve problems that they are either not capable of handling, or for which they would be overkill.

In many ways, a canoe cannot compare to a much larger, more powerful, and faster speed boat. Speed boats have comfortable seats, are much less susceptible to tipping over, have powerful engines, can tow water skiers, and are ideal for large, treacherous bodies of water that would swallow a canoe in a matter of minutes. A canoe, however, can go through narrow channels and shallow water that a larger boat never could, is much more nimble, can easily navigate through rocky whitewater rapids, and, if it hits a dry spot, can easily be picked up and carried to the water on the other side. Different tools are better for different problems.

VBScript is a worthy, and in some cases crucial, addition to any developers toolbox. Haven't you ever seen a speed boat towing a canoe behind it?

Other Languages, Other Platforms

As you've surely guessed by now, VBScript is not alone in the world of scripting languages. It's not even alone in the smaller world of scripting languages produced by Microsoft. Microsoft also produces and fully supports **JScript**, which can be used just about anywhere that VBScript can be used. Before VBScript version 5, JScript provided more features than VBScript. Awhile back, Microsoft pledged to keep VBScript on a par with JScript when it comes to features and capabilities. They will always remain separate languages, with different syntax and different ways of accomplishing the same thing, but Microsoft's goal is to make the choice of which Microsoft scripting language to use a matter of preference, not necessity.

JScript is closer in the nature of its syntax to C, and therefore C and C++ programmers might be more comfortable using JScript. JScript is also compatible with the **ECMAScript** standard. ECMAScript is a web-scripting standard that was developed by the European Computer Manufacturers Association (ECMA). The intent of ECMAScript is to provide a standard cross-platform scripting language, especially in the context of web scripting. The latest versions of Netscape's JavaScript and Microsoft's JScript are ECMAScript compatible, and in fact, both of these languages were used in the creation of the ECMAScript standard. You can download a description of the ECMAScript standard (ECMA-262) from
`http://www.ecma.ch/stand/ecma-262.htm`.

VBScript is not ECMAScript compatible, and therefore cannot generally be used in non-Microsoft operating systems (such as the many UNIX variants) or non-Microsoft web browsers (such as Netscape Navigator or Opera Software's Opera). That said, third party companies have developed tools that enable VBScript support in Netscape Navigator and in non-Windows operating systems. For example, NCompass Labs produces **scriptactive**, which is a 'plug-in' for Netscape Navigator that allows that browser to host VBScript code and ActiveX controls, which are not natively supported. You can reach NCompass Labs at http://www.ncompasslabs.com/default.htm.

On the Active Server Pages front (see Chapter 14), two companies offer products that allow you to develop VBScript ASP applications on several non-Windows platforms. The most well-known of these is Chili!Soft (http://www.chilisoft.com/), which produces **Chili!Soft ASP**. According to the Chili!Soft marketing literature 'Chili!Soft ASP provides full ASP support for Web servers from Apache, Lotus, Netscape, O'Reilly and Microsoft, running on Windows NT, Sun Solaris and IBM AIX, with other Web servers and Operating Systems coming soon.' Another player in this market is Halcyon Software (http://www.halcyonsoft.com/), which produces **Instant ASP**. According to the Halcyon marketing literature 'Halcyon's Instant ASP™ (iASP) provides Microsoft-compatible Active Server Pages (ASP) functionality and capability on all Web server, application server, and operating system platforms - from NT to Sun, Novell, AIX, AS/400, S/390, Apple, OS/2 and Linux to Apache, Netscape, Websphere, and more.'

What Can You Do With VBScript?

VBScript by itself is a powerful language, but you really can't do anything with it without a host. A host is an application that allows scripts written in VBScript to run within its context. Since VBScript cannot be compiled like a normal application and run on its own, it must have a host to read the script and compile it. This section contains a high level discussion of the many different ways you can use VBScript, and you'll find that these different capabilities are intrinsically tied to a particular host. Each of these subjects will be discussed in detail throughout the book.

The Windows Script Host

This Windows Script Host (WSH – formerly known as the Windows Scripting Host) is a scripting host that allows you to run scripts within the Windows operating system. This idea is very similar to UNIX Shell scripting and DOS batch files. These scripts can be run from the command line (in a DOS command shell window) or within native Windows. WSH is ideal for automating common tasks, writing network login scripts, and administering an NT network. Besides just executing the scripts you write, the WSH also includes and installs a set of objects that make it easy to access the Windows file system and environment. WSH scripts are not limited to those written in VBScript. It can execute scripts written in any language that conforms to the ActiveX Scripting specification, including JScript, Perl, and Python.

After covering the details of the VBScript language, this book will cover the Windows Script Host. The WSH is a great way to try out many of the sample scripts and code snippets that appear throughout the book. However, many of these examples will be dependent on a certain host. For instance, in order to try out some Active Server Pages scripts, you'll need to install Microsoft's Internet Information Server or Personal Web Server.

We will cover the Windows Script Host in Chapter 10.

Windows Script Components

A Windows Script Component (WSC) is a **COM component** that is written in a combination of script code and XML. They can be used on the server to execute **business logic**, read and write to databases, and even participate in **Microsoft Transaction Server** (MTS) transactions. You can even define events in a WSC. This is all functionality that was previously only available to C++, Visual Basic, and Delphi programmers, and is an exciting development.

In Chapters 5 and 6, you'll learn how, from VBScript, to use COM components and objects that are available from Microsoft and other companies. In Chapter 8 you'll learn how to create **classes** in VBScript. Then, in Chapter 9, we'll show how to group together one or more VBScript-based classes together into a Windows Script Component. Since a WSC is just like any other COM component, you can even use them from other COM-enabled languages such as Visual Basic and Delphi.

Client-Side Web Scripting

Client-side web scripting is something you probably encounter every day, and may not even know it. Even the simplest HTML pages on the web today often contain script code. Client-side web scripts are downloaded into the browser along with the HTML code that defines the layout of the web page. In fact, these scripts are embedded in (and are a part of) the HTML code.

Client-side web scripting is a fairly large subject, with many books dedicated to it, and we're going to cover as much of it as we can in this book. In Chapter 11, we'll talk about what we call 'general' client-side web scripting. This includes simple things like adding dynamic effects with `MouseOver` events, as well as validating and submitting forms to a web server. We use the term 'general' only because this type of scripting has been around awhile and become commonplace. Web browsers from Microsoft and Netscape going several versions back support general web scripting.

In Chapter 12, we'll introduce you to what we call 'high-powered' client side scripting. This includes subjects such as Dynamic HTML (DHMTL), Behaviors, and HTML Components (HTCs). These are powerful techniques and tools with which you can build rich web-based user interfaces that, besides looking great, help maximize server resources and network bandwidth. We'll also discuss the trade-offs of using VBScript and Microsoft's high-powered client-side scripting options, since these technologies are only supported by the latest versions of Microsoft's Internet Explorer (IE) web browser. (The IE-only limitation used to be a major drawback for someone considering writing a DHTML application, but HTML Applications now open up a whole world of possibilities for script authors.)

Server-Side Web Scripting

Server-side web scripting is accomplished with Microsoft's Internet Information Server (IIS) and Active Server Pages (ASP). Internet Information Server is the sophisticated web server that Microsoft ships with the Windows NT Option Pack, a free add-on for licensed users of Windows NT Version 4. Active Server Pages are essentially HTML pages with embedded script code. ASPs can include client-side web scripts that will be downloaded to the browser with the rest of the HTML, but also include scripts that are executed only in the web server. These embedded server-side scripts are executed *before* the page is released by the web server to be downloaded to the client's web browser. Using ASP scripts, you can dynamically change the content of the page as it is being built. For instance, you could store a user's profile and preferences in a database, and use these preferences to customize the content and appearance of the web page whenever the user requests it.

Don't dismay, though, if you are not lucky enough to have a dedicated NT Server with Internet Information Server installed on it. For no cost, you can download Microsoft's Personal Web Server (PWS), which runs on Windows 95 and Windows 98. Using Personal Web Server, you can develop your own Active Server Pages, and open them in any web browser. We'll cover ASP in Chapter 14.

Client-Server Web Scripting (Remote Scripting)

Remote Scripting is a cool new technology from Microsoft that allows you to treat ASP pages as if they were COM objects. From the client, you can 'call' the scripts embedded in an ASP page that's sitting on the server. This is important, because it means you can keep complicated, lengthy, and/or proprietary business logic on the server – it won't be downloaded to the browser, but client-side scripts in the browser can execute it as if it were. This also means less round trips to the server to reload entire pages. We'll discuss Remote Scripting in Chapter 12.

HTML Applications

An HTML Application (HTA) is one of the most exciting script-related technologies to come from Microsoft yet. Introduced with Internet Explorer Version 5, an HTML Application is a web page that runs in its own window – outside of the browser. The implications of this are significant. You can now use VBScript, HTML, DHTML, Cascading Style Sheets (CSS), HTML Components, Windows Script Components, and all the rest to build stand-alone graphical applications that do not require a web server or even a web or network connection to run. Also, since HTAs run outside the browser, they are considered 'trusted,' which means they are free of the security restrictions imposed by the browser. We predict that you will soon start seeing HTAs everywhere.

As Internet Explorer 5 becomes as ubiquitous as previous versions of Internet Explorer have become, script authors everywhere will be able to build and distribute non-web-dependent HTML Applications to users. This should be especially popular with the Windows Script Host authors who have previously been limited to lightweight popup dialog boxes for communicating with users. We'll cover HTAs in detail in Chapter 13.

Talking to Databases

Updating and reading information to and from databases is one of the most common needs of any developer, regardless of language or platform. Certainly, most applications written for business use depend on databases. VBScript developers are definitely not left out in the cold here. Microsoft's **Active Data Objects** (ADO) provide VBScript authors with full access to just about any data storage mechanism available, including relational databases (such as Access, SQL Server, and Oracle), object databases, flat files, and e-mail and groupware repositories. In Chapter 15, we'll introduce you to ADO and show you the basics of reading from and updating database tables, calling stored procedures, and more.

Adding Scripting to your Windows Applications

Adding scripting and 'macro' capability to a Windows application written in C++, Visual Basic, Delphi, and other languages used to be a complicated, often home-grown affair – no more. Using the free **Microsoft Script Control**, Windows developers can now extend their applications by adding support for VBScript, JScript, Perl, and other ActiveX-enabled scripting languages. Applications can expose objects to the scripting engine and allow end users and field implementers to customize the application, all with just a few extra lines of code. We'll show you how in Chapter 16.

What Tools Do You Need to Use VBScript?

In it's simplest form, all you need to create and run simple VBScript programs is a plain text editor (such as Windows Notepad) and the Windows Script Host. However, each of the many scripting hosts and components that we'll cover in this book require that you install certain applications and components on your PC or network. In order to keep you from having to jump all around the book to figure out what needs to be installed, each chapter will start with a section called *What Tools Do You Need?*

That said, one of the first questions most people ask is 'What editor should I use?' This is a matter of personal preference, and part of the decision hinges on whether or not you want to spend any money on an editor. There are commercial and shareware products available that provide sophisticated features that are especially useful for script developers. These features include color-coded syntax highlighting, automatic indenting, automatic backups, branch collapsing, super-charged clipboards, and macros. Some people prefer to use the simplest Windows text editor of them all, Notepad, which is usually installed automatically with Windows.

We do not endorse any particular editor (and this book will not use any examples that require you to use a certain editor), but here is a list of some 'free' and commercial products that you might want to consider. Most of the products have time – or functionality – limited demos that you can try for free. This is by no means a complete list (there are dozens of text editors on the market), and you might want to explore the Internet for more options. If you decide to use a shareware editor, we encourage you to register it and purchase a license.

These products are often a 'labor of love' for a programmer just like you, and registrations help keep the product alive:

❑ **PC Editor** – Freeware – Kazu Soft – `http://www.kazusoft.pair.com`

❑ **Programmer's File Editor** – Freeware – Alan Phillips – `http://www.lancs.ac.uk/people/cpaap/pfe/default.htm`

❑ **Edit Pad** – 'Postcardware' – JGSoft - `http://www.jgsoft.com`

❑ **GNU Emacs for Windows** – Open Source (freeware) – GNU – `http://www.cs.washington.edu/homes/voelker/ntemacs.html`

❑ **Codewhiz** – Shareware – Incatec – `http://www.incatec.com`

❑ **TextPad** – Shareware - Helios Software Solutions – `http://www.textpad.com`

❑ **UltraEdit-32** – Shareware – IDM Computer Services – `http://www.idmcomp.com`

❑ **Codewright** – Commercial – Premia Corporation – `http://www.premia.com`

❑ **HomeSite** – Commercial – Allaire – `http://www.allaire.com`

❑ **Multi-Edit** – Commercial – American Cybernetics – `http://www.amcyber.com`

❑ **PrimalScript** – Commercial – Sapien Technologies – `http://www.sapien.com`

Web scripters can also use two well-known products from Microsoft: Visual Interdev and FrontPage.

What's New in VBScript 5?

VBScript version 5 contains some significant new language features that should be most welcome to users of previous versions of VBScript. For the record, the last version of VBScript to receive general distribution was VBScript 3.1. Most people upgrading to version 5 will be coming from version 3.1. Version 4 of VBScript was distributed with Microsoft Visual Studio version 6, but did not contain any new language features. The changes between version 3.1 and 4 all had to do with IntelliSense and debugging features in Visual InterDev version 6.

If you're new to VBScript and not familiar with what we're talking about here – don't worry, we'll cover all of this later in the book.

Regular Expressions

VBScript now supports **regular expressions** through a new intrinsic VBScript object: RegExp. VBScript 5 developers can instantiate a RegExp object and use it to evaluate string data against a **pattern**, which is a kind of shorthand description of how a string of data might look. For example, the pattern "\w+\@[.\w]+" checks to see if a string looks like an e-mail address. Regular expression patterns are obviously rather strange looking, and can take some getting used to. However, regular expressions are a powerful way to check the validity of data (for instance, to see if your user entered a properly formatted e-mail address), or to search for all kinds of strings in text files or other text-based data.

The pattern syntax in the VBScript `RegExp` object is exactly the same as in JScript, which is in turn based on Perl regular expressions. JScript has supported regular expressions for a while, and adding this powerful feature to VBScript is Microsoft's fulfillment of a promise to keep VBScript and JScript 'in synch' feature-for-feature. We'll cover the `RegExp` object in Chapter 7.

Classes

The ability to define a class natively in VBScript is a welcome addition to VBScript 5. Classes are a great way to organize you code for readability, maintainability, and reusability. A class is a self-contained unit of code that acts as a template for an object. Classes are the building blocks of components.

Since scripts are generally self-contained units (with all of the code that makes up a script embedded in a single text file), and since, in languages such as VB and C++, classes are defined in their own separate text files, the VBScript development team had a bit of a challenge to give VBScript developers the ability to define a class. They solved the problem with the `Class` statement, which allows you to define a class within a script. You define the properties and methods (public and private) for a class between `Class` and `End Class` statements. You can then instantiate this class into an object variable and use it just like any other object. Writing classes is very straightforward. If you've had any experience writing classes in Visual Basic, you won't have any trouble. We'll show you the ins and outs of VBScript classes in Chapter 8.

With Statement

Visual Basic developers know how much coding time and processing time the `With` statement can save, but VBScript developers have, until now, been unable to take advantage of this great feature. The `With` statement is a shorthand, code blocking statement. Between `With <<object name>>` and `End With` statements, you don't have to repeat the name of an object every time you refer to one of its properties and methods. This saves you typing, and saves the compiler and runtime engine from having to resolve the reference to that object every time your code refers to it – and that makes your script run faster. Here's a quick example (we'll cover the `With` statement in Chapters 5 and 6):

Instead of typing this:

```
oCustomer.Name = "Mary Smith"
oCustomer.Address = "1234 Some Street"
oCustomer.ZipCode = "12345"
oCustomer.Update
```

You can type this:

```
With oCustomer
    .Name = "Mary Smith"
    .Address = "1234 Some Street"
    .ZipCode = "12345"
    .Update
End With
```

13

Eval, Execute, and ExecuteGlobal

These three new VBScript functions are included in version 5 to create compatibility with the JScript `Eval` method. They each do about the same thing, but which one you use depends on the scope of what it is your trying to do. The idea is to provide a way to evaluate and execute code 'on the fly' at runtime. For instance, your user could type in `x = (2 + 2) * 8`, which you would then send to the `Eval` function. `Eval` would tell you that this formula results in the number `32`.

`Execute` and `ExecuteGlobal` are for executing blocks of script code on the fly, whereas `Eval` is for executing single expressions such as the example we just used. Deciding whether to use `Execute` or `ExecuteGlobal` depends on the **namespace** that the script code you're executing needs to have access to, but we're not going to get into that here. We'll discuss these three new functions in Appendix A.

Function Pointers

The new `GetRef` function allows you to 'bind' a script procedure to any available object event in a DHTML page. Previously, this had to be accomplished through the `ObjectName_EventName` syntax or through an HTML tag. When the event occurs, the procedure name passed to the `GetRef` function will be executed. For example:

```
Set Window.OnLoad = GetRef("MyFunction")
```

When the `Window.OnLoad` event fires, `MyFunction` will be executed. We'll cover the `GetRef` function in Appendix A.

DCOM Support

Distributed COM (or DCOM) allows you to create and communicate with objects that live on another computer. Then, that computer's memory and processor handle the load of running that object. This is known as 'distributed processing'. Once a distributed object has been instantiated in your script, your code has no idea (nor does it care) that the object lives on another computer somewhere on your network. Microsoft added DCOM support to VBScript 5 by adding an additional optional argument to the `CreateObject` function. You pass the name of the computer on which the object is registered as the second argument to the `CreateObject` function. For example:

```
Set oCustomer = CreateObject("MyComponent.Customer", \\MyRemoteServer)
```

Code Conventions

We have used a number of different styles of text and layout in the book to help differentiate between the different kinds of information. Here are examples of the styles we use, and an explanation of what they mean:

Advice, hints, and background information comes in this type of font.

> **Important pieces of information come in boxes like this.**

Important words are in a bold type font.

Words that appear on the screen in menus, like **File** or **Window**, are in a similar font to the one that you see on the screen.

Keys that you press on the keyboard, like *Ctrl* and *Enter*, are in italics.

Code comes in a number of different styles. If it's something we're talking about in the text – when we're discussing the `MsgBox`, for example – it's in a fixed-width font. If it's a block of code from a program, then it's also in a gray box:

```
Dim varTest
varTest = "Hello There"
MsgBox TypeName(varTest)
```

Sometimes you'll see code in a mixture of styles like this:

```
Sub window_onload()
  On Error Resume Next
  x = 3/0
  Msgbox x
End Sub
```

The code with a white background is something that we've already looked at and don't wish to examine further.

These formats are designed to make sure that you know exactly what you're looking at. We hope that they make life easier.

Tell Us What You Think

We've worked hard on this book to make it enjoyable and useful. Our best reward would be to hear from you that you liked it and that it was worth the money you paid for it. We've done our best to try to understand and match your expectations.

Please let us know what you think about it. Tell us what you liked best and what we could have done better. If you think this is just a marketing gimmick, then test us out – drop us a line! We'll answer, and we'll take whatever you say on board for future editions. The easiest way is to use e-mail:

`feedback@wrox.com`

You can also find more details about Wrox Press on our web site. There you'll find the code from our latest books, sneak previews of forthcoming titles, and information about the authors and the editors. You can order Wrox titles directly from the site, or find out where your nearest local bookstore with Wrox titles is located. The address of out site is:

`http://www.wrox.com`

Customer Support

If you find a mistake in the book, your first port of call should be the errata page on our web site. If you can't find an answer there, send an e-mail to `support@wrox.com` telling us about the problem. We'll do everything we can to answer promptly. Please remember to let us know the book your query relates to, and if possible the page number as well. This will help us to get a reply to you more quickly.

A (Very) Short Introduction to Programming

In trying to squeeze the basics of writing computer programs into one chapter, we may be attempting the impossible, but we're going to do our best. The reason for including this chapter is that many people come to a scripting language, like VBScript, as their first language. Perhaps you're a network systems expert who wants to use VBScript and the Windows Script Host to write login scripts and automate administration tasks. Or perhaps you're a web designer who feels the need to branch out from the visual aspects of creating web pages and into writing scripts to drive content. Or perhaps you're just a person who wants to learn a programming language for the fun of it. Either way, you've come to the right place.

Programming – or "writing code," as some people like to call it – is a *huge* subject. Many volumes have been written about it. During this chapter, in a single paragraph, we might introduce multiple unfamiliar concepts. We're going to move pretty fast, but if you read along closely and try out the examples, you'll probably be just fine.

Keep in mind that even an in-depth discussion of how to write computer programs might not even begin to touch on subjects such as architecture, systems design, database design, testing, documentation, and all the rest of the subjects that an accomplished software developer must master. But don't let all that discourage you. Everyone starts somewhere, and this is a great place for you to start learning the art and science of making a computer sing. Consider this chapter a brief introduction to the important building blocks. It won't make you an expert overnight, but hopefully it will give you a the know-how you'll need in order to get the most out of the rest of the book.

Variables and Data Types

In this section, we're going to be moving quickly through some of the most basic concepts of programming: variables, comments, using built-in VBScript functions, and other syntax issues.

The first concept we're going to touch on is that of **variables**. Simply put, a variable is a place in memory where your script holds a piece (or a set) of information (we'll use the term **data** in place of "information" throughout most of this discussion). The data stored in a variable might be very simple, like the number 10,000, or very complex, such as a whole series of numbers, ranging from 1 to 10,000.

Behind the scenes, a variable is a reserved section of the computer's **memory**. Just to make sure we're clear, memory is temporary working space for the computer. Memory is transient – that is, things that are placed in memory are not stored there permanently. That's what the hard drive is for. Since memory is transient, and since variables are stored in the computer's memory, variables are by extension transient as well. Your script will use variables to temporarily store a piece of information that the script needs to keep track of. (If your script needs to store that information permanently, it would store it in a file on the hard disk, or in a database, which is also stored permanently on the hard drive.)

In order to make it easier for the computer to keep track of all the millions of pieces of information that might be stored in memory at any given moment, memory is broken up into chunks. Each chunk is exactly the same size, and each chunk is given an **address**. You don't need to worry about memory addresses, but it's useful to know that a variable is a reserved set of one or more chunks. Different types of variables take up different amounts of memory. In your VBScript program, you will **declare** (or "**dimension**") variables before you use them, and you will give them a name in the process. Here's an example of a variable declaration in VBScript:

```
Dim CustomerName
```

When you declare a variable like this, you are basically telling the computer "Reserve some memory for me, and please give that memory the name `CustomerName`." The computer (or, more precisely, the VBScript engine) keeps track of that memory for you, and whenever you use the variable name `CustomerName`, it will know what you're talking about.

> Note: it is not strictly required that you declare all of the variables you use. VBScript by default allows you to use undeclared variables. However, we strongly recommend that you declare all of the variables you use in your scripts. We'll cover this topic in more depth in Chapter 2.

Variables are essential to the activity of writing a VBScript program (or any program, for that matter). Without variables, you'd have no way of keeping track of all of the pieces of information your script is going to be manipulating, adding up, and displaying on the screen. Picture yourself at your desk keeping track of your household income and expenses in a paper-based ledger.

This process entails adding up and keeping track of multiple pieces of information: paychecks and other kinds of income, grocery expenses, automobile expenses, medical expenses, debt service, and so on. You'd keep each of these running totals in a separate column, and later you'd probably add them all up to create a view into your financial situation. If you were writing a computer program to keep up with all this information instead of using your paper-based ledger, you would probably store the permanent data in a database, but while your program was accepting input of the numbers and keeping track of the totals, it would use different variables to keep up with each different piece of information.

In VBScript, whenever you have a piece of information that you need to work with, you would declare a variable using the syntax we demonstrated a moment ago. At some point in your script, you're going to need to place a value in that variable — otherwise, what would be the point of declaring it? Placing a value in a variable for the first time is called **initializing** the variable. Sometimes you initialize a variable with a **default value**. Other times, you might ask the user for some information, and initialize the variable with whatever the user types in. Or you might open a database and use a previously-stored value to initialize the variable.

Initializing the variable gives you a starting point. After its been initialized, you can use the variable in calculations, store it in a database, or display it back to the user in another form. Here's a simple VBScript example:

```
Dim DateToday
'Initialize the variable
DateToday = Date
MsgBox "Today's date is " & DateToday & "."
```

Now we've opened up a bit of a can of worms. What's all that other stuff in this code? We'll look at it line-by-line. The first line is the variable declaration. We've asked the computer to reserve some memory for us, and to please remember the variable name `DateToday` for us.

All of the examples in this chapter are tailored so that they can be run by the **Windows Script Host**. The Windows Script Host is a scripting host that allows you to run VBScript programs within Windows. WSH will allow you to try these example programs out for yourself. You may already have WSH installed. To find out, type the above example script into a text editor, save the file as `TEST.VBS`, and double click the file in Windows Explorer. If the script runs, then you're all set. If Windows does not recognize the file, then you'll need to download and install WSH from `http://msdn.microsoft.com/scripting`.

If you like, you can skip ahead briefly and check out the beginning sections of Chapter 10. You don't need to read the whole chapter, just the first sections, which describe how to install the Windows Script Host, and how to use WSH to run scripts.

Let's get back to the code extract shown above. The second line is a **comment**. In VBScript, any text that follows the single quote character (') is treated as a comment. This means that the VBScript engine will ignore this text. This introduces an interesting point: if the script engine is going to ignore this text, why type it in at all? It doesn't contribute to the execution of the script, right? This is correct, but it excludes one of the most important principles of programming: it is equally important to write a script with human readers in mind as it is to write with the computer in mind.

Of course, when we are writing a script, we must write it with the computer (or, more specifically, the script engine) in mind, because if we don't type it in correctly (that is, if we don't use the correct **syntax**), the script engine won't execute the script. However, programming is an inherently human-involved activity. Once you've written some useful scripts, you're probably going to have to go back to make changes to a script you wrote six months ago. If you did not write that code with human readers in mind, it might be difficult to figure out what in the world you were thinking at the time you wrote the script. Worse yet, what happens when one of your co-workers has to go in and make changes to a script you wrote six months ago? If you did not write that script to be readable and maintainable, your co-worker will probably curse you as they try to decipher every line of your code.

Adding good comments to your code is only one aspect of writing readable, maintainable programs. We'll touch on some other principles later, such as choosing good variable names, indenting properly, using white space in a helpful way, and organizing your code clearly and logically. That said, keep in mind that adding too many comments, or adding comments that are not useful, can make a script almost as bad as one with no comments at all. Also, if you are scripting for a web page that must be downloaded to a user's browser, too many comments can affect the time that it takes to download the page.

We'll discuss some good commenting principles later in this chapter, but suffice it to say now that the comment in line two of our script is not really a good comment for everyday use. This is because, to any semi-experienced programmer, it is painfully obvious that what we are doing is initializing the `DateToday` variable. Throughout this book, you will often see the code commented this way. This is because the point of our code is to instruct you, the reader, in how a particular aspect of VBScript programming works.

Back to our example script. It should now be clear that what we're doing in line three is initializing the variable `DateToday`. To do this, we are using a built-in VBScript **function** called `Date`. A function is a piece of code that returns a value. VBScript comes with a lot of built-in functions. These functions are part of the language, and they're always available for your use. You can find a full listing of all of VBScript's built-in functions in Appendix A. The `Date` function is one such function that returns the current date according to the computer's internal clock. (In a few minutes, we'll get into the idea of writing your own functions.) In line three, we are telling the script engine, "Take the value returned by the `Date` function, and store it in the variable called `DateToday`." (Notice that we did not name the variable `Date`, but rather `DateToday`. This is necessary because, since `Date` is a built-in VBScript function, "date" is a **reserved word**. You cannot name your variables with the same name as a reserved word.)

In line four, now that we've initialized this variable, we're going to do something useful with it. `MsgBox` is another built-in VBScript function that you will use quite a bit. The `MsgBox` function is a good time to introduce the concept of **passing** function **parameters** (a.k.a. **arguments**). Some functions, such as the `Date` function, do not require you to pass parameters to them. This is because the `Date` function does not need any additional information from you in order to do its job. All it needs to know how to do is read the computer's clock and return the current date. The `MsgBox` function, on the other hand, displays a piece of information to the user in the form of a dialog box, like this:

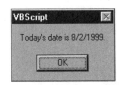

You have to pass `MsgBox` a parameter—otherwise, it would not have anything to display. The `MsgBox` function actually has several parameters, but we only used the first one. This is because the remaining parameters are **optional parameters**. You probably also noticed the ampersand (&) symbols in line four. The ampersand is a VBScript **operator**, and is used to **concatenate** text together. To concatenate means to "string together." This text can either take the form of a **literal**, or a variable. A literal is the opposite of a variable: a variable is so named because it can change throughout the **lifetime** of the script (a script's lifetime is the time from when it starts executing, to the time it stops executing). Unlike a variable, a literal cannot change during the lifetime of the script. Here is line four of the script again:

```
MsgBox "Today's date is " & DateToday & "."
```

The parts in bold are the literals. Notice how the concatenation of the `DateToday` variable results in the text "Today's date is 8/2/1999." in the resulting dialog box. An operator is a symbol or word that you use within your code, usually to change or test a value. Other operators include the standard mathematical operators (+, -, /, *), and the equals sign (=), which can actually be used in either a **comparison** or an **assignment**. Thus far, we've been using the equals sign as an **assignment operator**. We'll find out more about operators later on in this chapter.

> Here's something to confuse you: did you notice how we've been describing `MsgBox` as a function? Didn't we say that a function returns a value? What value is the `MsgBox` "function" returning? Good questions. Programming, and computing in general, is full of strange contradictions such as this. Without getting into too many details, the `MsgBox` function *does* return a value – we're just ignoring it in this case. By not capturing its return value into a variable, or otherwise doing something with it, we can ignore the return value. If you want to learn more about the various ways to use the `MsgBox` function, see Appendix A.

Let's take a closer look at variables. Remember that we said that a variable is a piece of reserved memory? Well, how does the computer know how large to make that piece of memory? Luckily, this is something that's handled automatically by the VBScript engine. You don't really have to worry too much about it. However, it's useful to know that the VBScript engine will dynamically change and reallocate the actual memory addresses that are used up by a variable. For example, take a quick look at this VBScript program:

```
'Declare the variable
Dim SomeText

'Initialize the variable
SomeText = "Hello there."
MsgBox SomeText

'Change the value of the variable
SomeText = "This is longer text which takes up more space in memory."
MsgBox SomeText

'Change it again
SomeText = "Shorter this time."
MsgBox SomeText
```

This is a bit of an oversimplification, but what happens here is that when we declare the variable, the script engine that is executing the script allocates a very minimal amount of memory. Since there's nothing stored in the variable yet, it doesn't require much space. When we initialize the variable with the simple text "Hello There," the script engine asks the computer for a little more space in memory to store this new value – but just enough to hold this short phrase. Then, when we assign the much longer text to the same variable, the script engine must allocate even more memory. Finally, when we assign the shorter string of text, the script engine can reduce the size of the variable in memory.

One final note about variables: once you've assigned a value to a variable, you don't have to throw it away in order to assign something else to the variable as well. Take a look at this script:

```
Dim SomeText

SomeText = "Hello There."
MsgBox SomeText

SomeText = SomeText & " I hope you're doing well today."
MsgBox SomeText
```

Notice how in this script, we're keeping the original value of the variable and adding some additional text to it. We told the script engine that this is what we wanted to do by also using the name of the SomeText variable on the right side of the equals sign, and then concatenating its existing value with an additional value using the ampersand (&) operator. Adding on to the original value works with numbers too, but we use the + operator instead:

```
Dim AnyNumber

AnyNumber = 100
MsgBox AnyNumber

AnyNumber = AnyNumber + 2
MsgBox AnyNumber
```

We're not going to get into it in this chapter, but variables can store all kinds of values in them, and be used in several different ways. We'll cover variables, **data types**, and **object variables** in Chapter 2.

Control of Flow

When you run a script that you have written, the code executes in a certain order. This order of execution is also known as **flow**. In simple scripts such as the ones we have been writing thus far, the statements execute from the top down – that is, the first statement in the script is executed first, then the next one, then the next one, and on and on until the script reaches the end. The execution occurs this way because the simple programs we've written so far do not contain any **branching** or **looping** code.

Branching

Take another look at this example script, which we were just using in the previous section:

```
Dim SomeText

SomeText = "Hello There."
MsgBox SomeText

SomeText = SomeText & " I hope you're doing well today."
MsgBox SomeText
```

If you save this script in a .vbs file, then execute it using the Windows Script Host, all of the statements will be executed in order from the first statement to the last. Note that we say that *all* of the statements will be executed. However, there are techniques that we can use to cause some statements to be executed, and some not, depending on certain **conditions**. This technique is called branching. VBScript supports a few different branching constructs, and we will cover all of them in detail in Chapter 3, but we're only going to cover the simplest and most common one here: the If...Else...End If construct.

Take a look at this modified version of our example script:

```
Dim Greeting
Dim UserName

UserName = InputBox("Please enter your name:")

UserName = Trim(UserName)
```

```
If UserName = "" Then
  Greeting = "Why won't you tell me your name? That's not very nice."
Else
  Greeting = "Hello, " & UserName & ", it's a pleasure to meet you."
End If

MsgBox Greeting
```

We've introduced a couple of built-in VB functions in this script (namely `InputBox` and `Trim`), but what is most important to this discussion is the `If…Else…End If` block of code. For the record, though, `InputBox` is a simple function that allows you to ask the user for some basic piece of information, such as her name, the location of a file, or just about anything else your script might need. The function expects one required parameter, the prompt text, and also accepts several optional parameters. We've only used the one required parameter. When this script is executed, the `InputBox` code will cause a dialog box like this to pop up:

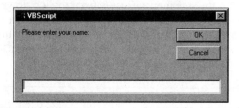

Note that the parameter text that we passed, "Please enter your name:", is displayed as a prompt for the dialog box. The `InputBox` function returns the value that the user types in, if any. If the user does not type anything in, or clicks the Cancel button, then `InputBox` will return a **zero-length string**, which is a strange kind of programming concept that basically means "text with no actual text in it." Our script stores the result of the `InputBox` function in the `UserName` variable.

This is where the branching comes in. Branching is very common when you are dealing with **input** to your script. Most programs take some sort of **input**, do something with it, and then produce an **output**. In our script, the input is the user's name, and the output is the greeting message that we display. The thing is that input is usually very unpredictable. We don't know what the user's going to do when they see this dialog box asking for his name. Will they enter their real name? Will they enter their name at all? Will they be offended and just click the Cancel button? Will they try and be cute and just hit the spacebar a few times before clicking the OK button? You just don't know.

So what your script must do is **test** the input, and then execute different code, depending on the result of that test. Hence the term branching – depending on our test of the input, the flow of execution is either going to go this way, or that way. Our script must adapt to the unpredictable nature of the input. For instance, wouldn't our script look pretty stupid if it looked like this:

```
Dim Greeting
Dim UserName

UserName = InputBox("Please enter your name:")
```

```
Greeting = "Hello, " & Trim(UserName) & ", it's a pleasure to meet you."

MsgBox Greeting
```

and produced this output:

This script does not contain any branching logic to test the input, so when the user does something unpredictable, like pressing the **Cancel** button, or not entering any name at all, the script does not have the ability to adapt. Our non-stupid script adapts to the unpredictability of input by testing it with If...Else...End If branching. Here's the branching code again:

```
UserName = Trim(UserName)
If UserName = "" Then
   Greeting = "Why won't you tell me your name? That's not very nice."
Else
   Greeting = "Hello, " & UserName & ", it's a pleasure to meet you."
End If
```

We use the Trim() function here to further insulate our script from unpredictability. The Trim() function takes any kind of text as a parameter, and returns the same text, but with any leading or trailing spaces removed. For example, the text " Hello " passed to the Trim() function would come back as just "Hello". We do this just in case the user enters a sequence of one or more spaces, which, for the purpose of our script, is equivalent to not having entered anything. Also, notice the double quotation marks ("") in the line If Trim(UserName) = "" Then. This is the way to express the "zero-length string" that we talked about earlier.

So if the user enters nothing (or a string of spaces), then the script will execute this line of code:

```
Greeting = "Why won't you tell me your name? That's not very nice."
```

Otherwise, it will execute this line of code:

```
Greeting = "Hello, " & UserName & ", it's a pleasure to meet you."
```

Notice that both lines of code assign a value to the Greeting variable. However, only one of these lines will actually execute. That's because our If...Else...End If block makes an either/or decision. Either a given condition is True, or it is False. It can't be both. If it is True, then we'll execute the code between the If and Else statements. If it is False, then we'll execute the code between the Else and End If statements.

Before we move on to looping, let's mention a couple other things about If...Else...End If.

First, the `If...Else...End If` construct is what's known as a **block** of code. A block is a section of code that has a beginning and an end, and usually contains keywords or statements at the beginning and the end. In the case of `If...Else...End If`, the `If` statements marks the beginning of the block, and the `End If` marks the end of the block. The script engine requires these beginning and ending statements, and if you omit them, the engine will not allow your script to execute. You will encounter lots of different code blocks in VBScript. That said, to confuse matters, the term "block of code" is often used informally to describe any group of lines of code.

Second, notice also that the lines of code inside the block are indented four spaces. This is an extremely important concept. It's not important for the script engine that these lines be indented, but for humans who are reading your code, proper indentation is essential. The script engine does not care whether your code has a pleasing appearance, or even that the visual presentation make any sense at all. For example, the following script is completely legal and will execute just fine:

```
Dim Greeting
    Dim UserName

        UserName = InputBox("Please enter your name:")

  If Trim(UserName) = "" Then
Greeting = "Why won't you tell me your name? That's not very nice."
    Else
       Greeting = "Hello, " & UserName & ", it's a pleasure to meet you."
          End If

       MsgBox Greeting
```

This might be fine for the script engine, but it's a nightmare for you and your fellow programmers to make sense of. Generally, you need to indent your code whenever a line or series of lines is subordinate to the lines above and below it. For example, the lines after the `If` clause and the `Else` clause belong *inside* the `If...Else...End If` block, so we indent them to visually suggest this.

This points up a very important programming principle: *the presentation of your code should visually suggest its logical structure*. In other words, without even reading it, we can look at the code and, consciously or unconsciously, get a sense for how it is organized and how it works. By detecting the indentations inside the `If...Else...End If` block, we can "see" the branching logic at that point in the code. Indenting is only one element of programming style, but learning and following proper style and layout is essential for any programmer who wants to be taken seriously.

Third, the `Else` part of the block is optional. Sometimes you want to test for a certain condition, and if that condition is `True`, execute some code – but if it's `False`, there's no code to execute. For example, we could add another `If...End If` block to our script:

```
Dim Greeting
Dim UserName

UserName = InputBox("Please enter your name:")

UserName = Trim(UserName)
```

```
If UserName = "" Then
  Greeting = "Why won't you tell me your name? That's not very nice."
Else
  Greeting = "Hello, " & UserName & ", it's a pleasure to meet you."
End If

If UserName = "Mike" Then
  Greeting = Greeting & " I like the name Mike."
End If

MsgBox Greeting
```

Fourth, If…Else…End If can be extended through the use of the ElseIf clause, and through **nesting**. Nesting is the technique of placing a block of code inside of another block of code of the same type. The following variation on our script illustrates both concepts:

```
Dim Greeting
Dim UserName

UserName = InputBox("Please enter your name:")

UserName = Trim(UserName)
If UserName = "" Then
  Greeting = "Why won't you tell me your name? That's not very nice."
ElseIf UserName = "go away" Then
  Greeting = "That's not very nice."
ElseIf UserName = "who's asking?" Then
  Greeting = "I asked you first."
Else
  Greeting = "Hello, " & UserName & ", it's a pleasure to meet you."

  If UserName = "Mike" Then
    Greeting = Greeting & " I like the name Mike."
  End If
End If

MsgBox Greeting
```

Once again, notice how the indenting identifies which lines of code are subordinate to the lines above them.

Finally (and this may seem obvious by now), even though branching logic tells the script to execute some lines of code and not others, the code that's not executed must still be interpreted by the script engine. If the code not executed contains syntax errors, the script engine will still produce a syntax error.

Looping

Branching allows you to tell the script to execute some lines of code, but not others. Looping, on the other hand, allows you to tell the script to execute some lines of code over and over again. This is useful in two situations: when you want to repeat a block of code until a condition is `True` or `False`, and when you want to repeat a block of code a defined number of times. In Chapter 3, we'll cover several different kinds of looping constructs, but here we're going to focus on only two: the basic `Do...Loop While` loop, and the basic `For...Next` loop.

First we're going to use the `Do...Loop While` construct to repeatedly execute a block of code until a certain condition is met. Take a look at this modification of out example script:

```
Dim Greeting
Dim UserName
Dim TryAgain

Do
  TryAgain = "No"

  UserName = InputBox("Please enter your name:")
  UserName = Trim(UserName)

  If UserName = "" Then
    MsgBox "You must enter your name."
    TryAgain = "Yes"
  Else
    Greeting = "Hello, " & UserName & ", it's a pleasure to meet you."
  End If

Loop While TryAgain = "Yes"

MsgBox Greeting
```

Notice the block of code that starts with the word `Do` and ends with the line that starts with the word `Loop`. The indentation should make this code block easy to identify. This is the definition of our loop. The code inside the loop will keep executing until at the end of the loop, the `TryAgain` variable equals `"No"`.

We are using the `TryAgain` variable to control the loop. The loop starts at the word `Do`. At the end of the loop, if the `TryAgain` variable equals `"Yes"`, then the code starting at the word `Do` will execute again. Notice that at the top of the loop we initialize the `TryAgain` variable to `"No"`. It is essential that this initialization take place inside the loop (that is, between the `Do` and `Loop` statements). This way, the variable is re-initialized every time a loop occurs. If we did not do this, we would end up with what's called an **infinite loop**.

Infinite loops are undesirable, and whenever you code any kind of loop, you need to take measures to make sure they do not produce an infinite loop. As the term suggests, an infinite loop is one that never stops. Remember that the computer will only do what your script tells it to do. If you tell it to keep looping forever, it will. As long as the loop keeps looping, the code that comes after the loop never gets executed. Let's take a look at why the `TryAgain = "No"` line is essential to preventing an infinite loop. We'll go through the script line by line.

```
Do
```

This starts the loop. This tells the script engine that we are starting a block of code that will define a loop. The script engine will expect to find a `Loop` statement somewhere further down in the script. This is similar to the `If...End If` code block: the script engine expects the block to be defined with beginning and ending statements. We'll get more into this in Chapter 3, but take note that the `Do` statement on a line all by itself means that the loop will execute *at least once*. Even if the `Loop While` statement at the end of the block does not result in a loop-around back to the `Do` line, the code inside this block is going to execute at least one time.

```
Do
    TryAgain = "No"
```

Here we are initializing our "control" variable. We call it the "control" variable because this variable will ultimately control whether or not the loop loops around again. We want to initialize this variable to `"No"` so that, by default, the loop will not loop around again. Only if a certain something occurs inside the loop will we set `TryAgain` to `"Yes"`. This is yet another strategy in our ever-vigilant desire to expect the unexpected.

```
Do
    TryAgain = "No"

    UserName = InputBox("Please enter your name:")
```

This should look familiar. We are using the `InputBox` function to ask the user for their name. We store the return value from the function in the `UserName` variable. Whatever the user types in, if anything, will be stored in this variable. Put another way, our script is receiving some external input – and remember that we said is always unpredictable.

```
Do
    TryAgain = "No"

    UserName = InputBox("Please enter your name:")

    If Trim(UserName) = "" Then
        MsgBox "You must enter your name."
        TryAgain = "Yes"
    Else
        Greeting = "Hello, " & UserName & ", it's a pleasure to meet you."
    End If
```

Now we are testing our input. The line `If Trim(UserName) = "" Then` tests to see if the user typed in their name. If they typed something in, the code immediately after the `Else` line will execute. If they did not (or if they clicked the Cancel button), then the `UserName` variable will be empty, and the code after the `If` line will execute instead. If the user did not type in their name, we display a message informing them that they have done something our script did not like. Then we set the `TryAgain` variable (our "control" variable) to `"Yes"`. This ensures that the loop will go around again, and then we'll ask the user for their name again.

If the user did type in their name, then we initialize our familiar `Greeting` variable. Note that in this case, we do not change the value of the `TryAgain` variable. This is because there is no need to loop around again – the user has obliged us and entered their name. The value of `TryAgain` is already equal to `"No"`, so there's no need to change it.

```
Do
  TryAgain = "No"

  UserName = InputBox("Please enter your name:")

  If Trim(UserName) = "" Then
    MsgBox "You must enter your name."
    TryAgain = "Yes"
  Else
    Greeting = "Hello, " & UserName & ", it's a pleasure to meet you."
  End If

Loop While TryAgain = "Yes"

MsgBox Greeting
```

Now we encounter the end of our loop block. What this `Loop` line is essentially telling the script engine is "If the `TryAgain` variable equals `"Yes"` at this point, then go back up to the `Do` line and execute all that code over again." If the user entered their name, then the `TryAgain` variable will be equal to `"No"`. Therefore, the code will not loop again, and will continue on to the last line: `MsgBox Greeting`, which we've seen before.

If the user did not enter their name, then `TryAgain` would be equal to `"Yes"`, which would mean that the code would jump back up to the `Do` line again. This is where the re-initialization of the `TryAgain` variable to `"No"` is essential. If we don't reset the value of `TryAgain`, then there's no way for `TryAgain` to ever equal *anything but* `"Yes"`. If `TryAgain` always equals `"Yes"`, then the loop keeps going around and around forever. This is disaster for your script, and for your user.

Next we'll take a quick look at another kind of loop: the `For...Next` loop. In this kind of loop, we don't need to worry about infinite loops. This is because the loop is predefined to only execute a certain number of times. Here's a simple (if not exactly useful) example:

```
Dim Index

MsgBox "Let's count to five. Ready?"

For Index = 1 to 5
  MsgBox Index
Next

MsgBox "Wasn't that fun?"
```

The beginning loop block is defined by the For statement, and the end is defined by the Next statement. This loop will go around exactly five times. The line For Index = 1 to 5 essentially tells the script engine, "Execute this block of code as many times as it takes to count from 1 to 5, and use the Index variable to keep track of your counting. When we've gone through this code five times, stop looping and move on." Notice that every time the loop goes around (including the first time through), the Index variable holds the value of the current count. The first time through, Index equals 1, the second time through it equals 2, and so on up to 5. It's important to note that *after* the loop is finished, the value of the Index variable will be 6, *one number higher* than the highest value in our For statement. This occurs because the Index variable is incremented at the end of the loop, after which the For statement tests the value of Index to see if it is necessary to loop again.

It's difficult to express the real-world usefulness of the For...Next loop without opening a can of worms on a lot of other subjects, but keep in mind that it is often used to traverse some sort of finite piece of data, such as a word, or a text file. For example, the word "elephant" has exactly eight letters. If you first calculated the number of letters in the word "elephant", you could use that number to drive a For...Next loop. Below is a simple example that uses the VBScript Len() function to calculate the length of the word "elephant." Inside the loop, it uses the Mid() function to pull one letter out of the word "elephant" at a time.

```
Dim Index
Dim WordLength

WordLength = Len("elephant")

For Index = 1 to WordLength
  MsgBox Mid("elephant", Index, 1)
Next

MsgBox "elephant"
```

Operators

An operator acts on one or more **operands** when comparing, assigning, concatenating, calculating, and performing logical operations.

Say, you want to calculate the difference between two variables A and B and save the result in variable C. These variables are the operands and to find the difference you use the subtraction operator like this:

```
C = A - B
```

Here we used the assignment operator (=) to assign the difference between A and B, which was found by using the subtraction operator (-).

Operators are one of the single-most important parts of any programming language. Without them, you would not be able to assign values to variables or perform calculations and comparisons! It would be a bit like a bicycle without pedals...

There are different types of operators and they each serve a specific purpose:

❑ The **assignment** (=) operator is the most obvious and is simply used for assigning a value to a variable or property.

❑ The **arithmetic** operators are all used to calculate a numeric value, and are normally used in conjunction with the assignment operator and/or one of the comparison operators.

❑ The **concatenation** operators are used to concatenate ("join together") expressions.

❑ The **comparison** operators are used for comparing variables and expressions against other variables, constants, or expressions.

❑ The **logical** operators are used for performing logical operations on expressions; all logical operators can also be used as bitwise operators.

❑ The **bitwise** operators are used for comparing binary values bit-by-bit; all bitwise operators can also be used as logical operators.

A comprehensive list of all operators, their full syntax for usage, an explanation, notes, sample codes, and exceptions can be found in Appendix A.

Operator Precedence

When more than one operation occurs in an expression they are normally performed from left to right. However, there are several rules.

Operators from the arithmetic group are evaluated first, then concatenation, comparison and finally logical operators.

This is the set order in which operations occur (operators in brackets have the same precedence):

^, -, (*, /), \, Mod, (+, -),
&,
=, <>, <, >, <=, >=, Is,
Not, And, Or, Xor, Eqv, Imp

This order can be overridden by using parentheses. Operations in parentheses are evaluated before operations outside the parentheses, but inside the parentheses, the normal precedence rules apply.
If we look at two statements:

```
A = 5 + 6 * 7 + 8
A = (5 + 6) * (7 + 8)
```

According to operator precedence, multiplication is performed before addition, so the top line gives A the value 55. By adding parentheses, we force additions to be evaluated first and A becomes equal to 165.

Organizing and Reusing Code

So far, the scripts we have been working with have been fairly simple in structure. The code has been all together in one unit. We haven't been doing anything all that complicated, so it has been easy to see all the code right there in front of you, all in a few lines. The execution of the code starts at the top, with the first line, and then continues downward until it reaches the last line. At some points, we have redirected the code using branching, or repeated sections of code using loops. Pretty straightforward.

However, when you actually sit down to write a script that will do something useful, chances are your code is going to get a bit more complex. As you add more and more code, it becomes harder and harder to read it all in one chunk. If printed on paper, your scripts would probably stretch across multiple pages. As the code gets more and more complex, it becomes easier and easier for bugs to creep in, which makes it harder and harder to find and fix those bugs. The most common technique that programmers use to manage complexity is called **modularization**. That's a big, fancy word, but the concept is simple really.

Modularization is the process of organizing your code into **modules**, which we can also think of as building blocks. You can apply the principles of modularity to create your own personal set of programming building blocks, which you can then use to build programs that are more powerful, more reliable, and easier for you and your fellow programmers to maintain. When you divide your code into modules, your goal is to create what are known as **black boxes**. A black box is any kind of device that has a simple, well defined interface and that performs some discrete, well defined function. A black box is so called because you don't need to see what is going on inside of it. All you need to know is what it does, what its inputs are, and (sometimes) what its outputs are.

We encounter black boxes every day. A wrist watch is a good example. A typical watch has some buttons or dials with which you can set the time (the inputs), and a face that you can read to determine the time at any given moment (the outputs). You don't need to know or care how all the gears and gizmos inside the watch are put together in order for the watch to be useful to you. Unless you're an aficionado or collector of watches, you don't really care if it has quartz movement or if there's a small rodent running around inside to keep the watch ticking. It's a black box. All that's important to you are that it works, and that you understand its inputs and outputs.

The most basic kind of black box programmers use to achieve modularity is the **procedure**. A procedure is a set of code that (ideally) performs a single function. We have been using procedures throughout this chapter, but they have been procedures that VBScript provides for us. Some of these procedures require input, some don't. Some of these procedures return a value, some don't. But all of the procedures we have used so far (MsgBox(), Trim(), InputBox(), etc.) are black boxes. They perform one single well defined function, and they perform it without your having to worry about *how* they perform their respective functions. In just a moment, we're going to learn how to extend the VBScript language by writing our own procedures.

First, though, let's get some terminology straight. "Procedure" is a generic term that can be used to describe either a **function** or a **subprocedure**. We touched on some of this confusing terminology earlier, but a function is a procedure that returns a value. Trim() is a function. You pass it some text, and it returns the same text back to you, but with the leading and trailing spaces stripped off. Functions do not always require input, but they often do.

A subprocedure is a procedure that does not return a value. We have been using MsgBox() as a subprocedure. We pass it some text, and it displays a message on the screen. It does not return any kind of value to our code. All we need to know is that it did what we asked it to do. Like functions, procedure may or may not require input.

> **More confusing terminology: the term "module" is often used generically to describe any set of code that is set off as its own black box. However, the term "module" has a specific meaning in some programming languages. For instance, in Visual Basic, a module is a set of related procedures that are all stored in one file with the extension .BAS. You have to determine the exact meaning from the context in which the term is used.**

Let's take some familiar code and turn it into a function.

```
Function GetUserName
   'Prompts the user for his name. If the user refuses to provide
   'his name five times, we give up and return a zero-length string.

   Dim UserName
   Dim TryAgain
   Dim LoopCount

   LoopCount = 1
   Do
     TryAgain = "No"

     UserName = InputBox("Please enter your name:")

     UserName = Trim(UserName)
     If UserName = "" Then
       If LoopCount > 5 Then
         UserName = ""
         TryAgain = "No"
       Else
         MsgBox "You must enter your name."
         TryAgain = "Yes"
       End If
     End If

     LoopCount = LoopCount + 1

   Loop While TryAgain = "Yes"

   GetUserName = UserName

End Function
```

The first thing to take note of here are the first and last lines. The first line defines the beginning of the function and gives it a name. The last line defines the end of the function. Based on our earlier discussion of code blocks, this should be a familiar convention by now. In a sense, a procedure is nothing but a special kind of code block. We have to tell the script engine where it begins, and where it ends. Notice that we have given the function a clear, useful name that precisely describes what this function does. Giving your procedures good names is a key to writing programs that are easy to read and maintain.

The code inside the function is very similar to the code we used in the discussion of loops. We have introduced one new element, though: the LoopCount variable. We are using this variable to count the number of times we go through the loop. Before we start the loop, we initialize LoopCount with the numeric value of zero. Then, at the beginning of each loop, we increment the value of LoopCount by 1. If we go through the loop more than five times without the user entering his name, we stop asking and set the user name to a blank string (represented by " ").

The reason we added the loop counter to the code is that our goal is to create a perfect black box. A perfect black box is very predictable. When we write a procedure, we want it to be as predictable as possible. The more predictable it is, the less the code that calls the procedure has to worry about it. If the user is being difficult and does not want to enter his name, we don't want to keep looping around forever, asking again and again. So after asking five times, the function gives up and returns a zero-length string.

We also added a comment to the beginning of the procedure to describe what it does. Notice that the comment does not describe *how* the function does what it does, only *what* it does. The code that uses this function does not care how the function accomplishes its task – it only cares about inputs, outputs, and predictability. It is very important that you add comments such as this to the beginning of your procedures, since they make it easy to determine what the function does. This comment also performs one other valuable service to you and any other developer who wants to call this function: it mentions that the function may return an zero-length string if the user is does not enter his name. It is important that a programmer knows the possible range of return values so they can write code to deal with those contingencies.

Finally, notice how, in the second to last line, we treat the function name GetUserName as if it were a variable. When using functions (as opposed to subprocedures, which do not return a value), this is how you give the function its return value. In a sense, the function name itself *is* a variable within the procedure.

Let's take a look at some code that uses the GetUserName function.

```
Dim Greeting
Dim AnyName

AnyName = GetUserName

If Trim(AnyName) <> "" Then
    Greeting = "Hello, " & AnyName & ". Glad to meet you."
```

```
Else
  Greeting = "I'm glad to meet you, but I wish I knew your name."
End If

MsgBox Greeting
```

If you are using the Windows Script Host to execute this code, keep in mind that the above code and the `GetUserName` function itself must be in the same `.vbs` file. As you can see, calling the `GetUserName` function is pretty straightforward. Once you have written a procedure, calling it is no different than calling a built-in VBScript procedure.

Breaking your code into modular procedures is a very good habit to pick up. Even though moving code to a procedure is not mandatory, it's seldom a bad idea. According to Steve McConnell (as stated in his landmark book, *Code Complete* – see the Suggestions for Further Reading section at the end of this chapter):

> *"Aside from the computer itself, the routine is the single greatest invention in computer science. The routine makes programs easier to read and easier to understand than any other feature of any programming language...The routine makes modern programming possible."*

(You can mentally insert the word "procedure" wherever he uses the word "routine." They are the same thing.) Procedures afford several key advantages which are beyond the scope of this discussion. However, here are a few of the most important ones:

❑   Code such as the code we put in the `GetUserName` function can be thought of as "generic," meaning that it can be applied to a variety of uses. Once you have a discreet, well defined, generic function such as `GetUserName`, you can reuse it any time you wish to prompt the user for their name. Once you've written a well-tested procedure, you never have to write that code again. Any time you need it, you just call the procedure. This is known as **code reuse**.

❑   When you call a procedure to perform a task rather than writing the code "in-line," it makes that code easier to read and maintain. Increasing the **readability**, and therefore the **maintainability**, of your code is a good enough reason by itself to break a block of code out into its own procedure. Not including the comments and blank lines, the `GetUserName` function contains 19 lines of code. By taking those 19 lines and moving them to their own procedure, we reduced the code from which we moved it by 19 lines. Less code + good procedure name = easier to read. If ever you're writing some code that is getting rather long, consider breaking one or more sections of it out into their own functions or subprocedures.

❑   When code is isolated into its own procedure, it greatly reduces the effects of changes to that code. This goes back to the idea of the black box. As long as the procedure itself maintains its predictable inputs and outputs, changes to the code inside of a procedure are insulated from harming the code that calls the procedure. If we decide we don't want to use a loop anymore in the `GetUserName` function, we can change the code to only ask the user his name once instead of five times. The code that calls the `GetUserName` function won't care.

Writing procedures in VBScript is a big subject that we will discuss further in Chapter 3.

Top-Down vs. Event Driven

Before we wrap up this fast-paced introduction to programming, it will be helpful to shed light on the fact that you will encounter two different "models" of programming in this book: top-down programs and event-driven programs. The differences between top-down and event-driven have to do with both the way you organize your code and how and when that code gets executed at runtime. As you get deeper into programming in general, and VBScript in particular, this will become more clear, so don't be alarmed if it does not completely sink in right now.

What we have been doing so far in this chapter is writing very simple top-down style programs. We write some code, save it in a script file, and use the Windows Script Host to execute the script. The Script Host starts executing at the first line and continues to the last line. If a script file contains some procedure definitions (such as our GetUserName function), then the Script Host will only execute those procedures if some other code calls them. Once the Script Host reaches the last line of code, the lifetime of the script ends.

Top-down programs are very useful for task-oriented scripts. For example, you might write a script to search your hard drive for all the files with the extension .DOC and copy them to a backup directory. Or you might write a script that gets executed every time Windows starts that randomly chooses a different desktop wallpaper bitmap file for that session of Windows. Top-down programming is perfect for these kinds of scripts.

Event driven code is different, and is useful in different contexts. As the name implies, event-driven code only gets executed when a certain "event" occurs. Until that event occurs, the code won't get executed. If a given event does not occur during the lifetime of the script, the code associated with that event won't get executed at all. If an event occurs, and there's no code associated with the event at all, the event is essentially ignored.

Event driven programming is the predominant paradigm in Windows programming. Most Windows programs that you use every day were written in the event driven model. This is because of the graphical nature of Windows programs. In a **graphical user interface** (GUI), you have all sorts of buttons, drop-down lists, fields in which to type text, etc. Every time a user clicks a button, chooses an item in a list, or types some text into a field, an event is "raised" within the script. The person who wrote that program may or may not have decided to write code in response to that event.

When a GUI-based program starts, there is almost always some top-down style code that executes first. This code would do things like connect to a database, prompt the user for a name and password, load some settings from a file or the Windows registry, etc. Then a "form" typically comes up. The form contains the menus, buttons, lists, and fields that make up the user interface of the program. At that point, the top-down style code is done, and the program enters what is known as a **wait state**. No code is executing at this point. The program is just sitting there, waiting for the user to do something. From here on in, it's all about events.

Lets say the user clicks on a button. Now the program comes to life again. The program raises the "Click" event for the button that the user clicked. The code that is attached to that event starts to execute, performs some operations, and when it's finished, the program returns to its wait state. Until another event occurs, the program just sits there.

As far as VBScript, the event driven model is used heavily in scripting for the World Wide Web. The scripts that run inside of HTML pages are all based on events. One script might execute when the page is loaded. Another script might execute when the user clicks on a button or graphic. These "mini scripts" are embedded in the HTML file, and are blocked out in a syntax very similar to the one we used to define the GetUserName function in the previous section of this chapter.

As you progress through the second half of this book, the finer points of event driven programming will become much clearer to you. However, just so you can see an example at this point, type the code below into your text editor, save the file with a .HTM extension, and then select Open from the File menu in Internet Explorer 4.0 or higher to open the file.

```
<HTML>
<HEAD>
<Script language="vbscript">
  Sub ButtonClicked
    window.alert("You clicked the button.")
  End Sub
</Script>
</HEAD>
<BODY>
  <BUTTON name="SomeButton" type=BUTTON onclick="ButtonClicked">
  Click Me
  </BUTTON>
</BODY>
</HTML>
```

Some Guidelines to Keep in Mind

It's a really good idea to start adopting good habits right from the beginning. Down the road, as you continue to hone your programming skills and even learn multiple languages, these habits will serve you well. Your programs will be easier for you and your fellow programmers to read, understand, and modify, and they will have fewer bugs. When you first get started writing code, you have to concentrate so hard on getting the syntax correct for the computer that its easy to lose sight of the things you need to do to make sure your programs are human friendly as well. However, diligence in this area will pay big dividends.

Expect the unexpected

Always remember that anything can and will happen. Code defensively. You don't need to obsess over contingencies and remote possibilities, but you can't ignore them either. You especially have to worry about the unexpected when receiving input from the user, from a database, or from a file. Whenever you're about to perform an action on something, ask yourself, "What could go wrong here? What happens if the file is flagged Read Only? What happens if the database table does not have any records? What happens if the registry keys I was expecting aren't there?" If you don't know what might go wrong with a given operation, find out through research or trial and error. Don't leave it up to your users to discover how gracefully your script reacts to the unexpected. A huge part of properly preparing for the unexpected is the implementation of proper **error handling**, which we discuss in detail in Chapter 4.

Always favor the explicit over the implicit

When you are writing code, constantly ask yourself, "Is my intent clear to someone reading this code? Does the code speak for itself? Is there anything mysterious here? Are there any hidden meanings?" Even though something is obvious in your mind at the moment you are typing in the code, that does not mean that it will be obvious to you six months from now, or to someone else tomorrow. Strive to make your code self-documenting, and where you fall short of that goal (which even the best programmers do – self-documenting code can be an elusive goal), use good comments to make things more clear.

Modularize your code into procedures, modules, classes, and components

When you are writing code, you should constantly evaluate whether any given block of code might be better if you moved it to its own function or subprocedure. Is the code you're working on rather complex? Break it into procedures. Are you using lots of `And`'s and `Or`'s in an `If...End If` statement? Consider moving the evaluation to its own procedure. Are you writing a block of code that you think you might need again in some other part of the script, or in another script? Move it to its own procedure. Are you writing some code that you think someone else might find useful? Move it.

Give variables and procedures a descriptive name

Giving the elements of your programs good names is one of the most important things you can do to ensure that your code will be readable and easily understood. Primarily, this applies to the names you give to variables and procedures.

When naming a variable, use a name that will make it clear what that variable is used for. Be careful using abbreviations, especially if you think programmers from other countries might need to read your code. Don't make variable names too short, but don't make them too long either (studies have shown that 10 to 16 characters is a good length, but ideal length is largely a matter of preference). Even though VBScript is not case-sensitive, use mixed case (for example, `UserName`) to make it easier to distinguish multiple words within the variable name.

When naming procedures, try to choose a name that describes exactly what the procedure does. If the procedure is a function that returns a value, indicate what the return value is in the function name (for example, `GetUserName`). Try to use good verb-noun combinations to describe firstly, what action the procedure performs, and secondly, what the action is performed on (for example `SearchDirectory`, `MakeUniqueFileName`, or `LoadSettings`). Studies show that, since procedures are generally more complicated than variables, good procedure names tend to be longer than good variable names. Don't go out of your way to make them longer, but don't be afraid to either. 15 to 30 characters for a procedure name is perfectly acceptable (they can be a bit longer since you generally don't type them nearly as much). If you are having trouble giving your procedure a good name, that might be an indication that the procedure is not narrow enough – a good procedure does *one* thing, and does it well.

That said, if you are writing scripts for web pages that will be downloaded to a user's browser, it is sometimes necessary to use shorter variable and procedure names. Longer names mean larger files to download. Even if you sacrifice some readability in order to make the file smaller, you can still make an effort to make the names as descriptive as possible.

Use the "Hungarian" variable naming convention

This is a bit out of scope of this introductory discussion, but it bears mentioning nonetheless. The concepts of variable **data types** and **scope** will be discussed in Chapter 2. The Hungarian naming convention involves giving variable names a prefix that indicates what the scope and data type of the variable are intended to be. So as not to confuse matters, we have not been using the Hungarian convention in this chapter, but you will find that most programmers prefer this convention. Properly used, it makes your programs more clear and easier to read and write. We list the standard prefixes for scope and data type in Appendix B.

Don't use one variable for multiple purposes

This is a common mistake of beginner and experienced programmers alike, but the fact that experienced programmers might have a bad habit does not make it any less bad. Each variable in your script should have *exactly one* purpose. It may be tempting to just declare a couple of generic variables with fuzzy names, and then use them for multiple purposes throughout your script – but don't do it! This is one of the best ways to introduce very strange, hard to track down bugs into your scripts. Giving a variable a good name that clearly defines its purpose will help prevent you from using it for multiple purposes.

Always indent your code properly, and use white space to make your code easier to read and understand

Keep in mind the power that the visual layout of your code has on its clarity. Without reading a single word, you should be able to look at the indentations of the lines to see which ones are subordinate to others. Keep related code together by keeping them on consecutive lines. Separate blocks of unrelated code by putting a blank line between them. Even though the script engine will let you, avoid putting multiple statements on the same line.

Use the line continuation character (_) to break long lines into multiple shorter lines. The importance of a clean layout that visually suggests the logic of the code cannot be overemphasized.

Use comments to make your code more clear and readable, but don't overuse them

When writing code, strive to make it self documenting. You can do this by following the guidelines above. However, self documenting code is elusive quarry. Like the pot of gold at the end of the rainbow, you can never quite reach it, even though it seems so close. The remedy for this is good comments. What separates a good comment from a bad comment?

Generally speaking, a good comment operates at the level of intent. A good comment answers the questions, "What was the programmer trying to do with this code? Where does this code fit in with the overall scheme of the script? Why does this code exist?" The answers to these questions fill in the blanks that can never be filled by even the best self-documenting code. Good comments are also generally "paragraph-level" comments. Your code should be clear enough that you do not need a comment for every line, but a comment that quickly and clearly describes the purpose for a block of code allows a reader to scan through the comments rather than reading every line of code. The idea is to keep the person who might be reading your code from having to pore over every line to try and figure out why the code exists.

Bad comments are generally redundant comments, meaning they repeat what the code itself already tells you. Try to make your code as clear as possible so that you don't need to repeat yourself with comments. Redundant comments tend to add clutter and do more harm then good. Reading the code tells you the *how*; reading the comments should tell you the *why*.

Finally, it's a good idea to get into the habit of adding "tombstone" or "flower box" comments at the top of each script file, module, class, and procedure. These comments typically describe the purpose of the code, the date it was created , the original author, and a log of modifications.

Suggestions for Further Reading

There are two areas you must concentrate on in order to become a great programmer: mastering the fundamentals of the art and science of programming, and mastering the particulars of the language and platform with which you are working. The goal of this book is to take care of the latter. We hope that this book will be a valuable tool for you as you learn VBScript, as well as an essential reference when you need to look up a specific piece of information.

However, the general art and science of software development is outside the scope of this book. These are the skills that stay with you no matter what language you are working with. We hope that this short chapter will enable you to get the most out of this book, VBScript, and Microsoft's awesome scripting technologies. However, if you crave more knowledge on the skills that separate the professionals from the pretenders, these sources should be of help. All of these resources are well worth your time, but if you only read one of them, make sure it's *Code Complete*.

- *Code Complete*, by Steve McConnell, Microsoft Press, 1993

- Rapid Development, by Steve McConnell, Microsoft Press, 1996

- Programming Pearls, by Jon Louis Bentley, Addison-Wesley, 1985

- The Psychology of Computer Programming, by Gerald Weinberg, Dorset House, "Silver Anniversary" edition released 1998

- The Mythical Man-Month, by Frederick Brooks, Addison-Wesley, "Anniversary Edition" released 1995

- Peopleware, by Tom DeMarco, Dorset House, 2nd edition released 1999

Variables and Data Types

This chapter will introduce VBScript variables and data types. If you feel you might need a primer on how programming in general is done, you might want to read Chapter 1 before starting here. Chapters 2 and 3 cover many of the same topics that Chapter 1 does, but in Chapters 2 and 3, we cover the specific VBScript elements that support variables, data types, and control of flow – the most basic building blocks of programming. Chapter 1 covers these topics in a more general way, with the aim of initiating someone who has never written any computer programs or scripts before. If you are already experienced with programming in another language, but have never used VBScript, you can probably skip Chapter 1, but Chapters 2 and 3 will cover essential VBScript-specific topics.

The Visual Basic Data Types

Strictly speaking, VBScript only has one data type: the Variant. The Variant is a special data type that can store many different **subtypes**. We're going to get to the Variant data type in the next section, but first we need to discuss the data types of VBScript's parent language, Visual Basic. You may be wondering why we need to discuss another language's data types when VBScript only supports the Variant. This is certainly a legitimate question.

The reason is that in order to fully understand the behavior of the Variant, it is essential that you understand that the Variant is merely a "container" for several different data types. Each of the Visual Basic data types listed below can be stored inside of the Variant as a **subtype**. A Variant's subtype changes automatically depending on what kind of value is stored in it, or you can manually set the subtype with one of the VBScript **conversion functions**. This becomes especially important when your VBScript programs need to interact with COM components that may have been written in VB or another COM-enabled language, such as C++ or Delphi. (We will cover VBScript interaction with COM objects in Chapters 5 and 6; and in Chapters 8 and 9, we'll show you how to build your own COM classes and components using VBScript and XML.)

The first question that needs answering is why a data type is important. Under the hood, data types are important because different data types are stored in different amounts of memory. As a VBScript programmer, you don't need to be concerned with this sort of detail, but it's useful to know that one data type might take more or less memory than another, which is one of the reasons Visual Basic developers will choose one data type over another – the less memory taken up, the better. Choosing a specific data type is also important to a Visual Basic developer because it helps make the program easier to understand. When you know what data type a variable or parameter is, you also know the limitations on what kind of data is meant to be stored in that variable.

A Visual Basic variable declared with one of the numeric data types would take up either one, two, or four bytes of memory, depending on whether it had the Byte, Integer, or Long data type, respectively. A Long variable with a value of 1 takes up the exact same four bytes of memory that a Long variable with a value of 2,000,000 does. What's different is the *range* of numeric values that each of the numeric types can support. Because a Long variable takes up more memory than an Integer variable, larger (and smaller, in the case of negative numbers) can be stored in a Long. The Visual Basic String data type, on the other hand, takes up a different amount of memory depending on how much text is stored in it. A small amount of text (such as the word "Hello") stored in a String variable would only take up a small amount of memory, whereas the a String variable with all of Shakespeare's sonnets stored in it would take up considerably more memory.

The data type is also important for another reason: certain types of operations can only be performed on certain data types. For example, before you can perform addition, subtraction, or multiplication on a variable, it must be a numeric data type. This allows the compiler and runtime engine to treat the variable as a number and perform mathematical operations on it. By declaring a variable with one of the numeric data types, you ensure that only numbers will be stored in it, and you can perform mathematical operations on that variable without having to worry about whether the variable actually has a numeric value.

So without further ado, here are the standard Visual Basic data types.

Data Type	Storage Required	Range of Allowable Values	Comments
Byte	1 Byte	0 to 255	Often used to store binary data in the form of a "Byte array"
Integer	2 Bytes	-32,768 to 32,767	None
Long	4 Bytes	-2,147,483,648 to 2,147,483,647	The most commonly used numeric data type

Data Type	Storage Required	Range of Allowable Values	Comments
`Single`	4 Bytes	**Negative values:** `-3.402823E38` to `-1.401298E-45`; **Positive values:** `1.401298E-45` to `3.402823E38`	For storing IEEE 32-bit single precision floating point numbers (in other words, numbers with decimals)
`Double`	8 Bytes	**Negative values:** `-1.79769313486232E 308` to `-4.94065645 841247E-324`; **Positive values:** `4.94065645841247 E-324` to `1.79769 313486232E308`	For storing IEEE 64-bit double precision floating point numbers; offers greater precision than the `Single`
`Currency`	8 Bytes	`-922,337,203,685, 477.5808` to `922,337 ,203,685,477.5807`	Automatically rounds to four decimal places

`Decimal`	14 Bytes	**with no decimal point:**
		
		`+/-79,228,162,514, 264,337,593,543, 950,335;`
		
		with 28 decimal places:
		
		`+/-7.9228162514264 337593543950335;`
		
		smallest non-zero number:
		
		`+/-0.000000000000 0000000000000001`
			Can only be stored in a variant; use when maximum floating point accuracy is needed

`Boolean`	2 Bytes	`True` or `False`	Only has two possible values; `False` can also be represented as zero (0), and `True` can also be represented as –1 (or, really, any non-zero value; Often used as a Success/Failure return value for functions; Also very common for routine parameters

Table Continued on Following Page

Data Type	Storage Required	Range of Allowable Values	Comments
String	10 Bytes + String Length	0 to approximately 2 billion	Can be used to store any kind of text characters, numbers, or symbols
Date	8 Bytes	January 1, 100 to December 31, 9999	When displayed, by default uses the Windows "Short Date" format setting
Object	4 Bytes	Any Object Reference	A generic data type that can hold a "late bound" reference to any COM object.
Variant	16 or 22 Bytes	Any data within the range of any of the above data types	Takes up 16 bytes when storing numeric data, 22 bytes when storing string data. Can have a different "subtype" depending on the type of value stored within it; also takes up a little more space when storing an array.

Note that the Object data type is generic and can hold a reference to any kind of object. Object references stored in a variable of the Object data type are said to be **late bound**, meaning that the object's interface cannot be resolved until runtime. Variables and routine parameters can also be declared as a specific object type. Variables of this sort are said to be **early bound**, meaning that the interface of the object was known at compile time. A late-bound Variant object variable can be passed to a VBScript procedure that uses an early bound parameter. That said, we are not going to be discussing objects in this chapter.

Also, if you are already familiar with the Visual Basic data types, you may have noticed that we did not include the "fixed length" String data type in our list. This is because fixed length strings cannot be stored in a Variant, and we are primarily interested in the data types that can be used as Variant subtypes.

In the next section you will see how these Visual Basic data types map to the subtypes of the Variant. Even though VBScript does not directly support declaring variables with these specific data types, you can use the Variant subtypes to simulate this feature.

The Variant: VBScript's Only Data Type

As we said in the previous section, the Variant is the only data type supported in VBScript. Programmers in another language who are accustomed to using a language that offers a wide range of data types might find this disconcerting. However, the good news is that the Variant is also very flexible. Because of the Variant's ability to store many different data types, your scripts can handle just about any kind of data you need: numbers, strings (text), and dates, plus other more complex data types such as objects and arrays.

This flexibility comes at a price, however. One downside of the Variant is that takes up more memory than many of the specific Visual Basic data types. For this reason, Visual Basic developers will normally only choose to declare a variable as a Variant when they specifically want that variable to be able to handle more than one data type. After all, why take up more memory than you have to?

Another downside of Variant variables is that you as a programmer must sometimes pay close attention to what the Variant subtype is at any given moment. This is because of something called **implicit type coercion**, which is what happens when a Variant variable changes its subtype automatically. Implicit type coercion occurs when you assign a new value to a Variant variable that is different than the value currently stored within it. The Variant variable "coerces" the subtype into another subtype based on the type of data assigned to it. Before we get into how and when Variant subtypes change, lets take a look at the possible subtypes a Variant can have.

Subtype	Visual Basic Data Type Equivalent	Conversion Function to Force the Subtype	Test Function (other than VarType and TypeName)	VarType() Function Return Value (with Named Constant Equivalent)	TypeName() Function Return Value
Empty	N/A	N/A	IsEmpty()	0 (vbEmpty)	Empty
Null	N/A	N/A	IsNull()	1 (vbNull)	Null
Long	Long	CLng()	IsNumeric()	2 (vbLong)	Long
Integer	Integer	CInt()	IsNumeric()	3 (vbInteger)	Integer
Single	Single	CSng()	IsNumeric()	4 (vbSingle)	Single
Double	Double	CDbl()	IsNumeric()	5 (vbDouble)	Double
Currency	Currency	CCur()	IsNumeric()	6 (vbCurrency)	Currency
Date	Date	CDate()	IsDate()	7 (vbDate)	Date
String	String	CStr()	None	8 (vbString)	String
Object	Object	N/A	IsObject()	9 (vbObject)	Object
Error	N/A	*	None	10 (vbError)	Error
Boolean	Boolean	CBool()	None	11 (vbBoolean)	Boolean
Variant	Variant	CVar()	None	12 (vbVariant)	Variant
Decimal	N/A	*	IsNumeric()	14 (vbDecimal)	Decimal$
Byte	Byte	CByte()	IsNumeric()	17 (vbByte)	Byte
Array	N/A	N/A	IsArray()	8192 (vbArray)*	Array

* - Visual Basic supports conversion functions for the Error and Decimal subtypes called CVErr() and CDec(), respectively. VBScript, however, does not support these conversion functions. See the sidebar later in this section for more information.

$ - Because of a bug in VBScript, the TypeName() function does not support the Decimal subtype (although VarType() does). See the sidebar later in this section for more information.

- This value is actually returned from the VarType() function in combination with the value for Variant (12). See the section on arrays at the end of this chapter.

We filled this table up with a whole bunch of information so that it will be available for your future reference, but for the moment, focus on just the first two columns. As you can see, there are sixteen subtypes that are supported by the VBScript Variant. Most of these correspond exactly to the Visual Basic data types that we looked at in the previous section. This is good news for you, because it means that if your VBScript code has to pass or receive values to or from a component written in Visual Basic (or another COM-enabled language), the Variant subtypes will be able to accommodate you.

Testing For and Coercing Subtypes

There are two built-in VBScript functions that allow you to check what the subtype is for any Variant variable. These functions are VarType() and TypeName(). These two functions do pretty much the same thing, but VarType() returns a numeric representation of the subtype and TypeName() returns a string representation. Take a look at the last two columns of this table and you'll see the different values that VarType() and TypeName() will return for each of the subtypes. Notice also that there are **named constant** equivalents for each of the values that VarType() returns.

> A named constant is similar to a variable, in that it represents a certain value, but constants cannot be changed at runtime like variables can. You can use a named constant in place of an actual value, which improves the understandability of your code. For example, it's much clearer to write
>
> ```
> If VarType(MyVariable) = vbString Then
> ```
>
> rather than
>
> ```
> If VarType(MyVariable) = 8 Then
> ```
>
> VBScript comes with some built-in named constants, and you can also declare your own. We cover constants later in this chapter.

As you can see in the third column of the table, VBScript also provides some functions that you can use to force (or "coerce") the Variant to have a specific subtype. These conversion functions are especially useful when you need to pass data of a certain data type to a VB/COM object that expects data of a specific data type. This is also useful when you want to ensure that the value stored in a Variant variable is treated in a certain way. For example, the value 12 can be stored in a Variant variable with either a String subtype or one of the numeric subtypes. If you want to make sure that the number 12 is treated as a number, and not a string, you can use the CLng() conversion function to make sure that the subtype is Long and not String.

A Variant variable automatically chooses its subtype whenever you place a new value into it. It does this by examining the value placed into and making its best guess as to what the appropriate subtype is. Sometimes, though, the Variant's "best guess" is not quite what you expect. However, you can control this by being careful and explicit in your code. Let's look at some code examples that will demonstrate the principles that we have been talking about here.

All of the examples in this chapter are tailored so that they can be run by the Windows Script Host. The Windows Script Host is a scripting host that allows you to run VBScript programs within Windows. WSH will allow you to try these example programs out for yourself. You may already have WSH installed. To find out, type the example script shown below into a text editor, save the file as TEST.VBS, and double click the file in Windows Explorer. If the script runs, then you're all set. If Windows does not recognize the file, then you'll need to download and install WSH from http://msdn.microsoft.com/scripting.

If you like, you can skip ahead briefly and check out the beginning sections of Chapter 10. You don't need to read the whole chapter, just the first sections, which describe how to install the Windows Script Host, and how to use WSH to run scripts.

```
Dim varTest
varTest = "Hello There"
MsgBox TypeName(varTest)
```

Running this code results in the following dialog box:

This makes sense. We placed a text (a.k.a. "string") value into the variable varTest, and VBScript appropriately decided that that the variable should have the String subtype.

You may have noticed that we named the variable in the above code example varTest. This might look strange if you have not seen "Hungarian Notation" before. Hungarian Notation defines the practice of placing prefixes in front of variable names in order to convey the data type of the variable, as well as its "scope". (We will discuss scope later in this chapter.) It might seem unnecessary to include a data type prefix since VBScript only supports one data type, the Variant. However, data type prefixes for Variant variables are just as useful and important, or even more so, as they are for languages that support specific data types. This is because Variant variables can hold virtually *any* kind of data.

Therefore, a data type prefix can tell you the programmer (and other programmers who are reading or modifying your code) what type of data you *intend* for a variable to hold. In other words, Variant variables *can* hold any kind of data, but in practice, any given variable *should* generally only hold one kind of data. This is not an absolute, as there are certainly legitimate circumstances under which you would intend for a variable to be able to hold multiple data types. By placing a data type prefix in front of your variable name, you make it absolutely clear what type of data you intend for that variable to hold, even if you intend for it to, or expect that it might need to, hold multiple types of data. Here is a short list of data type prefixes that are commonly used (see Appendix C):

```
var  - Variant
str  - String
int  - Integer
lng  - Long
byt  - Byte
sng  - Single
dbl  - Double
cur  - Currency
obj  - Object
bool - Boolean
```

The `var` prefix is best used when you don't know exactly what type of data might end up in the variable, or when you intend for that variable to hold all kinds of data. This is why we're using the `var` prefix often in this chapter where we're doing all sorts of playing around with data types.

Dealing with string values such as "Hello There" is generally straightforward – unless your string value looks like a number, as in the following examples.

```
Dim varTest
varTest = "12"
MsgBox TypeName(varTest)
```

Running this code results in the exact same dialog box:

Why does the `TypeName()` function return "String" when we clearly passed it a numeric value of 12? This is because we placed the value 12 in quotes. By placing it in quotes, we told VBScript to treat the value as a string, not a number. Here are three variations that will tell VBScript that we mean for the value to be treated as a number:

```
Dim varTest
varTest = 12
MsgBox TypeName(varTest)
```

```
Dim varTest
varTest = CInt("12")
MsgBox TypeName(varTest)
```

```
Dim varTest
varTest = "12"
varTest = CInt(varTest)
MsgBox TypeName(varTest)
```

All three of these examples result in the same dialog box:

All three of these examples achieve the same thing: coercing the `varTest` variable to have the `Integer` subtype. The first example results in the `Integer` subtype because we did not enclose the value 12 in quotes, as we did in the first example. This tells VBScript that we want the number to be treated as a number, not as text. The second example uses the `CInt()` conversion function to transform the string value `"12"` into an integer value *before* placing it in the variable. This tells the VBScript that we want the subtype to be `Integer` right from the start. The third example does the conversion after the fact. Any of these is a valid way to make sure that the value we are placing in the variable is treated as a numeric `Integer` value. However, the first example is might be better because it is theoretically faster because we're not making the extra call to the `CInt()` function.

Note that this code would be redundant:

```
Dim varTest
varTest = CInt(12)
```

Because we do not have quotes around the `12`, it will subtype will automatically be `Integer`. However, this code has a different effect:

```
Dim varTest
varTest = CLng(12)
```

This tells VBScript to make sure that the subtype of the variable is `Long`. The same numeric value of 12 is stored in the variable, but instead of being classified as an `Integer`, it is classified as a `Long`. This would be significant if you were passing the value to a VB/COM function that required a `Long`.

By default, the Variant subtype will be `Integer` when a whole number within the `Integer` range is placed in the variable. However, if you place a whole number outside of this range into the variable, it will choose the `Long` subtype, which has a much larger range (-2,147,483,648 to 2,147,483,647). You will find that the `Long` data type is used far more often than the `Integer` in VB/COM components and ActiveX controls, so you may need to use the `CLng()` function often to coerce your Variant subtypes to match, although this is not always necessary – when you are passing Variant variables to a COM/VB function, VBScript often takes care of the type coercion for you implicitly (more on this later in the chapter).

Given that VBScript chooses the `Integer` subtype by default instead of the `Long`, you would also expect it to choose the `Single` by default instead of the `Double` when placing floating point numbers into a Variant variable, since the `Single` takes up less resources than the `Double`. However, this is not the case. When floating point numbers (that is, numbers with decimal places) are assigned to a Variant variable, the default subtype is `Double`.

Also, as we'll see later, in the section called "Implicit Type Coercion", when you are placing the result of a mathematical expression into an uninitialized Variant variable, VBScript will choose the `Double` subtype.

Let's look at a similar example, this time using date/time values.

```
Dim varTest
varTest = "5/16/99 12:30 PM"
MsgBox TypeName(varTest)
```

Running this code results in the following dialog box:

The variable assignment results in a subtype of `String`, although you might expect it to be `Date`. We get the `String` subtype because we put the date/time value in quotes. We saw this principle in action in the previous set of examples when we put the number 12 in quotes in the variable assignment. Once again, there are different ways that we can force the subtype to be `Date` instead of `String`:

```
Dim varTest
varTest = #5/16/99 12:30 PM#
MsgBox TypeName(varTest)
```
Or:
```
Dim varTest
varTest = CDate("5/16/99 12:30 PM")
MsgBox TypeName(varTest)
```

Running either of these examples produces the following dialog box:

The first example surrounds the date/time value in # signs instead of quotes. This is the VBScript way of identifying a date **literal** (*VB/VBA uses this convention as well*). A literal is any value that's expressed directly in your code, as opposed to being expressed via a variable or named constant. The number 12 and the string "Hello There" that we used in previous examples are also literals. By enclosing the date/time in # signs rather than quotes, we are telling VBScript to treat the value as a date, not as a string. As a result, when the date literal gets stored in the variant variable, the subtype comes out as Date. The second example uses the CDate() conversion function to achieve the same thing. Once again, the first version is theoretically faster since it does not require an extra function call.

Often you are not exactly sure what type of data a variable might hold initially, and you need to be sure of what type of data it is before you try to use a conversion function on it. This is because using a conversion function on the wrong type of data can cause a runtime error. For example, try this code:

```
Dim varTest
varTest = "Hello"
varTest = CLng(varTest)
```

This code will cause a runtime error on line 3: "Type Mismatch". Not a nice thing to happen when your code is trying to accomplish something. Obviously, this little code sample is pretty silly, because we knew that the variable contained a String when we tried to convert it to a Long. However, you often do not have control over what value ends up in a variable. This is especially true when you are:

❑ accepting input from the user

❑ reading data from a database

❑ reading data from a file

You can often get around these Type Mismatch errors by using one of the "Is" functions that are listed in the fourth column of the variant subtypes table from a few pages back. For example, here is some code that asks the user his age. Since we don't have any control over what the user types in, we need to verify that he actually typed in a number:

```
Dim lngAge
lngAge = InputBox("Please enter your age in years.")
If IsNumeric(lngAge) Then
    lngAge = CLng(lngAge)
    lngAge = lngAge + 50
    MsgBox "In 50 years, you will be " & CStr(lngAge) & " years old."
Else
    MsgBox "Sorry, but you did not enter a valid number."
End If
```

Notice how we use the `IsNumeric()` function to test whether or not the user actually entered a valid number. Since we're planning to use the `CLng()` function to coerce the subtype, we want to avoid a Type Mismatch error. What we have not stated explicitly is that the subtype of the variable does not have to be numeric in order for `IsNumeric()` to return `True`. `IsNumeric()` examines the actual value of the variable, rather than its subtype. The subtype of the variable and the value of the variable are two different things. This behavior is actually what allows us to use `IsNumeric()` to avoid a Type Mismatch error. If `IsNumeric()` examined the subtype, it would not work as we have been using it. In line three of the above example, the subtype of the `lngAge` variable is `String`, yet `IsNumeric()` returns `True` if the variable has a number in it. That's because `IsNumeric()` is considering the value of `lngAge`, not the subtype. We can test the *value* before trying to convert the variable's subtype to a different subtype. The function `IsDate()` works in exactly the same way:

```
Dim datBirth
datBirth = InputBox("Please enter the date on which you were born.")
If IsDate(datBirth) Then
    datBirth = CDate(datBirth)
    MsgBox "You were born on day " & Day(datBirth) & _
        " of month " & Month(datBirth) & " in the year " & _
        Year(datBirth) & "."
Else
    MsgBox "Sorry, but you did not enter a valid date."
End If
```

`Day()`, `Month()`, and `Year()` are built-in VBScript functions that you can use to return the different parts of a date. These functions are covered in detail in Appendix A.

Note, however, that not all of the "Is" functions work strictly on the value, as `IsNumeric()` and `IsDate()` do. The functions `IsEmpty()`, `IsNull()`, and `IsObject()` examine the subtype of the variable, not the value. We will cover these three functions later in the chapter.

Please note that this line of code:

```
If IsNumeric(lngAge) Then
```

Is functionally equivalent to this line:

```
If IsNumeric(lngAge) = True Then
```

Likewise, this line:

```
If Not IsNumeric(lngAge) Then
```

Is functionally equivalent to this line:

```
If IsNumeric(lngAge) = False Then
```

However, when using the `Not` operator, you want to be sure you are only using it in combination with expressions that return the `Boolean` values `True` or `False` (such as the `IsNumeric()` function). This is because the `Not` operator can also be used as a "bitwise" operator (see Appendix A) when used with numeric (non-`Boolean`) values.

Implicit Type Coercion

So far, we have been discussing *explicit* type coercion using conversion functions. We have not yet discussed a phenomenon called *implicit* type coercion. Implicit type coercion is when a Variant variable changes its subtype automatically. Sometimes, this can work in your favor, and sometimes it can present a problem.

Remember the example code that asks the user for his age that we used in the previous section? Here it is again:

```
Dim lngAge
lngAge = InputBox("Please enter your age in years.")
If IsNumeric(lngAge) Then
    lngAge = CLng(lngAge)
    lngAge = lngAge + 50
    MsgBox "In 50 years, you will be " & CStr(lngAge) & " years old."
Else
    MsgBox "Sorry, but you did not enter a valid number."
End If
```

Notice how we use the `CLng()` and `CStr()` functions to explicitly coerce the subtypes. Well, in the case of this particular code, these functions are not strictly necessary. The reason is that VBScript's implicit type coercion would have done approximately the same thing for us. Here's the code again, without the conversion functions.

```
Dim lngAge
lngAge = InputBox("Please enter your age in years.")
If IsNumeric(lngAge) Then
    lngAge = lngAge + 50
    MsgBox "In 50 years, you will be " & lngAge & " years old."
Else
    MsgBox "Sorry, but you did not enter a valid number."
End If
```

Because of implicit type coercion, this code works the same way as the original code. Take a look at the fifth line. We did not explicitly coerce the subtype to `Long`, but the math still works as you'd expect. Let's run this same code, but with some `TypeName()` functions thrown in so that we can watch the subtypes change:

```
Dim lngAge
lngAge = InputBox("Please enter your age in years.")
MsgBox "TypeName After InputBox:  " & TypeName(lngAge)
If IsNumeric(lngAge) Then
```

```
    lngAge = lngAge + 50
    MsgBox "TypeName After Adding 50:  " & TypeName(lngAge)
    MsgBox "In 50 years, you will be " & lngAge & " years old."
Else
    MsgBox "Sorry, but you did not enter a valid number."
End If
```

Is the user enters, for example, the number 30, this code will result in the following dialog boxes (in this order):

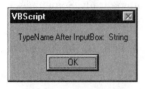

The first call to the `TypeName()` function shows that the subtype is `String`. That's because data coming back from the `InputBox` function is always treated as `String` data, even when the user types in a number. Remember that the `String` subtype can hold just about any kind of data. However, when numbers and dates and Boolean True/False values are stored in a variable with the `String` subtype, they are not treated as numbers or dates or as Boolean values – they are treated simply as strings of text with no special meaning. This is why, when our code tries to do math on the `String` value, VBScript must first coerce the subtype to a numeric one.

The second call to the `TypeName()` function comes *after* we add 50 to it, and shows that the subtype is `Double`. Wait a minute – `Double`? Why `Double`? Why not one of the whole number subtypes, such as `Integer` or `Long`? We didn't introduce any decimal places in this math? Why would VBScript implicitly coerce the subtype into `Double`? The answer is because VBScript determined that this was the best thing to do. Since we did not use a conversion function to explicitly tell VBScript to change the variable to one subtype or another, it evaluated the situation and chose the subtype that it thought was best. You have to be careful, because it can be tricky to predict exactly which subtype VBScript will choose.

However, does it really matter that VBScript coerced the variable into a `Double` instead of a `Long`? These are both numeric subtypes, and the math has exactly the same result. Why care? Well, it's not the end of the world, except that the `Double` subtype theoretically takes a little bit more processing power than the `Long`, because the `Double` is a floating point numeric subtype (floating point numbers require a greater degree of accuracy, and therefore the processor has to work a little harder to ensure that accuracy). If you were explicitly coercing the subtype, as in the code we started with, you might not choose the `Double`, because the `Double` is generally only used for very large or very small numbers. You might choose `Integer`, or `Long`, or even `Byte`. (That said, sometimes you need to care what the subtype is because you are planning to pass the variable to a method of a COM object that expects an explicit subtype.)

The point of this little exercise is not to debate whether one numeric subtype is better than another, rather to illustrate implicit type coercion. VBScript automatically knew that we wanted the value in the variable to be a number. It knew this because our code added 50 to the variable. VBScript says, "Oh, we're doing some math. I better change the subtype to a numeric one before I do the math, because I can't do math on strings." This is pretty straightforward. What isn't so straightforward is that it chose the `Double` subtype instead of `Long` or `Integer` or `Byte`.

We may never know the exact reason why VBScript chooses a `Double` in this situation, but it is probably a preventative measure. Other than the `Decimal` subtype, which is rarely used and only then for extremely large or extremely small numbers, the `Double` subtype is the most capable of holding large numbers. Rather than go to the trouble of figuring out the result of the math first, and then deciding on a subtype, VBScript just picks the most accommodating subtype, `Double`, so that it can be reasonably sure that the result of the math will fit in the variable. In other words, VBScript makes the safest choice.

> Before we move one, let's note that there is one other instance of implicit type coercion in our current example. The coercion is incidental, but useful to be aware of. It occurs on this line:
>
> ```
> MsgBox "In 50 years, you will be " & lngAge & " years old."
> ```
>
> At the time this line executes, we have just finished adding the number 50 to our variable, and the subtype is numeric. When we use the concatenation operator (&) to insert the value of the variable into the sentence, VBScript implicitly changes the subtype to `String`. This is similar to the way in which is changed the subtype from `String` to `Double` when we performed a mathematical operation on it. However, this coercion is not permanent. Since we did not assign a new value to the variable, the subtype does not change.

While you have to be aware of implicit type coercion, there is no reason to fear it. VBScript is not going to arbitrarily go around changing subtypes on you. Implicit type coercion only happens when you assign a new value to a variable that does not fit the current subtype. Generally, once a Variant variable has a subtype (based on the value first placed within it, or based on a subtype that your code explicitly coerced), it will keep that subtype as you place new values in the variable.

Where you do need to watch out for implicit type coercion is when you're dealing with a mixture of data types. We saw this in our example: when the data came back from the `InputBox()` function, it was a string. Then we did some math on it, which turned it into a number. Give this code a try:

```
Dim lngTest
lngTest = CLng(100)
MsgBox "TypeName after initialization: " & TypeName(lngTest)
lngTest = lngTest + 1000
```

```
MsgBox "TypeName after adding 1000: " & TypeName(lngTest)
lngTest = lngTest * 50
MsgBox "TypeName after multiplying by 50: " & TypeName(lngTest)
lngTest = "Hello"
MsgBox "TypeName after assigning value of 'Hello': " & TypeName(lngTest)
```

If you run this code, you'll see that the first three calls to the `TypeName()` function reveal that the subtype is `Long`. Then, after we change the value of the variable to "Hello", the subtype is automatically coerced into `String`. What this code illustrates is that, once the subtype is established as `Long`, it stays `Long` as long as we keep changing the value to other numbers. VBScript has no reason to change it, because the values we put in it remain in the range of the `Long` subtype. However, when we place text in the variable, VBScript sees that the new value is not appropriate for the `Long` subtype, so it changes it to `String`.

> This example reinforces the reason that we use the Hungarian subtype prefix in the variable name. By placing that `lng` prefix on the variable name, we indicate that we intend for this variable to hold `Long` numeric values only. The code at the end of our example violates this by changing the value to something non-numeric. VBScript allows this, but that's not the point. On the contrary, the fact the VBScript allows us to store any type of data we please in any variable increases the need for subtype prefixes. The point is to protect our code from strange errors creeping in. Six months from now, if we or someone else were modifying this code, the `lng` prefix would make it clear that the original intent was for the variable to hold `Long` numeric values.

Now give this code a try:

```
Dim intTest

intTest = CInt(100)
MsgBox "TypeName after initialization to 100: " & _
    TypeName(intTest)

intTest = intTest + 1000000
MsgBox "TypeName after adding 1,000,000: " & _
    TypeName(intTest)

intTest = intTest + 10000000000
MsgBox "TypeName after adding another 10,000,000,000: " & _
    TypeName(intTest)
```

Running this code results in the following three dialog boxes:

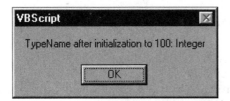 

Notice that we initialize the variable with a value of 100, and use the `CInt()` function to coerce the subtype into `Integer`. The first call to the `TypeName()` function reflects this. Then we add 1,000,000 to the variable. The next call to the `TypeName()` function reveals that VBScript coerced the subtype to `Long`. Why did it do this? Because we exceeded the upper limit of the `Integer` subtype, which is 32,767. VBScript will promote numeric subtypes when the value exceeds the upper or lower limits of the current numeric subtype. Finally, we add another ten billion to the variable. This exceeds the upper limit of the `Long` subtype, so VBScript upgrades the subtype to `Double`.

Throughout this chapter you have seen example code that uses the `&` operator to "concatenate" strings together. This is a very common operation in VBScript code. VBScript also allows you to use the + operator to concatenate strings. However, this usage of the + operator should be avoided. This is because the + operator, when used to concatenate strings, can cause unwanted implicit type coercion. Try this code:

```
Dim strFirst
Dim lngSecond
strFirst = CStr(50)
lngSecond = CLng(100)
MsgBox strFirst + lngSecond
```

The resulting dialog box will display the number 150, which means that it added the two numbers mathematically rather than concatenating them. Now, this is admittedly a very silly example, but it illustrates that the + operator has different effects when you are not using it in a strictly mathematical context. The + operator uses the following rules when deciding what to do:

❑ If both variables have the `String` subtype, then VBScript will concatenate them.

❑ If both variables have any of the numeric subtypes, then VBScript will add them.

❑ If one of the variables has a numeric subtype, and the other has the `String` subtype, then VBScript will attempt to add them. If the variable with the `String` subtype does not contain a number, then a "Type Mismatch" error will occur.

Your best bet is to not worry about these rules and remember only these:

❑ Use the + operator *only* when you explicitly want to perform math on numeric values.

❑ *Always* use the & operator to concatenate strings.

❑ Never use the + operator to concatenate strings.

Empty and Null

You may have noticed that we have not mentioned the first two subtypes in our table of subtypes: `Empty` and `Null`. These two subtypes are special in that they do not have a corresponding specific Visual Basic data type. In fact, it's a bit of a misnomer to call these subtypes, because they are actually special values that a Variant variable can hold. When the subtype of a variable is `Empty` or `Null`, its value is also either `Empty` or `Null`. This is different than the other subtypes, which only describe the *type* of value that the variable holds, not the value itself. For example, when the subtype of a variable is `Long`, the value of the variable can be 0, or 15, or 2,876,456, or one of about 4.3 billion other numbers (-2,147,483,648 to 2,147,483,647). However, when the subtype of a variable is `Empty`, it's value is also *always* a special value called `Empty`. In the same fashion, when the subtype of a variable is `Null`, the value is *always* a special value called `Null`.

`Empty` is a special value that can only be held in a Variant variable. In Visual Basic, variables declared as any of the specific data types cannot hold the value of `Empty` – only variables declared as Variant. In VBScript, of course, all variables are Variant variables. A Variant variable is "empty", and has the `Empty` subtype, after it has been declared, but before any value has been placed within it. In other words, `Empty` is the equivalent of "not initialized". Once any type of value has been placed into the variable, it will take on one of the other subtypes, depending on what the value is. Let's take a look at some examples:

```
Dim varTest
MsgBox TypeName(varTest)
```

This simple example results in the following dialog box:

The subtype is Empty because we have not yet placed any value in it. Empty is both the initial subtype and the initial value of the variable. However, Empty is not a value that you can really do anything with. You can't display it on the screen or print it on paper. It only exists to represent the condition of the variable not having had any value placed in it. Try this code:

```
Dim varTest
MsgBox CLng(varTest)
MsgBox CStr(varTest)
```

The code will produce the following two dialog boxes in succession:

The first box displays a 0 because Empty is 0 when represented as a number. The second box displays nothing because Empty is an "empty" or "zero length" string when represented as a String.

Once you place a value in a Variant variable, it is no longer empty. It will take on another subtype, depending on what type of value you place in it. This is also true when you use a conversion function to coerce the subtype. However, if you need to, you can force the variable to become empty again by using the Empty keyword directly:

```
varTest = Empty
```

You can also test for whether a variable is empty in either of two ways:

```
If varTest = Empty Then
    MsgBox "The variable is empty."
End If
```

Or:

```
If IsEmpty(varTest) Then
    MsgBox "The variable is empty."
End If
```

The IsEmpty() function returns a Variant value of the Boolean subtype with the value of True if the variable is empty, False if not.

The value/subtype of Null, in a confusing way, is similar to the value/subtype of Empty. The distinction may seem esoteric, but Empty indicates that a variable is uninitialized, whereas Null indicates the absence of valid data. Empty means that no value has been placed into a variable, whereas a Variant variable can only have the value/subtype of Null after the value of Null has been placed into it. In other words, a variable can only be Null if the Null value has explicitly been placed into it. Null is a special value that is most often encountered in database tables. A column in a database is Null when there is no data in it, and if you're code is going to read data from a database, you have to be ready for Null values.

Another way to think about it is that Empty generally happens by default – it is implicit, because a variable is Empty until you place something in it. Null, on the other hand, is explicit – a variable can only be Null if some code made it that way.

The syntax for assigning and testing for Null values is similar to the way the Empty value/subtype works. Here is some code that assigns a Null value to a variable:

```
varTest = Null
```

However, you cannot directly test for the value of Null in the same way that you can with Empty – you must use only the IsNull() function to test for a Null value. This is because Null represents invalid data, and when you try to make a direct comparison using invalid data, the result is always invalid data. Try running this code:

```
'This code does not work like you might expect
Dim varTest
VarTest = Null
If varTest = Null Then
    MsgBox "The variable has a Null value."
End If
```

You did not see any dialog box pop up did you? That's because the expression If varTest = Null *always* returns False. If you want to know if a variable contains a Null value, you must use the IsNull() function:

```
If IsNull(varTest) = True Then
    MsgBox "The variable has a Null value."
End If
```

As mentioned, often your code has to be concerned with receiving Null values from a database. The reason we say that you need to be concerned is that, since Null is an indicator of invalid data, Null can cause troubles for you if you pass it to certain functions or try and use it to perform mathematical operations. We saw this just a moment ago when we tried to use the expression If varTest = Null. This unpleasantness occurs in many contexts where you try to mix Null in with valid data. For example, try this code:

```
Dim varTest
varTest = Null
varTest = CLng(varTest)
```

Running this code produces an error on line 3: "Invalid Use of Null". This is a common error with many VBScript functions that don't like `Null` values to be passed into them. Take a look at the odd behavior that results from this code:

```
Dim varTest
Dim lngTest
varTest = Null
lngTest = 2 + varTest
MsgBox TypeName(lngTest)
```

Running this code results in the following dialog box:

Did you see what happened here? When we added the number 2 to the value `Null`, the result was `Null`. Once again when you mix invalid data (`Null`) with valid data (the number `2`, in this case), you always end up with invalid data.

The following code uses some ADO syntax that you might not be familiar with (see Chapter 15), but here's an example of the type of thing you want to do when you're concerned that a database column might return a `Null` value:

```
strCustomerName = rsCustomers.Fields("Name").Value
If IsNull(strCustomerName) Then
    strCustomerName = ""
End If
```

Here we are assigning the value of the "Name" column in a database table to the variable `strCustomerName`. If the Name column in the database allows `Null` values, then we need to be concerned that we might end up with a `Null` value in our variable. So we use `IsNull()` to test the value. If `IsNull()` returns `True`, then we assign an empty string to the variable instead. Empty strings are much more friendly than `Null`s. Here's a handy shortcut that achieves the same exact thing as the above code:

```
strCustomerName = "" & rsCustomers.Fields("Name").Value
```

Here we are appending an empty string to the value coming from the database. This takes advantage of VBScript's implicit type coercion behavior. Concatenating an empty string with a `Null` value transforms that value into an empty string, and concatenating an empty string to a valid string has not effect at all, so it's a win-win situation: if the value is `Null`, it gets fixed, and if it's not `Null`, it's left alone.

Here's a caution for you Visual Basic programmers who are accustomed to being able to use the `Trim$()` function to transform `Null` database values into empty strings. VBScript does not support the "$" versions of functions such as `Trim()`, `Format()`, and `Left()`. As you know, when you don't use the "$" versions of these functions in Visual Basic, they return a Variant value. This behavior is the same in VBScript, since *all* functions return Variant values. Therefore `Trim(Null)` always returns `Null`. If you still want to be able to trim database values as you read them in, you need to *both* append an empty string *and* use `Trim()`, like so:

```
strName = Trim("" & rsCustomers.Field("Name").Value)
```

The Object Subtype

So far, we have not discussed the `Object` subtype. As the name suggests, a variable will have the `Object` subtype when it contains a reference to an object. An object is a special construct that contains **properties** and **methods**. A property is analogous to a variable, and a method is analogous to a function or procedure. An object is essentially a convenient way of encompassing both data (in the form of properties) and functionality (in the form of methods). Objects are always created at runtime from a **class**, which is a template from which objects are created (or **instantiated**).

For example, you could create a class called "Dog". This Dog class could have properties called "Color", "Breed", and "Name", and it could have methods called "Bark" and "Sit". The class definition would have code to implement these properties and methods. Objects created at runtime from the Dog class would be able to set and read the properties and call the methods. A class typically exists as part of a component. For example, you might have a component called "Animals" that contains a bunch of different classes like "Dog", "Elephant", and "Rhino". The code to create and use a Dog object would look something like this:

```
Dim objMyDog
Set objMyDog = WScript.CreateObject("Animals.Dog")
objDog.Name = "Buddy"
objDog.Breed = "Poodle"
objDog.Color = "Brown"
objDog.Bark
objDog.Sit
```

Don't worry if this is going over your head at this point. We discuss objects classes and objects in much greater detail throughout the book, starting in Chapter 5. Our point in this section is simply to illustrate how variables with the object subtype behave. Let's look at some code that actually uses a real object, in this case the `FileSystemObject`, which is part of a collection of objects that allow your VBScript code to interact with the Windows file system. (We discuss `FileSystemObject` and its cousins in detail in Chapter 7, and we'll meet the `WScript.CreateObject` method in Chapter 10.)

```
Dim objFSO
Dim boolExists
Set objFSO = WScript.CreateObject("Scripting.FileSystemObject")
boolExists = objFSO.FileExists("C:\autoexec.bat")
MsgBox boolExists
```

In this code, we create a `FileSystemObject` object and store it in the variable called `objFSO`. We then use the `FileExists` method of the object to test for the existence of the `autoexec.bat` file. Then we display the result of this test in a dialog box. Note the use of the `Set` keyword. When changing the value of an object variable, you must use `Set`.

Now that you've seen an object in action, let's take a look at two concepts that are germane to this chapter: the `IsObject()` function, and the special value of `Nothing`.

```
Dim objFSO
Dim boolExists
Set objFSO = WScript.CreateObject("Scripting.FileSystemObject")
If IsObject(objFSO) Then
    boolExists = objFSO.FileExists("C:\autoexec.bat")
    MsgBox boolExists
End If
```

This illustrates the use of the `IsObject()` function, which is similar to the `IsNumeric()` and `IsDate()` functions that we met earlier in the chapter. If the variable holds a reference to an object, then the function will return `True`. Otherwise, it will return `False`.

`Nothing` is a special value that applies only to variables with the `Object` subtype. An object variable is equal to the value `Nothing` when the subtype is `Object`, but the object in the variable has either been destroyed or has not yet been instantiated. When testing for whether an object variable is equal to the value `Nothing`, you do not use the = operator, as you normally would to test for a specific value. Instead, you have to use the special operator `Is`. However, when you want to destroy an object, you have to use the `Set` keyword in combination with the = operator. If that sounds confusing, don't worry, because it is confusing. Let's look at an example:

```
Dim objFSO
Dim boolExists
Set objFSO = WScript.CreateObject("Scripting.FileSystemObject")
If IsObject(objFSO) Then
    boolExists = objFSO.FileExists("C:\autoexec.bat")
    MsgBox boolExists
    Set objFSO = Nothing
    If objFSO Is Nothing Then
        MsgBox "The object has been destroyed"
    End If
End If
```

Why would you want to destroy an object using the `Set <variable> = Nothing` syntax? It's a good idea to do this when you are done using an object, because destroying the object frees up the memory it was taking up. Objects take up a great deal more memory than normal variables. Also, for reasons that are too complex to go into here, not keeping object variables around longer than necessary can cause fatal memory errors. It's a good idea to develop a habit of setting all object variables equal to `Nothing` immediately after you are done with them.

The Error Subtype

We left the `Error` subtype for last because it is seldom used. However, there's a remote chance that you might end up coming across a component or function that uses the `Error` subtype to indicate that an error occurred in the function. We are not necessarily endorsing this methodology, but what you might encounter is a function that returns a Variant value that will either contain the result of the function, or an error number. Let's say it's a fictional function called `GetAge()` that returns a person's age in years. This function would take a date as a parameter, and return to you the person's age, based on the computer's current system date. If an error occurred in the function, then the return value would instead contain an error number indicating what went wrong. For example:

```
Dim datBirth
Dim lngAge
datBirth = InputBox("Please enter the date on which you were born.")
If IsDate(datBirth) Then
    lngAge = GetAge(datBirth)
    If Not IsError(lngAge) Then
        MsgBox "You are " & lngAge & " years old."
    Else
        If lngAge = 1000 Then
            'This error means that the date was greater
            'than the current system date.
            MsgBox "That date was greater than the current system date."
        Else
            'An unknown error occurred.
            MsgBox "The error " & lngAge & " occurred in the GetAge()"_
                            & "function"

        End If
    End If
Else
    MsgBox "You did not enter a valid date."
End If
```

Keep in mind that `GetAge()` is a totally fictional function, and you cannot actually run this code. The point here is only to illustrate how someone might use the `Error` subtype, and how your code might have to respond to it. You could not easily implement the use of the `Error` subtype yourself in VBScript because the VBScript does not support the `CVErr()` conversion function, as Visual Basic does. Therefore, without the aid of Visual Basic, you could never coerce the subtype of a variable to be `Error`.

VBScript does not fully support the Error and Decimal subtypes. In short, you can use them, but because conversion functions for them do not exist in VBScript, you cannot coerce the subtype of a variable to be either Error or Decimal. If you are dealing with a VB/COM component that returns a variable with either of these subtypes, you can use those variables with no problem. You just cannot create variables with these subtypes yourself, or coerce variables to have these subtypes.

Visual Basic has two conversion functions for coercing the subtype of a variable to be either Error or Decimal: CVErr() and CDec(), respectively. These functions do not exist in VBScript. You can, though, use the VarType() function to test whether a variable's subtype is either Error or Decimal. At the time of this writing, however, there is what appears to be a bug in the TypeName() function which prevents it from working with the Decimal subtype. If you try to use TypeName() on a variable with the Decimal subtype, you will get the following error:

```
Variable uses an Automation type not supported in
VBScript: 'TypeName'
```

Variables in VBScript

So far, we have been using a lot of variables in our sample code, but there are some topics which we have not explicitly discussed. These topics include rules for naming and declaring variables, as well as variable scope and lifetime.

Option Explicit

You might not be able to guess it based on the code examples we've presented so far, but declaring variables in VBScript is optional. That's right, you can just start using a new variable anywhere in your code without having declared it first. There is no absolute requirement that says that you must declare the variable first. As soon as VBScript encounters a new non-declared variable in your code, it just allocates memory for it and keeps going. Here's an example:

```
lngFirst = 1
lngSecond = 2
lngThird = lngFirst + lngSecond
MsgBox lngThird
```

You can type this code as-is into a script editor and run it with the Windows Script Host. Even though we did not explicitly declare any of the three variables, VBScript does not care. The code runs as you'd expect, and a dialog box comes up at the end displaying the number 3. Sounds pretty convenient, doesn't it. Well, maybe. This convenience comes at a very high price. Take a look at this code:

```
lngFirst = 1
lngSecond = 2
lngThird = lngFirst + lgnSecond
MsgBox lngThird
```

Isn't this the same code we just looked at? Look again. Do you notice the misspelling in the third line? An easy mistake to make while you're typing in line after line of script code. The trouble is that this misspelling does not cause VBScript any trouble at all. It just thinks the misspelling is yet another new variable, so it allocates memory for it and gives it the initial subtype of Empty. When you ask VBScript to do math on an empty variable, it just treats the variable as a zero. So when this code runs, the dialog box displays the number 1, rather than the number 3 we were expecting.

Easy enough to find the error and fix it in this simple do-nothing script, but what if this script contained dozens, or even hundreds of lines of code? What if instead of adding 1 to 2 to get 3, we were adding 78523.6778262 to 2349.25385 and then dividing the result by 4.97432? Would you be able to notice a math error by looking at the result? If you were storing these numbers in variables, and you accidentally misspelled one of the variables in your code, you could end up with a math error that you (or worse yet, your boss) might not notice for weeks.

So what can we do to prevent this? The answer is a statement called Option Explicit. What you do is place the statement Option Explicit at the top of your script file, before any other statements appear. This tells VBScript that our code requires that all variables be explicitly declared before they can be used. Now VBScript will no longer let you introduce a new variable right in the middle of your code without declaring it first. Here's an example:

```
Option Explicit

Dim lngFirst
Dim lngSecond
Dim lngThird

lngFirst = 1
lngSecond = 2
lngThird = lngFirst + lgnSecond
MsgBox lngThird
```

Notice that we have added the Option Explicit statement to the top of our code. Since we have added Option Explicit, we must now declare all of our variables before we use them, which is what you see on the three lines following Option Explicit. Finally, notice that we have left our misspelling on the second-to-last line. We did this in order to illustrate what happens when you try to use an undeclared variable. If we try and run this code, VBScript will halt the execution with the following error: Variable is undefined: 'lgnSecond'. This is a good thing. As long as we use Option Explicit, VBScript will catch our variable-related typing errors.

One thing that's very nice about Option Explicit is that it applies to the entire script file in which it resides. We have not discussed this too much so far in the book, but a single script file can contain multiple procedures, functions, and class definitions, and each class definition can itself contain multiple procedures and functions (we cover VBScript classes in Chapter 8). As long as you place Option Explicit at the top of the script file, all of this code is covered.

Start a good habit today: every single time you start a new script file, before you do anything else, type the words `Option Explicit` at the top of the file. This will prevent silly typing errors for seriously messing up your code, and your fellow script developers will appreciate it.

Naming Variables

VBScript has a few rules for what names you can give to a variable. The rules are pretty simple, and leave you plenty of room to come up with clear, useful, understandable variable names.

VBScript variable names must begin with an alpha character

An "alpha character" is any character between "a" and "z" (capital or lowercase). Non-alpha characters are pretty much everything else: numbers, punctuation marks, mathematical operators, and other special characters. For example, these are legal variable names:

❑ `strName`

❑ `Some_Thing`

❑ `Fruit`

And these are illegal variable names:

❑ `+strName`

❑ `99RedBalloons`

❑ `@Test`

Numbers and the underscore ("_") character can be used within the variable name, but all other non-alphanumeric characters are illegal.

VBScript does not like variable names that contain characters that are anything but numbers and letters. The lone exception to this is the underscore ("_") character. (Some programmers find the underscore character to be useful for separating distinct words within a variable name (e.g. `Customer_Name`), while other programmers prefer to accomplish this by letting the mixed upper and lower case letters accomplish the same thing (e.g. `CustomerName`).) For example, these are legal variable names:

❑ `lngPosition99`

❑ `Word1_Word2_`

❑ `bool2ndTime`

And these are illegal variable names:

❏   `str&Name`

❏   `SomeThing@`

❏   `First*Name`

VBScript variable names cannot exceed 255 characters
Hopefully your variable names will not exceed twenty characters or so, but VBScript allows them to be as long as 255 characters.

These rules for variable naming should be pretty easy to follow, but it is important to make a distinction between coming up with variable names that are legal, and coming up with variable names that are clear, useful, and understandable. The fact that VBScript will *allow* you to use a variable name such as `X99B2F012345` does not necessarily mean that it's a good idea to do so. A variable name should make the purpose of the variable clear. If you're going to store the user's name in a variable, a name like `strUserName` is a good one because it removes any doubt as to what the programmer intended the variable to be used for. Good variable names not only decrease the chances of errors creeping into your code, but they make the code itself easier for humans to read and understand.

The other principle that a large percentage of programmers have found useful is the "Hungarian naming convention," which we have mentioned a couple times before, and which we have been using throughout this chapter. This convention simply involves using a prefix on the variable name to indicate what type of data the programmer intends for that variable to store. For example, the variable name `strUserName` indicates not only that the variable should hold the user's name, but also that the subtype of the variable should be `String`. Similarly, the variable name `lngFileCount` indicates not only that the variable should hold a count of the number of files, but also that the subtype of the variable should be `Long`.

Appendix C of this book contains additional guidelines for naming variables, including a list of suggested data type prefixes.

Variable Declaration, Scope, and Lifetime

The issue of variable **scope** and **lifetime** are closely tied to the rules and guidelines that you should follow when declaring variables. A variable's scope is a boundary within which a variable is valid and accessible. The boundaries within which a variable is declared is directly related to the lifetime of that variable. Script code that is executing outside of a variable's scope cannot access that variable. There are three types of scope that a VBScript variable can have:

❏   **Script-level scope** – Script-level scope means that the variable is available to all of the scripts within a script file. Variables that are declared outside of the boundaries of a VBScript procedure, function, or class automatically have script-level scope.

❑ **Procedure-level scope** – Procedure-level scope (also known as "local" scope) means that the variable is only available within the procedure or function in which it is declared. Other code outside of the procedure, even if that code resides within the same script file, cannot access a procedure-level variable.

❑ **Class-level scope** – A Class is a special construct that contains a logic grouping of Properties and Methods. In VBScript, classes are defined within a script using the `Class...End Class` block definition statements. A variable that is declared using the `Private` statement within the class definition, but outside of any of the procedures or functions within the class, has class-level scope. This means that other code within the class can access the variable, but code outside of the class definition, even if that code resides in the same script file, cannot access the variable. (We cover VBScript classes in detail in Chapter 8.)

There are three statements that you can use to declare variables: `Dim`, `Private`, and `Public`. (`ReDim` also falls into this category of statements, but it is specifically used for the "re-dimensioning" of already declared array variables, and we'll cover it in the last section of this chapter, "Complex Data Types".) These declaration statements are used in different situations, depending on the scope of the variable being declared:

❑ `Dim` – This statement is generally used to declare variables at either the script-level or the procedure-level. Any variable declared at the script-level is automatically available to the entire script file, regardless of whether `Dim`, `Private`, or `Public` was used to declare it. In order to declare a variable inside of a procedure, you must use `Dim`. `Public` and `Private` are not valid inside of a procedure. If used at the class-level, then `Dim` has the exact same effect as `Public`.

❑ `Private` – The `Private` statement can be used at either the script-level or at the class level, but not inside of procedures or functions. If used at the script level, it has the exact same effect as using `Dim` or `Public`. Any variable declared at the script-level is automatically available to the entire script file, regardless of whether `Dim`, `Private`, or `Public` was used to declare it. Although VBScript does not require it, many programmers prefer to use the `Private` statement to declare variables at the script level, and to reserve `Dim` for use within procedures and functions. In order to declare a private class-level variable, you *must* use `Private`. Any variable declared at the class level with either `Dim` or `Public` is automatically available as a public property of the class.

❑ `Public` – The `Public` statement can be used to declare variables with script-level scope, but it has the exact same effect as either `Dim` or `Private`. The only place that `Public` is really meaningful is at the class level. A variable declared at the class level with `Public` is made available as a public property of the class. The reason that `Public` is not meaningful at the script level is that, with the exception of "script components" (see Chapters 9 and 12), variables within a script are not available outside the script file in which they reside. Therefore, the only place you will really use `Public` to declare variables is to create public properties for a class. However, note that many VBScript programmers discourage the use of `Public` variables in a class and prefer instead to use a combination of a `Private` class-level variable and `Property Let`, `Set` and `Get` procedures (see Chapter 8).

73

We packed a lot of rules into those three bullet items, so these guidelines might make it easier to keep track of when to use `Dim`, `Private`, and `Public`.

❑ Use `Dim` at the procedure level to declare variables that are local to that procedure. Even though `Dim` is legal at the script and class level, limiting its use to the procedure level can increase the clarity of your code.

❑ Use `Private` at the script level to declare variables that will be available to the whole script. Also use `Private` at the class level to declare variables that are only available within the class.

❑ Use `Public` only to declare public properties for a class, but consider also the option of using a `Private` variable in combination with `Property Let`/`Set` and `Get` procedures. Even though `Dim` has the same effect as `Public` at the class level, it is more explicit, and therefore preferable, to not use `Dim` at the class level.

Finally, a variable's lifetime is closely tied the variable's scope. Lifetime, as the term suggests, refers to the time that a variable is in memory and available for use. A variable with procedure-level scope is only alive as long as that procedure is executing. A variable with script level scope is alive as long as the script is running. A variable with class-level scope is only alive while some other code is using an object based on that class.

This points to an important principle: you should limit a variable's lifetime, and therefore its scope, as much as you can. Since a variable takes up memory, and therefore operating system and script engine resources, you should only keep it alive as long as you need it. By limiting a variable's scope, you also limit its lifetime. By declaring a variable within the procedure in which it will be used, you keep the variable from taking up resources when the procedure in which it resides is not being executed. If you had a script file that contained ten procedures and functions, and you declared all of your variables at the script level, you would not only create some pretty confusing code, but you would cause your script to take up more resources than necessary.

Let's look at an example:

```
Option Explicit

Private datToday

datToday = Date
MsgBox "Tommorrow's date will be " & AddOneDay(datToday) & "."

Function AddOneDay(datAny)

  Dim datResult

  datResult = DateAdd("d", 1, datAny)
  AddOneDay = datResult

End Function
```

This script contains a function called AddOneDay(). The variable datResult is declared with Dim inside the function and has procedure-level scope. The variable datToday is declared with Private and has script-level scope. The variable datResult will only be in memory while the AddOneDay() function is executing, whereas the datToday variable will be in memory for the entire lifetime of the script.

> **Just for the sake of clarity, please note that the above code example, like many code examples in this book, has some unnecessary variable declarations. These declarations are included in order to illustrate the concepts of declaring variables. Here is a much more compact version of the same script from the last example:**
>
> ```
> Option Explicit
>
> MsgBox "Tommorrow's date will be " & AddOneDay(Date()) & "."
>
> Function AddOneDay(datAny)
>
>   AddOneDay = DateAdd("d", 1, datAny)
>
> End Function
> ```

Let's finish off with some additional notes about variable declarations.

VBScript allows you to put more than one variable declaration on the same line. From a style standpoint, it is generally preferable to limit variable declarations to one-per-line, as our example scripts have, but this is not an absolute rule. Script programmers who are writing scripts that will be downloaded over the web as part of an HTML file often prefer to put multiple declarations on a single line since it makes the file a little smaller. Here is some examples:

```
Dim strUserName, strPassword, lngAge
```

```
Private strUserName, strPassword, lngAge
```

Note however, that, you cannot mix declarations of differing scope on the same line. If you wanted to declare some Private and Public variables within a class, for instance, you would have to have two separate lines:

```
Private strUserName, strPassword
Public lngAge, datBirthday, boolLikesPresents
```

Finally, VBScript does have limitations on the number of variables you can have within a script or procedure. You cannot have more than 127 procedure-level variables in any given procedure, and you cannot have any more that 127 script-level variables in any given script file. This should not cause you any trouble, however. If you are using this many variables within a script or procedure, you might want to rethink your design and break that giant procedure up into multiple procedures.

Literals and Named Constants

What is a Literal?

A literal is any piece of static data that appears in your code that is not stored as a variable or named constant. Literals can be strings of text, numbers, dates, or Boolean values. For example, the word "Hello" in the following code is a literal:

```
Dim strMessage

strMessage = "Hello"
MsgBox strMessage
```

The date 08/31/69 in the following code is also a literal:

```
Dim datBirthday

datBirthday = #08/31/69#
MsgBox "My birthday is " & datBirthday & "."
```

The string "My birthday is" is also a literal in this code. Literals do not need to be stored in a variable to be considered a literal. And for one more example, the value True in the following code is also a literal:

```
Dim boolCanShowMsg

boolCanShowMsg = True
If boolCanShowMsg Then
  MsgBox "Hello there."
End If
```

Many times, literals are just fine in your code. Programmers use them all the time. However, there are many instances when the use of a named constant is preferable to using a literal.

What is a Named Constant?

A named constant is similar to a variable, except that its value cannot be changed at runtime. A variable is transient. While the code is running, any code within a variable's scope can change the value of it to something else. A named constant, on the other hand, is static. Once defined, it cannot be changed by any code during runtime – hence the name "constant."

You define a constant in your code using the `Const` statement. Here's an example:

```
Const GREETING = "Hello there, "

Dim strUserName

strUserName = InputBox("Please enter your name.")
If Trim(strUserName) <> "" Then
  MsgBox GREETING & strUserName & "."
End If
```

If the user types in the name "William," then this code results in the following dialog box:

The `Const` statement defines the named constant called `GREETING`. The name of the constant is in all capital letters because this is the generally accepted convention for named constants. Defining constant names in all capital letters makes them easy to differentiate from variables, which are generally typed in either all lower case or mixed case. (Note however, that VBScript is *not* case sensitive. There is nothing in VBScript that enforces any capitalization standard. These are stylistic conventions only, adopted to make the code easier to read, understand, and maintain.) Additionally, since constants are usually written in all capital letters, distinct words within the constant's name are usually separated by the underscore ("_") character, as in this example:

```
Const RESPONSE_YES = "YES"
Const RESPONSE_NO = "NO"

Dim strResponse

strResponse = InputBox("Is today a Tuesday? Please answer Yes or No.")
strResponse = UCase(strResponse)
If strResponse = RESPONSE_YES Then
  MsgBox "I love Tuesdays."
ElseIf strResponse = RESPONSE_NO Then
  MsgBox "I will gladly pay you Tuesday for a hamburger today."
Else
  MsgBox "Invalid response."
End If
```

Constants also have scope, just like variables. While you cannot use the `Dim` statement to declare a constant, you can use `Private` and `Public` in front of the `Const` statement. However, these scope qualifications are optional. A constant declared at the script level automatically has script-level scope (meaning it is available to all procedures, functions, and classes within the script file.) A constant declared inside of procedure or function automatically has procedure-level scope (meaning that other code outside of the procedure cannot use the constant).

You can also declare multiple constants on one line, like so:

```
Const RESPONSE_YES = "YES", RESPONSE_NO = "No"
```

Finally, you cannot use variables or functions to define a constant. The value of a constant must be defined as a literal, as in the above examples.

When Should You Use Named Constants in Place of Literals?

Some programmers will answer this question with "always". There is a school of thought that says that your code should never contain any literals. Other programmers never use named constants, either out of a lack of knowledge of their benefits, or out of just plain laziness. However, there is a reasonable middle ground. In a moment, we will look at some guidelines that might help us find this middle ground. However, first, let's examine some of the benefits that named constants can afford your code:

❑ Named constants can decrease bugs. If you are repeating the same literal value many times throughout your code, the probability of misspelling that literal goes up every time you type it. If you type the constant's name in place of the literal throughout your code, you could just as easily misspell that, but the script engine would catch this error at runtime, whereas a misspelling of the literal itself might go unnoticed for quite some time.

❑ Named constants can increase clarity. Some of the literals we used in our previous examples were mostly clear all by themselves, and adding a constant did not really make their meaning more clear. However, using a literal in your code can often hide meaning when the purpose of the literal is not immediately apparent from reading the code. This is especially true with literals that are numbers. A number by itself does not suggest its purpose for being in the code, and using a constant in its place can make that meaning clear.

❑ If the literal being replaced by the constant is especially long, or otherwise cumbersome to type, then using the constant makes it a lot easier to type in your code. For example, if you needed to insert a large multi-paragraph legal disclaimer at various points in your scripts, it would be a good idea to replace that large block of text with a short named constant that's much easier to type.

> If you are only using a literal once, it's probably okay to use it instead of creating a named constant.

This statement is especially true when you consider constants used in HTML-embedded script code, which must be downloaded over the web. If you always used named constants in place of literals in client-side web scripting, you could easily increase the size of the file that the user has to download to a point that is noticeable. And even in a server-side web scripting scenario (where the script code is not downloaded to the user's browser), using constants everywhere can slow the script execution down considerably. This is because the script engine has to process all the constants before it can execute the code that uses them.

However, if you are using the same literal over and over throughout the script, then replacing it with a named constant can really increase the readability of the code, and reduce mistakes from misspellings of the literal. A great technique in server-side web ASP scripting (see Chapter 14) is to put named constants in an "include" file that can be re-used in multiple scripts. Named constants are important, but sometimes you have to weigh the trade-off.

> **If using the constant in place of a literal makes the meaning of the code more clear, use the constant.**

As we mentioned, this is especially true for literals that are numbers. If you are working with arrays with multiple dimensions (see the last section of this chapter), then using named constants in place of the array subscripts is a really good idea. If you are checking numeric codes that have different meanings based on the number, it's a great idea to use constants in place of the numbers, because the meaning of the numbers by themselves will probably not be clear. The same principle holds true of dates with a special meaning, or odd strings of characters whose meaning is not clear just from looking at them.

Built-In VBScript Constants

Many VBScript hosts, such as the Windows Script Host and Active Server Pages, support the use of constants that are built into VBScript. These are especially helpful for two reasons: first, it can be hard to remember a lot of the seemingly arbitrary numbers the many of the VBScript functions and procedures use as parameters and return values; and second, using these named constants makes your code a lot easier to read. We saw some examples of built-in named constants when we looked at the `VarType()` function earlier in this chapter.

Appendix D of this book contains a list of many of the named constants that VBScript provides for you for free. You'll notice that many of these constants are easy to identify by the prefix `vb`. Also, you'll notice that these constants are usually written in mixed case, rather than all upper case. By way of example, lets take a look at some constants you can use in an optional parameter of the `MsgBox()` function (see Appendix A for details of the `MsgBox()` function).

We have used the first parameter of `MsgBox()` multiple times throughout the book thus far. This first parameter is the message that we want displayed in the dialog box. The `MsgBox()` function also takes several optional parameters, the second of which is the "buttons" parameter, which lets you define different buttons and icons to appear on the dialog box. Here's an example:

```
MsgBox "The sky is falling!", 48
```

This code produces the following dialog box:

By passing the number 48 to the second parameter of `MsgBox()`, we told it that we wanted the exclamation point to appear on the dialog box. Instead of using the not-so-clear number 48, we could have used the `vbExclamation` named constant instead:

```
MsgBox "The sky is falling!", vbExclamation
```

This code results in the same exact dialog box, but it's much more clear from reading the code what we're trying to do.

Complex Data Types

Other than our brief discussion of objects in the previous section, we have so far been dealing only with very simple variables. The variables in our example code so far have held only one-dimensional values: a single number, a single date, a single string, etc. However, VBScript can work with two other types of data that are more complex than anything we've looked at so far: objects and **arrays**. We are not going to discuss objects here, since they are covered throughout the book, beginning in Chapter 5. However, we are going to take a detailed look at arrays.

What is an Array?

An array, as the name suggests, is a matrix of data. While a normal variable has one "compartment" in which to store one piece of information, an array has multiple compartments in which to store multiple pieces of information. As you can imagine, this comes in very handy. Even though you might not know it, you are probably already very familiar, outside the context of VBScript, with all sorts of matrices. A spreadsheet is a matrix. It has rows and columns, and you can identify a single "cell" in the spreadsheet by referring to the row number and column letter where that cell resides. A Bingo game card is also a matrix. It has rows of numbers that span five columns, which are headed by the letters B-I-N-G-O. A database table is a matrix – once again, rows and columns.

An array can be a very simple matrix, with a single column (which is called a **dimension**), or it can be much more complex, with up to 60 dimensions. Arrays are typically used to store repeating instances of the same type of information. For example, suppose your script needs to work with a list of names and phone numbers. An array is perfect for this. Rather than trying to declare separate variables for each of the names and phone numbers in your list (which would be especially challenging if you did not know in advance how many names were going to be in the list), you can store the entire list in one variable.

Arrays Have Dimensions

A VBScript array can have up to 60 **dimensions**. Most arrays have either one or two dimensions. A one-dimensional array is best thought of as a list of rows with only one column. A two-dimensional array is a straightforward list of values, with multiple columns (the first dimension) and rows (the second dimension). Beyond two dimensions, however, the grid analogy starts to break down, and the array turns into something much more complex. We're not going to discuss multi dimensional arrays much here. Luckily, for the needs of your average script, a two-dimensional array is absolutely sufficient.

Note that a two-dimensional array does not mean that you are limited to two columns. It only means that the array is limited to an x and a y axis. A one-dimensional array really does have two dimensions, but it is limited to a single column. A two-dimensional array can have as many columns and rows as the memory of your computer will allow. For example, here is graphical representation of a one-dimensional array, in the form of a list of colors:

Red
Green
Blue
Yellow
Orange
Black

And here is a two-dimensional array, in the form of a list of names and phone numbers:

Williams	Tony	404-985-6328
Carter	Ron	305-781-2514
Davis	Miles	212-963-5314
Hancock	Herbie	616-752-6943
Shorter	Wayne	853-238-0060

An array with three dimensions is more difficult to represent graphically. Picture a three-dimensional cube, divided up into sections. After three dimensions, it becomes even more difficult to hold a picture of the array's structure in your mind.

Array Bounds and Declaring Arrays

It's important to make a distinction between the number of dimensions that an array has, and the **bounds** that an array has. The phone list array above has two dimensions, but it has different upper and lower bounds for each dimension. The upper bound of an array determines how many "compartments" that dimension can hold. Each of the "compartments" in an array is called an **element**. An element can hold exactly one value, but an array can have as many elements as your computer's memory will allow. Here is the phone list array again, but with each of the elements numbered:

	0	1	2
0	Williams	Tony	404-985-6328
1	Carter	Ron	305-781-2514
2	Davis	Miles	212-963-5314
3	Hancock	Herbie	616-752-6943
4	Shorter	Wayne	853-238-0060

The lower bound of the first dimension (the columns) is 0, and the upper bound is 2. The lower bound of the second dimension (the rows) is once again 0, and the upper bound is 4. The lower bound of an array in VBScript is *always* 0 (unlike Visual Basic arrays, which can have any lower bound that you wish to declare). Arrays with a lower bound of 0 are said to be zero-based. This can become a bit confusing, because when you are accessing elements in the array, you have to always remember to start counting at 0, which is not always natural for people. So even though there are three columns in the first dimension, the upper bound is expressed as 2 – because we started numbering them at 0. Likewise, even though the there are five rows in the second dimension, the upper bound is expressed as 4.

When you declare (or "dimension") an array, you can tell VBScript how many dimensions you want, and what the upper bound of each dimension is. For example, here is a declaration for an array variable for the list of colors that we showed a picture of in the previous section:

```
Dim astrColors(5)
```

The list of colors was one dimensional (that is, it had only one column) and it had six elements. So the upper bound of the array is 5 – remember that we start counting at 0. Notice the Hungarian prefix (see Appendix C) that we used in our variable name: `astr`. For a normal string variable name, we would just use the `str` prefix. We add the additional a in order to convey that this variable is an array. For another example, an array of `Long` numbers would have this prefix: `alng`. For more information on subtypes and arrays, see the last section of this chapter.

Here is a declaration for an array variable for our phone list:

```
Dim astrPhoneList(2,4)
```

When we add another dimension, we add a comma and another upper bound definition to the declaration. Since our phone list has three columns, the upper bound of the first dimension is 2. And since it has five rows, the upper bound of the second dimension is 4. Note that you are not limited to using Dim to declare your array. You can use the Private and Public statements just as you would with any other variable.

But what happens when we don't know in advance how many elements we're going to need in our array? This is where the **dynamic array** comes in. A dynamic array is one that is not pre-constrained to have certain upper bounds, or even a certain number of dimensions. You can declare the array variable once at design time, then change the number of dimensions and the upper bound of those dimensions dynamically at runtime. In order to declare a variable as a dynamic array, you just use the parentheses without putting any dimensions in them:

```
Dim astrPhoneList()
```

This tells VBScript that we want this variable to be an array, we just don't know at design time how many elements we're going to need to store in it. This is a very common occurrence – perhaps more common than knowing in advance how many elements you're going to need. If you're going to open a file or database table and feed the contents into an array, how can you know at design time how many items will be in the file or database table? You can't know that. So the dynamic array solves that dilemma by allowing us to resize the array at runtime.

In order to change the number of dimensions, or the upper bounds of those dimensions, you have to use the ReDim statement. You can use the ReDim statement anywhere in any code that is in the same scope as the dynamic array variable. Here's an example:

```
Option Explicit

Private astrPhoneList()

FillPhoneList
AddToPhoneList "Ellington", "Duke", "856-963-7854"

Sub FillPhoneList
  ReDim astrPhoneList(2,4)
  <other code goes here to populate the array>
End Sub

Sub AddToPhoneList(strLast, strFirst, strPhone)

  Dim lngUBound
```

```
lngUBound = UBound(astrPhoneList) + 1
ReDim Preserve astrPhoneList(2, lngUBound)
astrPhoneList(0, lngUBound) = strLast
astrPhoneList(1, lngUBound) = strFirst
astrPhoneList(2, lngUBound) = strPhone

End Sub
```

Please note that this example has the exact same effect as our previous example, since we are still hard-coding the upper bound of the elements. In the real world, the whole point of using ReDim is that you have no idea at design time how many elements you would need, so you would use a variable to determine how many elements to declare. Later in the chapter, we'll have an example that uses ReDim inside of a loop to add the contents of a Recordset to a dynamic array.

Using ReDim all by itself completely resizes and clears out the array. If you stored some data in the array, and then used ReDim to resize it, all the data you previously stored in the array would be lost. That's where the Preserve keyword comes in. Using the Preserve keyword ensures that the data you've already stored in the variable stays there when you resize it. However, if you make the array smaller than it already was, you will of course lose the data that was in the elements you chopped off. Here's the syntax for the Preserve keyword:

```
ReDim Preserve astrPhoneList(2,5)
```

There is one caveat when using the Preserve keyword: you can only resize the last dimension in the array. If you attempt to resize any dimension other than the last dimension, VBScript will generate a runtime error. That's why, when working with two-dimensional arrays, it's best to think of the first dimension as the columns, and the second dimension as the rows. You will generally know how many columns you need in an array at design time, so you won't have to resize the columns dimension. It's the number of rows that you generally won't be sure about. For example, in our phone list array, we know that we need three columns: one for the last name, one for the first name, and one for the phone number. So we can hard code these at design time and dynamically resize the rows dimension at runtime. Regardless, make sure that the dimension you want to resize with ReDim Preserve is the last dimension in your array.

> Note that when you declare a variable with the parentheses at the end of the variable name – e.g. varTest() – that variable can *only* be used as an array. However, you can declare a variable *without* the parentheses at the end, and still use the ReDim statement later to turn it into a dynamic array. Then you can assign a normal number to the variable again to stop it from being an array. However, using a variable for multiple purposes in this manner can be confusing and might allow bugs to creep into your code. If you need a variable to be both an array and not an array, you might consider declaring two separate variables instead of using one variable for two purposes.

Accessing Arrays with Subscripts

In order to read from or write to an array element, you have to use a **subscript**. A subscript is similar to the column letter and row number syntax that you use in a spreadsheet program. Here's our phone list array again:

	0	1	2
0	Williams	Tony	404-985-6328
1	Carter	Ron	305-781-2514
2	Davis	Miles	212-963-5314
3	Hancock	Herbie	616-752-6943
4	Shorter	Wayne	853-238-0060

The last name "Williams" is stored in subscript 0,0. The first name "Miles" is stored in subscript 1,2. The phone number "305-781-2514" is stored in subscript 2,1. You get the idea. When reading or writing from or to a subscript, you would use this syntax:

```
astrPhoneList(0,0) = "Williams"
astrPhoneList(1,0) = "Tony"
astrPhoneList(2,0) = "404-985-6328"
MsgBox "The Last Name is: " & astrPhoneList(0,0)
MsgBox "The First Name is: " & astrPhoneList(1,0)
MsgBox "The Phone Number is: " & astrPhoneList(2,0)
```

Erasing Arrays

You can totally empty out an array using the `Erase` statement. The `Erase` statement has slightly different effects with fixed size and dynamic arrays. With a fixed size array, the information in the array elements is deleted, but the elements themselves stay there – they're just empty. With a dynamic array, the `Erase` statement completely releases the memory the array was taking up. The data in the array is deleted, and the elements themselves are destroyed. To get them back, you would have to use the `ReDim` statement on the array variable again. Here's an example:

```
Erase astrPhoneList
```

Populating and Looping Through Arrays

Let's look at an example script that declares a dynamic array variable, resizes it using the `ReDim` statement, populates the array with data, then loops through the array to retrieve all the information out of it:

```
Option Explicit

Private Const LAST_NAME = 0
Private Const FIRST_NAME = 1
Private Const PHONE = 2

Private astrPhoneList()

FillPhoneList
DisplayPhoneList

Sub FillPhoneList

  ReDim astrPhoneList(PHONE,4)

  astrPhoneList(LAST_NAME, 0) = "Williams"
  astrPhoneList(FIRST_NAME, 0) = "Tony"
  astrPhoneList(PHONE, 0) = "404-985-6328"

  astrPhoneList(LAST_NAME, 1) = "Carter"
  astrPhoneList(FIRST_NAME, 1) = "Ron"
  astrPhoneList(PHONE, 1) = "305-781-2514"

  astrPhoneList(LAST_NAME, 2) = "Davis"
  astrPhoneList(FIRST_NAME, 2) = "Miles"
  astrPhoneList(PHONE, 2) = "212-963-5314"

  astrPhoneList(LAST_NAME, 3) = "Hancock"
  astrPhoneList(FIRST_NAME, 3) = "Herbie"
  astrPhoneList(PHONE, 3) = "616-752-6943"

  astrPhoneList(LAST_NAME, 4) = "Shorter"
  astrPhoneList(FIRST_NAME, 4) = "Wayne"
  astrPhoneList(PHONE, 4) = "853-238-0060"

End Sub

Sub DisplayPhoneList

  Dim strMsg
  Dim lngIndex
  Dim lngUBound

  lngUBound = UBound(astrPhoneList, 2)
  strMsg = "The phone list is:" & vbNewLine & vbNewLine
  For lngIndex = 0 to lngUBound
    strMsg = strMsg & astrPhoneList(LAST_NAME, lngIndex) & ", "
    strMsg = strMsg & astrPhoneList(FIRST_NAME, lngIndex) & " - "
    strMsg = strMsg & astrPhoneList(PHONE, lngIndex) & vbNewLine
  Next

  MsgBox strMsg

End Sub
```

Running this script results in the following dialog box:

First, notice that we are using named constants for the subscripts of the columns of our phone list. These script-level constants are declared at the top of the script. This technique makes the code that accesses the array a lot more clear. Second, notice the use of the VBScript UBound() function in the DisplayPhoneList() procedure:

```
lngUBound = UBound(astrPhoneList, 2)
```

The first parameter of the UBound() function is an array variable. The second parameter is optional, and it is the number of the dimension that you want the upper bound of. The UBound() function returns the subscript of the upper bound of the dimension specified in the second parameter. If you do not provide the second parameter, it is assumed that you want the upper bound of the first dimension. Note that this second parameter is one-based, not zero-based. Use 1 for the first dimension, 2 for the second, and so on.

The DisplayPhoneList() procedure uses UBound() to determine how many times it needs to loop around in order to touch all the rows in the array. This is a very common technique since you usually won't know how many rows are in your array. Inside the For loop, DisplayPhoneList() uses the named constants and the lngIndex loop counter variable to access the elements in the array.

The example script still has one flaw, however: the FillPhoneList() procedure is hard coded to add five hard-coded items into the phone list. This is not very realistic, since the phone list would probably be stored in a file or a database table. So lets look at some code that uses the ActiveX Data Objects (ADO) Recordset object to populate the array. This technique uses the Preserve keyword with the ReDim statement. Try not to worry about the details of the ADO syntax if you are not familiar with it. We cover ADO in Chapter 15.

```
Sub FillPhoneList

    Dim lngCounter
    Dim rsList

    <code goes here to create and open the Recordset object>

    ReDim astrPhoneList(PHONE,0)
    lngCounter = 0
    Do While Not rsList.EOF
```

```
ReDim Preserve astrPhoneList(PHONE, lngCounter)

  astrPhoneList(LAST_NAME, lngCounter) = rsList.Fields("LastName").Value
  astrPhoneList(FIRST_NAME, lngCounter) = rsList.Fields("FirstName").Value
  astrPhoneList(PHONE, lngCounter) = rsList.Fields("Phone").Value

  lngCounter = lngCounter + 1
  rsList.MoveNext
Loop

End Sub
```

The `ReDim Preserve` code inside the loop, using the `lngCounter` variable, makes the array successively larger as the loop goes around and around.

> Note: you can also use the ADO `Recordset.GetRows()` method to achieve the same thing that the above example does. Using `GetRows()` would be much faster as well.

Using VarType() with Arrays

The Microsoft VBScript documentation has an error in its description of the `VarType()` function in regards to arrays. It states that when you use the `VarType()` function to determine the subtype of an array variable, the number returned will be a combination of the number `8192` and the normal `VarType()` return value for the subtype (see the table earlier in this chapter for a list of all the subtype return values and their named constant equivalents). The named constant equivalent for `8192` is `vbArray`. You can subtract `8192` from the `VarType()` return value to determine that actual subtype. This is only partially correct. The `VarType()` function does indeed return `8192` (`vbArray`) plus another subtype number – but that other subtype number will *always* be 12 (`vbVariant`). The subtype of a VBScript array can *never be anything but* `Variant`.

Give this code a try and you'll see that, no matter what types of values you try to place in the array (`String`, `Date`, `Long`, `Integer`, `Boolean`, etc.), you'll never get the message box in the `Else` clause to display:

```
Dim strTest(1)
Dim lngSubType

strTest(0) = CLng(12)
strTest(1) = "Hello"

lngSubType = VarType(strTest) - vbArray

If lngSubType = vbVariant Then
  MsgBox "The Subtype is Variant."
Else
  MsgBox "The subtype is: " & lngSubType
End If
```

Since we are discussing complex data types, Visual Basic developers take note that User Defined Types (UDTs) are not supported in VBScript. You cannot define UDTs with the Type statement, nor can you work with UDT variables exposed by VB components.

Summary

In this chapter we covered the ins and outs of VBScript variables and data types. VBScript supports only one data type, the Variant, but the Variant data type supports many "subtypes." Declaring and using VBScript variables properly requires a full understanding the multi-faceted Variant data type. In this chapter, we also discussed more complex data types, including objects and arrays.

Control of Flow

This chapter will pick up where Chapter 2 left off. Chapter 2 introduced VBScript variables and data types. This chapter will cover "control of flow", which involves the techniques of "branching" and "looping" in your VBScript code. If you feel you might need a primer on how programming in general is done, you might want to read Chapter 1 before starting here. Chapters 2 and 3 cover many of the same topics that Chapter 1 does, but in Chapters 2 and 3, we cover the specific VBScript elements that support variables, data types, and control of flow – the most basic building blocks of programming. Chapter 1 covers these topics in a more general way, with the aim of initiating someone who has never written any computer programs or scripts before. If you are already experienced with programming in another language, but have never used VBScript, you can probably skip Chapter 1, but Chapters 2 and 3 will cover essential VBScript-specific topics.

Branching Constructs

"Branching" is the process of making a decision in your code and then, based on that decision, executing one block of code, but not others. We will see the most common branching construct, If...End If, many times throughout this chapter, and we introduced it in Chapter 1. In this section, we will cover the If...End If construct in detail, as well as another branching construct, Select...End Select.

> In Chapter 1, we also introduced the idea of a code block, which is a section of code that is delimited by beginning and ending statements. In the case of an If block, the beginning of it is defined by an If statement, and the end is defined by an End If statement. VBScript requires that both the beginning and the ending statements be there. If you forget to include the ending statement, VBScript will produce a syntax error at runtime. It's a good idea to get in the habit of typing both the beginning and ending statements first, before you type the code that goes between them. This ensures that you will not forget to type the ending statement, especially if the code that goes between the statements is rather involved. This is also especially helpful if you're going to be nesting multiple code blocks within each other.

The "If" Branch

The If...End If construct can be very simple, or it can become fairly complicated. In its simplest form, it requires this syntax:

```
If <expression> Then
    <other code goes here>
End If
```

In place of <expression> you can use anything that results in a True or False answer (also known as a Boolean expression). This can be a mathematical equation:

```
If 2 + 2 = 4 Then
    <other code goes here>
End If
```

Or it can be a function that returns True or False:

```
If IsNumeric(varAny) Then
    <other code goes here>
End If
```

Or it can use more complicated Boolean logic:

```
If strMagicWord = "Please" And (strName = "Hank" Or strName = "Bill") Then
    <other code goes here>
End If
```

You can also use the Not statement to reverse the True or False result of the expression:

```
If Not IsNumeric(varAny) Then
    <other code goes here>
End If
```

We can add another dimension to the If construct by adding an Else block. The Else block will be executed if the result of the If expression is False:

```
If IsNumeric(varAny) Then
    <other code goes here>
Else
    <some other code goes here>
End If
```

Many times, however, the decision you are trying to make does not involve a simple either/or evaluation. In that case, you can add as many ElseIf blocks as you like:

```
If IsNumeric(varAny) Then
    <other code goes here>
ElseIf IsDate(varAny) Then
    <some other code goes here>
ElseIf IsEmpty(varAny) Then
    <some other code goes here>
Else
    <some other code goes here>
End If
```

If the first expression returns False, then the execution moves to the first ElseIf evaluation. If that returns False, then the execution moves on to the second ElseIf evaluation. If that returns False, then the execution falls into the code in the Else block. Note that the ElseIf line must end with the word Then, just as the initial If line must. Keep in mind that the Else block is always optional:

```
If IsNumeric(varAny) Then
    <other code goes here>
ElseIf IsDate(varAny) Then
    <some other code goes here>
ElseIf IsEmpty(varAny) Then
    <some other code goes here>
End If
```

You can also nest If...End If blocks within each other:

```
If IsNumeric(varAny) Then
    If varAny > 0 Then
       <code goes here>
    ElseIf varAny < 0 Then
       <code goes here>
    Else
       <code goes here>
    End If
Else
    <some other code goes here>
End If
```

You can nest as deeply as you like, but beware of nesting too deeply, because the code can become unmanageable and hard to follow.

Keep in mind that a Select...End Select block (which we introduce in the next section) is often an alternative to an If...End If block with a lot of ElseIf blocks in the middle. However, the ElseIf construct is more flexible, because each different ElseIf line can evaluate something totally different, whereas a Select...End Select block must consider different possible results to the *same* expression. Because the If...ElseIf...End If is more flexible, you can always use it in place of Select...End Select. However, the reverse is not true. Select...End Select can *only* be used to evaluate different variations of the *same* expression.

Here is a sequence of ElseIf blocks that evaluate totally different expressions:

```
If boolFirst Then
    <other code goes here>
ElseIf boolSecond Then
    <some other code goes here>
ElseIf boolThird Then
    <some other code goes here>
ElseIf lngTest = 1 Then
    <some other code goes here>
ElseIf strName = "Bill" Then
    <some other code goes here>
End If
```

93

The "Select Case" Branch

As we mentioned in the previous section, the `Select...End Select` construct is useful when you are evaluating different possible results to the *same* expression. `Select...End Select` has the following syntax:

```
Select Case <expression>
    Case <possibility 1>
        <code goes here>
    Case <possibility 2>
        <other code goes here>
    Case <possibility 3>
        <other code goes here>
    Case <possibility n>
        <other code goes here>
    Case Else
        <other code goes here>
End Select
```

Notice that we are evaluating the same expression multiple times, whereas the `If...ElseIf...End If` block allows you to evaluate different expressions. Notice also that after all of the tests are made, we can include an optional `Case Else` block that will be executed if none of the other possibilities return `True`. Let's look at a real example:

```
Select Case VarType(varAny)
    Case vbString
        <code goes here>
    Case vbLong
        <code goes here>
    Case vbBoolean
        <code goes here>
    Case Else
        <code goes here>
End Select
```

The first line evaluates the expression `VarType(varAny)`, then each subsequent `Case` statement checks for each of many possible results. Finally, if none of the `Case` statements evaluates to `True`, then the `Case Else` block will be executed. Note that we could accomplish this same thing with an `If...ElseIf...End If` block:

```
If VarType(varAny) = vbString Then
    <code goes here>
ElseIf VarType(varAny) = vbLong Then
    <code goes here>
ElseIf VarType(varAny) = vbBoolean Then
    <code goes here>
Else
    <code goes here>
End If
```

However, this has the disadvantage that the expression `VarType(varAny)` will be executed for *every* `ElseIf` block, whereas with the `Select...End Select`, it is only evaluated once.

It is a good idea to always consider including a `Case Else` block in your `Select Case` blocks – even if you cannot conceive of a situation where the `Case Else` would be executed. This is a good idea for two reasons:

❑ *If something somewhere changes unexpectedly, and the `Case Else` block does suddenly start executing, your code will catch it – whereas without the `Case Else` block you might never catch it .*

❑ *Including a `Case Else` block can add documentation to the code as to why the `Case Else` block is never intended to be executed.*

It's a common convention to include a `Case Else` block that contains nothing other than a comment stipulating why the programmer expects the `Else` condition to never exist. Here's an example:

```
Select Case lngColor
    Case vbRed
        <code goes here>
    Case vbGreen
        <code goes here>
    Case vbBlue
        <code goes here>
    Case Else
        'We never use anything but Red, Green, and Blue
        MsgBox "Illegal color encountered: " & lngColor, _
            vbExclamation
End Select
```

You can also nest `Select...End Select` blocks within one another, and you can nest `If...End If` blocks (or any other kind of code) inside the `Select...End Select` as well:

```
Select Case VarType(varAny)
    Case vbString
        Select Case varAny
            Case "Test1"
                If Trim(strUserName) = "" Then
                    <code goes here>
                Else
                    <code goes here>
                End If
            Case "Test2"
                <code goes here>
            Case "Test3"
                <code goes here>
        End Select
    Case vbLong
        <code goes here>
    Case vbBoolean
        <code goes here>
    Case Else
        <code goes here>
End Select
```

Loop Constructs

Whereas branching is the process of making a decision on whether to execute one block of code or another, looping is the process of repeating the same block of code over and over. VBScript provides four looping constructs that you can use in different situations. In most programmer's minds, however, one of these loop constructs, the While...Wend loop, has been supplanted by the more intuitive, powerful, and flexible Do...Loop loop. For this reason, in this chapter we will emphasize the remaining three loops. However, in the interest of completeness, we will cover the syntax for the While...Wend loop at the end of the chapter.

Once you remove While...Wend from consideration, each of the remaining three loop constructs is ideal for a different type of loop. Each of the following sections will explain the syntax for these loops, as well as when you would use one loop or another.

For...Next

The For...Next loop is ideal for two situations:

❑ *When you want to execute a block of code repeatedly a known, finite number of times.*

❑ *When you want to execute a block of code once for each element in a structure (other than a **collection**, which is what the For Each...Next loop is for).*

Let's first look at how to use the For...Next loop to execute a block of code a known number of times.

```
Dim lngIndex

For lngIndex = 1 To 5
    MsgBox "Loop Index: " & lngIndex
Next
```

Running this code produces the following five dialog boxes, in succession:

This is pretty straightforward. The first thing you'll notice is that, in order to use the For...Next loop, you need a loop variable – also known as a loop index. The variable lngIndex serves this purpose. The statement For lngIndex = 1 to 5 means that this loop will execute five times. As you can see from the dialog boxes that pop up, the value of lngIndex matches each step in the traversal from the number 1 to the number 5. After looping for the fifth time, the loop stops and moves on. Note that you don't need to start at one in order to loop five times:

```
Dim lngIndex

For lngIndex = 10 To 14
    MsgBox "Loop Index: " & lngIndex
Next
```

This will still loop five times, but instead of starting at 1, it will start at 10. Each time around, lngIndex will have a value of 10, then 11, then 12, and so on to 14. You can also use the Step keyword to skip numbers:

```
Dim lngIndex

For lngIndex = 10 To 18 Step 2
    MsgBox "Loop Index: " & lngIndex
Next
```

Once again, this will still loop five times, but, because we specified Step 2, it will skip every other number. On the first loop, lngIndex will have a value of 10, then 12, then 14, and so on to 18. You can use any increment you like with the Step keyword:

```
Dim lngIndex

For lngIndex = 100 To 500 Step 100
    MsgBox "Loop Index: " & lngIndex
Next
```

You can also use the Step keyword to cause the loop to go backwards:

```
Dim lngIndex

For lngIndex = 5 To 1 Step -1
    MsgBox "Loop Index: " & lngIndex
Next
```

Because we used a negative number with the Step keyword, the loop goes downward through the numbers. Notice that in order for this to work, the increment range must specify the larger number first.

You are not limited to using negative numbers with the Step keyword. The loop itself can loop through negative numbers, like this:

```
Dim lngIndex

For lngIndex = -10 To -1
    MsgBox "Loop Index: " & lngIndex
Next
```

Or like this:

```
Dim lngIndex

For lngIndex = -10 To -20 Step -2
    MsgBox "Loop Index: " & lngIndex
Next
```

You can also nest loops inside one another:

```
Dim lngOuter
Dim lngInner

For lngOuter = 1 to 5
    MsgBox "Outer loop index: " & lngOuter

    For lngInner = 10 to 18 Step 2
        MsgBox "Inner loop index: " & lngInner
    Next
Next
```

So what do you do when you don't know exactly how many times you want to loop? This is a common situation. It often comes up when you need to traverse an array (see the next section, "Complex Data Types"), a string, or any other kind of structure. Let's look at an example:

```
Dim lngIndex
Dim lngStrLen
Dim strFullPath
Dim strFileName

'This code will extract the filename from a path

strFullPath = "C:\Windows\Temp\Test\myfile.txt"
lngStrLen = Len(strFullPath)

For lngIndex = lngStrLen To 1 Step -1
    If Mid(strFullPath, lngIndex, 1) = "\" Then
        strFileName = Right(strFullPath, lngStrLen - lngIndex)
        Exit For
    End If
Next

MsgBox "The filename is: " & strFileName
```

Running this code produces the following dialog box:

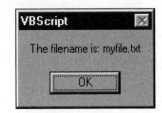

We've added some new elements in this example. The Len() function is a built-in VBScript function that returns the number of characters in a string. The Mid() function extracts one or more bytes from the middle of a string. The first parameter is the string to extract from; the second parameter is the character at which to start the extraction; the third parameter is how many characters to extract. The Right() function is similar to Mid(), except that it extracts a certain number of the rightmost characters in a string. Finally, the Exit For statement breaks you out of a loop. This is very handy when you know that you don't need to loop anymore.

Notice how we use the length of the strFullPath variable to drive how many times we need to loop. When we started, we did not know how many times we needed to loop, so we used the length of the structure we needed to traverse (in the case, a string) to tell us how many times to loop. Notice also how we loop backwards so that we can search for the last backslash character ("\") in the strFullPath variable. Once we've found the backslash, we know where the filename begins. Once we've used the Right() function to extract the filename into the strFileName variable, we don't need the loop anymore, so we use Exit For to break out of the loop. Exit For jumps the execution of the code to the very next line after the Next statement.

In the next section, "Complex Data Types", we'll show you how to use the For...Next loop to traverse an array.

> Note: the above example was provided for the purpose of demonstrating how to use a For...Next loop to move through a data structure of a size that is unknown at design time. This is not necessarily the best way to extract a filename from a full pathname. This, for example, would be much faster:
>
> ```
> Dim strFileName
> Dim strFullPath
>
> strFullPath = "C:\MyStuff\Documents\Personal\resume.doc"
>
> strFileName = Right(strFullPath, Len(strFullPath) -
> InStrRev(strFullPath,"\"))
>
> MsgBox "The filename is: " & strFileName
> ```

For Each...Next

The For Each...Next loop is a special kind of loop that is specifically used for traversing Collections. A Collection, as the name suggests, is a collection of data, almost like an array. A Collection is most often a collection of objects of the same type (even though Collections can be collections of virtually any kind of data). For example, the scripting Folder object has a Files Collection, which is exposed as a property on the Folder object. Inside the Folder.Files Collection are zero or more File objects. You can use a For Each...Next loop to move through each of the File objects in the Folder.Files Collection.

With the `For Each…Next` loop, you cannot directly control how many times the loop will go around. This is dependent upon how many objects are in the Collection you are traversing. However, you can still use the `Exit For` statement to break out of the loop at any time. You can figure out when to use `Exit For` by testing for some condition, or using an extra counter variable to count how many times you've gone through the loop. Let's look at an example that uses the `FileSystemObject` and related objects, which we introduce formally in Chapter 7. In this example, we will attempt to locate the `AUTOEXEC.BAT` file on our system. (Don't worry – it's safe to try out this code – there is no danger of harming your `AUTOEXEC.BAT` file.)

```
Dim objFSO
Dim objRootFolder
Dim objFileLoop
Dim boolFoundIt

Set objFSO = WScript.CreateObject("Scripting.FileSystemObject")
Set objRootFolder = objFSO.GetFolder("C:\")
Set objFSO = Nothing

boolFoundIt = False
For Each objFileLoop In objRootFolder.Files

    If UCase(objFileLoop.Name) = "AUTOEXEC.BAT" Then
        boolFoundIt = True
        Exit For
    End If

Next
Set objFileLoop = Nothing
Set objRootFolder = Nothing

If boolFoundIt Then
    MsgBox "We found your AUTOEXEC.BAT file in the C:\ directory."
Else
    MsgBox "We could not find AUTOEXEC.BAT in the C:\ directory."
End If
```

Try not to worry about the syntax that may be unfamiliar to you. Concentrate instead on the syntax of the `For Each…Next` loop block. The `objRootFolder` variable holds a reference to a `Folder` object. A `Folder` object has a `Files` collection. The `Files` collection is a collection of `File` objects. So what telling VBScript to do is "take a look at each `File` object in the `Files` Collection". Each time the loop goes around, the loop variable, `objFileLoop`, will hold a reference to a different `File` object in the `Files` collection. If the `Files` collection is empty, then the loop will not go around at all. Notice how we use the `Exit For` statement to break out of the loop once we've found the file we're looking for.

> Note: the above script example is intended to demonstrate the use of the **For Each…Next** loop to traverse a Collection of objects. This is not necessarily the best way to see if a file exists. For example, this is much faster and more compact:

```
Dim objFSO

Set objFSO =
WScript.CreateObject("Scripting.FileSystemObject")

If objFSO.FileExists("C:\AUTOEXEC.BAT") Then

    MsgBox "We found your AUTOEXEC.BAT file in the " _
        "C:\ directory."

End If

Set objFSO = Nothing
```

Before we move on to the Do loop, please note that even though the For Each...Next loop is most often used to loop through Collections, it can also be used to loop through all of the elements of an array. No matter how many elements or dimensions the array has, the For Each...Next loop will touch each and every one of them. Here is an example of using the For Each...Next loop to traverse a single dimension array:

```
Dim astrColors(3)
Dim strElement

astrColors(0) = "Red"
astrColors(1) = "Green"
astrColors(2) = "Blue"
astrColors(3) = "Yellow"

For Each strElement In astrColors
    MsgBox strElement
Next
```

Do...Loop

The Do...Loop is the most versatile of all of the loop constructs. This is because you can easily make it loop as many times as you like based on any criteria you like. (However, you'd have to jump through a few hoops to use it to traverse a collection – For Each...Next is much better for that.) The power of the Do loop is in the use of the While and Until keywords. You can use While or Until at either the beginning of the loop or the end of the loop to control whether the loop will go around again. Let's look at a simple script that uses a Do loop.

```
Dim boolLoopAgain
Dim lngLoopCount
Dim strResponse

boolLoopAgain = False
lngLoopCount = 0
Do
    boolLoopAgain = False
    lngLoopCount = lngLoopCount + 1
```

```
If lngLoopCount > 5 Then
        MsgBox "Okay, the word we wanted was 'Please.'"
    Else
        strResponse = InputBox("What is the magic word?")
        If UCase(Trim(strResponse)) = "PLEASE" Then
            MsgBox "Correct!  Congratulations!"
    Else
            MsgBox "Sorry, try again."
            boolLoopAgain = True
        End If
    End If

Loop While boolLoopAgain
```

Notice how the `Do` statement marks the beginning of the loop block, and how the `Loop` statement defines the end of the block. The `While` statement, however, places a condition on the `Loop` statement. The loop will only go around again if the expression following the `While` statement is `True`. In this case, our expression is a variable called `boolLoopAgain`, which has the `Boolean` subtype, but it could be any expression that evaluates to or returns a `True` or `False` response.

Notice also how we initialize the `boolLoopAgain` variable to `False` *before* the loop starts. This accomplishes two things: it establishes the subtype of the variable as `Boolean`, and it guarantees that the loop will only go around again if some piece of code inside the loop explicitly sets the variable to `True`. If the user guesses wrong, then we set `boolLoopAgain` to `True`, guaranteeing that the loop will go around at least one more time so we can ask the user to guess again. Finally, notice how we use a loop counter variable, `lngLoopCount`, to make sure that the loop does not go around forever and drive the user crazy if he can't guess the magic word. Using a loop counter variable is optional, and not part of the `Do`...`Loop` syntax, but it's a good idea if there's a chance that the loop might go around indefinitely.

Using this particular loop structure – with the `Do` statement by-itself at the beginning, and the `While` condition attached to the `Loop` statement at the end – has an important implication: because we did not place a condition on the `Do` statement, the code inside the loop is guaranteed to execute *at least once*. This is what we want in this case, because if we did not execute the code at least one time, the user would never get asked the question, "What is the magic word?"

Sometimes, though, you only want the code inside the loop to execute if some precondition is `True`; if that precondition is `False`, then you don't want the loop to execute at all. In that case, we can place the `While` statement at the beginning of the loop. If the `Do While` condition is `False`, then the loop will not go around even once. In the following example, we are going to use the `FileSystemObject` to open a text file. We will access the text file using a `TextStream` object. When you open a file in the form of a `TextStream` object, the `TextStream` object uses a "pointer" to keep track of it's place in the file as you move through it. When you first open the file, the pointer is at the beginning of the file. (The pointer is not physically placed in the file – it exists only in the `TextStream` object.) You can move through the file line-by-line using the `TextStream.ReadLine` method.

Each time you call ReadLine, the pointer moves one line down in the file. When the pointer moves past the last line in the file, the TextStream.AtEndOfStream property will have a value of True. That's when we know we are done reading the file. There is an issue though, that when we open a text file, we're not sure if it actually contains any data. It might be empty. If it is, then we don't want to call ReadLine, because this will cause an error. However, we'll know that the file is empty if the AtEndOfStream property is True right after opening the file. We can handle this nicely by placing the calls to ReadLine inside of a Do loop:

If you want to try out this code yourself, just create a text file and put the following lines in it:

```
Line 1
Line 2
Line 3
Line 4
Line 5
```

Save the file somewhere on your drive and make sure that the argument to the OpenTextFile method points to the file you created. The code for this is shown below (don't worry if you're not familiar with the particulars of the FileSystemObject and TextStream objects. They are covered in detail in Chapter 7):

```
Dim objFSO
Dim objStream
Dim strText

Set objFSO = WScript.CreateObject("Scripting.FileSystemObject")
Set objStream = objFSO.OpenTextFile("C:\temp\testfile.txt")
Set objFSO = Nothing

strText = ""
Do While Not objStream.AtEndOfStream
    strText = strText & objStream.ReadLine & vbNewLine
Loop
Set objStream = Nothing

If strText <> "" Then
    MsgBox strText
Else
    MsgBox "The file is empty."
End If
```

Running this code results in the following dialog box:

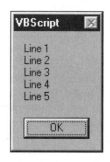

You can see that, by placing the While condition at the *beginning* of our loop, we can decide whether or not we want the loop to go around even once. If the file is empty, then we don't want to try reading any lines. Since there is no condition on the Loop statement, though, when the loop reaches the end, the code will jump back up to the Do line. However, if the Do While expression returns False, the loop will not execute again, and the code will jump back down to the line immediately following the Loop line.

For the record, note that we *could* have put the While statement with the Do in our first example and accomplished the same thing:

```
Dim boolLoopAgain
Dim lngLoopCount
Dim strResponse

boolLoopAgain = True
lngLoopCount = 0
Do While boolLoopAgain
    boolLoopAgain = False
    lngLoopCount = lngLoopCount + 1
    If lngLoopCount > 5 Then
        MsgBox "Okay, the word we wanted was 'Please.'"
    Else
        strResponse = InputBox("What is the magic word?")
        If UCase(strResponse) = "PLEASE" Then
            MsgBox "Correct!  Congratulations!"
        Else
            MsgBox "Sorry, try again."
            boolLoopAgain = True
        End If
    End If
Loop
```

Compare our first Do loop example with this one. Both examples accomplish exactly the same thing: the loop executes at least once, and it will only loop again if the code inside the loop says that we should. The difference with this second technique is that we started off by initializing boolLoopAgain to True, which guarantees that the loop will execute at least once. As you can see, the Do loop is quite versatile, and how you accomplish one thing or another is largely a matter of preference. That said, one could make a pretty good argument that the first version of this code is preferable because the Do statement all by itself makes it obvious that the loop is going to execute at least once, whereas this second example is a little bit tricky.

> **All else being equal, if there are two ways of coding something, the more explicit method is almost always preferable.**

So the first question you need to answer when considering the use of the Do loop is, do I want the code to execute at least once, no matter what? If the answer to that question is Yes, then it's best to place your condition at the end of the loop. Otherwise, put the condition at the beginning of the loop.

However, there is a second question: should you use the `While` statement for the condition, or its cousin, the `Until` statement? The answer to this second question is also largely a matter of preference. Although the `While` and `Until` statements are slightly different, they pretty much do the same thing. The main difference is one of semantics, and people generally fall into the habit of using one or the other, based on which syntax makes the most intuitive sense to them. However, one will usually tend to be more clear than another in a given situation.

Here's how Microsoft's VBScript documentation describes the `Do` loop (we added the **bold** emphasis):

> *"Repeats a block of statements **while** a condition is `True` or **until** a condition becomes `True`."*

As you can see, the distinction between `While` and `Until` is rather fuzzy. The easiest way to explain the difference is to look at our previous two examples, but using `Until` instead of `While`. You'll see that the consideration of whether to execute the loop *at least once* remains the same. However, the implementation is slightly different. Here's our first example, modified to use `Until`:

```
Dim boolLoopAgain
Dim lngLoopCount
Dim strResponse

boolLoopAgain = False
lngLoopCount = 0
Do
    boolLoopAgain = False
    lngLoopCount = lngLoopCount + 1

    If lngLoopCount > 5 Then
        MsgBox "Okay, the word we wanted was 'Please.'"
    Else
        strResponse = InputBox("What is the magic word?")
        If UCase(strResponse) = "PLEASE" Then
            MsgBox "Correct!  Congratulations!"
        Else
            MsgBox "Sorry, try again."
            boolLoopAgain = True
        End If
    End If

Loop Until boolLoopAgain = False
```

Looks like the same thing, no? The difference is that we must test for a `False` value in our `Until` clause, whereas we tested for a `True` value in our `While` clause. When you read the line `Loop While boolLoopAgain`, does it make more sense than `Loop Until boolLoopAgain = False`? If the `While` syntax makes more sense to you, maybe we can fix that by changing the name of our variable:

```
Dim boolStopLooping
Dim lngLoopCount
Dim strResponse
```

```
boolStopLooping = True
lngLoopCount = 0
Do

    boolStopLooping = True
    lngLoopCount = lngLoopCount + 1

    If lngLoopCount > 5 Then
        MsgBox "Okay, the word we wanted was 'Please.'"
    Else
        strResponse = InputBox("What is the magic word?")
        If UCase(strResponse) = "PLEASE" Then
            MsgBox "Correct!  Congratulations!"
        Else
            MsgBox "Sorry, try again."
            boolStopLooping = False
        End If
    End If

Loop Until boolStopLooping
```

Does the `Until` syntax make a little more sense now? The point is, you can use either `While` or `Until` to accomplish what you need to, it's just a matter of what makes more sense in a given situation. Let's look at our second example again, this time using `Until`:

```
Dim objFSO
Dim objStream
Dim strText

Set objFSO = WScript.CreateObject("Scripting.FileSystemObject")
Set objStream = objFSO.OpenTextFile("C:\temp\testfile.txt")
Set objFSO = Nothing

strText = ""
Do Until objStream.AtEndOfStream
    strText = strText & objStream.ReadLine & vbNewLine
Loop
Set objStream = Nothing

If strText <> "" Then
    MsgBox strText
Else
    MsgBox "The file is empty."
End If
```

What do you think? Does the `Until` syntax make this more clear? It just might. People sometimes have an easier time thinking in terms of positives, and the syntax `Do While Not objStream.AtEndOfStream` may be more or less clear to you than `Do Until objStream.AtEndOfStream`. It's up to you, though. VBScript doesn't care.

Before we move on to `While...Wend`, we need to mention the `Exit Do` statement. Like `Exit For`, you can use `Exit Do` to break out of a `Do` loop at any point. You can have as many `Exit Do` statements inside your loop as you like. Here's an example, yet another spin on our first example:

```
Dim boolStopLooping
Dim lngLoopCount
Dim strResponse

boolStopLooping = True
lngLoopCount = 0
Do
    lngLoopCount = lngLoopCount + 1

    If lngLoopCount > 5 Then
        MsgBox "Okay, the word we wanted was 'Please.'"
        Exit Do
    End If

    strResponse = InputBox("What is the magic word?")
    If UCase(strResponse) = "PLEASE" Then
        MsgBox "Correct!  Congratulations!"
        boolStopLooping = True
    Else
        MsgBox "Sorry, try again."
        boolStopLooping = False
    End If

Loop Until boolStopLooping
```

Instead of setting `boolStopLooping` to `True`, we just execute an `Exit Do`, which has the same effect. When the `Exit Do` statement executes, the code jumps out of the loop, to the line of code immediately following the last line of the loop block (in our example, there is not any code after our loop, so the script ends). Note that if you are working with nested loops, an `Exit Do` executed in the *inner* loop *does not* break out of the *outer* loop as well – only from the loop in which the `Exit Do` was executed.

While...Wend

As we mentioned at the beginning of the chapter, the While...Wend loop is an older loop syntax from early versions of BASIC and Visual Basic. The Do loop (see previous section) is almost universally preferred over the While...Wend loop, which is not nearly as versatile. This is not to say that it is not perfectly valid to use it. It works fine, it's simple, and Microsoft certainly has not given any indication that they plan to remove support for it. It has simply fallen out of vogue. In the interest of completeness, here's an example of the While...Wend syntax:

```
Dim lngCounter

lngCounter = 0
While lngCounter <= 20
    lngCounter = lngCounter + 1
    <other code goes here>
Wend
```

Unlike the Do loop, you do not have the option of using either While or Until, nor can you place the condition at the end of the loop. The condition for whether to loop again can only be placed at the beginning of the loop, as you see here. Finally, to put the nail in the coffin of the While...Wend loop, there is no equivalent to Exit For or Exit Do, meaning you cannot forcibly break out of the loop.

Summary

In this chapter we covered the topic of "control of flow", which involves branching and looping. Branching is the technique of checking conditions, making a decision, and executing (or not executing) a block of code based on that decision. Looping is the technique of repeating the same block of code over again.

Error Handling, Prevention and Debugging

Overview

Error handling, unlike some other features, has been one of the selling points of VBScript. In fact, until Version 5.0 of JScript had been released, VBScript held tremendous edge over JScript because of its error handling capabilities (at least on the server side of scripting). By now, you would expect volumes of literature on error handling to exist, but this couldn't be further from the truth. As the scripting hosts grow in their complexity, so do the general capabilities of scripted applications, and the end user's expectations. At the same time, however, the schedules get tighter and the workloads get bigger, making even ordinary bugs more difficult to catch. It seems that proper testing and error handling ends up on the back burner, and unjustifiably so, because simple error handling is not that difficult, as this chapter will show.

In this chapter, we will cover:

- ❏ How minute differences in hosts can affect runtime errors
- ❏ Different types of errors, and error display
- ❏ Basic handling of errors
- ❏ Strategies for handling errors in different situations
- ❏ Defensive coding strategies
- ❏ Debugging with Script Debugger and Visual InterDev
- ❏ Common errors and how to avoid them

Introduction

No matter how simple a VBScript project you are developing, there is always a need for effective error handling and debugging. If a project worked just fine the last time you tested it, it can be hard to see how error handling and debugging are at all relevant. In reality, script execution will depend on a variety of factors, starting with the user, and ending with the physical environment in which the project runs. To understand what the problems are, let's first consider the user.

Users rarely do what we expect them to do.

While many problems can be avoided by giving the user precise instructions and a clear interface in the first place, often the user does not take time to read the instructions, or does not understand them. So *you* understanding the way *your* project works might make it more difficult for *you* to anticipate the sort of mistakes a *user* might make. Thorough testing is therefore essential, especially when considering issues such as what happens if the user enters text when you are expecting numerical input? Does the script validate the data? Does the browser generate an error if the user clicks in the web page before a sub-procedure is completed? Even if all the user entered data is valid, there still exist possibilities that the user entered data may not work with other parts of the script – for instance, the data may represent a duplicate record, which will not be accepted by the database. Will the server script generate the error?

Next, the *dynamically* generated scripts which often depend on each other, are another common source of errors. What if one of the procedures does not perform exactly as in the test case or if the list box, containing an array of choices, is not present, or empty? Similarly, scripts depending on some components may not be able to access them. Perhaps the user has different *security preferences* than you anticipated, or does not have an appropriate component loaded on the system, or appropriate permissions to run it. What does your program do? Will your script attempt to log the error, or ask the user to file a report?

Finally, hardware issues may be responsible for serious deviations in script executions. The servers can be down, the client computer may be low on memory, or the disk that the script is trying to access may simply crash. Will an operator be alerted about a major malfunction?

In order to handle the error, you must anticipate it before it happens. Although defensive programming goes hand in hand with error handling, you'll have to figure out the trade offs, and choose the best technique for the situation.

Is there a part of the script that doesn't work *exactly* the way you expected it to and, while the user will quite probably discover it, you might not have noticed? These are all good reasons for emphasizing the following:

> **Thorough testing, debugging and error handling are vital for a project of any size.**

Undeniably, it is a chore to plan for errors before they happen, but in the long term, it is well worth the effort and is a valuable habit to get into. Note that there is more to error handling than the glorified `On Error` statement (dealt with later in this chapter). Before you rush out to use it, you should realize that it is as often used to handle errors as it is to cover up bugs and sloppy coding. Error handling is therefore also about good programming practices and testing methods, as well as using the `On Error` statement to handle the true exceptions.

Errors are not the evil we are led to believe and they can happen for bad or good reasons. As long as they are caught and handled properly (sometimes, you will not be able to correct an error), your programs will run smoothly. Understanding the differences in the types of errors, the situations in which they occur, and the simple error-handling techniques available, is paramount to graceful error handling. The environment that your script feeds from, the complexity and your own understanding of the language and the language's facilities, all combine to produce a vast source of possible errors.

> **Note that error handling associated with the Script Control (Chapter 16) is slightly different than with other hosts. Although error handling within the Script Control works similarly to other scripting hosts, there is also the possibility of handling errors via the host (e.g. the VB application itself), with a distinction between compilation and run-time errors. For more specific information, consult the above chapter on Script Control.**

Error handling and debugging can also give a much more professional finish to a project, as well as a sense of security that it will be able to stand up to at least some of what the users are going to throw at it. However, it is not only the user that can make mistakes: the errors can lurk in the script itself. Let's look at some other types of errors that can afflict your code.

Seeing the Error of your Ways

Error messages that are displayed by the host identify the line number and the nature of the error (see the figure below). Depending on the host, and on the nature of the error, the error code may be displayed as a decimal number (such as 1024) , a hexadecimal one (such as 800a0400), or simply as the text message identifying the error . If the error code is hexadecimal, and begins with 800A, it is thrown by the scripting engine, and the remaining four digits can be converted to its decimal representation. (They are covered in Appendix E, and are additionally listed in VBScript's help files, but without the hexadecimal representations.) Errors thrown by COM components and Windows are usually shown using hexadecimal codes.

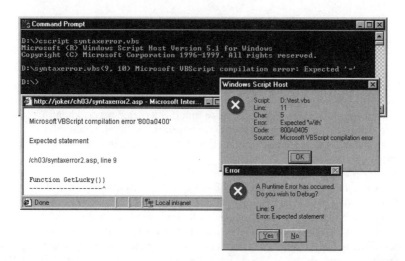

Now, to make things more complex for the beginner, sometimes these error messages will not show up, or will show up in a disguised format. These problems can be caused by the configuration of the host and, at least in the debugging stage of the project, the host ought to be configured to handle errors in the way you want it to behave. Only two of the hosts can change the way in which errors are displayed: the ASP engine (the IIS server) and IE5.

Enabling Error Display in IIS

Error handling in IIS is done on a Web application level (note: this does not apply to PWS). Generally, each Web application will have an application initialization file – the global.asa file – in its directory (see Chapter 14 for a description of this file and of ASP in general). If you are working with a newly installed server, there is no need to override any of the settings. If you are inheriting a server, or just an IIS application, and errors messages are not being displayed, you should edit the application's properties through the IIS' MMC (Microsoft Management Console) as shown in the figure below. In Windows 2000 it is called Internet Information Services. Other errors (especially HTTP) can also be configured using the Custom Errors tab (for more information you should consult an IIS reference available with installation of the Option Pack, or with Windows 2000).

Unfortunately, the error settings are hidden within the many options of the directory or file, or of the application, and to change the error options you have to locate the appropriate application, and then hit the **Configuration...** button to set the options available on the figure below. Obviously, in order to see the messages, the **Send detailed ASP error messages to client** option should be selected. Once your application is debugged and in production mode, the other option is preferred as occasionally an error may expose critical information about your system to the end user (e.g. critical variables, or a database name of the application), especially in a situation when custom error handlers are not available. Debugging flags, as seen on the screenshot, do not need to be modified as they are usually handled by Visual InterDev. If you are using the free debugger (downloadable from the Microsoft Scripting site), you must set the flags by yourself, and start the debugger before calling any of the ASP pages.

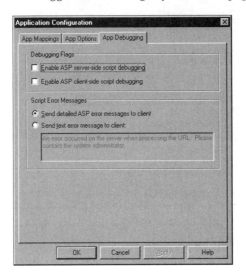

Enabling Error Display in IE 5.0

Although Internet Explorer 5.0 has an improved error display over previous versions, it has introduced several options that may cause some confusion. Essentially, there are two modes – 'debug' and 'run' – in which Internet Explorer can operate, each of which has certain quirks. The preferred mode of error display and debugging (at least, for developers in development mode) is the 'debug' mode with the use of the Script Debugger. However, when in 'production' and 'testing' modes, debugging should be disabled (see the note below). The standard (and free) script debugger may be downloaded from the Microsoft Scripting site:

```
http://msdn.microsoft.com/scripting/debugger/default.htm.
```

An alternative to the script debugger is the Visual InterDev application environment (which includes the script debugger), as well as the Microsoft Office 2000 element, the Microsoft Script Editor. Script debugger is also installed with Windows 2000. After the script debugger has been installed on the system, IE can display two different types of error messages, and allow the option of entering the debugger once the error has been found.

> With IE 4, similar steps can be taken to disable and enable debugging. There is no option to hide error display as in IE 5.

Internet Explorer error settings are neatly kept away from the end users and sometimes can be frustrating to locate. From the Tools menu you have to choose Internet Options... and then the Advanced tab to see the advanced IE settings as seen in the figure:

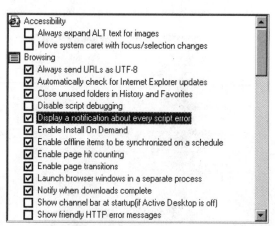

There are two options of interest to us: Disable script debugging and Display a notification about every script error.

With the first option selected, the debugger is disabled, and depending on the selection of the second option, either the so-called 'user friendly' error dialog box is set for the browser, or the error icon in the lower-left corner of the Internet Explorer. Although the dialog box shown below may be more *user* friendly, it may not be *programmer* friendly. The error code is not displayed (only the text of the error code – which forces you to dig through error code tables in case you would want to handle the error in code), but the line number is displayed correctly. The dialog box displayed below is for the same snippet of code as the dialog window shown in the following figure, but the line number in there is wrong (although after going into the debug mode the correct error is highlighted).

The disable script debugging option works only when the script debugger is installed on the system; and additionally the browser has to be restarted before changes to this option can take effect. Since this chapter will strictly work in developer mode, all of the IE errors will be presented in the 'debug' mode, as displayed in the figure below – do not check the Disable Script Debugging option:

The second option of interest – Display a notification about every script error – works when the debug option is de-selected (Disable script debugging), and it enables suppression of errors. When this option is cleared, an icon appears on the status bar to inform the user that an error has occurred; the error is then displayed by clicking on the icon. The yellow sign with an exclamation mark indicates that there was an error on the page, as seen in the snapshot below.

Obviously, this is the least desirable setup from the developer's point of view. However, it might be the default setup on your client's browser, which may prevent your client from reporting any unhandled errors back to you. When the Display Notification About Every Error option is checked, or the user clicks on the error icon (from the snapshot above), the following dialog will appear.

117

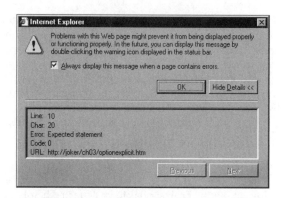

You should be aware of these subtle differences in error display, especially since this setting is in your end users' control. Your error handling mechanism may be disabled because of it, or the end user may not be able to see that an error has occurred, and be surprised that the page does not work.

> Note that when not 'debugging' scripts, the **Disable Script Debugging** option should be selected at all times. When in debug mode, the scripting engine, upon interception of an error, automatically invokes the debugger, and prompts the user if the debugger should be opened. Although this is nice, the standard client error handlers are ignored. Even if there is an error handler capable of correcting the error it will not be invoked. It would be nice if the debugger would start only as the last resort, but this is not the case. This problem does not apply to ASP's Visual InterDev debugging options.

Other hosts are 'dumber', in a sense that errors are always displayed (with the exception of WSH 2.0 – now in beta), and debugging is not possible. Different coding and debugging strategies are discussed later in this chapter.

Different Types of Errors

There are three types of errors that can burrow their way into your lovingly crafted VBScript (or any other scripting or programming language for that matter). The three types are not equally severe, the syntax errors will halt the execution of the script, run-time errors will invoke an error handler, and logical errors will most commonly contaminate data in your application, and often cause other run-time errors to occur.

Syntax Errors

VBScript, like all other programming or scripting languages, follows set rules for construction of statements. Before the script is run, the scripting engine parses all of the code, converting it into tokens. When an unrecognizable structure or an expression is encountered (for example, if you mistype a keyword or forget to close a loop), a syntax error is generated. Luckily, syntax errors can usually be caught during development phase, with minimal testing of the code.

> **In some programming environments, syntax errors are called pre-processor, compilation, or compile-time errors. If your script includes a syntax error, the script will not execute and the host immediately informs the user of an error.**

Those of you who are used to writing applications using Visual Basic will be used to having syntax errors highlighted by the interpreter in the IDE as soon as you move from the line containing the syntax error. This is a very useful feature that unfortunately is not available when using VBScript since the script is not interpreted until it is executed. What happens depends on what you are doing. If the syntax error is in a script being run at the server (as in an ASP-based application – see Chapter 14) then the error text is simply passed through and displayed in the client browser instead of the requested page, as shown in the figure below:

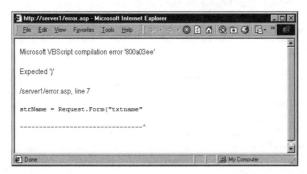

If the syntax error is in a client side script being run at the browser, the document loads but the script that contains the error prevents it from running properly.

What exactly happens depends on where in the script the error occurs. However, each time the script is run, the error message will be displayed. Here is the error message in Internet Explorer 4.0:

Here is the same error as seen by Internet Explorer 5.0. Notice how the syntax error is confusingly referred to as a run-time error:

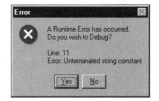

Syntax, and run-time errors are easier to spot than logic errors (which we will look at shortly) because they always result in an error message being generated. Needless to say, with proper understanding of VBScript, syntax errors are not a major concern.

Syntax errors tend to pop-up in several circumstances:

❑ When something is missing from the code – parentheses, keywords (especially in blocks), statement elements, or when the keywords are simply out of place.

❑ When a keyword is misspelled or used incorrectly.

❑ When you try to use a VB or VBA keyword that is not implemented by VBScript.

❑ When you use keywords that are not supported by the scripting engine (certain keywords may be phased out, and others added).

> Unfortunately, VBScript does not support conditional compilation (the ability to run different code depending on environment settings). Hence, when writing code for different versions of browsers, or scripting engines, you may either have to 'know-the-version', or use JScript.

As you may expect, code executed as part of `Eval()` or `Execute` and `ExecuteGlobalstatements` is not parsed before the script is run, and can generate runtime errors (but are exempt from the `Option Explicit` rules). Special attention has to be paid when generating dynamic code. Appendix E shows all 53 of VBScript's Syntax Errors and their codes. All of these errors, with an exception of the first two – Out Of Memory and Syntax Error – are relatively easy to diagnose and correct, but all of these errors (such as Expected '(' or Expected 'If') should really be caught when the program is run the first time.

Runtime Errors

The second, and most common type of error (at least to the general public), is the runtime error. A runtime error occurs when a command attempts to perform an action that is invalid. For example, a runtime error occurs if you try to divide by zero:

```
Sub window_onload()
Ans = 200/0
Msgbox Ans
End Sub
```

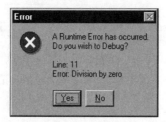

The various conditions that can result in runtime error depend on the language you are scripting with. A condition that might cause a runtime error in VBScript might not cause an error in JScript (for example, attempting to divide by zero in JScript doesn't generate an error). The result of a runtime error is similar to that of a syntax error – the script is halted and an error message is displayed.

Unlike the syntax errors, which pop-up when the script is loaded, runtime errors show up during script execution by the scripting engine. Runtime errors can occur as a result of bad coding (which should really be caught during the debugging and testing stage of the project), and as a result of unusual circumstances that may or may not be prevented. There are many factors that can contribute to a runtime error, all depending on the conditions under which the script is run.

The main reasons for these 'unusual circumstances' are:

❑   Certain security options may be turned on or off. For example, your script may try to access a component that has not been marked as "safe for scripting". In the tests you've carried out the Internet Explorer has been set to trust the component; however, during final release, the script crashes because of different security settings on client browsers.

❑   Components may or may not be available. Here, you might assume that a component is readily available on the client system, and not provide installation information when referencing the component. When the component is not available, the script will cause a run-time error.

❑   Platform differences. VBScript may be available on many platforms (including Unix, or Alpha) but the features supported by each platform may vary, especially when using external components.

❑   Configuration may be totally different (you should not expect an HTA based script to run 100% as an HTML based script).

❑   Finally, the computer might be under unusual stress. Scripts that use unusual amount of system resources (memory or CPU time, for example) may behave unexpectedly, especially when other scripts and applications contend for the same resources. Applications can often time out, and raise an error directly to the script, or, in other cases, terminate a script.

Technically, when the runtime error occurs, the script execution is stopped and the VBScript engine invokes an exception handler (it is considerably weaker in its functionality than the VB or VBA exception handler). There are several options at this point, but we will defer them to a later section – **What can we do about errors?**. The most essential error handler in question is the `On Error Resume Next` statement, which unfortunately requires a little foreknowledge into the possibility of an error occurring at the right time and at the right line of code (as you have to perform error testing immediately after the error occurs) in order to be able to use it. Internet Explorer additionally provides `window.onerror` and `element.onerror` events that can be bound to functions, which is covered in Appendix E. If no error handler is present, the error is reported back to the client.

Thus, runtime errors provide us with the possibility of taking some action. In order to correct the error in VBScript, you will need to know the decimal version of the error number (which is also provided as a hexadecimal code, for cases when VBScript throws an error, and passes it to the host): a full listing of VBScript runtime errors is provided in Appendix E. The majority of these errors (such as Division by zero or Variable is undefined), however, are simply a result of poor programming, and really should be caught during the debugging and testing stage of the project, rather than corrected by some overly complex error handler.

Non VBScript Runtime Errors

Usage of outside components and files (Automation Objects) can also be a cause of runtime errors. Although some of the errors listed below will be thrown in reference to improper usage of other components and files, you can also expect to see a lot of errors that may either be raised by the component or the operation system. For instance, the `ADODB.Recordset` component may raise the following error:

Microsoft OLE DB Provider for ODBC Drivers error '80004005' [Microsoft][ODBC Driver Manager] Data source name not found and no default driver specified

This is probably the most common COM failure error (which, in this case, actually has a useful description). This particular error – 80004005 (called SCODE) – is raised by a number of COM components, and sometimes contains useful information, as in the case above. Most of the time, though, you will end up scratching your head, wondering what the error message might mean. Good sources of information about errors are the appropriate documentation and Microsoft's Personal Online Support Site at `http://support.microsoft.com/support/search/`.

When trying to find out the meanings of error messages (after you realize it is not an error based in your VBScript), you may use the following list as a rule of thumb to identify a potential source of error:

8007xxxx	Windows errors (you may convert the xxxx hex code to decimal and use `net helpmsg dddd` in DOS window to find out the meaning of the error)
800Axxxx	ADO errors
80005xxx	ADSI errors

Knowledge of error codes thrown by components and windows is essential in the development of error handling functions, as the majority of error handling functions often rely on outside components.

> Additionally, some components, such as ADO, contain their own Errors collection, which may expose more than a single error that occurred. In case of ADO, the Errors collection contains information pertaining to a single operation involving a given provider. You should research a given component not only for the errors it might raise through automation, but also about its internal error handling capabilities.

Problems with Option Explicit

> If you come to VBScript with a good VB or VBA background, you are probably accustomed to the usage of `Option Explicit` statement as the very first line in your program. Kudos to you, but you should not expect the same behavior in VBScript. Expect a lot more work on your behalf. From now on this is a runtime error.

The Option Explicit statement is one of the many statements transplanted from VB into VBScript. It is particularly useful in identifying undeclared and misspelled variables, or variables that are being used beyond their scope. When a script contains the Option Explicit statement before any other statements, the scripting engine expects all variables to be declared explicitly by using any of the Dim, Private, Public, or ReDim statements, and only to be used within their scope (except for dynamically executed code associated with Eval, Execute and ExecuteGlobal). Unfortunately, unlike in VB or VBA, using Option Explicit causes the runtime error 500 Undeclared Variable; as you can imagine, this severely limits its usefulness when used in combination with the On Error Resume Next statement.

Let us demonstrate this with an example. The following code contains two undeclared variables, one that has global scope, and one within the scope of the GetLucky() function. The power of Option Explicit is easily identifiable:

```
<SCRIPT LANGUAGE=vbscript>
<!--
Option Explicit

Dim intMyNumber, intResult        ' Declare variables
intLucky = 10                     ' Undeclared variable generates syntax error
intMyNumber = 10                  ' Declared variable does not generate error
intResult = GetLucky()

Function GetLucky()
   Dim intMyNumber                ' Declare variable local in scope
   intLuck = 3                    ' Undeclared variable: wanted to change
                                  ' intLucky - error

   intMyNumber = 4 + intLucky     ' Now have 14 instead of 7 like we wanted
   GetLucky = intMyNumber
End Function
-->
</SCRIPT>
```

After the first run, we see that intLucky is not declared, and we proceed to fix the error:

```
Dim intMyNumber, intResult, intLucky                ' Declare variables
```

Now, as the screenshot below shows, we find another error (an undeclared or misspelled variable), which is easy to correct. Clearly, we wanted to change the global variable, intLucky, and the Option Explicit statement helps us to identify our mistake. Without the Option Explicit statement at the start of the script, various mistakes of this nature are likely to pass unnoticed, causing odd or unwanted results at runtime.

With the obvious usefulness of the Option Explicit statement, why should we be unhappy with it? Well, because it is a runtime error, and consequently, undeclared variables will not show up during parse stage, and its detection may even be negated by the use of On Error statement (with either Error being overwritten, or cleared) – something that is the opposite in the VB environment.

If the GetLucky() function had not been executed (some functions will not be called each time the script is run, depending on user responses), the undefined variable error would never have materialized. Secondly, it creates complications when you are creating error-handling functions. Essentially, when handling exceptions, you are expecting something more significant than an undeclared variable, in other words you are expecting a true exception, and not just a simple programming mistake.

Rarely will you try to correct this mistake, and you will probably have to consider an undeclared variable as a critical error, which should be caught early in the development stage. Unfortunately, this will throw you off because of the manner in which it will be introduced – the error may exist in a rarely accessed procedure, and the error reporting procedure may not be prepared to identify this type of error. Although error handling is discussed in more detail later in the chapter, consider a simple illustration of what might go wrong. Let us add On Error Resume Next – a footstep of error handling immediately after Option Explicit to the code above, as following:

```
Option Explicit
On Error Resume Next
```

Now, when running the script, Option Explicit is essentially neutralized, and the error is not easily caught. If a generic error handler were available, it would inform us that an error has occurred, but it would not tell us the line where the error occurred.

When writing an error handler, remember to provide reporting functionality for generic errors, including undefined variables. A callout label in such a handler may prove invaluable. Although you may not know the exact line number where the error occurred, at least you will be aware of its proximity.

In any way, when combining Option Explicit with On Error Resume Next you have to be extremely careful in the way you test for errors, create a scope for an exception handler, override the default exception handler, and, finally, clear the exception handler (via On Error Goto 0). More on Error Handling specifics is available in the Appendix E.

Logic Errors

Logic errors, or **bugs**, are the most difficult of all the errors to catch and track down. By their nature, these errors are caused when a valid script (no syntax, or runtime errors) produces undesirable results. For example, a script that asks for the user's password before letting them proceed, but which still allows them to proceed whether the password is correct or not, would have a logic error. Likewise a script that totaled-up an order form but which did not handle the tax right would be a logic error. A script might be designed to convert measurements from one unit to another (Fahrenheit to Celsius, for example) but if the formula is wrong, you have a logic error. In other words, VBScript will always do what you tell it to do, not what you thought or meant to tell it to do. The scripting engine will not generate an error message – your script will simply produce unexpected output; however, logic errors' side effects often include creation of other errors as well.

As always though, there are exceptions to the no-error-message rule for logic errors. This is in relation to infinite loops. For example:

```
Sub window_onload()
    Dim intX
    Do Until(intX)
        If intX < 10 Then
            inX = intX - 1
                'the above line has a mistake in the variable name
        End If
    Loop
End Sub
```

If your script contains a script that takes a long time to process then the VBScript DLL will eventually time out and display the following error message:

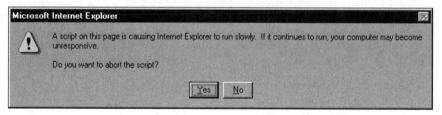

This allows you to stop the script before the system becomes unstable. However, it does not provide you with any clues as to what or where the error is.

Identification of logic errors is beyond the scope of this chapter. The most common types of errors will include bad calculation formulas, incorrect usage of operators, improper rounding, and generally problems with conditional statements, loops, and general lack of validation of data. The only way to reduce the occurrence of these is through full testing of borderline outcomes. There are testing tools, such as Visual Test, which will simplify repetitive testing processes (including regression testing), and the debugger (available with IE, or Visual InterDev), which will help you step through the code, look at the contents of variables, and the calling stack. In a proper test you will be required to feed the script a lot of data (good, borderline, and bad) and compare the output against the output you have calculated (or figured out) manually. Some tips on testing are:

❏ Check, double check, then recheck again any formulae you have used in your script, to make sure that they return the correct results.

❏ Work out the results that you expect – try out all the different combinations.

❏ Consider how the user might impact a calculation by, for example, entering zero or a negative number – does the script cope with this?

❏ Check that the knock-on effects of any actions are there – for example, if a customer deletes an item from their order, be sure to check that the item is removed AND the order total changed.

❏ Do not just check things to see if they work, also check what happens under circumstances where you know they should not work.

Only careful testing can help you spot logic errors in your projects.

Unfortunately, there are no other good techniques for catching logic errors. VBScript does not support anything like `Debug.Assert` which is found in its parent languages, and even though you might create an object with similar functionality on your own, you will also have to remove the additional code during the release stage on your own (this is not the case with VB and VBA). There are some guidelines we can follow:

❏ Testing (as mentioned above) is essential to eliminate logic and runtime errors.

❏ Use encapsulation within VBScript classes to reduce the chances of logic errors occurring.

❏ Whenever you can, re-use old code that has been thoroughly tested and that you know from experience works (one may say that the only good code is old code, which is crazy considering that the Internet reinvents itself every few months).

❏ Always adhere to coding conventions – these increase the overall clarity of your code.

❏ Adoption of good programming practices, particularly at design time, dramatically reduces the complexity of your code.

The only marginally practical technique is to treat possible logic errors as runtime errors, by raising an error. By testing and validating the critical values internally in the key subroutines and functions (at least, checking the input parameters), you may be able to find areas in which your code is producing an undesirable output. When you find that data is not valid within a certain predefined range, you may raise an error, and break execution within that procedure. This will, unfortunately, only cover a small percentage of logic errors; we re-emphasize that only a stringent testing method can identify all of the logic errors within your script.

Finally, logic errors are sometimes a by-product of a high degree of complexity. Proper encapsulation, variable scoping, and use of VBScript classes will undoubtedly reduce the likelihood of logic errors occurring. Following this to the extreme, the best approach is to simply re-use old and trusted code, whether by use of includes (in HTML and ASP) or through the use of various components (`.wsc`, `.htc`, `.dll`, `.ocx`).

What Can We Do About Errors?

There are two things we can do with an error:

❑ Get rid of it completely

❑ Handle it

Because it isn't possible to make a script completely bomb-proof (since errors can be caused not only by mistakes in the script itself but also by actions taken by the user), there is a real need to implement a method by which errors are dealt with more effectively than simply flashing the error message dialog box at the user.

> Remember that to most users the error messages will be incomprehensible.

We will look at how we get rid of errors later in this chapter, when we come to debugging, but for now let us look at what is meant by handling errors and how we go about doing it. Also take a look at Appendix E, which includes complete syntax, and many examples of error handling.

Handling Errors

The process of error handling involves detecting the error as it occurs and dealing with it effectively. How we choose to deal with errors depends on the type of error, what caused it and the consequences resulting from it. The simplest thing we can do with an error is ignore it and to do this we use the On Error Resume Next statement.

On Error Resume Next

The On Error statement enables error handling in the script that we are writing. The only thing that we can do with the On Error statement in VBScript is to Resume Next. What this means is that an error in the script in any procedure, instead of being fatal and causing the script execution to stop, is overlooked and the execution continues with the next statement following the error or with the statement following the most recent call out of the procedure containing the On Error Resume Next statement. In other words:

> On Error Resume Next is the VBScript equivalent of telling the interpreter to ignore any errors and carry on regardless!

The On Error Resume Next statement must come **before** any statements in the procedure you want it to protect. So for instance the following snippet of script, where we divide by zero, will not generate an error:

```
Sub window_onload()
On Error Resume Next
    x = 3/0
    Msgbox x
End Sub
```

127

It will simply resume execution of the script, in this case, by
displaying a message box with a meaningless result:

However, if we place the statement after the error, we lose all the protection that it offers
us:

```
Sub window_onload()
    x = 3/0
    Msgbox x
On Error Resume Next
End Sub
```

This time the error is handled by the host, and the
message is generated as normal:

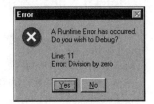

This statement might seem to be all we need to know for effective error handling – it
isn't. This is because it is really the error-handling equivalent of brushing dirt
underneath the carpet - sure, you don't see it, but the result isn't really ideal. Using it can
lead to some odd results, as the divide by zero example above shows. There are few
scripts that can be expected to function properly after one line has been ignored because
of an error: usually, this will cause another error further down the line.

Remember that when using the On Error Resume Next statement that the error has
still occurred. All it has done is hidden the standard error message response. While it is
useful at times to include the On Error Resume Next statement in code, a much
better way of dealing with errors is to actually *handle* them. To do that we use the Err
object.

Err Object

The Err object holds information about the last error that occurred. It is a feature that is
available for use at all levels of your script and there is no need to create an instance of it
in your code as it is an intrinsic object with global scope (see Appendix E for a more
detailed description). This object has five properties and two methods.

Err Object Properties

Property	Comment
Description	Sets or returns a descriptive string associated with an error.
HelpContext	Sets or returns a context ID for a topic in a help file.
HelpFile	Sets or returns a fully qualified path to a help file.
Number	Sets or returns a numeric value specifying an error – this is the Err object's default property. It can be used by automation objects (ActiveX) to return a SCODE (status code).
Source	Sets or returns the name of the object or application that originally generated the error.

Err Object Methods

Method	Comment
Clear	Clears all property settings of the Err object.
Raise	Used to generate a runtime error.

Using the Err Object

Let's look at how we can use the Description, Number and Source properties, and the Clear and Raise methods of the Err object. The other properties refer to custom help files that can be created for specific errors that the user might come across.

The first thing to remember about using Err to handle errors is that you need to have On Error Resume Next set before hand; otherwise, the script execution will be cut short and your error handling script will be wasted!

```
...
On Error Resume Next
...
```

Now we can set to work handling the error our way. The first thing to do is to generate an error, and to do this we could simply write a script with a deliberate error in it. However, we have no need as VBScript provides a way to generate errors on demand – the Raise method. Using this method we can generate any error we want, with just one line. All we need to know is the number of the error (given in Appendix E) that we wish to create.

So, if we want to generate an overflow error, for example, we raise error number 6:

```
On Error Resume Next
Err.Raise 6
```

Or, for a custom error, we can use `vbObjectError` constant. The programmer can define error numbers above this constant to create and handle errors specific to the script.

```
On Error Resume Next
Err.Raise vbObjectError + 1, "something is wrong", "Custom Error"
```

If you want to see the error messages generated by these, simply comment out the `On Error Resume Next` statement, or create a procedure to display the error.

Now we have our error, let's look at how we can handle it. The property to use is the `Description` property. This is used to set or return a textual description of the error. If we use the default description, we simply get the standard error message. For example, here is our error-handled divide by zero:

```
On Error Resume Next
Err.Raise 11
MsgBox (Err.Description)
```

Here is how it would be unhandled:

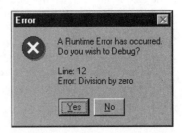

Not much of an improvement, is it? However, we can create a message that is a little more meaningful:

```
On Error Resume Next
Err.Raise 11
Err.Description = "You have attempted to divide by zero " _
    & "- please try another number"
MsgBox (Err.Description)
```

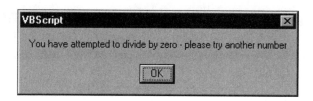

This example is preferable because it gives the user a clear and unambiguous explanation of what has happened and what they need to do next.

We can do the same thing with the error number, this time using the `Number` property:

```
On Error Resume Next
Err.Raise 11
Err.Description = "You have attempted to divide by zero " _
    & "- please try another number"
MsgBox (Err.Number & " " & Err.Description)
```

This property also allows us to set or return our own number to an error (setting your own number might be useful if you want to include an easy to use guide with your VBScript project). This is not the best way in which user-defined errors can be created, it is more advisable to use the `vbObjectError` constant, this is explained in Appendix E:

```
On Error Resume Next
Err.Raise 11
Err.Number = 1
Err.Description = "You have attempted to divide by zero " _
    & "- please try another number"
MsgBox (Err.Number & " " & Err.Description)
```

If we want to know what generated the error we can use the `Source` property:

```
On Error Resume Next
Err.Raise 11
Err.Number = 1
Err.Description = "You have attempted to divide by zero " _
    & "- please try another number"
MsgBox (Err.Number & " " & Err.Description & " - " & Err.Source)
```

131

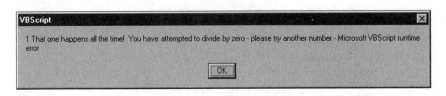

Using `Source` is helpful in tracking down errors when using VBScript to automate Microsoft Office tasks. For example, if using script to access Microsoft Excel, and it generates a division-by-zero error, Microsoft Excel sets `Err.Number` to its own error code for that error, and sets `Source` to `Excel.Application`. Note that if the error is generated in another object called by Microsoft Excel, Excel intercepts that error and re-sets `Err.Number` to its own code for division by zero. It does, however, leave the other `Err` object properties (including `Source`) as set by the object that generated the error.

Once the error is handled, we want to get rid of it completely. To do this, we use the `Clear` method:

```
On Error Resume Next
Err.Raise 11
Err.Number = 1
Err.Description = "That one happens all the time!" & _
      "You have attempted to divide by zero - please try another number"
MsgBox (Err.Number & " " & Err.Description & " - " & Err.Source)
Err.Clear
```

`Clear` is used explicitly to clear the `Err` object after an error has been handled. VBScript calls the `Clear` method automatically whenever any of the following statements are executed:

❑   `On Error Resume Next`

❑   `On Error Goto 0`

❑   `Exit Sub`

❑   `Exit Function`

> **Remember to remove any lines in your script that raise errors when you have finished testing your error-handling code!**

Remember that errors are like aches and pains - they point to something being wrong, either with the script itself or with the way it is being used. There is a tendency to think that, given all the power that VBScript has to offer, we should try to fix these problems 'on the fly'. So if someone divides by zero, it's easy to think that you could simply use VBScript to put another number into the sum. The danger here is that you create more problems in trying to 'fix' it, and this can lull the user into the false sense of security that everything is OK when it isn't. Only attempt this kind of error handling when you can be **absolutely sure** you know what the problem is.

A good alternative to using message boxes is to create custom help files and refer to these using the `Err` object properties `HelpContext` and `HelpFile`. These allow us to point to specific entries in a custom help file created for the project in question - giving the whole project a professional and polished feel.

For a project of any size, it is useful to log any errors that occur so that they can be studied later. This is particularly useful for large ASP-based projects, where the error might lurk otherwise undetected – although aggravated users can often points these out to you!

Handling Errors

So far we have identified the syntax and the simple techniques associated with error handling. Obviously, we cannot ever hope that errors "will just not happen", and even if it were possible to eliminate all of the errors from the code (through very defensive programming), the cost of developing such software would probably be quite prohibitive.

> Thou shall not underestimate the importance of error handling. Something *will* go wrong—will your program handle it gracefully when it does? A program can never be considered professionally done without a well thought-out and consistent error-handling scheme.

By now, based on the examples shown previously, we know that we can handle errors in three different ways:

- ❑ Ignore the errors altogether (the script stops), and allow the default error handler provided by the host to deal with the error.

- ❑ Try to intercept errors in-line, immediately after a suspect operation that could create an error.

- ❑ Push the error up the call stack, and create either generic error handlers, or procedure specific handlers that can anticipate the problems arising from the procedure.

If you are not familiar with the term "call stack", imagine that as each function or sub is called, it is placed on top of a stack. When a procedure calls another procedure (or even itself), the second procedure is placed on top of the stack. If the second procedure does not have an error handler and an error occurs (or `Err.Raise` is used), the error is pushed "up the call stack". The remaining piece of the second procedure is ignored, and the first procedure has a chance to handle the error. Since procedures are often nested, you can easily control errors by placing error handling routines in key procedures. You have to be aware that certain statements will reset the `Err` object, and your error handling has to come before that. Please see Appendix E for examples of using the calling stack to handle errors.

> Note that it is also a good idea to have a bottom-line, generic error handler available at all times. More often then not, the error handler will be written with a specific purpose in mind – checking whether a file exists, or whether an SQL string executed correctly. In such circumstances, there can be other errors that we have not accounted for – undeclared variables, bad parameters, etc. These should be either passed on up the call stack, by raising a custom error, or passed on to another, more generic procedure.

So, what can be done, after an error is intercepted? Perhaps the sky is the limit, and only creativity and limited time budget will prevent you from treating the error the way you want it treated – in other words fixed. There are no out-of-the-box solutions here, only loose guidelines. The simplest thing to do is obviously to display the error in the most meaningful way. As you go on, you should try to log the problem (if script is running unattended), or at least provide a simple facility for the end user to report the problem. Going further, you may try to fix the problem on the fly – perhaps it is just a simple exception (such as an out-of-bound array call), or a user error that can be retried. Then, if you can't fix it, gracefully fall back on the user-friendly error message, and log the error. More often than not, errors that cannot be easily handled will expose the weakness of your program, rather than a configuration problem that prevents the program from executing. Make the first few users your test subjects if you cannot test all of the exceptional permutations personally.

When writing an error handler, make sure it is bug proof. Test it more than any other procedure, preferably with the use of home-built test suites in order to see how it behaves with different data (either raise errors, or call it with simulated data), and in under different circumstances. Errors that are not found in development (computer low on memory, lack of appropriate permissions, etc) will unfortunately rear their ugly heads in production. Cross-application interactions as well as an increased user load on an IIS server may effectively disable some of the poorly written error handling procedures. It is also a good idea (or even standard practice) to get *someone else* to test it as thoroughly as possible as well.

Step #1: Diagnose What Went Wrong

Error diagnosis is obviously a large part of error handling and, unfortunately, there is no easy way to jump into error handling without making sacrifices. There are just too many error codes in VBScript alone for us to write code that will anticipate all of the possible errors, never mind writing code for all of the possible errors caused by outside components. The common technique is to debug early for the most common errors (bad parameters, undeclared variables, etc.) and write your error handling function around only those errors that you are anticipating.

For instance, working with ADSI (one of the common components automated by VBScript), we can pull out the most prevalent ADSI errors and put them into a common error handler, which may be invoked whenever an error is diagnosed. This may even happen when your script is executing correctly. For instance, if we want to add a new user to a domain, with a username that already exists, it will be less expensive in terms of programming and computer resources to check for an error when adding a new user rather than attempt to find out if the user exists.

The code below performs a select case against the Number property of the Err object, allowing the programmer to decide what happens when a given error occurs. Due to the number of possible errors, the listing is edited for brevity's sake; the snippet also adjusts for the poor error descriptions of ADSI:

```
<%
Sub adsiErr()
    Dim blnIsErrorFixed
    blnIsErrorFixed = False
    Select case Err.Number
        case &H80005000:                          ' Invalid ADSI pathname
            blnIsErrorFixed = fixErrorPath()
            case &H80005001:                      ' Unknown Domain Object
            call logError("Unknown Domain Object")
            call displayError("Unknown Domain Object")
            Err.Clear
' Bunch of case statements deleted, see real file
        case &H80004005:                          ' now the ambiguous COM Error
            call logError()
            call displayError()
            Err.Clear
        case &H800708B0:                          ' Unable to add, User Exists
            blnIsErrorFixed = fixUserExistsError()
        case else:                                ' unaccounted error, log it,
                                                  ' display it
            call logError()
            call displayError()
            Err.Clear
    End Select
    If Not blnIsErrorFixed Then Response.End
End Sub
%>
```

This semi-generic error-handling procedure is sufficient to cover the majority of errors that can be attributed to ADSI. It can be called in-line, as well as after a procedure call – the code below is slightly edited:

```
Option Explicit
Dim objComputer, objGroup, strGroupName
On Error Resume Next

' Get object for computer, call error handler inline
Set objComputer = GetObject("WinNT://" & Request.Form("DomainName"))
If Err Then adsiErr()

strGroupName = Request.Form("GroupName")


' Create the New Group, call error handler afterwards
Call createNewGroup( objComputer, objGroup, "group", strGroupName )
If Err Then adsiErr()
```

Regardless of whether or not the error handling routine is generic, the same principles will always apply, except when we're only interested in displaying and logging the error (where we would just use `case else:` from the previous code). The error identification template will always be the same, but with a specific error the template may be slightly smaller – and you may use a less generic function. For instance, because – after the call to the `createNewGroup()` subroutine – we were only expecting an **Unable to Add, User Exists** error (because we were already able to establish a connection with the domain) we could have automatically called `fixUserExistsError()` as it was the most likely error to occur.

Step #2: Attempt to Correct the Error

After you have identified the error, you should obviously attempt to fix it, if possible, if not, you may just follow the next two steps. In some circumstances, the error will be a result of a user action, or input. Since VBScript is commonly found in ASP type applications, the most common errors lie in the database or file handling, as a direct response to user interaction. We'll look at a detailed database and a COM object example at the end of the section. Here, this code allows the user to correct the error. In case of potential user errors, the best approach is to validate the data that will be used by the other components.

The code below tests if a string entered into an HTML form is a date. If the string entered is not a date, the procedure throws an error, and for practical purposes, invalidates the form, and displays a simple error message:

```
<%@ Language=VBScript %>
<%
Option Explicit
Dim strDate, strError, datDate, blnError, blnCanContinue
blnError = False
blnCanContinue = False
strDate = ""
strError = ""

Sub HandleError()                         ' this will handle Error string
    strError = "<font color=red><b>" & Err.description & "</b></font>"
    blnError = True
End Sub

Sub CheckDate                             ' Sub that checks the date
    strDate = Request.Form("strDate")
    If Not IsDate(strDate) Then Err.Raise vbObjectError + 1, , _
        "Not a Date<br>"
    datDate = CDate(strDate)
    blnCanContinue = True
End Sub

If Request.Form("strDate").Count = 1 Then  ' form was entered
    On Error Resume Next
    CheckDate
    If (Err.Number > vbObjectError) Then HandleError
End If

%>
```

```
<HTML>
<HEAD>
<TITLE>Try Again</title>
</HEAD>
<BODY>
<% If blnCanContinue = False Then
    If blnError = True Then Response.Write strError
%>
<form action="tryagain.asp" method="POST">
Enter a date: <INPUT type="text" id=strDate name=strDate value="<% = strDate
%>"><br>
</form>
<% Else %>
Date is OK: <% = strDate %>
<% End If %>
<P> </P>

</BODY>
</HTML>
```

Correction of run-time errors can be extremely difficult and is not really recommended – perhaps it is some other part of the script creating the error, and attempts at correcting it will cause more problems. As a rule of thumb, you should establish default values for critical variables, and check the validity of the variables used by procedures. When the variable is out of valid range, substitute it with the default value.

When attempting to correct the error you should think hard whether you can indeed fix it. Chances are that if you can anticipate it, you should be able to fix it. Perhaps a database server may be down, and you may be able to "switch" to a backup server, maybe user entered backward slashes "\" in a URL textbox instead of forward slashes "/", or simply an array is too small, and you might have to ReDim it. Usually, it is the unanticipated error that cannot be fixed with a backup plan.

Step #3: Come Up with a User-Friendly Error Message

A user-friendly error message goes a long way to show that you at least care a little bit. There is nothing more annoying than the default error message provided by the host. Not only is it more confusing to the user, but also offers no recourse of action. A user-friendly error message can contain some of the following information:

❑ An apology

❑ A plea to report the error, along with some nifty report form (or log the error, if possible)

❑ A more understandable explanation of the error

❑ Steps that the user can take to recover from the error

Obviously, the error message, as well as, any reporting utility will depend on the host and the nature of the error. With IE, it is fairly easy to create a new window with a form that would include an error reporting mechanism (shown in the code below). Other errors will require similar techniques, and may even include auto reporting via a logging mechanism.

```
<script language=VBScript>
Function onErrorHandler(message,url,line)
  dim strHTML, objWindow
  strHTML = "<HTML><HEAD>" & vbCrLf
  strHTML = strHTML & "<TITLE>An error has occurred!</TITLE></HEAD><BODY>" _
    & vbCrLf
  strHTML = strHTML & "<FONT FACE='sans-serif'>" _
    & "<FONT COLOR=darkred SIZE=+1>" & vbCrLf
  strHTML = strHTML & "<B>We are sorry!</B></FONT>" & vbCrLf
  strHTML = strHTML & "<FONT SIZE=-1><BR>Something went wrong " _
    & "while processing this page."
  strHTML = strHTML & "<P>To help the web administrator " _
    & "identify the problem," & vbCrLf
  strHTML = strHTML & "please provide a brief explanation of " _
    & "how the error occurred,"
  strHTML = strHTML & "and press the submit error button below. " _
    & "This will help us"
  strHTML = strHTML & "identify and fix the error." & vbCrLf
  strHTML = strHTML & "<FORM ACTION=""mailto:bugs@wrox.com"">" & vbCrLf
  strHTML = strHTML & "<Error Description:<BR><TEXTAREA NAME=desc ROWS=5"
  strHTML = strHTML & " COLS=30></TEXTAREA>" & vbCrLf
  strHTML = strHTML & "<INPUT TYPE=hidden name=error VALUE=""" _
    & message & """>" & vbCrLf
  strHTML = strHTML & "<INPUT TYPE=hidden name=file VALUE=""" _
    & url & """>" & vbCrLf
  strHTML = strHTML & "<INPUT TYPE=hidden name=line VALUE=""" _
    & line & """>" & vbCrLf
  strHTML = strHTML & "<P><INPUT TYPE=SUBMIT " _
    & "VALUE=""Submit Error Information"">" & vbCrLf
  strHTML = strHTML & "</FORM></FONT></FONT></BODY></HTML>"
  set objWindow = window.open("")
  objWindow.document.body.innerHTML= strHTML
  onErrorHandler = true
End Function

Set window.onerror = GetRef("onErrorHandler")
</script>
```

The code listing above is essentially suited to a fatal DHTML error, where script continuation may prove impossible. Other hosts will use a little variation on the theme above. A similar approach should be used in ASP, with an exception of automatic logging of the error, a few changes in an error message, and changes in the last few lines:

```
Response.Clear
Response.Write strHTML
Response.End
```

Other hosts may require a simple use of a MsgBox function, and logging of the error. The baseline attempt at displaying the error should contain the vital information. The following code function can be used to return information for errors that do not have a custom display. It can be used with practically any host, as the returning string can either be sent to the browser or another text handler.

```
Const cHTML = 1
Const cString = 2

Function UnknownError(intOutputConst)
   If Err = 0 Then UnknownError = ""
   Dim strOutput
   strOutput = ""
   If intOutputConstant = cHTML Then
      strOutput = strOutput & "<font name='sans-serif' color=red>"
      strOutput = strOutput & "<b>An Error Has Occurred</b><br>"
      strOutput = strOutput & "Error Number= #" & Err.number & "<br>"
      strOutput = strOutput & "Error Descr: " & Err.description & "<br>"
      strOutput = strOutput & "Error Source: " & Err.source & "<br>"
      strOutput = strOutput & "</font>" & vbCrLf
   Else
      strOutput = strOutput & "An Error Has Occurred" & vbCrLf & vbCrLf
      strOutput = strOutput & "Error Number= #" & Err.number & vbCrLf
      strOutput = strOutput & "Error Descr: " & Err.description & vbCrLf
      strOutput = strOutput & "Error Source: " & Err.source & vbCrLf
      strOutput = strOutput & vbCrLf
   End If
   Err.Clear
   UnknownError = strOutput
End Function
```

Step #4: Attempt to Log the Error

Contrary to popular opinion, error logging is actually easy to accomplish. There are several different ways in which it can be achieved and you may log to: the Windows log, a database, a file, or in some circumstances, via email. When the severity of an error is high (say, a hard drive failure), you should not just log the error (hoping that some day, someone will read it), but forward it to the operator or system administrator – email, SMS page, and netsend are just few of the possibilities. Under best circumstances, you could simply log the error, and the log monitoring software could decide about the severity of error, and appropriately relay the message to an available human operator.

When logging an error to a database, file or an e-mail, you can choose what information to include in the error log on top of the default information about the standard error information. Common information entities, which can be included, are:

❑ Date and time of the error

❑ File or application that created the error

❑ Scripting Engine information

❑ Account under which user is executing the script

❑ Key variables used by the script (a mini core dump)

Obviously, with the number of additional variables, you might end up building a fully-fledged help desk system, along with the tools to analyze the wealth of errors.

Instead of duplicating the article, you can download the source code for the logging component, compile it, and use it, simply by looking at the page140.vbs file in the downloadable source code for Chapter 4. Usage of the component is fairly simple:

```
Const cError = 1          ' define log constants
Const cWarning = 2
Const cInformation = 4

Sub LogError(intErrorType)
   Dim oEvent
   Set oEvent = Server.CreateObject("WroxLog.Event")
   oEvent.Application = "My ASP Script Name"
   oEvent.Description = Err.Description
   oEvent.EventID = Err.Number
   oEvent.LogType = intErrorType
   oEvent.WriteEvent
   Set oEvent = Nothing
   Err.Clear
End Sub

' Now Fake a call to the Sub
On Error Resume Next
Err.Raise 6
If Err Then Call LogError(cError)
```

Windows NT Log provides a neat summary of all errors that occurred on the computer, and include date, time, application name (source) and error ID. When the user double-clicks on the error, more detailed information, including error description (string insertion in our primitive case) is presented (although for a full, user friendly description, error IDs and their descriptions would have to be added to the registry).

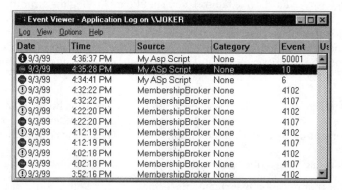

The last option is to use the Windows Script Host LogEvent method of the WshShell object. Error logging via WHS 2.0 (covered in Chapter 10) is simple (it can be done from any host except for IE), with the only drawback being the inability to change the source of the error, and the event ID (error number) – all of this data has to be included in the error description itself. Here is an ASP based sample, which can be used with the UnknownError function shown in the last snippet of code in **Step #3**:

```
Set WshShell = Server.CreateObject("WScript.Shell")
WshShell.LogEvent 1, UnknownError(cString)
```

The LogEvent method will use the same constants as shown in the code above. They are standard constants for writing to the NT log. Depending on the constant used, you will be able to identify errors through the NT log either visually (different icons), or by searching for particular errors:

Value	Description
0	Success
1	Error
2	Warning
4	Information
8	Audit Success
16	Audit Failure

Be More Aggressive with Reporting and Testing

Script debugging is an increasingly popular testing technique thanks to a fairly robust debugger included with Microsoft Visual InterDev, IE and Office 2000. Still, the process of starting the debugger (without even mentioning the horrors of installation), and stepping through the code may take the joy out of identifying errors. Often, you might create your own reporting functions, in order to speed up the process of testing.

General Environment Check-Up

The environment on which the script is deployed may be different from the development environment. Therefore, before you attempt to test the waters in real life, you should ensure that everything works, based on your own development platform. The following function checks the basics for you:

```
Function EnvironmentTest(sPad, blnShowServer)
    Dim strReport, oConn
    strReport = "Environment Report" & sPad
    strReport = strReport & "Scripting engine=" & ScriptEngine() & sPad
    strReport = strReport & "Buildversion = " & ScriptEngineBuildVersion() _
        & sPad
    strReport = strReport & "Majorversion = " & ScriptEngineMajorVersion() _
        & sPad
    strReport = strReport & "Minorversion = " & ScriptEngineMinorVersion() _
        & sPad

    strReport = strReport & sPad
    set oConn = Server.Createobject("ADODB.Connection")
    strReport = strReport & "ADO version = "
    strReport = strReport & oConn.version & sPad
    set oConn = Nothing
```

```
    If blnShowServer Then
        strReport = strReport & sPad
        strReport = strReport & "Server Software ="
        strReport = strReport & Request.Servervariables("server_software") _
            & sPad

        strReport = strReport &"Script Timeout = " & Server.ScriptTimeout _
            & " seconds" & sPad
        strReport = strReport & "Session Timeout = " & Session.Timeout _
            & " minutes" & sPad
    End If
    EnvironmentTest = strReport
End Function

Response.Write EnvironmentTest("<br>", True)
```

ADO Error Report

ADO always seems to create odd errors whenever you least expect it, perhaps because there are so many differences between providers. The function below alleviates the problem of trying to figure out what went wrong. This is probably the most useful reporting function, especially when working with a database application. As you attempt to carry out some dynamic SQL building, more often than not you discover that something is seriously wrong. The following function produces a neat report:

```
Function ErrorADOReport(strMsg, oConn, strSQL, sPad)
    ' produce a meaningful error report for an ADO connection object
    ' display title - strMsg, sql used - strSQL, and use different pad sPad
    Dim intErrors, i, strError
    strError = "Report for: " & strMsg & sPad & sPad
    intErrors = oConn.Errors.Count
    If intErrors = 0 Then
        ErrorADOReport = strError & "- no Errors" & sPad
        Exit Function
    End If
    strError = strError & "ADO Reports these Database Error(s) executing:" _
        & sPad
    strError = strError & strSQL & sPad
    For i = 0 To intErrors- 1
        strError = strError & "Err #" & oConn.errors(i).number
        strError = strError & " Descr:" & oConn.errors(i).description & sPad
    Next
    strError = strError & sPad
    ErrorADOReport = strError
End Function
```

This function simply looks at the errors collection of the ADO connection object to enumerate through all of the errors in the collection. The function can be used from other hosts, by passing a different line terminator, or "pad", as one of the arguments in order to achieve the appropriate formatting.

To continue with the listing, the following snippet of code shows how the function is called, and displays the results, by simulating an error in the SQL statement:

```
On Error Resume Next
Set objConn = Server.CreateObject("ADODB.Connection")
objConn.Open "DSN=pubs;uid=sa;pwd="
strSQL = "select * from authors where fafa < a"
Set objRS = Server.CreateObject("ADODB.Recordset")
objRS.Open strSQL, objConn

Response.Write ErrorADOReport("open authors table", objConn, strSQL, "<br>")
```

The results of the function clearly show what went wrong, displaying the SQL statement in question, as well as all of the errors associated with it (some people attempt to debug SQL statements without even dumping the SQL statement):

Report for: open authors table

ADO Reports these Database Error(s) executing:
select * from authors where fafa < a
Err #-2147217900 Descr:[Microsoft][ODBC SQL Server Driver][SQL Server]Invalid column name 'fafa'.
Err #-2147217900 Descr:[Microsoft][ODBC SQL Server Driver][SQL Server]Invalid column name 'a'.

COM Components

Another common script breaker is the failure of COM components referenced in the script. In order to test whether the components can be opened, you may create a mini-test studio that will attempt to create components, and if the component cannot be created, display the error. Changes in server configuration and installation of other components are frequent culprits of these errors. Your application may be working one day, but all of a sudden, it throws a number of errors:

```
Dim oDict, oTmp, strItem
Set oDict = Server.CreateObject("Scripting.Dictionary")
oDict.Add 1, "adodb.recordset"
oDict.Add 2, "adodb.connection"
oDict.Add 3, "adodb.command"
oDict.Add 4, "SoftArtisans.FileUp"
oDict.Add 5, "SoftArtisans.SACheck"
oDict.Add 6, "scripting.filesystemobject"
oDict.Add 7, "cdonts.newmail"

For Each strItem In oDict.Items
   On Error Resume Next
   Set oTmp = Server.CreateObject(strItem)
   If Err Then
      Response.Write strItem & " - failed. Error #" & Err.number _
         & " - " & Err.description & "<br>"
   Else
       Response.Write strItem & " - success<br>"
   End If
   Err.Clear
   oTmp = Nothing
Next
```

Similar component testing script can be developed for WSH by changing line breaks, output mechanism, and by changing `Server.CreateObject` to `Wscript.CreateObject`. Here is a sample output created by the script:

```
adodb.recordset - success
adodb.connection - success
adodb.command - success
SoftArtisans.FileUp - failed. Error #-2147319779 - 006~ASP 0177~Server.CreateObject
Failed~Library not registered.
SoftArtisans.SACheck - success
scripting.filesystemobject - success
cdonts.newmail - success
```

Defensive Programming

Probably the best way to prevent bugs is though defensive programming, combined with proper testing. Errors tend to occur as the complexity of the program increases. Unfortunately, full coverage of defensive programming is a topic for an entire book, not a sub-section of the chapter (see Code Complete by Steve McConnell, Microsoft Press, 1993 or Bug Proofing Visual Basic by Rod Stephens, John Wiley and Sons, 1998), or just stick to the following rules of thumb:

❑ Stick to a proper naming scheme.

❑ Validate data types using IsXXXX functions, such as IsDate, IsNumeric or IsObject, and create your own data validation functions such as IsEmail, IsCCNumber to make sure your procedures can actually handle the data.

❑ Use constants, not magic variables.

❑ Limit the scope of variables, objects and errors.

❑ Don't use clever programming when something obvious might suffice, even if it takes more programming.

❑ Reuse as much "stable" code as possible through includes, and components.

❑ Use parenthesis with complex expressions.

❑ Watch out for use of & and +.

❑ Watch out for variable scope.

❑ Watch out for array size.

❑ Declare and initialize your variables and objects.

❑ Watch out for endless loops.

❑ Encapsulate as much code as possible in VBScript Classes (covered in Chapter 8).

❑ Start with minimal functionality, and avoid optimization until later.

Debugging

> The term debugging has been wrongly attributed to the pioneer programmer, Grace Hopper. In 1944, Hopper, a young Naval Reserve officer, went to work on the Mark I computer at Harvard, becoming one of the first people to write programs for it. As Admiral Hopper, she later described an incident in which a technician is said to have pulled an actual bug (a moth, in fact) from between two electrical relays in the Mark II computer. In his book, *The New Hacker's Dictionary*, Eric Raymond reports that the moth was displayed for many years by the Navy and is now the property of the Smithsonian. Raymond also notes that Admiral Hopper was already aware of the term when she told the moth story.
>
> The word bug was used prior to modern computers to mean an industrial or electrical defect.

For a long time now, debugging has been the sore point of scripting languages. Even though the script debugger has been available for quite some time, it has been difficult to install and use. Needless to say, it has not gained too much popularity. Still, successful installation of ASP script debugging on your development server will pay for itself tenfold. There are two debuggers available, one that can be downloaded with Internet Explorer, and another that can be installed with Visual InterDev, or MS Office 2000. The freely downloadable script debugger is actually integrated into InterDev, however, the InterDev interface offers more choices, and it allows for smooth debugging of ASP scripts. In this section we will discuss the concepts behind the InterDev debugger, as it is more robust (includes the easiest ASP debugging) and more intuitive to use. Depending on your needs, you may use the MS Script Editor (which is similar in its functionality to InterDev), and its debugger, or the Script Debugger (which has only some of the options of InterDev) downloadable from the Microsoft Scripting site (`http://msdn.microsoft.com/scripting/`).

> To launch the free script debugger from Microsoft Internet Explorer, use the **View** menu, choose Script Debugger. Script Debugger starts, and then opens the current HTML source file.
>
> If you want to start the script editor from within Office 2000 applications, use the Tools menu, choose Macro, and then Microsoft Script Editor.

If you are interested in switching debuggers, you can manipulate the registry to do so:
`HKEY_CLASSES_ROOT\CLSID\{834128A2-51F4-11D0-8F20-00805F2CD064}\LocalServer32`

The default registry entry contains the path to the debugger, in case of the InterDev setup on my computer it is: `C:\WINNT\System32\mdm.exe` , to change it to the script debugger, I could enter `<path>\msscrdbg.exe` instead. In the registry, you can look for MDM Debug Session Provider Class.

145

Debugging with InterDev

In order to set up the debugging you have to follow the directions included in the set-up instructions, including those for the InterDev server components that are available later on during the set up of Visual Studio. The best conditions for the set-up are a local development Windows NT Server with IIS that doubles as your InterDev workstation. The applications set-up is fairly fast, and the debugging process is a lot smoother (as well as easier to set up) than if the server and client were set up separately. In order to enable ASP debugging, you must also choose the **Automatically Enable ASP server-side debugging on launch**, which is available in the Launch pad of the Project's Properties window. When you quit your debugging session, Visual InterDev restores the server debugging settings and out-of-process setting to their previous values.

Additionally, InterDev offers just-in-time debugging, and can go automatically into debug mode whenever an error is encountered when executing a client script.

> **Do NOT install a debugger, or debug, on a production machine. The InterDev Debugger uses incredible resources on the system, and runs the application out of process on a single thread. Essentially, changes are made to IIS and MTS that make them run very slow.**

Script debugging allows you to identify syntax, runtime and logic errors by inspection of both the script code and the contents of its variables during the execution of the script. Once your code is at a stage when it can be debugged, you'll be interested in setting up breakpoints (in order to pause the execution, or 'play', of the script), stepping through lines of script one by one, and inspecting the values of variables and objects.

There are several different ways in which these things can be accomplished. The two main ways are with the **Debug Menu**, which should switch on automatically once you start 'playing' the script, or can be switched on manually; and with the **Code Window** (or its shortcut menu). Let's take a look at the **Debug Menu** first:

The tables below contain a description of each group of buttons on the Visual InterDev **Debug Menu** shown above. Since the debug menu is also shared with Visual J++, some of the elements, related to threading etc. are not used when debugging with InterDev:

Group I	
Start	Begins debugging of the project by starting the script selected from the Project shortcut menu; this button can also be used to continue the running of the script.
Start Without Debugging	Project is executed, but the debugger is not started.

Group I	
Pause	Allows you to pause a running script at any time in order to start debugging it and/or to inspect the values of its variables.
Stop	Stops the debugging session altogether.
Detach All Processes	Used with J++
Restart	Restarts the application after any type of interruption.
Run To Cursor	After the execution has been paused, this allows you to set the point within your script where the execution will continue up to.

Group II	
Step Into	Allows you to execute the next line of code.
Step Over	Executes the next procedure as if it were a single line of code.
Step Out	Executes the remaining lines within a procedure.

Group III	
Insert Breakpoint	Inserts a breakpoint at the current line.
Enable/Disable Breakpoint	Toggles breakpoint status, allowing breakpoints to be turned 'on' or 'off'.
Clear All Breakpoints	Erases all of the breakpoints.
Breakpoints	Shows all of the breakpoints and their advanced properties within the Advanced Window.

Group IV	
Immediate	Opens the Immediate Window.
Autos	Opens the Autos Window.
Locals	Opens the Locals Window.
Watch	Opens the Watch Window.
Threads	Opens the Threads Window (only used with J++).

Table Continued on Following Page

Group IV	
Call Stack	Opens the Call Stack Window.
Running Documents	Opens the Running Documents Window.
Output	Opens the Output Window.

Group V	
Processes	Used with J++
Java Exceptions	Used with J++

The Code Window within Visual InterDev debugger (with some sample code) is shown below, this is the sample file created previously:

```
environmenttest.asp*                                            _ □ ×
<%@ Language=VBScript %>
<%
Function EnvironmentTest(sPad, blnShowServer)
    Dim strReport, oConn
    strReport = "Environment Report" & sPad
    strReport = strReport & "Scripting engine=" & ScriptEngine() & sP
    strReport = strReport & "Buildversion = " & ScriptEngineBuildVersi
    strReport = strReport & "Majorversion = " & ScriptEngineMajorVersi
    strReport = strReport & "Minorversion = " & ScriptEngineMinorVersi

    strReport = strReport & sPad
    set oConn = Server.Createobject("ADODB.Connection")
    strReport = strReport & "ADO version = "
    strReport = strReport & oConn.version & sPad
    set oConn = Nothing

    If blnShowServer Then

  Design    Source    Quick View
```

To get your program to pause automatically during a debug run, you have to set breakpoints. These can either be based on certain conditions (e.g. breakpoint reached 5 times, or a certain expression changes), or on a particular line of code. You may either click the mouse in the left-margin area of the window to toggle a breakpoint, or you can use either the Debug Menu or the Code Window shortcut menu:

When you right-mouse click in the **Code Window**, the shortcut menu shown in the screenshot above pops up. There are four interesting items here:

Insert Breakpoint	By clicking **Insert Breakpoint**, it automatically adds a breakpoint at the line where your cursor is located, unless the line is empty, a declaration, or a comment.
Add Watch	By clicking **Add Watch** over a variable, or an object, it automatically adds it to the **Watch Window**. It is a very useful feature, as it allows you to concentrate on the few variables that you are actually interested in examining, rather than looking at the entire stack of variables in the **Locals Window**.
Run To Cursor	The **Run To Cursor** option allows you to execute a number of lines of code between the current location and the line that the cursor is pointing to. This is similar to placing a temporary breakpoint, and then continuing execution of the code until that breakpoint. This is useful when you are tangled in a long, complex loop and simply want to get out of the loop as fast as possible.
Set Next Statement	The **Set Next Statement** option allows you to execute an arbitrary line of code.

In order to start debugging an individual page, a start page needs to be set in the project explorer window. If your script depends on other pages (e.g. you are testing a page that requires values from a form), set it to the first page that is needed for the script to run properly. First go to the project window, and select a file:

Afterwards, you can right-mouse click on the file for the pop-up menu to appear:

149

In order to start debugging, you should select the file as a **Start Page**. This is similar to VB's concept of a particular form (or code) being executed when the Start button is pressed.

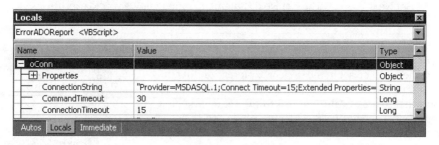

During the actual debugging process, the **Code Window** (above) comes alive. The majority of the features on the **Debug Menu** are available, and you can hover the mouse over variables to see their current values. Additionally, you may use some of the windows to perform specific actions. At this stage you may freely step though the code. Code stepping, like a dance, is a certain skill that needs to be acquired. First, you need to place your breakpoints in critical areas (or use the advanced breakpoints that can be set programmatically), and then test different 'stepping' possibilities - especially stepping over long routines, running to cursor, and finally, continuing the script to the next breakpoint (by pressing **Start**).

The **Locals Window** (above) is the most complex of all the windows and, in the long run, the least useful. It contains all the objects, variables, and object collections – along with their names, values and subtypes – that are currently within scope of reach (global and local variables), depending on your position in the script. Because some objects, such as the **Connection** object shown, may have many collections and properties, this window simply becomes too small for its own good. What normally happens is that you end up frantically chasing a few variables around with the use of the scrollbar. On the other hand, if you have only a few local variables, then it is very friendly and easy to use.

The **Immediate Window** (above) is the internal hacking tool for your script. With this window, you can inspect and change the values of variables within your script (if you'd rather not do this with either the **Locals** or **Watch Windows**), or run related or unrelated code. This window also provides a good opportunity to thoroughly test your scripts by feeding the procedures illegal values (by changing the value in the **Value** column), and then testing how the error handler will be able to cope with the problem. The **Immediate Window** can also give you a deeper insight into some of the interactions that occur between different variables that would otherwise be impossible, considering that many of the variables will only have values at runtime.

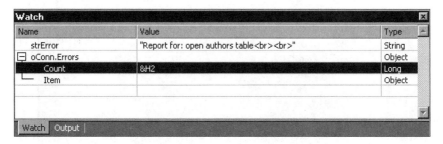

The **Watch Window** (above) is the user-friendlier version of the **Locals Window**, and has many of the same features. For example, you are able to inspect the types, names and values of specific variables, chosen by you, currently within scope. This has some benefits over the **Locals Window**, such as being able to observe when a particular variable comes into scope, as opposed to all of the variables that are displayed in locals window. Additionally, you may watch a particular property of a variable, which allows you to cut through the maze of + and - signs that would otherwise be displayed in the object model within the locals window. **Watch Window** can list a collection or a property of an object directly within the **Watch Window**, by specifying the member directly in the **Name** column. In the example above, the oConn.Errors collection is specified, as opposed to the entire oConn object. Entries within the **Watch Window** can be added directly from the **Code Window's** shortcut menu, and the values manipulated.

Advanced Breakpoints

The final interesting feature of the debugger is the ability to set smart breakpoints, by choosing **Breakpoint Properties** from the pop-up menu, available when your mouse is set over a breakpoint:

151

This is the same menu as seen previously, but based on the context, you have the capability of removing the breakpoint, disabling it, or setting some advanced properties, as seen in the screen below:

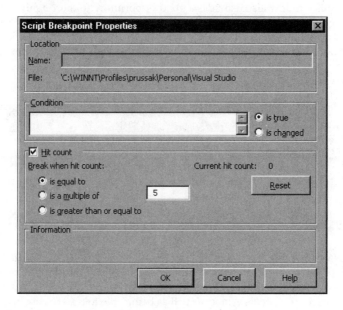

Although the location property is disabled in InterDev debugging, the other two properties make debugging smoother. You can:

- ❑ Define a conditional expression for the breakpoint. And pause execution when expression is true, or it changes.

- ❑ Specify the number of times a breakpoint should be hit before pausing code execution, using a variety of conditions. This property can also be changed when the script is paused, and the actual number of hits monitored.

Some other aspects of debugging not described here in detail are:

- ❑ Autos Window - displays variables within scope of the current line of execution.

- ❑ Output Window - displays status messages at runtime, not used.

- ❑ Call Stack - displays all procedures within the current thread of execution; useful when you want to jump between procedures, or stack frames.

- ❑ Threads Window - displays threads used by the application (for J++ debugging only).

Common Errors and How To Avoid Them

No matter what language you use or what you are doing, there are some errors that just keep on cropping up. Here are some of the more common ones, along with some good tips for avoiding them:

Problem	Suggestion for avoiding
Wrong data type in a variable, such as expecting a text value from a property instead of a number.	Explicitly declare variables, even if not required. In VBScript, use the `Dim` statement.
	Use naming conventions to help you remember variable types, such as `txtUserName` for a string, `fEnd` for a flag, and `intCounter` for an integer, etc.
Not understanding what objects are available in a given context, such as attempting to use the Internet Explorer object model in a script running on a different browser.	Be aware what objects your scripts have access to and what the scope or context is of an object. Be aware that objects (such as browser built-in objects) are not an inherent part of a language such as VBScript.
Not understanding a function or procedure or calling the incorrect function.	Double-check that the function you are calling performs the task you want it to.
Incorrect arguments for functions or arguments passed in the wrong order or not understanding what values a function or procedure returns.	Check syntax for functions whenever using them. Avoid relying on default argument values.
Not understanding a data structure, such as the object model for a browser, or trivial misunderstandings such as assuming that an array index begins with 1 instead of 0.	Check documentation for information about structure.
Typographic errors, such as misspelling a variable name or keyword, or forgetting to close a bracket.	Use consistent names to help avoid confusion. Type the closing portion of a statement as soon as you type the opening portion.
Unexpected data, such as a user typing in a string when prompted for a number.	Anticipate errors introduced by users and create error-handling routines.
Not understanding language conventions, such as using the wrong type of quotation marks to enclose literals. This is a really easy mistake to make when switching between languages.	Familiarize yourself with the operators and conventions of the language you are using.

Summary

In this chapter we looked at the process of handling errors and debugging VBScript code.

After configuring the host to display errors appropriately, we began by looking at the three types of error possible and how they are caused:

❑ Syntax errors.

❑ Runtime errors.

❑ Logic errors.

Having looked at the errors we then looked at how we can handle them. First, we looked at how we use the On Error Resume Next statement and then the Err object and its five properties and two methods. These methods and properties allow us to create a custom response to errors and also to Raise and Clear errors. We then briefly looked at other ways to handle errors, such as by creating custom help files to aid the user.

We then looked in more detail at the steps involved in dealing with errors:

❑ Diagnose what went wrong.

❑ Attempt to correct the error.

❑ Come up with a user friendly error message.

❑ Attempt to log the error.

We then covered some points on defensive programming before looking at the process of debugging VBScript code and how the InterDev debugger can help to make this vital process easier. Finally, we gave a list of some common errors to be aware of, and how to avoid them.

It is impossible to cover the whole topic of error handling and debugging in one chapter, or even in one book. Every script is different and so are the errors associated with it. This chapter's aim was to provide you with the basic strategies for finding and eliminating errors, and handling the remainder that the user might come across.

Using COM Components and Objects

Overview

In this chapter, we will introduce Microsoft's Component Object Model (COM). This will include a brief description of components, classes, and objects, how they 'interact' and how we use them. We'll also take a look under the surface of COM, which should help us to gain a better understanding when using them, but don't worry though — unless you plan to build your own COM components you won't need to remember all the fine details.

COM components are a great way of organizing functionality into logical units (or objects) so that you can '**component-ize**' your code and allow objects to interact with each other. COM components are both language and tool independent, so you can have a Visual C++ component work with a Visual Basic component that works with a Script component. COM allows all of these objects to work together even though they are very different in the way that they are created and developed. This means, for example, that a super fast C++ component can be incorporated into a web page and manipulated using VBScript.

COM components also give you the possibility of placing the workload on more than one machine, thus freeing up system resources where you need to — this is known as load balancing. They can also be used to break up the functionality of an application so that you have your database code in one object, the business logic of the application in another object, and then the user interface components in a third object. This is a useful technique, and is known as **three-tier development**.

After reading this chapter, you will understand some of the overall benefits of using COM components, but we will not be going into too much detail, as it is beyond the scope of this book.

If you want to find out more about COM, you should check out some of the material published on the Microsoft website such as http://www.microsoft.com/com or some of the many articles and whitepapers at the MSDN Online site at http://msdn.microsoft.com. You can find extensive coverage of COM programming in *VB COM*, from Wrox Press (ISBN 1861002130), which is an excellent resource for those new to COM from Visual Basic and VBScript.

Introduction to COM components and Objects

A COM component is a library most commonly used to organize functionality into logical objects. For instance, you may have a lot of functions that are used for calculations and complex mathematical functions. You could group these functions into a `Math` object that encapsulates all the functionality that you use. You could then use this common math object for all of you calculation needs. The advantage of this is that not only can your application then utilize this functionality, but all other COM compliant applications can also use your object seamlessly.

You may be wondering why this is relevant to you, as someone writing VBScript code, but these concepts are important in two ways:

❑   By understanding how COM works you can better utilize the technology. If you do not understand how COM works then you will spend a lot of time trying to figure out why some things work and others do not.

❑   In Chapter 9, you will see how you can build COM components though VBScript. Knowing the key concepts and terminology behind COM will help you understand the 'method in the madness' of COM components.

> There is one important concept to remember about COM: it is a *specification* for creating components and allowing components to interact, not a language or an implementation. Throughout this section remember that you are not 'programming COM' or 'adding COM', but you are complying with the COM specification.

Organizing functions into COM components particularly makes sense when you are planning to *reuse* code that you have created. If you have written some function in VBScript then you can include the code into other VBScript files, but what if you want to use the same code with a JScript module or in Visual Basic? What about that really cool function written in Visual C++ that you want to use? COM allows you to reuse all of this code regardless of what the code was created in and how the items are coded. You cannot use low-level items such as pointers in VBScript, but you could write a C++ component that does this for you.

Another common reason why COM components are used is that you can place the components on different machines from the one where the calling application resides. This is the case with most three-tier client-server solutions these days.

Although the developer has complete flexibility when creating COM objects, it is considered good design to logically organize the functions into groups. You should not need to call three different objects to get similar functions. A database object should not contain your function for generating an amortization schedule and the registry functions that you have created should not reside with your graphics routines. Imagine if you had to use Access to implement thesaurus functionality! Well-organized functions increase code reuse and allow developers to use your objects (and let you use other developer's objects) with a much lower degree of difficulty.

A component can be thought of as a container that holds one or more classes of functions. These classes encapsulate all the functionality, and you can use a class by instantiating it into an object. You can think of the class as the template or blueprint for the object. This object can then be referred to in your script code, thus enabling the language's functionality or the host environment to be easily extended. The set up for this is illustrated in the diagram below:

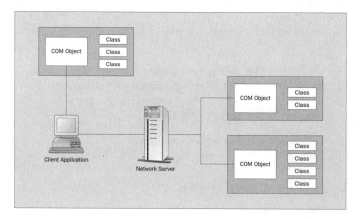

Before you can use a class you must create an object based on it and set a variable to reference or point to it, a process called **instantiation**. Once you have created an instance of a class object in your code, you can then set the properties and execute the methods on the object. The following code sample shows you how to do this. Please note that you must have Microsoft Word installed on your machine for this sample to work properly.

```
'Create the variables used for the code
Dim objWord
Dim objDocument

'Get an instance of the Word applicaiton and a document
Set objWord = CreateObject("Word.Application")
Set objDocument = CreateObject("Word.Document")

'Display Word
objWord.Visible = True

'Add a new document
Set objDocument = objWord.Documents.Add

'Set the text of the new Word document
objDocument.Content = "This iss a samplee document" & _
    " with some  errors."

'Call the spell checker
objDocument.CheckSpelling

'Save the document
objDocument.SaveAs "c:\temp\VBSDoc.doc"

'Clean up the memory used by the objects
Set objDocument = Nothing
Set objWord = Nothing
```

The new Word document you have just created will appear and you will see the spell check dialog. Once you finish the spell check, the code saves the file to `C:\temp`. The Microsoft Word application icon will be displayed in the Task Bar.

Object and Object Interfaces

All objects have one or more **interfaces**, which you use to establish communication between the object and your application. The interface defines the methods, properties and events that the component exposes and which you as a VBScripter can make use of.

An interface is a contract (or specification) that spells out how and what you can do with this object in a standard (COM) way. Standard is the keyword here, because it means that if two or more objects support the same interface, you can use these objects through this interface in the very same manner.

This is what an object interface contract specifies:

❑ The functions

❑ The parameter(s) the functions take

❑ The return value(s) from the functions

❑ A GUID (Globally Unique IDentifier)

The GUID is (as the name suggests) a globally unique ID used for identifying the interface.

As you can see from the interface contract, it does *not* specify how a function is implemented. Nor does it specify in what programming language it has been developed. This means that COM components can be developed in literally any programming language, and the functions can be implemented any way you like — as long as the objects within the component expose an interface in a standard way.

Registration of Components

All COM components must be registered within the Windows registry, before you can use them. When a component is registered, entries about the component are made in the Windows registry that helps applications find the component. Normally, a Setup program takes care of this for you when you buy your COM components from a vendor, but if you create them yourself or if something has screwed up one or more of the registry entries, you can register the component yourself.

In the Windows System folder, there is an executable file called `RegSvr32.exe`, which can be used from the command line (or from Start|Run) to register and unregister a COM component.

The command `RegSvr32 MyComponent.DLL` will register all the classes and their corresponding interfaces contained in `MyComponent.DLL` in the registry. The registry is the only place your application can get the information about a component from, so if is not in there, you will not be able to use it. If you need to unregister a component then you still use the `RegSvr32.exe` file, but you use the `/U` parameter to remove the data from the registry.

So, to register a component:

```
Regsvr32 <component>.dll
```

And to unregister a component:

```
Regsvr32 /u <component>.dll
```

Keep in mind that not all COM components come in DLL files. COM components can also run in EXE files. We will cover what the differences are later in this chapter, but it is important to note that you cannot use the RegSvr32 file with EXE components.

> *Note that we refer to a COM object residing in a DLL as an in-process server (or in-proc server) because the DLL is loaded into the same memory space as the client that calls it — that is, it shares the same process. A COM object that runs in an EXE is called an out-of-process server, because it runs in a separate process.*

In order to register an EXE you can simply run the EXE by double-clicking the file in the Windows Explorer or, using the more appropriate method you use to execute the file, with the /regserver parameter appended to it. If you want to unregister the EXE file, then you need to run the EXE with the /unregserver parameter. Both of these parameters operate in the same fashion as the RegSvr32 file.

IUnknown, IDispatch and Dual Interfaces

Before we get into the details of this section, it is important to note that although all of this information is really useful to know, is not required. This is very low-level COM information that is done for you by VBScript. Even using Visual Basic, you are shielded from implementing these interfaces or even being required to know that they exist! So, don't worry — this information will not be on the test.

The IUnknown interface is the most important interface in COM — it exists for all COM objects and it is used to find out if the object supports any other specific interface using the QueryInterface method. If it does, a pointer to the interface is returned.

IUnknown also has two other functions (AddRef and Release) that are used for reference counting. Every time you add a reference to an object (instantiate an object using the Set statement), a reference counter within the object is incremented, and when you destroy the reference (destroy the instantiated object using the Set <object> = Nothing syntax), the reference counter is decremented. This way the object can keep track of how many clients that are referencing it. When the reference count hits zero, the object unloads itself from memory. The IUnknown interface must be supported by all other interfaces that an object exposes and the functionality that is provided by IUnknown must be implemented. This is one of the rules of COM. Remember, though, that in VB and VBScript, all this is going on 'under the hood', so you don't need to worry about it.

To create objects in VBScript using the CreateObject function, the classes in the COM component *must* also support/expose the IDispatch (Automation) interface. Without this interface, the component is not accessible from VBScript (or any other scripting language). The IDispatch interface contains the following functions/methods:

❑ Invoke

❑ GetIDsOfNames

❑ GetTypeInfo

❑ GetTypeInfoCount

The GetTypeInfo and GetTypeInfoCount functions are used for browsing the properties and methods that the interface exposes. The other two functions are the ones needed for invoking a method and setting or retrieving a property.

Summarized below is how the IDispatch interface works when you need to invoke a function:

❑ Call GetIDsOfNames with the name of the function/method to get the dispatch ID

❑ The methods parameters/arguments are arranged in an array of variants

❑ Execute the function/method by using the Invoke function

Binding

When you instantiate a component you use a method called **binding**. Binding defines how and when you connect to an object. There are two types of binding: early and late.

Early binding declares a variable as an object type. For instance, you can early bind to Word by using the following syntax:

```
dim objWord as Word.Application
set objWord = new Word.Application
```

When this code is executed, a reference to the Word object is immediately set up. If we never use the objWord variable we still have the object. Early binding to an object is faster for accessing the properties and methods of the object. The reason why this is faster is due to the fact that early binding knows about the object ahead of time and the application stores information about the object. Once we cover the next type of binding you will see why this can be a good and a bad thing.

One very important thing you should note is that *we cannot early bind in VBScript*. The reason why we cannot early bind is because VBScript treats every variable as a variant data type. In order to work with early binding, we need to use a language such as Visual Basic that allows for strong typed variables. In VBScript, on the other hand, we need to call the CreateObject function to get a reference to our object.

That brings us to **late binding**. When we call `CreateObject` in VBScript, we are finding the object and getting the information about it. We would late bind to Word in VBScript using this code:

```
dim objWord
set objWord = CreateObject("Word.Application")
```

The major advantage of late binding is that we do not get a connection to the object until the `Set` statement is executed. If we were in an `If..Then` loop then we may never need this object, so we can conserve resources since we are using objects only as we need them.

The major disadvantage of using late bound objects is that we must do a lookup within the object on every call to the object. Early bound objects know more about the object because the application stores the structure of the object and other important information such as the GUIDs. Late bound objects are slower since they must access each method and property of an interface via `IDispatch`, using calls to the `GetIDsOfNames` and `Invoke` methods.

On the other hand, the way that early bound objects tie into the actual structure of the object means that we can easily break our applications. As such applications use the identifiers that uniquely identify an interface, our information about the object is no longer valid if we make changes to an interface and give it a new identifier. Late bound objects do not have these problems since they determine this information when the object is created and are tied to an item called the `ClassID` (discussed in more detail later) that is the programmatic name of the object.

So, let's look at the key advantages and disadvantages of early bound and late bound objects.

Early bound:

❏ Faster to use since they know the structure of the object

❏ Can easily be broken by modifying the object

❏ Requires more resources since the object must be created whether it is used or not

Late bound:

❏ Slower to use since the calls to the object must query the object first

❏ Use fewer resources since objects are created on demand and variables can be reused to create references to other objects

❏ Do not tie directly to the structure and unique identifiers within the objects, so the connections remain fairly stable even when the object changes

It may appear that VBScript actually does support early binding with internal classes. You can use a `Set obj = new internalclass` declaration to get a reference to an internal VBScript class. However, even though this may appear to be using early binding, it is actually using late binding. This call is the equivalent of calling `CreateObject` for an external object. This sometimes confuses developers that are new to COM and VBScript.

Since compile time and runtime is the same in VBScript, it will not help you discover invalid object references until runtime and thus result in a runtime error, but it will help you in the editors that support intellitype.

Dual Interfaces

Dual interfaces are mechanisms that allow us to take advantage of both early and late binding — giving us the best of both worlds; for example, a component that supports early interface binding, but also allows scripting languages (like VBScript) to access it using the slower `IDispatch` Automation interface. Dual interfaces are supported by most COM components and are supported by all COM components developed and compiled with Visual Basic.

New Component Version

In this section, we'll look at how we deal with versioning in COM. Note that when we are using VBScript, the versioning of our objects is not important since late binding is not affected by versioning issues. But, if you decide to move into Visual Basic for more of your component creation then this will be a bigger issue. I recommended that you look over this section and keep it in the back of your mind for later use.

The idea of interfaces is all very fine, but what happens when a new version of the component is released? Does this mean that we get a new interface? Well, yes and no. You see, in order for the component to be backwards compatible, an interface cannot be changed. Now, if you only change the implementation of the classes in the component, you don't need to change the interface, as it still uses the same methods and properties with the same arguments/parameters.

However, if you change the interface — by changing the parameters or adding/deleting a method or property — you are creating a new version of the interface. A second version, so to speak. The good thing about this is that a version of the 'old' interface is kept in the component as well as the new one. This means that existing applications relying on the old interface will continue to work, and new applications can take advantage of the new and hopefully improved interface (and implementation).

Compilers like VB will point out to you, if you are about to break backwards compatibility, and give you the options of reversing the changes or creating a new version of the interface. If you look at the ProgIDs in the Registry under `\HKEY_CLASSES_ROOT\`, you will find that many ProgIDs are entered a number of times, and some of them with a version number, like `Word.Document.8` (`\HKEY_CLASSES_ROOT\Word.Document.8`).

If you look closer, you will see that the CLSID for all these ProgIDs are the same, which means that they point to the same component. I realize that if you follow the example with the `Word.Document` ProgID, you will need to have installed more than one version of Microsoft Word on your system. If you haven't done that, just trust me on this one. Why not just use the ProgID with the version number then? Well, you can, but that would defeat the idea of versioning. If an application can run using version 1, it will also be able to use version 2 of the component. If you specified version 1 (`Word.Document.1`) as your ProgID, and you ran your application on a machine with only version 2, you would get an error.

So, leave out the version number from the ProgID, unless you need to make sure that a certain method or property, which only exists in this version or later, is supported. Under the Word.Document ProgID there is a CurVer subkey, which points to the very latest version of the component. So when you don't specify the version as part of the ProgID, the value of the CurVer subkey is used as a lookup value for finding the latest version.

Object Identifiers

A number of different ID's are used, when you instantiate an object in VBScript.

ProgID

You use a program Id (ProgID) when you call the CreateObject function. A ProgID consists of servername and typename, CreateObject(servername.typename). (See Appendix A for more information on this funtion.) You can find the ProgID in the registry under the \HKEY_CLASSES_ROOT hive.

\HKEY_CLASSES_ROOT\<ProgID> is the full path, where *ProgID* is the ProgID of the class you want. Word.Document is an example of a ProgID you can use to instantiate the Document class of the Microsoft Word COM component/server.

ClassID

Now, because COM classes can only be created from class Ids (CLSIDs), VBScript must use the ProgID to look up the class Id (CLSID) in the registry. This is done by calling the function CLSIDFromProgID, which is part of the COM library. This is a good example of a function name that actually says what it does.

If you want to perform this operation manually, you can look up the \HKEY_CLASSES_ROOT\Word.Document key in the Registry, where you will find a subkey called CLSID. Yes, you guessed it; that is our class ID.

GUID

A CLSID is a GUID (Globally Unique IDentifier), which means a 16-byte value that is globally unique. The reason why a GUID is globally unique is the way it is generated. The first part of the value is based on the MAC address of your network adapter, and MAC addresses are unique. The second part is generated by the compiler that compiles the COM component or a tool such at GUIDGen that generates a GUID for a developer.

Registry

Open up the Registry Editor (run the `RegEdit` executable, which is located in the main Windows folder. You can select the Run command from the Start menu in the Task Bar and type in `regedit`.), and select the **CLSID** subkey under the Word.Document ProgID key – you will see the Default value name on the right side of the tree view. It is of type REG_SZ, which means it is a string, and under the Data column, you can see the actual CLSID, which is 00020906-0000-0000-C000-000000000046.

> **ALWAYS back up the registry before you attempt to make any changes. Incorrectly modifying the registry can render your system inoperable. Deleting or modifying data can have unpredictable results.**

This ID is used to find the actual file on disk that holds the object and this is done by looking up the CLS ID in the registry under the key `\HKEY_CLASSES_ROOT\CLSID`. VBScript does it by calling the `CoCreateInstance` COM API with the CLSID as the only argument. When the CLSID has been found, the function looks for the `InProcServer32` or `LocalServer32` subkey in that order.

To do it manually, look up the Word.Document class, for which the full registry path is `\HKEY_CLASSES_ROOT\CLSID\00020906-0000-0000-C000-000000000046`. Under this key, you will find the subkey `LocalServer32` that indicates the location of the out-of-process (EXE file) server for this class. By location, I mean the full path, including the filename and even the server if you are using DCOM. The subkey `InprocServer32` will indicate the location of the in-process server (DLL file) for this class. If both are present, the `InprocServer32` will be chosen. If the server is out of process then the `LocalServer32` key indicates the location of the component.

Launch COM Component

Now that the location of the COM component server has been found, the server is launched. Depending on the server type, in-process or out-of-process, the server is loaded into the applications address space or launched with a call to the CreateProcess Windows API. Once this has been completed, COM will request an instance of the class and return a pointer to the `IUnknown` interface.

Default Interface

With the pointer to the `IUnknown` interface, VBScript queries for the default interface, which is the only interface VBScript can use. This interface is then assigned to the variable that you have specified on the left side of the assignment operator (=):

```
Set objDocument = CreateObject("Word.Document")
```

Set Statement

So, the `Set` statement is used for assigning class interfaces to an object variable. To the VBScript programmer this is easy, but try being a C++ programmer and doing all these steps yourself, plus a few more. COM is a very complex architecture, but it is extremely easy to use in VBScript, VB, and VBA. Actually, the `Set` statement can also be used to create an instance of an internal VBScript class as well, using the `New` keyword, like this:

```
Set objDocument = New clsDocument
```

This assumes you have declared a class named `clsDocument` in your script code.

What COM Components and Objects are Available?

In VBScript, we don't have a lot of information about what components we can use, besides the ones that come with VBScript. In other programming tools, such as Visual Basic, we can browse the components and objects that have been registered on our system, and find information about all the methods and properties as well as the arguments that they take. (Remember, however, we you can only use those COM components that support Automation from VBScript.)

You can of course always look in the registry yourself, but that is slow and painful process. You really need a tool for this. If you have Visual Basic installed on your system, I can recommend using the built-in Object Browser as well as the OLE View tool for checking out registered COM components. (To run OLEView select the Windows Start menu, Run and type `OLEView.exe`. You can consult the Visual Basic help files for more information.)

As part of installations such as Internet Explorer, you get the Scripting Runtime Library, which is in fact a COM component. It is installed and registered when you setup VBScript. The following classes exist in this library:

❑ Dictionary

❑ FileSystemObject

There are also some built-in objects:

❑ Err

❑ RegExp

See Chapter 7 *The Built-In and Scripting Runtime Objects* for a detailed description of these classes.

Objects and the Variant data type

Normally the Variant data type is very forgiving when it comes to conversion to and from various Variant data subtypes, but when dealing with objects, you need to be careful. The problems can occur when we pass arguments to an object that is instantiated from a class in a COM component.

The only data type in VBScript is the `Variant` and as we saw earlier, type coercion is normally applied automatically. An object's methods may be defined as having parameters passed by reference (`ByRef`) or by value (`ByVal`). If a parameter of an object's method is `ByVal` then VBScript will automatically handle any type conversions necessary. If the parameter has been defined as `ByRef` then VBScript won't do the conversion automatically and expects you as a VBScripter to know what the type is and convert (or Cast) to that type. Most components, if they have been written with scripting in mind, will be `ByVal` or use a `Variant` data type that VBScript understands.

Lets look at an example of a component method defined in Visual Basic.

First let's define one using `ByVal` parameters:

```
Public Function ToUpperCase(ByVal sString As String) As String
    ToUpperCase = Ucase(sString)
End Function
```

To use this component's method in VBScript:

```
Dim oMyObject
Set oMyObject = CreateObject("MyComponet.MyObject")

Dim sMyString
sMyString = "hello"
sMyString = oMyObject.ToUpperCase(sString)
```

Now let's look at the same method defined as `ByRef`. You'll see that there is no `ByVal` – the default in Visual Basic is `ByRef` unless we specify `ByVal`:

```
Public Function ToUpperCase(sString As String) As String
    ToUpperCase = Ucase(sString)
End Function
```

Now if we use the component with exactly the same script we'll get a type mismatch error. Why? Because our function is expecting a string but is being passed a `Variant` data type. VBScript has not performed the type conversion automatically as it does with `ByVal` parameter passing.

If we want to make this work then we have a number of choices. If we are the component developer then we could redefine our method so that it is 'script friendly' by making it `ByVal`. If we must use `ByRef` then we could define it as a `Variant` data type in our method.

If we are using someone else's component and are unable to change the parameter, then we need to do the type conversion ourselves by using VBScript's built in functions such as `CStr`, `Cint`, `Clng` and so on (see Appendix A for their details).

So our script would need to be re-written as:

```
Dim oMyObject
Set oMyObject = CreateObject("MyComponet.MyObject")

Dim sMyString
sMyString = "hello"
sMyString = oMyObject.ToUpperCase(CStr(sString))
```

Now it will work fine.

Properties and Methods

Nearly all classes in a COM component have public properties and/or methods. Without these, you wouldn't be able to access the functionality of the class. Some classes have private properties and methods and they are always inaccessible to the client. They are only used internally by the class itself.

There are two kinds of methods:

❑ The Sub procedure that performs a certain action

❑ The Function procedure that performs an action and then returns a value

They are not necessarily called Sub and Function procedures in the programming languages they were developed, but to keep things in Visual Basic terms, that is what we will call them here.

The examples in this section can be loaded into Internet Explorer 4 or 5, or you can just cut-and-paste the script part and use it in WSH. You'll need your browser settings at low, and when you load the page click **Yes** to the dialog box warning you about security.

The code below creates a FileSystemObject and sets oFileSys to reference it. Having checked that the folder exists using the FileSystemObject's FolderExists function, we then use the GetFolders function to return a Folder object. We pass the name of the folder we want the object to reflect as a parameter in the GetFolder method. I have used the C:\Temp directory as most Windows users have one – if you're the exception then change it to an alternative directory. We have set oFolder to reference our folder object.

Next, we need to get a list of files in the folder so that we can display their names and types in the page's text area. The Folder object's Files function returns a Files object – this is a collection of File objects, with each file object containing lots of useful information (such as name and type) about each file in the folder.

Rather than set oFile to reference each File object by using the Files collection object's Item property, the For Each...Next technique has been used. This does the hard work for us and is faster than accessing each item in the collection by its Index. It sets oFile to the first File object in the Files collection then, each time we loop, the oFile variable is set to the next File object until we have gone through the whole collection.

Finally, we make use of the `Folder` object's read-only `ParentDirectory` property to find out the parent directory's name and show it in a message box:

```html
<HTML>
<BODY>
<SCRIPT LANGUAGE="VBScript">
Sub Window_OnLoad

    ' Declare variable to reference FileSystemObject
    Dim oFileSys

    ' Create a FileSystemObject and Set oFileSys to point to it
    Set oFileSys = CreateObject("Scripting.FileSystemObject")

    Dim oFolder
    Dim oFiles

    ' The folder we will create a list of files in
    Dim sFolder
    sFolder = "C:\temp"

    ' Use FolderExists method of FileSystemObject to check its a valid folder
    If oFileSys.FolderExists(sFolder) Then
        ' GetFolder method of FileSystemObject returns a Folder Object,
        ' Set oFolder
        ' to point to it
      Set oFolder = oFileSys.GetFolder(sFolder)

        ' Folder Object's Files method returns a Files Object which is a
        ' collection of File Objects
        ' set oFiles to reference it
      Set oFiles = oFolder.Files

        ' For each allows us to loop through an array or collection
      For Each oFile in oFiles
            txtFiles.value = txtFiles.value & oFile.Name & "    " & oFile.Type
            txtFiles.value = txtFiles.value & "    " & oFile.Type & vbCrLf
      Next

        ' Use Folder Object's parentFolder property to find out name of
        ' parent directory
      MsgBox oFolder.ParentFolder

    Else
      txtFiles.value = sFolder & " does not exist"
    End If
End Sub
</SCRIPT>
<TEXTAREA rows=30 cols=80 id=txtFiles name=txtFiles>
</TEXTAREA>

</BODY>
</HTML>
```

Properties can be read-only, write-only or allow both read and write operations. A runtime error occurs if you try to read (`Get`) from a write-only property or write (`Set`) to a read-only property. For example the `ParentFolder` property of our `Folder` object is read-only.

COM components also have default properties and methods and this is valuable information, because it could improve the speed of your code or it could lead to unwanted errors. A default property is the property used if you fail to supply one when you reference the object. An example of this is the `Number` property of the built-in `Err` object.

```
MsgBox Err
MsgBox Err.Number
```

The above lines of code both display the same thing in a `MsgBox`: the last error. This is because they essentially reference the same property. There can actually be a substantial performance gain to be won by using default properties but at the cost of 'breaking' the readability of the code, especially for new programmers. For example, if we use `objTest = Err`, forgetting to put `Set` in front of it, and then try and use the variable as if it pointed to the `Err` object, then we will get difficult-to-track runtime errors. The code where it fails will, of course, be valid and this can cause confusion. You'll often have to backtrack to where the variable is assigned to check that the error is not there.

Object Scope, Lifetime and References

Scope

All variables have a scope, including variables used to reference objects. Scope defines which parts of your code can access the variable. All variables, including objects, in VBScript have one of the following scopes:

- ❏ Procedure-level, where the object is declared within a procedure, be it an `Event` procedure, or a `Function` or `Sub` procedure.
- ❏ Global-level, where the object is declared outside any procedure.

Objects with procedure-level scope can only be accessed within the procedure it is declared. The object goes out of scope when there are no longer any references to it, for example by using `Set object = Nothing`, or when the procedure exits.

Objects with script-level scope can be accessed within all the procedure in your script. The object goes out of scope when it is explicitly destroyed, by `Set object = Nothing`, or when your script ends.

Lifetime

The lifetime of an object depends on when it is instantiated and when it is destroyed. Unlike other variables, object variables must be instantiated using the `Set` statement before they can be used. The objects life begins when you instantiate it and ends when all references to the object have been released. References to an object are released when:

- ❏ You explicitly release it, using the `Set object = Nothing` statement
- ❏ It's a local variable inside a procedure and the procedure ends
- ❏ Your script ends (objects with script-level scope only)

171

Let's take a look at some examples of scope and lifetime.

The code below is an HTML page with four buttons and some VBScript:

```
<HTML>
<HEAD>
<META name=VI60_defaultClientScript content=VBScript>
<SCRIPT LANGUAGE="VBScript">
' Define a global (or page level) variable
Dim moGlobalDictionary

Sub Window_OnLoad()
    ' set our global or page level variable to reference a new instance of a
dictionary object
    Set moGlobalDictionary = CreateObject("Scripting.Dictionary")
End Sub

Sub cmdAccessGlobal_onclick
    ' Access the global variable's methods and properties
    moGlobalDictionary.Add CStr(moGlobalDictionary.Count + 1),"Another Item"
    MsgBox moGlobalDictionary.Count
End Sub

Sub cmdSetGlobalToNothing_onclick
    Set moGlobalDictionary = Nothing
End Sub

Sub cmdDefineAndSetLocal_onclick
    ' define a local variable
    Dim loLocalDictionary
    ' Set the local variable to reference a newly
    ' instantiated dictionary object

    Set loLocalDictionary = CreateObject("Scripting.Dictionary")
    loLocalDictionary.Add CStr(loLocalDictionary.Count + 1),"Another Item"
End Sub

Sub cmdAccessExternalLocal_onclick
    ' Try and access the local variable defined in button3_onclick
    loLocalDictionary.Add CStr(loLocalDictionary.Count + 1),"Another Item"
    MsgBox loLocalDictionary.Count
End Sub

Function ReturnADictionary()
    ' Define local variable
    Dim loLocalDictionary
    ' create dictionary object
    Set loLocalDictionary = CreateObject("Scripting.Dictionary")
    ' assign ReturnADictionary to return a reference to our local object
    Set ReturnADictionary = loLocalDictionary
End Function

Sub cmdSetGlobal_onclick
    ' Set global variable
    Set moGlobalDictionary = ReturnADictionary()
    MsgBox "Global Set"
End Sub


</SCRIPT>
</HEAD>
```

```
<BODY>
<INPUT type="button" value="Access Global Variable" name=cmdAccessGlobal>
<INPUT type="button" value="Set Global To Nothing"
name=cmdSetGlobalToNothing>
<INPUT type="button" value="Define variable and create local object"
name=cmdDefineAndSetLocal>
<INPUT type="button" value="Access externally defined local object"
name=cmdAccessExternalLocal>
<INPUT type="button" value="Set Global Using Function" name=cmdSetGlobal>
</BODY>
</HTML>
```

Let's examine how it works in some detail, paying particular attention to scope and lifetime.

We first define a global or page-level variable, moGlobalDictionary, which we will set to reference a Dictionary object. We create the Dictionary object in the Window_Onload() event that fires when we first browse the page. Note that moGlobalDictionary is a global variable because it has been defined outside of any sub or function procedure – and because it's global any Sub or Function can access it in the page.

If we click the button **Access Global Variable** then the code in Sub cmdAccessGlobal_onclick fires. This makes use of the methods of the Dictionary object to add a new item to it, and also displays the Count property. Click on this a few times and we'll see the count go up. Note that even when the Sub ends, the global variable continues to reference the Dictionary object we instantiated in the Window_OnLoad() event.

Now we click the **Set Global To Nothing** button – this will cause the Sub cmdSetGlobalToNothing_onclick to fire. This subprocedure de-references the global variable moGlobalDictionary by telling it to stop pointing to the Dictionary object that we created in Window_OnLoad() and, instead, point to nothing (the line Set moGlobalDictionary = Nothing). With no references to it, the Dictionary object's lifetime has come to an end. If we now click the **Access Global Variable** button, we'll see the following error message:

Although the variable still exists and is still valid, it no longer points to anything.

Next we click the **Define variable and create local object** button – this fires Sub cmdDefineAndSetLocal_onclick. This defines a variable, loLocalDictionary, and sets it to reference a new instance of the Dictionary object. However when the Sub ends the variable goes out of scope and, because it is local, no other references to the Dictionary object exist and so its lifetime comes to an end. If we click the **Access externally defined local object** button, we are trying to access the local variable from another subprocedure and so we get the following error message:

173

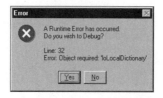

To show the importance of references and the effect they, in terms of un-freed resources, can have if we don't de-reference objects, let's look at the final button: **Set Global Using Function**. When this is clicked the code in Sub cmdSetGlobal_onclick fires. This calls the function ReturnADictionary() which defines a local variable (loLocalDictionary), sets it to reference a newly instantiated Dictionary object, then sets the return value of the function to reference the local variable and the Dictionary object it contains.

When the function finishes, the local variable loLocalDictionary goes out of scope and is no longer accessible. However, the Dictionary object is still referenced as it forms the return value of the function, so it's lifetime continues. Back in cmdSetGlobal_onclick, where we called the function, we set moGlobalDictionary to reference the Dictionary object returned and so its lifetime still continues. We can click the **Access Global Variable** button again without error as the global variable now points to a Dictionary object. The Dictionary object won't die unless we set it to nothing or the global variable goes out of scope, which will happen only when we leave the page.

References

When you instantiate an object, you effectively create a pointer, or a reference to an instance of a class in a COM component. This causes the COM component to be loaded into memory, if it hasn't already been loaded. The COM component keeps track of how many times it has been referenced, and if the reference counter hits zero, the component unloads itself from memory. This is something to keep in mind if you have more than one object variable referring to the same class. For example:

```
Dim objFirstDocument
Dim objSecondDocument

    ' Instantiate the Document class from the Word COM
    ' component/server on the local machine
    Set objFirstDocument = CreateObject("Word.Document")
    ' Let the second document reference the first document
    Set objSecondDocument = objFirstDocument
    ' Show the instance of Word
    objSecondDocument.ActiveWindow.Visible = True

    ' Destroy the first document after use
    objFirstDocument.Close
    Set objFirstDocument = Nothing
```

The Microsoft Word COM component is *not* unloaded after the last statement (Set objFirstDocument = Nothing) because another object variable is still referencing it. If you don't believe this, look at the **Processes** tab in the Task Manager (Windows NT only). It will list the out-of-process server for the Word.Document class, which is Winword.exe, until you explicitly destroy the second document or it goes out of scope.

Using the With Statement with Objects

Sometimes you refer to the same object many times within just a small piece of code:

```
Dim objDocument
Dim lngStatistics
Dim blnAutoHyphenate

    ' Instantiate the Document class from the Word COM
    ' component/server on the local machine
    Set objDocument = CreateObject("Word.Document")
    ' Show the Print preview window
    objDocument.PrintPreview
    ' Get the number of characters in the document
    lngStatistics = objDocument.ComputeStatistics( _
                    wdStatisticCharacters)
    ' Get the object's AutoHyphenation property
    blnAutoHyphenate = objDocument.AutoHyphenation
    ' Set the object's AutoHyphenation property
    objDocument.AutoHyphenation = True

    ' Destroy the object after use
    Set objDocument = Nothing
```

In this sample code the `objDocument` object variable is referenced five times after it has been instantiated. Now, this doesn't look too bad, but imagine that you needed to set 50 or perhaps 100 variables from your code. This is where the `With` statement comes in handy. The same piece of code can now look like this:

```
Dim objDocument
Dim lngStatistics
Dim blnAutoHyphenate

    ' Instantiate the Document class from the Word COM
    ' component/server on the local machine
    Set objDocument = CreateObject("Word.Document")

    With objDocument
        ' Show the Print preview window
        .PrintPreview
        ' Get the number characters in the document
        lngStatistics = _
            .ComputeStatistics(wdStatisticCharacters)
        ' Get the object's AutoHyphenation property
        blnAutoHyphenate =.AutoHyphenation
        ' Set the object's AutoHyphenation property
        .AutoHyphenation = True
        objDocument.Close
    End With

    ' Destroy the object after use
    Set objDocument = Nothing
```

Apart from saving you some typing, the With statement also adds to the readability of the code. The best thing, though, about using the `With` statement is the performance gain: the more times you access the object, the more you gain from using the `With` statement.

Create your own COM Objects

Even though you can do most things from your own script code, there are times when you should consider moving some of the code into a COM component. Since we already know VBScript, Visual Basic is a very good tool for this purpose.

Two advantages of placing your code in a COM component are the increase in performance, and the much better error handling. We get better performance from a VB COM component because the code is compiled, rather than interpreted as is the case with VBScript. When we place the code in a COM component, we can also use this component from various pieces of script code, without duplicating the code that's in the component. The fact that the code is placed in the component also makes it very hard to get at, which thus means better protection of proprietary code.

There are also things we cannot do in VBScript, but by moving the code to a component, we can overcome this limitation. One example is Windows API calls – these are not possible in VBScript because the Declare statement is 'missing'. Another example is workload on the machine. If you place the code in a component, you have the option of placing the component on a different machine and run it there. This might make sense if you can separate business logic into COM components and place them on a separate server as a middle-tier.

Note that with the advent of Windows Script Components, it is now possible to create COM components in VBScript! This is discussed in detail in Chapter 9.

Summary

In this chapter, we have looked at how we use COM components in our application. We took a closer look at interfaces (contracts/agreements), object identifiers (GUIDs, ClassIDs, ProgIDs), and different binding methods (early and late).

The Variant data type was discussed in regards to objects instantiated from classes in COM components, and we looked at default properties and methods and how they can cause problems if you are not aware of them. The use of the very powerful With statement was also discussed.

We also looked at object scope, lifetime, and references.

Last, but not least, we discussed why and when to create your own COM components. The why's includes greater speed, better error handling, reusability, and best of all; much better protection of your source code.

6

Using COM Components with MTS

Overview

In this chapter, we will introduce MTS (Microsoft Transaction Server) and how we place components in it. The advantages you can obtain by using MTS instead of just using DCOM on its own will be explained. We shall also look into what security models there are, and show an example on how to use a COM component in MTS from VBScript.

At the end of the chapter, there is a brief overview of COM+, the next generation of COM.

If you are new to COM components, I suggest you read chapter 5 *Using COM Components and Objects* prior to this chapter.

A Quick Introduction to MTS

What is MTS (Microsoft Transaction Server)? Well, that's a very good question, and to cut a long story short: MTS is a distributed application server.

Perhaps that was *too* short! Well, MTS is a middle-tier product that facilitates moving your business logic off the machine where you run your applications, and placing it instead in a distributed three-tier application model. This means that the front-end applications run on the user's machines and, instead of having all the business logic duplicated on all the user machines, it is now placed in MTS where all the front-end applications can access it.

This is illustrated in the diagram below:

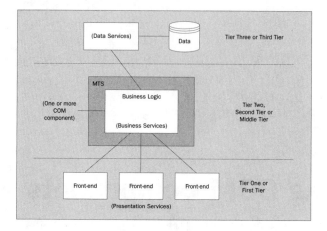

- ❏ The **First Tier** contains the front-end applications (which are usually placed on the user's machines) – they are primarily used for retrieving input from the user and presenting output to the user as requested

- ❏ The **Middle Tier** is where you place your business logic (sometimes called application logic) – this is normally a separate machine used as an application server

- ❏ The **Third Tier** is where you place you data services – the data services take care of manipulating and maintaining your data

This can also be done with the help of DCOM, but MTS brings a lot more than DCOM ever did. DCOM enables stand-alone COM objects to be part of a distributed application, but MTS also brings you the context, distributed transactions, role-based security, and synchronized concurrency. Now developers no longer have to spend time working on the application infrastructure under which the applications will run.

The context is an object, which is created for each instance of an object in MTS. It provides information about the environment in which the object executes, such as whether or not the object is part of a transaction and the identity of the object's creator. It also holds the object's security credentials, which can be checked when the object creates other MTS objects. When an object instance is part of a transaction, the corresponding context object collaborates with all other context objects within the same transaction to either commit or abort the transaction.

There are a number of things that you need to change when you move from either a single-user application (or a traditional two-tier) client-server solution to a multi-tier enterprise solution (like most web solutions). The application needs to be scalable and, at the same time, as robust as a single user application. Most single-user applications run on a single PC and are therefore not normally influenced by network breakdowns, etc.

Now, this is where MTS can help and make the transition a lot easier, especially if you are already using COM components, because MTS is a "component/object request broker with transactional capabilities" for the server part of your client-server application.

If you are currently using DCOM for your distributed applications, you will also gain from using MTS instead.

MTS provides a simple concurrency model for developing distributed applications that takes care of the synchronization between multiple threads on multiple machines. It is provided through activities, which are paths of execution that start when a client creates an object and end when that object is released. Within such an activity, the object might create other MTS objects and it is the responsibility of the activity to make sure that the objects don't run in parallel. So, an activity should be seen as a single logical thread of execution.

This frees you as a developer from dealing with the synchronization and leaves more time for developing the code (more often than not, this code is the business logic part of the three-tier model) your boss asked you to do.

MTS also takes care of managing resources (as in it maintains the durable state of an application), such as database connections and memory, for you. This is done through what is called Resource Managers. We saw earlier that MTS is a "component/object request broker with transactional capabilities", which means that if one of your components fails, then none of the work done in the activity will be committed. It is the all-or-nothing work management approach. Mind you, you can also place non-database and non-transactional components in MTS!

Packages

Components in MTS are grouped into packages of one or more components. This can be done using the MTS Explorer, and normally you group components that perform related functions because all components in a package run in the same MTS server process.

This is important because a package is the *trust boundary*, meaning that security authorization is checked whenever you pass the boundary of a package. This is when the client instantiates a class, or when one package calls another:

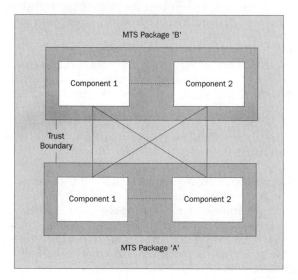

The dashed lines between the components indicate that no security check is performed, and the full lines indicate that security authorization is checked.

When you need to deploy your components, it is done by deploying a package file. This file is created using the export function in MTS Explorer.

In-Process Components Only

You should be aware that MTS only allows in-process components (DLL's) to run. You cannot register an out-of-process COM component (an EXE) with the MTS explorer. However, this does not mean that you cannot run the components as out-of-process servers. MTS enables the registered components to run in a separate process space by loading them into surrogate server processes. This is a neat little trick on behalf of MTS.

Advantages of using MTS

There are a number of advantages of using MTS when compared to using just DCOM. Below, we'll give you an overview of some of these.

Role-Based Security

In MTS, you can define roles. A role represents a logical group of users that are allowed to invoke the various interfaces on the classes in the components. The Windows NT user and group accounts are used for this purpose. Please be aware that because the security features are based on the Windows NT security model, these features are not available when you run MTS on Windows 9x.

You define a role by opening up the Microsoft Transaction Server Explorer and selecting the Roles icon under the Components you want to define the role(s) for:

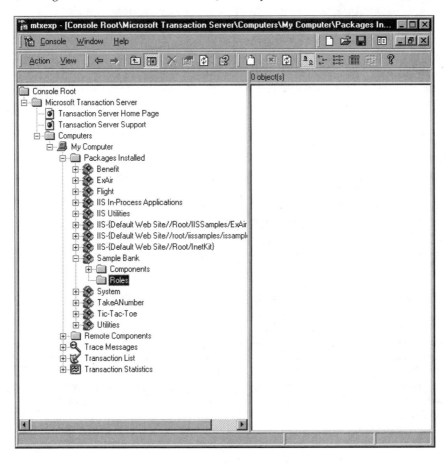

Right click on the `Roles` icon and select New|Role. Then enter the name of the role in the New Role dialog and click OK:

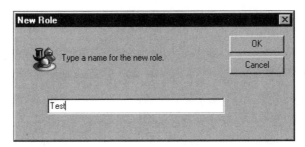

Once you have defined a role, and added the users, you can then map it to one or more classes or even a specific interface on a class, by adding the Role to the class/interface's Role Membership. Once this is done, MTS will take care of the security for you.

Can be Changed by an Administrator

Role-based security is much easier to manage than doing it from code, because when the security needs to be changed (an employee has left the company, and another one has taken his or her place), a System Administrator can deal with setting up the new employee.

If you base your roles entirely on Windows NT groups, so only NT groups and not individuals are added to a role, all that needs to be done when employees come and go is to add/delete Windows NT user accounts, and make sure new user accounts are added to the appropriate groups. Because the component(s) is already set up to use specific roles, no further setup is required on your part.

Declarative vs. Programmatic Security

What is described above is called *declarative security* because you declare or rather, define, who can invoke what interfaces. Declarative security is configured with MTS explorer.

Programmatic security is provided by the component itself. This means that the developer of a component must code the security into the component. Although this is much harder to maintain, it gives you the advantage of securing individual parts of your code. One example is if you want a manager to be able to authorize a higher amount than a normal user. This is done by using the `IsCallerInRole` method of the object context, which determines if the direct caller (the client/process that is currently accessing your component) is part of a specific role. Alternatively, you can use the `GetDirectCallerName` method of the `SecurityProperty` object.

It means that you can check the security credentials even when calling components within the same package.

What security model you should choose really depends on what kind of system you are building and how good you are at packaging the components.

Package Identity

Components traditionally use the identity of the calling client, but with MTS you can set the identity of a package and thus the identity of all components in the package. If the user/client Gregory calls component A, then component A impersonates Gregory when calling the object components, accessing files on disk, or updating data in SQL Server, and so on. This is not a good idea because this means that the Windows NT user account Gregory must have the proper access rights to all of this.

Maybe it is OK to give Gregory access rights to do this, but what happens when another user needs to perform the same tasks as Gregory from his/her machine? Well, you obviously need to grant him/her the same rights.

This is where package identity comes in handy when you set the identity of the package in which component A resides, all the calls component A makes take on the identity of the package. So, now you grant the proper access rights to the Windows NT user/group that you will use as the package identity. This means that all the user/group accounts that can access component A can also perform the external tasks performed by this component, without having the proper access rights themselves.

Pooling

Pooling is a way of recycling resources like database connections, and thus saving valuable resources. Object pooling was supposed to have been in MTS 2.0, but it never made it.

Connection Pooling

However, with the ODBC Driver Manager version 3.0 and later, you can pool your database connections. Database connections are scarce and expensive resources, and the creation and destruction of these uses up valuable time and network resources.

The ODBC Driver Manager maintains a pool of available (ODBC) database connections, and when your application opens a connection, this pool is searched for an available connection. If the connection meets your application's requirements, such as server name, cursor type etc., it is assigned to your application. Because an existing connection was used, you were saved the cost of establishing a new connection. Once your application releases the connection, it is returned to the pool.

The size of a pool grows dynamically, but it also shrinks when an inactivity timeout occurs for a connection.

JIT (Just-In-Time) Activation

Just-in-time activation is a feature of MTS to help reduce system resources consumption. This is done by activating objects only when you call them. When you create an instance of the class in your application, you are given a pointer to this object.

However, the object hasn't actually been created yet. This won't happen until the first time you call a property or method of the object. This means that the object doesn't take up any resources before you actually use it.

When the object finishes, it should call either the `SetComplete` or `SetAbort` method of the context object. This tells MTS to deactivate the object and free the resources used by it. When the object is deactivated, the object is destroyed but because MTS manages the pointer to the client application, the client won't know anything about what goes on.

This can lead to problems, because when the object is deactivated, its local state is lost. This means that all local variables and properties are reset. Therefore you should write *stateless* components if you want them to run in MTS.

This is one thing to keep in mind when you develop your components because if they are stateless, you cannot store instance data in the object. However, you can still store the state outside of the object, by using the **Shared Property Manager**.

The Shared Property Manager is used for sharing data between objects in the same server process and is called a **Resource Dispenser**, because it manages non-durable, shared-state data for the components in the same server process.

Easier Deployment

When you are ready to deploy your components, they can be deployed as packages. A package is a unit of deployment and you create your packages in the MTS Explorer, from where you also export them for deployment. It is easier to deploy a package consisting of several components than to manually deploy each component.

You might be forgiven for thinking that this could be a disadvantage, because a package cannot be split across multiple servers. Actually, this is not a problem, because you can deploy the same package to multiple servers and thus reap the benefits of load balancing.

When you export a package, MTS Explorer creates a package file that contains information about the components and, optionally, the roles (Windows NT user/group ID's) from the source package. To export a package, select the package in the MTS Explorer, right click on the package and select Export:

If you select the Save Windows NT user ids associated with roles checkbox, you will not have to set up the security on the deployment server. Please note, however, that this is only feasible if the deployment server is part of the same Windows NT domain and, thus, has the same user and group accounts. When you are ready to deploy the package on another server, you simply use the Package Wizard to import it, by right clicking on the Packages Installed node in MTS Explorer, and clicking on New|Package. In the Package Wizard dialog you click on the Install pre-built packages button:

In the **Select Package Files** dialog, you add the packages you want to import, and then click on the **Next >** button:

In the **Set Package Identity** dialog, you select the user ID you want to use when the components in the package are run:

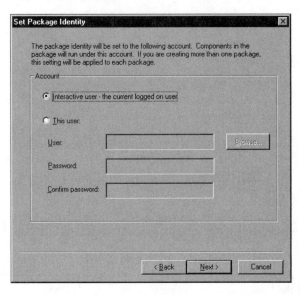

Finally, you enter the installation directory in the **Installation Options** dialog, and then click on the **Finish** button:

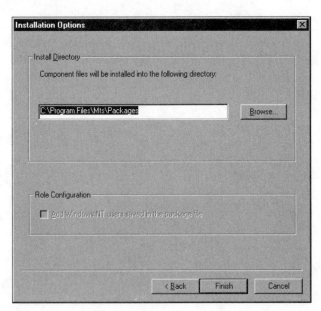

All this can even be automated using the scriptable administration objects that MTS provides. Check out the sample VBScript files (*.vbs) that come with Microsoft Transaction Server. They are located in the \Program Files\MTS\Samples folder.

Transaction Based (All-or-Nothing)

When you start an activity, which is what a set of objects executing on behalf of a base client application is called, everything is done in memory, i.e. it is not committed to disk. MTS automatically creates transactions for your components when you activate them.

This means that if one of your objects fails, regardless of what functions it performed, none of the changes made, by any of the objects in the activity, are committed. Actually, that is how it looks, but in fact MTS handles cleanup and rollbacks whenever necessary. MTS uses the MSDTC (Distributed Transaction Coordinator) for this task.

Only if all the objects in an activity complete successfully are the changes committed. This is the "all-or-nothing" approach and gives you better consistency, without writing any transactional code.

Sample

The first thing you need to do when you want to run your component in MTS is to open up the MTS Explorer (see figure below). Note that this is the MTS Explorer running in the Microsoft Management Console (MMC) on Windows NT. It looks quite similar on Windows 9x though.

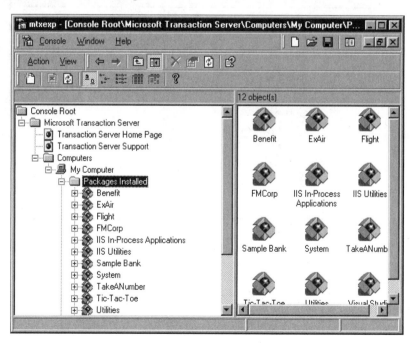

As you can see from this figure, we have expanded the **Packages Installed** node under **My Computer**. Here you can see all the packages installed on the selected machine.

Now you need to register your component as a package with the MTS Explorer. Right-click on the **Packages Installed** node, and click on **New|Package** in the **Context** menu.

When the **Package Wizard** appears, click on the **Create an empty package** button, and then you give the new package the name **Test**. Click **OK** and then you should see your package on the list. Expand the **Test** package and right-click on the **Components** node. Then select **New|Component** from the **Context** menu.

This brings up the **Component Wizard**, where you click on the **Install new component(s)** button. Click on **Add Files...** and add your component by browsing your system and selecting the component's DLL, which includes the Type Library. In the example below, we have added an **EventLog** component, which contains only one class, the **clsEventLog**.

If you expand the **Components** node, the MTS Explorer should look something like the figure below, depending on how many classes your component holds:

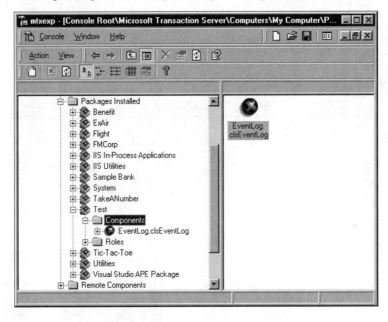

Because we want to use declarative security, we need to add a role to the component, so expand the **Component** node, right-click on the **Roles** node, and click **New|Role**.

Give the new role the name **Admin**. Expand the new **Admin** role, right-click on the **Users** tab and click **New|User**. Add the group from the **Add Users and Groups to Role** dialog and click **OK**. We added the **Admin** group for the local machine.

All you need to do now is to add the new role to the component. Right-click on the **Role Membership** node and click on **New| Role**. Then add the new **Admin** role and click **OK**.

Now the MTS Explorer should look like the figure below. Just leave all properties and settings at their default values. They are OK for now:

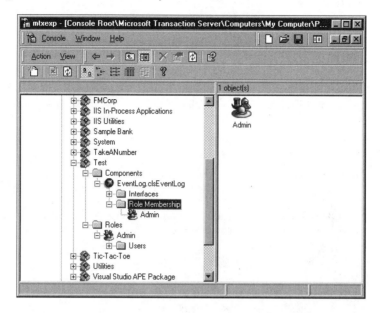

Run the VBScript code shown below to see how easy it is to communicate with a component in MTS. Remember that you'll need to change the names in the code to correspond to the names of your own component and class.

```vbscript
' Holds the transaction context
Dim objTxCtx
' Holds the MTS object
Dim objMTxAs
' Holds the event log object
Dim objEventLog
' Holds the error handler object
Dim objErrorHandler

  ' Get the reference to MTS
  Set objMTxAs = CreateObject("MTxAS.AppServer.1")
  ' Get the MTS Transaction context
  Set objTxCtx = objMTxAs.GetObjectContext

  ' Create an instance of the event log class
  Set objEventLog = objTxCtx.CreateInstance("EventLog.clsEventLog")
  ' Create an instance of the error handler class
  Set objErrorHandler = objTxCtx.CreateInstance( _
   "ErrorHandler.clsErrorHandler")

  ' Write an information event to the event log
  objEventLog.WriteEvent "VBScript", "VBScript", _
   INFORMATION_TYPE, 1003, "MYPC", 5
```

191

```
' Log an error message
objErrorHandler.LogError "modTest.Test", "This error occured", _
  PU_LNG_ERR_SHOW_MESSAGE

' ... Do all your other stuff here

' Abort the transaction
objTxCtx.SetAbort
```

Please be aware that there are many other things you need to consider when you place components in MTS. This is merely a quick example on how to do it:

1. Create a context in which your component(s) must run

2. Instantiate your objects using the context

The example below shows how to use MTS from within Active Server Pages (ASP) running on Microsoft Internet Information Server 4.0:

```
<%@ TRANSACTION=Required LANGUAGE="VBScript" %>

<HTML>
  <HEAD>
            <TITLE>Transactional Web Page</TITLE>
  </HEAD>

    <FONT size="10">
    <B>Transactional Web Page</B></FONT><BR>

    <HR>

This ASP page demonstrates how you can use the
transactional features of ASP to abort the
changes made to the Northwind database on a SQL
Server called DKTSNTS-1, using the Server and
the ObjectContext objects.

<%
Dim cnTest ' ADODB.Connection

  ' Create an instance of the ADODB.Connection
  Set cnTest = Server.CreateObject("ADODB.Connection")

  ' Open the connection
  cnTest.Open "Provider=SQLOLEDB.1;" & _
          "Persist Security Info=True;" & _
          "User ID=sa;Initial Catalog=Northwind;" & _
          "Data Source=DKTSNTS-1"

  cnTest.Execute "INSERT INTO Categories " & _
          "(CategoryName, Description) VALUES " & _
          "('Test', 'Test description')"

  ' Close the connection
  cnTest.Close

  ' Indicate to MTS that we need to rollback
  ' Comment out the next line to commit the changes
```

```
ObjectContext.SetAbort
 ' Indicate to MTS that all transactions went ok
 ' Uncomment the next line to commit the changes
 'ObjectContext.SetComplete
%>

 </BODY>
</HTML>
```

For more information about MTS, check out Visual Basic 6 MTS Programming, from Wrox Press (ISBN 1861002440).

Next Step: COM+

MTS has only been on the market a few years and already it is being replaced. Well, that is not quite true, because all of the functionality is being built into COM.

MTS + COM = COM+ ?

COM+, which is the new buzzword in town, is essentially the OLE 32 subsystem enhanced with the Context Concurrency Transactions features of MTS. In short, MTS COM, OLE DB and MSMQ (Microsoft Message Queue, used for asynchronous communication), plus some more, is what make up COM+!

MTS has been tightly integrated into the COM runtime, but it isn't just a simple merger. Everything has been improved and streamlined; for example, the COM API calls are now context aware, which means that you as a developer can forget about MTS.

Goodbye Middle-Tier Software

Up until now, you had to deploy some sort of middle-tier server software, like MTS, to get transaction-based features, but no longer. COM+ gives MTS and MSMQ a much needed improvement and integrates all of the functionality into COM+.

When

COM+ will hit the streets with the arrival of Windows 2000, as it is an integrated part of this new Operating System. Although Windows 2000 will be the first platform with COM+, it is unlikely to be the only. It will most likely be ported to various UNIX platforms, as Microsoft and its partners have done with previous versions of COM.

New Names

Not only have they changed the way they name the operating system from Windows NT to Windows 2000, but they have also changed many of the names you know from MTS. An MTS package is now called a **COM+ Application**; the different services provided by MTS are now as a whole called **COM+ Services** and **configured components** is the wording used about objects that use these services.

Extended Services

COM+ introduces some extra services that can be requested by a class at runtime using declarative attributes. The most important of these new services are summarized below.

Load Balancing

Unlike MTS that provides only basic load-balancing capabilities, COM+ comes with built-in dynamic application load balancing that can be split across servers. When a request, such as instantiating a class, comes in, it is redirected to a **Component Load Balancing** server that decides which system has the least load and then routes the request to that server.

COM+ acts as an object request broker, which makes COM+ components truly scalable.

Queued Components

This service (**Queued Component**) is an expansion of the capabilities we already know from MSMQ. This means that we are guaranteed delivery of information between two application components. This is true even when there is no network connection readily available. So now you can operate in a disconnected state and, when a connection is available, send the data asynchronously to the remote component. This is ideal for people who work in the field. The central database is offsite, which means that the transaction is created and queued, and then later it will be processed, when the system is online.

Object Pooling

This technique, which MTS never implemented, allows a certain number of objects to be created at the start of an application, and then they are recycled, all depending on the applications requirements. This is especially helpful if the startup time for an object is very long., If you are a VB COM component developer, you should be aware that components created in VB5 and VB6 cannot be recycled. This is because the current VB components have thread affinity due to TLS (Thread Local Storage) use. This will probably be resolved in the future versions of Visual Basic.

How to Make an Application COM+ "Compliant"

What about existing COM components, do they have to be rewritten? No,.is the short answer to that question.

In order to manage these non-COM+ components, a new registration database has been added. This database – called **RegDB** – stores the metadata that describes the components. This database is used instead of the system Registry and it is optimized for the information COM+ needs to activate the components. Every COM+ object stores metadata to describe the object itself, much the same way type libraries do today. The metadata is a superset of type libraries and it provides a more consistent definition across all types of COM+ objects.

COM+ is compatible with COM, as we know it, but if you want to make true COM+ components you will have to wait until the new developer tools, like the next Microsoft Visual Studio, hit the street. This will probably happen a short while after Windows 2000 has been released.

COM+ Uses Interception

Instead of trivial API calls, COM+ uses the concept of **interception**. Actually, MTS did this as well but with COM+ it is now integrated, which means no more calls to the infamous `SafeRef` function (used by an object to obtain a reference to itself). This is needed when the object needs to pass a safe reference to itself to another object or client outside the context.

What this means is that instead of coding some platform-dependent API calls into the component, you can describe the components requirements – such as transactions and resource pooling – by using declarative attributes. Remember that the declarative attributes are set after you have compiled your component, which means that it will be easy to change the requirements of a component once it has been compiled.

At activation time, COM+ retrieves information about the attribute values of a specific class. The **Catalog Manager** is responsible for looking up this information in the Catalog (which only holds information about COM+ components) and in the RegDB and Registry (where information about "normal" COM components can be found).

So, at activation time, COM+ looks in the Catalog to see if your class needs any extended services, and makes sure that the resulting object receives the requested services.

In other words, these interceptors exist to ensure a proper runtime environment, based on the class attributes in the Catalog. The runtime environment is also called a context.

Summary

In this chapter, we have looked at how we use COM components in MTS. We saw how MTS gave us a lot of extra features, such as:

❑ Transactions in an all-or-nothing framework

❑ Just-in-time activation for recycling of objects

❑ Easier deployment of components

❑ Declarative and programmatic security

This chapter is meant as a general overview, as an appetizer for getting started with MTS or COM+, there is a lot more to both than the coverage we have been able to provide here, so we can only suggest that you do some serious reading if you want to be at the forefront of the "Windows evolution".

Check out these web addresses; they are packed with more information about these subjects:

❑ http://www.microsoft.com/com/tech/COMPlus.asp – contains COM+ specific information, and a list of other websites that offer information about COM+

❑ http://www.microsoft.com/com – contains COM specific information, and a list of other websites that offer information about COM

❑ http://www.microsoft.com/com/tech/MTS.asp – contains MTS specific information, and a list of other websites that offer information about MTS

❑ http://www.comdeveloper.com – contains information about COM, DCOM, COM+ and other interesting material for "COM devotees"

The Built-In and Scripting Runtime Objects

In this chapter, we will be looking at two types of object available to VBScript: the built-in and runtime VBScript objects. We'll begin by looking at the differences between them, and then we'll take a tour through some of the objects available (with their various methods, properties and events), all the while concentrating on how we can utilize them in our scripts.

By the end of this chapter you'll know:

❑ The two kinds of objects that are included with all VBScript installations.

❑ How to use regular expressions to parse text strings and do powerful search-and-replace operations. Regular expressions are one of the major additions to VBScript 5.0.

❑ A way to create associative data structures, ones where you can store data by name, rather than by number as you do in an array. The Dictionary object does this for you and it can be used to maintain very flexible data structures.

❑ How to do all kinds of file manipulations with the FSO objects. If you're using VBScript with WSH to automate 'batch file' type operations, this is *your* chapter. If you're not using WSH to automate your computer functions, you should be!

Runtime vs. Built-In - What's the Difference?

The distinction between these two is subtle, especially because in current Microsoft products you always get both. But since Microsoft's documentation makes a distinction, we'll try to make the differences clear. Put simply, *built-in* objects are a part of the VBScript interpreter while *runtime* objects are supplied by an external DLL.

VBScript is designed to be a small and lightweight interpreted language, so it does not use strict data types (only Variants). In addition, because VBScript is intended to be a safe subset of Visual Basic, it does not include file I/O or direct access to the underlying operating system. This bare-bones VBScript functionality is provided by the VBScript engine DLL file (vbscript.dll).

However, the default scripting engines installed with current Microsoft products including Office 2000, Windows 98 and 2000, WSH and ASP 3.0 also provide a scripting runtime library in scrrun.dll. This library allows the VBScript programmer to reference a series of objects that provide file I/O, directory manipulation and an associative data structure that is much like a collection. This object library contains objects that are useful in VBA and any script language, which is why they are provided in a separate library. We'll look at Scripting Runtime Objects later in the chapter; first, let's look at the Built-In Objects.

Built-In Objects

VBScript comes equipped with the following objects:

❑ Err Object

❑ RegExp Object

❑ Match Objects

❑ Matches Collection - a collection of regular expression Match objects

The final three objects - RegExp, Match and the Matches collection - all form part of the regular expressions feature new to the VBScript 5 engine. We'll look at regular expressions in detail later.

The Err Object

The first of the built-in objects that we are going to look at is the Err object. This object contains information about runtime errors that occur in VBScript code during runtime.

The Err object is an intrinsic object with global scope – there is no need to create an instance of it in your code. The properties of the Err object are set by the generator of an error – Visual Basic, an Automation object, or the VBScript programmer.

This last point is important because you can explicitly force an error (called *raising* it). Before you raise an error, you can set some or all of Err 's properties. The resulting error then appears (to the user, or another scriptwriter's code) to be very similar to 'normal' errors raised by the system.

This object has five properties (Description, HelpContext, HelpFile, Number and Source) and two methods (Clear and Raise).

> **The Err object, its properties and methods are discussed in detail in Chapter 4** *Error Handling, Prevention and Debugging*, **and in Appendix E** *VBScript Error Codes and the Err Object*, **and are thus not discussed any further in this chapter.**

Regular Expressions

Since the next three objects – `RegExp`, `Match` and the `Matches` collection – all relate to regular expressions, we first need to look at what regular expressions are and why they are so important to us.

Regular Expressions – what are they?

The first thing to know is that regular expressions are new to the VBScript 5.0 engine - up until then VBScript had been sorely lacking this facility.

So what are regular expressions? Well, Perl, awk, and even JavaScript developers already know that regular expressions provide powerful facilities for character pattern-matching and replacing. Before the addition of regular expressions, performing a search-and-replace task throughout a string required a fair amount of code full of looping, `InStr`, and `Mid` functions. Now we can do it with one line of code using a regular expression.

But first a note to those experienced with regular expressions from other languages. VBScript *does not* support regular expression constants (like `/a pattern/`). Instead it uses text strings assigned to the `pattern` property of a `RegExp` object. In many ways this is superior to the traditional method because there is no new syntax to learn. But if you are used to regular expressions from other languages, especially client-side JavaScript, this can throw you.

Introduction to Regular Expressions

So let's look at a simple example of what you can do with regular expressions. The central concept in regular expressions is the *text pattern*. Regular expressions use text patterns in both searching and replacing. In VBScript we use a text string to represent a text pattern. For example, the following code uses the `Replace` method that we'll learn about in detail later.

```
Dim re, s
Set re = New RegExp
re.Pattern = "na"
s = "Spelling bana is easy, if you know when to stop."
MsgBox re.Replace(s, "nana")
```

In this example we first create a new regular expression object:

```
Set re = New RegExp
```

We then set the key property on that object, the pattern that it will match:

```
re.Pattern = "na"
```

The next line simply assigns a text sting and then the last line does the real work. It asks our regular expression object to find the first occurrence of 'na' (the pattern) within `s` and replace it with 'nana'. Once we've done that, we use a message box to show off our great spelling skills:

```
MsgBox re.Replace(s, "nana")
```

Obviously this is a very simple example, one we could probably do just as easily using VBScript's string manipulation functions. But what if we wanted to replace *all* occurrences of 'na'? Or what if we wanted to replace all occurrences of 'na' but only when they appear *at the end of a word*? Before looking at how we do this with regular expressions, take a minute to think about the code you'd need to handle this last case using string functions.

Would your solution handle both the occurrences in the string below?

```
Dim re, s
Set re = New RegExp
re.Pattern = "na\b"
re.Global = True
s = "May is National Bana Month. Eat a bana, everyday!"
MsgBox re.Replace(s, "nana")
```

This version has two key differences. First it uses a special sequence (\b) to match a word boundary (we'll explore all the special sequences available in the section *Regular Expression Characters*, below). Without this, the word 'National' would be changed to 'Nationanal'. Second, by setting the Global property we ensure that we match all the occurrences of 'na' that we want.

Regular expressions provide a very powerful language for expressing complicated patterns like these so let's get on with learning the objects we need that allow us to use them within VBScript.

The RegExp Object

The RegExp object provides simple regular expression support in VBScript:

```
Dim regEx
Set regEx = New RegExp
```

This object has three properties and three methods.

RegExp Properties

Let's take a look at the three properties associated with the RegExp object. These are:

❑   Global

❑   IgnoreCase

❑   Pattern

Global Property

The Global property is responsible for setting or returning a Boolean value that indicates whether or not a pattern is to match all occurrences in an entire search string or just the first occurrence.

```
object.Global [= value ]
```

object	Always a `RegExp` object.
value	There are two possible values, `True` or `False`.
	If the value of the `Global` property is `True` then the search applies to the entire string; if it is `False` then it does not. Default is `False`—not `True` as documented in some Microsoft sources.

Our example above used the `Global` property to ensure all occurrences of "bana" were corrected.

```
Dim re, s
Set re = New RegExp
re.Pattern = "na\b"
re.Global = True
s = "May is National Bana Month. Eat a bana, everyday!"
MsgBox re.Replace(s, "nana")
```

IgnoreCase Property

The `IgnoreCase` property sets or returns a Boolean value that indicates whether or not the pattern search is case-sensitive.

```
object.IgnoreCase [= value ]
```

object	Always a `RegExp` object
value	There are two possible values - `True` or `False`.
	If the value of the `IgnoreCase` property is `False` then the search is case sensitive, if it is `True` then it is case *in*sensitive. Default is `False`—not `True` as documented in some Microsoft sources.

Continuing our example above, if the string we want to match has 'BANA' capitalized, we need to tell VBScript to ignore case when it does the matching:

```
Dim re, s
Set re = New RegExp
re.Pattern = "na\b"
re.Global = True
re.IgnoreCase = True
s = "May is National BANA Month. Eat a bana, everyday!"
MsgBox re.Replace(s, "nana")
```

Pattern Property

The `Pattern` property sets or returns the regular expression pattern being searched.

```
object.Pattern [= "searchstring"]
```

`object`	Always a `RegExp` object
`searchstring`	Regular string expression being searched for. May include any of the regular expression characters - optional

We used the `Pattern` property in all of our examples above. In fact, you can't do very much with regular expressions without setting this property. But the real power of regular expressions comes from using special characters in the pattern so let's look at those next.

Regular Expression Characters

Character	Description
\	Marks the next character as either a special character or a literal.
^	Matches the beginning of input.
$	Matches the end of input.
*	Matches the preceding character zero or more times.
+	Matches the preceding character one or more times.
?	Matches the preceding character zero or one time.
.	Matches any single character except a newline character.
(pattern)	Matches *pattern* and remembers the match. The matched substring can be retrieved from the resulting **Matches** collection, using `Item` [*0*]...[*n*]. To match the parentheses characters themselves, precede with slash – use "\(" or "\)".
x|y	Matches either *x* or *y*.
{n}	Matches exactly *n* times (*n* is a nonnegative integer).
{n,}	Matches at least *n* times (*n* is a nonnegative integer – note the terminating comma).
{n,m}	Matches at least *n* and at most *m* times (*m* and *n* are nonnegative integers).
[xyz]	Matches any one of the enclosed characters (*xyz* represents a character set).
[^xyz]	Matches any character not enclosed (*^xyz* represents a negative character set).
[a-z]	Matches any character in the specified range (*a-z* represents a range of characters).

Character	Description
[^*m-z*]	Matches any character not in the specified range (^*m-z* represents a negative range of characters).
\b	Matches a word boundary, that is, the position between a word and a space.
\B	Matches a non-word boundary.
\d	Matches a digit character. Equivalent to [0-9].
\D	Matches a non-digit character. Equivalent to [^0-9].
\f	Matches a form-feed character.
\n	Matches a newline character.
\r	Matches a carriage return character.
\s	Matches any white space including space, tab, form-feed, etc. Equivalent to "[\f\n\r\t\v]".
\S	Matches any nonwhite space character. Equivalent to "[^ \f\n\r\t\v]".
\t	Matches a tab character.
\v	Matches a vertical tab character.
\w	Matches any word character including underscore. Equivalent to "[A-Za-z0-9_]".
\W	Matches any non-word character. Equivalent to "[^A-Za-z0-9_]".
$num	Matches *num*, where *num* is a positive integer. A reference back to remembered matches (note the $ symbol – differs from Microsoft documentation).
\n	Matches *n*, where *n* is an octal escape value. Octal escape values must be 1, 2, or 3 digits long.
\x*n*	Matches *n*, where *n* is a hexadecimal escape value. Hexadecimal escape values must be exactly two digits long.

Many of these codes are self explanatory, but some examples would probably help with others. We've already seen a simple pattern:

```
re.Pattern = "na"          'most characters match themselves
```

Often it's useful to match any one of a whole *class* of characters. We do this by enclosing the characters that we want to match in square brackets. For example, the following will replace any single digit with a more generic term:

```
Dim re, s
Set re = New RegExp
re.Pattern = "[0123456789]"
s = "May is National Banana Month. Eat 2 bananas, everyday!"
MsgBox re.Replace(s, "lots of")
```

In this case, the number '2' is replaced with the text 'lots of'. As you might hope, we can shorten this class by using a *range*. This pattern does the same as the one above but saves some typing.

```
Dim re, s
Set re = New RegExp
re.Pattern = "[0-9]"
s = "May is National Banana Month. Eat 2 bananas, everyday!"
MsgBox re.Replace(s, "lots of")
```

In fact, this pattern is used so often that there is a shortcut for it: \d is equivalent to [0-9]. But what if you wanted to match anything except a digit? Then we can use *negation*, which is indicated by a circumflex (^) used within the class square brackets. (Note that using ^ outside the square brackets has a totally different meaning and is discussed after the next example.) Thus to match any character other than a digit we can use any of the following patterns:

```
re.Pattern = "[^0-9]"    'the hard way
re.Pattern = "[^\d]"     'a little shorter
re.Pattern = "[\D]"      'another of those special characters
```

The last option above used another of the dozen or so special characters. In most cases these characters just save you some typing but a few, like matching tabs and other non-printable characters, can be very useful.

There are three special characters that *anchor* a pattern. They don't match any characters themselves but force another pattern to appear at the beginning of the input (^ used outside of [ ]), the end of the input ($) or at a word boundary (we've already seen \b).

Another way we can shorten our patterns is using *repeat counts*. The basic idea is to place the repeat after the character or class. For example, the following pattern matches both digits and replaces them:

```
Dim re, s
Set re = New RegExp
re.Pattern = "\d{2}"
s = "May is National Banana Month. Eat 19 bananas, everyday!"
MsgBox re.Replace(s, "lots of")
```

Without the repeat count, we'd leave the 9. Note we can't just set `re.Global=True` because we'd end up with two `'lots of'` phrases in the result. As the table above shows, we can also specify a minimum number of matches `{min,}` or a range `{min, max}`. Again there are a few repeat patterns that are used so often that they have special short cuts:

```
re.Pattern = "\d+"        'one or more digits, \d{1, }
re.Pattern = "\d*"        'zero or more digits, \d{0, }
re.Pattern = "\d?"        'optional: zero or one, \d{0,1}
```

The last special characters we should discuss are *remembered matches*. These are useful when we want to use some or all of the text that matched our pattern as part of the replacement text – see the `Replace` method below for an example of using remembered matches.

To illustrate this, and bring all this discussion of special characters together, let's do something more useful. We want to search an arbitrary text string and locate any URLs within it. To keep this example reasonable in size, we'll only search for http: protocols but we will handle most of the vulgarities of DNS names including an unlimited number of domain layers. Don't worry if you 'don't speak DNS,' just what you probably know from typing URLs into your browser will suffice.

Our code uses another of `RegExp` object's methods that we'll meet in more detail in the next section. For now, we just need to know that `Execute` simply performs the pattern match and returns each match via a collection. Here's the code:

```
Dim re, s
Set re = New RegExp
re.Global = True
re.Pattern = "http://(\w+[\w-]*\w+\.)*\w+"
s = "http://www.junk.com is a valid web address. And so is "
s = s & vbCrLf & "http://www.pc.ibm.com-even with 4 levels."
Set colMatches = re.Execute(s)
For Each match In colMatches
      MsgBox "Found URL: " & match.Value
Next
```

As we'd expect, the real work is done in the line that sets the pattern. It looks a little wild at first, but let's break it down. Our pattern begins with the fixed string `http://`. We then use parentheses to group the real workhorse of this pattern. The highlighted pattern below will match one level of a DNS name, including a trailing dot:

```
re.Pattern = "http://(\w[\w-]*\w\.)*\w+"
```

This pattern begins with one of the special characters, `\w`, which matches `[a-zA-Z0-9]` or in English, the alphanumeric characters. We next use the class brackets to match either an alphanumeric character or a dash. That's because DNS names can include dashes. Why didn't we use the same pattern before? Because DNS names can't begin or end with a dash. We allow zero or more characters from this expanded class by using the * repeat count:

```
re.Pattern = "http://(\w[\w-]*\w\.)*\w+"
```

After that, we again want strictly an alphanumeric character so our domain name doesn't end in a dash. The last pattern in the parentheses matches the dots (.) used to separate DNS levels. Note that we can't use the dot alone because that is a special character that normally matches any single character except a newline. Thus we 'escape' this character, by preceding it with a slash (\).

After wrapping all that in parentheses, just to keep our grouping straight, we again use the * repeat count. So the highlighted pattern below will match any valid domain name followed by a dot; in effect, one level of a fully qualified DNS name:

```
re.Pattern = "http://(\w[\w-]*\w\.)*\w+"
```

We end the pattern by requiring one or more alphanumeric characters for the top-level domain name (e.g., the com, org, edu, etc.):

```
re.Pattern = "http://(\w[\w-]*\w\.)*\w+"
```

Note this pattern doesn't allow dashes in the last level, which could, in theory, be there. Fortunately, none of the top-level domains we're interested in today use a dash. More seriously, in our zeal to avoid dashes as the first or last character of a domain name, we've excluded the possibility of a single character name. This is easily remedied using the 'or' operator (|). We'll leave it as the proverbial exercise for the reader to make this improvement.

RegExp Methods

Let's now look at the three methods associated with the RegExp object:

❑   Execute

❑   Replace

❑   Test

Execute Method

This executes a regular expression search against a specified string and returns a Matches collection..

```
object.Execute(string)
```

object	Always a RegExp object
string	The text string which is searched for - required

The actual pattern for the regular expression search is set using the Pattern property of the RegExp object:

```
Dim re, s
Set re = New RegExp
re.Global = True
```

```
re.Pattern = "http://(\w+[\w-]*\w+\.)*\w+"
s = "http://www.junk.com is a valid web address. And so is "
s = s & vbCrLf & "http://www.pc.ibm.com-even with 4 levels."
Set colMatches = re.Execute(s)
For Each match In colMatches
    MsgBox "Found URL: " & match.Value
Next
```

Note the difference with other languages that support regular expressions that treat the results of `Execute` as a Boolean to determine whether or not the pattern was found. As a result, you'll often see examples that are converted from other languages that simply don't work in VBScript – for example, in Microsoft's own documentation. Remember the result of `Execute` is always a collection (possibly empty) – you can use a test like `if re.Execute(s).count = 0`, or better yet use the `Test` method, which is designed for this purpose.

Replace Method

This method replaces text found in a regular expression search.

```
object.Replace(string1, string2)
```

object	Always a `RegExp` object
string1	This is the text string in which the text replacement is to occur – required
string2	This is the replacement text string – required

The `Replace` method returns a copy of `string1` with the text of `RegExp.Pattern` replaced with `string2`. If no match is found, a copy of `string1` is returned unchanged:

```
Dim re, s
Set re = New RegExp
re.Pattern = "http://(\w[\w-]*\w\.)*\w+"
s = "http://www.junk.com is a valid web address. And so is "
s = s & vbCrLf & "http://www.pc.ibm.com-even with 4 levels."
MsgBox re.Replace(s, "**Censored**")
```

The `Replace` method can replace sub-expressions in the pattern. For this we use the special characters $1, $2, etc. in the replace text. These 'parameters' refer to *remembered matches*. A remembered match is simply part of a pattern. We designate which parts we want to remember by enclosing them in parentheses, and refer to them sequentially as $1, $2, etc. In the following example we remember the first three words and then reverse two of them in the replacement text:

```
Dim re, s
Set re = New RegExp
re.Pattern = "(\S+)\s+(\S+)\s+(\S+)"
s = "The quick brown fox jumped over the lazy dog."
MsgBox re.Replace(s, "$1 $3 $2")
```

Test Method

The `Test` method executes a regular expression search against a specified string and returns a Boolean value that indicates whether or not a pattern match was found.

`object.Test(string)`

`object`	Always a `RegExp` object
`string`	The text string upon which the regular expression is executed - required

The `Test` method returns `True` if a pattern match is found and `False` if no match is found. This is the preferred way to determine if a string contains a pattern. Note we often must make patterns case insensitive as in the example below:

```
Dim re, s
Set re = New RegExp
re.IgnoreCase = True
re.Pattern = "http://(\w+[\w-]*\w+\.)*\w+"
s = "Some long string with HTTP://www.junk.com in it."
If re.Test(s) Then
     MsgBox "Found a URL."
Else
     MsgBox "Missing in action."
End If
```

The Matches Collection

The `Matches` collection is a collection of regular expression `Match` objects.

A `Matches` collection contains individual `Match` objects. The only way to create this collection is using the `Execute` method of the `RegExp` object. The `Matches` collection property is read-only, as are the individual `Match` objects.

When a regular expression is executed, zero or more `Match` objects result. Each `Match` object provides access to the string found by the regular expression, the length of the string, and an index to where the match was found. Remember to set the `Global` property to `True` or your `Matches` collection will never contain more than one member. This is an easy way to create a very subtle bug!

```
Dim re, objMatch, colMatches, sMsg
Set re = New RegExp
re.Global = True
re.Pattern = "http://(\w+[\w-]*\w+\.)*\w+"
s = "http://www.junk.com is a valid web address. And so is "
s = s & vbCrLf & "http://www.pc.ibm.com-even with 4 levels."
Set colMatches = re.Execute(s)
sMsg = ""
For Each objMatch in colMatches      'loop over matches
     sMsg = sMsg & "Match of " & objMatch.Value
     sMsg = sMsg & ", found at position " & objMatch.FirstIndex
     sMsg = sMsg & ". The length matched is "
     sMsg = sMsg & objMatch.Length & "." & vbCrLf
Next
MsgBox sMsg
```

Matches Properties

`Matches` is a simple collection and as such supports the standard two properties:

❑ `Count`

❑ `Item`

`Count` returns the number of items in the collection, and `Item` returns an item based on the specified key.

These two properties are self-explanatory and need no further discussion.

The Match Object

`Match` objects are the 'things' (more formally the members) in a `Matches` collection. The only way to create a `Match` object is by using the `Execute` method of the `RegExp` object. When a regular expression is executed, zero or more `Match` objects can result. Each `Match` object provides the following:

❑ Access to the string found by the regular expression

❑ The length of the string

❑ An index to where the match was found

See *The Matches Collection* section above for an example of using the `Match` object and its properties.

Match Properties

The `match` object has three properties, all of which are read-only:

❑ `FirstIndex`

❑ `Length`

❑ `Value`

FirstIndex Property

The `FirstIndex` property returns the position in a search string where a match occurs.

`object.FirstIndex`

`object`	Always a `Match` object

The `FirstIndex` property uses a zero-based offset from the beginning of the search string. In other words, the first character in the string is identified as character zero (`0`).

Length Property

This property returns the length of a match found in a search string.

`object.Length`

`object`	Always a `Match` object

Value Property

This property returns the value or text of a match found in a search string.

`object.Value`

`object`	Always a `Match` object

Scripting Runtime Objects

Now it's time to look at how the other half lives. You'll remember the objects in the scripting runtime library are made available to us by the Scripting Runtime Object Library `scrrun.dll`. As such these objects are available from any language that supports COM including JScript and Visual Basic for Applications and Windows.

> A complete listing of all the objects, properties and methods can be found in Appendix F - The Scripting Runtime Library Objects Reference.

The top-level objects in the Scripting Runtime Object library are the `Dictionary` object and the `FileSystemObject` object. We can use `CreateObject` to instantiate these two kinds of objects. There are seven other types of objects that we access via the `FileSystemObject`.

The following are the objects contained within the Scripting Runtime Object Library:

Object	Collection	Description
`Dictionary`		A top-level object. Similar to the VBA `Collection` object
`Drive`	`Drives`	Refers to a drive or collection of drives on the system
`File`	`Files`	Refers to a file or collection of files in the file system
`FileSystemObject`		A top-level object. Use this object to access drives, folders, and files in the file system

Object	Collection	Description
Folder	Folders	Refers to a folder or collection of folders in the file system
TextStream		Refers to a stream of text that is read from, written to, or appended to a text file

Let's take a closer look at how we can use the top-level objects, starting with the Dictionary object.

Dictionary Object

The Dictionary object provides an *associative array*, that is, a way to store key/item pairs. The item can be any type of data and the key can be any type except an array, although it is usually an integer or a string. When we store an item in a dictionary we must provide a unique key value with it. We can then look up the items by the key.

At first glance, a dictionary sounds like a collection, and they can often be used interchangeably but there are some differences:

❑ The Exists method returns whether or not a key exists in a dictionary. In fact, with a dictionary you can access a key that doesn't exist without raising an error. The corresponding entry is quietly added to the dictionary.

❑ A dictionary supports the CompareMode property to control whether a binary or text comparison is performed.

❑ A dictionary's Items and Keys methods return the data and key values, respectively, as an array. You can even use the Keys array to change the value of a key.

❑ The syntax is just different enough to take some getting used to. One advantage of the dictionary syntax is that you can retrieve the key value. With a collection, however, your retrieval is based on a key value and, given a member, there's no way to access what the key is (e.g. when iterating through the collection).

❑ You can't control the order of dictionary elements. In fact, there is no such thing as the concept of an 'order' as there is with a collection.

> Note: a Dictionary object is the equivalent of a PERL associative array.

There are several ways to add elements to a dictionary as the following example shows:

```
Dim dict
Set dict = CreateObject("Scripting.Dictionary")
dict.Add "1", "cat"          'Add keys and items.
dict.Add "Spot", "dog"
dict.Add 3, "goldfish"       'Note different key than "3"
dict.Item("Felix") = "cat"
dict("Flicka") = Array("Horse", 15, "15 hands, 3 in")
MsgBox "Do we have Spot here? " & dict.Exists("Spot")
```

The first three elements are added using the Add method (*syntax:* Add *key, item*). The thing to notice here is that the key does not have to be a specific type. In fact, the key 3 (the integer) is different from the key "3" (the text string). As noted above if we access a key that doesn't exist, the dictionary will quietly add one for us, as illustrated by the following two lines of code:

```
MsgBox dict("3") & " is different than " & dict(3)
MsgBox "But this created an entry for 3 (the string): " _
                        & dict.Exists("3")
```

The second message box tells us that an entry for "3" now exists. If we examined it, we'd discover dict("3") is empty. This can be a subtle source of bugs.

Usually we don't bother with the Add method, we simply set the Item property. And because Item is the default property we can use the natural syntax of the second line below:

```
dict.Item("Felix") = "cat"
dict("Flicka") = Array("Horse", 15, "15 hands, 3 in")
```

This line also illustrates that the element we place in our dictionary can be of any type. When we retrieve the value of "Flicka," we get an array. We can then index into that array. The following line illustrates doing this 'on the fly':

```
MsgBox "How tall is Flicka? " & dict("Flicka")(2)
```

The properties of the Dictionary object are:

❑ CompareMode – used to set whether a dictionary uses binary or text comparisons

❑ Count – the total number of elements in the dictionary

❑ Item – is an indexed property, as illustrated above. This is the default property.

❑ Key – is an indexed property, like Item but it is 'write only'. That is, use this property to change a key, rather than return it. For example:

```
dict.Key("Flicka") = "Man o' War"
MsgBox "How old is Man o' War? " & dict("Man o' War")(1)
```

The methods of the Dictionary object are:

❑ Add – to add a key, item pair to the dictionary

❑ Exists – tests whether or not a key exists in the dictionary

❑ Items – returns an array of the values in the dictionary

❑ Keys – returns an array of the keys in the dictionary

❑ Remove – removes one element (using its key) from the dictionary

❑ RemoveAll – removes all the elements from the dictionary

See Appendix E for their syntax details.

FileSystemObject Object

When writing scripts for Active Server Pages, the Windows Script Host, or other applications where VBScript can be used, it's sometimes important to be able to add, move, change, create, or delete folders (directories) and files. In addition, it may be desirable to get access to information drives attached to the system and have the ability to manipulate them on the fly.

The other runtime system object allows such access to drives, folders, and files using the `FileSystemObject` (FSO) object model.

When using VBScript on a web page, there are security issues concerning potentially unwelcome access to a client's local file system. Therefore Internet Explorer's default security settings do not allow client-side use of the `FileSystemObject` object. By overriding those defaults you are potentially allowing unwelcome access to the file system, which could result in the loss of file system's integrity, data loss or worse. The security issues are not as serious when FSO is used to manipulate the file system on a web server or via the WSH.

The FSO object model gives your server-side applications the ability to create, alter, move, and delete folders, or to find out if particular folders exist, and if so, where on the drive. You can also find out information about the folders, such as names, creation date or the last modified date.

The FSO object model also makes it easy to read and write text files via the `TextStream` object, which in simple cases may remove the need to use Access or SQL Server.

The FSO object model consists of the following objects and collections:

Object or Collection	Description
FileSystemObject	Main object.
	This contains methods and properties that allow you to create, delete, gain information about, and manipulate drives, folders, and files
Drive	Object.
	Contains methods and properties that allow you to access information about a drive attached to the system, such as share name and the amount of free space available.
	A drive can also be a CD-ROM drive or a RAM disk and doesn't need to be physically attached to the system but can be logically connected through a network

Table Continued on Following Page

Object or Collection	Description
Drives	Collection.
	Provides a list of the drives attached to the system, either physically or logically.
	All drives are included, regardless of type. Removable-media drives do not need to have media inserted to appear
File	Object.
	Contains methods and properties that allow you to create, delete, move a file, return a file name, path, and various other properties
Files	Collection.
	Provides a list of all files contained in a folder.
Folder	Object.
	Contains methods and properties that allow you to create, delete, move a folder, return a folder, path, and various other properties.
Folders	Collection.
	Provides a list of all the folders inside a folder.
TextStream	Object.
	Allows you to read and create text files.

> See Appendix E for a complete listing of the properties and methods, their required and optional parameters, for each object.

Using the FileSystemObject

To use the FSO object model you must:

❑ Use the CreateObject method to create a FileSystemObject object

❑ Use the appropriate method on the newly created object

❑ Access the appropriate properties on the object

Creating a FileSystemObject Object

The first thing we need to do is create an FSO by using the CreateObject method as follows:

```
Dim fso
Set fso = CreateObject("Scripting.FileSystemObject")
```

`Scripting` is the name of the type library and `FileSystemObject` is the name of the object that you want to create.

Use the Appropriate Method

Now you need to use the appropriate method of the FSO. If you want to create a new object, you can use either `CreateTextFile` or `CreateFolder`. To delete objects, use the `DeleteFile` and `DeleteFolder` methods of the FSO. Still other methods let you copy and move files and folders or 'walk' the file system starting with a drive letter.

> The FSO object model provides some redundancy. That is, there is often more than one way to do something. For example, you can copy a single file using the `CopyFile` method of the FSO or using the `Copy` method of the `File` object. Be aware that in some cases the differing ways of doing things have some subtle distinctions. In this example, `CopyFile` supports wildcards and copying of more than one file while `Copy` does not.

Accessing Existing Files, Folder and Drives

One of the simplest ways to access an existing file, folder or drive, is to use the appropriate `Get*` method of the `FileSystemObject` object:

❑ `GetDrive`

❑ `GetFolder`

❑ `GetFile`

For example, if you wanted to gain access to a file called `text.txt` in the root of the `C:\` drive, you could use something like the following:

```
Dim fso, file1
Set fso = CreateObject("Scripting.FileSystemObject")
Set file1 = fso.GetFile("c:\text.txt")
```

You do not need to use the `Get*` methods for objects that have just been created since these functions already return an object reference. Therefore, if you create a new folder using the `CreateFolder` method, you don't use the `GetFolder` method to access its properties. You simply set a variable to the `CreateFolder` method and then access its properties and methods. So if wanted to create `text.txt` in the root you would use:

```
Dim fso, file1
Set fso = CreateObject("Scripting.FileSystemObject")
Set file1 = fso.CreateFile("C:\text.txt")
```

You can also gain access to any drive, folder or file by 'walking the file system'. This begins with FSO's `Drives` collection. Each `Drive` object has a `RootFolder` property. And each `Folder` object has both a `SubFolders` and `Files` collection. The following example will get an object reference to the same file as the one above, but on every drive on the system:

```
Dim fso, drive, folder, file
Set fso = CreateObject("Scripting.FileSystemObject")
For Each drive in fso.Drives
    If drive.IsReady Then
            Set folder = drive.RootFolder
            Set file = folder.Files("text.txt")
            'Do something here...
            'Be sure to handle file not found errors...
    End If
Next
```

Accessing the Object's Properties

Once you have a reference to an object, you can access its properties; e.g. last time the file was modified:

```
Dim fso, file1
Set fso = CreateObject("Scripting.FileSystemObject")
Set file1 = fso.GetFile("c:\text.txt")
MsgBox "This file was last modified at " _
                        & file1.DateLastModified
```

The FSO Object Model

The FSO exposes a variety of objects for working with drives, folders and files. These all start from an FSO object.

FSO Objects

An FSO object has just one property:

Property	Information
Drives	Returns the collection of drives. As noted above this can be a starting point for 'walking' the file system.

In contrast, an FSO object exposes a rich selection of methods so we'll look at them in three groups. The methods in the first group are fairly self-explanatory and are similar across drives, folders, and files:

Drives	Folders	Files
DriveExists	FolderExists	FileExists
GetDrive	GetFolder	GetFile
GetDriveName	GetFileName (Note, not GetFolderName!)	GetFileName
	CopyFolder	CopyFile
	CreateFolder	CreateTextFile
	DeleteFolder	DeleteFile
	MoveFolder	MoveFile

The next set provides methods to parse paths:

Method	Information
BuildPath	Helps build a path by adding one level of folder or file name. BuildPath adds a path delimiter (\) if needed.
GetAbsolutePathName	Returns an unambiguous, fully qualified path name.
GetBaseName	Gets just the file/folder name, without any path or extension.
GetExtensionName	Gets the file/folder's extension, if any.

The final set provides miscellaneous methods:

Method	Information
GetParentFolderName	Given a path, returns its parent folder. See also the ParentFolder property of the File and Folder objects, below.
GetSpecialFolder	Returns the Windows, System or Temp folders. Note WSH provides much more powerful access to all the special folders if you are writing batch files.
GetTempName	Returns a randomly generated file or folder name.
OpenTextFile	Returns a TextStream object for doing file I/O. See File I/O, below.

Drive Objects

A wealth of information is available about the various drives attached to the system. The properties make available the following information (note that Drive objects have no methods):

Property	Information
TotalSize	Total drive space in bytes. Read only.
AvailableSpace, FreeSpace	Available space on drive in bytes. Read only.
DriveLetter	Letter assigned to the drive. Read only.
DriveType	Type of drive - such as removable, fixed, CD-ROM etc. Read only.

Table Continued on Following Page

Property	Information
SerialNumber	Drive's serial number. Read only.
FileSystem	Type of file system, such as FAT, FAT32, NTFS etc. Read only.
IsReady	Whether or not the drive is available. Read only.
ShareName	The share name. If the drive is not a mapped network drive or UNC, this property is the empty string. Read only.
VolumeName	The drive's volume name. Read or write.
Path, RootFolder	The path or root folder of the drive. Read only.

Working with Folders and Files

`Folder` and `File` objects provide ways to directly manipulate these elements of the file system. In many cases, their properties and method are similar:

Property	Information
Name	Sets or returns the folder's or file's name. Note this can be used to rename a folder or file. Read or write.
Path	Returns the full path. Read only.
Type	The file or folder's type (i.e. file extension).
ShortName, ShortPath	The 8.3 'DOS' name and path for the file or folder. Read only.
Drive, ParentFolder	The drive or parent folder that contains the object. Note, `ParentFolder` is undefined for a root folder (e.g. `C:\`). Read only.
DateCreated, DateLastAccessed, DateLastModified, Size	Set or returns the folder's or file's attributes. Read or write.
Files, Subfolders	Returns a collection of the files or subfolders in the folder. Only applies to `Folder` objects. Read only.
IsRootFolder	Returns `True` if the folder is the root of the drive. Returns `False` otherwise. Only applies to `Folder` objects. Read only.

Method	Information
Copy	Copies a folder or file. See also `FSO.CopyFolder` and `FSO.CopyFile`.
Delete	Deletes a folder or file. See also `FSO.DeleteFolder` and `FSO.DeleteFile`.
Move	Moves a folder or file. See also `FSO.MoveFolder` and `FSO.MoveFile`.
CreateTextFile (`Folder` object only)	Creates a new text file. See also `FSO.CreateTextFile`.
OpenTextFile (`Folder` object only)	Opens an existing file for I/O, which is detailed below. See also `FSO.OpenTextFile`.

File I/O

Now we are really getting down to the nitty-gritty, actually reading and writing the contents of a file. FSO only gives us access to text files (ADO 2.5 has more advanced facilities – see Chapter 15).

The object we use to actually read or write to a file is called a *text stream*. Note that a text stream is not the same thing as a file. More precisely, a text stream object is not a file object. They have very different properties and methods. Unfortunately some FSO methods blur this distinction; for example, OpenTextFile and CreateTextFile, both of which actually return a text stream object! Many examples in Microsoft's own documentation use variable names like file1 when the object is actually a text stream.

The properties of a TextStream object are straightforward:

Property	Information
AtEndOfLine, AtEndOfStream	True if the current position is at the end of a line (just before a end-of-line marker) or at the end of the file, respectively. Read only.
Column, Line	Returns the column or line number of the current position, respectively.

The methods of a `TextStream` object break down naturally into three groups plus `Close`:

Reading	Skipping	Writing	Information
Read	Skip	Write	Process as many bytes as in the method's argument. Doesn't add/strip any end-of-file markers.
ReadLine	SkipLine	WriteLine	Process one line, stripping the end-of-line marker on input and adding it on output.
ReadAll			Read the remainder of the stream (file).
		WriteBlankLines	Write the specified number of lines.

The `Close` method, as you might expect, will close a `TextStream`. Trying to do any I/O to a stream after it is closed will raise an error.

Creating Files

There are two ways that we can create an empty text file using the FSO:

❑ We can use the `FSO` or `Folder.CreateTextFile` method:

```
Dim fso, ts
Set fso = CreateObject("Scripting.FileSystemObject")
Set ts = fso.CreateTextFile("c:\text.txt", True)
```

❑ We can use the `FSO.OpenTextFile` method with the `ForWriting` flag set:

```
Const ForReading = 1, ForWriting = 2, ForAppending = 8
Dim fso, ts
Set fso = CreateObject("Scripting. FileSystemObject")
Set ts = fso.OpenTextFile("c:\text.txt", ForWriting, True)
```

Note that in both cases we've set the last parameter, `OverWrite`, to `True`. This ensures we'll create a new file if one already exists.

> **See Appendix F - The Scripting Runtime Library Objects Reference for information on `ForWriting` and `OverWrite`**

Opening Files

Similarly there are two ways we can open an existing file using the FSO:

❑ Again we can use the FSO.OpenTextFile method, this time with OverWrite = False:

```
Const ForReading = 1, ForWriting = 2, ForAppending = 8
Dim fso, ts
Set fso = CreateObject("Scripting.FileSystemObject")
Set ts = fso.OpenTextFile("c:\text.txt", ForWriting, False)
```

❑ We can use File.OpenAsTextStream method with the ForWriting flag set:

```
Const ForReading = 1, ForWriting = 2, ForAppending = 8
Dim fso, ts
Set fso = CreateObject("Scripting.FileSystemObject")
Set ts = fso.OpenAsTextStream("c:\text.txt", ForWriting, False)
```

In both these cases, if we want to read the file we use ForReading as the second parameter.

Adding Data to the File

Now that we have opened our text file, we can add data to it.

To write data to an open text stream, use the Write, WriteLine, or WriteBlankLines methods, depending on the action we want to carry out.

When you're done, don't forget to Close the TextStream object.

Here is an example that opens a file, uses all three write methods and closes the file:

```
Dim fso, ts
Set fso = CreateObject("Scripting.FileSystemObject")
Set ts = fso.CreateTextFile("c:\text.txt", True)
ts.WriteLine("Calling the Doc")       'write a line incl. newline
ts.WriteBlankLines(5)                 'write 5 newlines
ts.Write ("This is a test.")          'writes w/o newline
ts.Write(" And this is on the same line")
ts.Close
```

Reading Files

To read data from a text file, we use the Read, ReadLine, or ReadAll methods of the TextStream object. The resulting text of the read methods is stored in a string, which can then be used as required.

If you use the `Read` or `ReadLine` method and want to skip to a particular part of the data, you can use the `Skip` or `SkipLine` method.

```
Const ForReading = 1, ForWriting = 2, ForAppending = 8
Dim fso, ts, strg
Set fso = CreateObject("Scripting.FileSystemObject")
Set ts = fso.OpenTextFile("c:\text.txt", ForReading)
strg = ts.ReadAll
MsgBox "File data is: '" & strg & "'"
ts.Close
```

Note this technique reads the entire file into a single variable. Often you want to work line by line. `ReadLine` works fine for this but you can only move forward through a `TextStream` object. If you need to work back and forth, it may be easier to read the file into an array. While you can do this with a loop, it's faster to use:

```
arLines = Split(ts.ReadAll, vbCrLf)
```

Summary

This chapter has covered a lot of objects, their methods and properties. All the objects are included with every (current) VBScript installation, although technically some are built-in and some are provided by the separate Scripting Runtime file.

Of the built-in objects, the three that implement regular expressions are probably the most flexible, and hence difficult to completely master. But hopefully this introduction to regular expressions has shown that you don't have to be an 'RE guru' to save yourself a lot of coding whenever you need to search or replace text strings.

The Scripting Runtime library exposes two very different top-level objects. The `Dictionary` object provides an easy way to create 'super collections.' You can use these objects to store all kinds of data and access it flexibly. Many scripting applications need a little 'database power' and `Dictionary` is often the way to provide an in-memory database with all the searching you could want.

The other top-level object in the Scripting Runtime is the `FileSystemObject`, universally abbreviated as `FSO`. `FSO` is actually a gateway to four other objects (three of which have corresponding collections). These other objects are `Drive`, `Folder`, `File` and `TextStream`. All together these objects let us perform basic file manipulation, read and write text files, and automate many tasks that previously required a 'real' programming language. For system administrators who need to automate setup and maintenance procedures – or anyone tired of 1980's-era batch files – the `FSO` objects along with WSH are a major improvement.

Classes in VBScript
(Writing Your Own COM Objects)

One of the most exciting features added to the VBScript Version 5 is the ability to write classes. This is functionality that was previously reserved for programmers of full-blown compiled languages like Visual Basic, C++, Java, Visual FoxPro, and Delphi. Before we get too far into how to write your own classes in VBScript, and where you can make use of them, let's detour for a moment to cover some terminology. (By the way, if you've skipped previous chapters and are not familiar with how to use COM objects from VBScript, then you might benefit from reading Chapter 5 before tackling this one. This chapter will assume that you are familiar with the basics of instantiating objects and calling their properties and methods.)

Classes vs. Objects vs. Components

Few terms have been misused, obscured, and confused more than "class", "object", and "component". Mainly what has happened is that the term "object" has become a generic term to mean all three of these. This drives object-oriented purists crazy. Let's clear the fog a little bit:

A **class** is a template for an **object**. A class is something that you work with at design time: if you want to be able to use an object at runtime, you have to first define a class at design time. Objects are created at runtime based on templates provided by classes. An object is a temporary construct that lives in memory while your application or script is using it, whereas a class is a persistent template for an object. If you create a thousand separate customer objects during the lifetime of your script, each of those separate objects has its origins in a single class definition.

One of the reasons that the term "class" has been overrun by the term "object" is that a large percentage of the "objects" that people use were not written by themselves. Instead, they are binary "objects" distributed in the form of **components**. So they do not think of them as classes. On the other hand, when you are coding your own "objects", you are actually writing "classes", so people find it easier to think of the "objects" that they wrote themselves as "classes", but tend to think of other people's "objects" as just that – objects. Is this confusing? Don't worry. Just remember that when you are writing code to define an object, you are writing a class. And when you use a class at runtime, you are using it in the form of an object.

A component is nothing more than a packaging mechanism. When you write some classes, and you want people to be able to use them as objects at runtime, you package them in a component. A component is a way of compiling one or more related classes into a binary file that can be distributed to one or more computers. Components are not the only way to make use of classes, however. In a Visual Basic application, for example, you can write classes that are compiled within the application itself, and are never exposed to the outside world. The classes exist only inside that application, and the sole purpose is to serve the needs of that application. However, people are finding that it is often much more productive and forward-thinking to package their classes into a component that can exist outside of the application. The thinking is that you might find a use for one or more of those classes later, and having them in a more portable component makes them much easier to reuse.

When you are writing VBScript code to instantiate (see Chapter 5) an object – be it the scripting `FileSystemObject` object (Chapter 7) or the ADO `Recordset` object (Chapter 15) – that object is available to your script because it was packaged in the form of a component.

The Class Statement

The key to creating VBScript classes is the `Class` statement. Similar to the way the `Function...End Function` or `Sub...End Sub` statement pairs are used to block off the boundaries of a procedure, the `Class` statement, and its companion `End Class` statement, are used to block off the boundaries of a class. You can use multiple blocks of `Class...End Class` blocks in a single script file to define multiple classes. If you are coming to VBScript from another language, such as Visual Basic, you are probably accustomed to classes being stored in their own separate files. However, this is not the case with VBScript classes. In general, a VBScript class must be defined in the same script file as the script code that creates an instance of it.

This may seem like a pretty big limitation – since part of the purpose of creating a class is easy code portability and centralized reuse – but there are some other options. First, you can package one or more VBScript classes in a Windows Script Component (WSC), which we discuss in detail in Chapter 9. Second, you can use the Active Server Pages (ASP) `#INCLUDE` directive to include VBScript classes in your ASP scripts, which we discuss in Chapter 14. Third, when the 2.0 version of the Windows Script Host (WSH) ships with Windows 2000, you will also be able to include external script files in your WSH scripts. In this chapter, however, we are going to limit ourselves to the discussion of classes that are defined within the same Windows Script Host script file as the script code that uses the class.

Other than this same-script-file difference, Visual Basic programmers will not have any trouble adjusting to VBScript classes. Except for the differences between the VB and VBScript languages, the structure and techniques for VBScript classes are pretty much the same as for VB.

Here is the syntax for the `Class` statement:

```
Class MyClass

    <rest of the class code will go here>

End Class
```

You would, of course, replace `MyClass` with the name of the class you are defining. This class name must be unique within the script file, as well as within any classes that are brought into the same scope through "include" directives (see Chapters 9 and 14). The class name must also not be the same as any of the VBScript reserved words.

Defining Properties

When a script creates an object based on a class, properties are the mechanisms through which data is:

❑　passed into the object

❑　read from the object

Private Property Variables

The best way to store the value of a property is in a private property variable. This is a variable that is defined at the class level (at the beginning of the class). This variable is private (that is, it is not directly accessible to code outside of the class) and holds the actual value of the property. Code that is using a class will use `Property Let`, Set, and `Get` procedures to interact with the property, but these procedures are merely gatekeepers for the private property variable.

You define a private property variable like so:

```
Class Customer

    Private mstrName

    <rest of the class code will go here>

End Class
```

In order for the variable to have private, class-level scope, it must be declared with the `Private` statement. The m prefix is the "Hungarian" notation to indicate that the scope of the variable is "module level", which is another way of saying "class level". Some texts will advocate the use of the c prefix (as in `cstrName`) to indicate class level scope. However, we do not recommend this approach as it is easily confused with the prefix that Visual Basic programmers often use for the `Currency` data type.

Property Let

A `Property Let` procedure is a special kind of procedure that allows code outside of a class to place a value in a private property variable. A `Property Let` procedure is similar to a VBScript `Sub` procedure in that it does not return a value. Here is the syntax:

```
Class Customer

    Private mstrName

    Public Property Let CustomerName(strName)

        mstrName = strName

    End Property

End Class
```

Notice that instead of using the `Sub` or `Function` statements to define the procedure, `Property Let` is used instead. A `Property Let` procedure must accept at least one parameter. To leave this parameter out would defeat the whole purpose of the `Property Let` procedure, which is to allow outside code to store a value in the private property variable. Notice how the code inside the property procedure saves that `strName` value passed into the procedure in the private property variable `mstrName`. You are not required to have any code at all inside the procedure, but not storing the value passed into the procedure in some sort of class-level variable or object would tend to, once again, defeat the whole purpose of the `Property Let` procedure.

Conversely, you can have as much additional code in the procedure as you like. In some cases, you might wish to do some sort of validation before actually assigning the passed-in value in the private property variable. For example, if the length of the customer name value was not allowed to exceed 50 characters, you could verify that the `strName` parameter value does not exceed 50 characters, and, if it did, use the `Err.Raise` method (see Chapter 4/Appendix E) to inform the calling code of this violation.

Finally, a property procedure must end with the `End Property` statement (just as a `Function` procedure ends with `End Function`, and a `Sub` procedure ends with `End Sub`). If you wished to break out of a property procedure, you would use the `Exit Property` statement (just as you would use `Exit Function` to break out of a `Function`, and `Exit Sub` to break out of a `Sub`).

Property Get

A `Property Get` procedure is the inverse of a `Property Let` procedure. While a `Property Let` procedure allows code outside of your class to write a value to a private property variable, a `Property Get` procedure allows code outside of your class to read the value of a private property variable. A `Property Get` procedure is similar to a VBScript `Function` procedure in that it returns a value. Here is the syntax:

```
Class Customer

    Private mstrName

    Public Property Let CustomerName(strName)

        mstrName = strName

    End Property

    Public Property Get CustomerName()

        CustomerName = mstrName

    End Property

End Class
```

Like a VBScript `Function` procedure, a `Property Get` procedure returns a value to the calling code. This value will typically be the value of a private property variable. Notice how the name of the `Property Get` procedure is the same as the corresponding `Property Let` procedure. The `Property Let` procedure stores a value in the private property variable, and the `Property Get` procedure reads it back out.

The `Property Get` procedure does not accept any parameters. VBScript will allow you to add a parameter, but if you are tempted to do this, then you will also have to add an additional parameter to the property's corresponding `Property Let` or `Property Set` procedure (if there is one). This is because a `Property Let/Set` procedure must always have *exactly one more* parameter than its corresponding `Property Get` procedure. Adding an extra parameter to a `Property Let/Set` procedure is extremely awkward, and asking the code that uses your class to accommodate more than one parameter in a `Property Let` procedure is very bad form. If you feel you have a need for a `Property Get` procedure to accept a parameter, you are much better off adding an additional property to fulfill whatever need the `Property Get` parameter would have fulfilled.

If your `Property Get` procedure returns a reference to an object variable, then you may wish to use the `Set` statement to return the value. For example:

```
Class FileHelper

    'Private FileSystemObject object
    Private mobjFSO

    Public Property Get FSO()

        Set FSO = mobjFSO

    End Property

End Class
```

However, since all VBScript variables are `Variant` variables, the `Set` syntax is not strictly required. This syntax would work just as well:

```
Class FileHelper

    'Private FileSystemObject object
    Private mobjFSO

    Public Property Get FSO()

        FSO = mobjFSO

    End Property

End Class
```

It's a good idea to use the `Set` syntax, though, since it makes it clearer that the `Property Get` procedure is returning a reference to an object variable.

Property Set

A `Property Set` procedure is very similar to a `Property Let` procedure, but the `Property Set` procedure is used exclusively for object based properties. When the property needs to store an object (as opposed to a variable with a numeric, `Date`, `Boolean`, or `String` subtype), you can provide a `Property` Set procedure instead of a `Property Let` procedure. Here is the syntax for a `Property Set` procedure:

```
Class FileHelper

    'Private FileSystemObject object
    Private mobjFSO

    Public Property Set FSO(objFSO)

        Set mobjFSO = objFSO

    End Property

End Class
```

Functionally, `Property Let` and `Property Set` procedures do the same thing. However, the `Property Set` procedure has two differences:

❑ it makes it clearer that the property is an object-based property (more explicit = good)

❑ code outside of your class must use the `Set Object.Property = Object` syntax in order to write to the property (also a good thing, since this is the typical way of doing things)

For example, here is what code that is using an object based on the above class might look like:

```
Dim objFileHelper
Dim objFSO

Set objFSO = WScript.CreateObject("Scripting.FileSystemObject")
Set objFileHelper = New FileHelper
Set objFileHelper.FSO = objFSO
```

Notice that when the last line writes to the FSO property, it uses the Set statement. This is required because the FileHelper class used a Property Set procedure for the FSO property. Without the Set statement at the beginning of the last line, VBScript would produce an error. When a property on a class is object-based, it is typical to use a Property Set procedure. Most programmers using your class will expect this. That said, since all VBScript variables are Variant variables, it is perfectly legal to use a Property Let procedure instead. However, if you provide a Property Let procedure *instead* of a Property Set procedure, code that is using your class will not be able to use the Set statement to write to the property (VBScript will produce an error if they do), and this will be a trip-up for programmers who are accustomed to using the Set syntax. If you want to be very thorough, and cover both bases, you can provide both a Property Let and a Property Set for the same property, like so:

```
Class FileHelper

    'Private FileSystemObject object
    Private mobjFSO

    Public Property Set FSO(objFSO)

        Set mobjFSO = objFSO

    End Property

    Public Property Let FSO(objFSO)

        Set mobjFSO = objFSO

    End Property

End Class
```

The Set syntax inside of the Property Set and Let is optional. Since you are writing directly to the Variant private property variable, you can use either. This example is the functional equivalent of the previous example:

```
Class FileHelper

    'Private FileSystemObject object
    Private mobjFSO

    Public Property Set FSO(objFSO)

        mobjFSO = objFSO

    End Property

    Public Property Let FSO(objFSO)
```

233

```
        mobjFSO = objFSO

    End Property

End Class
```

Making a Property Read-Only

You can make a property on a class read-only in one of two ways:

❑ by providing only a `Property Get` procedure for the property

❑ by declaring the `Property Get` procedure `Public` and the `Property Let` procedure `Private`

Here is the first method:

```
Class Customer

    Private mstrName

    Public Property Get CustomerName()

        CustomerName = mstrName

    End Property

End Class
```

Notice the absence of a `Property Let` procedure. Since we have not provided a `Property Let` procedure, code outside of the class cannot write to the `CustomerName` property.

Here is the second method:

```
Class Customer

    Private mstrName

    Private Property Let CustomerName(strName)

        mstrName = strName

    End Property

    Public Property Get CustomerName()

        CustomerName = mstrName

    End Property

End Class
```

The Property Get procedure is declared with the Public statement, and the Property Let procedure is declared with the Private statement. By declaring the Property Let as Private, we have effectively hidden it from code outside of the class. Code inside of the class can still write to the property through the Property Let procedure, but in our simple example, this is of limited usefulness. This is because code inside of the class can write directly to the private property variable, so there is little need for the private Property Let procedure. The exception to this would be when there is code inside of the Property Let procedure that is performing validations and/or transformations on the value being placed in the property. If this were the case, then there might be a benefit in code inside the class using the private Property Let procedure rather than writing directly to the private property variable.

The first method (providing only a Property Get) is the more typical method of creating a read-only property.

Making a Property Write-Only

The two techniques for making a property write-only are the exact reverse of the two techniques for making a property read-only (see previous section):

❑ you can omit the Property Get procedure and provide only a Property Let procedure

❑ you can declare the Property Let procedure with the Public statement, and declare the Property Get with the Private statement

Public Properties without Property Procedures

You can provide properties for your class without using Property Let, Set, and Get procedures at all. This is accomplished through the use of public class-level variables. For example, this:

```
Class Customer

    Private mstrName

    Public Property Let CustomerName(strName)

        mstrName = strName

    End Property

    Public Property Get CustomerName()

        CustomerName = mstrName

    End Property

End Class
```

is the functional equivalent of this:

```
Class Customer

    Public Name

End Class
```

The second option looks a lot more attractive, doesn't it? It's a lot less code. From a functionality and syntax standpoint, the second option is perfectly legal. However, many VBScript programmers strongly prefer using private property variables in combination with `Property Let`, `Set`, and `Get` procedures, as we have discussed in the previous sections. Other programmers prefer to use public class-level variables instead of `Property Let`, `Set`, and `Get` procedures. The main advantage to using public class-level variables to create class properties is that this method takes a lot less code. However, not using `Property Let`, `Set`, and `Get` procedures also has some serious disadvantages that you should consider:

❑ Unless you want the code that uses your class to use awkward syntax like `objCustomer.mstrName = "ACME Inc."`, you cannot use Hungarian scope or subtype prefixes on your class-level variables. If you agree with the theory that Hungarian prefixes (see Appendix C) add value to your code, this tends to make the code less readable and understandable.

❑ You cannot use the techniques described in previous sections of this chapter for making properties read-only or write-only.

❑ Code outside of your class can write to any property at any time. If there are certain circumstances where it is valid to write to a certain property, and other circumstances where it is invalid to write to a certain property, the only way you can enforce this is through `Property Let` procedures that have code in them to check for these valid and invalid circumstances. You never know when code outside the class might be changing the values of properties.

❑ Without `Property Let` procedures, you cannot write code to validate or transform the value being written to a property.

❑ Without `Property Get` procedures, you cannot write code to validate or transform the value being read from a property.

That said, if you can live with the first disadvantage in this list, you certainly can declare your properties as public class-level variables and change them to use `Property Let`, `Set`, and `Get` procedures later if the need arises. However, one could make an argument that it's better to do it the "right" way from the start. This is one of those issues where good programmers will simply have a difference of opinion, but we think you'll find more programmers who prefer `Property Let`, `Set`, and `Get` procedures over public class-level variables.

Defining Methods

How do you declare methods for your classes and what scope will they have? Read on.

Function and Sub

A method on a class is nothing more than a normal Function or Sub procedure. If you know how to write Function and Sub procedures (see Chapter 3), then you know how to write methods for a class. There is no special syntax for methods, as there is for properties. Your primary consideration is whether to declare a Function or Sub in a class as Public or Private.

Public and Private

Simply put, a class method that is declared with the Public statement will be available to code outside or inside the class, and a method that is declared with the Private statement will be available only to code inside the class. Here is a sample class with both public and private methods:

```
Class Greeting

    Private mstrName

    Public Property Let Name(strName)
        mstrName = strName
    End Property

    Public Sub ShowGreeting(strType)
        MsgBox MakeGreeting(strType) & mstrName & "."
    End Sub

    Private Function MakeGreeting(strType)
        Select Case strType
            Case "Formal"
                MakeGreeting = "Greetings, "
            Case "Informal"
                MakeGreeting = "Hello there, "
            Case "Casual"
                MakeGreeting = "Hey, "
        End Select
    End Function

End Class
```

Code that is outside of this class can call the ShowGreeting method, which is public, but cannot call the MakeGreeting method, which is private for internal use only. Here is some example code that makes use of this class:

```
Dim objGreet
Set objGreet = New Greeting

With objGreet
    .Name = "Dan"
    .ShowGreeting "Informal"
    .ShowGreeting "Formal"
    .ShowGreeting "Casual"
End With
Set objGreet = Nothing
```

237

> Note to Visual Basic programmers: VBScript does not support the
> `Friend` statement.

Class Events

Any VBScript class that you write automatically supports two events:
`Class_Initialize` and `Class_Terminate`. Implementing these events is optional.
The sample classes we have been using so far have not contained code to implement
these events.

The Class_Initialize Event

The `Class_Initialize` event "fires" in your class when some code instantiates an
object that is based on your class. It will always fire when an object based on your class
is instantiated, but whether your class contains any code to respond to it is up to you.
If you do not wish to respond to this event, then you can simply choose to omit an
"event handler" for the event. An event handler is a `Sub` procedure that is called
automatically whenever the event that it is tied to fires. Here is an example class that
contains a `Class_Initialize` event handler:

```
Class FileHelper

    'Private FileSystemObject object
    Private mobjFSO

    Private Sub Class_Initialize

        Set mobjFSO = WScript.CreateObject("Scripting.FileSystemObject")

    End Sub

    '<rest of the class goes here>

End Class
```

As in this example, initializing class-level variables is a fairly typical use for a
`Class_Initialize` event handler. If you have a variable that you want to make sure
has a certain value when your class first starts, you can initialize it in the
`Class_Initialize` event handler. You might also use the `Class_Initialize`
event to do other preliminary things such as opening a database connection, or
opening a file.

The syntax for blocking off the beginning and ending of the `Class_Initialize`
event handler must be exactly as you see it in this example. Your code can do just
about whatever you please inside the event handler, but you do not have the flexibility
of giving the procedure a different name. The first line of the handler must be
`Private Sub Class_Initialize`, and the last line must be `End Sub`. Really, the
event handler is a normal VBScript `Sub` procedure, but with a special name.
(Technically, the event handler could also be declared with the `Public` statement (as
opposed to `Private`), but event handlers are generally private. If you were to make it
public, then code outside of the class could call it like any other method any time it
liked.)

There can only be exactly one Class_Initialize event handler in a given class. You can omit it if you don't need it, but you can't have more than one.

The Class_Terminate Event

The Class_Terminate event is the inverse of the Class_Initialize event (see previous section). Whereas the Class_Initialize event fires whenever an object based on your class is instantiated, the Class_Terminate event fires whenever an object based on your class is destroyed. An object can be destroyed in either of two ways:

❑ when some code explicitly sets the object variable equal to the special value Nothing

❑ when the object variable goes out of scope

When either of these things occurs, the Class_Terminate event will fire right before the object is actually destroyed. Here is the example FileHelper class that we saw in the previous section, this time with a Class_Terminate event handler added:

```
Class FileHelper

    'Private FileSystemObject object
    Private mobjFSO

    Private Sub Class_Initialize

        Set mobjFSO = WScript.CreateObject("Scripting.FileSystemObject")

    End Sub

    Private Sub Class_Terminate

        Set mobjFSO = Nothing

    End Sub

    '<rest of the class goes here>
End Class
```

In this example, we are using the Class_Terminate event handler to destroy the object that we instantiated in the Class_Initialize event. This is not strictly necessary, since when the FileHelper object is destroyed, the private mobjFSO variable will go out of scope and the script engine will destroy it for us. However, some programmers prefer to explicitly destroy all objects that they instantiate. You might also use the Class_Terminate event to close a database connection, close a file, or save some information in the class to a database or file. The same syntactical restrictions that apply to Class_Initialize event handlers apply to Class_Terminate event handlers.

> Note: do not be confused by earlier versions of the Microsoft HTML-
> based VBScript documentation that misspelled the names of the
> `Class_Initialize` and `Class_Terminate` events.
> `Class_Initialize` and `Class_Terminate` are the correct spellings.
> The VBScript documentation on the Microsoft site
> (`http://msdn.microsoft.com/scripting`) appears to now be
> corrected.

Regarding Class-Level Constants and Arrays

VBScript Version 5 (as well as the forthcoming Version 5.1) has two "behaviors" that may throw you for a loop. The first is that any constants declared at the class level are ignored by the VBScript engine. The engine does not produce a compile or runtime error – it simply ignores the value of the constant. It is unclear if this is a bug or a designed behavior. Here is an example:

```
Option Explicit

Dim objTest

Set objTest = new ConstTest
objTest.SayHello
Set objTest = Nothing

Class ConstTest

    Private Const TEST_CONST = "Hello there."

    Public Sub SayHello
        MsgBox TEST_CONST
    End Sub

End Class
```

Running this code with the Windows Script Host will not produce an error, but the message box that the `SayHello` method displays will be empty. You can work around this "behavior" with the following trick:

```
Option Explicit

Dim objTest

set objTest = new ConstTest
objTest.SayHello

Class ConstTest

    Private TEST_CONST

    Private Sub Class_Initialize
        TEST_CONST = "Hello there."
    End Sub
```

```
        Public Sub SayHello
            MsgBox TEST_CONST
        End Sub

End Class
```

This work-around creates a pseudo-constant. Instead of declaring TEST_CONST with the Const statement, we declare it as a normal, private class-level variable. Then in the Class_Initialize event handler, we give the TEST_CONST variable the "constant" value that we want. There is a danger in this, however, because code inside your class can still change the value of the TEST_CONST variable, but using the all-caps naming convention might help prevent this from happening (most programmers are accustomed to equating all-caps with a constant). You'll just have to make sure the code inside the class behaves itself.

Class-level arrays are also ignored by the VBScript engine. The variables themselves are not ignored, but the fact that you have declared them as arrays is. This occurs with variables declared as fixed or dynamic arrays. Take a look at this code:

```
Option Explicit

Dim objTest
Set objTest = New ArrayTest
objTest.ShowGreeting 1

Class ArrayTest

    Private mastrGreetings(3)

    Private Sub Class_Initialize

        'Populate the greetings
        mastrGreetings(0) = "Hello"
        mastrGreetings(1) = "Hey"
        mastrGreetings(2) = "Yo"
        mastrGreetings(3) = "What's up?"

    End Sub

    Public Sub ShowGreeting(intGreetingID)

        MsgBox mastrGreetings(intGreetingID)

    End Sub

End Class
```

Attempting to run this code will produce the runtime error Type mismatch: 'mastrGreetings' on the line mastrGreetings(0) = "Hello" in the Class_Initialize subprocedure. The type mismatch occurs because the VBScript engine fails to recognize that you have declared the variable mastrGreetings as an array. This is a pretty serious limitation. There is a way to get around it, however:

```
Option Explicit

Dim objTest
Set objTest = New ArrayTest
objTest.ShowGreeting 1


Class ArrayTest

    Private mastrGreetings

    Private Sub Class_Initialize

        'Make the variable an array
        ReDim mastrGreetings(3)

        'Populate the greetings
        mastrGreetings(0) = "Hello"
        mastrGreetings(1) = "Hey"
        mastrGreetings(2) = "Yo"
        mastrGreetings(3) = "What's up?"

    End Sub

    Public Sub ShowGreeting(intGreetingID)

        MsgBox mastrGreetings(intGreetingID)

    End Sub

End Class
```

This code works as expected. In this workaround, we do not declare
mastrGreetings as an array variable. We just declare it as a normal variable. Then,
in the Class_Initialize event handler procedure, we use the ReDim statement to
turn the variable into an array. Once again, not ideal, but it works.

Note that local constants and arrays (that is, those declared inside of class methods or
property procedures) work fine. It's only class-level arrays and constants that will
cause these problems for you. If you are using a version of VBScript higher than 5.1
(5.0 was the highest version available at the time of writing), you might try and see if
this behavior has changed.

Building and Using a Sample VBScript Class

In this section will we will develop a VBScript class called FolderSummary. The
purpose of this class will be to summarize the contents of any folder (a.k.a. "directory")
on your system. The class will make use of the Scripting Runtime
FileSystemObject (and some of its related objects) which we covered in detail in
Chapter 7. You will need to feed the class a FileSystemObject and a folder name,
and the Summarize method of the class will provide some statistics for that folder:
how many files there are, the date of the oldest and newest files, whether there are any
hidden files, etc. The real-world usefulness of this class is debatable, but it should give
us a context in which to illustrate the thought process and syntax of building a
VBScript class.

Let's start out by defining the skeleton for our class. (Keep in mind that we will be operating under the assumption that this class and the example code that uses it are all in the same .VBS script file. We will be using the Windows Script Host for our example, but you should be able to adapt this to other hosts quite easily.)

```
Class FolderSummary

    <rest of the class code will go here>

End Class
```

This is the basic block structure for a VBScript class. All of the code in our class will go between the Class and End Class statements. You need to give your class a name after the Class statement. The name of our class is FolderSummary. It's a good idea to pick a name that is not the same as any of the built-in VBScript classes, or the classes provided by any of the common scripting hosts, such as the Scripting Runtime, the Windows Script Host, Active Server Pages, or Active Data Objects. Note also that there is an alternative naming convention that some programmers like to use. It involves placing the letter C in front of the class name, like so:

```
Class CFolderSummary

    <rest of the class code will go here>

End Class
```

Another common convention is the cls prefix, which is closer to the three-letter Hungarian prefixes that this book advocates in Appendix C.

Giving a class name a prefix is optional, and we will not be using the class name prefix convention in this chapter.

Let's define the first property for our class:

```
Class FolderSummary

    'Private property variables
    Private mstrFolderPath

    Public Property Let FolderPath(strFolderPath)
        mstrFolderPath = strFolderPath
    End Property

    Public Property Get FolderPath
        FolderPath = mstrFolderPath
    End Property

End Class
```

We have added a property called FolderPath to our class. There are two elements that make this property work.

The first element is the private variable called `mstrFolderPath`. Because we used the `Private` statement to define this variable, it will be available to all of the code within the class, but no code outside of the class will be able to read from or write to this variable directly. (Another way to say this would be to say that the variable has "private class-level scope".) In order to achieve private class-level scope for this variable, we *must* use the `Private` statement to declare it. Class-level variables declared with the `Dim` statement will have public scope, meaning the all of the code in the script will be able to access the variable directly.

The second element of the property are the `Property Let` and `Property Get` procedures. These procedures are how we give outside code access to our private property variable `mstrFolderPath`. The key here is that, by using a private property variable and `Property Let` and `Property Get` procedures, *we* control access to the property variable. If we want to put extra code in the `Property Let` and `Get` procedures, we can. For example, we might want to put some code in the `Property Let` procedure to make sure that a valid value is being sent to the property. Also, we can choose to omit either the `Property Let` or `Property Get` procedure. (In a minute we'll see how we can selectively use the `Property Let` and `Get` procedures to make a property either write-only or read-only.)

The `Property Let` and `Get` procedures act as a gatekeeper between outside code and the actual property variable. When outside code passes a folder pathname to our `Property Let` procedure, the value is stored in the private class-level variable `mstrFolderPath`. Then, when outside code wants to read this property, the `Property Get` procedure passes the value back out.

> There is an alternative to using `Property Let` and `Get` procedures to allow outside code to have access to our class property. That alternative is to use public variables. If a class-level variable is public, then code that is using our class can access that variable as a property. However, we then give up the control over how, what, and when outside code can read from or write to our property. Using `Property Let` and `Get` procedures is generally preferable, but here is an example of this alternate syntax:
>
> ```
> Class FolderSummary
>
>     'Using a public variable for our property.
>     'It is preferable to make this Private and
>     'use Property Let and Get procedures instead.
>     Public FolderPath
>
> End Class
> ```

Let's add another property to our class.

```
Class FolderSummary

    'Private property variables
    Private mstrFolderPath
    Private mobjFSO
```

```
Public Property Let FolderPath(strFolderPath)
    mstrFolderPath = strFolderPath
End Property

Public Property Get FolderPath
    FolderPath = mstrFolderPath
End Property

Private Sub Class_Initialize

    'This forces the subtype of this variable
    'To be "Object".
    Set objFSO = Nothing

End Sub

Public Property Set FSO(objFSO)

    If objFSO Is Nothing Then
        Err.Raise 32000, "FolderSummary", _
            "The objFSO parameter of the FileSystemObject class " & _
            "may not be Nothing."
    End If
    If TypeName(objFSO) <> "FileSystemObject" Then
        Err.Raise 32000, "FolderSummary", _
            "The objFSO parameter of the FileSystemObject class " & _
            "may not be Nothing."
    End If

    Set mobjFSO = objFSO

End Property

End Class
```

We still have our FolderPath property, but now we've added another property called FSO, which is short for FileSystemObject. This is the object we're going to use to access the folder specified by the FolderPath property. We implemented this new property a little bit differently than the FolderPath property, however. The first difference is that we used a Property Set procedure instead of a Property Let procedure. This is because this property holds an object variable, and whenever you have an object-based property, you should (in general – see the "Property Set" section earlier in this chapter) use Property Set instead of Property Let. The second difference is that we did not include a Property Get procedure. We did this so that the property would be write-only. Since the code that uses this class will be providing the FileSystemObject for us, there's probably not a reason for that code to need to read this property back, so we make it write-only. It becomes write-only by virtue of the fact that there is no Property Get procedure.

The third difference is that we've put some extra code in the Property Set procedure. This type of validation code is very common in Property Let and Set procedures. The purpose of the validation code is to allow the rest of the class to operate under the assumption that the properties are valid. As you'll see later, though, we're still going to need to test the properties again in the Summarize method. This is because we can't guarantee that the outside code is going to set the properties before it calls the Summarize method.

Basically what we're doing is enforcing proper use of the class and attempting to provide the outside code with helpful error messages when they deviate from this proper use. You'll see more of this as we continue to build the class. (If you are not familiar with the `Err.Raise` code that we're using, you might want to review Chapter 4 and Appendix E.)

Finally, notice that we added a `Class_Initialize` event handler to the class. The purpose of the code in this procedure is to coerce the subtype of the `objFSO` variable to be object. We do this so that we can legitimately use the `Is Nothing` check later, in the `Property Set FSO` procedure. Trying to use the `Is Nothing` test on a non-object variable will cause a runtime error.

Now let's add the rest of the properties that we'll need for the results of the `Summarize` method:

```
Class FolderSummary

    'Private property variables
    Private mstrFolderPath
    Private mobjFSO
    Private mlngFileCount
    Private mlngSubFolderCount
    Private mboolHasHiddenFiles
    Private mdatOldestFile
    Private mdatNewestFile

    Public Property Let FolderPath(strFolderPath)
        mstrFolderPath = strFolderPath
    End Property
    Public Property Get FolderPath
        FolderPath = mstrFolderPath
    End Property

    Public Property Set FSO(objFSO)
        If objFSO Is Nothing Then
            Err.Raise 32000, "FolderSummary", _
                "The objFSO parameter of the FileSystemObject class " & _
                "may not be Nothing."
        End If
        If TypeName(objFSO) <> "FileSystemObject" Then
            Err.Raise 32000, "FolderSummary", _
                "The objFSO parameter of the FileSystemObject class " & _
                "may not be Nothing."
        End If

        Set mobjFSO = objFSO

    End Property

    Public Property Get FileCount
        FileCount = mlngFileCount
    End Property
    Public Property Get SubFolderCount
        SubFolderCount = mlngSubFolderCount
    End Property
    Public Property Get HasHiddenFiles
        HasHiddenFiles = mboolHasHiddenFiles
    End Property
```

```
    Public Property Get OldestFileDate
        OldestFileDate = mdatOldestFile
    End Property
    Public Property Get NewestFileDate
        NewestFileDate = mdatNewestFile
    End Property

End Class
```

We added five new properties, which represent statistics for this folder that we're going to gather with the Summarize method: FileCount, SubFolderCount, HasHiddenFiles, OldestFileDate, and NewestFileDate. Each of these properties has a corresponding private property variable, just like our other properties. This time, however, we only added Property Get procedures for these properties. This makes the properties read-only. There is no reason to provide Property Let procedures for these properties since the Summarize method populates them internally.

Now let's tie it all together with the Summarize method (For the sake of brevity, the code below only includes the Summarize method. If we were to show the whole class, this code would go right after the property procedures, but before the End Class statement – although technically it could go anywhere in the class after the variable declarations section.):

```
Public Sub Summarize

        Const ERR_INVALID_PATH = 76
        Const ATTR_HIDDEN = 2

        Dim objFolder
        Dim objFiles
        Dim objFileLoop

        If mobjFSO Is Nothing Then
            Err.Raise 32001, "FolderSummary.Summarize", _
                "You cannot call the Summarize method without first " & _
                "setting the FSO property to a valid FileSystemObject."
        End If
        If Len(Trim(mstrFolderPath)) = 0 Then
            Err.Raise 32002, "FolderSummary.Summarize", _
                "You cannot call the Summarize method without first " & _
                "setting the FolderPath property to a valid path."
        End If

        On Error Resume Next
        Set objFolder = mobjFSO.GetFolder(mstrFolderPath)
        If Err.Number = ERR_INVALID_PATH Then
            Err.Raise 32003, "FolderSummary.Summarize", _
                "The '" & mstrFolderPath & "' path does not appear to be " & _
                "valid.  The Summarize method failed."
        ElseIf Err.Number <> 0 Then
            Err.Raise 32004, "FolderSummary.Summarize", _
                "There was an error accessing the folder '" & mstrFolderPath & _
                "': " & Err.Number & " - " & Err.Description & vbNewLine & _
                vbNewLine & "The Summarize method failed."
```

```
    Else
        On Error GoTo 0
    End If

    'Now that we know that all is well with the Folder, let's summarize.

    'Initialize the stats
    mlngFileCount = 0
    mlngSubFolderCount = 0
    mboolHasHiddenFiles = False
    mdatOldestFile = #12/31/2999#
    mdatNewestFile = #01/01/1900#

    'First get the file and subfolders counts
    mlngFileCount = objFolder.Files.Count
    mlngSubFolderCount = objFolder.SubFolders.Count

    'Next process the files
    Set objFiles = objFolder.Files
    For Each objFileLoop In objFiles
        With objFileLoop
            If .DateCreated < mdatOldestFile Then
                mdatOldestFile = .DateCreated
            End If
            If .DateCreated > mdatNewestFile Then
                mdatNewestFile = .DateCreated
            End If
            If .Attributes And ATTR_HIDDEN Then
                mboolHasHiddenFiles = True
            End If
        End With
    Next
    Set objFileLoop = Nothing
    Set objFiles = Nothing
    Set objFolder = Nothing

End Sub
```

As you can see, a method is nothing more than a normal procedure. The procedure can be either a Function or a Sub. As long as the procedure is declared with the Public statement, it becomes a method that is available to outside code. (You can also declare procedures within a class with the Private statement, which means that outside code will not be able to call the procedure.) We won't go into describing all of the code within in this method, but here are a couple things to take note of:

❑   At the beginning of the procedure, we do some checking to make sure that it's valid for someone to be calling the Summarize method. In order for the Summarize method to work, we need two things: a FileSystemObject object and a valid folder path. So before we get into the meat of the procedure, we test these two things. It's not absolutely required for us to do this, but it's a good idea because it provides the calling code with useful error messages in case the class is being used improperly.

❑   Throughout the procedure, we read from and write directly to the private property variables. Since we are inside the class, we can do this. Code inside the class is not required to use the Property Let, Set, and Get procedures. However, it is perfectly valid to do so, but usually unnecessary. One exception to this is when the Property Let, Set, or Get procedure is doing something to validate or transform the value of the property. In this case, it might be advantageous to use the property procedures so that this validation/transformation code would get executed. To access the property procedures from within the class, you can either call them directly, just like any other procedure, or use the Me keyword in front of the procedure name, as in Me.FSO or Me.FileCount. Using the Me keyword within a class refers to the object itself.

More facts about the Me keyword:

❑   It can be used to pass the current object itself to another procedure as a parameter. For example, if we were to develop another class that required a FolderSummary class as a property, we could have code like this within the class: Set objWhatever.FoldSumm = Me.

❑   It can also be used in regular (non-class) VBScript code to refer to the currently running script.

Now that we've built our class, how about some code to make use of it:

```
Option Explicit

Dim objFSO
Dim objFoldSumm
Dim strSummary

Set objFoldSumm = New FolderSummary
Set objFSO = WScript.CreateObject("Scripting.FileSystemObject")
Set objFoldSumm.FSO = objFSO
Set objFSO = Nothing

With objFoldSumm
    .FolderPath = "C:\bin"
    .Summarize

    strSummary = "Summary for " & .FolderPath & ":" & vbNewLine & vbNewLine
    strSummary = strSummary & "Number of Files:  " & .FileCount & vbNewLine
    strSummary = strSummary & "Number of SubFolders:  " & _
        .SubFolderCount & vbNewLine
    strSummary = strSummary & "Has Hidden Files:  " & .HasHiddenFiles & _
        vbNewLine
    strSummary = strSummary & "Oldest File Date:  " & .OldestFileDate & _
        vbNewLine
    strSummary = strSummary & "Newest File Date:  " & .NewestFileDate & _
        vbNewLine
End With
Set objFoldSumm = Nothing

MsgBox strSummary
```

Running this code produces a dialog box similar to this:

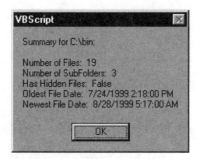

Design Note:

The design decisions for the FolderSummary class were made primarily to illustrate the elements of the creating a VBScript class. One could easily make an argument for alternative design strategies.

For example, instead of making the FolderPath and FSO properties, we could have made them parameters of the Summarize method instead. We implemented them as properties in order to demonstrate the Property Let, Set, and Get techniques and syntax.

Also, there is no real reason to ask the outside code to provide a FileSystemObject for us. The Summarize method could just as easily create one for itself. We implemented it the way we did so that we could illustrate object-based properties and the Property Set statement.

Also, the code that generates the summary message to display the folder summary in a message box would have been better implemented as a method of the class, but we wanted to demonstrate how to read properties from outside the class.

Finally, if you were going to implement this class over the web, through Distributed COM, or in Microsoft Transaction Server (in which case you would also want to convert the class to the "stateless" paradigm), you might decide to return the statistics as elements of an array, which would greatly reduce the number of times the outside code would need to access the class, thereby trading some ease of use for an increase in performance. When designing a class, there are usually multiple ways of formulating the design, and you have to consider the benefits and tradeoffs of designing it one way or another.

Summary

In this chapter we explained how to develop classes in native VBScript. We covered the use of

- the Class statement
- Property Let, Set, and Get procedures
- the Class_Initialize and Class_Terminate events
- and class methods

We also developed a working sample class called FolderSummary, which makes use of all the VBScript class features we discussed.

Windows Script Components

In this chapter, we'll be looking at Windows Script Components. We'll examine their structure and see how to create and register them. Later in the chapter, we'll see how we can use classes in our components. Our first job is to see just what Windows Script Components are.

What Are Windows Script Components?

Windows Script Components are interpreted COM components. Structurally, they're XML-based files that contain script code. Within them, you can use VBScript, JScript, Python, PERLScript, or any other scripting language. We will focus on using VBScript in this chapter (for obvious reasons), but you can actually use the script language of your choice.

The script components are interpreted by the **Script Component Runtime** which exposes the internal properties and methods, fires the events, and makes the component look like a compiled COM component to the calling application. We will look at the Script Component Runtime in more detail in the next section.

Script components are full COM components, and have the ability to call other COM components. Script components have some built-in interfaces into the Active Server Pages library and Internet Explorer DHTML behaviors that make it very easy to build these components for the Web.

> **Script components are not designed for use as early bound objects. If you reference a script component as an early bound component then your application will generate a runtime error. This is a common issue with using script components – so keep them late bound and you will have fewer problems with implementing them.**

So, why would you want to use these when you could use Visual Basic to build a standard COM component instead? Well, Windows Script Components don't require a compiler. Basically all you need to build script components is Notepad. Script components are also an easy way to encapsulate some of the functions and routines that you write in VBScript – this gives you a way to create a library of your source code. Finally, the ASP interfaces allow you to directly access the Active Server Pages library for quick and easy integration with your Internet or intranet sites.

> *If you're not familiar with ASP, don't worry – Chapter 14 is an introduction to that subject.*

What Tools Do You Need?

You can create Windows Script Components with nothing more than Notepad and your imagination, but you may find that it's a bit tedious to do it by hand. Microsoft provides the Script Component Wizard (which you can find at `http://msdn.microsoft.com/scripting/scriptlets/wz10en.exe`) to help speed up the creation of the script component framework. You need to have the VBScript 5.0 libraries on your machine to run script components properly. Script components use the Windows Script Host when they run, so you'll also need that. Luckily, it comes with the scripting libraries.

Here's a list of items that you *must* have to create script components.

❑ VBScript 5.0 libraries
(`http://msdn.microsoft.com/scripting/vbscript/download/x86/sce10en.exe`)

❑ Internet Explorer 5.0 (`http://www.microsoft.com/ie`)

The next items are optional but will make the process of creating script components much easier:

❑ The Script Component Wizard
(`http://msdn.microsoft.com/scripting/scriptlets/wz10en.exe`)

❑ A copy of the Script Component documentation
(`http://msdn.microsoft.com/scripting/scriptlets/serverdocs.htm`)

The Script Component Runtime

The Script Component Runtime (`scrobj.dll`) is the interpreter used to marshal calls between clients and script components. The runtime implements the basic COM interfaces for the component (`IUnknown`) and handles some of the basic COM methods (`QueryInterface, AddRef`) in the same way that the Visual Basic runtime handles the low-level COM routines of Visual Basic components.

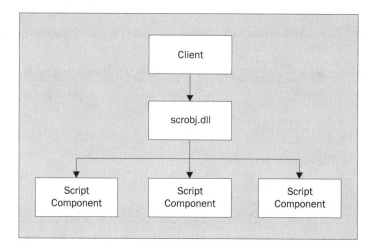

Since we are running though an interpreter, our script components will look different from other COM components in the registry. Let's examine this in a bit more detail.

We will assume that our object is called "Math.WSC" and that we are calling this object through script:

```
Set objMath = CreateObject("Math.WSC")
```

The first thing that happens is that the registry will be searched for the Math.WSC entry under HKEY_CLASSES_ROOT:

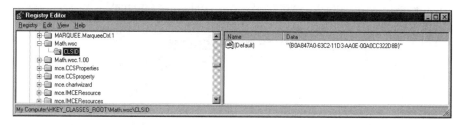

If we look up the GUID (**G**lobally **U**nique **ID**entifier) under HKEY_CLASSES_ROOT\CLSID then it brings us to our information for our COM component. Notice that the InprocServer32 key is actually scrobj.dll, not the script component file itself. We are actually creating the scrobj.dll component when we call our CreateObject statement.

The `scrobj.dll` file knows to look at the `ScriptletURL` key for the location of our component. It now knows that we need to look at that path for the actual object for the method calls.

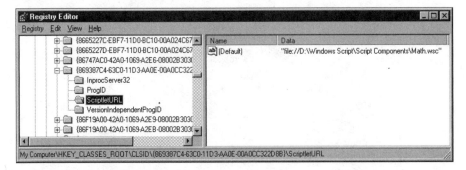

Notice that the key is named `ScriptletURL`. This implies that these can be called over the Internet. Don't get too excited about this just yet, because we don't cover this little tidbit of information until later in the chapter. There is a bit more to know about script components first.

Script Component Files

Now let's see how to create script components. You can build script files by hand, but Microsoft ships a free wizard for building a script component file. What this essentially does is to build the XML framework that defines your component. There's nothing at all to stop you creating this yourself if you know how it's done. Of course, the best way to find out how it's done is to use the wizard first, so let's do that.

The Script Component Wizard

We invoke the wizard from the Start > Programs > Microsoft Windows Script > Windows Script Component Wizard shortcut. First we will tell the wizard the name of the component along with the ProgID of the component. One thing to note is that script components use a special ProgID that defines the component. By default, the ProgID of the component will be *componentname*.WSC. This can be changed in this step or after the component file has been created. Script components can also maintain version information just like any other COM component, as you can see in the Version field.

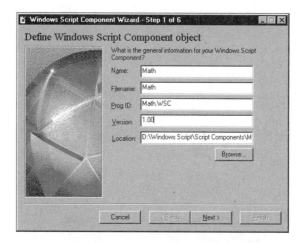

Note that the Location in this dialog is simply the location of the source files that the wizard produces. The location of the source files will not be important to Windows until you register the component.

Once you are satisfied with the settings, select the Next button to go to the second step of the wizard.

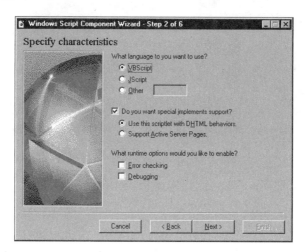

Windows Script Components can use VBScript or JScript natively, but other scripting platforms such as Python and PERL can be used as well if the proper interpreter is installed on the computer. There are two options under the implements section that need a little extra background information: DHTML behaviors and Active Server Pages.

DHTML behaviors are simple, lightweight components that interface with some of the DHTML objects and events of Internet Explorer. DHTML components are beyond the scope of this chapter, but for more information you can refer to the Microsoft Scripting site and the MSDN Web Workshop (http://msdn.microsoft.com/workshop).

257

Active Server Pages support will be covered in more detail in this chapter, and ASP itself will be covered in Chapter 14. Basically, ASP support allows a script component to gain direct access to the ASP object model. The ASP object model exposes the vast ASP `Request`, `Response`, `Application`, `Session`, and `Server` objects.

Finally, error checking and debugging can be selected as options. If you select debugging, you'll be allowed to use the script debugger. The script debugger can be found at `http://msdn.microsoft.com/scripting/debugger/dbdown.htm`, and it's one of the only ways to debug a script component. It gives you the ability to check variables and view data, in a similar way to the Visual Basic debugging tools.

When you have selected the options that you want, select the **Next** button to move to step 3 of the wizard.

This screen allows you to define the properties of your object. You are able to define the name, type, and default values for the component. The **Type** setting is not the data type, but the property type, which can be one of the following:

- ❑ Read/Write
- ❑ Read-Only
- ❑ Write-Only

The **Default** entry allows you to specify a default value for the property. The code listing below shows a read/write property with a default value of 5:

```
Dim ReadWriteProperty
ReadWriteProperty = 5
```

Note that this is how the wizard declares a variable that will be accessed by a property. This should be changed to read:

```
Private ReadWriteProperty
ReadWriteProperty = 5
```

This will make sure that the variable is private to the script component. Otherwise the variable will be public, as will the property that is accessing it.

Press the **Next** button to proceed to the next step in the wizard.

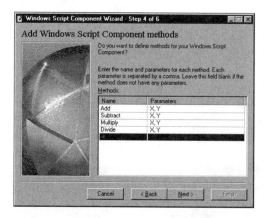

The fourth step of the wizard brings us to the methods of our component. You can specify the name of the method as well as the parameters list. When adding parameters, be sure to separate them with a comma, so that the parameter list looks like the following:

```
param1, param2, param3, ...
```

Again, remember that VBScript uses only variants, so you don't need to specify a type. Actually, if you try to specify a type you'll get an error. For similar reasons, you can't specify a return type. The use of variant data types does reduce overall performance somewhat because variants are the largest data type that can be used, and are designed to represent any other data type, so each time a variant is called the application must decide what format the variable should be in. But there's nothing we can do about that.

We will add a few methods here for our Math component. The Script Component Wizard will generate all methods as functions, but you can manually change these to subprocedures later if you don't need return values.

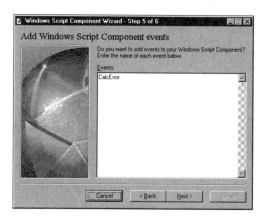

The fifth step of the wizard allows us to specify the events for our component. This is one of the most exciting areas of script components. We will see a little more on events in script components later in this section. Our Math component won't actually use events as such.

If you do want to have any events in your objects, enter one event name per line. Once you are satisfied with the layout of the events, press the **Next** button to move to the final step of the wizard.

> **The current version of the Script Component Wizard has a bug that ignores any entries in this section. You will need to add events in manually once the component has been created. We will go into more detail later in this chapter.**

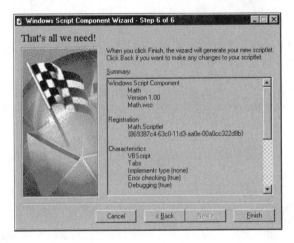

The final step of the wizard gives us some information about our component and some of the settings that we have selected. If you find any errors or omissions at this point then you can press the **Back** button to return to the previous steps and make the necessary changes.

Once we click **Finish**, the wizard will create a skeleton component like that in the code sample below:

```
<?xml version="1.0"?>
<component>

<registration
  description="Math"
  progid="Math.WSC"
  version="1.00"
  classid="{87ea3720-7ca8-11d3-8ecc-00104bdc2e9c}"
>
</registration>
```

```
<public>
  <property name="ReadOnlyProperty">
    <get/>
  </property>
  <property name="WriteOnlyProperty">
    <put/>
  </property>
  <property name="ReadWriteProperty">
    <get/>
    <put/>
  </property>
  <method name="Add">
    <PARAMETER name="X"/>
    <PARAMETER name="Y"/>
  </method>
  <method name="Subtract">
    <PARAMETER name="X"/>
    <PARAMETER name="Y"/>
  </method>
  <method name="Multiply">
    <PARAMETER name="X"/>
    <PARAMETER name="Y"/>
  </method>
  <method name="Divide">
    <PARAMETER name="X"/>
    <PARAMETER name="Y"/>
  </method>
</public>

<script language="VBScript">
<![CDATA[

dim ReadOnlyProperty
dim WriteOnlyProperty
dim ReadWriteProperty

function get_ReadOnlyProperty()
  get_ReadOnlyProperty = ReadOnlyProperty
end function

function put_WriteOnlyProperty(newValue)
  WriteOnlyProperty = newValue
end function

function get_ReadWriteProperty()
  get_ReadWriteProperty = ReadWriteProperty
end function

function put_ReadWriteProperty(newValue)
  ReadWriteProperty = newValue
end function

function Add(X, Y)
  Add = "Temporary Value"
end function

function Subtract(X, Y)
  Subtract = "Temporary Value"
end function
```

261

```
function Multiply(X, Y)
  Multiply = "Temporary Value"
end function

function Divide(X, Y)
  Divide = "Temporary Value"
end function

]]>
</script>

</component>
```

Great! You have now created a Windows Script COM Component. Now let's take a look at it in a little more detail.

Exposing Properties, Methods, and Events

The next thing to do is to actually define the properties, methods, and events that your component needs to contain.

Properties

Properties within script components can be read/write, read-only, or write-only. They are implemented within the script file using <property></property> tags. Within these tags you set the get and put options for the property. Gets are used for reading the values and puts are for writing to the properties. The code sample below lists the structure that's created to first 'declare' the three types of properties:

```
<property name="PropReadOnly">
  <get/>
</property>
<property name="PropReadWrite">
  <get/>
  <put/>
</property>
<property name="PropWriteOnly">
  <put/>
</property>
```

The properties are then actually defined within script code later in the script file:

```
<script language="VBScript">
<![CDATA[

Private PropReadOnly
Private PropReadWrite
Private PropWriteOnly

Function get_PropReadOnly()
  get_PropReadOnly = PropReadOnly
End Function

Function get_PropReadWrite()
  get_PropReadWrite = PropReadWrite
End Function
```

```
Function put_PropReadWrite(newValue)
  PropReadWrite = newValue
End Function

Function put_PropWriteOnly(newValue)
  PropWriteOnly = newValue
End Function

]]>
</script>
```

You can script any additional logic within the get and put functions of the properties. For this example, we haven't included any real properties. Later on, when we look at classes, we'll actually see an example that does use properties.

Remember that script components can implement other COM objects, so you can create an ADO component, access LDAP and Exchange, or even call Excel and Word. The sky is the limit with script components!

Methods

Methods in script components are defined in <method></method> tags in the object definition section of the script file. Parameters for a method use a <parameter> definition for the values, as you can see in the following code sample:

```
<public>
  <method name="mNoParameters">
  </method>
  <method name="mWithParameters">
    <PARAMETER name="var1"/>
    <PARAMETER name="var2"/>
  </method>
</public>
```

The <parameter> tag simply defines the name of the input parameters. Remember that everything from the Script Component Wizard is a function by default within the script components and no return type is specified since all variables are of the variant data type. We can also use subprocedures as our methods in place of functions.

The actual method code is within the script tags of the script component:

```
<script language="VBScript">
<![CDATA[

Function mNoParameters()
  mNoParameters = "Temporary Value"
End Function

Function mWithParameters(var1, var2)
  mWithParameters = "Temporary Value"
End Function

]]>
</script>
```

Note that all methods that are created though the Windows Script Component Wizard return the value "Temporary Value". You will probably want to change this (unless you really *need* a function that returns "Temporary Value"...). You will also want to declare any temporary variables before the function definitions.

While we're here, let's add our real methods to our Math component.

```
<script language="VBScript">
<![CDATA[

function Add(X,Y)
  Add = X + Y
end function

function Subtract(X,Y)
  Subtract = X - Y
end function

function Multiply(X,Y)
  Multiply = X * Y
end function

function Divide(X,Y)
  Divide = X / Y
end function

]]>
</script>
```

Something that is not documented in the WSC documentation (because it's specific to the scripting language you use) is that you can use the `byval` (by value) and `byref` (by reference) keywords within the parameter declaration of the method. By default in VBScript all values are passed `byref`, so any changes to the variables in the method will change the underlying value in the calling function.

> *Just by the way, JScript variables are all passed* `byval` *since JScript cannot pass a variable* `byref`.

Events

Events are defined within `<event></event>` tags within the object definition of the script file. There is a bug in the current Windows Script Component Wizard which means that it does not create the events you specify. All event declarations must be created manually within a script file.

```
<public>
  <method name="mNoParameters">
  </method>
  <event name="MethodCalled">
  </event>
</public>
```

The event is actually fired through the `FireEvent()` method. `FireEvent()` is called within the script of the script component. The event itself should be described here as well, using the form *ComponentName_EventName*:

```
<script language="VBScript">
<![CDATA[

function mNoParameters()
  FireEvent("MethodCalled")
  mNoParameters = "Temporary Value"
end function

sub MyComponent_MethodCalled()
  'some event handling code
end sub

]]>
</script>
```

Script components can also handle events using an `<implements>` tag within the script definition. The syntax for capturing events in a script component is defined as:

```
<implements type="COMHandlerName" [id="internalName"] [default=fAssumed]>
  handler-specific information here
</implements>
```

The `COMHandlerName` is the name of the handler (ASP or behavior) or the COM object that is being handled. `InternalName` is an optional parameter that allows you to define a variable name for the COM handler. The `fAssumed` property is a Boolean flag (default = `True`) that indicates `InternalName` is assumed in scripts. You would set this to `False` to hide some members in the `<implements>` tag.

There are two built-in COM handlers: ASP and behaviors. We will look at the ASP COM handler later in this section.

Creating Registration Information

In order to register a Windows Script Component you need to have the Script Component Runtime (`scrobj.dll`) on your machine and have it properly registered. This file is automatically registered when you download and install the VBScript or JScript libraries.

Once you have the scripting runtime and a valid script component (`.wsc`) file then you can register the component. There are three methods available for properly registering a WSC file.

The easiest way to register and unregister a script component is to right-click the component file in Windows Explorer and select **Register** or **Unregister** from the popup menu.

In the event that you need to manually register and unregister a file you can still use the old standby of `regsvr32.exe`. If you are using an old version of `regsvr32` that comes with Windows or Visual Studio then you can use the command:

```
regsvr32 scrobj.dll /n /i:Path/component_name.wsc
```

New versions of `regsvr32` that ship with the script component packages can directly register the script component file:

```
regsvr32 path/component_name.wsc
```

You can also add a registration entry into the script component that defines the registration behavior. You can add the `<registration>` tag to the component as defined below:

```
<registration progid="progID" classid="GUID" description="description"
   version="version" [remotable=remoteFlag]>
<script>
  (registration and unregistration script)
</script>
</registration>
```

Within the `<script>` tags you can add a `Register()` and `Unregister()` event that is fired whenever the component is registered or unregistered on the system. The `progID` attribute is optional, but you must have data for either the `classid` or `progID` in order for the component to register. If you leave either `classid` or `progID` out then it will be automatically generated when the component is registered.

All of these methods will properly register a script component file on your system. This is nice, but does not address the need for remote components. More and more components are moving toward an n-tier architecture where a component resides on a middle tier server so all applications can access the component. Microsoft is really practicing what they preach when it comes to the DNA (**Distributed interNet Application**) initiative and distributed components because Windows Script Components can be registered remotely. Yes, you may want to read that last line again – Windows Script Components can be registered *remotely*.

In order to make the components DCOM-ready, you need to follow these steps:

1. Determine the `progid` and `clsid` of the component. Local components do not need an entry for a `clsid` in the object definition section of the script file. The absence of a `clsid` line tells the component to create a `clsid` entry at registration time.

2. On each local machine that needs to access the component, add an entry into the registry under `HKEY_CLASSES_ROOT\componentProgID`. `ComponentProgID` is the `ProgID` of the script component.

3. Under this entry, create a `CLSID` key and set the value to the `CLSID` of the script component.

4. Set `remotable=true` in the `<registration>` tags of the component.

You can make this process easier by registering the component on the server and exporting the registry key information through `regedit`. You can then copy the `.reg` file that was created from `regedit` to each machine that needs the component. Once the file has been copied to the local machine, double-click the `.reg` file to merge the data into the registry.

You now have a DCOM-ready script component that can be used throughout the enterprise.

Let's quickly test the component with a short test script. Save the following code as a file called `testmath.vbs` and then run it after you've registered your Math component:

```
dim obj

set obj = wscript.createobject("math.wsc")

msgbox obj.add(2, 7)

set obj = nothing
```

Creating the Script Component Type Library

Script components can have type libraries generated just as other COM components would. A type library is used in some environments (such as Visual Basic) for enabling events or for enabling the use of IntelliSense by programs such as Visual InterDev. Type libraries contain the descriptions of the COM components. They also help with early binding of objects or using tools such as `OLE2VIEW` to view the declarations and constants in a component.

To generate a type library for a script component, simply right-click on the script component file and select the **Generate Type Library** option from the popup menu.

That's all there is to generating a type library for a component. Don't you wish everything was this easy?

There is one other way to generate a type library within a script component. Script components can automatically generate a type library when the Register method is called. When this method is called, the component uses the information that is set up within <registration> tags. As we saw above, the syntax of the <registration> tag is as follows:

```
<registration progid="progID" classid="GUID" description="description"
   version="version" [remotable=remoteFlag]>
   <script>
   (registration and unregistration script)
   </script>
</registration>
```

Both the progID and classid items are optional, but one of the two must be specified for the tags to be valid. The progID is the component name and the classid entry is for the GUID of the component. If the classid entry is left blank, then a GUID will be assigned to the component at registration time. Description and version are optional as well. If we used a registration entry with our Math component above, then we would add the following <registration> tags:

```
<registration
   description="My Math Component"
   progid="Math.WSC"
   version="1.0"
   classid="{2154c700-9253-11d1-a3ac-0aa0044eb5f}">
   <script language="VBScript">
<![CDATA[
   Function Register()
      Set oComponent = CreateObject("Scriptlet.GenerateTypeLib")
      oComponent.AddURL "d:\components\Math.wsc"
```

AddURL allows us to add other component files into the type library. If we used or exposed other components then we would want to add them into one type library rather than tracking multiple files.

```
      oComponent.Path = "d:\components\Math.tlb"
```

We add the path that we plan on writing the component to. If we leave this blank then we will write the type library to the current location of the script component.

```
      oComponent.Doc = "Math component typelib" ' Documentation string.
      oComponent.GUID = "{a1e1e3e0-a252-11d1-9fa1-00a0c90fffc0}"
      oComponent.Name = "MathComponent" ' Internal name for tlb.
      oComponent.MajorVersion = 1
      oComponent.MinorVersion = 0
      oComponent.Write
```

Here we are writing the type library to the disk.

```
    oComponent.Reset
  End Function
]]>
  </script>
</registration>
```

If we were planning on using this component through DCOM, then we would add the line:

```
    remotable=true
```

This tells the component that it needs to set itself up in the registry for DCOM.

Referencing Other Components

A script component file can have more than one component inside it. You can create a library of components just like in Visual Basic. You cannot use the Windows Script Component Wizard, though. The script components use a series of `<package></package>` tags to create script libraries. For instance, you can define a series of components within a file:

```
<package>
  <component id="COMObject1">

  </component>

  <component id="COMObject2">

  </component>
</package>
```

Within each script you can create your properties, methods, and events for each component along with the necessary registration information.

You can reference another component within the package by using the `CreateComponent` function. If we want to reference `COMObject1` in code, we would set a reference to an object using `CreateComponent`:

```
Set oComponent = CreateComponent("COMObject1")
```

This will give us a runtime reference of `COMObject1`. This allows you to add components that implement ASP interfaces and DHTML behaviors as well as expose properties and methods to other client applications. Your ASP and DHTML components can access all of the properties and methods of the COM component and will reduce your amount of redundant code.

One easy way to create this package is to use the Windows Script Component Wizard to build the individual objects. Once all of the objects have been created then you can build a package and copy/paste the contents of the individual files.

Interface Handlers

Windows Script Components can implement two specific interface handlers: ASP and DHTML behaviors. The ASP interface handler gives the script component a hook into the Active Server Pages library, and the DHTML behaviors interface can link the script component to specific events within Internet Explorer.

Creating ASP Script Components

ASP script components include the functionality of the Active Server Pages library to allow for web enabled script components. These script components can be called from within ASP pages and can greatly increase code reuse of ASP components and business logic. In order to set up a script component to be ASP-enabled, you add an <implements> tag with a reference to the ASP COM handler.

```
<implements type="ASP">
</implements>
```

Once the <implements> tag has been set up, the script component will have a reference to ASP and can make use of the Response, Request, Session, Application, and Server ASP objects. For instance, we can have a component that outputs the current date and time to an ASP page. The script component would be created:

```
<component id="ASPDateTimeObject">
<registration progid="ASPDateTimeObject"/>

<public>
  <method name="OutputDateTime"/>
</public>

<implements type="ASP"/>
<script language="VBScript">
<![CDATA[

Sub OutputDateTime()
  Response.Write("Is is currently " & Time & " on " & Date)
End Sub

]]>
</script>
</component>
```

Our HTML and ASP code would create this object and call the OutputDateTime method:

```
<HTML>
<HEAD>
<TITLE>Using ASP Script Objects</TITLE>
</HEAD>

<H1>Using ASP Script Objects</H1>
```

```
<%

Set objDateTime = CreateObject("ASPDateTimeObject")%>

objDateTime.OutputDateTime()

set objDateTime = nothing

%>

</BODY>
</HTML>
```

An ASP script component can also contain complex database functions that can be re-used for generic database output. Since script objects can call other COM components, we have access to all ADO functions, Office COM libraries, and third party objects.

So, how do ASP script components operate? When the script object is called from an ASP page, the script object is run in the same **namespace** (or **process space**) as the calling page. This gives the script component direct access to the page, so it can use all of the intrinsic ASP objects and all output back to ASP is directed back to the page. The script component and the ASP page see exactly the same objects. This is similar to creating a Visual Basic COM component that implements the `OnStartPage` method. When a Visual Basic COM component has this method, ASP will call it automatically and send a reference to the ASP library, thus giving Visual Basic full control over ASP.

So, why is this better than using `#include` directives? Whenever you include a library into ASP files, the entire contents of the file are merged with the source file. Let's say that you have a library with 20 functions that are relatively complex. A library like this could easily contain several hundred lines of source code. If you only use one function out of the 20 then you are still forced to add all of the remaining code to the ASP page for processing. What if you don't happen to use any of the functions due to the way the page is processed? Too bad, because ASP must still merge all of the included files in order to process the page.

An ASP script component, on the other hand, can contain all of the library functions that you use, but is only loaded and used when needed. If the page logic does not require a function then the object is never loaded and the page is smaller and faster. ASP script components are a better design choice for ASP pages because you can organize individual components with related functions, you're not required to add `#include` directives for every page that might need a function, and you can remotely execute complex scripts on middle tier servers. Included files run directly on the web server and cannot take advantage of n-tier architectures in intranet and Internet applications.

Compile-time Error Checking

When you register your script component the syntax is validated and you will receive error messages if there are scripting errors or if the XML cannot be validated. The error messages are not very verbose and give you little more than a position in the file and possibly a snippet of the affected code. As an example, I've added a semi-colon to my script (let's pretend we were converting the source from JScript):

```
function Add(X,Y)
  Add = X + Y;
end function
```

What we get when we register the component are the following dialogs:

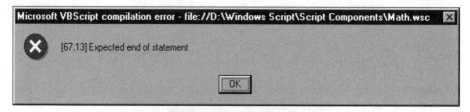

The text [67,13] is the approximate location (line, column) of the error in the component. Unfortunately this is not usually completely accurate, but it's close. For example, the location quoted above is actually pointing to the plus sign in our code, rather than the semi-colon at the end of our line.

Compile-time error checking is not perfect, but it will point you in the general direction of your errors. When verifying the source of your component it is handy to have an editor such as the default editor in Visual Studio that can give you the line and column location of your cursor.

Using VBScript Classes in Script Components

As you saw in the last chapter, VBScript now includes the ability to declare classes and class constructs. You can integrate a standard VBScript class into a Windows Script Component within the `<script></script>` tags in the data portion of the XML file. You still use the standard construct for classes:

```
class <classname>

  <internal class declaration>

end class
```

For a full description of the VBScript class constructs refer to Chapter 8.

Limitations of VBScript Classes

There is one key limitation of using VBScript classes in Windows Script Components that you should be aware of: the class information is not exposed automatically. In essence, script components know nothing about the structure of an internal class. In order to expose the class to the outside world you must wrap the class information around methods and properties declared in the script component file.

So, why use a class in a script component? Well, classes will not provide a lot of functionality for a small component, but a complex component can benefit from a class by helping a developer to organize the object structure in a more meaningful way. Large script components can get very complex due to the reliance on XML parsing, so your component may become harder to maintain over time. A well-defined class will always provide a more familiar structure to developers.

As we will see later in this section, you can include external source files. If you have defined many classes you can simply include the source file and provide a COM wrapper for the class definition. Remember that VBScript classes cannot be exposed automatically to COM, so you must provide a mechanism for other objects to access your class.

Using Internal Classes

Internal classes in script components need a class construct and a series of methods and properties that wrap the internal class. We can take the Math component that we built earlier in the chapter and use it as a class wrapper. Initially our script component had the following form:

```xml
<?xml version="1.0"?>
<component>

<?component error="true" debug="true"?>

<registration
  description="Math"
  progid="Math.Scriptlet"
  version="1.00"
  classid="{b0a847a0-63c2-11d3-aa0e-00a0cc322d8b}"
>
</registration>

<public>
  <method name="Add">
    <PARAMETER name="X"/>
    <PARAMETER name="Y"/>
  </method>
  <method name="Subtract">
    <PARAMETER name="X"/>
    <PARAMETER name="Y"/>
  </method>
  <method name="Multiply">
    <PARAMETER name="X"/>
    <PARAMETER name="Y"/>
  </method>
```

```
  <method name="Divide">
    <PARAMETER name="X"/>
    <PARAMETER name="Y"/>
  </method>
</public>

<script language="VBScript">
<![CDATA[

function Add(X,Y)
  Add = X + Y
end function

function Subtract(X,Y)
  Subtract = X - Y
end function

function Multiply(X,Y)
  Multiply = X * Y
end function

function Divide(X,Y)
  Divide = X / Y
end function

]]>
</script>

</component>
```

Within our `<script>` tags we can build a class that handles the methods of the script component.

```
<script language="VBScript">
<![CDATA[

Class clsMath

  Public Function Add(X, Y)
    Add = X + Y
  End Function

  Public Function Subtract(X, Y)
    Subtract = X - Y
  End Function

  Public Function Multiply(X, Y)
    Multiply = X * Y
  End Function

  Public Function Divide(X, Y)
    Divide = X / Y
  End Function

End Class

Private oMath
set oMath = new clsMath
```

```
Function Add(X,Y)
  Add = oMath.Add(X,Y)
End Function

Function Subtract(X,Y)
  Subtract = oMath.Subtract(X,Y)
End Function

Function Multiply(X,Y)
  Multiply = oMath.Multiply(X,Y)
End Function

Function Divide(X,Y)
  Divide = oMath.Divide(X,Y)
End Function

]]>
</script>
```

You can see that we have built a VBScript class and we have wrapped the functionality into the script component. This can provide a new level of flexibility to a script component, as you will see in the next section.

Including External Source Files

We are not required to have our class declarations (or our source for that matter) in the file itself. There is a declaration within the <script> tag that allows us to include an external source file. The src= declaration acts as an include for another file. This gives us the ability to move our class declarations to a .vbs (or .txt) file for later use. We can then leverage our external source files across both the Windows Script Host as well as within Active Server Pages and script components.

We can move the class declaration from our math sample to math.vbs. The text of math.vbs is simply the entire class declaration:

```
Class clsMath

  Public Function Add(X, Y)
    Add = X + Y
  End Function

  Public Function Subtract(X, Y)
    Subtract = X - Y
  End Function

  Public Function Multiply(X, Y)
    Multiply = X * Y
  End Function

  Public Function Divide(X, Y)
    Divide = X / Y
  End Function

End Class
```

We then change the text of the Math component to include the new source file:

```
<script language="VBScript" src="math.vbs">
<![CDATA[

private oMath
set oMath = new clsMath
```

When the component is instantiated we parse the script file, add any included files into the <script> tag and continue processing. As far as COM is concerned, the internal class declaration and the external class declaration are identical.

Let's look at a more practical example of where we would use this technique. We introduced a class for gathering folder information in Chapter 8. If we wanted to build a script component out of this file we would have to add the source of the file into the script component or rebuild the script component through the logic of the class. Instead we can wrap the functions of the class into the component.

The FolderSummary.vbs file contains the FolderSummary class from Chapter 8. We like this class, but it requires us to send a reference to the Scripting.FileSystem object. We can build this step into our script component to further simplify the usage of the object.

We use the Script Component Wizard to build our object, containing the properties: FileCount, SubFolderCount, HasHiddenFiles, OldestFileDate, NewestFileDate, and the method Summarize which takes the folder path as a parameter. This is a slightly different declaration than our original object. This shows us that we can extend and simplify the interfaces of other objects through our own custom objects.

The Script Component Wizard returns the following skeleton file:

```
<?xml version="1.0"?>
<component>

<?component error="true" debug="true"?>

<registration
  description="FolderSummary"
  progid="FolderSummary.WSC"
  version="1.00"
  classid="{4038d41e-7b94-11d3-aa5f-00a0cc322d8b}"
>
</registration>

<public>
  <property name="FileCount">
    <get/>
  </property>
  <property name="SubFolderCount">
    <get/>
  </property>
  <property name="HasHiddenFiles">
    <get/>
```

```
  </property>
  <property name="OldestFileDate">
    <get/>
  </property>
  <property name="NewestFileDate">
    <get/>
  </property>
  <method name="Summarize">
    <PARAMETER name="sFolderPath"/>
  </method>
</public>

<script language="VBScript">
<![CDATA[

dim FileCount
dim SubFolderCount
dim HasHiddenFiles
dim OldestFileDate
dim NewestFileDate

Function get_FileCount()
  get_FileCount = FileCount
End Function

Function get_SubFolderCount()
  get_SubFolderCount = SubFolderCount
End Function

Function get_HasHiddenFiles()
  get_HasHiddenFiles = HasHiddenFiles
End Function

Function get_OldestFileDate()
  get_OldestFileDate = OldestFileDate
End Function

Function get_NewestFileDate()
  get_NewestFileDate = NewestFileDate
End Function

Function Summarize(sFolderPath)
  Summarize = "Temporary Value"
End Function

]]>
</script>

</component>
```

We now need to include the source file and populate the function and property prototypes with the wrapper code for our object. Once we add this into our <script> tags we get our complete and ready to run wrapper object. The shell generated by the Wizard becomes:

```
<script language="VBScript" src="FolderSummary.vbs">
<![CDATA[
```

277

```
Private FileCount
Private SubFolderCount
Private HasHiddenFiles
Private OldestFileDate
Private NewestFileDate

Private oFolderSummary
Set oFolderSummary = new FolderSummary

Private oFSO
Set oFSO = CreateObject("Scripting.FileSystemObject")

Function get_FileCount()
  get_FileCount = oFolderSummary.FileCount
End Function

Function get_SubFolderCount()
  get_SubFolderCount = oFolderSummary.SubFolderCount
End Function

Function get_HasHiddenFiles()
  get_HasHiddenFiles = oFolderSummary.HasHiddenFiles
End Function

Function get_OldestFileDate()
  get_OldestFileDate = oFolderSummary.OldestFileDate
End Function

Function get_NewestFileDate()
  get_NewestFileDate = oFolderSummary.NewestFileDate
End Function

Function Summarize(sFolderPath)
  Set oFolderSummary.FSO = oFSO
  oFolderSummary.FolderPath = sFolderPath
  Summarize = oFolderSummary.Summarize
End Function

]]>
</script>
```

As you can see, we use our Summarize() method to handle several functions and hide them from the user. This gives us the power and the flexibility to take complex functions and classes and create easy to use objects that can be tailored to our needs.

> Note that in this example it was necessary to change the
> Wscript.CreateObject statement in the FolderSummary.vbs file to
> read simply CreateObject. The presence of the
> Wscript.CreateObject statement causes an exception error to occur.

We can test the functionality of our component by using a slightly modified version of the test file from Chapter 8:

```
Option Explicit

Dim objFSO
Dim objFoldSumm
Dim strSummary
dim sFolderPath

Set objFoldSumm = CreateObject("FolderSummary.wsc")

sFolderPath = InputBox("Enter the path")

With objFoldSumm
  .Summarize sFolderPath

  strSummary = "Summary for " & sFolderPath & ":" & vbNewLine & vbNewLine
  strSummary = strSummary & "Number of Files: " & .FileCount & vbNewLine
  strSummary = strSummary & "Number of SubFolders: " _
    & .SubFolderCount & vbNewLine
  strSummary = strSummary & "Has Hidden Files: " _
    & .HasHiddenFiles & vbNewLine
  strSummary = strSummary & "Oldest File Date: " _
    & .OldestFileDate & vbNewLine
  strSummary = strSummary & "Newest File Date: " _
    & .NewestFileDate & vbNewLine
End With
Set objFoldSumm = Nothing

MsgBox strSummary
```

When I ran the test script against C:\WinNT, the same dialog box that we saw in Chapter 8 popped up:

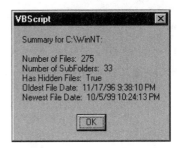

So, even though script components do not directly access a VBScript class construct, we can still use VBScript classes to extend the functionality and maintainability of our script components while leveraging existing VBScript classes that are used in other areas of our business.

279

Summary

Windows Script Components provide added flexibility to web pages and can tightly integrate into your ASP code. You can use these objects as stand alone COM components or you can have them interact directly with ASP pages. A generous portion of scripting, a dash of XML, some Script Component Wizard, and a quick run through `regsvr32` and you have a perfectly formed and ready-to-run script component!

10

The Windows Script Host

Perhaps you noticed that the title of this section of the book is "VBScript in Context". You may be comfortable using VBScript for scripting client-side Web pages; or perhaps for Active Server Pages development – these are nothing more than **contexts** where VBScript can be used for problems in need of scripting solutions. Since VBScript is designed as an ActiveX Scripting engine, it can be used to provide scripting capability for any ActiveX Scripting host environment. Active Server Pages and Internet Explorer are two such host environments. However, both of these hosts come with certain limitations. For instance, Internet Explorer does not provide a capability for interacting with the local computer (such as file system access, etc.) unless the user explicitly sets permissions for this (doing so can cause a security risk; for this reason, this is usually done only for trusted sites and Intranets). That's where Windows Script Host (WSH) comes in. WSH is a scripting language-neutral host interface that works with any ActiveX Scripting Engine, which means that developers can use VBScript, JScript, PerlScript or any other scripting language that expose the ActiveX Scripting interfaces. The WSH host interface thus provides Windows platforms with an easy-to-use yet powerful scripting platform, available from both the Windows GUI and the command prompt.

In this chapter, we will examine the following aspects of Windows Script Host:

- ❑ Tools required for WSH development
- ❑ What WSH can be used for
- ❑ The two execution environments for WSH scripts
- ❑ The use of .WSH files to customize script behavior
- ❑ The WSH object model
- ❑ The .WSF file format, used for creating more advanced scripts
- ❑ Using WSH for network administration

What Tools Do You Need?

In order to begin building solutions using WSH, you need only a few things:

❑ The WSH engine, which comes in both console-style and Windows-based flavors

❑ A text editor, such as Notepad, although one that is designed with programming in mind may be more useful

❑ If you wish to use a scripting language other than VBScript or JScript, you will also need to download and install the proper ActiveX Scripting engine (such as PerlScript from ActiveState, `http://www.activestate.com`)

If your operating system is Windows 98, Windows NT 4.0 with Option Pack 4 installed, or Windows 2000, then you may already have Windows Script Host (WSH 1.0 is provided as an optional component for Win98 and WinNT). However, you may want to ensure that you have the latest version in order to run the scripts included in this chapter. You can download it from the Microsoft Scripting Technologies Web site at `http://msdn.microsoft.com/scripting/windowshost/`. Version 5.1 of the Windows Script engines for JScript and VBScript are included with WSH 2.0.

In addition, you may wish to install the WSH references locally; the aforementioned site provides all of the necessary WSH documentation in a single HTML Help file. When you branch out into using external objects to develop your WSH scripts, you may want to make sure that you have local references for the object model(s) specific to the area of development. There is a great deal of reference documentation available in the MSDN Online Library: `http://msdn.microsoft.com/library/` (this material is also available on the MSDN Library CD, which is included with Microsoft's Visual Studio tools and is also available by separate subscription).

What is the Windows Script Host?

WSH is a technology that exposes some of the underlying functionality of the Microsoft Windows family of operating systems to script developers. By itself, it provides very little other than potential; however, when coupled with VBScript or other scripting languages, WSH provides scriptable access to the Component Object Model (COM) architecture with which many Windows applications are built. This includes applications such as Internet Explorer and the tools which comprise the Microsoft Office suite – any application that exposes an Automation interface can be scripted via WSH. Technically this is a COM IDispatch interface (for those unfamiliar with COM interfaces, IDispatch exposes objects, properties and methods from one application to be used by other tools or applications). Since it is script language-independent, WSH also provides the facility to write scripts in JScript, Perl, Python or any other ActiveX Scripting Language (only VBScript and JScript are available from Microsoft – other ActiveX Scripting engines are available from third parties).

In addition, WSH provides network administrators with a handy toolkit to use for access to machines scattered across a network of computers running various flavors of the Windows operating system family. Much of this access comes through the use of Active Directory Service Interfaces (ADSI) and Windows Management Instrumentation (WMI). ADSI provides a single set of COM interfaces that can be used with multiple directory services, such as the Lightweight Directory Access Protocol (LDAP), the Windows NT directory service, and Novell's Netware and NDS services. WMI is Microsoft's implementation of Web-Based Enterprise Management (WBEM), a standard method of providing access to management information such as applications installed on a given client, system memory, and other client information.

By developing WSH scripts that take advantage of ADSI and WMI, administrators can develop scripts that make it very easy to perform the following tasks and more:

❑   Access and manipulate Web servers

❑   Identify objects as nodes in a network based on properties of the object in question without knowledge of the objects name: "List all computers in domain DomainName"

❑   Add and remove users or change user passwords

❑   Add network file shares

Windows Script Host 2.0 is currently in beta release as of this writing; the final release is scheduled to ship with Windows 2000. Once completed, WSH 2.0 will be available to download for other 32-bit Windows platforms as well. WSH 2.0 offers many new features and is a considerable improvement over WSH 1.0. A few of the new features (many of which were added based on user requests) are:

❑   Support for file inclusion

❑   Ability to use multiple languages within the same script

❑   Support for drag-and-drop functionality

❑   Enhanced access to external objects and type libraries

❑   Stronger debugging capability

❑   A mechanism for pausing script execution (useful for sinking events raised by controlled objects)

❑   Standard input/output and standard error support (only available via console-mode execution with cscript.exe)

WSH 1.0 operated by simply associating the file extension for VBScript (.vbs) and JScript (.js) files with the script host itself, such that if you were to double-click on a script file, it would automatically execute. However, many developers expressed their frustration that this association model did not allow for the use of code modules or for intermixing multiple languages in a single script project. In order to remedy these and other concerns, Microsoft has introduced a new type of script file (.WSF) in WSH 2.0, which utilizes an XML syntax that provides much of the new functionality listed above. This schema includes the tags <script>, <object> and <job>, among others. We'll look at the way this all works toward the end of the chapter.

Note that the file extension `.WSF` will not be available until the final release of WSH 2.0, concurrent with the release of Windows 2000. For developers working with the beta releases of WSH 2.0, the correct file extension to use is `.WS`. This documentation will use the extension `.WSF` exclusively.

Running Scripts with Windows Script Host

WSH provides two interfaces that allow us to execute scripts either on the command line, or from within the Windows environment. Both `cscript.exe` and `wscript.exe` are host programs for the VBScript interpreting engine. The reason there are two is because `cscript.exe` is designed for use from a console window (basically, an MS-DOS box within Windows) while `wscript.exe` is intended to interface directly with the Windows GUI itself. There's not much difference between them.

Command-line Execution

The console interface for executing script files, `cscript.exe`, is called as follows:

Open the Run dialog (Start I Run) or a command window (in Windows 9x, this is done via Start I Programs I DOS Prompt – or in Windows NT via Start I Programs I Command Prompt in Windows NT)

Execute your script as follows:

```
cscript c:\folderName\scriptName.vbs
```

If you run `cscript.exe` with no arguments directly from an MS-DOS window, you will simply get the usage notes:

The following command-line options are provided by `cscript.exe` to allow you to control various settings for the WSH environment:

`//B`	Batch mode – errors and dialogs will not be displayed
`//D`	Enables debugging for current script

`//E:engine`	Executes script, using *engine* (VBScript, JScript, etc.) Allows you to use custom file extensions, while controlling the language engine
`//H:CScript`	Configures `CScript.exe` as default script host
`//H:WScript`	Configures `WScript.exe` as default script host (default)
`//I`	Interactive mode (default, opposite of `//B`)
`//Job:xxxx`	Execute a single job within a `.WSF` file that defines multiple jobs (*see Using .WSF Files for More Advanced Scripts*, near the end of this chapter, for more information on defining jobs)
`//Logo`	Display version and copyright information for scripts executed via `CScript.exe` (default)
`//Nologo`	Prevent logo information from being displayed.
`//S`	Save user-specified command-line options. Overrides default options
`//T:nn`	Set timeout period, where `nn` is the delay in seconds. Scripts will automatically exit if timeout period elapses before execution has completed.
`//X`	Launch script in debugger (as opposed to executing within `cscript/wscript`)

Execution within Windows

The Windows GUI interface for executing script files, `wscript.exe`, allows us to execute files in several ways:

❑   If the file type is registered to execute within WSH, the script can be run by simply double-clicking on its icon in any folder-view window.

❑   Using the Run command dialog, simply type in the full path and name of the script.

❑   Also from the Run dialog, we can invoke `wscript.exe`:

```
wscript c:\folderName\scriptName.vbs
```

If you run `wscript.exe` from an MS-DOS window, you'll get no output in the MS-DOS window; instead you'll see the following dialog box, which provides minimal customization options:

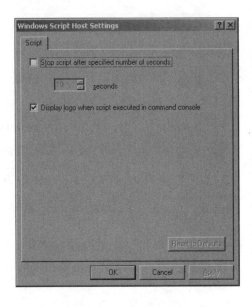

When you click **OK**, nothing happens – the only way to customize script behavior on a system level is through the **cscript** options detailed above. This dialog is used for individual script customization through `.WSH` files, which we'll cover next.

> The difference between cscript and wscript becomes important when debugging a faulty script because sending error messages to a console window can be a lot easier to deal with than the error pop-ups produced by wscript. Thus, cscript is recommended for use when debugging scripts, and it is best to use the Echo method of the WScript object when printing debug output.

Using .WSH Files to Launch Scripts

Perhaps you don't need or want to modify the settings for every script you execute, but you do need to be able to control individual files. This is made possible by creating control files, which have the extension `.WSH`, that allow us to control settings for individual scripts. A `.WSH` file is a small configuration file roughly following the `.INI` file format of past Windows versions. These files are good for customizing the way a script is started up – you can have several different `.WSH` files for the one script.

To create a .WSH file, right-click on a file associated with Windows Script Host (i.e., a file with a .js, .vbs, or .WSF extension), select **Properties**, and then the **Script** tab from the dialog box that appears:

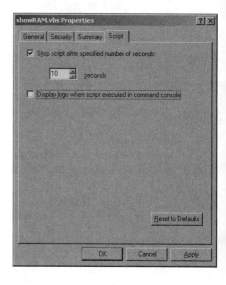

This dialog box allows you to change the timeout default setting and whether or not logo information should be displayed when the script is executed on the command-line. When you apply or accept any changes you have made, a new file will be created, with the same name as the script in question, but containing the extension .WSH. This new file will record these custom settings in a format which the host engines use to set runtime options. Here is what a hypothetical .WSH file created from a script named hello.vbs might look like (in order to execute the script with these options, you would run the hello.wsh file):

```
[ScriptFile]
Path=C:\wsh\hello.vbs

[Options]
Timeout=15
DisplayLogo=1
BatchMode=0
```

Windows Script Host Intrinsic Objects

Every programming environment provides an Object Model that developers can use to implement solutions, and Windows Script Host is no different. WSH contains a core set of objects, containing properties and methods, which can be used to access other computers on a network, import external scriptable objects for use within an application, or connect with Windows or the Windows shell.

The WScript Object

The root of the WSH object model is the WScript object. This object provides properties and methods that allow developers to access name and path information for the script file being executed, determine which version of the Microsoft Scripting engines is currently installed, work with external objects, provide user interaction (as we have already seen) and delay or terminate script execution.

WScript Properties

Application

Exposes the WScript object's **IDispatch** interface, which provides programmatic access to an Automation server application's internal objects, properties and methods.

Syntax
```
Set foo = WScript.Application
```

Arguments

Returns a collection of all arguments passed to the current script either on the command line or in the shortcut used to access the file.

Syntax
```
Set collArgs = WScript.Arguments
```

FullName

Returns a string containing the complete path to the host executable file (`wscript.exe` or `cscript.exe`), `WshShortcut`, or `WshUrlShortcut` object (more on these later).

Syntax
```
strExePath = WScript.FullName
```

Interactive

Sets or retrieves the interaction state (batch or interactive).

Syntax
```
WScript.Interactive = true
boolInteract = WScript.Interactive
```

Name

Returns a string containing the friendly name of the `WScript` object ("Windows Script Host").

Syntax
```
strName = WScript.Name
```

Path

Returns a string containing the parent directory of the active WSH environment (`cscript.exe` or `wscript.exe`).

Syntax
```
strPath = WScript.Path
```

ScriptFullName
Returns a string containing the complete path to the script currently executing.

Syntax

```
strFullName = WScript.ScriptFullName
```

ScriptName
Returns a string containing the file name of the script currently executing.

Syntax

```
strSrcName = WScript.ScriptName
```

StdErr
Provides access to scripts error output stream. This stream is write-only. Only available to scripts being executed from within the command-line host environment `cscript.exe`.

StdIn
Provides access to scripts input stream. This stream is read-only. Only available to scripts being executed from within the command-line host environment `cscript.exe`.

StdOut
Provides access to scripts output stream. This stream is write-only. Only available to scripts being executed from within the command-line host environment `cscript.exe`.

> Note: `StdErr`, `StdIn` and `StdOut` are all implemented as `TextStream` objects. See Chapter 7 for properties and methods exposed by the `TextStream` object. These objects are designed only for use within `cscript`, and will result in a runtime error if executed within `wscript`.

The following example makes use of all three of the built-in stream types to print a list of all files matching a particular extension. This is implemented by piping the output from the DOS `dir` command into the filter script, with an extension string passed as an argument:

```
' Usage:   dir | cscript filter.vbs ext
'          ext: file extension to match
'
Dim streamOut, streamIn, streamErr
Set streamOut = WScript.StdOut
Set streamIn  = WScript.StdIn
Set streamErr = WScript.StdErr

Dim strExt, strLineIn
Dim intMatch
strExt = WScript.Arguments(0)
intMatch = 0
```

```
Do While Not streamIn.AtEndOfStream
  strLineIn = streamIn.ReadLine
  If 0 = StrComp(strExt, Right(strLineIn, Len(strExt)), _
                vbTextCompare) Then
    streamOut.WriteLine strLineIn
    intMatch = intMatch + 1
  End If
Loop

If 0 = intMatch Then
  streamErr.WriteLine "No files of type '" & strExt & "' found"
End If
```

Since this example uses StdIn, StdOut and StdErr for all messaging, you could use it to not only print out matching files to the screen, but also to send output to a text file or another application with redirection or additional piping. For example, you could create a file containing all .vbs files in an entire directory tree, including all subdirectories, with the following command:

```
C:\wsh>dir /s | cscript filter.vbs vbs >> vbsfiles.txt
```

Timeout

Sets or retrieves current timeout length, nDelay, in seconds.

Syntax

```
WScript.Timeout = nDelay
```

Version

Returns a string containing the version number of Windows Script Host.

Syntax

```
strVer = WScript.ScriptVersion
```

WScript Methods

ConnectObject

Used to hook into the event model of an object previously created via the CreateObject or GetObject methods or, if working with the new Windows Script file format, the <object> tag (all of the tags supported by .WSF files will be covered in detail towards the end of the chapter). The object thus connected is required to provide enumeration of its event model for external usage.

Syntax

```
WScript.ConnectObject strObjName, strPrefix
```

strObjName	Name of object to connect
strPrefix	Event function prefix

The following example presumes the existence of a COM object with the progID
`"MyObj.Object"`, which exposes the event `MyEvent`:

```
Set obj = WScript.CreateObject("MyObj.Object")
WScript.ConnectObject(obj, "MyObj")

Sub MyObj_MyEvent()
    ' do something to handle event
End Sub
```

CreateObject

Creates an instance of an Automation object from a passed progID. This instance allows
you to access properties and call methods of the created object. In addition, this method
accepts an optional second argument, which is used as a way to sink events from the
object in order to handle them in your own application.

Syntax

```
Set objFoo = WScript.CreateObject( strProgID [, strPrefix] )
```

`strProgID`	String containing objects program identifier (ProgID).
`strPrefix`	If specified, `strPrefix` provides script developers a hook into the event model of the controlled object. Allows a developer to create event handlers for the internal events raised by the object. If `strPrefix` is set to `"MyObject_"`, and if the application fires an event named "Open", WSH will look for an event handler named `"MyObject_Open"` in the script. Optional.

Example (requires Word 97 or greater)

```
Set objWord = WScript.CreateObject( "Word.Application" )
objWord.Visible = true;
```

DisconnectObject

Disconnects event source object from your script. Inverse of `ConnectObject`. The
object itself is not affected.

Syntax

```
WScript.DisconnectObject objID
```

`objID`	Reference to active object instance.

Example

```
...
WScript.DisconnectObject(objWord)
```

Echo

Provides host-dependent user feedback. If `cscript.exe` is host, arguments to `Echo` are displayed on the command line. If `wscript.exe` is host, arguments are displayed in a Windows pop-up dialog. Comma-separated arguments are displayed as a string with spaces separating the arguments.

Syntax

```
WScript.Echo arg1 [, ... argN]
```

`arg1 [, ... argN]`	String or numeric data.

Example

```
WScript.Echo "foo", "bar", "baz", 123
```

GetObject

Similar to `CreateObject`. Retrieves an instance of an Automation object from a file or progID. This gives you access to an object that already exists somewhere on your computer – like an already running version of some program, or an application with an unknown automation interface. By passing `strProgID`, you can access a specified Automation object from the single call, and by passing `strPrefix`, you can sink the application's events for handling on your own, as with `ConnectObject` and `CreateObject`.

Syntax

```
Set obj = WScript.GetObject(strPath [,strProgID] [,strPrefix])
```

`strPath`	Full path and file name of object to retrieve.
`strProgID`	String containing objects program identifier (ProgID). Optional.
`strPrefix`	See description of `strPrefix` in `CreateObject` notes, above. Optional.

Examples (require Word 97 or greater)

```
' simple example
' retrieves interface through document
Set objDoc = WScript.GetObject( "c:\wsh\test.doc" )
objDoc.Application.Visible = true


' example using strProgID
' iterates through all built-in properties after
' retrieving the 'Word.Document' exposed interface
Set objWord = WScript.GetObject( "c:\test.doc", "Word.Document" )
strProps = ""
For Each Prop in objWord.BuiltInDocumentProperties
  strProps = strProps & Prop.Name & vbCrLf
Next
WScript.Echo strProps
```

Quit

Terminates host execution and returns the argument as an error code. In other words, it kills the `cscript` or `wscript` instance. The optional argument allows you to set an error code for the process' exit. If not included, the return value is 0.

Syntax

```
WScript.Quit [numErrCode]
```

numErrCode	If specified, WSH returns the value as an exit code; otherwise, WSH returns (0) as the process exit code. Optional.

Example

```
If Err.Number <> 0 Then
   WScript.Quit 1    ' some failure indicator
Else
   WScript.Quit 0    ' success
End If
WScript.Quit 1
```

Sleep

Suspends execution of active script for time specified (in milliseconds). After `intDelay` has passed, control is returned to the script.

Syntax

```
WScript.Sleep intDelay
```

intDelay	Delay in milliseconds.

Example

```
WScript.Sleep 1000    ' wait one second
```

Some of the previous methods take a unique identifier (a program identifier, or progID) for the object in question as an input argument and return a reference to an instance of that object, which you can store for later reference. Finding a list of all of these progIDs and their uses is a bit of a voyage of discovery. We're not going to go into in the details of the Microsoft Windows component object model (COM) management facilities as this subject can fill an entire book in itself. Here are two relatively easy methods of discovering progID values for programs installed on a particular computer:

❑ Run `regedit` and look at the second half of the long list under the top level item `HKEY_CLASSES_ROOT`

❑ Get the **OLEView** tool from Microsoft and become familiar with that. You can obtain it via the web from
`http://www.microsoft.com/com/resource/oleview.asp`.

You'll also need proper documentation on the objects you intend to use, in order to take advantage of the features offered by scripted objects. Much of this documentation can be found online or on permanent media (for example, the MSDN Library – both CD and online versions – contains a complete reference for scripting the individual applications which make up the Microsoft Office 2000 suite). Of course, other Wrox publications, such as *Professional IE4 Programming, ISBN 1861000707,* also provide good reference documentation.

The WshArguments Object

The use of arguments in programming tasks is a very useful mechanism for providing your script with input upon which it can act. Consider for a moment what it's like to work at a DOS prompt. Most command-line executables use arguments in order to determine the right thing to do. For example, navigating within a directory structure:

```
c:\>cd wsh
```

In this instance, cd is the name of a DOS command (for change directory), while wsh is the name of the directory activated – it is an argument passed to cd.

Creating scripts that work with arguments is a good step towards writing reusable code. Take the sample code for the description of the WScript.Std* (*=Err, In, Out) properties above. It could have been written to simply filter for a specific file type, but then would have to be changed in order to be useful for other file types. By using the WshArguments object, this script provides much more usefulness.

Developers creating scripts designed to execute on the command-line may immediately see the benefits of working with the Arguments property. However, within WSH, there is another good reason to use this object – that is how drag-and-drop functionality is implemented.

A final justification for the use of this object is that it allows developers to reuse script code within other scripts, by running the script in question as if it were executing on the command-line, passing whatever arguments may be necessary at run-time.

Accessing the WshArguments object

Use WScript.Arguments property:

```
Set collArgs = WScript.Arguments
```

WshArguments Properties

Since the WshArguments object returns a collection, it merely exposes all of the properties of the WshCollection object, which is detailed later in this chapter. All internal collections exposed by Windows Script Host are implemented as WshCollection objects.

The following sample simply loops through the `WshArguments` collection, displaying each in turn.

```
Set collArgs = WScript.Arguments
For inx = 0 To collArgs.Count - 1
  WScript.Echo collArgs(inx)
Next
```

The interesting thing here is that this works in both `cscript` and `wscript`. Try it yourself – save the sample as `echoargs.vbs`, then execute on the command line, passing a few arguments:

```
c:\wsh\echoargs foo bar baz
```

Here's the output from this simple script:

Now try opening up your test folder, and dragging a file or two, then dropping them on `echoargs.vbs`. If you drag a file named `testme.txt` onto your `echoargs.vbs` file, you should see the following:

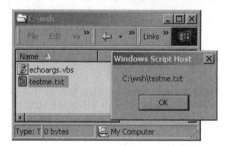

The WshShell object

Windows Script Host provides a convenient way to gain access to system environment variables, create shortcuts, access Windows special folders such as the Desktop, and add or remove entries from the registry. In addition, it is possible to create more customized dialogs for user interaction by using features of the Shell object.

Accessing the WshShell object

Developers should create an instance of the object `WScript.Shell` in order to work with the properties listed below. Further references to the `WshShell` object will refer to this created instance.

```
Set WshShell= WScript.CreateObject( "WScript.Shell" )
```

WshShell Properties

Environment

Returns a handle to the `WshEnvironment` object. Usage of this object is described in the section on the `WshEnvironment` object, below.

Syntax

```
Set WshEnvironment = WshShell.Environment [("ENV_VAR")]
```

> Note: excluding the parameter returns **PROCESS** environment variables by default on Windows 9x, and **SYSTEM** by default on Windows NT 4 / Windows 2000.

SpecialFolders

Returns a handle to the `WshSpecialFolders` object. Usage of this object is described in the section on the `WshSpecialFolders` object, below.

Syntax

```
// retrieve entire collection of folders
Set WshFolders = WshShell.SpecialFolders
// retrieve a single folder
objDesktop = WshShell.SpecialFolders("Desktop")
```

Example

```
// echo all special folders in collection
Set WshShell = WScript.CreateObject("WScript.Shell")
str = ""
For Each Folder In WshShell.SpecialFolders
  str = str & Folder & vbCrLf
Next
WScript.Echo str
```

WshShell Methods

AppActivate

Activates an application window, based on passed `strTitle`. Returns success or failure.

Syntax

```
' capturing return
retval = WshShell.AppActivate(strTitle)
' not capturing return
WshShell.AppActivate strTitle
```

strTitle	If strTitle exactly matches that of a current running application window, that window will be activated; otherwise, the title of each active window will be checked to see if it begins with strTitle. If still no match is found, all windows will be checked again to determine whether they end with strTitle.

Example

```
...
WshShell.Run "notepad"
retval = WshShell.AppActivate("Notepad")
If retval Then
  WshShell.SendKeys "Hello, World!"
End If
```

CreateShortcut

Returns a handle to a WshShortcut or WshUrlShortcut object, depending on the extension of the created shortcut. Shortcuts created with the extension .LNK become WshShortcut objects, which are intended for linking files on a local system or LAN. Those created with the extension .URL are WshUrlShortcut objects, designed to provide links to Web pages on the Internet or a company intranet.

Syntax

```
Set objLink = WshShell.CreateShortcut(strPath)
```

strPath	Path and file name of shortcut being created.

Examples of usage will follow in the sections on WshShortcut and WshUrlShortcut objects.

ExpandEnvironmentStrings

Returns a string representing the expanded value of the requested environment string. Variables passed into the method are surrounded with the % character.

Syntax

```
str = WshShell.ExpandEnvironmentStrings("%strEnv%")
```

strEnv	Name of desired environment variable.

Example

```
Set WshShell = CreateObject("WScript.Shell")
strWinDir = WshShell.ExpandEnvironmentStrings("%WinDir%")
WScript.Echo "Your Windows directory is: " & strWinDir
```

Chapter 10

LogEvent

Writes an event to the event log. In Windows NT, this is written to the NT Event log. In Windows 9x, this is written to the file `WSH.log` in the `%windir%` directory.

Syntax

```
WshShell.LogEvent intType, strMsg [,strTarget]
```

intType	Number corresponding to the type of the event (see next table for possible values).
strMsg	Text to be entered into the log.
strTarget	Name of system where event should be logged (defaults to local system). Optional. (Windows NT only, ignored on Windows 9x.)

The following table lists the possible values that can be used as the first argument to `LogEvent`, along with their predefined meanings:

0	Success
1	Error
2	Warning
4	Information
8	Audit_success
16	Audit_failure

Example

```
Set WshShell = WScript.CreateObject("WScript.Shell")
' assume that boolRet contains a return code
' from another application
If boolRet Then
  WshShell.LogEvent 0, "Application success"
Else
  WshShell.LogEvent 1, "Application failure"
End If
```

Popup

Shows a modal dialog window containing script-defined settings – message, title and display characteristics. The button that is clicked in the window determines the return value from `Popup`. See the Microsoft Scripting documentation for detailed information regarding return values (`http://msdn.microsoft.com/scripting/windowshost/`).

Syntax

```
intReturn = WshShell.Popup strMsg [,intDelay] [,strTitle] [,intFeatures]
```

`strMsg`	Message to be displayed.
`intDelay`	The number of seconds to wait before closing the pop-up window. Optional. If using `strTitle` and `intFeatures`, this should be set to zero (0) if you do not want the window to dismiss itself.
`strTitle`	The text to appear in the windows title bar. Optional.
`intFeatures`	Display features for the window, to include icons and buttons. Optional.

The actual values of features set using `intFeatures` are determined by comparison to the Windows operating system internal values. Listed below are a few examples; see Appendix D for a complete list.

0	Button: OK
1	Button: OK and Cancel
3	Button: Yes, No, and Cancel
16	Icon: Stop sign
32	Icon: Question Mark
48	Icon: Exclamation Mark

Example

```
Set WshShell = WScript.CreateObject("WScript.Shell")
strMsg = "Hello from Windows Script Host!"
strTitle = "WSH Popup dialog"
intReturn = WshShell.Popup(strMsg, 0, strTitle, 48 + 3)
WScript.Echo "Return value: " & intReturn
```

RegDelete
Removes keys or values from the Windows registry. Under Windows NT and Windows 2000, it is not possible to delete keys that contain sub-keys.

Syntax

```
WshShell.RegDelete strKeyValue
```

`strKeyValue`	Name of key or value to delete.

RegRead
Reads keys or values from the Windows registry. `RegRead` is unable to read a key unless its default value is set; attempting to do so will generate a runtime error number (identical to the error generated if the key doesn't exist -- checking `err.description` will yield the difference). In addition, `RegRead` cannot read valid named values containing "\" in the value name; the slash is interpreted as delimiting nodes in the key string.

Syntax

```
WshShell.RegRead(strKeyValue)
```

strKeyValue	Name of key or value to read. Supports the following data types: REG_SZ, REG_EXPAND_SZ, REG_DWORD, REG_BINARY, and REG_MULTI_SZ; returns DISP_E_TYPEMISMATCH for other data types.

RegWrite

Writes keys or values to the Windows registry.

Syn tax

```
WshShell.RegWrite strName, anyValue [,strType]
```

strName	Name of key or value where data should be written.
anyValue	Value to write into the key or value.
strType	Data type for value being stored in the registry. Optional. Valid values for strType are REG_SZ, REG_EXPAND_SZ, REG_DWORD, and REG_BINARY, and returns E_INVALIDARG if other data types are passed.

Example (shows use of all registry methods)

```
Set WshShell = WScript.CreateObject("WScript.Shell")
WshShell.Popup "Setting registry value"
WshShell.RegWrite "HKCU\WSHTestKey", "WSH test value"
WshShell.Popup "Reading registry value" & vbCrLf & _
               "Value: " & WshShell.RegRead("HKCU\WSHTestKey")
WshShell.Popup "Deleting registry value"
WshShell.RegDelete "HKCU\WSHTestKey"
```

> **Note: It is important to be very careful when modifying registry settings. Making incorrect changes to the registry can cause your system to become unstable or unusable. If you are not familiar with the inner workings of the registry, you are strongly advised to do some reading on the subject before beginning to experiment on your own.**

If we had wanted to set an actual registry key, as opposed to a simple value, we could have done this quite easily as well, by ending the string passed as an argument to RegWrite with a backslash:

```
WshShell.RegWrite "HKCU\WSHTestKey\", "WSH test value"
```

Run

Execute an application in a new process.

Syntax

```
WshShell.Run(strCmd [,intWinStyle] [,boolWait])
```

strCmd	String containing the application name and path, or other command (such as a DOS command) to execute.
intWinStyle	Sets window style of program being executed. Optional.
boolWait	If not passed, or passed as false, immediately resumes script execution, and returns 0 (zero).
	If set to true, the Run method waits for the child process to end and returns any error code from the application.

Example

```
Set WshShell = WScript.CreateObject("WScript.Shell")
strScript = WScript.ScriptFullName

' if not capturing return value, call as Sub
WshShell.Run "notepad " & strScript, 1, TRUE

' if capturing return value, call as Function
return = WshShell.Run("%windir%\notepad " & strScript, 1, TRUE)
```

Note that in the second call (where the return value is captured), Run is executed as a function; the arguments passed are contained in a set of parentheses. However, when not capturing the return value, Run is called as a subprocedure, without parentheses. In addition, note that the second example contains an environment string – this is automatically expanded by the host before execution, so that the call receives a complete argument.

SendKeys
Programmatically sends keystroke sequences to the active application (most likely activated through the AppActivate method) as if the input were entered from a keyboard. The host will not allow the sequence " ^%{DEL} ", which represents *CTRL+ALT+DEL*, to be sent, so programmatic rebooting of servers is not possible using this technique.

Syntax

```
WshShell.SendKeys strKeys
```

| strKeys | String representation of keystrokes to send to active application. See WSH documentation for complete list of specific key codes used. |

Example

This example shows the `Run`, `AppActivate` and `SendKeys` methods together.

```
...
WshShell.Run "Notepad"
WshShell.AppActivate("Notepad")
WScript.Sleep 500
WshShell.SendKeys "Hello, Wodlr!"
WScript.Sleep 500
WshShell.SendKeys "{LEFT 4}"
WScript.Sleep 500
WshShell.SendKeys "{DEL 3}"
WScript.Sleep 500
WshShell.SendKeys "rld"
```

The WshNetwork Object

Windows Script Host is commonly used for creating login scripts for computers that are part of a corporate network. These scripts can make it easier for users to get their important work done by mapping to commonly used network file servers and connecting to one or more network printers. This is where the `WshNetwork` object comes in handy. This object provides important functionality to be used for many network connectivity needs.

Accessing the WshNetwork Object

Accessed by creating an instance of `WScript.Network`.

```
Set WshNetwork = WScript.CreateObject("WScript.Network")
```

WshNetwork Properties

ComputerName
Returns a string containing the computer name.

Syntax

```
strCompName = WshNetwork.ComputerName
```

UserDomain
Returns a string containing the user domain.

Syntax

```
strDomain = WshNetwork.UserDomain
```

UserName
Returns a string containing the username. Commonly used in network logon scripts. Under Windows 9x, logon scripts runs before the user is fully logged on, so scripts should query the `UserName` property in a loop until it contains a non-blank string.

Syntax

```
strName = WshNetwork.UserName
```

WshNetwork Methods

AddPrinterConnection

Maps a network printer to a printer port on a local computer, allowing you to send print jobs from your computer to a remote printer. Printers connected using this method are only recognized in DOS (they do not show up under Settings|Printers from the Start menu).

Syntax

```
WshNetwork.AddPrinterConnection strPort, strPrinterName _
                            [,boolUpdate] [,strUser] [,strPassword]
```

strPort	Printer port to connect (such as LPT1:)
strPrinterName	Network share for remote printer
boolUpdate	If true, printer mapping stored in user profile. Optional.
strUser, strPassword	Used when mapping a shared network resource for someone other than currently logged-on user. Optional.

Example

```
WshNetwork.AddPrinterConnection _
    "LPT1:", "\\printserver\printername"
```

AddWindowsPrinterConnection

Maps a network printer to a printer port on a local computer, allowing you to send print jobs from your computer to a remote printer. Printers added using this method are available to Windows applications (appear under Start|Settings|Printers).

Syntax (Windows NT/Windows 2000)

```
WshNetwork.AddWindowsPrinterConnection(strPrinter)
```

Example

```
strPath = "\\printserver\printername"
WshNetwork.AddWindowsPrinterConnection(strPath)
```

Syntax (Windows 9x)

```
WshNetwork.AddWindowsPrinterConnection(strPrinter, strDriver [,strPort])
```

Example

```
strPath = "\\printserver\printername"
strDriver = "HP DeskJet 890C"
WshNetwork.AddWindowsPrinterConnection(strPath, strPort, "LPT1:")
```

strPrinter	Network share for remote printer
strDriver	Name of printer driver. Required on Windows 95/98 (driver must be already installed); ignored if used on Windows NT/Windows 2000.
strPort	Printer port to connect (defaults to LPT1). Ignored if used on Windows NT/Windows 2000. Optional.

EnumNetworkDrives
Returns a collection containing current network drive mappings.

Syntax
```
collDrives = WshNetwork.EnumNetworkDrives
```

EnumPrinterConnections
Returns a collection containing current network printer mappings.

Syntax
```
collDrives = WshNetwork.EnumNetworkPrinters
```

Note: the two methods `EnumNetworkDrives()` and
`EnumPrinterConnections()` have somewhat unusual return values, in
that values are returned in pairs. The first is the local resource (drive
letter or port) while the second is the mapped network share. Thus, in the
example below, `collNetDrive(0)` will contain `"Q"`, and
`collNetDrive(1)` will contain `"\\server\share"`.

MapNetworkDrive
Maps a network shared resource to a local drive letter.

Syntax
```
WshNetwork.MapNetworkDrive strDrive, strSharePath _
                          [,boolUpdate] [,strUser] [,strPassword]
```

Parameters

strDrive	Local drive letter to use for mapping
strSharePath	Network share
boolUpdate	If true, mapping stored in user profile. Optional.
strUser and strPassword	Used when mapping a shared network resource for someone other than currently logged-on user. Optional.

Example
```
WshNetwork.MapNetworkDrive "Q:", "\\server\share"
```

RemoveNetworkDrive

Removes a network drive, either mapped to a local drive letter or merely remotely connected.

Syntax

```
WshNetwork.RemoveNetworkDrive strName [,boolForce] [,boolUpdate]
```

strName	If mapping exists between local name (drive letter) and network share, then strName is the local name. If no local name (drive letter) mapping exists, strName is the remote name.
boolForce	If true, connection will be removed whether in use or not. Optional.
boolUpdate	If true, mapping stored in user profile. Optional.

Example (based on MapNetworkDrive example)

```
WshNetwork.RemoveNetworkDrive "Q:"
```

RemovePrinterConnection

Removes a networked printer connection, either mapped to a local port or remotely connected.

Syntax

```
WshNetwork.RemovePrinterConnection strName [,boolForce] [,boolUpdate]
```

strName	If mapping exists between local port (such as LPT1) and network share, then strName is the local name. If no port mapping exists, strName is the remote name.
boolForce	If true, connection will be removed whether in use or not. Optional.
boolUpdate	If true, mapping stored in user profile. Optional.

Example (based on AddPrinterConnection example)

```
WshNetwork.RemovePrinterConnection "LPT1:"
```

SetDefaultPrinter

Establishes printer connection as default printer.

Syntax (based on AddPrinterConnection example)

```
WshNetwork.SetDefaultPrinter strName
```

strName	Remote printer name or local printer port.

Example (based on AddPrinterConnection example)

```
WshNetwork.SetDefaultPrinter "LPT1:"
```

307

The following example uses all properties and methods of the `WshNetwork` object:

> **Please note that this example requires an active network connection to work correctly. In addition, running this script on your computer may end up modifying your existing settings.**

```
Dim strShare, strPrint
strShare = "\\fileserver\share"
strPrint = "\\printserver\printer"
Dim WshNetwork, collNetDrive, collNetPrint
Set WshNetwork = WScript.CreateObject("WScript.Network")

' map network share, printer, set printer default
WScript.Echo vbCrLf & "Mapping network drive: " & strShare
WshNetwork.MapNetworkDrive "Z:", strShare
WScript.Echo vbCrLf & "Mapping printer share: " & strPrint
WshNetwork.AddWindowsPrinterConnection strPrint
WshNetwork.SetDefaultPrinter strPrint

WScript.Echo vbCrLf & _
  "Computer Name: " & WshNetwork.ComputerName & _
  vbCrLf & "Current User: " & WshNetwork.UserName & _
  vbCrLf & "User Domain: " & WshNetwork.UserDomain

' get network drives and printers collections
Set collNetDrive = WshNetwork.EnumNetworkDrives
Set collNetPrint = WshNetwork.EnumPrinterConnections

' echo all networked drives and printers
For i = 0 To collNetDrive.Count - 1
  WScript.Echo vbCrLf & collNetDrive(i) & " > " & collNetDrive(i+1)
  i = i + 1
Next
For j = 0 To collNetPrint.Count - 1
  WScript.Echo vbCrLf & collNetPrint(j) & " > " & collNetPrint(j+1)
  j = j + 1
Next

' remove mapped drive and printer
WshNetwork.RemoveNetworkDrive "Z:"
WshNetwork.RemovePrinterConnection "LPT1:"
```

The WshShortcut Object

The same method of the `WshShell` object is used for creating both `WshShortcut` and `WshURLShortcut` objects – the primary difference being the file extension given to the actual shortcut file: A **WshShortcut** object is created when the extension is `.lnk`, and a `WshURLShortcut` object is created when the extension is `.url`.

The standard `WshShortcut` object can be used to create shortcuts to any system resource such as a file or folder, or even to a Web address.

Accessing the WshShortcut object

To create an instance of the `WshShortcut` object, use the `CreateShortcut` method of `WshShell`. The path specified must be a complete path to the shortcut location.

WshShortcut Properties

Arguments
Text string of arguments to be passed to the application defined in `TargetPath` property.

Description
Sets or retrieves descriptive text representing the shortcut.

Syntax
```
objShortcut.Description = str
```

str	String to assign description value to.

Example
```
...
Set objShortcut = WshShell.CreateShortcut "foo.lnk"
objShortcut.Description = "This is a link to foo."
```

FullName
Returns a read-only string containing the complete path to the file being executed.

Syntax
```
retval = objShortcut.FullName
```

Example
```
...
WScript.Echo objShortcut.FullName
```

Hotkey
Allows a keyboard shortcut to be created for the `WshShortcut` object. Hotkeys can only activate shortcuts which exist on the Windows desktop or the Start menu.

Syntax
```
objShortcut.Hotkey = strHotkey
```

Possible values for `strHotKey` are as follows (`Hotkey` values are case-sensitive):

Meta Keys	Standard Keys
ALT+	*A...Z*
CTRL+	*0...9*
SHIFT+	*Back*
EXT+	*Tab*
	Clear
	Return
	Escape
	Space
	Prior
	...

Example

```
objShortcut.Hotkey = "CTRL+SHIFT+Z"
```

IconLocation

Assigns an icon to the `WshShortcut` object.

Syntax

```
objShortcut.IconLocation = strIconLocation
```

strIconLocation	String in the form location, index as in example below.

Example

```
...
objShortcut.IconLocation = "C:\explorer.exe, 0"
```

TargetPath

Assigns path to executable with which the shortcut is associated.

Syntax

```
objShortcut.TargetPath = strPath
```

strPath	Path to which shortcut should resolve.

Example

```
objShortcut.TargetPath = "C:\foo.exe"
```

WindowStyle
Assigns window style to shortcut.

Syntax
```
objShortcut.WindowStyle = intStyle
```

Possible values for `intStyle` are as follows:

1	Sets window active, restoring original size and position if applicable.
3	Maximized window.
7	Minimized window.

Example
```
objShortcut.WindowStyle = 3
```

WorkingDirectory
Sets active directory for the shortcut object.

Syntax
```
objShortcut.WorkingDirectory = strPath
```

`strPath`	Initial directory for shortcut.

Example
```
objShortcut.WorkingDirectory = "c:\"
```

WshShortcut Method

Save
Saves shortcut object to location specified by argument to `CreateShortcut`. This method is required to complete creation of a new shortcut.

Syntax
```
objShortcut.Save
```

The following sample makes use of all of the `WshShortcut` properties as well as its `Save` method.

```
Set WshShell = WScript.CreateObject("WScript.Shell")
strLink = WshShell.SpecialFolders("Desktop") + "WSHtest.lnk"
Set WshShortcut = WshShell.CreateShortcut(strLink)
WshShortcut.Description = "Test shortcut created from WSH."
WshShortcut.TargetPath = "notepad.exe"
WshShortcut.IconLocation = "notepad.exe, 0"
WshShortcut.Hotkey = "CTRL+SHIFT+X"
WshShortcut.WindowStyle = 1
WshShortcut.WorkingDirectory = "C:\"
WshShortcut.Save
```

The WshUrlShortcut Object

This object provides a means to create a special shortcut type: a reference to a Web page on the Internet or a company Intranet. Remember that creating a URL shortcut is differentiated from creating a regular shortcut by the different file extension used in the call to `CreateShortcut`. To create a `WshUrlShortcut` object, you would use the extension .URL instead of .LNK. Another difference is that this object exposes far fewer properties than does the `WshShortcut` object.

Accessing the WshUrlShortcut object

Same as `WshShortcut`, above.

WshUrlShortcut Property

TargetPath
See descriptions for these properties under the `WshShortcut` object, above.

WshUrlShortcut Method

Save
See description for `WshShortcut` object, above.
Here's a quick example showing the creation of a URL shortcut on the Desktop, pointing to the Wrox home page:

```
Set WshShell = WScript.CreateObject("WScript.Shell")
strURL = WshShell.SpecialFolders("Desktop") + "Wrox Home.url"
Set WshShortcut = WshShell.CreateShortcut(strPath)
WshShortcut.TargetPath = "http://www.wrox.com/"
WshShortcut.Save
```

The WshCollection Object

This object is the base representation for all collections returned by objects, properties or methods internal to Windows Script Host.

Accessing the WshCollection object

There are five ways to retrieve collections under WSH:

- ❑ The *Arguments* property of *WScript*
- ❑ The *EnumNetworkDrives* method of *WshNetwork*
- ❑ The *EnumPrinterConnections* method of *WshNetwork*
- ❑ The *SpecialFolders* property of *WshShell*
- ❑ The *WshEnvironment* object.

WshCollection Properties

Item

Returns an item from a collection, by index. This is the default property for all collections exposed as part of the Windows Script Host object model.

Length

Returns the number of items in the collection. Return value is identical to return value from `Count`. Implemented for JScript compatibility.

Count

Returns the number of items in the collection. Return value is identical to return value from `Length`.

```
Set collArgs = WScript.Arguments
For inx = 0 To collArgs.Count - 1
  WScript.Echo collArgs.Item(inx)
Next
```

The WshEnvironment Object

When a developer needs to access system specifics such as the operating system version or information pertaining to processor type, the place to look is within the system's environment variables, stored as a collection of unique `name=value` pairs.

Accessing the WshEnvironment Object

WSH provides a method to get this information through the `Environment` property of the `WshShell` object:

```
Set WshEnvironment = WshShell.Environment
```

There are four sets of Environment variables available: `System`, `User`, `Volatile`, and `Process`. Accessing a variable set other than the default is shown in the example below.

> Note: if you wish to access the default set of environment variables, do not use an empty set of parentheses after the `Environment` keyword – doing so will generate a script error.

WshEnvironment Properties

The `WshEnvironment` object contains all the properties exposed by `WshCollection`.

WshEnvironment Methods

Remove

Deletes environment variable specified as argument to method.

Syntax

```
WshEnvironment.Remove(strEnvVar)
```

strEnvVar	Environment variable

Example

```
Set WshShell = WScript.CreateObject("WScript.Shell")
Set WshEnvironment = WshShell.Environment("process")
WshEnvironment.Remove("Example_Env_Var")
```

The following is a brief example showing how to access specific process variables:

```
Set WshShell = WScript.CreateObject("WScript.Shell")
Set WshEnvironment = WshShell.Environment("process")
WScript.Echo WshEnvironment("WINDIR")
WScript.Echo WshEnvironment("PATH")
```

This example shows how to iterate over the entire collection, followed by its output under Windows 2000:

```
Set WshShell = CreateObject("Wscript.Shell")
Set WshEnvironment = WshShell.Environment
For Each var In WshEnvironment
  strEnv = strEnv & var & vbCrLf
Next
WScript.Echo strEnv
```

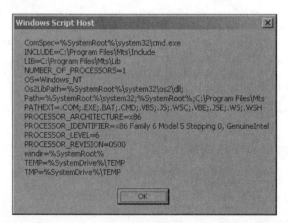

Note: due to the internal structure of Windows NT 4 and Windows 2000, much more information is available when accessing system environment information under these systems than when using Windows 95/98.

Windows NT/Windows 2000:
All Environment variable types are available: `System`, `User`, `Volatile`, and `Process`. If no type is passed, the default is `System`.

Windows 95/Windows 98:
Only Environment variables of type `Process` are available. This will be the default if no value is specified.

The WshSpecialFolders Object

This object provides access to Windows shell folders, which is a group of various folders used by the operating system for storage of items needed for proper system operation, such as the Start menu, Favorites folder, and the Windows Desktop. The actual file locations of Windows special folders are dependent on the operating system and location of the default Windows installation directory, so they may not be in the same place on one computer that they are on another. The `WshSpecialFolders` collection helps developers get around this, making it very easy to access these folders.

Why would you want to use this object? Here's an example: perhaps your company wants to add a standard set of Favorites to the Favorites menu (exposed by Internet Explorer, among other applications). This is a perfect use for the `WshSpecialFolders` object. We can get a reference to the object (shown below), retrieve from it the path to the Favorites folder, which can then be used in conjunction with the `GetFolder` method of the `FileSystemObject` (features of the Scripting Runtime library, documented in Chapter 7) to get a reference to the actual folder. Once this reference is attained, you can add URL shortcuts and/or folders to it.

Remember that the file locations to which these shortcuts resolve is dependent upon the actual user profile in use when the shortcut is created. This is a consideration by default when using Windows NT 4.0 or Windows 2000, and will be an issue if user profiles are active on an installation of Windows 9*x*.

Accessing the WshSpecialFolders Object

The `WshSpecialFolders` object is available via the `SpecialFolders` property of `WshShell`.

```
Set WshSpecialFolders = WshShell.SpecialFolders
```

WshSpecialFolders Properties

Since the `WshSpecialFolders` object returns a collection, it exposes all of the properties of the `WshCollection` object, which is detailed above.

The following sample prints out all members of the `WshSpecialFolders` collection:

```
Set WshShell = WScript.CreateObject("WScript.Shell")
Set WshSpecialFolders = WshShell.SpecialFolders
For intx = 0 To WshSpecialFolders.Count - 1
    WScript.Echo WshSpecialFolders.Item(intx)
Next
```

Here's the output of the above script, when executed using `cscript`:

Using .WSF Files for More Advanced Scripts

With WSH 1.0, developers were limited to using a single scripting language to access the system - the host determined the appropriate action based on the extension of the file being executed. Thus, in the case of a VBScript file, Windows mapped its `.vbs` extension to WSH, which controlled its execution, passing the contents of the file off to the VBScript engine for interpretation and execution.

The features available in WSH 2.0 are quite an improvement over version 1.0, primarily due to the fact that, in addition to JScript and VBScript files, the host now recognizes a new file type: Windows Script (`.WSF`) file (remember, `.WS` is the extension used in beta releases of WSH 2.0).

The Windows Script file provides increased functionality and flexibility over that available from `.js` and `.vbs` files, using a simple XML syntax. The following description of the XML elements available in the WSH schema assumes some familiarity with tag-based markup and container models such as that used in HTML.

Unless stated otherwise, all of these tags are container tags, meaning that each requires matching opening and closing tags, as follows:

```
<tag>
  your content here
</tag>
```

If you are new to XML, please note one crucial difference from HTML syntax. All empty elements in XML require a terminating slash in order to be recognized as valid elements by the XML parsing engine:

```
<element attrib="value"/>
```

Empty elements exist in HTML as well - such as `<IMG>` and `<BR>`. Since HTML is not as rigid a syntax as XML, empty HTML elements do not need the terminating slash. The reason for the difference is that, in the interest of having a small, clean parsing engine, XML requires that every opening tag have a corresponding closing tag. In the case of empty elements, the open and close are the same.

<?xml?>

Standard XML declaration - forces WSH to parse the file rigidly as XML, enforcing case-sensitivity. This is an empty element. This element is optional, and must be the first tag to appear when used. Note, the standalone attribute is not required, and `"yes"` is the only valid value for this attribute.

Syntax

```
<?xml version="1.0" [standalone="yes"]?>
```

<?job?>

This element is a processing instruction that specifies error-handling attributes. This is an empty element, and should appear prior to the opening `<job>` or `<package>` tag. The `error` attribute should be set to true to allow the script to raise error messages, and the `debug` attribute should be true to enable debugging (setting otherwise will prevent the script from running in the script debugger).

Syntax

```
<?job error="true|false|1|0" debug="true|false|1|0"?>
```

<package>

Provides a way for developers to include the necessary code for multiple jobs within a single file. All multi-job files must have this element as the root. Optional.

Syntax

```
<package>
<job id="job1">
  <!-- do something -->
</job>
<job id="job2">
  <!-- do something else -->
</job>
</package>
```

<job>

Provides a method for defining multiple jobs within a single file, used in conjunction with the `<package>` tag.

Syntax

```
<job [id="jobID"]>
  <!-- do something -->
</job>
```

<object>

Used to define scriptable external objects without the use of methods such as `CreateObject` and `GetObject`. Objects defined using the `<object>` tag are available globally. This is an empty element. Optional. Child of `<job>`.

Syntax

```
<object
  id="objID"
  [classid="clsid:GUID" | progid="programID"]/>
```

<reference>
Provides an inclusion mechanism to be used as a way to access type library information without having to create an instance of an object. This is an empty element. Optional. Child of <job>.

Syntax

```
<reference
   [object="progID"|guid="typelibGUID"]
   [version="version"]/>
```

<resource>
Allows a developer to declare string or numeric data to be used within a WSH application, while keeping this data separate from the actual script code. Commonly used for strings that require localization. Optional. Child of <job>. Note; evidently support for <resource> was added as of WSH 2.0 beta 2, and documentation of this tag was not included in the HTML Help file available for the beta release. This situation will be remedied for the final release.

Syntax

```
<job>
  <resource id="resErr">
    An error has occurred in this script.
  </resource>
  <script language="VBScript">
    ' catch an error
    WScript.Echo getResource("resErr")
  </script>
</job>
```

<script>
Uses the familiar HTML syntax. Can be used for external script inclusion by setting the src attribute to a valid file or UNC path, or for embedding script code directly into your WSH application. Child of <job>.

Syntax

```
<script [language="VBScript"] [src="strFilePath"]>
  ' script code here ...
</script>
```

When WSH scripts are being developed with strict adherence to XML conventions enabled (due to the inclusion of the <?xml?> processing instruction), inline script should be wrapped in a CDATA section. Otherwise special characters within the script code cause trouble when parsing the XML structure, as these characters may also have specific but conflicting meanings in XML. For example, the less than (<) symbol may be interpreted as starting a new element, while bitwise or Boolean and operations (& or &&) may be interpreted as unrecognized external entities. In order to avoid these problems, use this syntax when following XML-based lexical rules:

```
<?xml version="1.0"?>
<job>
  <script language="VBScript"><![CDATA[
    ' script code here
  ]]></script>
</job>
```

Including the CDATA processing instruction informs the XML parser that all information included within the CDATA block should be treated as literal Character DATA, not as characters that the parser needs to recognize. For more information on CDATA, see the World Wide Web Consortium's XML 1.0 Recommendation at http://www.w3.org/TR/1998/REC-xml-19980210.

The following is a brief example of the .WSF format, which shows how this new file type can be used to combine multiple script languages into a single larger functional script:

```
<?xml version="1.0" standalone="yes"?>
<job>
  <script language="VBScript">
  <![CDATA[
     Function ShowInputBox(str)
        ShowInputBox = InputBox(str)
     End Function
  ]]>
  </script>
  <script language="JScript">
  <![CDATA[
     var sMsg = "hello from a VBS InputBox";
     var sInput = ShowInputBox(sMsg);
     WScript.Echo(sInput);
  ]]>
  </script>
</job>
```

For additional documentation on the optional attributes of these elements, see the online documentation available on the Microsoft Scripting Technologies Web site (http://msdn.microsoft.com/scripting/windowshost/). Full documentation in the HTML Help format is also available for download from this site.

Network Administration with Windows Script Host

Windows Script Host offers a great deal of power and flexibility for network administrators who wish to automate routine tasks such as managing user accounts; starting, stopping or pausing Internet Information Services, or creating and deleting file shares.

> Note: This section will focus primarily on network administration using Active Directory Service Interfaces (ADSI) 2.5. If you are interested in using WSH in conjunction with Windows Management Instrumentation (WMI), please consult the WMI documentation included in the MSDN Library (http://msdn.microsoft.com/library/) under the **Platform SDK | Management Services** node.

ADSI 2.5 is available as part of a default install of Windows 2000, and the product is available for download for other 32-bit Windows platforms from the Microsoft Web site http://www.microsoft.com/ntserver/nts/downloads/other/adsi25/default.asp along with documentation and SDK.

Before we go too far here, let's get a better understanding of the territory. A `directory` contains information about objects in a distributed network, such as printers, databases, and other users. A `directory service` contains both the directory and the services that make these objects available to users and network administrators.

Briefly, ADSI allows you to interact with disparate directory services by providing a common set of interfaces that can be used for interaction with multiple providers. Consider how a Java compiler translates from Java code to machine-specific instructions. ADSI works similarly – it allows you to connect to various different providers with similar code, whereas previously you would have been required to learn many different techniques for connecting to the namespaces of various providers. Providers included with ADSI 2.5 include the following – please be aware that these names are *case-sensitive*, and require the terminating colon:

`WinNT:`	Connection to Windows NT4.0 domain controllers.
`LDAP:`	Connection to Lightweight Directory Access Protocol servers, which include Windows 2000 Active Directory and Exchange 5.
`NDS:`	Connection to Novell Directory Services servers.
`NWCOMPAT:`	Connection to NetWare servers.
`IIS:`	Connection to Internet Information Services Administration objects.

The rest of this section will briefly cover how to undertake a few common network administration tasks via provider connections using the `WinNT:` protocol. This is not intended to be a thorough examination of ADSI, or even of the `WinNT:` subset; such an undertaking would require an entire volume unto itself. All of the code samples presented here are using simple, standard ADSI functionality – there's no WSH magic being performed. The samples could easily be used in an ASP page or in a Visual Basic application.

The following table covers a few of the connection types available when using the `WinNT:` binding string:

`WinNT://DomainName`	Binds to root of `DomainName`
`WinNT://ServerName/Users`	Binds to `Users` collection on `ServerName`
`WinNT://DomainName/JohnDoe,user`	Binds to user `DomainName\JohnDoe`
`WinNT://DomainName/DC/GroupName,group`	Binds to `GroupName` on the DC domain controller
`WinNT://ComputerName,computer`	Binds to computer `ComputerName`

Binding to ADSI objects is accomplished with the `GetObject` method, as shown here. This example creates a binding to the group `DomainName\Users`, and lists all users in the group:

```
' Enumerate members of group "Users"
Set objGroup = GetObject("WinNT://DomainName/Users")
For Each Member in objGroup.Members
  WScript.Echo Member.Name
Next
```

Here are some code snippets for common administrivia.

A simple example of creating a new user in a domain, and adding to the group `Users`:

```
Set objDomain = GetObject("WinNT://DomainName")
Set objUser   = objDomain.Create("user", "JohnDoe")
    objUser.FullName = "John Q.Doe"
    objUser.SetInfo
Set objGroup = GetObject("WinNT://DomainName/Users")
    objGroup.Add("WinNT://" & strDomain & "/" & strUser)
```

The following example generates a file containing all the groups in the domain, and all of the users in each group. Due to the file redirection the script performs, it is designed to only run from `cscript.exe` executing in a console window. Rather than 'error out' if running under `wscript.exe`, the script verifies that it is executing in the correct environment; if not, it prompts the user, suggesting the proper behavior.

```
' Usage: ADSI_EnumDomGrp >> GroupList.txt
If 0 = Instr(LCase(WScript.Fullname), "cscript") Then
  Set WshShell = WScript.CreateObject("WScript.Shell")
  strMsg = "This script must be executed in a console window,"
  strMsg = strMsg & "using cscript.exe." & vbCrLf & vbCrLf
  strMsg = strMsg & "To execute, enter the selected text"
  strMsg = strMsg & "at a command prompt."
  strExec = "cscript " & WScript.ScriptFullname
  strExec = strExec & " >> GroupList.txt"
  InputBox strMsg, , strExec
Else
  Dim objDomain
  Set objDomain = GetObject("WinNT://stuartu")
    objDomain.Filter = Array("group")
  For Each Group In objDomain
    WScript.Echo vbCrLf & Group.Name
    For Each User In Group.Members
      WScript.Echo vbTab & User.Name
    Next
  Next
End If
```

Creating and removing file shares:

```
' Create a file share
Set objComp = GetObject("WinNT://ComputerName/lanmanserver")
Set objShare = objComp.Create("fileshare","WSH")
    objShare.Path  = "c:\projects\wsh"
    objShare.SetInfo
Set objShare = Nothing
Set objComp = Nothing
' Remove a file share
Set objComp = GetObject("WinNT://ComputerName/lanmanserver")
    objComp.Delete("fileshare","WSH")
Set objComp = Nothing
```

This is obviously a very brief introduction into the world of network administration with Windows Script Host. There is a great deal of power available to administrators who decide to make WSH a part of their toolkit. Take the time to experiment and figure out how it all works; there is much more than can be done than what was presented here.

Summary

By now, you should realize that Windows Script Host 2.0 is a good technology with which to familiarize yourself. From the improvements offered over version 1, to the new XML-based file format to the flexibility provided by automation of COM objects and the use of administration tools such as ADSI, WSH has much to offer to the scripter who is ready to move beyond client and server development alone.

Here's a recap of the topics covered in this chapter:

- ❑ The tools needed to get started writing scripts with Windows Script Host

- ❑ Ways in which WSH can be used, including the creation of custom solutions which integrate scripting with COM components

- ❑ The cscript and wscript execution environments, and how they differ

- ❑ How to customize the behavior of individual scripts through the use of .WSH configuration files

- ❑ A detailed examination of the object model available to WSH developers

- ❑ A reference of the elements used in the authoring of the more robust .WSF file format

- ❑ A brief introduction to the world of network administration using WSH in conjunction with ADSI

Additional Resources

Usenet

Microsoft Windows Script Host Newsgroup:
news://msnews.microsoft.com/microsoft.public.scripting.wsh

WWW

WSH FAQ:
http://wsh.glazier.co.nz/

Win32 Scripting:
http://cwashington.netreach.net/

Born's Windows Scripting Host Bazaar:
http://ourworld.compuserve.com/homepages/Guenter_Born/index0.htm

Windows Script Technologies:
http://msdn.microsoft.com/scripting/

OLE/COM Object Viewer:
http://www.microsoft.com/com/resource/oleview.asp

Active Directory Services Interfaces
http://www.microsoft.com/ntserver/nts/downloads/other/adsi25/

Print

Windows Script Host Programmer's Reference (*Wrox Press ISBN 1861002653*).

General Client-Side Web Scripting

Still on the subject of VBScript context, we're going to take a look at the area of client-side web scripting, where the client's browser interprets the script you write. This chapter will serve as a quick look at some of the uses of client-side scripting.

What Tools Do You Need?

Creating HTML web pages requires a text editor to type in your HTML and a browser to view it. To check that visitors to your web site see things the way you intend, you'll need to use the same browser (or browsers) as your users. This is fairly easy with Netscape Navigator, as you can have different versions installed on the same machine. But because Internet Explorer (IE) couples so tightly with the operating system you can only have one version of IE per machine, although IE5 has a compatibility mode which allows you to launch IE5 acting as IE4. To use IE5's IE4 compatibility mode you'll actually need to have IE4 installed on the machine *prior* to installing IE5, and choose the IE4 compatibility mode option during the IE5 setup.

To thoroughly test your web pages you need to test using the same operating systems as your users. The same version of a browser may support different features or behave differently depending on the operating system. For example, IE4 on the Mac does not support ActiveX.

It's possible to create all your pages using Notepad. This has the advantage of being simple to use and it's free with Windows. However, scripting a whole web site using just Notepad is unnecessarily complicated when there are plenty of tools available specifically for web page creation.

Most seasoned web designers have some kind of HTML editor that they swear by. If you're expecting to do a lot of VBScripting and haven't decided on a tool to use, the sort of features you should look for are syntax highlighting, automatic code completion, and help with event scripting. Syntax highlighting makes code easier to read by color-coding language keywords. Automatic code completion gives a list of available properties and methods associated with a HTML tag or an ActiveX control. Event scripting lists the events available for a particular tag or ActiveX control and will write the code framework to handle the event.

Some WYSIWYG page design tools also have a tendency to rearrange your carefully hand-crafted tags and code. Because of this, many developers start by building the web site using a WYSIWYG page design tool, but then switch back to Notepad to hand-code the script.

How Browser Scripting Works

Client-side scripting allows the web developer to manipulate elements within an HTML page and interact with the user. It also provides a glue with which to bind and work with ActiveX components embedded in the page.

Client-side scripting, in the form of JavaScript 1.0, first emerged with the release of Netscape Navigator 2. Although primitive in comparison to the scripting capabilities of modern browsers, it did mean that an HTML page was no longer just a set of information passively viewed by the user, but was now active and able to act more like a conventional program.

Prior to DHTML, the most important use of scripting was in form validation. Forms have been supported since the very first browsers, back in the days when just having text and images on the same page was considered exciting.

However, there was no way to check that what (if anything) the user had entered on a form was actually valid until *after* they had submitted it to the server. On receiving the submit form, we could check the validity of the data with a server-side component (say a CGI program). It would be more user-friendly, though, to catch as many form errors as possible before this stage, so that we can notify the user of any mistakes before they submit the form. With client-side scripting we can do just that.

Scripting in the earlier browsers also enabled simple special effects, such as scrolling text in the status bar and image rollover. However, once a page was loaded it was essentially static – some reaction to user interaction with elements in the page was possible, but the elements themselves could not be changed, nor was it possible to add new elements.

As you will see in the next chapter, all this was to change with DHTML, particularly that supported by Microsoft's Internet Explorer 4 and 5.

Including script into your page just involves using the <SCRIPT> tag. In theory you can generally put script anywhere in the page, but it's common to place it inside the <HEAD> tag of a page.

As a very simple example, the following script shows a message box when the page is loaded. Note that we use the LANGUAGE attribute to tell the browser to interpret the script as VBScript.

```
<HTML>
<HEAD>

<SCRIPT LANGUAGE="VBScript">
  MsgBox "Hello World"
</SCRIPT>

</HEAD>

<BODY>
<H3>A page with script</H3>
</BODY>

</HTML>
```

The script is not connected to any event in the browser but fires as the browser reaches it when parsing the page.

The Various Scripting Languages – What's Best for the Browser

The browser wars between Netscape and Microsoft have left us with a (sometimes confusing) array of scripting languages and standards.

The table below details which browser supports which languages. (for a more detailed breakdown of what is supported, see Appendices H and I):

Browser Version	Microsoft	Netscape
2	None	JavaScript 1.0
3	JScript 1, VBScript 1	JavaScript 1.1
4	JScript 3, VBScript 3	JavaScript 1.2
5	JScript 5, VBScript 5	

Your choice of scripting language is usually limited by which browsers your pages must be compatible with. Though it is possible to include different client-side scripting languages in a page, it can quickly become confusing.

JavaScript, JScript, and ECMAScript

JavaScript was first developed by Netscape and was first supported in Netscape Navigator 2. Although named JavaScript, it in fact has no connection with the development of the Java language, although its syntax often resembles Java's. To be honest, one of the reasons they called it JavaScript was because it sounded cooler than its original name, LiveScript.

Because Netscape owned the name JavaScript, when Microsoft released its version of JavaScript with Internet Explorer 3 it had to be called something else. Microsoft chose **JScript**. JScript 1.0 has a similar feature set to JavaScript 1.0. Microsoft jumped a version to JScript 3, which is very similar to (though not totally compatible with) JavaScript 1.2. Internet Explorer 5 saw the release of JScript 5, which incorporates some of the features of JavaScript 1.3. Netscape will release JavaScript 1.3 with Netscape Communicator 5.

All the subtle (and sometimes less subtle) differences between Netscape's and Microsoft's versions of JavaScript produce headaches for developers who just want to get the job done up to the maximum potential of the languages available. There's nothing more frustrating than spending a day designing an all-singing, all-dancing web page, only to find that it needs to be significantly amended to run on browser X, version Y, and platform Z.

To aid the developer, steps have been made towards compatibility between the various dialects of JavaScript, in the form of **ECMAScript**. The European Computer Manufacturers Association (ECMA) have released a standard for JavaScript ECMA-262, hence ECMAScript. Microsoft's JScript 5 is fully compatible with ECMA-262, and Netscape's JavaScript 1.2 is *almost* compliant (how's that headache?). The future promises an updated ECMAScript (likely to be similar to JavaScript 1.3).

VBScript

Given the existence of JavaScript in all its forms, why use VBScript?

Well, firstly, if you're a Visual Basic or VBA developer then you'll feel right at home with VBScript, which is a subset of VBA. With such similarity (and this book...), you'll quickly be ready to start creating sophisticated web applications. JavaScript's syntax is arguably less intuitive than VBScript, and tends to be less forgiving of 'mistakes' such as case sensitivity.

In terms of what VBScript and JavaScript can actually *do*, there is little to choose between the two. Most of what can be achieved in one can be achieved in the other, though sometimes a clever workarounds is necessary. Although not compliant with the ECMA standard at all (because it's a different language), Microsoft have made clear their intention that VBScript will continue to match JavaScript in terms of functionality.

There are important differences between VBScript and VBA. VBScript is an **untyped** language, which means that all variables are variants and don't have an explicit type (such as **integer** or **string**).

> *In fact, they do have subtypes and you can (and often need to) use conversion functions such as* CLng, CStr, *and* CInt *to make explicit the subtype you're dealing with.*

You'll also find VBScript's error handling less powerful than VBA's.

Responding to Browser Events

Much of the client-side scripting you do will be to handle events raised by objects in the page. It could be the onSubmit event of a form, the onClick event of an image, or an event raised by an ActiveX control that you have embedded in your page. The reference section of the book includes a listing of objects and the events they support.

Adding an Event Handler

The easiest way to add an event handler in Internet Explorer is to define a Sub or Function to handle it inside a <SCRIPT> block. The name for the Sub or Function must be of the form *elementName_eventname*. Also note in the example below the use of the VBScript Me object, which references the object (for example, an HTML tag or ActiveX control) that caused the event to fire.

```
<HTML>
<HEAD>
<SCRIPT LANGUAGE="VBScript">
  Sub cmdFire_onclick
    MsgBox Me.Name & " made me do this"
  End Sub
</SCRIPT>
</HEAD>

<BODY>
<INPUT TYPE="BUTTON" NAME="cmdFire" VALUE="Fire">
</BODY>
</HTML>
```

An alternative way of doing the same thing is to use the FOR and EVENT properties of the <SCRIPT> tag. All the code inside the <SCRIPT> tags will execute when the event fires.

```
<HTML>
<HEAD>
<SCRIPT FOR="cmdFire" EVENT="onclick" LANGUAGE="vbscript">
  MsgBox Me.Name & " made me do this"
</SCRIPT>
</HEAD>

<BODY>
<INPUT TYPE="BUTTON" NAME="cmdFire" VALUE="Fire">
</BODY>
</HTML>
```

Adding an Event Handler That Passes Parameters

If you want to pass parameters to your event handling subroutine, then you must define a Sub or Function and call that in your element's onEvent embedded inside the tag. You must not name your Sub routine *elementName_EventName* or the browser will get confused with the first way we saw above of defining the event.

Because we are calling a separate subroutine (and not directly defining an event handler), the Me object if used *inside* our subroutine won't point to the element that caused the event to fire. It will, however, behave 'correctly' in the procedure that calls the function, so from here we can pass Me to our Sub as one of its parameters.

> With Internet Explorer 3 there is no other way of finding out which element fired the Sub routine. Internet Explorers 4 and above have the Event object which you will find out more about in the next chapter.

```
<HTML>
<HEAD>
<SCRIPT LANGUAGE="VBScript">
Sub DoSomething(theElement,theNumber)
  MsgBox theElement.Name & " made me fire"
  MsgBox "Today's number is the number " & theNumber
End Sub
</SCRIPT>
</HEAD>

<BODY>
<INPUT TYPE="BUTTON" NAME="cmdFire" VALUE="Fire"
  onClick="DoSomething Me,1">
</BODY>
</HTML>
```

Here, our subroutine is called DoSomething, and it's called from the onclick event of our INPUT button with our two parameters. Me works fine in the event handler, but if we were to try to refer directly to Me in the DoSomething procedure, it would have no meaning since the DoSomething procedure is a stand-alone Sub.

Canceling Events

Certain events, such as those associated with link tags and forms, can be cancelled. If, for example, the user has entered an invalid value in a form, then we don't want the form to submit because we know that it will fail. Rather, we want to stop the event and notify the user. To do this we normally need to return a value of False to cancel the action. As only functions (not subroutines) can have return values, we need to define our event handler code as a function.

```
<HTML>
<HEAD>
<SCRIPT LANGUAGE="VBScript">
Function form1_onsubmit()
  ' Has something been entered?
```

```
  If form1.txtNumber.value = "" Then
    MsgBox "You must enter a value"
    form1_onsubmit = false
  ' Is it a valid number?
  ElseIf Not IsNumeric(form1.txtNumber.value) Then
    MsgBox "You must enter a number"
    form1_onsubmit = false
  ' Is the value in range?
  ElseIf form1.txtNumber.value > 10 Or _
      form1.txtNumber.value < 1 Then
    MsgBox "Invalid number"
    form1_onsubmit = false
  Else
    'Form submit can continue
    MsgBox "Valid Number"
  End If
End Function
</SCRIPT>
</HEAD>

<BODY>
  <FORM action="" method=POST id=form1 name=form1 >
    Enter a number from 1 to 10
    <INPUT type="text" id=txtNumber name=txtNumber>
    <BR>
    <INPUT type="submit" value="Submit" id=submit1 name=submit1>
  </FORM>
</BODY>
</HTML>
```

The Order of Things

With many events it's obvious when they will fire. You click a button, and the onclick event fires. However, some events don't fire as a direct response to user interaction. The window_onload event is a good example of this. Any script in your page outside of a subprocedure or function will fire as the page is parsed by the browser. But which comes first, the window_onload or the parsed code? Also if you have a frameset and frames, what will be the order the window_onloads fire?

Let's take a look at a simple example. You'll need to create 3 HTML pages: a page containing the frameset tags and a page for each of the frames.

First we have the frameset page, which we'll call EventOrder.htm.

```
<HTML>
<HEAD>
<SCRIPT LANGUAGE="VBSCRIPT">
Dim sEventTracker
Dim iEventOrder
iEventOrder = 0

window.Parent.iEventOrder = window.Parent.iEventOrder + 1
window.Parent.sEventTracker = window.Parent.sEventTracker _
  & window.Parent.iEventOrder _
  & " Frameset - First code in Page" & Chr(13) & Chr(10)
```

```
Sub window_onload
  iEventOrder = iEventOrder + 1
  sEventTracker = sEventTracker & iEventOrder _
    & " Frameset window_onload" & Chr(13) & Chr(10)
End Sub
</SCRIPT>
</HEAD>
<FRAMESET rows=50%,*>
  <FRAME SRC="top.htm" id=fraTop name=fraTop>
  <FRAME SRC="bottom.htm" id=fraBottom name=fraBottom>
</FRAMESET>
</HTML>
```

Next we create the top frame page. Save this page as top.htm.

```
<HTML>
<HEAD>
<SCRIPT LANGUAGE="VBScript">
window.Parent.iEventOrder = window.Parent.iEventOrder + 1
window.Parent.sEventTracker = window.Parent.sEventTracker _
  & window.Parent.iEventOrder _
  & " Top frame - First code in Page" & Chr(13) & Chr(10)

Sub cmdCheckForm_onclick
  window.Parent.iEventOrder = window.Parent.iEventOrder + 1
  window.Parent.sEventTracker = window.Parent.sEventTracker _
    & window.Parent.iEventOrder _
    & " Top frame - cmdCheckForm_onclick" & Chr(13) & Chr(10)
  form1.txtEvents.Value = window.Parent.sEventTracker
End Sub

Sub window_onload
  window.Parent.iEventOrder = window.Parent.iEventOrder + 1
  window.Parent.sEventTracker = window.Parent.sEventTracker _
    & window.Parent.iEventOrder _
    & " Top frame - window_onload" & Chr(13) & Chr(10)
End Sub

</SCRIPT>

</HEAD>
<BODY>
<FORM action="myform_handler.asp" method=post id=form1 name=form1>
<TEXTAREA cols=60 name=txtEvents rows=10></TEXTAREA>
<INPUT type="button" value="List Events" name=cmdCheckForm>
</FORM>

<SCRIPT LANGUAGE="VBScript">
window.Parent.iEventOrder = window.Parent.iEventOrder + 1
window.Parent.sEventTracker = window.Parent.sEventTracker _
  & window.Parent.iEventOrder _
  & " Top frame - Second code in Page" & Chr(13) & Chr(10)
</SCRIPT>
</BODY>
</HTML>
```

Finally, the page for the bottom frame. Save this as `bottom.htm`.

```
<HTML>
<HEAD>
<SCRIPT LANGUAGE="VBScript">
window.Parent.iEventOrder = window.Parent.iEventOrder + 1
window.Parent.sEventTracker = window.Parent.sEventTracker _
   & window.Parent.iEventOrder _
   & " bottom frame - First code in Page" & Chr(13) & Chr(10)

Sub window_onload
   window.Parent.iEventOrder = window.Parent.iEventOrder + 1
   window.parent.sEventTracker = window.Parent.sEventTracker _
      & window.Parent.iEventOrder _
      & " bottom frame - window_onload" & Chr(13) & Chr(10)
End Sub
</SCRIPT>

</BODY>
</HTML>
```

If you load the page containing the frameset, then click the list events button, the text area will be filled with details of the `window_onload` events and embedded scripts, listed in the order they fired.

It's perhaps worth noting that the differences between browsers include not just the events each HTML tag has but the order they fire in. For example, If you try this on IE3 you'll find the order in which events fire is different from that of IE4 and 5. Though the events we've used in our examples are the same for IE4 and IE5, you will find other differences between them.

Validating Forms

To obtain information from the user we need to use an HTML form populated with form elements. In scripting the HTML form can be manipulated and examined using its form object. An HTML page can have one or more forms which we can either reference by name or using the document object's `forms` array. In most cases it's easier just to refer to a form by name.

To insert an HTML form into a page the `<FORM>` tag is used along with the corresponding `</FORM>` close tag.

The most important properties of the `<FORM>` tag are `Action` and `Method`. The `Action` property is the URL where the form will post to, for example an ASP page or a CGI script. The `Method` property can be either `post` or `get`, and determines how the form's data is transmitted to the server when the form is submitted. If the `Method` property is set to `get`, then the data in the form's elements will be appended to the URL that was specified in the `Action` property. A form `Method` of `post` sends the form's data as a data stream to the server along with the http header.

Generally speaking the form `post` method is used, and indeed the `get` method has been depreciated in HTML 4.0. This is because `Get` places a limit on how much data can be sent and is actually visible in the URL for your users to see, something which you may not want.

Having defined our form tags, we can then populate the form with the HTML controls (also referred to as **elements**) available. The most common controls are input boxes, radio buttons and select controls. The next thing we need to worry about is how we make sure what the user submits is valid data.

Validating Numerical Input Box Values

The most common criteria for validation of an input box that's being used for the entry of numerical data are:

❑ that the field has been completed

❑ that it contains a numeric value

❑ that the numeric value is within an acceptable range

❑ that it is an integer

We saw a simple example of this earlier on. The example below describes another approach. If the value entered by the user into form1's element text1 is an integer between 1 and 10, then a message box tells us that it's valid. At this point (in real life...) you would actually submit the form rather than inform the user the way we do here. The line 'form1.submit' (which is currently commented out) in the code below will do this, although to use the code as supplied here you'll need to create the page myform_handler.asp yourself.

If the user has entered invalid data then the ValidInteger function returns a message describing the problem.

```
<HTML>
<HEAD>
<SCRIPT LANGUAGE="VBScript">
Function ValidInteger(sNumber, iMin, iMax)
  Dim iNumber
  ' Is it a number?
  If IsNumeric(sNumber) Then

    ' Is it a whole number (no decimal place)?
    If InStr(sNumber,".") = 0 Then

      ' Is it in range?
      If CLng(sNumber) >= iMin And CLng(sNumber) <= iMax Then
        ValidInteger = ""
      Else
        ValidInteger = "You must enter a number between " _
          & iMin & " and " & iMax
      End If
    Else
      ValidInteger = "You must enter a whole number"
    End If

  Else
    ValidInteger = "You must enter a number"
  End If
End Function
```

```
Sub cmdCheckForm_onclick
  Dim sValidity
  sValidity = ValidInteger(form1.text1.value,1,10)
  If sValidity = "" Then
    MsgBox "Valid"
    'form1.submit
  Else
    MsgBox sValidity
  End If

End Sub
</SCRIPT>
</HEAD>

<BODY>
<FORM action="myform_handler.asp" method=POST id=form1 name=form1>
  <INPUT id=text1 name=text1>
  <INPUT type="button" value="Button" id=cmdCheckForm name=cmdCheckForm>
</FORM>
</BODY>
</HTML>
```

Validating Radio Buttons

The only check for validity you can make with a radio button group is that one element has been selected by the user. You could define one of the elements to be checked by default, simply by putting CHECKED inside one of the radio buttons' tags.

Note that to define a group of radio buttons we simply create a number of radio buttons and give them the same name.

Some things are too important to be left to defaults, though. Take the example of a radio group for selecting a credit card type. By not using a default, you know that the user has made a positive choice in setting their credit card type. Otherwise there is a danger that they could have missed the question, and we would end up with invalid information.

```
<HTML>
<HEAD>
<SCRIPT LANGUAGE="VBScript">

Function RadioGroupValid(radGroup)
  Dim iElement
  RadioGroupValid = False
  ' Loop through the radio buttons in the group
  For iElement = 0 To radGroup.Length - 1
    ' If one is checked then we have validity
    If radGroup(iElement).Checked = True _
      Then RadioGroupValid = True
  Next
End Function

Sub cmdCheckForm_onclick
  Dim sValidity
  If RadioGroupValid(form1.radCreditCard) Then
    MsgBox "Valid"
    'form1.submit
```

```
    Else
       MsgBox "Invalid"
    End If
End Sub

</SCRIPT>
</HEAD>
<BODY>
<FORM action="myform_handler.asp" method=post id=form1 name=form1>
    Visa
    <INPUT type="radio" id=radCreditCard name=radCreditCard value="Visa">
    <BR>
    American Express
    <INPUT type="radio" id=radCreditCard name=radCreditCard value="Amex">
    <BR>
    Master Card
    <INPUT type="radio" id=radCreditCard name=radCreditCard value="MasterCard">
    <BR>
    <INPUT type="button" value="Test" id=cmdCheckForm name=cmdCheckForm>
</FORM>
</BODY>
</HTML>
```

We loop through each of the radio buttons in the group and check if one is selected. We can find out how many elements there are in a group using the `length` property. When the form is actually posted the value sent will only be the value of the selected radio button. So if radio button 3 is selected then `radio1=MasterCard` will be submitted to the server.

Validating Select Controls and Dates

An HTML SELECT element can be used like either a Visual Basic combo box or a list box, depending on its `size` property. If you set the `size` property to 1 then it acts like a drop-down combo box, but if its `size` is set to more than one then it becomes a list box.

A common use of the `select` element is to allow the user to enter a date. Its advantage over using a text box for dates is its clarity for the user. For example, American and British formatting of dates differs and can cause problems. In Britain 11/07/1999 is the 11th day of July, and in America this is interpreted as the 7th day of November. Using `select` controls you can unambiguously pass the date you mean without trusting the user to get it the right way around.

In the next example we validate the date defined by the user selecting from `select` boxes. We need to ensure that they don't select the 31st April or the 29th of Feb in a non-leap year.

I've deliberately not fully populated the select boxes to save space and time. In practice you could use ASP server-side code to dynamically populate them with day and year values.

```
<HTML>
<HEAD>
<SCRIPT LANGUAGE="VBScript">

Function CheckDate(sDay, sMonth, sYear)
  On Error Resume Next
  Dim Date1
  ' If invalid date an error will be raised
  Date1 = CDate(sDay & "/" & sMonth & "/" & sYear)
  ' If error number not 0 then invalid date
  If Err.number <> 0 Then
    Err.Clear
    ' Calc days in month by going to next month then
    ' subtract 1 day
    Date1 = DateAdd("m",1,sMonth & "/" & sYear)
    Date1 = DateAdd("d",-1,Date1)
    CheckDate = "There are only " & Day(Date1) _
      & " days in " & sMonth
  Else
    CheckDate = ""
  End If
End Function

Sub cmdCheckForm_onclick
  sDateValidityMessage = CheckDate(form1.cboDay.Value, _
    form1.cboMonth.Value, form1.cboYear.Value)
  If sDateValidityMessage <> "" Then
    MsgBox sDateValidityMessage
  Else
    MsgBox "That date is valid"
    'form1.submit
  End If
End Sub
</SCRIPT>
</HEAD>

<BODY>
<FORM action="myform_handler.asp" method=post id=form1 name=form1>
<SELECT id=cboDay name=cboDay size=1>
<OPTION value=28>28
<OPTION value=29>29
<OPTION value=30>30
<OPTION value=31>31
</SELECT>

<SELECT id=cboMonth name=cboMonth size=1>
<OPTION value=Jan>Jan
<OPTION value=Feb>Feb
<OPTION value=Mar>Mar
<OPTION value=Apr>Apr
</SELECT>

<SELECT id=cboYear name=cboYear size=1>
<OPTION value=1999>1999
<OPTION value=2000>2000
<OPTION value=2001>2001
</SELECT>

<BR>
```

```
<INPUT type="button" value="Test" id=cmdCheckForm name=cmdCheckForm>
</FORM>
</BODY>
</HTML>
```

Finally, we'll take a look at an important aid to scripting – the Document Object Model, which allows us to access all the objects and tags in our pages in our script.

The Document Object Model

VBScript doesn't exist in a vacuum. It's a tool with which to manipulate the environment of its current context, whether that's WSH and the Windows system, ASP and Internet Information Server, or a web browser and web pages. But what are we actually manipulating? The answer is the Document Object Model.

The Document Object Model (DOM) is an all-encompassing term for the programmatic interface to the hierarchy of objects available within a browser and the web page it displays. It maps out each object's associated properties, methods and events. Objects include the browser itself, a frame's window, the document or web page within that frame, and the HTML and XML tags within the page, as well as any plugins or embedded ActiveX controls. The DOM also includes a number of collections of objects, such as the forms collection we have already seen in use.

Every browser version has its own DOM, and they vary considerably between Microsoft's Internet Explorer and Netscape's Navigator. There is also considerable variation between different versions of the same browser.

In an effort to bring about a common standard for the DOM, the W3C (the body which deals with Web standards) has released a number of standards for defining the DOM. The W3C's DOM (Level 0) approximated to the level supported by version 3 browsers.

Level 1 DOM specifications, released in October 1998, struck a balance between Internet Explorer 4's DOM and that of Netscape 4's, though IE4's was much closer to the spec. The changes from the Level 0 DOM to Level 1, particularly those supported by IE4, were quite dramatic. The Level 1 spec makes every element within a page a programmable object and exposes its attributes as properties. Microsoft's DOM in IE4 went even further, allowing pages to be updated even after they have been loaded. This puts the 'Dynamic' in Dynamic HTML. Prior to this (with the exception of images), once the page was loaded into a browser no further changes were possible.

Level 2 is still a working draft and reflects developments in the latest browsers, as well as looking ahead to the future. Appendices H and I detail the DOM implementations of Internet Explorer 4 and 5. You can find the latest information on DOM specification developments on the W3C's web site at http://www.w3.org/DOM/. Although IE5's version of the DOM is already out, it has been submitted to the W3C for inclusion in their specification, and it is hoped that Netscape will live up to its promises to implement the W3C level 2 DOM in its forthcoming Communicator 5.

The new DOM supported by IE5 is a significantly evolutionary move on from that supported by IE4. In IE4 *almost* all tags were programmable; in IE5 *all* tags are. Also, new methods introduced in IE5's DOM make dynamically manipulating the page easier than it was with IE4.

The DOM In Practice

DOM specifications are all well and good, but as programmers it's the practical implementation we're interested in. Before leaving this chapter it's worth taking a look at the DOM as implemented by IE4 and IE5. We'll just take a broad overview here; you can find the full object models in the appendices.

The Window Object

At the top of the HTML DOM hierarchy is the `window` object. If your page has no frames then there is just one `window` object; if there *are* frames, then each frame has its own `window` object.

Each `window` object within a frameset has a parent `window` object which is the `window` object of the page defining the frames. You can access any of the other `window` objects from script inside a page by using the `window` object's `parent` property. Once you have a reference to the parent `window` object you can use that to access not only the `window` object's properties and methods, but also those of any HTML tags inside that window. You can also use it to access any global VBScript variables or functions.

Let's take a look at a simple frameset example. We will create 3 pages, the first defines a frameset, the second is the left window's page and the third the right window's page.

Save the first page as `TopFrame.htm`:

```
<HTML>
<SCRIPT LANGUAGE="VBSCRIPT">
Dim sName
sName = "Top Frame"

Sub SayWhoIsThis()
  MsgBox "This is the top frame's subprocedure " _
    & "window.SayWhoIsThis"
End Sub
</SCRIPT>
<FRAMESET COLS="50%,*">
  <FRAME SRC="LFrame.htm" NAME="LFrame">
  <FRAME SRC="RFrame.htm" NAME="RFrame">
</FRAMESET>
</HTML>
```

Save this next page as `Lframe.htm`:

```
<HTML>
<HEAD>
<SCRIPT LANGUAGE="VBSCRIPT">
Dim sName
sName = "Left Frame"

Sub SayWhoIsThis()
  MsgBox "This is LFrame's subroutine window.SayWhoIsThis"
End Sub
</SCRIPT>
<TITLE>Left</TITLE>
</HEAD>
```

```
<BODY>
<H2>LEFT FRAME</H2>
</BODY>
</HTML>
```

Save the final page as `Rframe.htm`:

```
<HTML>
<HEAD>
<META name=VI60_defaultClientScript content=VBScript>
<SCRIPT LANGUAGE="VBSCRIPT">
Dim sName
sName = "Right Frame"

Sub SayWhoIsThis()
  MsgBox "This is RFrame's subroutine window.SayWhoIsThis"
End Sub

Sub button1_onclick
  MsgBox "window.sName = " & window.sName
  window.SayWhoIsThis
End Sub

Sub button2_onclick
  MsgBox "window.Parent.sName = " & window.parent.sName
  window.Parent.SayWhoIsThis
End Sub

Sub button3_onclick
  MsgBox "window.parent.LFrame.sName = " & window.Parent.LFrame.sName
  window.Parent.LFrame.SayWhoIsThis
End Sub

Sub button4_onclick
  MsgBox "window.Parent.LFrame.sName = " & window.Parent.frames(0).sName
  window.Parent.frames(0).SayWhoIsThis
End Sub
</SCRIPT>
</HEAD>

<BODY>
<H2>RIGHT FRAME</H2>
<INPUT type="button" value="window" name=button1>
<INPUT type="button" value="window.Parent" name=button2>
<INPUT type="button" value="window.Parent.LFrame" name=button3>
<INPUT type="button" value="window.Parent.frames(0)" name=button4>
</BODY>
</HTML>
```

If you load `Topframe.htm` into your browser you can try out the buttons in the right frame. These demonstrate accessing script in the window object of the right frame, its parent's window and the left frame.

In the first button's `on_click` we are accessing the window of the current frame so we normally don't need to explicitly say it's the `window` object we are referring to as this is implied – `sName` is the same as `window.sName`. In some contexts you will need to explicitly state it's the `window` object you are referring to.

When the second button is clicked, the top frame page (in other words, the right window's parent object), is referenced. This is very handy for defining global variables and functions when you have a multi-frame page.

For the third button we access the sName and SayWhoIsThis function contained in the left frame. When the button is clicked we do this by referencing the frame named Lframe contained by the right window's parent window object. As you can see navigating the DOM can get a little complex.

The fourth button does exactly the same as the third but in a different way to demonstrate another of the DOM's important features: **collections**.

Collections

The window object has not only properties, methods and events, but like many other objects in the DOM it also has collections. We know from the example above that a window object can have many child window objects, but where are these contained? The answer is in the frames collection. The frames collection is a zero-based array containing references to the frames defined by that window. So in button4's code, you see that the left frame is window.parent.frames(0) which is exactly the same as window.parent.Lframe.

Moving down the DOM hierarchy, we come to the document object. Each window object contains a document object, which can be referenced using the window object's document property. The document object acts as a container for all the document objects, such as HTML tags, ActiveX controls, inside your page. Like the window object it has a large number of collections associated with it.

Let's take a look at an example. Here we create a simple page with a paragraph and a table. Using script we access collections and properties in the DOM. I have used the document.all collection to set references to various document objects in the page. An alternative would be to give all the tags names and use them instead, but you'll find that there are times when you're not in a position to know the name of a tag and need to access it using collections such as the all collection.

```
<HTML>
<HEAD>
<TITLE>Navigating the DOM</TITLE>
<SCRIPT LANGUAGE="VBScript">
Sub button1_onclick
  Dim theWindow
  Dim theDocument
  Dim thePara
  Dim theTable
  Dim theRow
  Dim theCell

  Set theWindow = window

  Set theDocument = theWindow.document
  MsgBox theDocument.title

  Set thePara = theDocument.all(5)
  MsgBox thepara.innerText
```

```
    Set theTable = theDocument.all(6)
    MsgBox theTable.tagName

    Set theRow = theTable.rows(1)
    MsgBox theRow.name

    Set theCell = theRow.all(1)
    MsgBox theCell.innertext
End Sub</SCRIPT>
</HEAD>
<BODY>
  <P>A Paragraph</P>
  <TABLE BORDER=1 NAME="table1">
    <TR>
      <TD>Cell 1</TD>
      <TD>Cell 2</TD>
    </TR>
    <TR NAME="second_row_in_table1">
      <TD>Cell 3</TD>
      <TD>Cell 4</TD>
    </TR>
  </TABLE>
<INPUT type="button" value="document.all" name=button1>
</BODY>
</HTML>
```

First we dimension some variables which we will set to reference document objects. We could reference the objects directly, but creating variables to reference them does make your code easier to read if you are accessing the property numerous times. Creating the reference to the window and document object is unnecessary for this example, but we've done it to emphasize what it is we are referencing in the DOM.

We set the variable theWindow to reference the window object for our page. Then we use object's document property to set a reference to the document for that page and to display the page's title.

We set the variable thePara to reference our paragraph contained in the document object. Why document.all(5) and not document.all(0)? Well, the all collection of an object references all objects contained by that object. Here it's the document and the document includes the html tag, head tags, the script tags, the body tags and so on. The collection starts at zero and as our paragraph is the sixth tag in the page it is document.all(5).

We then use the message box to show the innerText property of the paragraph object.

Next, we set theTable to reference the table in the page. It's the next tag after the paragraph, so it corresponds to document.all(6). We show a message box with the table's tagName property. The tagName is simply the tag definition, so for <TABLE> it's TABLE, for a <P> it's P, and so on.

Next we set theRow to reference the second row in the table. We do this using the rows collection of the table object.

Finally we obtain a reference to the second cell in the row by using the `all` collection of the row object. We could have used the `cells` collection, but this example demonstrates that it's not just documents which have the `all` collection. In fact all objects have it if they contain other objects.

Hopefully the examples in this section have demonstrated how to access objects in the DOM, and also shown that the DOM is a hierarchical collection of objects, with each object in the hierarchy being both an object inside another object and also a container for other objects.

Summary

In this chapter we have taken a brief look at what client-side scripting is for. We saw how to connect events raised by HTML objects to VBScript code. We noted relationship between VBScript and JavaScript. In reality neither language is better than the other, it's really determined by what browsers your pages must support and what your previous programming experience is. VBScript makes an excellent choice for Visual Basic and MS Office VBA programmers who are writing for Internet Explorer.

Validating forms client-side using VBScript was also demonstrated with various controls and types of data. Finally, we examined the Document Object Model and the various standards associated with it, including those laid out by the W3C and implemented by Microsoft and Netscape.

In the next chapter you'll be shown lots of exciting techniques using the latest technologies available with Internet Explorer 5.

12

High-Powered Client Scripting

In this chapter, we'll continue looking at client-side scripting. But we'll look at more advanced technologies that give much needed functionality and extensibility to client-side pages: scriptlets, behaviors, HTML components, and remote scripting (which allows your client page to execute a method on the server). Each of these subjects could be (and are) covered in books of their own, so we'll focus on small, well-tested samples (code examples) that hit all the major techniques required to enable these technologies. In reality, to achieve maximum gain from these technologies you'd have to read masses of documentation – most of which is very poor. We'll show you here what is possible and how to go about doing it. We'll have achieved what we set out to do if, when you finish this chapter, you are able to make any sense of the documentation! (http://msdn.microsoft.com/scripting)

Technology Requirements

Even though these are advanced applications and tools, you still need a good text editor to manage these technologies. The following table lists the applications you need to make use of the technologies:

Technology	Requirements	
Scriptlets	IE4 or IE5	
Behaviors/HTML Components	IE5	
Remote Scripting	Client Side:	IE4 or IE5
	Server Side:	IIS 4.0
		Microsoft Remote Scripting 1.0a

Importance of Browser Security Settings

The browser is a security-aware application. Every component contained within the browser is subject to the security settings defined for it. For information about security settings refer to the documentation for your browser(s). Typically, the zone containing the components-server should be Medium (Medium-Low in IE5) or Low. If the security level is more restrictive the components will not download on the client computer. It is especially important to verify security settings when distributing an application that uses components.

Scriptlets – Ancestors of Behaviors

Introduced in IE4, the scriptlet mechanism was the first browser technology to permit the design of components using DHTML. While developing a web or an intranet project, you usually produce a lot of HTML and scripting functionalities. Without a technology to implement components, you're limited to reusing your code by cutting it from a source file and pasting it into another file (or you can include external scripting files using the SRC attribute of the <SCRIPT> tag: a useful facility, not a component-based technology). Furthermore, to cut and paste code usually requires lot of adaptations to make the code work in the new context. On the other hand the usage of a component is straightforward. You include it in your context using its public interface made of properties, methods, and events – the usual stuff expected by an object oriented programmer.

What is a Scriptlet?

Conceptually a scriptlet is a component developed using DHTML. Physically a scriptlet is an HTML file with a few extensions to allow the definition of properties, methods and events that permit its use as a component.

The Hello World Scriptlet

To quickly show what a scriptlet is, we'll introduce the classic minimal application "Hello World". The application's task is just to output the "Hello World" message using the technology under examination. To implement Hello World two files are required:

❏   the component file: HELLO.HTM

❏   the client file: CLIENT01.HTM

The following code shows the content of CLIENT01.HTM.

```
<html>
<head>
<SCRIPT LANGUAGE="VBScript">

Sub Hello()
        Document.All.myScriptlet.Hello
End Sub
```

```
</SCRIPT>
</head>

<body onload="Hello()">

<OBJECT ID="myScriptlet"
    TYPE="text/x-scriptlet"
    DATA="hello.htm"
    HEIGHT="0" WIDTH="0">
</OBJECT>

</body>
</html>
```

The scriptlet is identified by the name `myScriptlet`. This name has been used as the ID of an OBJECT tag included in the HTML file. The details of this tag are:

```
<OBJECT ID="myScriptlet"
    TYPE="text/x-scriptlet"
    DATA="hello.htm"
    HEIGHT="0" WIDTH="0">
</OBJECT>
```

> **Note: the HEIGHT and WIDTH parameters of the <OBJECT> tag have been set to zero to make the object invisible. It could make sense to have a visible object if the scriptlet contains visible objects as well – not the case in this sample.**

The following line calls the scriptlet code:

```
Document.All.myScriptlet.Hello
```

This line will require a scriptlet that exposes a `Hello` method. This very simple scriptlet is stored in the `HELLO.HTM` file:

```
<SCRIPT LANGUAGE="VBScript">

Sub public_Hello()
    MsgBox "Hello World!"
End Sub

</SCRIPT>
```

So, what does our scriptlet comprise? An HTML file encapsulating the scripting code inside a <SCRIPT> tag – in our case containing just one VBScript function defined as `public_Hello`.

Points to note from this example:

❑ The <OBJECT> tag permits us to insert a scriptlet into an HTML document using a special object type defined as "text/x-scriptlet".

❑ The scriptlet code is contained in an HTML file specified in the DATA attribute of the <OBJECT> tag.

❑ The scriptlet is accessed for scripting through the ID specified for the <OBJECT> tag (in other words `myScriptlet` in the sample).

347

The Prefix "public_" Exposes Scriptlet Members

VBScript offers a very simple way to define which code is exposed by the scriptlet to the container: a naming convention.

❑ The procedures and functions become public methods of the scriptlet if their names are prefixed with **public_**.

❑ The global variables in the code become properties of the scriptlet if their names are prefixed with **public_** as well.

> Note: JScript (JavaScript) offers a further mechanism called "Public Description Object" to define the public interface of a scriptlet. JScript is outside the scope of this book and, anyway, we don't need it to implement scriptlets.

Further naming conventions:

Prefix:	Used to expose:
public_	variables as read/write properties, procedures or functions as methods
public_get_	functions as readable properties
public_put_	functions as writable properties

When a scriptlet member is exposed, its name in the host application does not have the prefix. Remember that the Hello function in the HELLO.HTM scriptlet was defined as public_Hello:

```
Sub public_Hello()
```

While the public_ prefix has been removed in the method call made by the host file CLIENT01.HTM:

```
Document.All.myScriptlet.Hello ' and not Document.All.myScriptlet.public_Hello
```

Scriptlets use prefixes to expose their public interface, but the host applications don't use the prefixes to access that interface. Quite an ambiguous syntax to declare a public interface.

Packaging Code in a Scriptlet for Reuse

Scriptlets are a good mechanism to package reusable code into one module. The next page sees the start of a more complex example that exposes a few methods and a property:

The Cookies Manager

The Cookies Manager is a scriptlet that exposes the following interface:

Member Type	Name	Description
Property	`KeyExists`	True if the cookie key exists. Usually checked after calling `GetCookieKey` or `RemoveCookieKey`.
Method	`SetCookieKey ( Key, Value )`	Stores a value in a cookie, associating it with a specific key.
Method	`GetCookieKey ( Key )`	Returns the value of a specific key in a cookie.
Method	`RemoveCookieKey ( Key )`	Removes a specific key from a cookie.

Using this interface, the client can store, read or remove a specific key in a cookie.

> Note: an HTTP cookie is a small file stored on a client machine. Using cookies, you can implement persistency among different sessions (so a user returning to the page will still find the values previously stored in the cookie).

The content of `COOKIESMANAGER.HTM` (the scriptlet) is:

```
<SCRIPT LANGUAGE="VBScript">
<!--

Dim public_KeyExists

Sub public_SetCookieKey(sKey, sValue)
  Dim ck
  ck = sKey & "=" & sValue
  ck = ck & ";Expires=Fri 01-Jan-2010 13:00:00 GMT"
  Document.Cookie = ck
End Sub

Function public_GetCookieKey(sKey)

  public_KeyExists = True

  Dim iLoc
  iLoc = Instr(Document.Cookie, sKey)

  If iLoc = 0 Then
    public_GetCookieKey = ""
    public_KeyExists = False
  Else
    Dim sTemp
    sTemp = Right(Document.Cookie, Len(Document.Cookie) - iLoc + 1)
```

```
    Dim iKeyLen
    iKeyLen = Len(sKey)

    If Mid(sTemp, iKeyLen + 1, 1) <> "=" Then
      public_GetCookieKey = ""
      public_KeyExists = False
    Else
      Dim iNextSep
      iNextSep = Instr(sTemp, ";")

      If iNextSep = 0 Then iNextSep = Len(sTemp) + 1
      If iNextSep = (iKeyLen + 2) Then
        public_GetCookieKey = ""
      Else
        Dim iValLen
        iValLen = iNextSep - iKeyLen - 2
        public_GetCookieKey = Mid(sTemp, iKeyLen + 2, iValLen)
      End If
    End If
  End if

End Function

Sub public_RemoveCookieKey(sKey)
  Document.Cookie = sKey & "=NULL;Expires=Fri 01-Jan-1980 13:00:00 GMT"
End Sub

-->
</SCRIPT>
```

We need a new host application to display an example of using the Cookies Manager scriptlet. This is the content of the sample file CLIENT02.HTM:

```
<html>
<head>
<SCRIPT LANGUAGE="VBScript">
<!--

  Sub btnGetName_onClick
    Dim sValue
    sValue = InputBox("Enter your name:")
    Document.All.myScriptlet.SetCookieKey "Name", sValue
    Document.All.Message.InnerHTML = "And now reload the page please..."
  End Sub

-->
</SCRIPT>

<SCRIPT LANGUAGE="VBScript" FOR="window" EVENT="onload">
<!--
  Dim sValue
  sValue = Document.All.myScriptlet.GetCookieKey("Name")

  If Document.All.myScriptlet.KeyExists Then
    Document.All.Main.InnerHTML = "Hello " & sValue & "!"
  End If
-->
</SCRIPT>
```

```
</head>
<body>

<OBJECT ID="myScriptlet"
  TYPE="text/x-scriptlet"
  DATA="cookiesManager.htm"
  HEIGHT="0" WIDTH="0">
</OBJECT>

<div id="Main">
<input TYPE='BUTTON' NAME='btnGetName' VALUE='Give me your name'>
</div>

<br>

<div id="Message">
</div>

</body>
</html>
```

The first time you load the
CLIENT02.HTM file in the
browser, you will just see a
button:

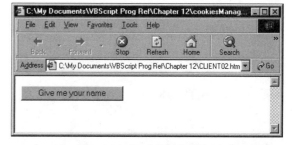

Pushing the button results in
a dialog box asking for your
name:

After giving your name, the
document will be updated
informing you to reload the
page:

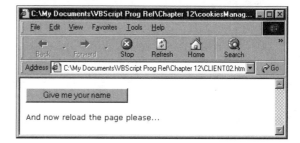

Reloading the page will demonstrate that you added persistence to the page using the Cookies Manager:

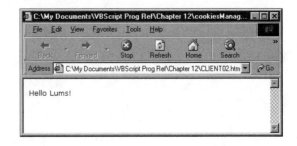

What Has Really Happened?

The first time you load the page there is no cookie storing your name. The following <DIV> tag will show the button:

```
<div id="Main">
<input TYPE='BUTTON' NAME='btnGetName' VALUE='Give me your name'>
</div>
```

Once you've completed the process by giving your name and then reloading the page, the same <DIV> will be dynamically filled with a different content by the VBScript code:

```
sValue = Document.All.myScriptlet.GetCookieKey("Name")

If Document.All.myScriptlet.KeyExists Then
        Document.All.Main.InnerHTML = "Hello " & sValue & "!"
End If
```

Using the Cookies Manager, your name has been stored in a cookie (very originally called "Name").

The Cookies Manager sample extends the "Hello World" sample showing:

❑   How to implement properties (KeyExists)

❑   How to pass variables to methods (SetCookieKey, GetCookieKey, RemoveCookieKey)

❑   How to retrieve values from methods (GetCookieKey)

> **Note: the algorithms in the scriptlet can be improved sensibly. The Cookie Manager is just a sample to show how code can be conveniently packaged into scriptlets.**

Managing Events

When the scriptlet is used in a host document, the host document can be notified about events raised from the scriptlet. The scriptlet can raise two types of events:

❑ Standard DHTML events.

❑ Custom events (not standard events defined by the scriptlet).

Event Handlers' Relationships

Handlers have a one-to-one relationship with each other: one event handler is in the scriptlet and raises the event, another event handler is in the host document to capture the event raised by the scriptlet.

Standard Events

The standard DHTML events exposed by the scriptlet are:

❑ onclick

❑ ondblclick

❑ onkeydown

❑ onkeypress

❑ onkeyup

❑ onmousedown

❑ onmousemove

❑ onmouseup

The following sample shows the implementation of an event handler in the scriptlet for the onclick event:

```
<IMG SRC="some.gif" ONCLICK="BubbleOnClick()">

<SCRIPT LANGUAGE="VBScript">

Function BubbleOnClick()
    ' do something before raising event in the container object if required
    ' usually check the frozen property to be sure that the container
    ' object is ready to handle events
    Window.External.BubbleEvent
    ' do something after raising the event if required
End Function

</SCRIPT>
```

The sample shows:

❑ How to access the object container through the `External` property of the `Window` object

❑ How to raise the event in the object container using the `BubbleEvent` method

If the scriptlet does not implement an event handler for a standard event using the `BubbleEvent` method, that event will not be passed to the host application.

> **Note: in a COM development environment the scriptlet container object will expose all standard events at design time, even if the scriptlet does not handle all of them.**

In this context the scriptlet container object is the HTML document. The `Event` object is accessed through the `Window.Event` property. The `Event` object properties will give additional information on the specific event.

The following sample shows how to access the event additional information using the `Window.Event` property:

```
<SCRIPT LANGUAGE="VBScript" FOR="document" EVENT="onkeydown">
    Window.Status = "Key code = " & Window.Event.KeyCode
Window.Status = Window.Status & "Shift status  = " & Window.Event.ShiftKey
</SCRIPT>
```

Custom Events

Custom events are used:

❑ to expose more information about a standard event

❑ to notify the host document about DHTML events that are not among the events handled by the `BubbleEvent` method

❑ to notify the host document about changes in the internal state of the scriptlet

The following sample shows how to notify an event in the last case:

```
<SCRIPT LANGUAGE="VBScript">

Function public_put_Title(sNewTitle)
    public_Title = sNewTitle
    Window.External.RaiseEvent ("event_ontitlechange", Window.Document)
End Function

</SCRIPT>
```

The sample shows that:

- ❑ to raise an event from the scriptlet the `RaiseEvent` method is required
- ❑ there is a naming convention: the exposed event name is prefixed with `event_`
- ❑ the object involved is passed as an argument to the `RaiseEvent` method

A special event is captured in the host document to run the host event handler: `onscriptletevent`. The following sample shows the technique:

```
<SCRIPT LANGUAGE="VBScript" FOR="myScriptlet"
                        EVENT=onscriptletevent(EventName, EventData)>
    MsgBox "The scriptlet raised the following event: " & EventName
</SCRIPT>
```

All the custom events are then handled by the `onscriptletevent`. As a result, a `Select Case` structure is usually used in the `onscriptletevent` handler to take different actions based on different events.

Determining When the Scriptlet is Ready

To make sure everything works fine, the container object implements the property `ReadyState` and the event `onreadystatechange` to be used to ensure that specific code will be executed only when the scriptlet has been completely loaded into the container object. The `onreadystatechange` event is fired multiple times while the scriptlet is loading. The last time, it indicates that the scriptlet's `.htm` page is fully loaded and its scripts can be called. The `ReadyState` property is used to test the current state. This property is read-only and it is available only at runtime. The `ReadyState` property returns an integer value indicating the loading state of the scriptlet:

Value	Description
1,2	Still loading
3	Scriptlet has been loaded, but the page might not yet be fully functional.
4	Scriptlet is completely loaded

Scriptlet Model Extensions

Specific extensions have been introduced into the Dynamic HTML Object Model to facilitate the design and implementation of scriptlets. All these extensions are available in the DHTML `Window.External` object.

Properties	Methods
Frozen	BubbleEvent
SelectableContent	RaiseEvent
Version	SetContextMenu

The above properties and methods are considered in more detail below:

Frozen Property

Description	Indicates whether the scriptlet container object is ready to handle events.
Syntax	`Variable = Window.External.Frozen`
Remarks	While this property is True, events will not be received by the scriptlet container object. When the container is ready the variable is set to False. The property is read-only.

SelectableContent Property

Description	Specifies whether the user can select the contents of the scriptlet.
Syntax	`Window.External.SelectableContent = boolean`
Remarks	By default, the value of this property is False and the user can click the objects in the scriptlet but not select them. If this property is True, the user can select text or objects in the scriptlet.

Version Property

Description	Returns the version and platform of the scriptlet container object. (sample: "5.0 Win32" is the value returned by the Version property when the scriptlet is hosted by IE5 for Windows95/98/NT)
Syntax	`ver = Window.External.Version`

Remarks	Version is returned in the format N.nnnn platform where N is an integer representing the major version number, nnnn is any number of characters (except a space) representing the minor version number, and platform is the platform (win32, mac, alpha, and so on). The following is an example version number: 2.0b win32
	The version property can be used to determine whether the page is being used as a scriptlet or as a standalone Web page. The following sample shows the technique:
| | ```
Mode = ( TypeName( Window.External.Version) = "String" )
``` |
| | If the value of Mode is True, the page is being used as a scriptlet. Otherwise the page is being used as a standalone page. |

BubbleEvent Method

Description	Sends event notification for a standard event to the host document.
Syntax	`Window.External.BubbleEvent`
Remarks	Use this method to pass a standard DHTML event (as they have been defined previously in this chapter) from the scriptlet to the host document

RaiseEvent Method

Description	Passes a custom event notification from the scriptlet to the host document.
Syntax	`Window.External.RaiseEvent EventName, EventObject`
Parameters	**EventName** is a string identifying the event that is being passed.
	EventObject is a variant type that typically includes a reference to the object on the scriptlet that triggered the event.
Remarks	This method is used to notify the host document about a non-standard event. The onscriptletevents event is strictly related to this method.
```

SetContextMenu Method

Description	Creates a context menu that is displayed when a user right-clicks a scriptlet in the scriptlet container object.
Syntax	`Window.External.SetContextMenu MenuDefinition`
Parameters	**MenuDefinition** defines the command text and commands contained in the context menu. A one-dimensional array in which the menu items are defined using sequences of two elements, *n* and *n+1*.

Element *n* is the command text. Shortcut keys are defined by preceding a letter with "&".

Element *n+1* The method to be called when the command is chosen. You cannot pass parameters to the method.

For example, the following script defines a context menu with two commands: |

```
<SCRIPT LANGUAGE="VBScript" FOR="Menu"
EVENT="onClick">

Dim MenuItems(4)

MenuItems(0) = "&Red Background"
MenuItems(1) = "SetRedBackground"
MenuItems(2) = "&Green Background"
MenuItems(3) = "SetGreenBackground"

Window.External.SetContextMenu MenuItems

</SCRIPT>
```

Scriptlets are Deprecated in IE5

This chapter shows examples of scriptlets that contain code only (no visible HTML tags). Originally scriptlets were introduced to contain HTML visible tags as well. You can actually use it adopting the same techniques we've shown thus far. The only thing to remember is to not set the `WIDTH` and `HEIGHT` parameters of the `<OBJECT>` tag to zero. If the scriptlet has visible parts then it will occupy a visible place in the layout of the HTML page that contains the component. The examples display thinking in "behaviors terms". At the end of 1998, Microsoft deprecated the scriptlets technology. You can still use this technology but Microsoft suggests replacing it in your applications with HTC components (aka behaviors). As we will see later in this chapter, behaviors have a strong influence during the design of an application, suggesting the separation of the code that defines the behavior of an HTML tag from the tag itself (that's the reason why they're called behaviors!). We have presented scriptlets as the original approach; these evolved into behaviors (aka HTML components) and are still an influent technology. (Behaviors are not supported in IE4.)

Behaviors

Introduced with the advent of Internet Explorer 5.0, behaviors are a fascinating mechanism that have the potential to bring a new programming paradigm in the DHTML world.

The behaviors technology is based on a concept: the behavior. The previous sentence could appear to be a truism, but it introduces a major point. As we will see, Microsoft overused the term behavior in different contexts (to indicate a concept, a technology label, and a keyword). We are now focusing on the first and most important occurrence: the behavior concept.

Unlike scriptlets that were created to group HTML elements and scripts together in an external HTML file, the behavior concept emphasizes the separation of script from HTML elements.

The behavior concept is implemented as an encapsulated component that is associated to an HTML element or, more frequently, to a (CSS) class of HTML elements. The following diagrammatically emphasizes this concept:

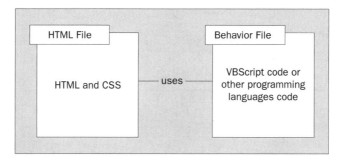

Which Technologies Implement Behaviors?

Currently two technologies allow us to implement behaviors:

- HTCs – HTML Components
- binary behaviors

The following diagram represents the relationship between a behavior and an HTC:

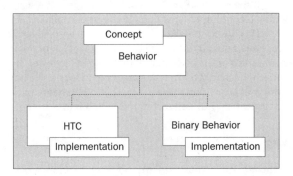

While HTML components are text files with an HTC extension containing code scripts (VBScript or JScript), binary behaviors are built using compiled languages such as C++ or Visual Basic. Binary behaviors do not fall within the scope of this book; they have been introduced to further clarify the relationship between the behavior concept and an HTML component: the HTML component is one of the possible implementations of the behavior concept, binary behaviors are an alternative implementation of the same concept.

When the encapsulated component implementing a behavior is applied to an HTML element, that component extends the behavior of the HTML element (that's where the term behavior comes from).

Applying a Behavior to an HTML Element

There are two major approaches to apply a behavior to an HTML element:

- **Statically** by using a CSS class
- **Dynamically** by using scripting

Applying a Behavior Statically

In IE5 you can define a CSS class using a new property: behavior (the property is currently a Microsoft proposal to W3C). The following code defines a simple CSS class that will be used to apply a behavior to HTML elements:

```
<STYLE>
.myClass {
    behavior: url(somebehavior.htc);
}
</STYLE>
```

After the declaration of such a class, your HTML file could contain different tags, as in:

```
<UL class="myClass">
    <LI> item </LI>
    <LI> item </LI>
</UL>

<DIV class="myClass">just a div</DIV>
```

In the last sample a behavior has been applied to two different HTML elements: <UL> and <DIV>. The behavior of both HTML elements will be extended by the code (possibly VBScript code) that is in the somebehavior.htc file.

The CSS property named behavior can be defined inline using the <STYLE> attribute. In this case the programmer doesn't even need to declare a CSS class to apply the behavior, furthermore a single specific element can be addressed. The following sample shows this technique:

```
<DIV STYLE="behavior: url(somebehavior.htc)">just another div</DIV>
```

Applying a Behavior Dynamically

A behavior can be applied through scripting in two different ways:

❑   using the AddBehavior method

❑   modifying the Behavior property of the Style object

The following code shows both options:

```
<SCRIPT LANGUAGE="VBSCript">
    Sub ApplyOption1()
        Document.All.oMyDiv.AddBehavior("somebehavior.htc");
    End Sub

    Sub ApplyOption2()
        Document.All.oMyDiv.Style.Behavior = "url(somebehavior.htc)";
    End Sub
</SCRIPT>

.............................................................

<DIV ID="oMyDiv">yet another div</DIV>
```

> Note: the Behavior property still expects the syntax
> "url(somebehavior.htc)" while the AddBehavior method doesn't
> require it.

Remove a Behavior Attached Dynamically

An interesting point to consider is the lifecycle of the relationship between an attached behavior and the HTML elements. Behaviors attached employing CSS classes are automatically detached from the elements as soon as the elements are removed from the document tree. Attaching behaviors using any other method (including specifying the behavior statically using the inline technique), will require using the `RemoveBehavior` method. In all these cases it is not enough to remove the elements from the document tree. They will still maintain all the style sheet rules defined programmatically or by inline definitions (including the behavior rule itself).

So far, we have looked at what a behavior is as a concept and in what ways it is used to enhance HTML elements. We haven't examined any behavior implementation yet. We discovered that behaviors could be implemented using VBScript through HTML components. It is time to consider HTML components.

HTML Components

Conceptually an HTML component is an encapsulated component, which implements a behavior. Physically it is a file with an HTC extension. An HTC file contains VBScript code wrapped by a few tags that define the public interface of the component.

Extending HTML Elements Behavior

It is not too difficult to confuse HTML components with scriptlets. Microsoft recommends replacing scriptlets with HTML components because they are a better evolution of this technology. HTML components are evolving into something very different from their ancestor. The behavior concept (discussed earlier) is what makes the difference – a great difference.

The goal of both scriptlets and HTML components is to facilitate code reuse – this produces the misconception that HTML components should replace scriptlets. However, they capture different code aspects and *both* of them should be used in large projects that are component-based. In contrast to scriptlets, the goal of HTML components is to extend HTML elements' behavior. Let's examine a few techniques to extend HTML elements using HTML components:

- ❑ Adding Properties
- ❑ Adding Methods
- ❑ Exposing Component's Events
- ❑ Handling HTML Element's Events

Let's start by taking a look at a basic "Hello World" HTML component to get a taste of how this technology works

The HTML component is stored in the HELLO.HTC file:

```
<ATTACH EVENT="ondocumentready" ONEVENT="Hello()" />

<SCRIPT LANGUAGE="VBScript">

Function Hello()
      MsgBox "Hello World!"
End Function

</SCRIPT>
```

The component has one line of code more than the analogue scriptlet sample, but perhaps it is more important to notice that the prefix "public_" is not required (prefix naming conventions are not required for HTML components).

In the case of this minimal sample, you will certainly find it more interesting to have a look at the HTML file that uses the component CLIENT03.HTM:

```
<html>
<head>

<style>

.myClass   {
      behavior: url(hello.htc);
}

</style>

</head>

<body class="myClass">

</body>
</html>
```

As promised previously, there is a total separation between scripting code (on one side) and HTML+CSS (on the other side). If you think this minimalism was exaggerated, have a look to the following alternative for the client file (CLIENT04.HTM):

```
<html>
<body style="behavior: url(hello.htc)">
</body>
</html>
```

Extreme minimalism! You must be starting to perceive the potential of the behavior paradigm, just looking at the tiny file above.

Enhancing I: Adding Properties

An HTML component can expose properties to the containing document by using the <PROPERTY> element.

The following example implements an HTML component which has a public interface made of only one property called `CryptedKey`. The example captures the essentials of the technique to exposes properties. The HTML component is contained in a file named `CRYPTED.HTC`:

```
<PROPERTY NAME="CryptedKey" PUT="PutCK" GET="GetCK" />

<SCRIPT LANGUAGE="VBScript">

Dim cKey

Function PutCK(ByVal newValue)
    cKey = newValue Xor 43960
End Function

Function GetCK()
    GetCK = cKey Xor 43960
End Function

</SCRIPT>
```

This sample shows:

❑ How to declare the name of the property through the NAME attribute of the `<PROPERTY>` tag

❑ How to declare a function to make the property writable using the PUT attribute

❑ How to declare a function to make the property readable using the GET attribute

The example uses the `Xor` function to crypt/decrypt the value of the property. Applying this crypt/decrypt transformation the example shows how it is possible to use read/write property functions that actually do something more than simply give access to an internal variable.

A client sample that uses the HTML component is shown next (`CLIENT05.HTM`):

```
<html>
<head>

<STYLE>

.myClass  {
    background: red;
    behavior: url(crypted.htc);
}

</STYLE>

<SCRIPT LANGUAGE="VBScript">

Sub WriteProp()
    Dim iKey
```

```
      iKey = CInt(InputBox("Enter the a number:"))
      Document.All.myDIV.CryptedKey = iKey
End Sub

Sub ReadProp()
    MsgBox Document.All.myDiv.CryptedKey
End Sub

</SCRIPT>

</head>
<body>

<DIV CLASS="myClass" ID="myDIV">This div has been enhanced with a Crypted
property</DIV>

<INPUT TYPE="Button" onclick="VBScript:WriteProp" VALUE="Change
Property"></INPUT>
<INPUT TYPE="Button" onclick="VBScript:ReadProp" VALUE="Read
Property"></INPUT>

</body>
</html>
```

The sample applies the behavior to a <DIV> element, identified by the "myDIV" ID.
As you can see from the line:

```
MsgBox Document.All.myDiv.CryptedKey
```

The HTML component has actually enhanced the <DIV> adding to it the CryptedKey
property that behaves as implemented. To check this you could generate an error by
choice, changing a letter in the same line, as in:

```
MsgBox Document.All.myDiv.CryptedKei
```

If you then push the button
labeled **Read Property** you
will see the following error
message:

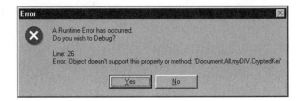

The system is telling you that the CryptedKei property it is not supported by the
object: further evidence that you can actually extend HTML elements using behaviors.

Overriding Standard Properties

It is possible to override the element's default behavior by specifying a name for the
property that is the same as that of a property already defined for the element.

Notify the HTML Element that the Property Value has Changed

When the value of the property has changed, the HTML element can be notified by firing the onpropertychange event calling the FireChange method:

```
Function PutCK(ByVal newValue)
    cKey = newValue Xor 43960
    oCryptedKey.FireChange
End Function
```

The oCryptedKey identifier indicates the ID of the PROPERTY element that has been specified:

```
<PROPERTY NAME="CryptedKey" PUT="PutCK" GET="GetCK" ID="oCryptedKey" />
```

To verify that the event has fired effectively, modify the <DIV> definition in the client:

```
<DIV CLASS="myClass" ID="myDIV" onpropertychange="MsgBox('!')">This div has
been enhanced with a Crypted property</DIV>
```

Enhancing II: Adding Methods

To add new methods to an HTML element using an HTML component is easier than to add properties. Let's modify the CRYPTED.HTC component to expose a method named DisplayCryptedValue which displays the internal value of the CryptedKey property in a dialog. A further element named METHOD (!) is available to expose methods. The resulting CRYPTED.HTC contains the following code:

```
<PROPERTY NAME="CryptedKey" PUT="PutCK" GET="GetCK" ID="oCryptedKey" />
<METHOD NAME="DisplayCryptedValue" />

<SCRIPT LANGUAGE="VBScript">

Dim cKey

Function PutCK(ByVal newValue)
    cKey = newValue Xor 43960
    oCryptedKey.FireChange
End Function

Function GetCK()
    GetCK = cKey Xor 43960
End Function

Sub DisplayCryptedValue()
    MsgBox cKey
End Sub

</SCRIPT>
```

Obviously the host application requires modification to use the
`DisplayCryptedValue` method. The new host application is (`CLIENT06.HTM`):

```
<html>
<head>

<STYLE>

.myClass  {
     background: red;
     behavior: url(crypted.htc);
}

</STYLE>

<SCRIPT LANGUAGE="VBScript">

Sub WriteProp()
     Dim iKey
     iKey = CInt(InputBox("Enter a number:"))
     Document.All.myDIV.CryptedKey = iKey
End Sub

Sub ReadProp()
     MsgBox Document.All.myDiv.CryptedKey
End Sub

Sub DisplayCV()
     Document.All.myDIV.DisplayCryptedValue
End Sub

</SCRIPT>

</head>
<body>

<DIV CLASS="myClass" ID="myDIV">This div has been enhanced with a Crypted
property</DIV>

<INPUT TYPE="Button" onclick="VBScript:WriteProp" VALUE="Change
Property"></INPUT>
<INPUT TYPE="Button" onclick="VBScript:ReadProp" VALUE="Read
Property"></INPUT>
<INPUT TYPE="Button" onclick="VBScript:DisplayCV" VALUE="Display Crypted
Value"></INPUT>

</body>
</html>
```

Enhancing III: Exposing Component's Events

An HTML component can define its own events and expose them through the
<EVENT> element. This mechanism of exposing custom events is clearly more
powerful than the one offered by scriptlets (previously described in this chapter).
Actually, scriptlets expose only one event (`onscriptletevent`). With HTML
components you can expose any kind of event you want to the containing document.
We are going to enhance our CRYPTED.HTC sample with an OnReadWarning event,
which informs the container that somebody has accessed the CryptedKey property:

```
<PROPERTY NAME="CryptedKey" PUT="PutCK" GET="GetCK" ID="oCryptedKey" />
<METHOD NAME="DisplayCryptedValue" />
<EVENT NAME="OnReadWarning" ID="orw" />

<SCRIPT LANGUAGE="VBScript">

Dim cKey

Function PutCK(ByVal newValue)
    cKey = newValue Xor 43960
    oCryptedKey.FireChange
End Function

Function GetCK()
    Dim oEvent
    Set oEvent = CreateEventObject()
    orw.Fire(oEvent)
    GetCK = cKey Xor 43960
End Function

Sub DisplayCryptedValue()
    MsgBox cKey
End Sub

</SCRIPT>
```

This code shows the technique to fire a component event in:

```
Dim oEvent
Set oEvent = CreateEventObject()
orw.Fire(oEvent)
```

The CreateEventObject function is required to create an event object. The event object becomes the parameter of the Fire method of the <EVENT> element. The <EVENT> element is identified by its ID attribute (orw). The <EVENT> element defines the name of the exposed event as well:

```
<EVENT NAME="OnReadWarning" ID="orw" />
```

It is necessary to modify only one line of code in the CLIENT06.HTM to test this new event:

```
<DIV CLASS="myClass" ID="myDIV" onreadwarning="MsgBox('Somebody is reading
the property')">This div has been enhanced with a Crypted property</DIV>
```

To generate the event we launch the client application, assign a value to the property, and then read that value.

The onreadwarning event will be raised and the application will inform you with the following dialog:

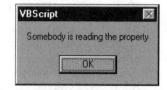

Enhancing IV: Handling HTML Element's Events

HTML components offer a further mechanism to enhance HTML elements: they can attach handlers for the HTML element's events using the <ATTACH> element. The CRYPTED.HTC sample is going to be enhanced to handle the onclick event of the HTML elements to which the behavior is attached:

```
<PROPERTY NAME="CryptedKey" PUT="PutCK" GET="GetCK" ID="oCryptedKey" />
<METHOD NAME="DisplayCryptedValue" />
<EVENT NAME="OnReadWarning" ID="orw" />
<ATTACH EVENT="onclick" ONEVENT="ClickHandler()" />

<SCRIPT LANGUAGE="VBScript">

Dim cKey

Function PutCK(ByVal newValue)
    cKey = newValue Xor 43960
    oCryptedKey.FireChange
End Function

Function GetCK()
    Dim oEvent
    Set oEvent = CreateEventObject()
    orw.Fire(oEvent)
    GetCK = cKey Xor 43960
End Function

Sub DisplayCryptedValue()
    MsgBox cKey
End Sub

Function ClickHandler()
    MsgBox "You clicked on an element enhanced by the CRYPTED behavior"
End Function

</SCRIPT>
```

The handler for the onclick event is declared in the line:

```
<ATTACH EVENT="onclick" ONEVENT="ClickHandler()" />
```

No modifications are required in the host application.

To test the handler, click on the div to run the handler that will produce the following dialog:

Note that when the specified event fires on the element, to which the behavior is attached, the behavior's handler is called after the element's event handler (if any).

Attach Event Handlers Through Scripting

Timing becomes a very critical issue when dealing with event handlers. Sometimes you need to an attach an event handler responding to specific events. It is possible to attach handlers through scripting using the `AttachEvent` method instead of the `<ATTACH>` element. The general technique to deal with dynamically attached event handlers is shown in the following lines of code:

```
<ATTACH EVENT="ondetach" ONEVENT="DetachEvents()" />

<SCRIPT LANGUAGE="VBScript">

Function DetachEvents()
    DetachEvent('onevent1', EvH1)
    DetachEvent('onevent2', EvH2)
End Function

Function EvH1()
    ' do something
End Function

Function EvH2()
    ' do something
End Function

Function SomeTimeInTheBehavior()
    AttachEvent('onevent1', EvH1)
    AttachEvent('onevent2', EvH2)
    ' do something
End Function

</SCRIPT>
```

A `DetachEvent` method and an `ondetach` event are introduced above. Event handlers attached using the `AttachEvent` method must call the `DetachEvent` method to stop receiving notifications. The HTML component will be notified with the `ondetach` event from the page to actually detach all the handlers attached through scripting. The handlers attached the declarative way, using the `<ATTACH>` element, do not need to call the `detachEvent` method.

Multiple Behaviors

It is possible to apply multiple behaviors to an element using the `AddBehavior` method multiple times or using the syntax shown in the following sample:

```
<style>

.myClass {
    behavior: url(bhv-one.htc), url(bhv-two.htc), url(bhv-three.htc);
}

</style>
```

Regarding conflicts resulting from applying multiple behaviors to an element, the following resolution rule is defined: **each succeeding behavior takes precedence over the previous behavior in the order in which the behavior is applied to the element.**

Name Clashing Resolution and the COMPONENT Element

A further element can actually be helpful in the case of multiple behaviors. The
<COMPONENT> element allows us to give a name to the HTML component that can be
used to access properties and methods though scripting (solving name clashing issues
whenever multiple behaviors are applied to the same element). Our sample
component CRYPTED.HTC will be completed using the COMPONENT element to
encapsulate the previous code and give a scripting name to the behavior:

```
<COMPONENT NAME="Crypted">

<PROPERTY NAME="CryptedKey" PUT="PutCK" GET="GetCK" ID="oCryptedKey" />
<METHOD NAME="DisplayCryptedValue" />
<EVENT NAME="OnReadWarning" ID="orw" />
<ATTACH EVENT="onclick" ONEVENT="ClickHandler()" />

<SCRIPT LANGUAGE="VBScript">

Dim cKey

Function PutCK(ByVal newValue)
    cKey = newValue Xor 43960
    oCryptedKey.FireChange
End Function

Function GetCK()
    Dim oEvent
    Set oEvent = CreateEventObject()
    orw.Fire(oEvent)
    GetCK = cKey Xor 43960
End Function

Sub DisplayCryptedValue()
    MsgBox cKey
End Sub

Function ClickHandler()
    MsgBox "You clicked on an element enhanced by the CRYPTED behavior"
End Function

</SCRIPT>

</COMPONENT>
```

After using the <COMPONENT> element it is possible to access the component
properties and methods using the component name:

```
Sub ReadProp()
    MsgBox Document.All.myDiv.Crypted.CryptedKey
End Sub
```

This definitively solves the name clashing issue. Suppose we want to apply two
behaviors (named, for example, Bh1 and Bh2) that both define a Description
property to the same element (myDiv), it is possible to access both properties:

```
MsgBox Document.All.myDiv.Bh1.Title & Document.All.myDiv.Bh2.Title
```

The goal of this section was to introduce all the fundamental techniques to start you on your way using behaviors and HTML components. Experimenting with the code and concepts discussed above can only help to further your understanding of these topics. OK, let's look at a technology that extends the functionality of your page beyond the browser.

Remote Scripting

Remote scripting was created to make web applications substantially more powerful and to make them more closely resemble client/server applications developed using languages like C++, Visual Basic, or Java – thereby overcoming the inherent limitations of web applications. Without remote scripting, a web browser has only one way to request new information from the server: to load an entirely new page. With remote scripting it becomes possible for the client page to execute a method on an ASP page without navigating away from the page itself. More importantly, the requested data is available as the return value of the remote method called by the client page.

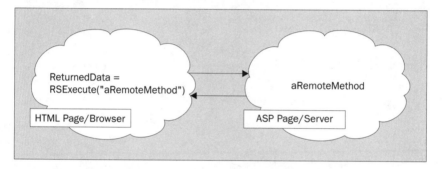

Combined with DHTML, this technology heavily simplifies all the applications that were forced to use cookies, hidden HTML input fields or other dirty tricks to rebuild the new page as similar as possible to the previous one.

Influence of JScript on Remote Scripting

Unfortunately for VBScript users, the current remote scripting (version 1.0a) was created for JavaScript (or JScript to use its Microsoft equivalent). Microsoft developed remote scripting as part of a larger project called Microsoft Scripting Library. In fact the current implementation is a library of functions to enable remote scripting features, plus something more: a Java applet. Three files constitute the implementation of the remote scripting technology:

❑   RS.HTM (a collection of JScript functions to be used on the client page)

❑   RS.ASP (a collection of JScript functions to be used on the server ASP page)

❑   RSPROXY.CLASS (a Java applet that plays the main role)

These files, along with the official documentation, can be downloaded from the Microsoft Scripting Technologies Site
(http://www.msdn.microsoft.com/scripting/).

What is the Role of Remote Scripting Files?

Staying within the scope of this chapter (and this book), let's look at the role of the three files listed above, so we can get a clearer idea of what is 'under the hood' of remote scripting:

❏ The Java applet RSPROXY.CLASS is inserted automatically in the client page during initialization by the RSEnableRemoteScripting function. The role of the Java applet is to send the HTTP request to the server and receive the response.

❏ The RS.HTM file implements functions that marshal the remote method name and parameters into a buffer to be sent "over the wire".

❏ RS.ASP implements functions that unmarshal such data from the receiving buffer. In a complementary way the returned value is marshaled by RS.ASP function and unmarshaled by RS.HTM functions.

The following pictures illustrates the mechanism:

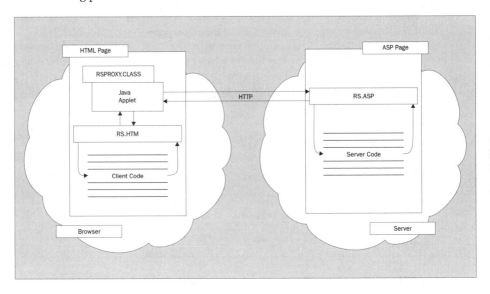

Can Remote Scripting be used by VBScript users?

The answer is obviously positive, otherwise you would not have found this section in a book about VBScript. The remainder of this chapter provides a few guidelines to permit VBScript developers to use remote scripting in a profitable way, avoiding features that have been proved to work with JScript only. The guidelines are on how to:

❑ install the remote scripting files

❑ enable the remote scripting engine on the server side

❑ enable the remote scripting engine on the client side

❑ call a remote method from a client page using VBScript

❑ fetch the data returned from the remote method call

❑ transform an ASP page into a VBScript remote object

Luckily the major benefits of remote scripting are available to VBScript users as well. To achieve them, the following step should be followed carefully.

Installing Remote Script on the Server

The default location for the remote scripting files is in a directory called `_ScriptLibrary` that must be located in the root directory of your Web Server. All the samples in this section will assume that the files using remote scripting are located in a directory located in the root directory of your Web Server as well. The remote scripting files can be located elsewhere but then you have to specify which is the location while initializing the remote scripting engine both on client and server side. To avoid any problem, follow this format while building your first remote scripting project:

If the root directory of your Web Server is:	`c:\inetpub\wwwroot\`
The three remote scripting files (`rs.htm`, `rs.asp`, `rsproxy.class`) should be located in the directory:	`c:\inetpub\wwwroot\ _ScriptLibrary`
Any file in your project using remote scripting should be located in a directory like:	`c:\inetpub\wwwroot\ YourProject`

Enabling Remote Scripting on the Server

On the server your code will be included inside an ASP page. I suggest you use the following skeleton to encapsulate your server side scripting code and at the same time enable remote scripting:

```
<%@ LANGUAGE=VBSCRIPT %>
<%

' ...write your VBScript remote methods here...

' remember to call RSDispatch to initialize the remote scripting engine
RSDispatch

%>
<!-- #INCLUDE FILE="../_scriptlibrary/rs.asp" -->
```

As you can see, two steps are required:

- ❑ To invoke the function RSDispatch once in the lifetime of the ASP page to initialize the remote scripting engine

- ❑ To include the file RS.ASP that contains the implementation of the RSDispatch function.

Enabling Remote Scripting on the Client

The remote scripting engine must be initialized on every client page that needs to call remote methods. In this case there is a standard header to be applied just after the <BODY> html element:

```
<BODY>
<SCRIPT language="JavaScript" src="../_ScriptLibrary/rs.htm"></SCRIPT>
<SCRIPT
language="JavaScript">RSEnableRemoteScripting("../_ScriptLibrary");</SCRIPT>
```

This is the only place in which we will use JavaScript in this chapter. It is necessary because the file RS.HTM is a file of Javascript functions despite its .HTM extension. Furthermore, RSEnableRemoteScripting is an initializing function contained in that file.

Invoking a Remote Method

Once the remote scripting has been properly initialized we can start invoking VBScript remote methods, entering the sample "Hello (Remote) World!" The sample requires two files that should be located in the same directory on your Web Server. For example they could be located at:

```
D:\inetpub\wwwroot\rs\04\rsclient01.htm
D:\inetpub\wwwroot\rs\04\hello.asp
```

While the remote scripting library (rs.htm, rs.asp and rsproxy.class) is located in:

```
D:\inetpub\wwwroot\rs\_ScriptLibrary
```

The ASP page that hosts the remote method is called HELLO.ASP, its source code is:

```
<%@ LANGUAGE=VBSCRIPT %>
<%

Function HRW()
     HRW = "Hello Remote World!"
End Function

RSDispatch
```

```
%>
<!-- #INCLUDE FILE="../_scriptlibrary/rs.asp" -->

<SCRIPT RUNAT=SERVER LANGUAGE="JavaScript">

   var public_description = new ExposeRemoteMethods();

   function ExposeRemoteMethods()
   {
      this.HRW = Function( 'return HRW()' );
   }

</SCRIPT>
```

A bit of JavaScript is used to build this sample and make it as simple as possible, for now. But we'll get rid of this need for JavaScript after introducing VBScript classes. JavaScript is needed to expose the HRW method as a remote function. VBScript cannot expose remote functions, but it can expose remote objects (with their methods), that give us more power and flexibility. By the way, the remote method is called HRW (and stands for "Hello Remote World"):

```
Function HRW()
     HRW = "Hello Remote World!"
End Function
```

A client page named RSCLIENT01.HTM calls the remote method. Its source code is:

```
<HTML>
<HEAD>
<SCRIPT language="VBScript">

Function InvokeHRW()
     Dim retObj
     set retObj = RSExecute("http://me/rs/04/hello.asp", "HRW")
     MsgBox retObj.return_value
End Function

</SCRIPT>
</HEAD>

<BODY onload="InvokeHRW">

<SCRIPT language="JavaScript" src="../_ScriptLibrary/rs.htm"></SCRIPT>
<SCRIPT
language="JavaScript">RSEnableRemoteScripting("../_ScriptLibrary");</SCRIPT>

</BODY>
</HTML>
```

The remote method is called by the VBScript function:

```
Function InvokeHRW()
     Dim retObj
     Set retObj = RSExecute("http://me/rs/04/hello.asp", "HRW")
     MsgBox retObj.return_value
End Function
```

The function RSExecute is implemented in the RS.HTM file and gives the developer the power to invoke remote methods on the server without leaving the current client page. It returns an object with a very important property called return_value. *This property contains the data retrieved from the server without loading a new page* (!).

The remote method HRW simply returns a constant string "Hello Remote World", but it could be attached to a database via ADO, or it could have retrieved data on the server by other means, returning more meaningful and critical information.

We are now going to introduce a technique to get rid of the Javascript public_description object, using VBScript classes.

Transforming an ASP Page into a VBScript Object

In the former sample code a little JavaScript was required. So, let's get rid of the JavaScript, introduce a fully VBScript sample, and then discuss the importance and benefits of this approach. Let's call the sample "Hello (VBScript Remote) World!" Changes are required in both the client and the server page. Using our model directory structure, the two new files could be located in the directories:

```
D:\inetpub\wwwroot\rs\05\rsclient02.htm
D:\inetpub\wwwroot\rs\05\vbhello.asp
```

While the remote scripting library (rs.htm, rs.asp and rsproxy.class) are still located in:

```
D:\inetpub\wwwroot\rs\_ScriptLibrary
```

Here's the server page, so you can immediately appreciate that there is no more JavaScript. The VBHELLO.ASP code is:

```
<%@ LANGUAGE=VBSCRIPT %>
<%

Class clsHello
    Public Function HRW()
        HRW = "Hello Remote World!"
    End Function
End Class

Set public_description = New clsHello

RSDispatch

%>
<!-- #INCLUDE FILE="../_scriptlibrary/rs.asp" -->
```

In this version the HRW remote method has become a method of a VBScript (5!) class named clsHello. The nice issue is that VBScript classes can be used to define a working public_description object.

Modifications are required in the client page. Now we must invoke a VBScript object and not just a remote function. The `RSCLIENT02.HTM` code is:

```
<HTML>
<HEAD>
<SCRIPT language="VBScript">

Function InvokeHRW()
     Dim aspObj
     Dim retObj
     Set aspObj = RSGetASPObject("vbhello.asp")
     Set retObj = aspObj.HRW()
     MsgBox retObj.return_value
End Function

</SCRIPT>
</HEAD>

<BODY onload="InvokeHRW">

<SCRIPT language="JavaScript" src="../_ScriptLibrary/rs.htm"></SCRIPT>
<SCRIPT
language="JavaScript">RSEnableRemoteScripting("../_ScriptLibrary");</SCRIPT>

</BODY>
</HTML>
```

In this case we are no more using `RSExecute` but a different function available in the remote scripting engine: `RSGetASPObject`. As you can see from the line:

```
     Set aspObj = RSGetASPObject("vbhello.asp")
```

The `RSGetAspObject` function takes only one parameter that is our ASP page. It actually converts an ASP page into a remote object; in fact, we can call the `HRW` remote method without using `RSExecute`:

```
     Set retObj = aspObj.HRW()
```

All those who are used to implementing the object oriented model will immediately understand the benefits coming from this technique. The functionality of an ASP page can be divided in remote methods and encapsulated inside an object. On the client side all the scripting code will invoke remote methods as if they were local:

```
     aspObj.aRemoteMethod
```

The number of applications of this technique are then just limited by your imagination. Once again, experimentation is the mother of learning *and* invention. Enjoy!

Summary

The goal of this chapter is to give you an understanding of how much farther (than a static web page) VBScript can take you. There are sufficient code samples for you to reuse or adapt to your own needs. We have looked at the evolution of scriptlets into behaviors and their use through HTML components. With regard to scriptlets we saw how to:

❑   implement properties

❑   pass variables to methods

❑   retrieve values from methods

❑   manage events statically

❑   manage events dynamically

❑   use custom events

We then moved on to look at behaviors and saw how to:

❑   apply a behavior statically

❑   apply a behavior dynamically

❑   remove attached behaviors

This led us to learn that the goal of HTML components is to extend HTML elements' behavior. And, with regard to HTML components, we also looked at:

❑   adding properties

❑   adding methods

❑   exposing events

❑   handling HTML element's events

❑   enhancement techniques

Finally, we looked at how to make web applications using VBScript perform like applications developed using more complicated compiled languages. Specifically, we looked at using remote scripting technologies and saw how to:

❑   install the remote scripting files

❑   enable the remote scripting engine on the server side

❑   enable the remote scripting engine on the client side

❑   call a remote method from a client page using VBScript

❑   fetch the data returned from the remote method call

❑   transform an ASP page into a VBScript remote object

Again, remember that whole volumes can (and have!) been devoted to the topics we have considered in this chapter and, so, refer to more specialized sources to further your learning.

13

HTML Applications (HTAs)

The previous chapters focused on web development, but there are times when you don't want your application to look like a web page with all of the browser components exposed, like toolbars and so on. In the past, C/C++, Java, and Visual Basic programmers had the market cornered for traditional Windows applications. With the introduction of HTML applications in Internet Explorer 5, though, that has changed. Now you can use the knowledge that you already have of DHTML, CSS, and scripting to write Windows applications.

HTML applications are often referred to as HTAs. This refers to the file extension (.hta) that HTML applications use. We'll be using both 'HTA' and 'HTML application' interchangeably throughout the chapter.

What Tools Do You Need?

❑   A text editor

❑   Version 5 of the Script Engines (download free from http://msdn.microsoft.com/scripting)

❑   Internet Explorer 5 (HTAs are supported automatically when you install Internet Explorer 5. Previous versions of Internet Explorer do not support HTAs.)

What is an HTML Application?

An HTML application is essentially what it sounds like. It is an HTML-based application. The parent process of mshta.exe (the application that actually runs an HTA) is Internet Explorer 5, so almost anything (we'll talk about exceptions later) that you can do with Internet Explorer 5, you can do in HTA. That includes scripting, CSS, behaviors, XML, and XSL.

You can control everything that is shown on the screen with an HTA. You don't have to see Internet Explorer menus or toolbars if you don't want to. For example, take a look at the simple application that we will use to help us explore HTAs in this chapter. All it does is navigate to a few select sites, but as you can see, this application really doesn't look like it's running under IE5 at all. There's no toolbars or menus.

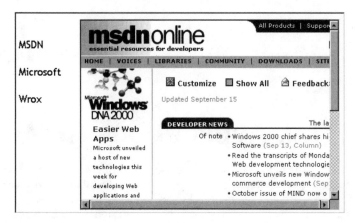

You may be thinking, that's great, but what about the security warnings that come up when you embed other objects in a browser? The great thing about HTAs is that they are **fully trusted** applications. All of the restrictions that you worry about with a web page are not a problem with HTAs. You can even modify the registry while running an HTA. But keep in mind that if you don't have standard security restrictions, you need to be aware of the problems that may arise from your code or another site that is used within the HTA. We'll look into security issues in more depth later in this chapter.

Ok, that's all good, but how do we run an HTA? All you need is Internet Explorer 5, and you're ready. Once you have an HTA, you can simply double-click on the file and the application will run, just like any other program. HTAs can be run from a server as well as a client machine, as we'll see later on.

I hope that you are now as excited about HTAs as I am. Now let's learn how to make them work.

How to Create a Basic HTA

It's actually very simple. All you need to do is change the file extension of your HTML file to hta. That's pretty easy, right? Let's look at an example.

Sample HTML File

We'll start with an HTML file that navigates a frame to a web site. Since it's a normal HTML file at the moment, it'll have the file extension .htm. There are three SPANs that, when clicked, navigate the IFRAME (which will act as our viewer). The three web sites we'll be using are www.wrox.com, www.microsoft.com, and msdn.microsoft.com. When the page is loaded, we navigate to MSDN by default.

```
<HTML>
<HEAD>

<TITLE>Sample HTML Application</TITLE>

<LINK rel="stylesheet" type="text/css" href="HTA.css">
</HEAD>
<BODY>

<BR>
<BR>
<SPAN
  onclick="Viewer.document.location.href='http://msdn.microsoft.com'">
  MSDN</SPAN>
<BR>
<BR>
<SPAN
  onclick="Viewer.document.location.href='http://www.microsoft.com'">
  Microsoft</SPAN>
<BR>
<BR>
<SPAN
  onclick="Viewer.document.location.href='http://www.wrox.com'">
  Wrox</SPAN>

<IFRAME ID=Viewer src="http://msdn.microsoft.com">
</IFRAME>

</BODY>
</HTML>
```

Now we have to create the `HTA.css` file. Here's the code:

```
BODY
{
  FONT-FAMILY: 'Trebuchet MS';
  FONT-SIZE: 18px;
  POSITION: absolute
}
SPAN
{
  CURSOR: hand;
  POSITION: absolute;
  WIDTH: 15%
}
IFRAME
{
  HEIGHT: 95%;
  LEFT: 15%;
  OVERFLOW: scroll;
  POSITION: absolute;
  TOP: 5%;
  WIDTH: 80%
}
```

Our stylesheet sets the default font as Trebuchet MS with a font size of 18 pixels. We define positioning as absolute. For our spans, we turn the mouse pointer into a hand.

We refer to a number of size parameters in percentages. This sets the dimension as a percentage of the size of its parent element. If the length of the parent element changes, the length of the child element will be changed as well. Say we give the parent element a width of 900px (pixels). If the width of the child element is 10%, then the absolute width of the child element will be 90px.

Our web page looks like the picture below. Note that we have all of the standard Internet Explorer toolbars and menus.

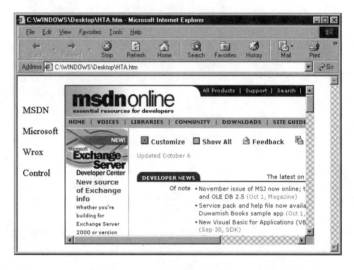

Although the script may look correct, we do have a few problems. When an HTML file has a FRAME or IFRAME, there are some security restrictions that aren't necessarily obvious right away.

If a frame navigates away from the domain in which the original file is located, the properties and methods of the frame, and the elements within it, are no longer accessible to the parent element. For example, once the IFRAME has been navigated to another URL, such as the MSDN site, we can't change the document.location of the IFRAME. In fact the document of the IFRAME is not accessible at all. This caused me quite a few headaches before I figured it out.

Thus, if I try to click on MSDN or any other link, I receive an error message. This restriction is there to limit the ability of one site to track your subsequent navigation.

This might not seem reasonable, but let's think about it a little bit more. Let's say that you have search results in one panel of a page, generated from a search engine. The search panel can know where you are going from the IFRAME, but once you get to the site in the opposite frame, the search engine can't track anything else. It's a privacy thing – do you really want Yahoo to know about everything that you do on the Internet?

Making an HTML File into an HTML Application

Let's try renaming our file from HTA.htm to HTA.hta. This small change now gives our application an entirely different look. By default, we have a title bar and minimize, maximize and restore buttons, but we don't have any of the Internet Explorer toolbars. The title bar of the application even picked up the title that we put in. You can also navigate to other sites through the main application. That was a quick fix to some painful problems.

Now, that's sweet. All we needed to do was change the file extension, and our file is recognized as an application. We don't have to deal with all the security issues any more. But we might want to get rid of the title bar, or have the application launch in full screen.... Well, we can solve those problems, too. Let's look at the HTA:APPLICATION tag.

The <HTA:APPLICATION> Tag

We want to modify the look of our application even further. Fortunately, there is an HTML tag called HTA:APPLICATION. With this tag we can choose not to display a caption, or to maximize the window, as well as a few other things. In our sample application, let's try some of these options.

You can embed the HTA:APPLICATION tag anywhere within the document, but for performance reasons, it's recommended that you embed it within the head of the document. Since the browser parses information in the order that it is found on the page, if you place the HTA tag at the end of the document, the browser won't recognize the HTA attributes that you have set until it has completely parsed the document. For example, let's say that you have sized elements by percentages. The browser will now need to calculate these parameters over again.

An end tag is not required. We'll set the `Caption` attribute to `no` and the `windowState` attribute of the `HTML` tag to `maximize`. Now our application loads in full screen mode without a title bar. We can close the application through the Windows task bar.

```
<HTML>
<HEAD>

<TITLE>Sample HTML Application</TITLE>

<HTA:APPLICATION
  Caption="no"
  windowState="maximize">

<LINK rel="stylesheet" type="text/css" href="HTA.css">
</HEAD>
<BODY>

<BR>
<BR>
<SPAN
  onclick="Viewer.document.location.href='http://msdn.microsoft.com'">
  MSDN</SPAN>
<BR>
<BR>
<SPAN
  onclick="Viewer.document.location.href='http://www.microsoft.com'">
  Microsoft</SPAN>
<BR>
<BR>
<SPAN
  onclick="Viewer.document.location.href='http://www.wrox.com'">
  Wrox</SPAN>

<IFRAME ID=Viewer src="http://msdn.microsoft.com">
</IFRAME>

</BODY>
</HTML>
```

And here's our new look.

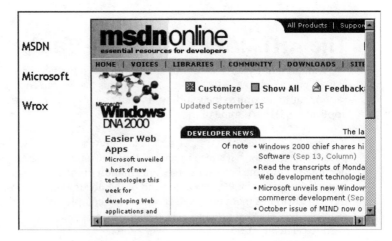

Do File Extensions Still Matter?

If you use an `.htm` file extension, but an `HTA` tag is embedded, will the application act like an HTML application? The answer is no. Without the `.hta` file extension, the `HTA:APPLICATION` tag is not recognized. The file extension is the only thing that truly defines an HTML application.

Changing Parameters from the Command Line

Let's try launching an HTA from the command line. First, we need to have an ID for our HTA to be able to access attributes of our HTA through script. We are also going to put our caption back in, but we'll talk about that sort of thing further in the next section.

We'll also create a script that creates an array from our `commandLine` property. The `commandLine` property is only available through scripting. It returns the location of the HTA launched and any other parameters specified on the command line. It cannot be specified within the `HTA:APPLICATION` tag. Please note that this script requires that there are no spaces in the name of the location used to launch the application. You can use this in your existing HTA if you simply replace the existing HTA tag with the one below, and add the script under the new HTA tag:

```
<HTA:APPLICATION
  ID=MySampleHTA
  Caption="yes"
  windowState="maximize">

<SCRIPT LANGUAGE="VBScript">
  Option Explicit

  Sub LoadPage

    Dim cmdLineArray
    Dim WebSite

    ' fill array with elements of commandLine attribute
    cmdLineArray = Split(MySampleHTA.commandLine)

    ' check if first element of array is equal to commandLine attribute
    ' if so, no web site was specified, so go to MSDN.
    If cmdLineArray(0) = MySampleHTA.commandLine Then
      WebSite = "http://msdn.microsoft.com"

    ' Otherwise, there is a specified web site. Need to see
    ' if it's properly formatted. If :// isn't present in
    ' the second element of the array, we add http://
    ElseIf InStr(1, cmdLineArray(1), "://" ) = 0 Then
      WebSite = cmdLineArray(1)
      WebSite = "http://" & WebSite
    Else
      WebSite = cmdLineArray(1)
    End If

    Viewer.document.location.href = WebSite

  End Sub

</SCRIPT>
```

You'll also need to change your HTML BODY tag to read:

```
<BODY onload="LoadPage">
```

Now, when we launch the application from the command line with:

```
d:\wrox\hta\hta.hta www.wrox.com
```

...the Wrox site will be displayed in the IFRAME. If a specific web site is not specified at the command line, the default will be MSDN. Let's just see how we did that. First, this line:

```
cmdLineArray = Split(MySampleHTA.commandLine)
```

...creates an array that accesses the commandLine attribute of our HTA and splits it into separate pieces wherever it finds a space. Then, we check to see if the first element of the array is the same as the commandLine attribute of the HTA. If it is, that means that the string had no spaces, which in turn means that no web site was specified. So we go to the MSDN site.

```
If cmdLineArray(0) = MySampleHTA.commandLine Then
    WebSite = "http://msdn.microsoft.com"
```

Otherwise, we know that a web site *has* been specified, so we need to see if it is properly formatted. If we don't find '://' in the second element of the array, we'll add 'http://'.

```
ElseIf InStr(1, cmdLineArray(1), "://" ) = 0 Then
    WebSite = cmdLineArray(1)
    WebSite = "http://" & WebSite
```

Finally, what if the URL *is* formed correctly? Here, we assume that if the Else statement is hit, then the command line must contain a properly formatted URL, so we use that.

```
Else
    WebSite = cmdLineArray(1)
```

After we've done all that, we send the IFRAME to the web site we specified.

```
Viewer.document.location.href = WebSite
```

And that's it!

All HTA:APPLICATION Attributes

There are a number of other properties that we can access for the HTA:APPLICATION tag. The full list of properties for the HTA:APPLICATION tag appears in the table below.

Property	Values	Description
ID	User-defined string	ID that can be used to access the HTA through script.
applicationName	User-defined string	Sets the name of the HTA.
border	thick (Default) thin none dialog	The border size for the application. Experiment to see what they all look like!
borderStyle	normal (Default) static raised sunken complex	The style of the border. The static border style is normally used for windows that don't allow user input.
caption	yes (Default) no	Displays a caption in the title bar.
commandLine	N/A	Path used to launch the HTA. This is a read-only property.
icon	Path to .bmp or.ico file	Icon to be displayed in the task bar and title bar when the application is running.
maximizeButton	yes (Default) no	Displays the maximize button.
minimizeButton	yes (Default) no	Displays the minimize button.
showInTaskBar	yes (Default) no	Shows the application running in the task bar. Even if this property is set to no, the application is still seen when using *Alt+Tab* or *Ctrl+Alt+Del*.

Property	Values	Description
singleInstance	no (Default) yes	Determines whether more than one instance of the program can run at a time.
sysMenu	yes (Default) no	System menu is displayed when clicking on the title bar or by right clicking on the application in the task bar. The system displays resizing options, such as minimize and maximize
version	User defined	Version number. This attribute is available for display, but has no effect on the application itself
windowState	normal (Default) minimize maximize	The normal state will size the window to the same size Internet Explorer starts up at, whatever that may be.

Interdependent Attributes

A number of attributes are dependent upon each other. If the `border` attribute is not set to thick, the HTA cannot be resized. If the ID of the application is not specified, other attributes of the HTA cannot be accessed.

- ❑ If the `caption` is set to `no`, then the minimize and maximize buttons aren't displayed, the system menu is not available, and the program icon is not seen in the title bar.

- ❑ If the system menu is turned off, then the minimize and maximize buttons are not visible. The icon in the title bar won't be visible either.

- ❑ If you choose not to display a border, there is no title bar, and so the minimize and maximize buttons (along with the title bar icon in the title bar) are not visible.

This may seem a little confusing, but the goal was to match the current Windows user interface.

Examples of Interdependency

Let's look at a few examples. We'll start by setting the minimize and maximize buttons, add an icon, a caption, a border, and a system menu. We can also see the system menu from the task bar. This is all done by changing the `HTA:APPLICATION` tag as seen next.

```
<HTML>
<HEAD>
<META NAME="GENERATOR" Content="Microsoft Visual Studio 6.0">

<TITLE>Sample HTML Application</TITLE>
<HTA:APPLICATION
  ID=MySampleHTA
  icon="hta.ico"
  caption="yes"
  minimizeButton="yes"
  maximizeButton="yes"
  sysMenu = "yes"
  border="thick"
  windowState="maximize">

<SCRIPT LANGUAGE="VBScript">
  Option Explicit
```

Now let's try setting the `sysMenu` property to no, as shown:

```
<HTA:APPLICATION
  ID=MySampleHTA
  icon="hta.ico"
  caption="yes"
  minimizeButton="yes"
  maximizeButton="yes"
  sysMenu = "no"
  border="thick"
  windowState="maximize">
```

With this simple change, our HTA no longer displays the icon in the title bar and in the taskbar; we aren't able to resize our window; and the minimize, maximize and close buttons are no longer visible.

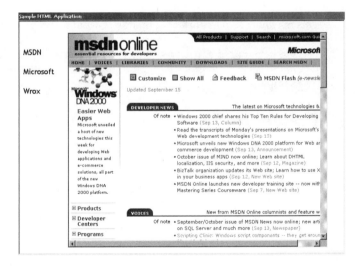

Now let's change the `sysMenu` attribute back to `yes`, but set the `caption` to no. Now we can no longer see the minimize, maximize and close buttons. This time, since the `windowState` is also set to `maximize`, the task bar is no longer visible.

```
<HTA:APPLICATION
  ID=MySampleHTA
  icon="hta.ico"
  caption="no"
  minimizeButton="yes"
  maximizeButton="yes"
  sysMenu = "yes"
  border="thick"
  windowState="maximize">
```

Finally, we'll set the caption attribute back to yes, and see what happens when we set the border to none. In fact, we have the same result as if we set the caption attribute to no.

```
<HTA:APPLICATION
  ID=MySampleHTA
  icon="hta.ico"
  caption="yes"
  minimizeButton="yes"
  maximizeButton="yes"
  sysMenu = "yes"
  border="none"
  windowState="maximize">
```

There isn't a way to specifically set the close button on the application. Although the minimize and maximize button can be set to no without losing the close button, if the caption or the system menu are set to no or if the border is set to none, the close button will not be visible.

This may not seem important at first glance, but if you choose certain options, you will have to close the application using *Ctrl+Alt+Del*. You probably don't want all of your users to be required to use this method. Thus, you will need to provide another method to close your application through scripting, with the window.close function for example.

Helpful Hints

Some of the references that I found said that yes/no values could be replaced by true or false. I tried this, but with no success. I recommend using yes or no.

I have read other sources which say the title bar is not immediately loaded, and that the more logic you perform within a document, the longer it takes the title to appear. A simple solution is to limit the amount of logic that is performed prior to the onload event firing, although I haven't found this to be a major issue.

The document's location href is not updated until the application is completely loaded. If you try to access this property before the onload event fires, you will be given the href of the previous frame. It's recommended that you use the document.URL property if you need access to the location of the document before it is loaded. For example, you could use document.URL and retrieve the same result you'd have expected from the document.location.href property.

HTAs and Security

We've already seen that HTAs aren't limited by browser security because the executable file that runs the HTA (`mshta.exe`) disables Internet Explorer's standard security. HTAs are considered fully trusted applications, and all of the restrictions on the client machine and its file system are removed. The registry of the client machine is even accessible.

> *If this seems like a very unsafe thing to you, bear in mind that the same power is available to standard programs written in C++ and Visual Basic, for example.*

ActiveX controls can be embedded without warnings. This is extremely helpful when using even standard scripting controls such as the `FileSystemObject` or the XMLDOM. Keep in mind when disabling security warnings, though, that you should make sure that security issues won't be a problem.

But what if you want to apply some restrictions when navigating to another web site? There are certainly no guarantees that the site you are navigating to doesn't have a virus or some other problem.

Typically, FRAMEs or IFRAMEs are used to navigate to another site within a document. These tags are generally used because they can have a source. In fact, frames have their own document object. DIVs, SPANs, and other frequently used tags do not have this capability. Let's look at security for frames.

Frames Without Trust

In the past, FRAMEs and IFRAMEs have supported an attribute called TRUSTED to indicate if normal browser security would apply to a frame. With Internet Explorer 5, the TRUSTED attribute is no longer functional. Although there is still quite a bit of documentation that refers to the TRUSTED attribute, I tried it out and it doesn't work.

Well, that's great. How are you supposed to change a frame's security options in Internet Explorer 5? First of all, when you are not using a frame within an HTML application, the answer is that you can't.

> **All FRAMEs and IFRAMEs not in HTML applications are considered untrusted. Normal browser security applies to the frame.**

But what if you *are* in an HTML application? You may want a frame to be trusted. How are you going to do that? Well, that's where the APPLICATION attribute of the frames comes in.

APPLICATION Attribute

The APPLICATION attribute has been added to the FRAME and IFRAME tags. The APPLICATION attribute indicates whether a frame should be treated like an HTML application, disabling security warnings. The possible values for the attribute are **yes**, meaning the application is trusted, or **no** (the default), meaning that standard security warnings apply.

If, by default, frames are untrusted, how did we avoid the security issues in the example above by simply changing the file extension? That's because untrusted frames in an HTA are unaware of both the parent window and the URL that opened the external frame. The untrusted content then can't use that information in any way. When the document within the untrusted frame tries to access the top element of the document, the frame's window is returned. That way, there are no access violations that would occur in the HTML file with frames in different domains.

> If frames within an html document are in different URL domains, the script for one domain cannot access the properties and methods in another domain.

The HTA itself is considered trusted, and does have access to the frame's properties and methods.

Let's take a look at a page that contains an ActiveX control. We'll create a simple VBScript object, the FileSystemObject. This is just a simple demonstration page, though, and we aren't going to actually use the FileSystemObject in any way. We'll call this page ActiveXControl.htm.

```
<HTML>
<HEAD>

<TITLE>ActiveX Control</TITLE>

<LINK rel="stylesheet" type="text/css" href="HTA.css">

<SCRIPT Language="VBSCRIPT">

  Dim FileSystem
  ' Creates the FileSystemObject
  Set FileSystem = CreateObject("Scripting.FileSystemObject")

</SCRIPT>
</HEAD>

<BODY>

This page contains the ActiveX control FileSystemObject.

</BODY>
</HTML>
```

Let's look at what happens when we try to load this page into the browser. We get a security warning that asks the user if they want to download the ActiveX control:

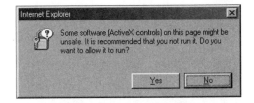

After we answer yes, our page looks like the picture below.

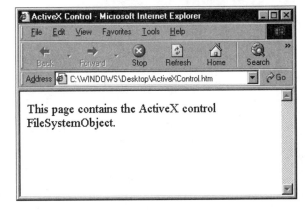

Let's try adding this page into our HTA and see what happens. We'll add a fourth span that is linked to our new page. For now, everything else will stay the same. Just add these lines under the other 3 spans.

```
<BR>
<BR>
<SPAN
    onclick="Viewer.document.location.href='ActiveXControl.htm'">
    Control</SPAN>
```

When we click on our new span, we see the same security warning. But now let's set our IFRAME's APPLICATION attribute to yes.

```
<IFRAME ID=Viewer APPLICATION="yes">
</IFRAME>
```

Now when we navigate to our new page, we don't see any security warnings. The resulting HTA should look like the following picture.

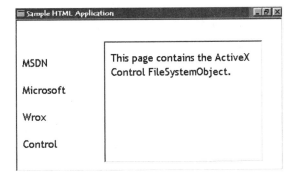

Nested Frames

What if you want to have nested frames? Let's add an `IFRAME` into the body of
`ActiveXControl.htm`. The source for the `IFRAME` will be `NestedFrame.htm`.

```
<HTML>
<HEAD>
<TITLE>ActiveX Control</TITLE>

<LINK rel="stylesheet" type="text/css" href="HTA.css">

<SCRIPT Language="VBSCRIPT">

  Dim FileSystem
  ' Creates the FileSystemObject
  Set FileSystem = CreateObject("Scripting.FileSystemObject")

</SCRIPT>
</HEAD>

<BODY>

<IFRAME src="NestedFrame.htm">
</IFRAME>

</BODY>
</HTML>
```

Let's create `NestedFrame.htm`. This file also creates the `FileSystemObject`. The
body of the document contains text. Now when we try to load the file
`ActiveXControl.htm`, we receive two security warnings, one for each frame.

```
<HTML>
<HEAD>
<TITLE>ActiveX Control</TITLE>

<LINK rel="stylesheet" type="text/css" href="HTA.css">

<SCRIPT Language="VBSCRIPT">

  Dim FileSystem
  ' Creates the FileSystemObject
  Set FileSystem = CreateObject("Scripting.FileSystemObject")

</SCRIPT>
</HEAD>

<BODY>
This page contains the ActiveX control FileSystemObject.
</BODY>
</HTML>
```

Now let's try loading the frame from the HTA. Since we already changed the
`APPLICATION` attributes of the `IFRAME` in the HTA to `yes`, we'll only see one
warning; if we hadn't, we'd have seen two.

Interestingly, if we set the APPLICATION attribute of the IFRAME in the HTA to no, and the one in the ActiveXControl to yes, we still get two sets of security warnings, because the APPLICATION attribute isn't recognized by Internet Explorer unless the parent element is an APPLICATION.

> **For nested frames, the application attribute will not recognized, and will mean the frame is untrusted, if its parent window is not trusted.**

Now if we set *both* APPLICATION attributes to yes, we won't have any security warnings at all.

HTA Deployment Models

HTAs are very exciting, but by now you're probably wondering how you can distribute them. It's actually fairly simple. HTAs can be accessed in a couple of ways: either through the web, or as a package with all of the referenced files in the HTA (in much the same way that you would install a standard Windows application). You can even create a combination of the two. Let's look at all these models in more depth.

Web Model

In a web model, an HTA can be referenced just as you might reference any other file with a URL. The user is asked to verify that they want to download the file, and no further security warnings occur. The application, and any other relevant files, are downloaded by the browser and cached.

Since the files live on the server, the user will always receive the most recent version when they download it. If the user elects to run from the current location, they don't even need to install or configure anything. The browser will do all of the work. The application doesn't even need to be uninstalled.

The server does need to have the MIME type "application:hta" registered for the file to be successfully downloaded through the http: protocol. Keep in mind that the client machine must also be running Internet Explorer 5. Currently, this is the only browser that supports HTAs.

Web Model Issues

When you are thinking about running the application from the server, there are few things to consider:

- ❏ Since you have to go to the server to retrieve the application, the application isn't available when the user isn't connected to the Internet. If your network isn't that reliable, that is certainly going to be an issue.

- ❏ If you aren't on a high-speed network, and particularly if your application is large, the speed of your application is going to suffer. While DSL and ADSL are starting to replace standard modems, the new technology hasn't reached everyone yet....

- ❏ Every time the application is run, the user is prompted with a screen about downloading the file. This can get pretty frustrating if the application is started frequently.

However, on a high speed corporate intranet where all users have Internet Explorer 5, the web model is extremely useful. Changes can be made to code without any of the hassles that are seen with traditional Windows applications.

Package Model

An HTML application doesn't need to run through the web. In many cases, that's not necessary at all. All that is required is Internet Explorer 5. Since an HTML application is a set of files, the files can be installed on a user's local drive or even at a network location. If your application doesn't contain custom ActiveX controls, you can use a simple zip file to place the files on the client's machine.

If you *do* have custom Active X controls, you will need to register them. You could use applications such as Wise or InstallShield to register controls and create an installation process.

The advantages of this model are that you don't need to be online, the application will run faster, and you don't need to deal with security warnings after the initial installation.

Package Model Issues

The disadvantage of using a package model is that the updates are not automatically transferred to the user like they are in the web model. You would need to manually update the files on the local machine.

Also, if you do have ActiveX controls to register, you will need to provide a way to uninstall the controls. If you choose to install controls, you will probably want to use programs that have uninstall utilities, such as Wise or InstallShield.

Hybrid Model

You can also combine the two models, forming a kind of 'hybrid' model. You can install part of the application locally, and part of the application on the server. Anything that you want to reference on the server, such as images, stylesheets, sources for frames, XML data, and so on can be referenced from the HTML application on the client machine.

Our example application could be seen as a kind of hybrid-model HTA, as it accesses URLs on the Internet, while the application and corresponding stylesheet are stored locally. Using an approach such as this one may better meet your needs.

For example, if your concern is speed, you might choose to store larger files locally. If you want to limit the number of updates that are manually sent to the user, you might choose to make your HTA file fairly simple, possibly by using frames which have their sources on the server. That way, any content changes can be made to the frame files in their central location.

What Isn't Supported With HTAs?

Many of the references on HTML applications state that all of the features available in Internet Explorer 5 are also available in HTAs. This isn't exactly true. For example, the HTA doesn't know anything about the application or site that launched the HTA. As a result, there are a number of properties and methods of the window object that aren't available within the HTA. There are also some default behaviors that aren't supported. I'm not sure if all of these are by design or not. I guess we'll find out in Internet Explorer 6.

The Window Object

The window object's opener property is not available to the user. The external property (which normally allows the window access to its referring window) is also unavailable, as is the menuArguments property.

Most of the methods that aren't available are those that would give the HTA unreasonable access to other programs, like Internet Explorer. Since an HTA is in fact an application, it makes sense that the user wouldn't have access to another application, even Internet Explorer. Here's a list of the unavailable methods in HTAs.

Method	Description
AddChannel	Presents a dialog box that allows the user to either add the channel specified, or change the channel URL if it is already installed.
AddDesktopComponent	Adds a web site or image to the Microsoft Active Desktop.
AddFavorite	Adds a page to the Favorites list.
AutoCompleteSaveForm	Saves the form to the auto complete data.
AutoScan	Tries to connect to the web server with queries.
ImportExportFavorites	Imports or exports Internet Explorer's favorites list.
IsSubscribed	Indicates if a user is subscribed to an Active Channel.
NavigateAndFind	Opens a web page, and highlights a specific string.
ShowBrowser	Opens the browser's dialog box.

Default Behaviors

There are also a few default behaviors in Internet Explorer 5 that are not available within a HTML application. As in the previous section, they are related to browser modifications and involve data storage by the browser. They include:

❑ saveFavorite

❑ saveHistory

❑ saveSnapshot

❑ userData

Summary

I'm sure that you are now quite the expert on HTML applications. They provide a simple way to get the most out of HTML and script, and they give you even more control over the user interface of your application.

HTML applications are a powerful technique for quickly developing Windows applications. They provide a great way for HTML and other programming languages to come together. They are also a good way for you to use your skills on both the server and client machines. The standard security warnings that are usually encountered with browsers are no longer a problem.

In addition to creating full-blown Windows applications, HTAs are an excellent tool for prototyping. Application designers can easily build an interface, and demonstrate the interactions that they want built without having to learn C++ or VB.

Anyway, have fun creating your HTML applications. The next chapter will introduce server-side programming with Active Server Pages.

14

Server-Side Web Scripting With ASP

Up until this chapter, we've been focusing mainly on client-side scripting and applications. Now it's time to take a look at the server side. Creating web sites with only client-side scripting is all well and good, but your functionality is severely limited. By adding server-side scripting, you gain a huge advantage. You are able to draw upon the wealth of data available to you on the server and across the enterprise in various databases (more on databases in Chapter 15). You are able to customize pages to the needs of each different user that comes to your web site. In addition, by keeping your code on the server-side you can build a library of functionality. This library can be drawn from again and again to further enhance other web sites. Best of all, using server-side script libraries will allow your web sites to scale to multi-tier, or distributed, web applications.

To do this, you'll need a good understanding of the HTTP protocol, and how an HTTP server interacts with a browser. This model is important to understand when developing web applications that exist on the client and server side.

Next, we'll introduce you to Active Server Pages, or ASP. ASP is Microsoft's server-side scripting environment. It can be used to create everything from simple, static web pages, to database-aware dynamic sites, using HTML and scripting. Its other important use is as a programming "glue". Through the use of ASP, you can create and manipulate server-side components. These components can perhaps provide data to your application such as graphic image generation, or maybe link to a mainframe database. The important thing is that the ASP code does nothing more than facilitate the use of these components on the Web.

ASP comes with some built-in objects that are important to understand before their full potential can be unleashed. We will cover these objects in depth.

Finally, we'll look at some real-world examples of using ASP on a web site. These should give you some idea of the power and beauty of server-side scripting with ASP.

The Anatomy of the HTTP Protocol

As you know, surfing the web is as simple as clicking a link on your browser. But do you know what really goes on beneath the hood of your web browser? It can be quite complex, but isn't too difficult to understand. More importantly, it will help you to understand the intricacies of client and server side scripting.

Overview

The **Hypertext Transfer Protocol**, or **HTTP**, is an *application level* TCP/IP protocol. An application level protocol is one that travels on top of another protocol. In this instance, HTTP travels on top of TCP, which is also a protocol. When two computers communicate over a TCP/IP connection, the data is formatted and processed in such a manner that it is guaranteed to arrive at its destination. This elaborate mechanism is the TCP/IP protocol.

HTTP takes for granted, and largely ignores, the entire TCP/IP protocol. It relies instead on text commands like GET and PUT. Application level protocols are implemented, usually, within an application (as opposed to at the driver level), hence the name. Some other examples of application level protocols are the **File Transfer Protocol** (FTP) and the mail protocols, **Standard Mail Transfer Protocol** (SMTP) and the **Post Office Protocol** (POP3). Pure binary data is rarely sent via these protocols, but when it is, it is encoded into an ASCII format. This is inefficient at best, and future versions of the HTTP protocol will rectify this problem. The most up-to-date version of HTTP is version 1.1, and almost all web servers available today support this version.

There is also a new HTTP protocol in the works called HTTP-NG, or HTTP-Next Generation. This newer, robust protocol will utilize bandwidth more efficiently and improve on many of the original HTTP's shortcomings. The biggest improvement in the new protocol is that data will be transferred in binary as opposed to text, thus making transactions quicker. More technical information about HTTP-NG is available from the W3C at http://www.w3.org/Protocols/HTTP-NG.

The HTTP Server

To carry out an HTTP request, there must be an HTTP or web server running on the target machine. This server is an application that listens for and responds to HTTP requests on a certain TCP port (by default, port 80). An HTTP request is for a single item from the web server. The item may be anything from a web page to a sound file. The server, upon receipt of the request, attempts to retrieve the data asked for. If the server finds the correct information, it formats and returns the data to the client. If the requested information could not be found, the server will return an error message.

Pulling up a single web page in your browser may cause dozens of HTTP transactions to occur. Each element on a web page that is not text needs to be requested from the HTTP server individually. The main point of all this is that each HTTP transaction consists of a request and a response:

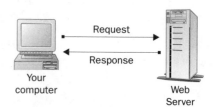

And it is in this transaction model that you must place yourself when you are programming web applications.

Protocol Basics

There are four basic states that make up a single HTTP transaction. They are:

- ❑ *The Connection*
- ❑ *The Request*
- ❑ *The Response*
- ❑ *The Disconnection*

A client connects to a server and issues the request. It waits for a response, then disconnects. A connection typically lasts only for a few seconds. On web sites like Yahoo where the data is not laden with graphics, and the information is fairly static, requests last less than one second.

The Connection

The client software, a web browser in this case, creates a TCP/IP connection to an HTTP server on a specific TCP/IP port. Port 80 is used if one is not specified. This is considered the default port for an HTTP server. A web server may, however, reside on any port allowed. It is completely up to the operator of the web server, and port numbers are often deliberately changed as a first line of defense against unauthorized users.

The Request

Once connected, the client sends a request to the server. This request is in ASCII, and must be terminated by a carriage-return/line-feed pair. Every request must specify a method which tells the server what the client wants. In HTTP 1.1, there are eight methods: OPTIONS, GET, HEAD, POST, PUT, DELETE, TRACE, and CONNECT. For more information about the different methods and their use, please check out the HTTP specification on the W3C web site. For the purpose of this chapter, we are going to focus on the GET method.

The GET method asks the web server to return the specified page. The format of this request is as follows:

```
GET <URL> <HTTP Version>
```

You can make HTTP requests yourself with the **telnet** program. Telnet is a program that is available on most computer systems and it was originally designed for use on UNIX systems. Since basic UNIX is character-based, one could log in from a remote site and work with the operating system. Telnet is the program that allows you to connect to a remote machine and all versions of Windows come with a telnet program. The figure overleaf shows what it looks like.

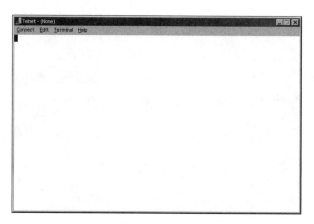

Microsoft's telnet program leaves much to be desired. Thankfully, a company called Van Dyke Technologies (www.vandyke.com) created an excellent telnet program called CRT. In fact, the above is a screen shot of CRT.

Telnet defaults to TCP/IP port 23. On UNIX systems, in order to telnet into a machine, that machine must be running a telnet server. This server listens for incoming telnet connections on port 23. However, almost all telnet programs allow you to specify the port on which to connect. It is this feature that we can utilize to examine HTTP running under the hood.

If you choose not to download the Van Dyke telnet client, you can test this by running Window's own telnet. Windows has no predefined menu item for this program, but on NT it can usually be found at C:\WINNT\system32\Telnet.exe. To run it, press the Start button and select Run. Type in telnet and press ENTER. You should see a telnet window similar to the one above above.

Select Remote System from the Connect menu and you'll be presented with the following dialog:

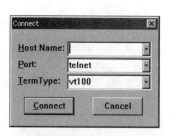

Type in the name of any web server; we chose http://www.mindbuilder.com. Then enter the web server's port. This is almost always 80.

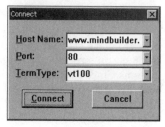

Once you are connected, the title bar will change to contain the name of the server to which you are connected. There is no other indication of connection. It is at this point that you need to type in your HTTP command. Type in the following, all in upper case:

```
GET / HTTP/1.0
```

Please note that unless you have turned on **Local Echo** in the **Preferences**, you will not see what you type. After you've entered the command you must send a carriage return (*Ctrl-M*) followed by a line feed (*Ctrl-J*). What is returned is shown as follows, and is the response to your HTTP request.

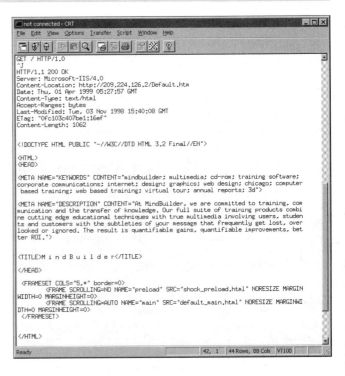

The Response

Upon receipt of the request, the web server will answer. This will most likely result in some sort of HTML data as shown previously. However, you may get an error as in the following example:

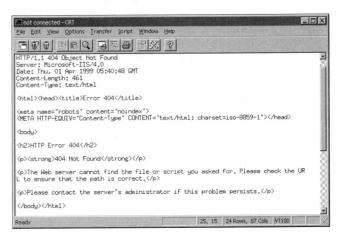

Again, the response is in HTML, but the code returned is an error code (404) instead of an OK (200).

HTTP Headers

What was actually returned is a two-part response. The first part consists of HTTP headers. These headers provide information about the actual response to the request, the most important header being the `status` header. In the listing above, it reads HTTP/1.1 404 Object Not Found. This indicates the actual status of the request.

The other headers that were returned with this request are `Server`, `Date`, `Content-Length`, and `Content-Type`. There are many different types of headers, and they are all designed to aid the browser in easily identifying the type of information that is being returned.

The Disconnect

After the server has responded to your request, it closes the connection thus disconnecting you. Subsequent requests require you to re-establish your connection with the server.

Introducing Active Server Pages

With the HTTP architecture laid out in the last section, you can clearly see that the real heart of the HTTP protocol lies in the request and the response. The client makes a request to the server, and the server provides the response to the client. What we're looking at here is really the foundations of client/server computing. A client makes a request from a server and the server fulfills that request. We see this pattern of behavior throughout the programming world today, not only in Web programming.

Microsoft recognized this pattern and developed a new technology that rendered web programming a much more accessible technique. This technology is **Active Server Pages** or **ASP** for short. ASP is a server-side scripting environment that comes with Microsoft's Internet Information Services. ASP allows you to embed scripting commands inside your HTML documents. The scripting commands are interpreted by the server and translated into the corresponding HTML and sent back to the server. This enables the web developer to create content that is dynamic and fresh. The beauty of this is that it does not matter which browser your web visitor is using, because the server returns only pure HTML. Sure you can extend your returned HTML with browser specific programming, but that is your prerogative. By no means is this all that ASP can do, but we'll cover more of its capabilities like form validation and data manipulation later on in this chapter.

Although you can use languages such as JavaScript or even Perl, by default the ASP scripting language is...yes, you've guessed it, VBScript.

How the Server Recognizes ASPs

ASP pages do not have an `.html` or `.htm` extension; they have a `.asp` extension instead. The reason for this is twofold. First, in order for the web server to know to process the scripting in your web page, it needs to know that there is some in there. Well, by setting the extension of your web page to `.asp`, the server can assume that there are scripts in your page.

A nice side effect of naming your ASP pages with the .asp *extension is that the ASP processor knows that it does not need to process your HTML files. It used to be the case, as in ASP 2.0, that any page with the* .asp *extension, no matter whether it contained any server side scripting code or not, was automatically sent to the server, and would thereby take longer to process. With the introduction of ASP 3.0 in Windows 2000, the server is able to determine the presence of any server side code and process or not process the page accordingly. This increases the speed of your HTML file retrieval and makes your web server run more efficiently.*

Secondly, using an .asp extension (forcing interpretation by the ASP processor every time your page is requested) hides your ASP scripts. If someone requests your .asp file from the web server, all he is going to get back is the resultant processed HTML. If you put your ASP code in a file called mycode.scr and requested it from the web server, you'll see all of the code inside.

ASP Basics

ASP files are really just HTML files with scripting embedded within them. When a browser requests an ASP file from the server, it is passed on to the ASP processing DLL for execution. After processing, the resulting file is then sent on to the requesting browser. Any scripting commands embedded from the original HTML file are executed and then removed from the results. This is excellent in that all of your scripting code is hidden from the person viewing your web pages. That is why it is so important that files that contain ASP scripts have an .asp extension.

The Tags of ASP

To distinguish the ASP code from the HTML inside your files, ASP code is placed between <% and %> tags. This convention should be familiar to you if you have ever worked with any kind of server-side commands before in HTML. The tag combination implies to the ASP processor that the code within should be executed by the server and removed from the results. Depending on the default scripting language of your web site, this code may be VBScript, JScript, or any other language you've installed. Since this book is for the VBScript programmer, all of our ASP scripts will be in VBScript.

In the following snippet of HTML, you'll see an example of some ASP code between the <% and %> tags:

```
<TABLE>
<TR>
<TD>
<%
    x = x + 1
    y = y - 1
%>
</TD>
</TR>
</TABLE>
```

<SCRIPT> Blocks

You may also place your ASP code between `<SCRIPT></SCRIPT>` blocks. However, unless you direct the script to run at the server level, code placed between these tags will be executed at the client as normal client-side scripts. To direct your script block to execute on the server, use the `RUNAT` command within your `<SCRIPT>` block as follows:

```
<SCRIPT Language="VBScript" RUNAT="Server">
… Your Script …
</SCRIPT>
```

The Default Scripting Language

As stated previously, the default scripting language used by ASP is VBScript. However, you may change it for your entire site, or just a single web page. Placing a special scripting tag at the beginning of your web page does this. This tag specifies the scripting language to use for this page only.

```
<%@ LANGUAGE=ScriptingLanguage %>
```

`"ScriptingLanguage"` can be any language for which you have the scripting engine installed. ASP comes with JScript, as well as VBScript.

You can set the default scripting language for the entire application by changing the **Default ASP Language** field in the Internet Service Manager on the **App Options** tab. Though why you would want to do this is questionable!

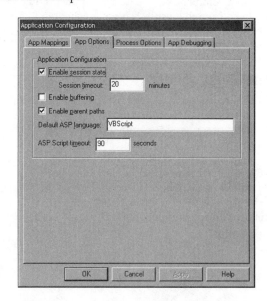

Mixing HTML and ASP

You've probably guessed by now that one can easily mix HTML code with ASP scripts. The power of this feature is phenomenal! VBScript, as you know, has all of the control flow mechanisms like `If Then`, `For Next`, and `Do While` loops. But with ASP you can selectively include HTML code based on the results of these operators. Let's look at an example.

Suppose you are creating a web page that greets the viewer with a "Good Morning", "Good Afternoon", or "Good Evening" depending on the time of day. This can be done as follows:

```
<HTML>
<BODY>
<P>The time is now <%=Time()%></P>
<%
   Dim iHour

   iHour = Hour(Time())

   If (iHour >= 0 And iHour < 12 ) Then
%>
Good Morning!
<%
   ElseIf (iHour > 11 And iHour < 5 ) Then
%>
Good Afternoon!
<%
   Else
%>
Good Evening!
<%
End If
%>
</BODY>
</HTML>
```

First we print out the current time. The `<%=` notation is shorthand to print out the value of an ASP variable or the result of a function call. We then move the hour of the current time into a variable called `iHour`. Based on the value of this variable we write our normal HTML text.

Notice how the HTML code is outside of the ASP script tags. When the ASP processor executes this page, the HTML that lies between control flow blocks that aren't executed is discarded, leaving you with only the correct code. Here is the source of what is returned from our web server after processing this page:

```
<HTML>
<BODY>
<P>The time is now 7:48:37 PM</P>

Good Evening!

</BODY>
</HTML>
```

As you can see, the scripting is completely removed leaving only the HTML and text.

The other way to output data to your web page viewer is using one of ASP's built-in objects called `Response`. We'll cover this approach in the next section as you learn about the ASP object model.

Commenting Your ASP Code

As with any programming language, it is of the utmost importance to comment your ASP code as much as possible. However, how many times have you come across a piece of code and said "eh?" Someone once told me that the only purpose comments served were to amuse the compiler. In some instances, he may have been correct. However, unclear comments are not worth putting in your code.

Comments in ASP are identical to comments in VBScript. When ASP comes across the single quote character it will graciously ignore the rest of the line:

```
<%
Dim iLumberJack

'I'm a comment and I'm O.K.
iLumberJack = iLumberJack + 1
%>
```

The Active Server Pages Object Model

ASP, like most Microsoft technologies, utilizes the Component Object Model (as discussed in Chapter 5), or COM, to expose functionality to consumer applications. ASP is actually an extension to your web server that allows server-side scripting. At the same it also provides a compendium of objects and components, which manage interaction between the web server and the browser. These objects form the **Active Server Pages Object Model**. These 'objects' can be manipulated by scripting languages. Take a look at the following diagram:

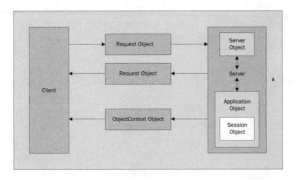

ASP neatly divides up into six objects, which manage their own part of the interaction between client and server. As you can see in the diagram, at the heart of the interaction between client and server are the Request and Response objects, which deal with the HTTP request and response; but we will be taking a quick tour through all of the different objects and components that are part of ASP.

Four of the six core objects of the object model (the Request, Response, Application, and Session objects) can use collections to store data. Before we look at each object in turn we need to take a quick overview of collections.

Collections

Collections in ASP are very similar to their VBScript namesakes. They act as data containers that store their data in a manner close to that of an array. The information is stored in the form of name/value pairs.

The `Application` and the `Session` objects have a collection property called `Contents`. This collection of variants can hold any information you wish to place in it. Using these collections allow you to share information between web pages.

To place a value into the collection, simply assign it a key and then assign the value:

```
Application.Contents("Name") = "Evil Knievil"
```

Or

```
Session.Contents("Age") = 25
```

Fortunately for us, Microsoft has made the `Contents` collection the default property for these two objects. Therefore the following shorthand usage is perfectly acceptable:

```
Application("Name") = "Evil Knievil"
Session("Age") = 25
```

To read values from the `Contents` collections, just reverse the call:

```
sName = Application("Name")
sAge = Session("Age")
```

Iterating the Contents Collection

Because the `Contents` collections work like regular VBScript collections, they are easily iterated. You can use the collections `Count` property, or use the `For Each` iteration method:

```
for x = 1 to Application.Contents.Count
    ..
next

for each item in Application.Contents
    ..
next
```

> Please note that the Contents collections are 1 based. That is to say that the first element in the collection is at position 1, not 0.

To illustrate this, the following ASP script will dump the current contents of the `Application` and `Session` objects' `Contents` collections:

```
<HTML>
<BODY>
<P>The Application.Contents</P>
<%
    Dim Item

    For Each Item In Application.Contents
      Response.Write Item & " = [" & Application(Item) & "]<BR>"
    Next
%>
<P>The Session.Contents</P>
<%
    For Each Item In Session.Contents
      Response.Write Item & " = [" & Session(Item) & "]<BR>"
    Next
%>
</BODY>
</HTML>
```

Removing an Item from the Contents Collection

The `Application` Object's `Contents` collection contains two methods, and these are `Remove` and `RemoveAll`. These allow you to remove one or all of the items stored in the `Application.Contents` collection. At the time of writing, there is no method to remove an item from the `Session.Contents` collection.

Let's add an item to the `Application.Contents` collection, and then remove it.

```
<%
    Application("MySign") = "Pisces"
    Application.Contents.Remove("MySign")
%>
```

Or we can just get rid of everything...

```
<%
    Application.Contents.RemoveAll
%>
```

Not all of the collections of each object work in this way, but the principles remain the same and we will explain how each differs when we discuss each object.

The Request Object

When your web page is requested, along with the HTTP request, information such as the URL of the web page request and the format of the data requested is passed. It can also contain feedback from the user such as the input from a text box or drop down list box. The `Request` object allows you to get at information passed along as part of the HTTP request. The corresponding output from the server is returned as part of the `Response`. The `Request` object has several collections to store information that warrant discussion.

The Request Object's Collections

The `Request` object has five collections. Interestingly, they all act as the default property for the object. That is to say, you may retrieve information from any of the five collections by using the abbreviated syntax:

```
ClientIPAddress = Request("REMOTE_ADDR")
```

The `REMOTE_ADDR` value lies in the `ServerVariables` collection. However, through the use of the collection cascade, it can be retrieved with the above notation. Please note that for ASP to dig through each collection, especially if they have many values, to retrieve a value from the last collection is inefficient. It is always recommended to use the fully qualified collection name in your code. Not only is this faster, but it improves your code in that it is more specific, and less cryptic.

ASP searches through the collections in the following order:

- ❏ *QueryString*
- ❏ *Form*
- ❏ *Cookies*
- ❏ *ClientCertificate*
- ❏ *ServerVariables*

If there are variables with the same name, only the first is returned when you allow ASP to search. This is another good reason for you to fully qualify your collection.

QueryString

This contains a collection of all the information attached to the end of an URL. When you make an URL request, the additional information is passed along with the URL to the web page appended with a question mark. This information takes the following form:
`URL?item=data[&item=data][...]`

The clue to the server is the question mark. When the server sees this, it knows that the URL has ended, and variables are starting. So an example of a URL with a query string might look like this:
`http://www.buythisbook.com/book.asp?bookname=VBScriptProgrammersRef`
`erence`

We stated earlier that the collections store information in name/value pairs. Despite this slightly unusual method of creating the name/value pair, the principle remains the same; `bookname` is the name and `VBScriptProgrammersReference` is the value. When ASP gets hold of this URL request, it breaks apart all of the name/value pairs and places them into this collection for easy access. This is another excellent feature of ASP. Query strings are built up using ampersands to delimit each name/value pair so if you wished to pass the user information along with the book information, you could pass the following:
`http://www.buythisbook.com/book.asp?bookname=VBScriptProgrammersRef`
`erence&buyer=JerryAblan`

Query strings can be generated in one of three ways. The first is, as discussed, by a user typed URL. The second is as part of a URL specified in an Anchor tag.

```
<A HREF="book.asp?bookname=VBScriptProgrammersReference">Go to book buying
page</A>
```

So when you click on the link, the name/value pair is passed along with the URL. The third and final method is via a form sent to the server with the GET method.

```
<FORM ACTION="book.asp" METHOD="GET">
Type your name: <INPUT TYPE="TEXT" NAME="buyer"><BR>
Type your requested book:  <INPUT TYPE="TEXT" NAME="bookname" SIZE=40><BR>
<INPUT TYPE=SUBMIT VALUE=Submit>
</FORM>
```

You input the information onto the text boxes on the form and the text is submitted when you click on Submit and two query strings are generated.

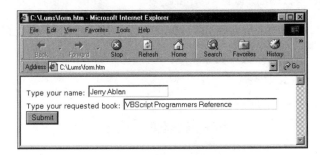

Next you need to be able to retrieve information, and you use this technique to retrieve from each of the three methods used to generate a query string.

```
Request.QueryString("buyer")
Request.QueryString("bookname")
```

Please note that these lines won't display anything by themselves, you need to add either the shorthand notation (equality operator) to display functions in front of a single statement, or when a number of values need displaying then use Response.Write *to separately display each value in the collection. For example:*

```
<%=Request.QueryString("buyer")%> or
Response.Write(Request.QueryString("bookname") )
```

The first of the two Request object calls should return the name of Jerry Ablan on the page and the second of the two should return VBScript Programmers Reference. Of course you could always store this information in a variable for later access.

```
sBookName = Request.QueryString("bookname")
```

Form

Contains a collection of all the form variables posted to the HTTP request by an HTML form. Query strings aren't very private as they transmit information via a very visible method, the URL. If you want to transmit information from the form more privately then you can use the form collection to do so which sends its information as part of the HTTP Request body. The easy access to form variables is one of ASP's best features.

If we go back to our previous example, the only alteration we need to make to our HTML form code is to change the METHOD attribute. Forms using this collection must be sent with the POST method and not the GET method. It is actually this attribute that determines how the information is sent by the form. So if we change the method of the form as follows:

```
<FORM ACTION="book.asp" METHOD="POST">
Type your name: <INPUT TYPE="TEXT" NAME="buyer"><BR>
Type your requested book:  <INPUT TYPE="TEXT" NAME="bookname" SIZE=40><BR>
<INPUT TYPE=SUBMIT VALUE=Submit>
</FORM>
```

Once the form has been submitted in this style, then we can retrieve and display the information using the following:

```
=Request.Form("buyer")
```

Cookies

Contains a read-only collection of cookies sent by the client browser along with the request. Because the cookies were sent from the client, they cannot be changed here. You must change them using the Response.Cookies collection. A discussion of cookies can be found in the discussion of the Response object.

ClientCertificate

When a client makes a connection with a server requiring a high degree of security, either party can confirm who the sender/receiver is by inspecting their digital certificate. A digital certificate contains a number of items of information about the sender, such as the holder's name, address and length of time the certificate is valid for. A third party, known as the Certificate Authority or CA, will have previously verified these details.

The ClientCertificate collection is used access details held in a client side digital certificate sent by the browser. This collection is only populated if you are running a secure server, and the request was via an https:// call instead of an http:// call. This is the preferred method to invoke a secure connection.

ServerVariables

When the client sends a request and information is passed across to the server, it's not just the page that is passed across, but information such as who created the page, the server name, and the port that the request was sent to. The HTTP header that is sent across together with the HTTP request also contains information of this nature such as the type of browser, and type of connection. This information is combined into a list of variables that are predefined by the server as environment variables. Most of them are static and never really change unless you change the configuration of your web server. The rest are based on the client browser.

These server variables can be accessed in the normal method. For instance, the server variable HTTP_USER_AGENT, which returns information about the type of browser being used to view the page, can be displayed as follows:

```
<%=Request.ServerVariables("HTTP_USER_AGENT")%>
```

Alternatively you can printout the whole list of server variables and their values with the following code:

```
For Each key in Request.ServerVariables
    Response.Write "<B>" & (Key) &"</B> "
    Response.Write (Request.ServerVariables(key)) & "<BR>"
Next
```

This displays each of the `ServerVariables` collection in bold, and the contents of the key (if any) after it. The final product looks like this:

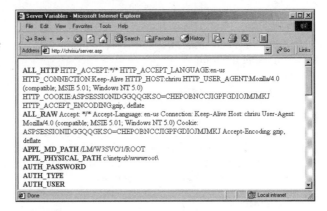

Server variables are merely informative, but they do give you the ability to customize page content for specific browsers, or to avoid script errors that might be generated.

Request Object Properties and Methods

The `Request` object contains a single property and a single method. They are used together to transfer files from the client to the server. Uploading is accomplished using HTML forms.

TotalBytes Property

When the request is processed, this property will hold the total number of bytes in the client browser request. Most likely you'd use it to return the number of bytes in the file you wish to transfer. This information is important to the `BinaryRead` method.

BinaryRead Method

This method retrieves the information sent to the web server by the client browser in a `POST` operation. When the browser issues a `POST`, the data is encoded and sent to the server. When the browser issues a `GET`, there is no data other than the URL. The `BinaryRead` method takes one parameter, the number of bytes to read. So if you want it to read a whole file, you pass it the total number of bytes in the file, generated by the `TotalBytes` property.

It's very rarely applied because `Request.QueryString` and `Request.Form` are much easier to use. That's because `BinaryRead` wraps its answer in a safe array of bytes. For a scripting language that essentially only handles variants, that makes life a little complicated. However this format is essential for file uploading. You can find full details on how to upload files and then decode a safe array of bytes in an excellent article at 15seconds.com (`http://www.15seconds.com/Issue/981121.htm`.)

The Response Object

After you've processed the request information from the client browser, you'll need to be able to send information back. The `Response` object is just the ticket. It provides you with the tools necessary to send anything you need back to the client.

The Response Object's Collection

The `Response` object contains only one collection: `Cookies`. This is the version of the `Request` object's `Cookies` collection that can be written to.

If you've not come across them before, cookies are small (limited to 4kb of data) text files stored on the hard drive of the client that contain information about the user, such as whether they have visited the site before and what date they last visited the site on. There are lots of misapprehensions about cookies being intrusive as they allow servers to store information on the user's drive. However you need to remember that firstly the user has to voluntarily accept cookies or activate an Accept Cookies mechanism on the browser for them to work, secondly this information is completely benign and cannot be used to determine the user's e-mail address or such like. They are used to personalize pages that the user might have visited before. Examples of things to store in cookies are unique user IDs, or user names; then, when the user returns to your web site, a quick check of cookies will let you know if this is a return visitor or not.

You can create a cookie on the user's machine as follows:

```
Response.Cookies("BookBought") = "VBScript Programmers Reference"
```

You can also store multiple values in one cookie using an index value key. The cookie effectively contains a VBScript `Dictionary` object and using the key can retrieve individual items. Its functioning is very close to that of an array.

```
Response.Cookies("BookBought")("1") = "VBScript Programmers Reference "
Response.Cookies("BookBought")("2") = "Instant HTML"
```

A cookie will automatically expire – disappear from the user's machine – the moment a user ends their session. To extend the cookie beyond this natural lifetime, you can specify a date with the `Expires` property. The date takes the following format WEEKDAY DD-MON-YY HH:MM:SS

```
Response.Cookies("BookBought").Expires = #31-Dec-99#
```

The # sign can be used to delimit dates in ASP (as in VBScript).

Other properties that can be used in conjunction with this collection are:

❑   *`Domain`: a cookie is only sent to page requested within the domain from which it was created*

❑   *`Path` : a cookie is only sent to pages requested within this path*

❑   *`HasKeys`: specifies whether the cookie uses an index/dictionary object or not*

❑   *`Secure`: specifies whether the cookie is secure. A cookie is only deemed secure if sent via the HTTPS protocol.*

You can retrieve the cookies information using the `Request` object cookies collection, mentioned earlier. To do this you could do the following:

```
You purchased <%=Request.Cookies("BookBought")%> last time you visited the
site.
```

If there were several cookies in the collection you could iterate through each cookie and display the contents as follows:

```
For Each cookie in Request.Cookies
    Response.Write (Request.Cookies(cookie))
Next
```

The Response Object's Methods

To understand what the `Response` Object's methods and properties do, we need to examine the workings of how ASP sends a response in more detail. When an ASP script is run, an **HTML output stream** is created. This stream is a receptacle for the web server to store details and create the dynamic/interactive web page in. As mentioned before, the page has to be created entirely in HTML for the browser to understand it (excluding client-side scripting, which is ignored by the server).

The stream is initially empty when created. New information is added to the end. If any custom HTML headers are required then they have to be added at the beginning. Then the HTML contained in the ASP page is added next to the script, so anything not encompassed by `<% %>` tags is added. The `Response` object provides two ways of writing directly to the output stream, either using the `Write` method or it's shorthand technique.

Write

Probably the most used method of all the built-in objects, `Write` allows you to send information back to the client browser. You can write text directly to a web page by encasing the text in quotation marks:

```
Response.Write "Hello World!"
```

Or to display the contents of a variant you just drop the quotation marks:

```
sText = "Hello World!"
Response.Write sText
```

For single portions of dynamic information that only require adding into large portions of HTML, you can use the equality sign as shorthand for this method, as specified earlier, e.g.

```
My message is <% =sText %>
```

This technique reduces the amount of code needed, but at the expense of readability. There is nothing to choose between these techniques in terms of performance.

AddHeader

This method allows you to add custom headers to the HTTP response. For example, if you were to write a custom browser application that examined the headers of your HTTP requests for a certain value, you'd use this method to set that value. Usage is as follows:

```
Response.AddHeader "CustomServerApp", "BogiePicker/1.0"
```

This would add the header `CustomServerApp` to the response with the value of `BogiePicker/1.0`. There are no restrictions regarding headers and header value.

AppendToLog

Calling this method allows you to append a string to the web server log file entry for this particular request. This allows you to add custom log messages to the log file.

BinaryWrite

This method allows you to bypass the normal character conversion that takes place when data is sent back to the client. Usually, only text is returned, so the web server cleans it up. By calling `BinaryWrite` to send your data, the actual binary data is sent back, bypassing that cleaning process.

Clear

This method allows you to delete any data that has been buffered for this page so far. See discussion of the `Buffer` property for more details.

End

This method stops processing the ASP file and returns any currently buffered data to the client browser.

Flush

This method returns any currently buffered data to the client browser and then clears the buffer. See discussion of the `Buffer` property for more details.

Redirect

This method allows you to relinquish control of the current page to another web page entirely. For example, you can use this method to redirect users to a login page if they have not yet logged on to your web site:

```
<%
If (Not Session("LoggedOn") ) Then
    Response.Redirect "login.asp"
End If
%>
```

The Response Object's Properties

Buffer

You may optionally have ASP buffer your output for you. This property tells ASP whether or not to buffer output. Usually, output is sent to the client as it is generated. If you turn buffering on (by setting this property to `True`), output will not be sent until all scripts have been executed for the current page, or the `Flush` or `End` methods are called.

`Response.Buffer` has to be inserted after the language declaration, but before any HTML is used. If you insert it outside this scope you will most likely generate an error. A correct use of this method would look like:

```
<@ LANGUAGE = "VBSCRIPT">
<% Response.Buffer = True %>
<HTML>
. . .
```

The `Flush` method is used in conjunction with the `Buffer` property. To use it correctly you must set the `Buffer` property first and then at places within the script you can flush the buffer to the output stream, while continuing processing. This is useful for long queries, which might otherwise worry the user that nothing was being returned.

The `Clear` method erases everything in the buffer that has been added since the last `Response.Flush` call. It erases only the response body however and leaves intact the response header.

CacheControl

Generally when a proxy server retrieves an ASP web page, it does not place a copy of it into its cache. That is because by their very nature ASP pages are dynamic and, most likely, a page will be stale the next time it is requested. You may override this feature by changing the value of this property to `Public`.

Charset

This property will append its contents to the HTTP content-type header that is sent back to the browser. Every HTTP response has a content-type header that defines the content of the response. Usually the content-type is "text/html". Setting this property will modify the type sent back to the browser.

ContentType

This property allows you to set the value of the content-type that is sent back to the client browser.

Expires

Most web browsers keep web pages in a local cache. The cache is usually as good as long as you keep your browser running. Setting this property allows you to limit the time the page stays in the local cache. The value of the `Expires` property specifies the length of time in minutes before the page will expire from the local cache. If you set this to zero, the page will not be cached.

ExpiresAbsolute

Just like the `Expires` property, this property allows you to specify the exact time and date on which the page will expire.

IsClientConnected

This read-only property indicates whether or not the client is still connected to the server. Remember that the client browser makes a request then waits for a response? Well, imagine you're running a lengthy script and during the middle of processing, the client disconnects because he was waiting too long. Reading this property will tell you if the client is still connected or not.

Status

This property allows you to set the value returned on the status header with the HTTP response.

The Application and Session Objects

The `Application` and `Session` objects like `Request` and `Response` work very closely together. `Application` is used to tie all of the pages together into one consistent application, while the `Session` object is used to track and present a user's series of requests to the web site as a continuous action, rather than an arbitrary set of requests.

Scope Springs Eternal

Normally, you will declare a variable for use within your web page. You'll use it, manipulate it, then perhaps print out its value, or whatever. But when your page is reloaded, or the viewer moves to another page, the variable, with its value, is gone forever. By placing your variable within the `Contents` collection of the `Application` or `Session` objects, you can extend the life span of your variable!

Any variable or object that you declare has two potential scopes: procedure and page. When you declare a variable within a procedure, its life span is limited to that procedure. Once the procedure has executed, your variable is gone. You may also declare a variable at the web page level but like the procedure-defined variable, once the page is reloaded, the value is reset.

Enter the `Application` and `Session` objects. The `Contents` collections of these two objects allow you to extend the scope of your variables to session-wide, and application-wide. If you place a value in the `Session` object, it will be available to all web pages in your site for the life span of the current session (more on sessions later). Good session scope variables are user IDs, user names, login time, etc., things that pertain only to the session. Likewise, if you place your value into the `Application` object, it will exist until the web site is restarted. This allows you to place application-wide settings into a conveniently accessible place. Good application scope variables are font names and sizes, table colors, system constants, etc., things that pertain to the application as a whole.

The global.asa File

Every ASP application may utilize a special script file. This file is named `global.asa` and it must reside in the root directory of your web application. It can contain script code that pertains to the application as a whole, or each session. You may also create ActiveX objects for later use in this scripting file.

The Application Object

ASP works on the concept that an entire web site is a single web application. Therefore, there is only one instance of the `Application` object available for your use in your scripting at all times. Please note that it is possible to divide up your web site into separate applications, but for the purposes of this discussion we'll assume there is only one application per web site.

Collections

The `Application` object contains two collections: `Contents` and `StaticObjects`. The `Contents` collection is discussed above. The `StaticObjects` collection is similar to `Contents`, but only contains the objects that were created with the `<OBJECT>` tag in the scope of your application. This collection can be iterated just like the `Contents` collection.

> *You cannot store references to ASP's built-in objects in* `Application`*'s collections.*

Methods

The `Application` object contains two methods as detailed below.

Lock	The `Lock` method is used to "lock-down" the `Contents` collection so that it cannot be modified by other clients. This is useful if you are updating a counter, or perhaps grabbing a transaction number stored in the `Application`'s `Contents` collection.
Unlock	The `Unlock` method "unlocks" the `Application` object thus allowing others to modify the `Contents` collection.

Events

The `Application` object generates two events: `Application_OnStart` and `Application_OnEnd`. The `Application_OnStart` event is fired when the first view of your web page occurs. The `Application_OnEnd` event is fired when the web server is shut down. If you choose to write scripts for these events they must be placed in your `global.asa` file.

The most common use of these events is to initialize application-wide variables. Items such as font names, table colors, database connection strings, perhaps even writing information to a system log file. The following is an example `global.asa` file with script for these events:

```
<SCRIPT LANGUAGE=VBScript RUNAT=Server>
Sub Application_OnStart
    'Globals…
    Application("ErrorPage") = "handleError.asp"
    Application("SiteBanAttemptLimit") = 10
    Application("AccessErrorPage") = "handleError.asp"
    Application("RestrictAccess") = False

    'Keep track of visitors…
    Application("NumVisits") = Application("NumVisits") + 1
End Sub
</SCRIPT>
```

The Session Object

Each time a visitor comes to your web site, a Session object is created for the visitor if the visitor does not already have one. Therefore, there is an instance of the Session object available to you in your scripting as well. The Session object is similar to the Application object in that it can contain values. However, the Session object's values are lost when your visitor leaves the site. The Session object is most useful for transferring information from web page to web page. Using the Session object, there is no need to pass information in the URL.

The most common use of the Session object is to store information in its Contents collection. This information would be session-specific in that it would pertain only to the current user.

Many web sites today offer a "user personalization" service. That is, to customize a web page to their preference. This is easily done with ASP and the Session object. The user variables are stored in the client browser for retrieval by the server later. Simply load the user's preferences at the start of the session and then, as the user browses your site, utilize the information regarding the user's preferences to display information.

Suppose your web site displays stock quotes for users. You could allow users to customize the start page to display their favorite stock quotes when they visit the site. By storing the stock symbols in your Session object, you can easily display the correct quotes when you render your web page.

This session management system relies on the use of browser cookies. The cookies allow the user information to be persisted even after a client leaves the site. Unfortunately, if a visitor to your web site does not allow cookies to be stored, you will be unable to pass information between web pages within the Session object.

Collections

The Session object contains two collections: Contents and StaticObjects. The Contents collection we discussed above. The StaticObjects collection is similar to Contents, but only contains the objects that were created with the <OBJECT> tag in your HTML page. This collection can be iterated just like the Contents collection.

425

Properties

Below are the properties that the `Session` object exposes for your use:

CodePage	Setting this property will allow you to change the character set used by ASP when it is creating output. This property could be used if you were creating a multi-national web site.
LCID	This property sets the internal locale value for the entire web application. By default, your application's locale is your server's locale. If you server is in the U.S., then your application will default to the U.S. Much of the formatting functionality of ASP utilizes this locale setting to display information correctly for the country in question. For example, the date is displayed differently in Europe versus the U.S. So based on the locale setting, the date formatting functions will output the date in the correct format.
	You can also change this property temporarily to output data in a different format. A good example is currency. Let's say your web site had a shopping cart and you wanted to display totals in U.S. dollars for U.S. customers, and Pounds Sterling for U.K. customers. To do this you'd change the LCID property to the British locale setting, and then call the currency formatting routine.
SessionID	Every session created by ASP has a unique identifier. This identifier is called the `SessionID` and is accessible through this property. It can be used for debugging ASP scripts.
Timeout	By default, an ASP session will timeout after 20 minutes of inactivity. Every time a web page is requested or refreshed by a user, his internal ASP time clock starts ticking. When the time clock reaches the value set in this property, his session is automatically destroyed. You can set this property to reduce the timeout period if you wish.

Methods

The `Session` object contains a single method, `Abandon`. This instructs ASP to destroy the current `Session` object for this user. This method is what you would call when a user logs off your web site.

Events

The `Session` object generates two events: `Session_OnStart` and `Session_OnEnd`. The `Session_OnStart` event is fired when the first view of your web page occurs. The `Session_OnEnd` event is fired when the web server is shut down. If you choose to write scripts for these events they must be placed in your `global.asa` file.

The most common use of these events is to initialize session-wide variables. Items like usage counts, login names, real names, user preferences, etc. The following is an example `global.asa` file with script for these events:

```
<SCRIPT LANGUAGE=VBScript RUNAT=Server>
Sub Session_OnStart
     Session("LoginAttempts") = 0
     Session("LoggedOn") = False
End Sub

Sub Session_OnEnd
     Session("LoggedOn") = False
End Sub
</SCRIPT>
```

The Server Object

The next object in the ASP object model is the `Server` object. The `Server` object enables you to create and work with ActiveX controls in your web pages. In addition, the `Server` object exposes methods that help in the encoding of URLs and HTML text.

Properties

ScriptTimeout

This property sets the time in seconds that a script will be allowed to run. The default value for all scripts on the system is 90 seconds. That is to say that if a script has run for longer than 90 seconds, the web server will intervene and let the client browser know something is wrong. If you expect your scripts to run for a long time, you will want to use this property.

Methods

CreateObject

This method is the equivalent to VBScript's `CreateObject`, or using the `New` keyword - it instantiates a new instance of an object. The result can be placed into the `Application` or `Session Contents` collection to lengthen its life span.

Generally you'll create an object at the time the session is created and place it into the `Session.Contents` collection. For example, let's say you've created a killer ActiveX DLL with a really cool class that converts Fahrenheit to Celsius and vice versa. You could create an instance of this class with the `CreateObject` method and store it in the `Session.Contents` collection like this:

```
Set Session("MyConverter") = Server.CreateObject("KillerDLL.CDegreeConverter")
```

This object would be around as long as the session is and will be available for you to call. As you'll see in later chapters, this method is invaluable when working with database connections.

ASP comes with its own built in set of components that you can create instances of using the `CreateObject` method. These are:

❏ **Ad Rotator** – *used to display a random graphic and link every time a user connects to the page.*

❏ **Browser Capabilities** – *manipulates a file* `browscap.ini` *contained on the server computer to determine the capabilities of a particular client's browser.*

❏ **Content Linker** – *provides a central repository file from where you manage a series of links and their URLs, and provide appropriate descriptions about them.*

❏ **Content Rotator** – *a cut down version of the Ad Rotator that provides the same function but without optional redirection.*

❏ **Page Counter** – *Counts the number of times a page has been hit.*

❏ **Permission Checker** – *checks to see if a user has permissions before allowing them to access a given page.*

❏ **Counters** – *counts any value on an ASP page from anywhere within an ASP application.*

❏ **MyInfo** – *can be used to store personal information about a user within an XML file.*

❏ **Status** – *used to collect server profile information.*

❏ **Tools** – *a set of miscellaneous methods that are grouped under the generic heading of* Tools.

❏ **IIS Log** - *allows you to create an object that allows your applications to write to and otherwise access the IIS log.*

Execute

This method executes an ASP file and inserts the results into the response. You can use this call to include snippets of ASP code, like subroutines.

GetLastError

This method returns an `ASPError` object that contains all of the information about the last error that has occurred.

HTMLEncode

This method encodes a string for proper HTML usage. This is useful if you want to actually display HTML code on your web pages.

MapPath

This method returns a string that contains the actual physical path to the file in question. Subdirectories of your web site can be virtual. That is to say that they don't physically exist in the hierarchy of your web site. To find out the true whereabouts of a file, you can call this method.

Transfer

The `Transfer` method allows you to immediately transfer control of the executing page to another page. This is similar to the `Response.Redirect` method except for the fact that the `Transfer` method makes all variables and the `Request` collections available to the called page.

URLEncode

This method, as the title says, encodes a URL for transmission. This encoding includes replacing spaces with a plus sign (+) and replacing unprintable characters with hexadecimal values. You should always run your URLs through this method when redirecting.

The ObjectContext Object

The final object we shall consider is the `ObjectContext` object, which comes into play when you use transactions in your web page. When an ASP script has initiated a transaction, it can either be committed or aborted by this object. It has two methods to do this with.

SetAbort

`SetAbort` is called when the transaction has not been completed and you don't want resources updated.

SetComplete

`SetComplete` is called when there is no reason for the transaction to fail. If all of the components that form part of the transaction call `SetComplete`, then the transaction will complete.

Using Active Server Pages Effectively

Is it true that a little bit of knowledge is a bad thing? In the realm of ASP, I think not. A little bit of knowledge is probably just piquing your interest. For the final part of this chapter we're going to build a web site to demonstrate some of the features of ASP. This sample site will demonstrate many of the ASP features and principles described earlier in this chapter.

Designing the Site

Before we start creating our new web site, we should discuss the design. For your first ASP application, we'll keep it quite simple. What we want to create is an HTML form that accepts for input the following information: first name, last name, and e-mail address. After the user submits the form, our ASP page will reformat the first and last name, and check the e-mail address for proper syntax.

The user will be given three attempts to enter the information correctly or else a warning message will display at the bottom of the screen:

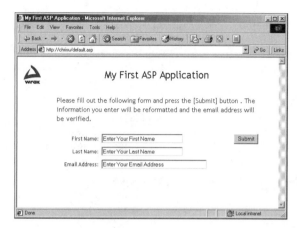

Creating the global.asa file

The first step in creating a new ASP application is to create your `global.asa` file. This is the file that houses your event handlers for the `Application` and `Session` objects. In addition, in this file you may set application, and session-wide variables to their default values. To create this file, in the root of your web server directory create a file called `global.asa`. Here is the content of our sample `global.asa`:

```
<SCRIPT LANGUAGE=VBScript RUNAT=Server>
Sub Application_OnStart
    Application("AllowedErrorsBeforeWarning") = 3
End Sub

Sub Session_OnStart
    Session("ErrorCount") = 0
End Sub

Sub Session_OnEnd
    'Nothing to do here...
End Sub

Sub Application_OnEnd
    'Nothing to do here...
End Sub
</SCRIPT>
```

Our file has handlers defined for `Application_OnStart`, `Application_OnEnd`, `Session_OnStart`, and `Session_OnEnd`. The `Application_OnEnd` and `Session_OnEnd` events are not used in this example, but shown above for completeness.

We want to set a limit on the number of submissions the user gets before a warning message is shown. Since this is a feature of the application and affects all users, we will store this constant in the `Application.Contents` collection. This is done in the `Application_OnStart` event. We add to the collection an item named `AllowedErrorsBeforeWarning` and set its value to 3.

Now that we know how many times a user can *try* to get it right, we need a place to store the number of times the user has *tried* to get it right. Since this counter is different for each user, we'll place this into the `Session.Contents` collection. We initialize our variable to 0. This is done in the `Session_OnStart` event. We add to the collection an item named, appropriately, `ErrorCount`, with a value of 0.

Creating our Main Page

Now that we've laid the groundwork for our ASP application, it's time to build the main page. Since this is a simple example, we will only utilize a single web page. Let's begin by creating this single page.

Create a new web page on your site and name it `default.asp`. This is the file name used by IIS as the default web page. The default web page is the page that is returned by a web server when no web page is specified. For example, when you call up `http://www.wrox.com/`, you aren't specifying a web page. The server looks through its list of default file names and finds the first match in the web site's root directory.

The following shows the contents of your `default.asp` page:

```
<%@ Language=VBScript %>
<%
Dim txtFirstName, txtLastName, txtEmailAddr
Dim sMessage

'*****************************************************************************
'* Main
'*
'* The main subroutine for this page...
'*****************************************************************************

Sub Main()
  'Was this page submitted?
  if ( Request("cmdSubmit") = "Submit" ) Then
    'Reformat the data into a more readable format...
    txtFirstName = InitCap(Request("txtFirstName"))
    txtLastName = InitCap(Request("txtLastName"))
    txtEmailAddr = LCase(Request("txtEmailAddr"))

    'Check the email address for the correct components...
    if (Instr(1, txtEmailAddr, "@") = 0 _
        or Instr(1, txtEmailAddr, ".") = 0 ) Then
      sMessage = "The email address you entered does not " _
        & "appear to be valid."
    Else
      'Make sure there is something after the period..
      if ( Instr(1, txtEmailAddr, ".") = Len(txtEmailAddr) _
      or Instr(1, txtEmailAddr, "@") = 1 or _
      (Instr(1, txtEmailAddr, ".") = Instr(1, txtEmailAddr, "@") + 1) ) Then
        sMessage = "You must enter a complete email address."
      end if
    End If
```

```
    'We passed our validation, show that all is good...
  if ( sMessage = "" ) Then
    sMessage = "Thank you for your input. All data has " _
      & "passed verification."
  else
    Session("ErrorCount") = Session("ErrorCount") + 1

    if ( Session("ErrorCount") > _
        Application("AllowedErrorsBeforeWarning") ) then
      sMessage = sMessage & "<P><Font Size=1>You have exceeded " _
        & "the normal number of times it takes to get this right!</Font>"
    end if
  End If
Else
  'First time in here? Set some default values...
  txtFirstName = "Enter Your First Name"
  txtLastName = "Enter Your Last Name"
  txtEmailAddr = "Enter Your Email Address"
End If
End Sub


'**************************************************************************
'* InitCap
'*
'* Capitalizes the first letter of the string
'**************************************************************************

Function InitCap(sStr)
  InitCap = UCase(Left(sStr, 1)) & LCase(Right(sStr, Len(sStr) - 1))
End Function


'**************************************************************************
'* Call our main subroutine
'**************************************************************************

Call Main()
%>

<html>
<head>
  <meta NAME="GENERATOR" Content="Microsoft FrontPage 3.0">
  <title>My First ASP Application</title>
</head>

<body>

<table border="0" cellPadding="0" cellSpacing="0" width="600">
<tbody>
  <tr>
    <td width="100"><a href="http://www.wrox.com" target="_blank" border=0
alt><img border=0 title="Check out the Wrox Press Web Site!"
src="images/wroxlogo.gif" WIDTH="56" HEIGHT="56"></a></td>
    <td width="500"><center><font size="5" face="Trebuchet MS">My First ASP
```

```
Application</font></center></td>
   </tr>

   <tr>
      <td width="100"> </td>
      <td width="500" align="left"><font face="Trebuchet MS"><br>
      Please fill out the following form and press the [Submit] button. The
information you enter will be reformatted and the email address will be
verified.</font><form action="default.asp" id="FORM1" method="post"
name="frmMain">
         <table border="0" cellPadding="1" cellSpacing="5" width="100%">
         <tr>
            <td width="100" nowrap align="right"><font size="2" face="Trebuchet
MS">First Name:</font></td>
            <td width="350"><font size="2" face="Trebuchet MS">
            <input title="Enter your first name here" name="txtFirstName"
size="30" value="<%=txtFirstName%>" tabindex="1"></font></td>
               <td width="50"><div align="right"><font size="2" face="Trebuchet MS">
               <input type="submit" title="Submit this data for processing..."
value="Submit" name="cmdSubmit" tabindex="4"></font></td>
            </tr>

            <tr>
            <td width="100" nowrap align="right">
            <font size="2" face="Trebuchet MS">Last Name:</font></td>
            <td width="400" colspan="2">
            <font size="2" face="Trebuchet MS">
            <input title="Enter your last name here" name="txtLastName"
size="30" value="<%=txtLastName%>" tabindex="2"></font></td>
            </tr>

            <tr>
            <td width="100" nowrap align="right"><font size="2" face="Trebuchet
MS">Email Address:</font></td>
            <td width="400" colspan="2"><font size="2" face="Trebuchet MS"><input
title="Enter your valid email address here" name="txtEmailAddr"
            size="40" value="<%=txtEmailAddr%>" tabindex="3"></font></td>
            </tr>
            <tr>
            <td nowrap width=500 colspan="3" align="center"><font face="Trebuchet
MS"><br>
               <strong><%=sMessage%></strong> </font></td>
            </tr>
         </table>
      </form>
      <p> </td>
   </tr>
</tbody>
</table>
</body>
</html>
```

As you can see, the page is quite long. But it breaks logically into two distinct sections: the ASP/VBScript portion, and the HTML portion. Let's examine each section individually.

The ASP/VBScript Section

The top half of our file is where the ASP code lives. This is the code that is executed by the server before the page is returned to the browser that requested it. Any code, as you've seen, that is to be executed on the server before returning is enclosed in the special `<%` and `%>` tags.

For clarity (and sanity!), the ASP code has been divided into subroutines. This not only makes the code more readable, but also will aid in its reuse. Our code has two routines: `Main`, and `InitCap`.

Before we do anything however, we declare some variables:

```
Dim txtFirstName, txtLastName, txtEmailAddr
Dim sMessage
```

When variables are declared outside of a subroutine in an ASP page, the variables retain their data until the page is completely processed. This allows you to pass information from your ASP code to your HTML code as you'll see.

After our variables have been declared, we have our `Main` routine. This is what is called by our ASP code every time a browser retrieves the page. The `Main` subroutine is not called automatically: we must explicitly call it ourselves.

```
'*****************************************************************
'* Main
'*
'* The main subroutine for this page...
'*****************************************************************

Sub Main()
    '   Was this page submitted?
    if ( Request("cmdSubmit") = "Submit" ) Then
    ' Reformat the data into a more readable format...
        txtFirstName = InitCap(Request("txtFirstName"))
        txtLastName = InitCap(Request("txtLastName"))
        txtEmailAddr = LCase(Request("txtEmailAddr"))

        '   Check the email address for the correct components...
        if ( Instr(1, txtEmailAddr, "@") = 0 or Instr(1, txtEmailAddr, ".") _
            = 0 ) Then
          sMessage = "The email address you entered does not appear to be valid."
        Else
            '   Make sure there is something after the period..
            if ( Instr(1, txtEmailAddr, ".") = Len(txtEmailAddr) & _
                or Instr(1, txtEmailAddr, "@") = 1 or & _
                (Instr(1, txtEmailAddr, ".") = Instr(1, txtEmailAddr, "@") + 1) ) _
                Then
              sMessage = "You must enter a complete email address."
            end if
        End If
```

```
'    We passed our validation, show that all is good...
   if ( sMessage = "" ) Then
       sMessage = "Thank you for your input. All data has " _
          & "passed verification."
   else
       Session("ErrorCount") = Session("ErrorCount") + 1

       if ( Session("ErrorCount") > _
            Application("AllowedErrorsBeforeWarning") ) then
            sMessage = sMessage & "<P><Font Size=1>You have exceeded " _
               & "the normal number of times it takes to get this right!</Font>"
       end if
   End If
   Else
      'First time in here? Set some default values...
      txtFirstName = "Enter Your First Name"
      txtLastName = "Enter Your Last Name"
      txtEmailAddr = "Enter Your Email Address"
   End If
End Sub
```

First we see if the form was actually submitted by the user, otherwise we initialize our variables. To determine if the page has been submitted, we check the value of the cmdSubmit Request variable. This is the button on our form. When pressed, the form calls this page and sets the value of the cmdSubmit button to Submit. If a user just loads the page without pressing the button, the value of cmdSubmit is blank (" "). There are other ways to determine if a web page was submitted, but this method is the simplest.

After we have determined that the page was in fact submitted, run the names through the second function on this page: InitCap. InitCap is a quick little function that will format a word to proper case. That is to say that the first letter will be capitalized, and the rest of the word will be lowercase. Here is the function:

```
'******************************************************************
'* InitCap
'*
'* Capitalizes the first letter of the string
'******************************************************************

Function InitCap(sStr)
    InitCap = UCase(Left(sStr, 1)) & LCase(Right(sStr, Len(sStr) - 1))
End Function
```

Now that we've cleaned up the names, we need to check the e-mail address for validity. To do this we ensure that it contains an "@" sign and a period (.). Once past this check, we make sure that there is data after the period and that there is data before the "@" sign. This is 'quick and dirty' e-mail validity checking.

If either of these checks fail, we place a failure message into the string sMessage. This will be displayed in our HTML section after the page processing is complete.

Now, if our e-mail address has passed the test, we set the message (sMessage) to display a thank you note. If we failed our test, we increment our error counter that we set up in the global.asa file. Here we also check to see if we have exceeded our limit on errors. If we have, a sterner message is set for display.

435

Finally, the last thing in our ASP section is our call to `Main`. This is what is called when the page is loaded:

```
'**********************************************************************
'* Call our main subroutine
'**********************************************************************

Call Main()
```

The HTML Section

This section is a regular HTML form with a smattering of ASP thrown in for good measure. The ASP that we've embedded in the HTML sets default values for the input fields, and displays any messages that our server side code has generated.

The most important part of the HTML is where the ASP code is embedded. The following snippet illustrates this:

```
<input title="Enter your first name here" name="txtFirstName" size="30"
  value="<%=txtFirstName%>" tabindex="1">
```

Here we see a normal text input box. However, to set the value of the text box we use the `Response.Write` shortcut (`<%=`) to insert the value of the variable `txtFirstName`. Remember that we dimensioned this outside of our ASP functions so that it would have page scope. Now we utilize its value by inserting it into our HTML.

We do exactly the same thing with the Last Name and Email Address text boxes:

```
<input title="Enter your last name here" name="txtLastName" size="30"
  value="<%=txtLastName%>" tabindex="2">
<input title="Enter your valid email address here" name="txtEmailAddr"
  size="40" value="<%=txtEmailAddr%>" tabindex="3">
</tr>
```

The last trick in the HTML section is the display of our failure or success message. This message is stored in the variable called `sMessage`. At the bottom of the form, we display the contents of this variable like so:

```
<td nowrap width=500 colspan="3" align="center">
  <font face="Trebuchet MS">
  <br>
  <strong>
  <%=sMessage%>
  </strong>
  </font>
</td>
```

The beauty of this code is that if `sMessage` is blank then nothing is shown, otherwise the message is displayed.

Summary

You should have learned much in this chapter. We first learned how HTTP is the transaction system that sends web pages to requesting clients. It is a very important piece of the puzzle. We then discussed Active Server Pages, or ASP. You learned how ASP pages are created, and what special HTML tags you need to include in your files to use ASP. We looked through the ASP object model and saw that the Request and Response objects are used to manage details of the HTTP request and responses. We saw that the Application object is used to group pages together into one application and we saw that the Session is used to create the illusion that the interaction between user and site is one continuous action. Finally we created a small application that demonstrates two uses for ASP: form validation and data manipulation.

Note that you can find full details of the ASP object model in Appendix J.

15

Talking to Databases: ActiveX Data Objects

In this chapter, you will be introduced to ADO (ActiveX Data Objects). ADO provides a COM-based way of accessing data of many kinds, whether or not the data can be considered to be a 'database' in the standard sense. That said, we'll be concentrating on relational database access in this short introduction. We'll see how to use the various objects (`Connection`, `Command`, `Recordset` and `Error`) that ADO exposes.

This chapter won't teach you database access from scratch. Databases are a huge topic, and we'll barely scratch the surface of ADO as it is. There's too much to learn. If you already know a little about databases, though, you should be able to see how ADO works at its most basic level.

What Tools Do You Need?

ADO is COM-based, which means that you can use ADO with any development tool that can take advantage of COM components (also called ActiveX components). These tools include Microsoft Visual Basic, Microsoft Visual C++, Borland Delphi, and of course you can also use ADO in VBScript, which is why we're all here.

The Windows Script Host (WSH) can be used to run the samples in this chapter (see Chapter 10 for more information on this). Microsoft Internet Information Server (IIS) on Windows NT/2000, Microsoft Personal Web Server (PWS) on Windows 9x, and Microsoft Internet Explorer can also be used as hosts for running the samples. If you want to experiment with the samples, you can use any text editor, like Notepad, to edit them.

ADO itself is free of charge and the latest version can be downloaded from Microsoft's website, http://www.microsoft.com/data. We will be talking about ADO version 2.1 in this chapter. Version 2.5 of ADO is available with Windows 2000 and Appendix K provides detailed reference to the objects, constants and data types therein.

The Evolution of ADO

Before ADO came along, we had (from a Visual Basic/VBScript developer's perspective) DAO and RDO. Just for a minute, let's take a short look at these two technologies and see where ADO came from.

DAO

DAO is based on the JET database engine and it is more or less perfect for Access/Jet databases. It lets you perform any database-related function you can do in Microsoft Access, such as creating a new database, compacting a database, adding/deleting tables, changing the table structure, and so on.

DAO uses an object model that is based on the DBEngine and WorkSpace objects. This means that all other objects are related to these objects. ADO, on the other hand, has a 'flatter' object model, where most objects can be used on their own without having to create their base objects. This means that fewer steps are needed when you write your code using ADO.

DAO doesn't give you the ability to perform asynchronous operations, to use disconnected recordsets (where you work with a local copy of the data) or to respond to various events within the object model. There are other things that DAO is not able to do, like data shaping (hierarchical recordsets) and persistent data (good for the Web).

Even after the arrival of ADO, though, DAO is probably still the best database engine for use with Access/Jet databases that are placed locally or on a network server in a LAN. This is because DAO has been optimized for use with the Jet engine, whereas ADO is a database-independent engine. With a little tweaking and fine-tuning, you can get almost the same and (in some areas better) result with ADO, as of version 2.1. Who knows, it might actually be that version 2.5, which ships with Windows 2000, is better overall than DAO....

Although DAO can use ODBCDirect to access remote servers and thus skip the overhead of using the Jet engine, it is largely the same as using RDO, but with a little less functionality.

RDO

RDO (Remote Data Objects) was created as a way of dealing with ODBC data without using the ODBC API calls. It was created with VB programmers in mind, and it is simple to use compared to using ODBC API calls. RDO is based on a programming model that is very similar to the DAO one, but it is intended to be used with intelligent database servers, such as Microsoft SQL Server and Oracle (hence the word Remote). RDO only ships with Enterprise editions of Visual Basic and Visual Studio, and as such is not a product you can use as a VBScript developer, unless you are using the script engine with one of these development environments.

ADO

ADO is COM-based and, unlike DAO and RDO, it is not specifically designed to access ISAM or relational databases. Nor is it specifically designed to use either local or remote data sources. Whatever data source you are using, you will be able to use the same code and simply change the data provider. This is what makes ADO so exciting. Mind you, there can be a few minor differences, so keep your eyes open.

What Are ActiveX Data Objects?

ADO is part of Microsoft's **UDA** (Universal Data Access) strategy. UDA is Microsoft's strategy for access to information across an enterprise. It gives you access to a variety of relational databases, as ODBC have done in the past, but also to non-relational information sources, like e-mail and file systems that are normally organized hierarchically. This, of course, also means that you can access hierarchical databases such as IBM's IMS and Microsoft Index Server.

In fact, ADO is actually part of **MDAC** (Microsoft Data Access Components), which is the UDA enabling technology. MDAC includes the following components: ADO, **RDS** (Remote Data Services, for use with disconnected data sources like servers on the Web), various OLEDB providers, ODBC Driver Manager and various ODBC drivers, and the Jet engine.

If you're not confused enough already, ADO is actually a wrapper around OLEDB, which makes it easier for application developers to use UDA. ADO is the *application-*level programming interface, whereas OLEDB is the *system-*level programming interface to data access. The diagram shows how this works. As you can see, some low-level languages (like C++ and Java) can deal directly with OLEDB. As a VBScript programmer, though, it's highly unlikely that you'd ever want to deal directly with OLEDB. ADO wraps up the functionality of OLEDB and provides you with an object model that is much easier to use than OLEDB itself.

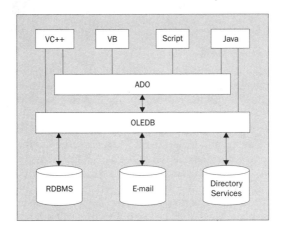

In order for you to get access to a data store, you will need an OLEDB **data provider**. A provider is anything that provides data – not the physical source of the data, but the mechanism that connects to the physical store.

The **data consumer** is any application or system that needs access to the data, so the data consumer uses the data provider to retrieve and manipulate the wanted data. In a much more abstract sense, you can say that *you* are the consumer using the provider to get to your data. Strictly, ADO itself is actually a consumer as well, because it uses data provided by OLEDB.

The ADO Objects

The following diagram shows the relationships between the main ADO objects. Although the Connection object is nominally at the head of the hierarchy, the Command and Recordset objects can actually exist separately in their own right, without having to create a (permanent) Connection object. That means that you can create whatever object you really need without having to litter the place with too many extra objects.

In the diagram below, what look like piles of pages represent **collections**, which contain zero or more instances of the objects under them. For example, the Errors collection may have a number of Error objects in it.

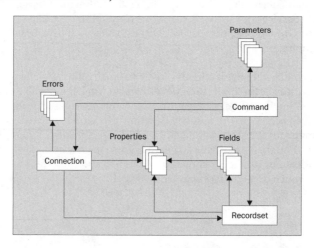

For the rest of the chapter, we're going to examine the ADO objects in some detail. We've presented the examples in Access, mostly because we had to present them in *something*, and because it was the most likely 'normal' database that you'd have lying around. But ADO is so versatile that we could have chosen practically anything. The examples are really only designed to give you a brief introduction to ADO, which is a big topic. If you're serious about getting into ADO in more depth, consider picking up the most recent ADO Programmer's Reference by Wrox Press – at the time of writing, this was ADO 2.1.

Not all the examples will visibly do something. They're there so you can see how to structure each statement. Most of these examples connect to the same database in the same way, so much of the code will remain the same – the changed areas will be highlighted. Let's look at the Connection object first.

The Connection Object

What is a `Connection` object? Well, the `Connection` object is actually the only object that is always required in the ADO programming model, and even this is not quite true, as we've seen. It *is* required that you have a connection to a data source, but you don't have to have a *permanent* connection; rather, you can choose to have a *temporary* connection that closes when the requested operation has been performed. If you're going to be using the same connection a lot, it's faster to explicitly create the `Connection` object than to create a separate temporary connection each time.

The `Connection` object itself is created like this:

```
Dim cnNorthwind

' Create the connection object
Set cnNorthwind = CreateObject("ADODB.Connection")
```

Note that this isn't actually connected to anything. At this point, we have the object, but we haven't pointed it at anything yet.

The `Connection` object can perform the following operations (remember that we're working with an Access database):

- Open or close a connection to a database
- Execute a query
- Cancel a connection

If you're using SQL Server or another database that supports transactions, you'll also be able to begin, commit, and rollback transactions using the `Connection` object.

Opening a Connection

This code opens the connection to the `Northwind.mdb` database found with Visual Studio and various versions of Microsoft Office packages. If you're trying this out yourself, make sure the path to the database is correct. If you don't have this database, you can supply the path to any other Access database and follow on from there. You'll have to alter the later examples to point to tables in your own database, though.

Don't forget to create the `Connection` object in your code before trying to execute these lines...

```
' Set the connection string
cnNorthwind.ConnectionString = "Provider=Microsoft.Jet.OLEDB.3.51;" _
    & "User ID=Admin;Data Source=c:\Program Files\Microsoft Visual " _
    & "Studio\VB98\Nwind.mdb"
' Open the connection
cnNorthwind.Open
```

We'll be using this same code for most of the examples in this chapter.

Note that the connection string could have been specified as an argument of the Open method instead, so the above code would simply become:

```
cnNorthwind.Open("Provider=Microsoft.Jet.OLEDB.3.51;" _
    & "User ID=Admin;Data Source=c:\Program Files\Microsoft Visual" _
    & "Studio\VB98\Nwind.mdb")
```

Instead of specifying the name of an OLEDB provider and the name and location of physical storage, you can also supply the name of an ODBC **DSN** (Data Source Name) Data Source Names are set up from the Control Panel, under ODBC Data Sources. Once you've pointed a DSN at a database, you don't have to keep supplying the full connection string each time, you can simply use:

```
cnNorthwind.Open("DSN=Nwind")
```

...assuming you've created a DSN called Nwind.

Closing a Connection

```
' Close the connection
cnNorthwind.Close
```

This will also close any recordsets that have been opened using the connection.

Executing a Query

```
Dim cnNorthwind
Dim rsCategory

    ' Create the connection object
    Set cnNorthwind = CreateObject("ADODB.Connection")
    ' Set the connection string
    cnNorthwind.ConnectionString = "Provider=Microsoft.Jet.OLEDB.3.51;" & _
        "User ID=Admin;Data Source=c:\Program Files\Microsoft Visual " & _
        "Studio\VB98\Nwind.mdb"
    ' Open the connection
    cnNorthwind.Open

    ' Get the recordset returned from a select query
    Set rsCategory = cnNorthwind.Execute("SELECT CategoryName " & _
        & "FROM Categories WHERE CategoryID = 2")

    MsgBox rsCategory.GetString

    ' Close and destroy the connection object
    cnNorthwind.Close
    Set cnNorthwind = Nothing
```

Note that you can also execute a query that doesn't return any records, which is called an action query. Action queries include adding and deleting records.

Cancel a Connection While Executing a Query

```
Dim cnNorthwind

'Connection info is here

' Execute an action query asynchronously
cnNorthwind.Execute "DELETE FROM Categories " & _
"WHERE CategoryID = 100", , adAsyncExecute
' Cancel the execution of the action query
cnNorthwind.Cancel
```

.
.
.

It's important to note that you can only cancel the Open and Execute methods when they have been executed asynchronously (at the same time as other commands are running). That's what adAsyncExecute is doing here – that's how we say that we want to execute the action asynchronously. If we hadn't, we'd have got a run-time error.

The Command Object

The Command object is used much the same way as the Execute method of the Connection object – it lets you execute a command against your database. It's easier to work with, though, and the Command object also has an associated Parameters collection, which you can use for specifying the name, size, direction and value of the parameters that a stored procedure or query takes. In fact, whenever you use a stored procedure (note that Access doesn't support stored procedures) or query that takes parameters, you need to be using the Command object.

The Command object is created like this:

```
Dim cmNorthwind

' Create the command object
Set cmNorthwind = CreateObject("ADODB.Command")
```

The Command object can perform the following operations:

❑   Execute the command

❑   Cancel the command

❑   Create a parameter

We won't cover parameters here.

Executing the Command

This first example shows the `Command` object in its usual habitat. After creating and opening our (by now familiar) connection, we then create the `Command` object, assign it to the connection we've opened, and then set the `CommandText` property. This is the property that contains the substance of the command itself. When the `Execute` method of the `Command` object is invoked, it's this text that will be run.

```
Dim cmNorthwind
Dim cnNorthwind

   ' Normal connection   code goes here

   ' Create the command object
   Set cmNorthwind = CreateObject("ADODB.Command")
   ' Set the command connection
   cmNorthwind.ActiveConnection = cnNorthwind
   ' Set the command text
   cmNorthwind.CommandText = "DELETE FROM Categories WHERE " & _
      "CategoryID = 100"
   ' Execute the command
   cmNorthwind.Execute

   ' Destroy the command object
   Set cmNorthwind = Nothing
   ' Close and destroy the connection object
   cnNorthwind.Close
   Set cnNorthwind = Nothing
```

Our command here specifies the deletion of a certain record in the Northwind Categories table. To try it out, you should insert a new record into this table, and note down the `CategoryID` that is assigned to it (it's an Autonumber field). Then modify your code to delete that record.

Also note that instead of creating a 'full' connection, as we have done above, you can actually supply a connection string in the line that specifies the `ActiveConnection` property of the `Command`, like this:

```
cmNorthwind.ActiveConnection = "Provider=Microsoft.Jet.OLEDB.3.51;" _
   & "User ID=Admin;Data Source=c:\Program Files\Microsoft Visual " _
   & "Studio\VB98\Nwind.mdb"
```

This way a temporary connection is opened and closed again when the command is finished.

If the `Execute` method performs a row-returning query (the one above simply deleted a record, so no data was actually returned), you need to specify a `Recordset` object that can hold the returned rows. We'll see how to work with `Recordset` objects later on. This example, though, works in a similar way to the first example we used when we looked at the `Connection` object – you `Set` the `Recordset` equal to the result of executing the command.

```
' code to create recordset and command...
' Set the command text
cmNorthwind.CommandText = "SELECT * FROM Categories WHERE " & _
    "CategoryID = 100"
' Execute the command
Set rsCategory = cmNorthwind.Execute
' ...
```

Canceling the command

```
Dim cmNorthwind
Dim cnNorthwind
Dim rsCategory

    'normal connection code goes here

    ' Create the command object
    Set cmNorthwind = CreateObject("ADODB.Command")
    ' Set the command connection
    cmNorthwind.ActiveConnection = cnNorthwind
    ' Set the command text
    cmNorthwind.CommandText = "SELECT * FROM Categories WHERE " & _
    & "CategoryID = 100"

    ' Execute the command asynchronously
    Set rsCategory = cmNorthwind.Execute(, , adAsyncExecute)

    ' Check if the command is still executing
    If CBool(cmNorthwind.State And adStateExecuting) Then
        ' Cancel the pending command
        cmNorthwind.Cancel
    End If

    ' Destroy the command object
    .
    .
    .
```

You can only cancel commands that are executed asynchronously. The Cancel command is ignored if it is executed after an asynchronous command has completed or if the command wasn't executed asynchronously. If the command is still executing, the Cancel command works like a rollback feature. This means that if the query is deleting records, these won't actually be deleted from the database.

Above, we checked whether the command was still executing – if so, we cancelled it. If it was already finished, it would be too late to cancel it anyway.

The Recordset Object

The Recordset object is a representation of a base table, the result of a query or SELECT statement, or the result of an executed command (see the Command object). The Recordset object is the object that represents the actual data you are presented with. For example, if you execute a query that asks for people whose last names begin with G, you'll get a recordset back containing just those records where that's the case. Then you can actually get down to manipulating them in some way.

When you want to manipulate similar rows individually, you cannot use a SQL statement, because that will treat all the selected rows equally. Instead, you use the `Recordset` object to hold all the similar rows and then you perform the operations on the individual rows, either by moving sequentially through the recordset or by searching for a specific row.

Also, you might want to use a **disconnected** recordset, which means that a recordset is dissociated from the server, and can be re-associated at a later time. You can also save them locally, make changes, and update the data source later. This is one of the very valuable new features of ADO, and it is extremely useful for Internet applications.

The `Recordset` object is created like this:

```
Dim rsCategory

    ' Create the recordset object
    Set rsCategory = CreateObject("ADODB.Recordset")
```

The `Recordset` object is what you'll use to work with your actual data. Here's a list of what you can do with the `Recordset` object:

❑   Open and close the recordset

❑   Add a new row to the recordset

❑   Delete from a recordset

❑   Cancel the recordset

❑   Save/persist the recordset to a file

❑   Open a persisted recordset from a file

❑   Move to a different record

❑   Locate a specific record

Opening a Recordset

```
Dim cnNorthwind
Dim rsCategory

    ' Create the connection object
    Set cnNorthwind = CreateObject("ADODB.Connection")
    ' Set the connection string
    cnNorthwind.ConnectionString = "Provider=Microsoft.Jet.OLEDB.3.51;" _
        & "User ID=Admin;Data Source=c:\Program Files\Microsoft Visual "& _
        & "Studio\VB98\Nwind.mdb"

    ' Open the connection
    cnNorthwind.Open

    ' Create the recordset object
    Set rsCategory = CreateObject("ADODB.Recordset")
    ' Open the Categories table
    rsCategory.Open "Categories", cnNorthwind, , , adCmdTable
```

```
' Close and destroy the recordset object
rsCategory.Close
Set rsCategory = Nothing
' Close and destroy the connection object
cnNorthwind.Close
Set cnNorthwind = Nothing
```

The Open method takes several arguments (source, activeconnection, cursortype, locktype, and options), but only two of them are needed (source, activeconnection). The last three arguments all have default values, if you don't specify them.

Take note of the options argument, however, as it might save you some connection time if you do specify it. The default value for the options argument is adCmdUnknown, which means that ADO needs to make an extra round trip to the provider, in order to find out if source is a table name, a stored procedure, or an SQL statement. We've told it in advance that it's a table.

When you open a recordset, the cursor is always placed on the first record, if the recordset is not empty. If it is empty, the BOF and EOF (beginning and end of file) properties are both set to True.

The Close method takes no arguments. When you close an open recordset, any lock you might have placed on the data source is released.

Adding a New Row to the Recordset

Access supports this method, however it will return an error saying 'the provider does not support the requested operation' if the correct lock type (adLockOptimistic) is not specified. If you have SQL Server you can connect to that version of the Northwind database to try this out (this assumes the server is called TESTPC; you should substitute your own machine name here):

```
Dim cnNorthwind
Dim rsCategory

    ' Create the connection object
    Set cnNorthwind = CreateObject("ADODB.Connection")
    ' Set the connection string
    cnNorthwind.ConnectionString = "Provider=SQLOLEDB.1;" _
        & "User ID=sa;Initial Catalog=Northwind;Data Source=TESTPC"

    ' Open the connection
    cnNorthwind.Open

    ' Create the recordset object
    Set rsCategory = CreateObject("ADODB.Recordset")
    ' Open the Categories table
    rsCategory.Open "Categories", cnNorthwind, , , adCmdTable
    ' Add an empty row to the recordset
    rsCategory.AddNew
    ' Update the fields in the empty row
    rsCategory.Fields("CategoryName").Value = "Test"
    rsCategory.Fields("Description").Value = _
        "This is a sample description"
    ' Update/save the row to the recordset
    rsCategory.Update
```

449

```
' Close and destroy the Recordset object
   .
   .
   .
```

If the recordset is disconnected, the update will not happen in the database itself until you reconnect and use the UpdateBatch method to synchronize the recordsets.

As you can see, we've added an empty row to the recordset, populated the fields, and then saved the row. You can actually do this in another way:

```
'  Connect to SQL DB as above...
'  Create the recordset object
Set rsCategory = CreateObject("ADODB.Recordset")
' Open the Categories table
rsCategory.Open "Categories", cnNorthwind, , , adCmdTable
' Add a new row to the recordset
rsCategory.AddNew Array("CategoryName", "Description"), _
   Array("Test", "This is sample description")

' Close and destroy the recordset object
   .
   .
   .
```

The AddNew method can only be used on an updateable recordset. You can use the Supports method to check if you can add new records to an existing recordset:

```
' Is the recordset updateable?
If rsCategory.Supports(adAddNew) Then
   ' Do your stuff here...
Else
   MsgBox "This recordset doesn't support that method"
End If
```

Deleting From a Recordset

Again Access will return an error saying 'the provider does not support the requested operation' if the correct lock type (adLockOptimistic) is not specified. We will demonstrate the use of the Delete method using the SQL Server Northwind database.

```
Dim cnNorthwind
Dim rsOrderDetails

   ' Connection to SQL DB as above

   ' Create the recordset object
   Set rsOrderDetails = CreateObject("ADODB.Recordset")
   ' Open the Order Details table
   rsOrderDetails.Open "[Order Details]", cnNorthwind, , , adCmdTable
   ' Delete the first row from the recordset
   rsOrderDetails.Delete

   ' Close and destroy the Recordset object
   .
   .
   .
```

The `Delete` method can take the `affectrecords` argument that tells ADO what records to delete. The default (when the argument is omitted) is to delete the current record. You can also specify to delete all records in the recordset, delete all records that have been filtered using the `Filter` property, and to delete all chapter records. If the recordset is disconnected, the deletion will not happen in the database itself, until you reconnect and use the `UpdateBatch` method to synchronize the recordsets.

You should be aware that after you have deleted the current record, it remains active until you move to another record. This can cause run-time errors, if you forget to move to a different record before you start inspecting the field values or otherwise manipulate the current record.

Canceling the Recordset

For this example, we've gone back to the Access database.

```
Dim cnNorthwind
Dim rsCategory

    ' Create the connection object
    Set cnNorthwind = CreateObject("ADODB.Connection")
    ' Set the connection string
    cnNorthwind.ConnectionString = "Provider=Microsoft.Jet.OLEDB.3.51;" _
        & "User ID=Admin;Data Source=c:\Program Files\Microsoft Visual " _
        & "Studio\VB98\Nwind.mdb"
    ' Open the connection
    cnNorthwind.Open

    ' Create the recordset object
    Set rsCategory = CreateObject("ADODB.Recordset")
    ' Open the Categories table asynchronously
    rsCategory.Open "Categories", cnNorthwind, ,, adCmdTable + adAsyncExecute
    ' Cancel the opening of the recordset
    rsCategory.Cancel

    ' Close and destroy the recordset object
    .
    .
    .
```

You can only cancel the `Open` method if it has been executed asynchronously. A run-time error occurs otherwise.

Save/Persist the Recordset to a File

```
' Connect as usual
' Create the recordset object
    Set rsCategory = CreateObject("ADODB.Recordset")
    ' Open the Categories table
    rsCategory.Open "Categories", cnNorthwind, , , adCmdTable
    ' Save the recordset
    rsCategory.Save "C:\Category.ado"

    ' Close and destroy the recordset object
    .
    .
    .
```

The above piece of code saves the recordset to the file `C:\Category.ado`, in a proprietary format, but you can also save it in XML format using the `adPersistXML` constant as the second argument. You can only use the `Save` method on an open recordset.

Open a Persisted Recordset from a File

This code opens the saved recordset from the file `C:\Category.ado`.

```
' Connect as usual
' Create the recordset object
Set rsCategory = CreateObject("ADODB.Recordset")

' Open the recordset from file
rsCategory.Open "C:\Category.ado", , , , adCmdFile
' ... Do your other stuff here

' Close and destroy the recordset object
.
.
.
```

Moving to a Different Record

```
' Connect as usual

' Create the recordset object
Set rsCategory = CreateObject("ADODB.Recordset")
' Open the Categories table
rsCategory.Open "Categories", cnNorthwind, , , adCmdTable
' Move to the last record
rsCategory.MoveLast
' Move to the previous record
rsCategory.MovePrevious
' Move to the next record
rsCategory.MoveNext
' Move to the first record
rsCategory.MoveFirst
' Move five records ahead of the current one
rsCategory.Move 5

' Close and destroy the recordset object
.
.
.
```

The above piece of code moves the cursor around the recordset. Note that you can use the `Move` method to move backwards as well; just supply a negative number as the argument.

Locating a Specific Record

Note that if you've tried out all the previous examples, you may find that the record specified here has been deleted. If that's the case, either add a new record that satisfies the criteria, or change the criteria to point to a record that does exist.

```
' Connect as usual

' Create the recordset object
Set rsCategory = CreateObject("ADODB.Recordset")
' Open the Categories table
rsCategory.Open "Categories", cnNorthwind, , , adCmdTable
```

```
' Locate the record with the category Beverages
' starting from the current record searching forwards
rsCategory.Find "CategoryName='Beverages'"

' Use the Filter property to find a specific record using more
' than one criterion
rsCategory.Filter = "CategoryName='Condiments' AND CategoryID=2"
' Remove the filter
rsCategory.Filter = adFilterNone
```

```
' Close and destroy the recordset object
```

The above piece of code locates two different records in two different ways. Use the Find method when you only need to specify one criterion, and use the Filter property if you need to specify more than one criterion. Setting the Filter property might "return" more than one record. Don't forget to remove the filter once you are done. There is also the Seek method, which can be used for searching using an index, but this method is not currently supported by all providers.

Without going into too much detail in this chapter, there are also ways of creating disconnected recordsets that are useful when the server isn't always available. Disconnected means that the connection to the data store is "cut", by setting the Connection property to Nothing. You then perform your actions on the data in the disconnected recordset and use the UpdateBatch method to synchronize once you have reconnected to the data store.

The Error Object

The Error object is the place to look if you want to see what (if anything) went wrong with the outcome of an action you have performed. The Connection object holds an Errors collection, which is made up of Error objects.

If the operation you perform generates an error, one or more Error objects are placed in the Errors collection. Note that if there is no valid Connection object, you can still retrieve the error from the VBScript Err object instead.

You don't have to instantiate the Error object; the Connection object controlling the Errors collection for the specified provider automatically does that. The key here is the connection, because there is an Errors collection for each connection you have.

> If you have more than one connection, you must make sure you examine the correct Errors collection.

You can perform the following operations on the Errors collection/ Error object:

❑ Inspect the Errors collection
❑ Clear the Errors collection

Inspecting the Errors Collection

```
Dim cnNorthwind
Dim errNorthwind

    'Connect as usual
    ' ...
    ' Do your other stuff here
    ' ...
    ' Inspect the Errors collection
    If cnNorthwind.Errors.Count > 0 Then
      ' Loop through the Errors collection
      For Each errNorthwind In cnNorthwind.Errors
        ' Display the error number for the current Error object
        MsgBox "Error number: " & errNorthwind.Number
      Next
    End If

    ' Close and destroy the connection object
    cnNorthwind.Close
    Set cnNorthwind = Nothing
```

It is important that you check the Errors collection after performing a series of methods on any of the objects attached to a Connection object. You could create a subprocedure that takes the Collection name as an argument and then put your error handling code in this procedure. That would make it easier for you to handle errors and not duplicate the code.

When you inspect the Errors collection and you find some Error objects in it, you should loop through the collection and examine the Error objects one by one:

```
Dim cnNorthwind
Dim errNorthwind

    ' Disable error handling
    On Error Resume Next

    'Connect as usual
    ' ...
    ' Do your other stuff here
    ' ...
    ' Inspect the Errors collection
    If cnNorthwind.Errors.Count > 0 Then
      ' Loop through the Errors collection
      For Each errNorthwind In cnNorthwind.Errors
        ' Display all the error properties
        MsgBox "Error description: " & errNorthwind.Description & _
            vbNewLine & "Error number" & errNorthwind.Number & _
```

```
        vbNewLine & "Native error (from provider)" & _
        errNorthwind.NativeError & vbNewLine & "Source" & _
        errNorthwind.Source & vbNewLine & "SQL state" & _
        errNorthwind.SQLState
  Next
End If

' Close and destroy the connection object
cnNorthwind.Close
Set cnNorthwind = Nothing
```

We've disabled error handling here so that the program doesn't break when an error is found, but carries on.

The following properties have been used in the piece of sample code shown above:

❑   **Description** – returns a brief description of the error that occurred. This is provided by ADO or the OLEDB provider.

❑   **Number** – returns a number that uniquely identifies an `Error` object.

❑   **NativeError** – returns the provider-specific error code for the `Error` object.

❑   **Source** – returns the name of the object or application that originally generated the `Error` object.

❑   **SQLState** – returns the SQL state for the `Error` object. This is a five-character string holding the error code that follows the ANSI SQL standard.

Clearing the Errors Collection

```
Dim cnNorthwind

' Disable error handling
On Error Resume Next

'Connect as usual
' Do your other stuff here
...
' Inspect the Errors collection
If cnNorthwind.Errors.Count > 0 Then
  '...
  ' Clear the Errors collection
  cnNorthwind.Errors.Clear
End If

' Close and destroy the connection object
cnNorthwind.Close
Set cnNorthwind = Nothing
```

If, for example, you had an error logging system that wrote errors to a database file somewhere, you could clear the `Errors` collection once the errors had been dealt with.

That concludes our introduction to ADO. Hopefully this short tour has shown you a little bit about how versatile it can be.

Summary

In this chapter, we have taken a very quick look at the world of ADO. We've looked at how you use the ADO `Connection`, `Command`, `Recordset`, and `Error` objects when you manipulate the data in your database. Hopefully you can start to see how simple ADO is to use. Believe me, whole books have been (and are being) written on this subject. We've only scratched the surface here, but hopefully you now have a taste for ADO.

In the next chapter, we'll see how to add scripting to Visual Basic programs.

16

Microsoft Script Control

By now, it should be clear that VBScript can be used in pretty much anything that is related to Windows. Not surprisingly, along with a variety of different technologies, Microsoft provides yet another component capable of supporting VBScript – the Script Control. Although the name may suggest that 'Script Control' may be a tool for movie writers that want to control the rights to their script, it couldn't be further from the truth. This ActiveX control provides a simple way for your application to host a scripting environment, allowing you, or your users, to further customize your application.

In the past, programmers had to struggle to provide customizability to their projects, or pay through their nose to license other products such as VBA. In 1997, Microsoft released basic interfaces to scripting engines, and eventually followed up with Script Control. Although Windows Script Interfaces provide greater control over the Script Control, they require great C++ skills to accomplish most of the tasks that can easily be carried out with the Script Control, which we'll discuss throughout this chapter.

Why Script your Application?

Scripting parts of the application can open many opportunities not only to you, the programmer (as you may not have to go through the standard rewrite, recompile and redistribute routine), but also to the end users, who will be able to do more with your application. The possibilities of scripting are almost endless, but, as usual, adding this capability to your application will take a lot more design, testing and occasionally, frustration. Before you set out to use the Script Control, you should consider simpler alternatives – Script Components, Windows Script Host and HTML Applications – all of which can provide some form of scripting to your application.

In its simplest form, the Script Control will allow you to use functionality that is beyond VB, such as the ability to evaluate expressions entered by users at runtime, as illustrated in the code extract below. Following this example, you may extend your VB application with few interchangeable routines that can be executed when a certain events occurs (in some cases it might be easier to use the scripting options mentioned above). In more advanced cases, you can add the object model of your ActiveX component to the control, and allow the user to more effectively automate your application, from writing a customizable report to adding a macro language.

The following example shows just how easy it is to evaluate a mathematical expression in VB with a little help from the Script Control. Although a step-by-step introduction to the Script Control is available later in the chapter, the code snippet shows how to calculate a user-entered expression with the use of the `Eval` method:

```
MsgBox objSC.Eval(InputBox$( _
        "Enter Numeric Expression", _
        "Power of Eval", "5 * 3 - 1"))
```

> The Script Control supports any ActiveX scripting engine, including the default VBScript and JScript. Should your competency gear towards other languages, discussion in this chapter will still be relevant. Additionally, the Script Control can be used with other COM capable development tools. If, on the other hand, your application requires "scripting speed", consider licensing other tools (and paying for them), including Microsoft VBA, Cypress Enable, or Sax Basic Engine from the respective vendors.

What tools do you need?

Microsoft Script Control is provided for free from the Microsoft Scripting Technologies Web Site (you may have to register prior to downloading the component): http://msdn.microsoft.com/scripting/scriptcontrol/default.htm Once you download sct10en.exe (or whatever the current version might be) from the downloads section of the Script Component site, you may install it and use it with any ActiveX scripting engine available on the computer. The installation program is not very sophisticated, and once you confirm that you'd like to install the Script Control, choose the installation directory, and accept the license: it will automatically install and register the control for you. Note that the Script Control may already be installed with other applications, so you can perform a search for the component before committing to a download and installation.

Essentially, three files are installed in your Windows' System32 directory, or the directory of your choice (keep that in mind if you want to find the help files, there are no shortcuts placed in your **Program Files** menu). These are

❑   Msscript.cnt – the help context file

❑   Msscript.hlp – the help file

❑   Msscript.ocx – the Script Control

After the installation, you are ready to use the control in any COM enabled language. Help files are rather chunky (old help format, huge, multiple windows, etc.), and occasionally, short on implementation detail. We'll use the VB6 IDE as the development environment; but you can search through the scarce resources available on the Internet that show you how to use the Script Control in other environments (e.g. Delphi).

During installation, familiarize yourself with the licensing agreement, especially if you plan on redistributing the Script Control with your application. Your application should provide a similar agreement:

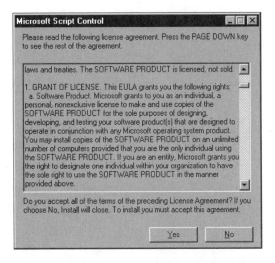

Although the component is free, you should be aware of the licensing restrictions placed upon the Script Control, especially when redistributing this component with your software. Although you should read the licensing agreement carefully by yourself, the most important points of the agreements are:

❑ You may redistribute `msscript.ocx` in the form as provided, given that it adds significant functionality to your application

❑ Include a copyright in your application (so that others may not redistribute the control), and indemnify Microsoft from any legal action

❑ You can't use Microsoft trademarks to market your application

❑ You can't export your application to certain countries

In most circumstances, you'll have to include some licensing agreement, which the user should accept prior to the installation of the application, and give credit to Microsoft in the **About Box** of your application.

Since the use of Script Control also depends on the scripting engines (which may already be present as part of the Internet Explorer), you may also have to redistribute the scripting engines along with the application. Distribution of the scripting engines may additionally prevent script incompatibilities, especially in cases where IE 5 is not present on the client computer.

Adding Script Control to VB Application

Script Control can be easily added to a VB project as an ActiveX Control or as an Automation Object. If you plan on using several instances of the Script Control in a project, you should probably add it as a reference. If you are not accustomed to working with VBScript, you should remember to account for all of its limitations, especially the fact that `variant` is the only data type, that no optional arguments are allowed, and that there are no built-in collections.

You can add the Script Control as a Component (ActiveX Control) or as a Reference by choosing References... or Components from the Project menu in VB IDE:

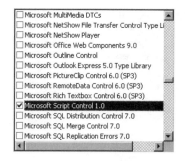

When working in other circumstances (such as WSH), or even in VB, you may use the Script Control in a late-bound mode. This way, you don't need to add it through the VB IDE:

```
Set objSC = CreateObject("MSScriptControl.ScriptControl")
```

When the Script Control is added as a control, it can be used on a form, as seen here, or simply declared and initialized through VB code, as above.

The control itself is invisible at runtime, and some of the properties that are available through the Properties dialog (Index, Left, Tag, Top) as seen in the screenshot below, are simply not available. Key properties can be set at both design and run time, but more properties and methods are available at run time.

Several of the properties should be set before the real use of the Script Control begins, such as Language, Timeout, AllowUI, and UseSafeSubset. If you are happy with the defaults (as shown here), you can start scripting and programming:

Note that we use the default properties throughout this chapter.

When adding the Script Control to the form, it acts like any other control sited in a form: it is automatically instantiated, and is capable of raising events (such as Timeout and Error) to the form. The same functionality can be achieved when the Script Control, added as a component, is declared WithEvents through code:

```
Private WithEvents objSC As ScriptControl
```

There are no strict guidelines for naming your Script Control objects, but it is customary to prefix object names with obj (hence objSC – see Appendix C for notes on Hungarian notation), but when it is added as a control, a prefix of sc is also common. Both styles are used throughout this chapter.

Once your Script Control is initialized you may use it to evaluate expressions, add the script directly (through VB code), or load an external script and add it to the Script Control. Other than evaluating expressions, the Script Control simply requires some form of script in order to be useful to you. First, let's revisit the evaluation example. After you place a command button on your form (cmdEval), this will be the code executed as a result of a click (you also need an objSC – the Script Control, which is also placed on the form):

```
Private Sub cmdEval_Click()
    MsgBox objSC.Eval(InputBox$( _
        "Enter Numeric Expression", _
        "Power of Eval", "5 * 3 - 1")), vbOKOnly, "Eval"
End Sub
```

Although the results are not spectacular, try achieving this in VB alone. Here we have the expression window, and the results:

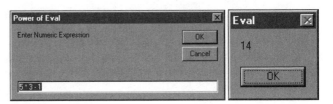

Next, you might want to add some code to the Script Control, in order to do something more fun. The Script Control object model (which is described later on in the chapter) organizes script code into modules (these are distinct scripts that do not share namespace) with the default Global module, with the latter being referenced directly through the Script Control. Modules can be further broken down into procedures – you can add procedures (as well as variables and constants) through the AddCode method. The following code illustrates how to add procedures and how to execute them:

```
' Add some procedures to the Global Module.
strCode = "Function Cube(a): Cube = a * a * a"
strCode = strCode & ": End Function"
objSC.AddCode strCode

strCode = "Sub MsgCube(a): MsgBox ""Cube "" & (a * a * a)"
strCode = strCode & " : End Sub"
objSC.AddCode strCode

' Run those procedures
MsgBox objSC.Run("Cube", 5)
objSC.Run "MsgCube", 5
```

Both procedures calculate 5^3, but the resulting calls to the procedures are quite different, and are worth looking at. The first procedure, a function, must be called according to the syntax used to call functions (brackets used), but you can call it through the Run method of the ScriptControl object (also take a look at CodeObject, which simplifies calls to procedures, and effectively bypasses the awkward 'Run' syntax). The first parameter of the Run method is the procedure name, and the remaining parameters (optional) are arguments that can be passed to the procedure. Hence our call to Cube(5) looks like:

```
MsgBox objSC.Run("Cube", 5)
```

The results are passed to the MsgBox, and then displayed.

The second procedure, MsgCube subroutine, uses VBScript's MsgBox to display the results of its calculation. In this case, the AllowUI property is set to true, which means that the script can use visual functions such as MsgBox and InputBox to communicate with the user directly. Note that the calling syntax for subs is a little different (unless you use Call) – since they do not return values, the brackets are not required:

```
objSC.Run "MsgCube", 5
```

And the results are almost identical (other than the default window title).

Additional examples are dispersed throughout this chapter, either in the syntax section, or in two projects that are available at the end of the chapter.

You may additionally check the mode of the ScriptControl object, and its ability to handle events generated by objects added through the AddObject method by checking the state property. Support for sinking events for VB forms and VB's intrinsic controls can be achieved through the class wrapper technique that would handle encapsulated object events and re-raise them as class events. This is beyond the scope of this chapter.

Macro and Scripting Concepts

Basic use of the Script Control in VB is fairly straightforward; however, it is important to conceptualize the capacity in which the Script Control can be used inside an application. Before we look at the object model of the Script Control, let's take a look at the major differences between this and other forms of scripting.

The script is not necessarily executed in-line, as is commonly done in ASP or WSH, and you might be forced to alter your coding convention to fit the need of the application. Unlike other hosts, which tend to execute the script from top to bottom, scripting an application will require a different approach. Most likely, you'll be required to load the code from an external file (or add it dynamically though user interaction), and call script procedures as results of application-generated events. Because of that, you might have to rethink your strategy, properly initialize script variables, reset them when required, and avoid calling external components due to inherent disadvantage of calling them through script – slower, more error prone, etc. If you want, you can create some standard procedures that initialize the script (e.g. Main() or Init()), and keep track of the changes in the script – after all, your ASP or WSH script is (more or less) likely to be run only once.

Evaluation of dynamically generated expressions is one of the most difficult tasks, and thus, custom calculations (as entered by the user) can become a breeze when used combined with the Script Control. Examples provided with the chapter provide the foundation for basic communication between the application and the script. The **Scavenger** project, which extracts data from an HTML document, provides a very simple use of the Script Component, feeding, and retrieving the data to and from the application. Another example of dynamically generated expressions (Customizable Calculator) has been published in the July '99 issue of Microsoft Internet Developer, *Exploring the Microsoft Script Control* by Francesco Balena, 2/7/99 (July) Vol. 4, No. 7. You can download the code for the article from
`http://www.microsoft.com/mind/0799/code/mind0799.zip`

Finally, a more advanced application will want to open up its object model to the script to provide a macro-type capability. In order for the application to open its object model, the application must be an ActiveX DLL or an EXE server, and must provide a mechanism to expose its object model to the script. Most commonly, this is achieved through direct sharing of a form through the `AddObject` method of the Script Control:

```
objSC.AddObject "Form", frmForm, False
```

Also, you can use a shared class module that exposes the application's object model through its members, as shown in the code listing below. This approach allows you to share additional class modules, and may provide additional functionality that may not be accessible via the VB form alone:

```
Private m_Form As Form

Public Property Get Form() As Object
    Set Form = m_Form
End Property

Friend Property Set Form(ByVal newValue As Object)
    Set m_Form = newValue
End Property
```

Listing above shows how to share a single VB form, and its members, with the Script Control. When the class is available, you may use the `AddObject` method of the Script Control to expose the members of the shared class, as shown below:

```
Dim objShared As New CShared
objSC.AddObject "objShared", objShared, True
```

A more complete example of this is provided as a sample project (**ComplexSC Project**) towards the end of this chapter, which allows the script to access elements on a VB form.

Still, some difficulties exist. Processing events, adding controls dynamically (from the script) is not an easy task. Although the **ComplexSC Project** shows how static events (we know about them at design time) can be handled by the script, adding controls to the application, and processing of *ad-hoc* events is simply beyond the scope of this chapter.

For a more advanced coverage of the Script Control look to Visual Basic Developer's Journal: the February 99 issue contains an advanced example (*Write a Macro Language Add-In* by R. Mark Tucker) of building a macro language for VB IDE. Another article is on its way (Late 99, Early 2000), which builds a framework for script-driven applications, allowing for smooth integration with the host application: creation of new controls, and easy event trapping for new and existing controls.

The Script Control Object Model

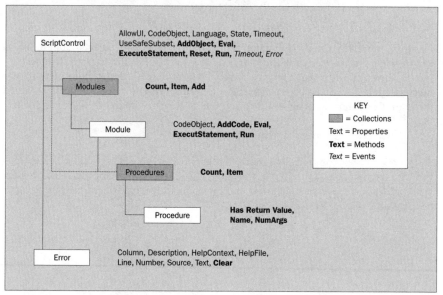

Objects and Collections

ScriptControl

`ScriptControl` is the main element that enables scripting in an application. It provides a simple interface for hosting scripting engines such as VBScript or JScript. All of the members depend on an instance of the `ScriptControl`. `ScriptControl` can be instantiated in three different ways:

- ❑ early bound, on a form (add it through the **Components** dialog)
- ❑ early bound, through code (add it through the **References** dialog)
- ❑ late bound (at any time)

Syntax

Early Bound (add Microsoft Script Control 1.0 as a reference)
```
Dim|Private|Public [WithEvents] objSC As
[MSScriptControl.]ScriptControl
```

```
Set objSC = New [MSScriptControl.]ScriptControl
```

Late Bound (will not handle events, control does not have to be referenced in the Project)

```
Dim|Private|Public objSC [As Object|Variant]
```

```
Set objSC = CreateObject("[MSScriptControl.]ScriptControl")
```

Error Object

The `Error` object provides information about syntax and runtime errors associated with the Script Control. Although information provided by the `Error` object is similar to that of the `Err` object in VB, there are additional properties (`Column`, `Text`, `Line`) that are invaluable when diagnosing problems associated with the script. Take a look at *Error Trapping with Script Control* for additional information about error handling strategies later in the chapter, as well as Chapter 4 and Appendix E, regarding error handling within VBScript. You should be aware of the fact that script debuggers (such as Visual InterDev) have a tendency to get in the way of error handling, which may impact if the error is handled via VB's error handler, or intercepted by the debugger.

Unlike VB's `Err` object, the `Error` object is not global in scope and only handles errors associated with a single instance of the Script Control. It behaves just like any other object (e.g. ADO `Error` collection) that is capable of its own error handling. The `Error` object is reset each time the `Language` property of the `ScriptControl` is changed, or calls to `Reset`, `AddCode`, `Eval`, `ExecuteStatement` and `Clear` methods are made. The `Clear` method is used to explicitly reset the `Error` object properties. Runtime errors handled internally by the script will not be raised to the application level.

Although it is possible to declare and initialize the `Error` object in VB, it is common to access members of the `Error` object directly through the Script Control.

Module Object

The `Module` object, a member of the `Modules` collection, contains procedure, type and data declarations used in a script. The script control has a default `Global` module, which is automatically used unless specific member calls are made to other modules that have been added. You can add code to the module using the `AddCode` method. Individual `Module` objects, on the other hand, are added by using the `Add` method of the `Modules` collection. Code used by other modules is private in scope, and essentially allows you to reuse variable and procedure names between modules, load separate scripts, and functions as a script namespace mechanism within the instance of the Script Control object.

Syntax

```
Dim|Private|Public objModule [As
[MSScriptControl.]Module|Object]
```

Example of non-global `Module` use:

```
Set objModule = objSC.Modules.Add("NewModule")
objModule.AddCode "Sub Test(): 'just comment : End Sub"
objModule.Run "Test"
```

Modules Collection

The `Modules` collection contains all the `Module` objects in a Script Control and includes the default `Global` module. Calls to the members of the `Global` module can be made directly through the `ScriptControl` object without iterating through the `Modules` collection. It also has an index of the constant `GlobalModule`.

`Module` objects can be added using the `Add` method (see example above), and specific `Module` objects accessed using the default `Item` method. The `Count` property provides the number of items in the collection. The entire collection can be iterated in various ways, most commonly, using the `For Each...Next` loop. Since there is no way of deleting individual modules, you will have to use the `Reset` method of the `ScriptControl` object to delete unwanted modules, and clear the entire collection.

Example of accessing the `Global` module directly (can be used with other named modules):

```
Set objModule = sc.Modules("Global")
```

Example of iterating through the `Modules` collection:

```
For Each objModule In objSC.Modules
    strReport = strReport & vbNewLine & objModule.Name
    For intCounter = 1 To objModule.Procedures.Count
        strReport = strReport & vbNewLine & Space(10)
        strReport = strReport & objModule.Procedures.Item(intCounter).Name
    Next
Next
```

Procedure Object

The `Procedure` object defines a logical unit of code, which in case of VBScript can be either a `Sub` or a `Function`. The `Procedure` object contains a number of useful properties that allow us to inspect a procedure's name, the number of arguments, and whether or not the procedure returns any values. Entry to the script code is provided via the `Procedure` object.

Syntax

```
Dim|Private|Public objProc [As
[MSScriptControl.]Procedure|Object]
```

Adding procedures, and executing procedure code

When adding code to the Script Control, you should be aware of the fact that the script control resolves variables, constants and procedures on a 'last one wins' basis, meaning that previously added code with the same name will not be used. The code below illustrates adding and running procedures (a `Function` and a `Sub`).

Procedure object's properties

`Name`, `HasReturnValue` and `NumArgs`, (discussed later) provide insight into the procedure's interface.

Procedures Collection

The `Procedures` collection holds all of the procedures in a given `Module` object (maybe `Global` module). It provides a convenient way to iterate all of the procedures; however, individual procedures are added through the `Module` object's `AddCode` method. You can't remove an individual procedure from your code (there is no `Remove` method as in other collections), but you may either reset the entire script, or overwrite the procedure with something else.

Below is an example showing how to iterate through `Procedure` objects in the `Procedures` collection:

```
' Check if objProcedure has a return value and arguments.
strMsg = ""
For Each objProcedure In objModule.Procedures
    intArgCount = objProcedure.NumArgs
    strMsg = strMsg & objProcedure & " requires " & intArgCount

    If intArgCount > 1 Then
        strMsg = strMsg & " arguments."
    Else
        strMsg = strMsg & " argument."
    End If

    If objProcedure.HasReturnValue Then
        strMsg = strMsg & " It has a return Value."
    End If

    strMsg = strMsg & vbCrLf
Next objProcedure
```

Constants

GlobalModule value = 'Global'

Scripting Engines such as VBScript or JScript that support more than one module use the `GlobalModule` constant to identify the index of the Global Module object in the `Modules` collection. When the language is set to VBScript or JScript, this value is `'Global'` and helps you identify the built-in global module in the `Modules` collection.

NoTimeout: value = -1

This constant can be used to set the `Timeout` property (10000 milliseconds is the default) of the `ScriptControl` object, and prevent the execution from timing out. Please refer to the `Timeout` property for more specifics.

States

These constants define the Script Control states, which can be accessed through the `State` property of the `ScriptControl` object.

Initialized: value = 0

The scripting engine is initialized, and the code will execute but will not sink events generated by shared objects.

Connected: value = 1

The scripting engine is initialized and the ScriptControl will sink events generated by shared objects. See the AddObject method for discussion about sharing objects between the application and the script.

Properties

> Note that although we are able to view the procedure's interface, there are no properties that allow us to inspect the script code itself.

AllowUI

The AllowUI property sets or returns the value of the ScriptControl, indicating whether or not the user-interface elements such as Error messages, MsgBox or InputBox can be displayed. When this is set to False, the only way to notify the user is directly through the application. When designing applications for unattended execution, it is best to have the application cause an error rather than wait indefinitely for user input.

Syntax

obj.AllowUI [= *booleanexpression*]

Name	Description
obj	This is the ScriptControl object
booleanexpression	Boolean expression or value that is true when user interface elements are allowed, false otherwise.

```
Dim strCode As String
strCode = "Sub Test: MsgBox ""UI call"": End Sub"

objSC.AllowUI = False
objSC.Language = "VBScript"
objSC.AddCode strCode
On Error Resume Next
objSC.Run "Test"
If objSC.Error.Number = 70 Then
    MsgBox "UI disabled, press OK to continue"
    objSC.AllowUI = True
    objSC.Run "Main"
End If
```

CodeObject

The CodeObject property returns an object that is used to call the public members of a Module object, or the Script Control's Global module. This is a late bound object, but it is useful, as it allows direct calls to procedures in the script, without using the Run method.

Syntax

```
Dim|Private|Public objCode [As Object]
Set objCode = obj.CodeObject
```

Name	Description
obj	This is the ScriptControl or Module object

Retrieving the CodeObject property from the Module object, and calling code members

Note that calling procedures is more natural, and perhaps more readable (procedures act as methods of the CodeObject) than with using the ScriptControl's Run method.

```
Set objModule = objSC.Modules.Add("TestMod") ' New module.

objModule.AddCode "Sub Sub1 : MsgBox ""Sub1"": End Sub"
objModule.AddCode "Function Func1(a): Func1 = a*a: End Function"
' Set reference to CodeObject.
Set objCodeObject = objModule.CodeObject

' Run public member of Module1.
objCodeObject.Sub1
lngVal = objCodeObject.Func1(2)
```

Column

The Column property returns a long value indicating the place where the syntax error has occurred while adding script code.

Syntax

```
Error.Column
```

The *Error Trapping* section in this chapter contains examples of this property.

Count

The Count property returns a long value representing the number of items in a collection

Syntax

```
obj.Count
```

Name	Description
obj	This is Modules or Procedures collection

```
objSC.AddCode "Sub Sub1 : MsgBox ""Sub1"": End Sub"
objSC.AddCode "Function Func1(a): Func1 = a*a: End Function"
lngValue = objSC.Procedures.Count
```

Description

Returns a string associated with the `Error` object. This is a zero-length string when `Err.Number = 0`.

Syntax

```
Error.Description
```

The *Error Trapping* section in this chapter contains examples of this property.

Error

The `Error` property returns an `Error` object associated with the `ScriptControl` object. See the `Error` object reference, and the *Error Trapping* section for details.

Syntax

```
obj.Error
```

Name	Description
obj	This is a `ScriptControl` object

HasReturnValue

`HasReturnValue` returns a Boolean value indicating whether or not the procedure in question returns any values. Since JScript only uses 'functions', this is always true when the language property is set to 'JScript'.

Syntax

```
obj.HasReturnValue
```

Name	Description
obj	Name or `Reference` to `Procedure` object

Shown below is an example of an iteration through procedures in a `Module` object, and use of the `HasReturnValue` property:

```
For Each objProcedure In objModule.Procedures
    intArgCount = objProcedure.NumArgs
    strMsg = strMsg & objProcedure.Name

    If objProcedure.HasReturnValue Then
        strMsg = strMsg & " has a return Value."
    End If

    strMsg = strMsg & vbCrLf
Next objProcedure
```

HelpContext

HelpContext returns the context ID associated with a help topic in a help file. This number can be set by the script using Err.Raise, or by an ActiveX component (script, or component utilized by the script).

When an error occurs, and a HelpContext and a HelpFile are set by Err.Raise, the user has a chance to open the help file associated with the error.

Syntax

Error.HelpContext

HelpFile

This returns the file name associated with a help file. This can be set by script using Err.Raise, or by an ActiveX component (script, or component utilized by the script).

Syntax

Error.HelpFile

Language

This properly sets or returns the name of the scripting language used by the ScriptControl object. 'VBScript' and 'JScript' can be used by default, and other languages, when they are installed, e.g. 'PerlScript'. Setting this property resets all members of the ScriptControl.

Syntax

obj.Language [=language]

Name	Description
obj	This is the ScriptControl object
language	String associated with the Scripting Language, e.g. "VBScript"

Line

The Line property returns a long value indicating the place where the syntax or runtime error has occurred while adding or executing script code.

Syntax

Error.Line

The *Error Trapping* section in this chapter contains examples of this property.

Modules

The Modules property returns the Modules collection of the ScriptControl object. The Modules collection always has a default Global module. For more information, see the Modules collection and Module object.

Syntax

obj.Modules

Name	Description
obj	This is the ScriptControl object

Name

The Name property returns the name of a module, procedure or ScriptControl object, depending on what it references. The name of an object must be unique within the namespace in question (procedures, modules), and is established when the object is added to the Script Control using the Add or the AddCode methods. Host objects added using the AddObject method are always added to the global namespace. You must be careful when adding objects and code to your Script Control so as not to overwrite each other. This may be a potential source of errors, considering that your host application is not aware of the objects that have been added to the script control.

Syntax

obj.Name

Name	Description
obj	This can be a ScriptControl, Module or Procedure object

NumArgs

The NumArgs property returns a long number associated with the number of arguments required by a procedure.

Syntax

obj.NumArgs

Name	Description
obj	This can be a Procedure object, or its reference

Here is an example of iterating through the `Procedures` collection, and inspecting the `NumArgs` property

```
For Each objProcedure In objModule.Procedures
    intArgCount = objProcedure.NumArgs
    strMsg = strMsg & objProcedure & " requires " & intArgCount

    If intArgCount > 1 Then
        strMsg = strMsg & " arguments."
    Else
        strMsg = strMsg & " argument."
    End If
    strMsg = strMsg & vbCrLf
Next objProcedure
```

Number

This returns a long number associated with a syntax or runtime error from the script. `Number` is the default property of the `Error` object.

Syntax

`Error[.Number]`

The *Error Trapping* section in this chapter contains examples of this property.

Procedures

The `Procedures` property returns the `Procedures` collection associated with a `Module` object, or with `ScriptControl`.

Syntax

`obj.Procedures`

Name	Description
obj	This can be a `Module` object, its reference, or `ScriptControl` (i.e. `Global` module)

SitehWnd

`SitehWnd` sets or returns a long pointer to the parent window used by the executing code. When the Script Control is used as an ActiveX Control, placed on a form, the default value of `SitehWnd` is the `hWnd` property of the container of the control. Otherwise, when `ScriptControl` is an Automation Object, `SitehWnd` is 0, which corresponds to the Desktop. This property may impact on which window (or control) has UI control over the scripted UI elements. You may change this property to make the Script Control dependent upon a specific window, rather than, in some cases, the Desktop (for example, you might want the Script Control to freeze a part of your application, and not the Desktop).

Syntax

obj.SitehWnd [=*lptr*]

Name	Description
obj	This is always the ScriptControl object
lptr	This can be 0 or a valid hWnd value

Source

Source returns a string specifying the type of error that occurred within the script. This property helps you distinguish whether a runtime or syntax error has occurred, and additionally provides information about the scripting language used. Please see the *Error Trapping* section later in the chapter.

Syntax

Error.Source

State

The State property sets or returns the mode of the ScriptControl object, based on the valid state constant discussed in the Constants section. For instance, when this value is set to Connected (=1), the ScriptControl will be able to sink events generated by objects added using the AddObject method. Thus, changing the state gives you some control over the handling of events.

Syntax

obj.State [=*value*]

Name	Description
obj	This is always the ScriptControl object
value	This is one of the constants: Initialized or Connected

The code below shows how to toggle the state of the ScriptControl object:

```
' Toggle ScriptControl's state.
If Not IsObject(objSC) Then
    Set objSC = CreateObject("ScriptControl")
End If
objSC.State = objSC.State Xor 1
```

Text

The Text property returns a string containing a snippet of code where a script syntax error has occurred. The Text property only provides a context of the syntax error, and its main use is in reporting errors, and debugging scripts.

Syntax

```
Error.Text
```

An example of this property is provided in the *Error Trapping* section of this chapter.

Timeout

The `Timeout` property sets or returns a long number representing time in milliseconds, which serves as a script break for code execution. This property can be set to a constant `NoTimeout` (-1) which removes time restrictions placed on the execution of script code. The default value is 10000 milliseconds (10 seconds). When the timeout expires, a `Timeout` event may occur (depending on whether or not the `ScriptControl` can handle events), and at that time, if the `ScriptControl` has the `AllowUI` property enabled, the user is alerted with a dialog box, permitting the user to continue execution of the script. Otherwise, the script is terminated and an error is raised.

When this property is set to 0, a `Timeout` event occurs as soon as the script stops Windows messaging for slightly more than 100 milliseconds.

Syntax

```
obj.Timeout [=value]
```

Name	Description
obj	This is always the `ScriptControl` object
value	Long number representing time in milliseconds, or the `NoTimeout` constant (-1)

UseSafeSubset

The `UseSafeSubset` property sets or returns a Boolean value indicating whether or not the Script Control may run components that are not marked as 'Safe for Scripting', such as the `FileSystemObject`, which is a part of the scripting engines. You may set this property to true when you are concerned about the ability of the script to create damage on the client computer. When the Script Control is used in a host that requires that components are 'Safe for Scripting', this property defaults to `True` and is read-only.

Syntax

```
obj.UseSafeSubset [=value]
```

Name	Description
obj	This is always the `ScriptControl` object
value	Boolean, indicates if access to components that are not marked as 'Safe for Scripting' is allowed.

Methods

Add

The Add method is used to add new modules to the Modules collection.

Syntax

obj.Modules.Add (*name* [,*object*])

Name	Description
obj	This is always the ScriptControl object
name	This is a string name of the module being added
object	This argument is optional – it is the name of the object associated with the module, and when an object is specified, event-handling code can be written for the object and its subordinates.

Modules allow use of separate scripts, and provide separate namespaces:

```
Set objModule = objSC.Modules.Add("Maine")
' Add code to modules, use same sub names.
objModule.AddCode "Sub Main : MsgBox ""In Maine"" : End Sub"
Set objModule = objSC.Modules.Add("Ohio")
objModule.AddCode "Sub Main : MsgBox ""In Ohio"" : End Sub"
```

AddCode

The AddCode method allows us to add code to the Module object or to the ScriptControl object. This is the primary method of adding script to the Script Control. When adding code for entire procedures and blocks of code, the code must be added in a single call to the AddCode method. Each statement in the block can be separated by colons (:) or the new line character variations: vbCr, vbLf, vbCrLf and vbNewLine.

Syntax

obj.AddCode *code*

Name	Description
obj	This is the ScriptControl or Module object
code	This is a string containing the code to be added.

Variables and procedures can be added in several steps with the AddCode method:

```
strCode = "Option Explicit" & vbNewLine & "x = 15"
objSC.AddCode strCode
strCode = "y=2"
objSC.AddCode strCode
strCode = "Function getX(): getX = x * y: End Function"
objSC.AddCode strCode
```

AddObject

The AddObject method allows the script to access the host's runtime object model (including other components that may be members of your host) exposed by the object being added. Objects added to the ScriptControl are available globally. An optional addmemebers parameter indicates whether or not the members of the added object are also available to the ScriptControl. By placing the shared objects in their own VBClass, you may expose the host's objects in a variety of ways, and by building custom Property Let/Get/Set procedures, you may easily share variables, constants and methods. Although you may also directly share a form in an ActiveX EXE project, a shared class can give you greater control, and might prevent an accidental circular reference (especially when the script would be placed on the same form that was shared).

See the example application provided at the end of this chapter for an illustration of the use of this method.

Syntax

obj.AddObject (*name* ,*object*[, *addmembers*])

Name	Description
obj	This is always the ScriptControl object
name	This is a string name of the object being added
object	This is an actual reference to the object being added
addmembers	This is a Boolean value indicating whether *object*'s members are accessible to the ScriptControl

Here is the code required in a *SharedClass* (this is a read/write shared form object):

```
Private m_Form As Form
Public Property Get Form() As Object
    Set Form = m_Form
End Property

Friend Property Set Form(ByVal newValue As Object)
    Set m_Form = newValue
End Property
```

And here is the code required to add the Form to `ScriptControl`:

```
Dim objCS AS ScriptControl
Dim objShare As New CShareClass
Set objSC = New ScriptControl
objCS.Language = "VBScript"
' link it an instance of the shared class
Set objShare.Form = Form
objSC.AddObject "share", objShare, True
```

Clear

The `Clear` method resets the `Error` object. This method should be used after an error is handled. The `Error` object is also reset when `Reset`, `AddCode`, `Eval`, or `ExecuteStatement` methods are called.

Syntax

`Error.Clear`

Eval

The `Eval` method evaluates an expression similar to the `Eval` function in VBScript. This is one of the best ways to evaluate dynamic expressions provided by the user. When comparing `Eval` to the `ExecuteStatement` method, you should be aware that certain operators, such as '=' will be treated as comparison operators when used with `Eval`. Hence, x = y will evaluate to a Boolean subtype when used with `Eval`, but when used with `ExecuteStatement`, the value of y will be assigned to variable x, and nothing will be returned. The `Eval` method may be used against the `ScriptControl` or `Module` object, and take advantage of its members.

Syntax

`obj.Eval (expression)`

Name	Description
obj	This is the `ScriptControl` or `Module` object
expression	This is a string containing expression to be evaluated

`Eval` is simple but effective, capable of achieving tasks nearly impossible in VB:

```
MsgBox objSC.Eval(InputBox$( _
        "Enter Numeric Expression", _
        "Power of Eval", "5 * 3 - 1"))
```

ExecuteStatement

Unlike the `Eval` method, `ExecuteStatement` only executes a statement, and does not return any value. Additionally, `ExecuteStatement` will assign values to variables when '=' is used in a statement. The statement executed can take advantage of any members within scope of the object context. In order to obtain a return value from a procedure, you should use either the `Eval` or `Run` method.

Syntax

obj.ExecuteStatement *statement*

Name	Description
obj	This is the ScriptControl or Module object
statement	This is a string containing *statement* to be executed

ExecuteStatement should be used to execute a statement within the context of a given object:

```
objModule.AddCode "Private x"
objModule.AddCode "x = 1"
objModule.ExecuteStatement("x = 3")
objModule.Eval("x")
```

Item

The Item method returns a member of a collection either by the index number or the key (name of the member). The Item method can be used on its own, when the index or key is known, or as part of collection's enumeration. Individual Procedure and Module objects can be retrieved from their respective collections.

Syntax

obj.Item(*index*)

Name	Description
obj	This is the Modules or Procedures collection
index	This is either a string representing the key, or long integer representing the index

Reset

The Reset method discards all the members of the ScriptControl object, and initializes them to their default state. When the Reset method is called, the state property is set to Initialized (0), and should be set to Connected (1) if required.

Syntax

obj.Reset

Name	Description
obj	This is always the ScriptControl object

Run

The Run method allows you to run a procedure in the ScriptControl or Module objects. It allows you to specify the procedure name and its arguments at runtime. A call to the Run method may return a value, depending on the nature of the procedure called.

Alternatively, procedures whose names and signatures are known ahead of time may be executed directly using the CodeObject object.

Syntax

obj.Run (procedureName [, paramArray()])

Name	Description
obj	This is the ScriptControl or Module object
procedureName	This is a string name of the procedure being called
paramArray()	This is an optional array containing parameters required by the procedure. To find out the number of parameters required by the procedure, you may use the object's NumArgs property.

Depending upon the type of a procedure, you may call the Run method in several different ways, depending on return values and parameters:

```
strCode = "Sub TwoArg(a,b): MsgBox ""TwoArg "" & CInt(a + b)"
strCode = strCode & " : End Sub"
objSC.AddCode strCode
objSC.Run "TwoArg", 1, 2

strCode = "Function ManyArg(a,b,c,d): ManyArg= a * b + c - d"
strCode = strCode & ":  End Function"
objSC.AddCode strCode
MsgBox objSC.Run("ManyArg", 1, 2, 3, 4)
```

Events

Error

The Error event occurs in response to a syntax or a runtime error, when the ScriptControl is instantiated early bound and with events (when used as a component).

Syntax

Private|Public Sub obj_Error()

Name	Description
obj	This is the always the ScriptControl object

Timeout

The Timeout event occurs when script execution exceeds the time allotted in the Timeout property, and the user decides to stop the execution of the script. When several ScriptControl objects are present, a Timeout event will occur only for the first ScriptControl object to time out.

Syntax

Private | Public Sub *obj*_Timeout *( )*

Name	Description
obj	This is the always the ScriptControl object

Other Scripting Elements

Besides the Script Control, VB (as well as other languages and environments) can easily be enhanced with other scripting objects, without the necessity of using the Script Control, WSH or Windows Script Components. Most of these components can be instantiated directly in VB – and not only can you gain the advantage of early binding but also greater programming control through VB IDE. Please refer to other chapters of this book for their complete documentation. Currently the FileSystemObject as well as regular expression objects are becoming very popular 'tools' used directly in VB. However, keep in mind that the following should be referenced directly by VB and properly declared, giving you the speed provided by early binding, and the additional functionality provided by IntelliSense and direct debugging:

❑   Dictionary object

❑   FileSystemObject object

❑   RegExp object

❑   Objects exposed by WSH except for wscript and cscript objects (objects implemented in wshom.ocx with Wscript.xxx progids)

Some of the elements mentioned above can really simplify development because of the simplicity of their object models and the functionality they posses. Previously, this was only available through the use of API functions and through other components.

> Please note that similar licensing agreements apply to the above components as to the Script Control. You should include appropriate information regarding the use of these components when redistributing your application.

Error Trapping with Script Control

Error handling can never be underestimated, especially when dealing with several sources of code. This is especially true for dynamically generated scripts, and user entered expressions. In order to handle the errors, you may have to work with both VB's Err object and the Script Control's Error object. If you are working with several instances of the Script Control, each will have a separate Error object. When an error occurs, and you have a proper strategy to handle the error, you may always clear the error and continue execution of the program.

As usual, you should use all possible script error-handling techniques in your scripts (especially the scripts you load from files), and handle them internally as much as possible (see Chapter 4 and Appendix E for more information).

> Note: depending on VB's settings, your error handlers may not work
> properly in debug mode (check **Break on Unhandled Errors** in IDE's
> **General Options** tab). Additionally, error handlers in script will depend
> on the **Disable Script Debugging** option set in Internet Explorer, and on
> the availability of the debugger. Script errors may automatically invoke
> the debugger, bypassing your error handling code. Consult Chapter 4 for
> more information.

The Script Control is bound to raise several types of errors when setting global properties:

Error	Description
Can't execute; script is running	An attempt has been made to modify one of Script Control object's members while the script is running.
Can't set UseSafeSubset property	Application hosting Script Control may force it into safe mode.
Executing script has timed out	Script execution has ended because it went over the time allotted in the Timeout property.
Language property not set	Certain properties can only be set after the Language property is set.
Member is not supported by selected scripting engine	When working with languages other than VBScript or JScript, not all of the properties and methods may be supported.
Object is no longer valid	When Script Control is reset, objects that have been set previously are released.

These errors can most probably be avoided by careful programming, and should not be a big factor of your error handling strategy. The two cases when errors will be a major nuisance are when adding the scripting code to the Script Control (syntax errors), and when executing it. You may inspect both error objects; however, Script Control's `Error` object provides additional information about the nature of the error. The example below shows hypothetical error handling through VB:

```
Dim strCode As String
Dim strValue As String
sc.Reset
On Error GoTo SyntaxErrorHandler
strCode = InputBox("Enter Function (name it Test(a))", _
    "Syntax Error Testing", _
    "Sub Test(a): MsgBox ""Result: "" & CStr(a*a): End Sub")

sc.AddCode strCode
On Error GoTo RuntimeErrorHandler
strValue = InputBox("Enter a Value for Test function", _
    "Runtime Error Testing", _
    "test")
sc.Run "Test", strValue

Exit Sub
SyntaxErrorHandler:
    MsgBox "Error # " & Err.Number & ": " & _
        Err.Description, vbCritical, "Syntax Error in Script"

Exit Sub
RuntimeErrorHandler:
    MsgBox "Error # " & Err.Number & ": " & _
        Err.Description, vbCritical, "Runtime Error in Script"
```

There are several different ways in which VB can handle errors: through use of the `Goto` *label* and, as in VBScript, through `Resume Next`, and immediate testing of `Err` object. The example below illustrates the use of `On Error Resume Next`, combined with an inspection of the `Err` object as well as Script Control's `Error` object, which provides us with more information:

```
On Error Resume Next
    sc.AddCode strCode
    If Err Then
        With sc.Error
            MsgBox "Error # " & .Number & ": " _
                & .Description & vbCrLf _
                & "At Line: " & .Line & " Column: " & .Column _
                & " : " & .Text, vbCritical, "Syntax Error"
        End With
    Else
        MsgBox "No Error, result: " & CStr(sc.Run("Test", _
            strValue))
        If Err Then
            With sc.Error
                MsgBox "Error # " & .Number & ": " _
                    & .Description & vbCrLf _
                    & "At Line: " & .Line _
                    , vbCritical, "Runtime Error"
            End With
        End If
    End If
```

485

Finally, you may also use two of the events exposed by the Script Control, Event and Timeout, to handle some of the errors; however, in some circumstances it may be a nuisance, and the use of the On Error... statement is preferred because:

❑ The Timeout event will only occur for the initial ScriptControl object

❑ Script Control either has to be used as a VB 'Component', or has to be initialized 'With Events' as a reference

❑ You may lose the granularity required when executing certain 'likely to cause errors' procedures

You should use the Error event when you do not plan on adding any other error-handling script code to your application, as the example code shows below:

```
Private Sub sc_Error()
    Dim strMsg As String

    With sc.Error
        strMsg = "Script error has occurred:" & vbCrLf & vbCrLf
        strMsg = strMsg & .Description & vbCrLf
        strMsg = strMsg & "Line # " & .Line
        ' Syntax errors have additional properties
        If InStr(.Source, "compilation") > 0 Then
            strMsg = strMsg & ", Column# " & .Column
            strMsg = strMsg & ", Text: " & .Text
        End If
        strMsg = strMsg & vbCrLf
    End With

    MsgBox strMsg, vbCritical, "Script Error"
    sc.Error.Clear
End Sub
```

> Note: When using the ScriptControl Error event, the error handler is invoked before any On Error... code. Hence, use of both error-handling techniques may produce double error messages, and disable any effective error handling.

Help with Debugging

The ability to step through code is one of the most valuable resources made available by Microsoft's IDEs. Although the debugger can be obnoxious at times (especially when you want the custom error handler to 'kick-in'), there are circumstances where you need it more than anything.

When working with Script Control, and a custom script, you may either invoke the debugger by raising an error from your script (it might be difficult to find later), or use the Stop command in VBScript to start the debugger (use Debugger when working with JScript). This technique is an equivalent of placing a breakpoint in VB or Visual InterDev (for more information on how to use the debugger, please see Chapter 4 where the basics of debugging are covered).

Sample Applications

The Script Control is unfortunately one of the lesser children of Microsoft – examples of its use, other than the references provided, are scarce. Because of that, I have provided two examples of Script Control use – the **Scavenger Project**, and the **ComplexSC Project** – that go beyond the little snippets of code that are usually provided in a reference manual. Note that these examples can be downloaded from the Wrox web site at `http://www.wrox.com`.

Scavenger Project

Data retrieval from a web page can be quite easily achieved by the simple automation of Visual Basic's Inet Control. Unfortunately web pages tend to change their internal structures, with the result that your carefully created and compiled data parsing routines produce nothing but garbage.

This is where the Script Control can save your life. In this project, the Script Control works in conjunction with the Inet Control and other elements of the project to retrieve the correct data. The illustration above shows the target of our interest – the Top 50 stocks – that can be considered as the input for our application.

The page contains a lot of information but we are only interested in retrieving certain values provided in one of the tables of the document, to produce our own sample output as shown below:

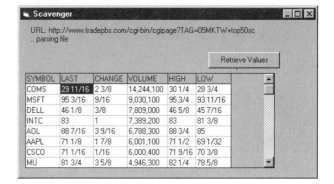

The entire project, aside from the intricacies of retrieving web documents and parsing, is very simple. Here is the flow of the program:

1. Initialize the Script Control

2. Initialize the hidden form with the Inet Control (to receive events, etc)

3. Load the script

4. Initialize values in Script Control

5. Retrieve URL and feed it to the Inet Control

6. Wait until the web file is retrieved

7. Feed the file to the script function

8. The script parses the file according to its own rules

9. The script returns a Variant array

10. Array values are placed on a grid

The concepts and the actions carried out are quite simple. Use of the script provides you with the flexibility to easily change the URL or the parsing routine associated with a particular web document. The project shows a very simple communication structure between the script and the application, without the unnecessary complications of shared application objects.

Here are the key actions (omitting the retrieval of the file).

The code below shows how the script can be initialized in a standard EXE application, at the time when the main form is loaded:

```
Private Sub Form_Load()
    Set objSC = InitScriptControl()
    objSC.ExecuteStatement "Init"
End Sub
```

Next, a generic routine to load a script from a file (scavenger.scp) that is called by the code above. After the file is loaded, the reference to the ScriptControl is returned to the form:

```
Function InitScriptControl() As ScriptControl
    Dim objSC As ScriptControl
    Dim fileName As String, intFnum As Integer

    ' create a new instance of the control
    Set objSC = New ScriptControl
    objSC.Language = "VBScript"


    ' load the code into the script control
    fileName = App.Path & "\scavenger.scp"
    intFnum = FreeFile
    Open fileName For Input As #intFnum
    objSC.AddCode Input$(LOF(intFnum), intFnum)
    Close #intFnum

    ' return to the caller
    Set InitScriptControl = objSC
End Function
```

The URL is stored in the script, and can be easily retrieved by the application:

```
strURL = objSC.Run("getURL")
```

And by the `getURL` function inside the script:

```
Function getURL()
    getURL = strURL
End Function
```

Finally, after the HTML document is retrieved by the Inet Control (as a buffer) it is passed to the parsing function (`getValues()`), which returns a Variant array:

```
arrResults = objSC.Run("getValues", Buffer)
```

The technical details of the parsing function (shown below) are somewhat complex, but they are obviously suited to that particular document. After the irrelevant information is stripped from the top and bottom of the file, the remaining information is split into a table of 50 elements. Afterwards, each single element, representing data about a single stock, is split into the `Matches` collection (see the section on regular expressions in Chapter 7), and individual matching elements entered into table cells.

When the table is built, it is returned back to the application, as shown in the code below:

```
Function getValues(strHTML)
    Dim arrValues(5,50), i, j, regEx, regMatches, strTmp
    Dim strTmp2, intPos

    ' get rid of all data in front of table
    ' we are only interested in top 50 stocks
    ' top 50 stocks are in the last table on the page,
    strTmp2 = "<TABLE BORDER=0 WIDTH=100%>"
    intPos = InStrRev(strHTML, strTmp2)
    strTmp = Right(strHTML, _
        Len(strHTML) - intPos - Len(strTmp2) + 1)

    strTmp2 = "</TR>"
    intPos = InStr(strTmp, strTmp2)
    strTmp = Right(strTmp, Len(strTmp) - _
        intPos - Len(strTmp2) + 1)

    ' get rid of all data after table
    strTmp2 = "</TABLE>"
    intPos = InStr(strTmp, strTmp2)
    strTmp = Left(strTmp, intPos - 1)

    ' split all rows in the table - replace "</tr> with "@"
    ' I'm assuming there are no "@" anywhere, if there were,
    ' replace them with &atsymbol; or something, and replace
    ' &atsymbol; after the split is made
    Set regEx = new RegExp
    regEx.pattern = "</TR>"
    regEx.IgnoreCase = True
    regEx.Global = True
```

```
' and now each company is in a separate row...
strTmp = regEx.replace(strTmp, "@")
arrCompanies = Split(strTmp, "@")

' initialize table headings
arrValues(0,0) = "SYMBOL"
arrValues(1,0) = "LAST"
arrValues(2,0) = "CHANGE"
arrValues(3,0) = "VOLUME"
arrValues(4,0) = "HIGH"
arrValues(5,0) = "LOW"

' put the values from the HTML file into our two
' dimensional table - there are also other values,
' but we're ignoring them, choosing 6 columns

For i = 1 To UBound(arrValues,2)

        ' put the company into a temp string
        strTmp = arrCompanies(i-1)

        ' get the stuff from interesting fields
        ' they all are: words: \w, spaces: \s and "/",
        ' all of them end with</FONT>)
        regEx.pattern = "[\w\s/,.]+</FONT>"
        Set regMatches = regEx.execute(strTmp)
        For j = 0 To Ubound(arrValues,1)
                ' now get rid of </font> (7 chars) and trim
                arrValues(j,i) = _
                        Trim(Left(regMatches.Item(j), _
                        Len(regMatches.Item(j)) -7))
        Next
    Next
    getValues = arrValues

End Function
```

This project shows how simple the script can actually be, and how it can enhance the application. Although the script will treat all of its values as Variants, passing and retrieving different objects is not difficult. In this case, we returned a simple array, but we could have used a custom COM component, and XML document, or even a recordset to return the values to the application. This way you can extend either your application, or VBScript, almost indefinitely – either by providing access to data that is difficult to achieve with VBScript, or by providing the flexibility of scripting to your application.

Encrypted Scripts and Script Control

In some circumstances, you may not be interested in sharing the source code of your script. Perhaps your parsing routine may be more high-tech than the one above. Luckily you may use the Script Encoder provided by Microsoft on the scripting site. After using the encoder (as shown below) we end up with an encoded script that we can still use provided we make a few changes:

```
screnc scavenger.scp scavenger.enc /e vbs
```

One would assume that all we have to do is to change the `Language` property to `VBScript.Encode`. However, all that happens is that the file loading routine crashes while reading the encrypted file. Luckily, the FSO (File System Object) has no problems opening the encrypted file. Only the script loading procedure has to be altered to accommodate for the encoded script:

```
Function InitScriptControl() As ScriptControl
    Dim objSC As ScriptControl, fso as Scripting.FileSystemObject
    Dim  tsInput, scriptSrc

    ' create a new instance of the control
    Set objSC = New ScriptControl

    Set fso =New Scripting.FileSystemObject
    Set tsInput = fso.OpenTextfile(App.Path & "\scavenger.enc", 1)
    scriptSrc = tsInput.ReadAll
    objSC.Language = "VBScript.Encode"
    objSC.AddCode scriptSrc

    ' return to the caller
    Set InitScriptControl = objSC

End Function
```

And the encrypted file (`scavenger.enc`) remains encrypted and relatively protected from prying eyes – here are the first few characters from the file:

```
#@~^HAoAAA==9b:~kYMjId@#@&@#@&UE8P&xrOv#@#@&7B,qx,^C/•PDtnPi
```

ComplexSC – Connection Registration

The second sample project, ComplexSC, demonstrates how the application can share its objects with the script, and pass static events – because of this requirement, the project is an ActiveX EXE type.

When building database applications that depend on an outside database, we always encounter the problem of feeding the application the connection string associated with the appropriate database and the appropriate server. Most commonly, this information is retrieved from the system registry, identifying the software author and the application, and then by the custom key:

Sample Registry SubPath: SOFTWARE\Company Name\App Name\
Sample Key Name: MyAppConnection

The problem lies with the fact that ordinarily, you'd have to provide a custom application to the end user with the values hard coded within the application (or try something like WSH and make things complex). Through the use of Script Control, you can create a basic registration utility that can be distributed along with a customized script. The script can automate your application providing important values when they are needed, depending on user input:

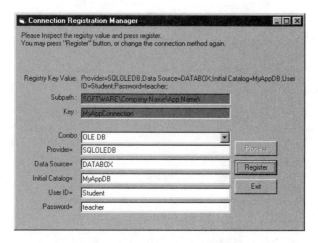

The possibilities here are almost endless: by exposing the objects in the application, and passing some of the events to the script, the script can act as a macro, and adapt to your needs. There are some idiosyncrasies, especially when it comes to passing events between the form and the script. To make this possible, all of the controls are placed on the form at design time, some of them in control arrays. The script can easily control all of the properties and methods of all controls, but when the control arrays (optional connection string tags and their values) are used, dynamic modification of the form members is simplified. Here, depending on the choice of connection (OLE DB, ODBC, and DSN) we can display different labels and editable values associated with the connection type.

Sharing of the form members is easily achieved through the `CShared` class, which allows us to share the main `Form` and all of its members, with a script (shown below). Although we could expose individual elements as opposed to the entire form, and prevent the script from manipulating any of the elements we want protected, in the case of this application it is simply not necessary:

```
Option Explicit

Private m_Form As Form

Public Property Get Form() As Object
    Set Form = m_Form
End Property

Friend Property Set Form(ByVal newValue As Object)
    Set m_Form = newValue
End Property
```

With the `CShared` class in place, we need to use the `AddObject` method of the Script Control to share the `Form` with the script. This is done via a slightly modified `InitScriptControl` procedure, which is executed when the form is loaded. We are passing the reference to the VB form, which in turn, becomes the `Form` in the `CShared` class:

```
Private Sub Form_Load()
    Set objScript = InitScriptControl(Me)
    objScript.Run "init"
End Sub
```

The modified `InitScriptControl` procedure takes on the additional requirement of setting up the `CShared` class. Because we set the third parameter of the `AddObject` method to true, all of the members of the existing form are shared too:

```
Function InitScriptControl(frmForm As Form) As ScriptControl
    Dim objSC As ScriptControl
    Dim fileName As String, intFnum As Integer
    Dim objShare As New CShared

    ' create a new instance of the control
    Set objSC = New ScriptControl
    objSC.Language = "VBScript"
    objSC.AllowUI = True
    Set objShare.Form = frmForm
    objSC.AddObject "share", objShare, True

    ' load the code into the script control
    fileName = App.Path & "\regeditor.scp"
    intFnum = FreeFile
    Open fileName For Input As #intFnum

    objSC.AddCode Input$(LOF(intFnum), intFnum)
    Close #intFnum

    ' return to the caller
    Set InitScriptControl = objSC

End Function
```

After the script is initialized, we call the `Init` procedure in the script, which sets up all of the necessary controls on the form. In actuality, some of the controls are pre-set with certain properties (such as background color, enabled, etc.), while others are initialized by the script, by accessing the members of the shared `Form`, as shown in the code below:

```
Sub Init()
    Dim i, strTmp
    Form.Caption = "Connection Registration Manager"
    strTmp = "This application saves the database connection"
    strTmp = strTMP & string in the registry. " & vbCrLf
    Form.lblExplanation = strTmp
    Form.lblRegistry.Caption = ""
    ' this information should be reflected in your application
    ' the standard is to store the registry keys in subhives
    ' for different companies and projects
```

```
      Form.txtSubpath.Text = "SOFTWARE\Company Name\App Name\"
      ' finally the name of the key
      ' you could similarly extend this application so it would
      ' work like a wizard, and register several keys
      Form.txtKey.Text = "MyAppConnection"
      Form.lblRegistry.Caption = ""
      Form.cmdRegister.Enabled = False
      Form.cmdProcess.Enabled = True
      For i = 0 To 5
              Form.lblLabel(i).Visible = False
              Form.txtText(i).Visible = False
      Next
      Form.cboCombo.Clear
      Form.cboCombo.AddItem "OLE DB"
      Form.cboCombo.AddItem "ODBC"
      Form.cboCombo.AddItem "DSN"
End Sub
```

Next, we need to respond to events generated by the application. In this simple case
(for a more complex case, look for an article in VBPJ by Francesco Balena, unpublished
at the time of this printing), we simply pass the events as intercepted by the
application directly to the script. Hence, our application may have the following events
passed to the script:

```
Private Sub cboCombo_Click()
    objScript.Run "cboCombo_Click"
End Sub

Private Sub txtText_KeyPress(Index As Integer, KeyAscii As Integer)
    KeyAscii = objScript.Run("txtText_KeyPress",Index, KeyAscii)
End Sub
```

As the example shows, we pass the events directly to the script, optionally passing
along the parameters generated by the event. Because in certain cases we might want
to modify one of the parameters, we should treat the event-handling procedure as a
function, which would return the modified value. This is probably the simplest
mechanism for modifying such parameters. Although this functionality is not required
by our application, the following function inside the script would capitalize each
character entered into one of the text boxes:

```
Function txtText_KeyPress(Index , KeyAscii)
    txtText_KeyPress = Asc(Ucase(Chr(KeyAscii)))
End Function
```

This approach is a little different than what you'd expect in VB code, because even if
we pass the value of `KeyAscii` by reference (normal VB Code would be `KeyAscii =
Asc(Ucase(Chr(KeyAscii)))`), the script will not update this value back in VB.
Hence, we employ a simple work around using the script `Function` procedure.

It is also possible to 'override' the default event handling, or to provide 'optional' event handling in the script. When the script does not have the member procedure, an error is generated, which provides us with a possibility of either ignoring events or providing default events, in case the script does not have an appropriately named procedure. The example below shows the simplest error trapping, which allows us to create a default event handler. Additionally, when the Error handler is not enabled (as On Error Resume Next below), the script must contain an appropriately named procedure with the correct number of parameters:

```
Private Sub cboCombo_Click()
    On Error Resume Next
    objScript.Run "cboCombo_Click"
    If Err = 0 Then Exit Sub
    ' default event handler goes here...
End Sub
```

Details of the application lie in the script itself, so rather than copy the entire code listing, the example below only shows partial implementation of the cboCombo_Click procedure within the script. After the key controls are reset, we set up values of the labels and the associated text that would correspond to an OLE DB type connection string:

```
Sub cboCombo_Click()
    Dim strComboSelection, strTmp

    ' Clean Up in case this was pressed already
    Form.cmdRegister.Enabled = False
    Form.cmdProcess.Enabled = True
    Form.lblRegistry.Caption = ""
    For i = 0 To 5
            Form.lblLabel(i).Visible = False
            Form.txtText(i).Visible = False
    Next

    strComboSelection = _
            Trim(Form.cboCombo.List(Form.cboCombo.ListIndex))
    Select Case strComboSelection
            Case "OLE DB"
                    For i = 0 To 4
                            Form.lblLabel(i).Visible = True
                            Form.txtText(i).Visible = True
                    Next
                    Form.lblLabel(0).Caption = "Provider="
                    Form.lblLabel(1).Caption = "Data Source="
                    Form.lblLabel(2).Caption = "Initial Catalog="
                    Form.lblLabel(3).Caption = "User ID="
                    Form.lblLabel(4).Caption = "Password="
                    Form.txtText(0).Text = "SQLOLEDB"
                    Form.txtText(1).Text = "DATABOX"
                    Form.txtText(2).Text = "MyAppDB"
                    Form.txtText(3).Text = "Student"
                    Form.txtText(4).Text = "teacher"

    [...]
```

```
        End Select
        strTmp = "Please Fill In Remaining Values in the available"
        strTmp = strTmp & " text boxes. " & vbCrLf
        strTmp = strTmp & "You may press ""Proceed"" button, or"
        strTmp = strTmp & " change the connection method again. "
        strTmp = strTmp & "Leaving User ID empty will leave out"
        strTmp = strTmp & " user infromation from registry"
        Form.lblExplanation = strTmp
End Sub
```

The remainder of the application responds to the end-user events, and builds the connection string as required by the core application, enabling and disabling controls, and modifying values on the form, depending on the 'stage'. The last action is actually carried out directly by the application itself – a value is written to the registry based on the string that is stored in one of the labels on the form.

This little application can be further extended to take advantage of several scripts, and provide wizard-like functionality that can easily be scripted.

Summary

The Script Control is a free control provided by Microsoft that enables your application to host a scripting engine. Uses of the script control can range from simple dynamic evaluation of expressions, to a fully-fledged macro language add-on capable of automating your applications.

We looked at the benefits of scripting, licensing issues, full syntax of the Script Control within the VB environment, and finally at some sample mini-apps (applications) that utilize the Script Control in different ways.

You can use the `ScriptControl` to perform tasks that may be difficult to achieve directly in VB, such as:

❑   Evaluate Dynamic Expressions

❑   Execute script code from a file, or a database

❑   Integrate your application with the Script Control, and expose its objects to the script

❑   You may also encode the script if necessary

❑   Finally, you may use other scripting objects such as File System Object and Regular Expression Object through a script, or directly in VB

Visual Basic Functions and Keywords

Overview

This Appendix contains a complete reference of functions and keywords in VBScript 5. You will also find a list of the VB/VBA functions and keywords that are not supported in VBScript. Where appropriate an alternative to an unsupported function or keyword is shown.

The function and keyword references are grouped in categories and they include the full syntax, an explanation, notes, sample code, and a "See also" list. The function references also include a list of named constants and their values.

Please note that there are a number of VB constructs that are not supported in VBScript. This includes File I/O (for security reasons), the Debug and Collection objects, some conversion functions, and the complete set of financial functions. For a complete list, see "Differences Between VB/VBA and VBScript" in Appendix B.

Operators

An operator acts on one or more operands when comparing, assigning, concatenating, calculating, and performing logical operations.

Say you want to calculate the difference between two variables A and B and save the result in variable C. These variables are the operands and to find the difference you use the subtraction operator like this:

```
C = A - B
```

Here we used the assignment operator (=) to assign the difference between A and B, which was found by using the subtraction operator (-). Operators are one of the single-most important parts of any programming language. Without them, you would not be able to assign values to variables or perform calculations and comparisons! It would be a bit like a bicycle without pedals...

There are different types of operators and they each serve a specific purpose, as you will see from the following.

Assignment Operator

The assignment operator is simply used for assigning a value to a variable or property. See the **Set** keyword for an explanation of how to reference and assign objects.

=	Name	**Assignment**
	Description	Assigns the result of an expression, the value of a constant, or the value of another variable to a variable or property.
	Syntax	**Variable = value**

Arithmetic Operators

The arithmetic operators are all used to calculate a numeric value, and are normally used in conjunction with the *Assignment Operator* and/or one of the *Comparison Operators*; they are listed in order of *Operator Precedence*.

^	Name	**Exponentiation**
	Description	Raises a number to the power of an exponent.
	Syntax	**Result = number ^ exponent**
		number and *exponent* is any valid numeric expression.
	Example	`MsgBox 5 ^ 5`
		MsgBox displays *3125*, which is the result of raising the number 5 to the exponent 5.

*	Name	**Multiplication**
	Description	Multiplies two numbers.
	Syntax	**Result = number1 * number2**
		number1 and *number2* is any valid numeric expression.
	Example	`MsgBox 5 * 5`
		MsgBox displays *25*, which is the result of multiplying the number 5 by 5.

500

/	Name	**Floating Point Division**
	Description	Returns a floating point result when dividing two numbers.
	Syntax	`Result = number1 / number2`
		number1 and *number2* is any valid numeric expression.
	Example	`MsgBox 5 / 4`
		MsgBox displays *1.25*, which is the result of dividing the number 5 by 4.

\	Name	**Integer Division**
	Description	Returns the integer part of the result when dividing two numbers.
	Syntax	`Result = number1 \ number2`
		number1 and *number2* is any valid numeric expression.
	Example	`MsgBox 5 \ 4`
		MsgBox displays *1*, which is the integer part of the result, when dividing the number 5 with 4.
	Note	The numeric expressions are rounded to `Byte`, `Integer`, or `Long` subtype expressions, before the integer division is performed. They are rounded to the smallest possible subtype, i.e. a value of 255 will be rounded to a `Byte`, and 256 will be rounded to an `Integer` and so on.

Mod	Name	**Modulus Division**
	Description	Returns the remainder when dividing two numbers.
	Syntax	`Result = number1 Mod number2`
		number1 and *number2* is any valid numeric expression.
	Example	`MsgBox 5 Mod 4`
		MsgBox displays *1*, which is the remainder part of the result, when dividing the number 5 with 4.

Table Continued on Following Page

Note	The numeric expressions are rounded to `Byte`, `Integer`, or `Long` subtype expressions, before the modulus division is performed. They are rounded to the smallest possible subtype, i.e. a value of 255 will be rounded to a `Byte`, and 256 will be rounded to an `Integer` and so on.

+	Name	**Addition**
	Description	Sums two expressions.
	Syntax	**Result = expression1 + expression2**
		expression1 and *expression2* is any valid numeric expression.
	Example	`MsgBox 5 + 5`
		MsgBox displays *10*, which is the result of adding the expression 5 to 5.
	Note	If one or both expressions are numeric, the expressions will be summed, but if both expressions are strings, they will be concatenated. This is important to understand, especially if you have a Java background, in order to avoid runtime errors. In general use the **&**operator (*see under **Concatenation Operators***), when concatenating and the + operator when dealing with numbers.

-	Name	**Subtraction**
	Description	Subtracts one number from another or indicates the negative value of an expression.
	Syntax (1)	**Result = number1 − number2**
		number1 and *number2* is any valid numeric expression.
	Example (1)	`MsgBox 5 - 4`
		MsgBox displays *1*, which is the result of subtracting the number 4 from 5.
	Syntax (2)	**−number**
		number is any valid numeric expression.
	Example (2)	`MsgBox -(5 - 4)`
		MsgBox displays *-1*, which is the result of subtracting the number 4 from 5 and using the unary negation operator (-) to indicate a negative value.

Concatenation Operators

Concatenation operators are used for concatenating expressions; they are listed in order of *Operator Precedence*.

&	Name	Ampersand
	Description	Concatenates two expressions.
	Syntax	Returns the concatenated expressions: `Result = expression1 & expression2`
	Example	If *expression1* is "WROX " and *expression2* is " Press" then the result is "WROX Press".
	Note	The expressions are converted to a String subtype, if they are not already of this subtype.

+	Name	+ Operator
	Description	Does the same as the & operator if both expressions are strings.
	Syntax	Returns the concatenated or summed expressions: `Result = expression1 + expression2`
	Example	1 + "1" = 2 "1" + "1" = "11"
	Note	If one or both expressions are numeric, the + operator will work as an arithmetic + operator and sum the expressions. A runtime error occurs if one expression is numeric and the other a string containing no numbers. It is recommended that + should only be used for numeric addition and never for concatenation purposes (use & instead).

Comparison Operators

The comparison operators are used for comparing variables and expressions against other variables, constants or expressions; they are listed in order of *Operator Precedence*.

One important thing to remember when comparing strings is case sensitivity. You can use the *UCase* and *LCase* functions to make sure that the strings you compare are the same case; the *StrComp* function offers another way of dealing with case sensitivity (*see under String Functions*). In VB/VBA you have the Option Compare statement, but this is not supported in VBScript. So keep in mind, when using the operators listed below, that if you compare strings (when both expressions are strings), a binary comparison is performed on the sequences of characters. A binary comparison is always case sensitive. If only one of the expressions is a string and the other is numeric, the numeric expression is always less than the string expression.

Null is returned if either expression is Null. If either expression is Empty, it is converted to the value 0 if the other expression is numeric, and to an empty string ("") if the other expression is a string. In the case where both expressions are Empty, they are obviously equal.

The **Is** operator is for dealing with objects and Variants.

=	Name	**Equal to**
	Description	Returns true if *expression1* is equal to *expression2*; false otherwise.
	Syntax	`Result = expression1 = expression2`

<>	Name	**Not equal to (different from)**
	Description	Returns true if *expression1* is not equal to *expression2*; false otherwise.
	Syntax	`Result = expression1 <> expression2`

<	Name	**Less than**
	Description	Returns true if *expression1* is less than *expression2*; false otherwise.
	Syntax	`Result = expression1 < expression2`

>	Name	**Greater than**
	Description	Returns true if *expression1* is greater than *expression2*; false otherwise.
	Syntax	`Result = expression1 > expression2`

<=	Name	**Less than or equal to**
	Description	Returns true if *expression1* is less than or equal to *expression2*; false otherwise.
	Syntax	`Result = expression1 <= expression2`

>=	Name	**Greater than or equal to**
	Description	Returns true if *expression1* is greater than or equal to *expression2*; false otherwise.
	Syntax	`Result = expression1 >= expression2`

Is	Name	Compare objects
	Description	Returns true if *object1* and *object2* refers to the same memory location (if they are in fact the same object).
	Syntax	`Result = object1 Is object2`
	Note	Use the **Not** operator (*see* under ***Logical Operators***) with the **Is** operator to get the opposite effect:
		`Result = object1 Not Is object2`
		Use the **Nothing** keyword with the **Is** operator to check if an object reference is valid. Returns true if object has been destroyed (`Set object = Nothing`):
		`Result = object Is Nothing`
		Be careful, **Nothing** is NOT the same as **Empty**. **Nothing** references an invalid object reference, whereas **Empty** is used for any variable, which has been assigned the value of Empty, or has not yet been assigned a value.

Logical Operators

The logical operators are used for performing logical operations on expressions; they are listed in order of ***Operator Precedence***. All logical operators can also be used as bitwise operators (*see* under ***Bitwise Operators***).

Not	Used to	Negate the expression.
	Returns	Returns the logical negation of an expression.
	Syntax	`Result = Not expression`
	Note	Result will be true if *expression* is false; and false if *expression* is true. `Null` will be returned if expression is `Null`.

And	Used to	Check if both expressions are true.
	Returns	Returns true if both expressions evaluate to true; otherwise, false is returned.
	Syntax	`Result = expression1 And expression2`

Or	Used to	Check if one or both expressions are true.
	Returns	Returns true if one or both expressions evaluate to true; otherwise, false is returned.
	Syntax	`Result = expression1 Or expression2`

Xor	Used to	Check if one and only one expression is true.
	Returns	Null will be returned if either expression is Null.
	Syntax	**Result = expression1 Xor expression2**
	Note	Returns true if only one of the expressions evaluates to true; otherwise, false is returned.

Eqv	Used to	Check if both expressions evaluate to the same value.
	Returns	Returns true if both expressions evaluate to the same value (true or false).
	Syntax	**Result = expression1 Eqv expression2**
	Note	Null will be returned if either expression is Null.

Imp	Used to	Perform a logical implication.
	Returns	Returns these values:
| | | ```
true Imp true = true
false Imp true = true
false Imp false = true
false Imp Null = true
Null Imp true = true
true Imp false = false
true Imp Null = Null
Null Imp false = Null
Null Imp Null = Null
``` |
| | Syntax | **Result = expression1 Imp expression2** |

Bitwise Operators

Bitwise operators are used for comparing binary values bit-by-bit; they are listed in order of *Operator Precedence*. All bitwise operators can also be used as logical operators (*see under Logical Operators*).
```

Not	Used to	Invert the bit values.
	Returns	Returns 1 if bit is 0 and vice versa.
	Syntax	`Result = Not expression`
		If *expression* is 101 then *result* is 010.

And	Used to	Check if both bits are set to 1.
	Returns	Returns 1 if both bits are 1; otherwise, 0 is returned.
	Syntax	`Result = expression1 And expression2`
		If *expression1* is 101 and *expression2* is 100 then *result* is 100.

Or	Used to	Check if one of the bits is set to 1.
	Returns	Returns 1 if one or both bits are 1; otherwise, 0 is returned.
	Syntax	`Result = expression1 Or expression2`
		If *expression1* is 101 and *expression2* is 100 then *result* is 101.

Xor	Used to	Checks if one and only one of the bits are set to 1.
	Returns	Returns 1 if only one bit is 1; otherwise, 0 is returned.
	Syntax	`Result = expression1 Xor expression2`
		If *expression1* is 101 and *expression2* is 100 then *result* is 001.

Eqv	Used to	Checks if both bits evaluate to the same value.
	Returns	Returns 1 if both bits have the same value (0 or 1).
	Syntax	`Result = expression1 Eqv expression2`
		If *expression1* is 101 and *expression2* is 100 then *result* is 110.

Imp	Used to	Performs a logical implication on two bits.
	Returns	Returns these values:
		0 Imp 0 = 1
		0 Imp 1 = 1
		1 Imp 1 = 1
		1 Imp 0 = 0
	Syntax	`Result = expression1 Imp expression2`
		If *expression1* is 101 and *expression2* is 100 then *result* is 110.

Operator Precedence

When more than one operation occurs in an expression they are normally performed from left to right. However, there are several rules.

Operators from the arithmetic group are evaluated first, then concatenation, comparison and logical operators.

This is the complete order in which operations occur (operators in brackets have the same precedence):

^, -, (*, /), \, **Mod**, (+, -),
&,
=, <>, <, >, <=, >=, **Is**,
Not, And, Or, Xor, Eqv, Imp

This order can be overridden by using parentheses. Operations in parentheses are evaluated before operations outside the parentheses, but inside the parentheses, the normal precedence rules apply.

Unsupported Operators

The following VB/VBA operator is not supported in VBScript:

Like

Math Functions

Every now and then, depending on what kind of applications you design, you will need to do some math calculations and VBScript goes a long way towards helping you here. There are a number of intrinsic functions, but it is also possible to derive many other math functions from the intrinsic ones. Math functions are especially helpful when you need to display graphics, charts etc; the listing is in alphabetical order.

Abs	Returns the absolute value of a number, i.e. its unsigned magnitude.
Syntax	`Abs(number)`
	number is any valid numeric expression.
Note	`Null` will be returned if *number* contains `Null`.
Example	`Abs(-50)  '  50` `Abs(50)   '  50`
See Also	*Sgn*

Atn	Returns the arctangent of a number as Variant subtype `Double` (5).
Syntax	`Atn(number)`
	number is any valid numeric expression.
Note	This function takes the ratio of two sides of a right-angled triangle (*number*) and returns the corresponding angle in radians. The ratio is the length of the side opposite the angle divided by the length of the side adjacent to the angle. The range of the result is -pi/2 to pi/2 radians.
Example	

```
Dim dblPi

        ' Calculate the
        ' value of Pi
        dblPi = 4 * Atn(1)
```

See Also	*Cos, Sin* and *Tan*

Cos	Returns the cosine of an angle as Variant subtype `Double` (5).
Syntax	`Cos(number)`
	number is any valid numeric expression that expresses an angle in radians.
Note	This function takes an angle and returns the ratio of two sides of a right-angled triangle. The ratio is the length of the side adjacent to the angle divided by the length of the hypotenuse (`dblSecant`). The result is within the range -1 to 1, both inclusive.
Example	

```
Dim dblAngle, dblSecant
Dim dblLength

    dblLength = 10
            ' Convert 30° to radians
    dblAngle = (30 * 3.14 / 180)
    dblSecant = dblLength / Cos(dblAngle)
```

Here the **Cos** function is used to return the cosine of an angle.

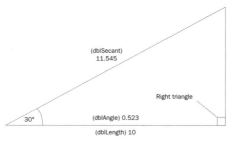

See Also	*Atn, Sin* and *Tan*

Exp	Returns a Variant subtype `Double` (5) specifying *e* (the base of natural logarithms) raised to a power.
Syntax	`Exp(number)`
	number is any valid numeric expression.
Note	A runtime error occurs if *number* is larger than 709.782712893. *e* is approximately 2.718282.
	Sometimes this function is referred to as the *antilogarithm,* and complements the action of the ***Log*** function.
| Example | ```
Dim dblAngle, dblHSin

    dblAngle = 1.3
    dblHSin = (Exp( dblAngle) - Exp( -1 * dblAngle)) / 2
``` |
| | Here the ***Exp*** function is used to return *e* raised to a power. |
| See Also | ***Log*** |

Fix	Returns the integer part of a number.
Syntax	`Fix(number)`
Note	***Fix*** is internationally aware, which means that the return value is based on the locale settings on the machine.
	`Null` is returned if *number* contains `Null`. The data type returned will be decided from the size of the integer part. Possible return data types in ascending order: `Integer`, `Long`, and `Double`.
	If *number* is negative, the first negative integer equal to or greater than *number* is returned.
| Example | ```
Dim vntPosValue
Dim vntNegValue

    vntPosValue = Fix(5579.56)
    vntNegValue = Fix(-5579.56)
``` |
	`vntPosValue` now holds the value 5579, and `vntNegValue` the value -5579.
	Fix is the equivalent of Int when dealing with non-negative numbers. When you handle negative numbers, Fix returns the first negative integer, greater than, or equal to the number supplied.
See Also	***Int***, ***Round*** and the ***Conversion Functions CInt*** and ***CLng***

Int	Returns the integer part of a number.
Syntax	`Int(number)` *number* is any valid numeric expression.
Note	*Int* is internationally aware, which means that the return value is based on the locale settings on the machine. `Null` is returned if *number* contains `Null`. The data type returned will be decided from the size of the integer part. Possible return data types in ascending order: `Integer`, `Long`, and `Double`. If *number* is negative, the first negative integer equal to or less than *number* is returned.

Example	```
	Dim vntPosValue
	Dim vntNegValue
	
	  vntPosValue = Int(5579.56)
	  vntNegValue = Int(-5579.56)
	``
	
	`vntPosValue` now holds the value 5579, and `vntNegValue` the value -5580.
	
	Int is the equivalent of Fix when dealing with non-negative numbers. When you handle negative numbers, Int returns the first negative integer, less than, or equal to the number supplied.

See Also	*Fix*, *Round* and the *Conversion Functions CInt and CLng*

Log	Returns the natural logarithm of a number.
Syntax	`Log(number)` *number* is any valid numeric expression greater than zero.
Example	``` Dim vntValueBase10 vntValueBase10 = Log(5) / Log(10) ``` The above sample code calculates the base-10 logarithm of the number 5, which is *0.698970004336019*.
See Also	*Exp*

Randomize	Initilizes the random number generator, by giving it a new seed-value. A seed-value is an initial value used for generating random numbers.
Syntax	`Randomize [number]` *number* is any valid numeric expression.
Note	You can repeat a sequence of random numbers, by calling the Rnd function with a negative *number*, before using the Randomize statement with a numeric argument.
Example	

```
Const LNG_UPPER_BOUND = 20
Const LNG_LOWER_BOUND = 1

Dim intValue
Dim lngCounterIn
Dim lngCounterOut

   For lngCounterOut = 1 To 3
      Rnd -1
      Randomize 3

      For lngCounterIn = 1 To 3
         intValue = Int((LNG_UPPER_BOUND - LNG_LOWER_BOUND + 1) * _
         Rnd + LNG_LOWER_BOUND)
         MsgBox intValue
      Next
   Next
```

	The above sample has an inner loop that generates three random numbers and an outer loop that calls the Rnd function with a negative number, immediately before calling Randomize with an argument. This makes sure that the random numbers generated in the inner loop will be the same for every loop the outer loop performs.
See Also	*Rnd*

Rnd	Returns a random number, less than 1 but greater than or equal to 0.
Syntax	`Rnd[(number)]` *number* (Optional) is any valid numeric expression that determines how the random number is generated; if *number* is: **< 0** – uses same number every time, **> 0 or missing** – uses next random number in sequence, **= 0** – uses most recently generated number.

Note	Use the *Randomize* statement, with no argument, to initialize the random-number generator with a seed based on the system timer, before calling *Rnd*.
	The same number sequence is generated for any given initial seed, because each successive call to *Rnd* uses the previous number as the seed for the next number in the sequence.
	Call *Rnd* with a negative argument immediately before using *Randomize* with a numeric argument, in order to repeat sequences of random numbers.
Example	``` Const LNG_UPPER_BOUND = 20 Const LNG_LOWER_BOUND = 1 Dim intValue Dim lngCounter For lngCounter = 1 To 10 intValue = Int(_ (LNG_UPPER_BOUND - _ LNG_LOWER_BOUND + 1) * _ ‡ Rnd + LNG_LOWER_BOUND) MsgBox intValue Next ```
	This produces 10 random integers in the range 1-20.
See Also	*Randomize*

Round	Returns a number rounded to a specified number of decimal places as a Variant subtype `Double` (5).
Syntax	`Round(number, [numdecimalplaces])`
	number is any valid numeric expression.
	numdecimalplaces, (Optional) indicates how many places to the right of the decimal separator should be included in the rounding.
Note	An integer is returned if *numdecimalplaces* is missing.
Example	``` Round(10.4) ' Returns 10 Round(10.456) ' Returns 10 Round(-10.456) ' Returns -10 Round(10.4, 1) ' Returns 10.4 Round(10.456, 2) ' Returns 10.46 Round(-10.456, 2) ' Returns -10.46 ```
See Also	*Int* and *Fix*

Sgn	Returns an integer indicating the sign of a number.
Syntax	`Sgn(number)`
	number is any valid numeric expression.
Note	*Sgn* returns the following when number is:
	< 0 – -1 **= 0 – 0** **> 0 – 1**

Example	```Sgn(10.4) ' Returns 1```
	```Sgn(0) ' Returns 0```
	```Sgn(-2) ' Returns -1```

See Also	*Abs*

Sin	Returns a Variant subtype `Double` (5) specifying the sine of an angle.
Syntax	`Sin(number)`
	number is any valid numeric expression that expresses an angle in radians.
Note	This function takes an angle and returns the ratio of two sides of a right-angled triangle. The ratio is the length of the side opposite the angle (`dblCosecant`) divided by the length of the hypotenuse (`dblSecant`). The result is within the range -1 to 1, both inclusive.

Example	```Dim dblAngle, dblCosecant```
	```Dim dblSecant```
	``` dblSecant = 11.545```
	``` ' Convert 30° to radians```
	``` dblAngle = (30 * 3.14 / 180)```
	``` dblCosecant = dblSecant * Sin(dblAngle)```

Here the *Sin* function is used to return the sine of an angle.

See Also	*Atn*, *Cos* and *Tan*

Sqr	Returns the square root of a number.
Syntax	`Sqr(number)`
	number is any valid numeric expression greater than or equal to zero.
Example	`Sqr(16) ' Returns 4`

Tan	Returns a Variant subtype `Double` (5) specifying the tangent of an angle.
Syntax	`Tan(number)`
	number is any valid numeric expression that expresses an angle in radians.
Note	This function takes an angle and returns the ratio of two sides of a right-angled triangle. The ratio is the length of the side opposite the angle (`dblCosecant`) divided by the length of the side adjacent to the angle (`dblLength`), - see diagram of Sin function.
	The result is within the range -1 to 1, both inclusive.

Example	`Tan(10.4) ' Returns 1.47566791425166`
	`Tan(0)    ' Returns 0`
	`Tan(-2)   ' Returns 2.18503986326152`

See Also	*Atn*, *Cos* and *Sin*

Date and Time Functions and Statements

There are a number of ways to display and represent dates and times. This includes date literals, which are valid date expression, enclosed in number signs (#). You need to be careful when using date literals because VBScript only lets you use the US-English date format, mm/dd/yyyy. This is true even if a different locale is being used on the machine. This might lead to problems when trying to use date literals in other formats, because in most cases the date will be accepted although converted to a different date. #10/12/1997# will be interpreted as October 12, 1997, but you might in fact want December 10, 1997, because your locale settings interprets dates as dd/mm/yyyy. `Date` literals only accept the forward slash (/) as the date separator.

The data range for a date is January 1, 100 to December 31, 9999, both inclusive. Internally, dates are stored as part of real numbers or to be more specific as a Variant subtype `Double` (5). The digits to the left of the decimal separator represent the date and the digits to the right of the decimal separator represent the time. Negative numbers are used internally for representing dates prior to December 30, 1899.

Below is a list of functions used for converting and formatting dates and times.

CDate	Returns an expression converted to Variant subtype `Date` (7).
Syntax	`CDate(date)`
	date is any valid `Date` expression.
Note	**CDate** is internationally aware, which means that the return value is based on the locale settings on the machine. Dates and times will be formatted with the appropriate time and date separators, and for dates the correct order of year, month and day are applied. Date and time literals are recognized.

Example	`Dim dtmValue`
	
	`    dtmValue = CDate( #12/10/1997#)`
	
	`dtmValue` now holds the value "10-12-97", if your locale settings use the dash (–) as the date separator and the short date format is dd/mm/yy.

See Also	*IsDate*

Date Syntax	Returns a Variant subtype `Date` (7) indicating the current system date. `Date`
Example	`MsgBox Date` Assuming that today is July 29 1999, the `MsgBox` now displays **29-07-99**, if your locale settings use the dash (–) as the date separator and the short date format is dd/mm/yy.
See Also	*Now* and *Time*

DateAdd	Adds or subtracts a time interval to a specified date and returns the new date.	
Syntax	`DateAdd(interval, number, date)`	
	interval can have these values:	
	d	Day
	h	Hour
	m	Month
	n	Minute
	q	Quarter
	s	Second

w	Weekday
ww	Week of year
y	Day of year
yyyy	Year

number is a numeric expression that must be positive if you want to add or negative if you want to subtract.

number is rounded to the nearest whole number if it's not a `Long` value.

Note

date must be a Variant or `Date` literal to which *interval* is added. **DateAdd** is internationally aware, which means that the return value is based on the locale settings on the machine. Dates and times will be formatted with the appropriate time and date separators and for dates the correct order of year, month and day are applied. An error occurs if the date returned precedes the year 100.

Example

```
MsgBox DateAdd("m", 3, "1-Jan-99")
```

This will add 3 months to January 1, 1999 and the `MsgBox` now displays 01-04-99, if your locale settings use the dash (–) as the date separator and the short date format is dd/mm/yy.

See Also ***DateDiff, DatePart***

DateDiff   Returns the interval between two dates.

Syntax

```
DateDiff(interval, date1, date2, [firstdayofweek],
[firstweekofyear])
```

interval can have these values:

d	Day
h	Hour
m	Month
n	Minute
q	Quarter
s	Second
w	Weekday
ww	Week of year
y	Day of year
yyyy	Year

date1 and *date2* are date expressions.

firstdayofweek (Optional) specifies the first day of the week. Use one of the following constants:

Table Continued on Following Page

517

vbUseSystemDayOfWeek   **0**   (National Language Support (NLS) API setting. NLS functions help Win32-based applications support the differing language- and location-specific needs of users around the world.)

vbSunday	**1** (default)
vbMonday	**2**
vbTuesday	**3**
vbWednesday	**4**
vbThursday	**5**
vbFriday	**6**
vbSaturday	**7**

firstweekofyear (Optional) specifies the first week of the year. Use one of the following constants:

vbUseSystem	**0** (Use NLS API setting)
vbFirstJan1	**1** (default) Week in which January 1 occurs.
vbFirstFourDays	**2** First week in the new year with at least four days.
vbFirstFullWeek	**3** First full week of the new year.

Note   A negative number is returned if *date1* is later in time than *date2*.

Example
```
MsgBox DateDiff("yyyy", #11-22-1967#, Now)
```

This will calculate the number of years between 11/22/1967 and now. In 1999, the `MsgBox` will display 32.

See Also   ***DateAdd, DatePart***

DatePart   Returns a specified part of a date.

Syntax
```
DatePart(interval, date, [firstdayofweek],
[firstweekofyear])
```

interval can have these values:

d	Day
h	Hour
m	Month
n	Minute
q	Quarter
s	Second
w	Weekday
ww	Week of year
y	Day of year
yyyy	Year

date is a date expression.

firstdayofweek (Optional) specifies the first day of the week. Use one of the following constants:

vbUseSystemDayOfWeek	**0** (NLS API setting)
vbSunday	**1** (default)
vbMonday	**2**
vbTuesday	**3**
vbWednesday	**4**
vbThursday	**5**
vbFriday	**6**
vbSaturday	**7**

firstweekofyear (Optional) specifies the first week of the year. Use one of the following constants:

vbUseSystem	**0** (Use NLS API setting)
vbFirstJan1	**1** (default) Week in which January 1 occurs.
vbFirstFourDays	**2** First week in the new year with at least four days.
vbFirstFullWeek	**3** First full week of the new year.

Example

```
MsgBox DatePart("ww", Now, vbMonday, vbFirstFourDays)
```

This will extract the week number from the current system date. On July 29, 1999 the `MsgBox` will display **30**.

See Also   ***DateAdd, DateDiff***

DateSerial   Returns a Variant subtype `Date` (7) for the specified year, month and day.

Syntax   **DateSerial(year, month, day)**

year is an expression that evaluates to a number between 0 and 9999. Values between 0 and 99, both inclusive, are interpreted as the years 1900 – 1999.

month is an expression that must evaluate to a number between 1 and 12.

day is an expression that must evaluate to a number between 1 and 31.

Note   If an argument is outside the acceptable range for that argument, it increments the next larger unit. Specifying 13 as the month will automatically increment year by one and subtract 12 from month leaving a value of 1. The same is true for negative values and a value of 0. However, instead of incrementing, the next larger unit is decremented.

Table Continued on Following Page

An error occurs if any of the arguments is outside the Variant subtype `Integer` range, which is -32768 – +32767. The same is true if the result is later than December 31, 9999. If you specify the year as 0, and the month and day as 0 or a negative value, the function wrongly assumes that the year is 100 and decrements this value.
So `DateSerial(0, 0, 0)` returns 11/30/99.

Example

```
MsgBox DateSerial( 1999, 07, 29)
```

The `MsgBox` will display 29-07-99, if your locale settings use the dash (–) as the date separator and the short date format is dd/mm/yy.

See Also

Date, *DateValue*, *Day*, *Month*, *Now*, *TimeSerial*, *TimeValue*, *Weekday* and *Year*

DateValue

Returns a Variant subtype `Date` (7).

Syntax

`DateValue(date)`

date is an expression representing a date, a time, or both, in the range January 1, 100 – December 31, 9999.

Note

Time information in *date* is not returned, but invalid time information will result in a runtime error. *DateValue* is internationally aware and uses the locale settings on the machine, when recognizing the order of a date with only numbers and separators. If the year is omitted from *date*, it is obtained from the current system date.

Example

```
DateValue("07/29/1999")
DateValue("July 29, 1999")
DateValue("Jul 29, 1999")
DateValue("Jul 29")
```

All of the above will return the same valid date of 07/29/99.

See Also

Date, *DateSerial*, *Day*, *Month*, *Now*, *TimeSerial*, *TimeValue*, *Weekday* and *Year*

Day

Returns a number between 1 and 31 representing the day of the month.

Syntax

`Day(date)`

date is any valid date expression.

Note

A runtime error occurs if *date* is not a valid date expression. `Null` will be returned if *date* contains `Null`.

Example

```
MsgBox Day("July 29, 1999")
```

The `MsgBox` will display 29.

See Also

Date, *Hour*, *Minute*, *Month*, *Now*, *Second*, *Weekday* and *Year*

FormatDateTime	*See under **String Functions***

Hour	Returns an integer between 0 and 23, representing the hour of the day.
Syntax	`Hour(time)`
	time is any valid time expression.
Note	A runtime error occurs if *time* is not a valid time expression. `Null` will be returned if *time* contains `Null`.
Example	`MsgBox Hour("12:05:12")`
	The `MsgBox` will display 12.
See Also	***Date, Day, Minute, Month, Now, Second, Weekday** and **Year***

IsDate	Returns a Variant subtype `Boolean` (11) indicating whether an expression can be converted to a valid date.
Syntax	`IsDate(expression)`
	expression is any expression you want to evaluate as a date or time.
| Example | ```
MsgBox IsDate(Now)          ' true
MsgBox IsDate("")           ' false
MsgBox IsDate(#7/29/1999#)  ' true
``` |
| See Also | ***CDate, IsArray, IsEmpty, IsNull, IsNumeric, IsObject** and **VarType*** |

Minute	Returns a number between 0 and 59, both inclusive, indicating the minute of the hour.
Syntax	`Minute(time)`
	time is any valid time expression.
Note	A runtime error occurs if *time* is not a valid time expression. `Null` will be returned if *time* contains `Null`.
Example	`MsgBox Minute("12:45")`
	The `MsgBox` will display 45.
See Also	***Date, Day, Hour, Month, Now, Second, Weekday** and **Year***
```

Month	Returns a number between 1 and 12, both inclusive, indicating the month of the year.
Syntax	`Month(date)`
	date is any valid date expression.
Note	A runtime error occurs if *date* is not a valid date expression. `Null` will be returned if *date* contains `Null`.
Example	`MsgBox Month(#7/29/1999#)`
	The `MsgBox` will display 7.
See Also	*Date*, *Day*, *Hour*, *Minute*, *Now*, *Second*, *Weekday* and *Year*

MonthName	Returns a Variant subtype `String` (8) for the specified month.
Syntax	`MonthName(month, [abbreviate])`
	month is a number between 1 and 12 for each month of the year beginning with January.
	abbreviate (Optional) is a boolean value indicating if the month name should be abbreviated or spelled out (default)
Note	A runtime error occurs if *month* is outside the valid range (1-12). *MonthName* is internationally aware, which means that the returned strings are localized into the language specified as part of your locale settings.
Example	`MsgBox MonthName(2)        ' February` `MsgBox MonthName(2, true)  ' Feb`
See Also	*WeekdayName*

Now	Returns the system's current date and time.
Syntax	`Now`
Example	`Dim dtmValue` `        dtmValue = Now`
	`dtmValue` now holds the current system date and time.
See Also	*Date*, *Day*, *Hour*, *Month*, *Minute*, *Second*, *Weekday* and *Year*

Second	Returns a Variant subtype Date (7) indicating the number of seconds (0-59) in the specified time.
Syntax	`Second(time)`
	time is any valid time expression.
Note	A runtime error occurs if *time* is not a valid time expression. Null will be returned if *time* contains Null.
Example	`MsgBox Second("12:45:56")`
	The MsgBox will display **56**.
See Also	*Date*, *Day*, *Hour*, *Minute*, *Month*, *Now*, *Weekday* and *Year*

Time	Returns a Variant subtype Date (7) indicating the current system time.
Syntax	`Time`
Example	`Dim dtmValue` `        dtmValue = Time`
	dtmValue now holds the current system time.
See Also	*Date*, *Now*

Timer	Returns a Variant subtype Single (5) indicating the number of seconds that have elapsed since midnight. This means that it is "reset" every 24 hours.
Syntax	`Timer`

Example	`Dim dtmStart, dtmStop`
	
	`        dtmStart = Timer`
	`        ' Do processing here`
	`        dtmStop = Timer`
	`        ' Display how many`
	`        ' seconds the operation`
	`        ' took`
	`        MsgBox dtmStop - dtmStart`

TimeSerial	Returns a Variant subtype Date (7) for the specified hour, minute and second.

Table Continued on Following Page

523

Syntax	`TimeSerial(hour, minute, second)`
	hour is an expression that evaluates to a number between 0 and 23.
	minute is an expression that must evaluate to a number between 0 and 59.
	second is an expression that must evaluate to a number between 0 and 59.
Note	If an argument is outside the acceptable range for that argument, it increments the next larger unit. Specifying 61 as *minute* will automatically increment *hour* by one and subtract 60 from *minute* leaving a value of 1. The same is true for negative values and a value of 0. However, instead of incrementing, the next larger unit is decremented.
	An error occurs if any of the arguments is outside the Variant subtype `Integer` range, which is -32768 – +32767.
Example	`MsgBox TimeSerial(23, 07, 29)`
	The `MsgBox` will display 23:07:29.
See Also	*Date*, *DateSerial*, *DateValue*, *Day*, *Month*, *Now*, *TimeValue*, *Weekday* and *Year*

TimeValue	Returns a Variant subtype `Date` (7) containing the time.
Syntax	`TimeValue(time)`
	time is an expression in the range 0:00:00 – 23:59:59.
Note	Date information in *time* is not returned, but invalid date information will result in a runtime error. `Null` is returned if *time* contains `Null`. You can use both 24 and 12-hour representations for the *time* argument.
Example	`TimeValue("23:59")` `TimeValue("11:59 PM")`
	Both will return the same valid time.
See Also	*Date*, *DateSerial*, *DateValue*, *Day*, *Month*, *Now*, *TimeSerial*, *Weekday* and *Year*

Weekday	Returns a number indicating the day of the week.
Syntax	`Weekday(date, [firstdayofweek])`
	date is any valid date expression.
	firstdayofweek (Optional) specifies the first day of the week. Use one of the following constants:

vbUseSystemDayOfWeek	**0** (Use NLS API setting)
vbSunday	**1** (Default)
vbMonday	**2**
vbTuesday	**3**
vbWednesday	**4**
vbThursday	**5**
vbFriday	**6**
vbSaturday	**7**

Note	`Null` is returned if *date* contains `Null`. A runtime occurs if *date* is invalid. Possible return values are:

vbSunday	**1**
vbMonday	**2**
vbTuesday	**3**
vbWednesday	**4**
vbThursday	**5**
vbFriday	**6**
vbSaturday	**7**

Example	`Weekday(#July 29, 1999#)`
	Returns 5 for Thursday.
See Also	*Date*, *Day*, *Month*, *Now* and *Year*

WeekdayName	Returns a Variant subtype `String` (8) for the specified weekday.
Syntax	`WeekdayName(weekday, [abbreviate], [firstdayofweek])`
	weekday is a number between 1 and 7 for each day of the week. This value depends on the *firstdayofweek* setting.
	abbreviate (Optional) is a boolean value indicating if the weekday name should be abbreviated or spelled out (default)
	firstdayofweek (Optional) is a numeric value indicating the first day of the week. Use one of the following constants:

Table Continued on Following Page

	vbUseSystemDayOfWeek	**0** (Use NLS API setting)
	vbSunday	**1** (Default)
	vbMonday	**2**
	vbTuesday	**3**
	vbWednesday	**4**
	vbThursday	**5**
	vbFriday	**6**
	vbSaturday	**7**
Note	A runtime error occurs if *weekday* is outside the valid range (1-7). ***WeekdayName*** is internationally aware, which means that the returned strings are localized into the language specified as part of your locale settings.	
Example	`WeekdayName(2, , vbSunday) ' Monday` `WeekdayName(1, , vbMonday) ' Monday`	
See Also	***MonthName***	

Year	Returns a number indicating the year.
Syntax	`Year(date)`
	date is any valid date expression.
Note	A runtime error occurs if *date* is not a valid date expression. `Null` will be returned if *date* contains `Null`.
Example	`MsgBox Year(#7/29/1999#)`
	The `MsgBox` will display 1999.
See Also	***Date, Day, Month, Now*** and ***Weekday***

Unsupported Date Functions and Statements

The following VB/VBA statements are not supported in VBScript:

Function/Statement Name	Alternative
Date statement	Sets the system date, which is not possible in VBScript.
Time statement	Sets the system time, which is not possible in VBScript.

Array Functions and Statements

One major difference between VB/VBA and VBScript is the way you can declare your arrays. VBScript does not support the `Option Base` statement and you cannot declare arrays that are not zero-based. Below is a list of functions and statements that you can use for array manipulation in VBScript.

Array	Returns a comma-delimited list of values as a Variant subtype `Array` (8192).
Syntax	`Array(arglist)`
	arglist is a comma-delimited list of values that is inserted into the one dimensional array in the order they appear in the list
Note	An array of zero length is created if *arglist* contains no arguments.
	All arrays in VBScript are zero-based, which means that the first element in the list will be element 0 in the returned array.

Example	```
	Dim arrstrTest
	
	    ' Create an array with three elements
	        arrstrTest = Array(_
	                    "Element0", "Element1", "Element2")
	    ' Show the first list element
	    ' now in the array
	    MsgBox arrstrTest(0)
	``

	`MsgBox` displays **Element0**
See Also	***Dim***

Erase	Reinitializes the elements if it is a fixed-size array and de-allocates the memory used if it is a dynamic array.
Syntax	`Erase array`
	array is the array to be reinitialized or erased.
Note	You must know if you are using a fixed-size or a dynamic array, because this statement behaves differently depending on the array type.
	Because the memory is de-allocated when using ***Erase*** with dynamic arrays, you must re-declare the array structure with the ***ReDim*** statement, before you use it again.
	Fixed-size arrays are reinitialized differently depending on the contents of the elements:
	Numeric Set to 0. Strings Set to "" Objects Set to `Nothing`.

Table Continued on Following Page

527

| Example | ```
Dim arrstrDynamic()
Dim arrstrFixed(3)

        ' Allocate space for the
        ' dynamic array
        ReDim arrstrDynamic(3)
        ' Free the memory used by
        ' the dynamic array
        Erase arrstrDynamic
        ' Reinitialize the elements
        ' in the fixed-size array
        Erase arrstrFixed
``` |
|---|---|
| See Also | **_Dim_** and **_ReDim_** |

For Each Performs a group of statements repeatedly for each element in a collection or an array.

Syntax

```
For Each element In group

    [statements]

    [Exit For]

Next [element]
```

element is a variable used for iterating through the elements in a collection or an array.

group is the name of the object or array.

statements is one or more statements you want to execute on each item in the group.

Note The **_For Each_** loop is only entered if there is at least one element in the collection or array. All the statements in the loop are executed for all the elements in the group. You can control this by executing the `Exit For` statement if a certain condition is met. This will exit the loop and start executing on the first line after the `Next` statement.

The **_For Each_** loops can be nested, but you must make sure that each loop element is unique.

Example

```
Dim arrstrLoop
Dim strElement

        ' Create the array
        arrstrLoop = Array( "Element0", "Element1", "Element2")
        ' Loop through the array
        For Each strElement In arrstrLoop
                ' Display the element content
                MsgBox strElement
        Next
```
```

IsArray	Returns a Variant subtype `Boolean` (11) indicating if a variable is an array.
Syntax	`IsArray(varname)`
	varname is a variable you want to check is an array.
Note	Only returns true if *varname* is an array.
Example	```Dim strName
Dim arrstrFixed(3)

        strName = "WROX rocks!"
        MsgBox IsArray(strName)   ' false
        MsgBox IsArray(arrstrFixed)   ' true``` |
| See Also | *IsDate, IsEmpty, IsNull, IsNumeric, IsObject* and *VarType* |

LBound	Returns the smallest possible subscript for the dimension indicated.
Syntax	`LBound(arrayname[, dimension])`
	arrayname is the name of the array variable.
	dimension is an integer indicating the dimension you want to know the smallest possible subscript for. The dimension starts with 1, which is also the default that will be used if this argument is omitted.
Note	The smallest possible subscript for any array is always 0 in VBScript. *LBound* will raise a runtime error if the array has not been initialized.
Example	```Dim arrstrFixed(3)

        MsgBox LBound(arrstrFixed)```

`MsgBox` displays 0. |
| See Also | *Dim, ReDim* and *UBound* |

ReDim	This statement is used to size or resize a dynamic array.

Syntax	`ReDim [Preserve] varname(subscripts[,`
	`varname(subscripts)]...)`
	
	Preserve (Optional) is used to preserve the data in an existing array, when you resize it. The overhead of using this functionality is quite high and should only be used when necessary.
	
	varname is the name of the array variable.
	
	subscripts is the dimension of the array variable *varname*. You can declare up to 60 multiple dimensions. The syntax is:
	
	upper[, upper]...
	
	where you indicate the upper bounds of the subscript. The lower bound is always zero.

Note	A dynamic array must already have been declared without dimension subscripts, when you size or resize it. If you use the `Preserve` keyword, only the last array dimension can be resized and the number of dimensions will remain unchanged. Since an array can be made smaller when resizing, you should take care that you don't lose any data already in the array.

Example	`Dim arrstrDynamic()`
	
	` ' Size the dimension to`
	` ' contain one dimension`
	` ' with 3 elements`
	`ReDim arrstrDynamic(3)`
	` ' Put data in the array`
	`arrstrDynamic(0) = "1"`
	`arrstrDynamic(1) = "2"`
	`arrstrDynamic(2) = "3"`
	` ' Resize the array, but`
	` ' keep the existing data`
	`ReDim Preserve arrstrDynamic(5)`
	` ' Display the 3rd element`
	`MsgBox arrstrDynamic(2)`
	
	`MsgBox` displays 3.

See Also	*Dim* and *Set*

UBound	Returns the largest possible subscript for the dimension indicated
Syntax	`UBound(arrayname[, dimension])`
	arrayname is the name of the array variable.
	dimension is an integer indicating the dimension you want to know the largest possible subscript for. The dimension starts with 1, which is also the default that will be used if this argument is omitted.
Note	*UBound* will raise a runtime error if the array has not been initialized. If the array is empty, -1 is returned.
Example	```
Dim arrstrFixed(3)
        MsgBox UBound(arrstrFixed)
```
`MsgBox` displays 3. |
| See Also | *Dim* statement, *UBound* and *ReDim* statement |

# Unsupported Array Functions and Statements

The following VB/VBA constructs are not supported in VBScript:

**Option Base**

# String Functions and Statements

Whatever your application does, you are likely to use string manipulation. By string manipulation we mean things like extracting a name from a string, checking if a particular string is part of another string, formatting numbers as strings with delimiters, and so on. Below is a list of the various string functions in VBScript.

Some functionality is not exposed as functions, but as methods of objects. For Example, the `RegExp` object exposes regular expression support. *See Chapter 7 The Built-In and Scripting Runtime Objects*.
```

Format Currency	Formats an expression as a currency value with the current currency symbol. The currency symbol is defined in Regional Settings in the Control Panel
Syntax	`FormatCurrency(expression [,numdigitsafterdecimal [,includeleadingdigit [,useparensfornegativenumbers [,groupdigits]]]])`

expression is the expression that you want formatted.

numdigitsafterdecimal (Optional) is a numeric value that indicates how many places to the right of the decimal separator should be displayed. If you omit this argument, the default value (-1) will be assumed and the settings from Control Panel will be used.

includeleadingdigit (Optional) indicates if a leading zero is displayed for fractional values. Use one of the following constants:

vbUseDefault	2 (Uses the settings from the Number tab in Control Panel)
vbtrue	-1
vbfalse	0

useparensfornegativenumbers (Optional) indicates if negative numbers are enclosed in parentheses. Use one of the following constants:

vbUseDefault	2 (Uses the settings from the Regional Settings tab in Control Panel)
vbTrue	-1
vbFalse	0

groupdigits (Optional) indicates if numbers are grouped using the thousand separator specified in Control Panel. Use one of the following constants:

vbUseDefault	2 (Uses the settings from the Regional Settings tab in Control Panel)
vbtrue	-1
vbfalse	0

Note	The way the currency symbol is placed in relation to the currency value is determined by the settings in the Regional Settings tab in Control Panel. (Is the currency symbol placed before the number, after the number, is there a space between the symbol and the number and so on.)
Example	

```
MsgBox FormatCurrency(7500)
MsgBox FormatCurrency(7500, , vbtrue)
MsgBox FormatCurrency(7500, 2, vbtrue)
```

If the currency symbol is a pound sign (£), the thousand separator a comma (,), and the currency symbol placed in front of the number with no spaces between, then `MsgBox` will display £7,500.00 in all of the above statements.

See Also	*FormatDateTime*, *FormatNumber* and *FormatPercent*

FormatDateTime	Returns a string formatted as a date and/or time.
Syntax	`FormatDateTime(date, [namedformat])`
	date is any valid date expression.
	namedformat (Optional) is a numeric value that indicates the date/time format used. Use one of the following constants:

vbGeneralDate	0	Format date (if present) and time (if present) using the short date and long time format from the machine's locale settings.
vbLongDate	1	Format date using the long date format from the machine's locale settings.
vbShortDate	2	Format date using the short date format from the machine's locale settings.
vbLongTime	3	Format time using the long time format from the machine's locale settings.
vbShortTime	4	Format time using the short time format from the machine's locale settings.

Note	A runtime error occurs if *date* is not a valid date expression. `Null` will be returned if *date* contains `Null`.
Example	```MsgBox FormatDateTime(Now, vbShortDate)```
	On July 29, 1999 the `MsgBox` will display **07/29/99**, if the locale settings use mm/dd/yy as the short date order and the forward slash (/) as the date separator.
See Also	*FormatCurrency*, *FormatNumber*, and *FormatPercent*

FormatNumber	Returns a string formatted as a number.

Syntax	```FormatNumber (expression,```
	 ```[, numdigitsafterdecimal```
	 ```[, includeleadingdigit```
	 ```[, useparensfornegativenumbers [,```
	 ```groupDigits]]]])```

	expression is the expression that you want formatted.
	numdigitsafterdecimal (Optional) is a numeric value that indicates how many places to the right of the decimal separator should be displayed. If you omit this argument, the default value (-1) will be assumed and the settings from Control Panel will be used.

Table Continued on Following Page

533

includeleadingdigit (Optional) indicates if a leading zero is displayed for fractional values. Use one of the following constants:

vbUseDefault	2 (Uses the settings from the Number tab in Control Panel)
vbtrue	-1
vbfalse	0

useparensfornegativenumbers (Optional) indicates if negative numbers are enclosed in parentheses. Use one of the following constants:

vbUseDefault	2 (Uses the settings from the Regional Settings tab in Control Panel)
vbtrue	-1
vbfalse	0

groupdigits (Optional) indicates if numbers are grouped using the thousand separator specified in Control Panel. Use one of the following constants:

vbUseDefault	2 (Uses the settings from the Regional Settings tab in Control Panel)
vbtrue	-1
vbfalse	0

Note   The Number tab in Regional Settings in Control Panel supplies all the information used for formatting.

Example
```
MsgBox FormatNumber("50000", 2, vbtrue, vbfalse, vbtrue)
MsgBox FormatNumber("50000")
```

The MsgBox will display 50,000.00, if the locale settings use a comma (,) as the thousand separator and a period (.) as the decimal separator.

See Also   ***FormatCurrency*, *FormatDateTime*, and *FormatPercent***

FormatPercent   Returns a string formatted as a percentage, like 50%.

Syntax
```
FormatPercent(expression,
[, numdigitsafterdecimal
[, includeleadingdigit
[, useparensfornegativenumbers [,groupDigits]]]])
```

expression is any valid expression that you want formatted.

numdigitsafterdecimal (Optional) is a numeric value that indicates how many places to the right of the decimal separator should be displayed. If you omit this argument, the default value (-1) will be assumed and the settings from Control Panel will be used.

includeleadingdigit (Optional) indicates if a leading zero is displayed for fractional values. Use one of the following constants:

vbUseDefault	2 (Uses the settings from the Number tab in Control Panel)
vbtrue	-1
vbfalse	0

useparensfornegativenumbers (Optional) indicates if negative numbers are enclosed in parentheses. Use one of the following constants:

vbUseDefault	2 (Uses the settings from the Regional Settings tab in Control Panel)
vbtrue	-1
vbfalse	0

groupdigits (Optional) indicates if numbers are grouped using the thousand separator specified in Control Panel. Use one of the following constants:

vbUseDefault	2 (Uses the settings from the Regional Settings tab in Control Panel)
vbtrue	-1
vbfalse	0

Note   The Number tab in Regional Settings in Control Panel supplies all the information used for formatting.

Example

```
MsgBox FormatPercent(4 / 45)
MsgBox FormatPercent(4 / 45, 2, vbtrue, vbtrue, vbtrue)
```

The `MsgBox` will display 8.89%, if the locale settings use a period (.) as the decimal separator.

See Also   *FormatCurrency*, *FormatDateTime*, and *FormatNumber*

InStr   Returns an integer indicating the position for the first occurrence of a sub string within a string.

Syntax   `InStr([start,] string1, string2[, compare])`

start (Optional) is any valid non-negative expression indicating the starting position for the search within *string1*. Non-integer values are rounded. This argument is required if the compare argument is specified.

string1 is the string you want to search within.

string2 is the sub string you want to search for.

compare (Optional) indicates the comparison method used when evaluating. Use one of the following constants:

| Syntax | **vbBinaryCompare** | 0 (Default) Performs a binary comparison, i.e. a case sensitive comparison. |
| | **vbTextCompare** | 1 Performs a textual comparison, i.e. a non-case sensitive comparison. |

Note

A runtime error will occur, if *start* contains Null. If *start* is larger than the length of string2 (> Len(*string2*)) 0 will be returned.

Possible return values for different *stringx* settings:

string1	zero-length	**0**
string1	Null	**Null**
string2	zero-length	*start*
string2	Null	**Null**
string2	not found	**0**
string2	found	**Position**

Example

```
Dim lngStartPos
Dim lngFoundPos
Dim strSearchWithin
Dim strSearchFor

    ' Set the start pos
    lngStartPos = 1
    ' Initialize the strings
    strSearchWithin = "This is a test string"
    strSearchFor = "t"
    ' Find the first occurrence
    lngFoundPos = InStr( lngStartPos, strSearchWithin, strSearchFor)
    ' Loop through the string
    Do While lngFoundPos > 0
        ' Display the found position
        MsgBox lngFoundPos
        ' Set the new start pos to
                ' the char after the found position
        lngStartPos = lngFoundPos + 1
        ' Find the next occurrence
        lngFoundPos = InStr( lngStartPos, strSearchWithin, strSearchFor)
    Loop
```

The above code finds all occurrences of the letter t in *string1*, at position 11, 14 and 17. Please note that we use binary comparison here, which means that the uppercase T will not be "found". If you want to perform a case-insensitive search, you will need to specify the *compare* argument as **vbTextCompare**.

See Also

InStrB, InStrRev

InStrB	Returns an integer indicating the byte position for the first occurrence of a sub string within a string containing byte data.
Syntax	`InStrB([start,] string1, string2[, compare])`
	start (Optional) is any valid non-negative expression indicating the starting position for the search within *string1*. Non-integer values are rounded. This argument is required, if the compare argument is specified.
	string1 is the string containing byte data you want to search within.
	string2 is the sub string you want to search for.
	compare (Optional) indicates the comparison method used when evaluating. Use one of the following constants:
	vbBinaryCompare – 0 (Default) Performs a binary comparison, i.e. a case sensitive comparison.
	vbTextCompare – 1 Performs a textual comparison, i.e. a non-case sensitive comparison.
Note	A runtime error will occur, if *start* contains `Null`. If *start* is larger than the length of string2 (> `Len(string2)`) 0 will be returned.
	Possible return values for different *stringx* settings:

string1	zero-length	**0**
string1	Null	**Null**
string2	zero-length	*start*
string2	Null	**Null**
string2	not found	**0**
string2	found	**Position**

Example	

```
Dim lngStartPos
Dim lngFoundPos
Dim strSearchWithin
Dim strSearchFor

    ' Set the start pos
    lngStartPos = 1
    ' Initialize the strings
    strSearchWithin = "This is a test string"
    strSearchFor = ChrB(0)

    ' Find the first occurrence
    lngFoundPos = InStrB( lngStartPos, strSearchWithin, strSearchFor)
    ' Loop through the string
    Do While lngFoundPos > 0
        ' Display the found position
        MsgBox lngFoundPos
        ' Set the new start pos to
            ' the char after the found position
        lngStartPos = lngFoundPos + 1
        ' Find the next occurrence
        lngFoundPos = InStrB( lngStartPos, strSearchWithin, strSearchFor)
    Loop
```

The above code finds all occurrences of the byte value 0 in *string1*, at position 2, 4, 6, ...40 and 42. This is because only the first byte of the Unicode character is used for the character. If you use a double-byte character set like the Japanese, the second byte will also contain a non-zero value.

See Also	*InStr*, *InStrRev*

InStrRev	Returns an integer indicating the position of the first occurrence of a sub string within a string starting from the end of the string. This is the reverse functionality of **InStr**.
Syntax	`InStrRev(string1, string2[, start[, compare]])` *string1* is the string you want to search within. *string2* is the sub string you want to search for. *start* (Optional) is any valid non-negative expression indicating the starting position for the search within *string1*; –1 is the default and it will be used if this argument is omitted. *compare* (Optional) indicates the comparison method used when evaluating. Use one of the following constants: **vbBinaryCompare** – 0 (Default) Performs a binary comparison, i.e. a case sensitive comparison. **vbTextCompare** – 1 Performs a textual comparison, i.e. a non-case sensitive comparison.
Note	A runtime error will occur, if *start* contains `Null`. If *start* is larger than the length if string2 (`> Len(string2)`) 0 will be returned. Possible return values for different *stringx* settings:

string1	zero-length	**0**
string1	Null	**Null**
string2	zero-length	***start***
string2	Null	**Null**
string2	not found	**0**
string2	found	**Position**

InStrRev and InStr do not have same syntax!

Example	

```
Dim lngStartPos
Dim lngFoundPos
Dim strSearchWithin
Dim strSearchFor

    ' Set the start pos
    lngStartPos = -1
    ' Initialize the strings
    strSearchWithin = "This is a test string"
    strSearchFor = "t"

    ' Find the first occurrence
    lngFoundPos = InStrRev( strSearchWithin, strSearchFor, lngStartPos)
    ' Loop through the string
    Do While lngFoundPos > 0
        ' Display the found
        '   position
        MsgBox lngFoundPos
        ' Set the new start pos to
        '   the char before the found position
        lngStartPos = lngFoundPos - 1
        ' Find the next occurrence
        lngFoundPos = InStrRev( strSearchWithin, strSearchFor,-
                                lngStartPos)
    Loop
```

The above code finds all occurrences of the letter t in *string1*, at position 17, 14 and 11. Please note that we use binary comparison here, which means that the uppercase T will not be "found". If you want to perform a case-insensitive search, you will need to specify the *compare* argument as **vbTextCompare**.

See Also   *InStr, InStrB*

Join	Joins a number of substrings in an array to form the returned string.
Syntax	`Join(list[, delimiter])`

list is a one dimensional array that contains all the substrings that you want to join.

delimiter (Optional) is the character(s) used to separate the substrings. A space character " " is used as the delimiter if this argument is omitted.

Note   All the substrings are concatenated with no delimiter if a zero-length string is used as *delimiter*. If any element in the array is empty, a zero-length string will be used as the value.

Example
```
Dim strLights
Dim arrstrColors(3)

    ' Fill the array
    arrstrColors(0) = "Red"
    arrstrColors(1) = "Yellow"
    arrstrColors(2) = "Green"

    ' Join the array into a string
    strLights = Join( arrstrColors, ",")
```

strLights contains "Red,Yellow,Green".

See Also   *Split*

LCase	Converts all alpha characters in a string to lowercase.
Syntax	`LCase(string)`

string is the string you want converted to lowercase.

Note   `Null` is returned if *string* contains `Null`. Only uppercase letters are converted.

Example
```
                MsgBox LCase("ThisIsLowerCase")
```

MsgBox displays thisislowercase

See Also   *UCase*

Left	Returns *length* number of leftmost characters from *string*.
Syntax	`Left(string, length)`

string is the string you want to extract a number of characters from.

length is the number of characters you want to extract starting from the left. The entire *string* will be returned if *length* is equal to or greater than the total number of characters in *string*.

Table Continued on Following Page

Note	Null is returned if *string* contains Null.

Example	``` Dim strExtract ```
	 ``` strExtract = "LeftRight" ```
	 ``` MsgBox Left(strExtract, 4) ```

	MsgBox displays **Left**.
See Also	***Len***, ***LenB***, ***Mid***, ***MidB*** and ***Right***

Len	Returns the number of characters in a string.
Syntax	**Len(string)**
	string is any valid string expression you want the length of.
Note	Null is returned if *string* contains Null.

Example	``` Dim strLength ```
	 ``` strLength = "1 2 3 4 5 6 7 8 9" ```
	 ``` MsgBox Len(strLength) ```

	MsgBox displays **17**.
See Also	***Left***, ***LenB***, ***Mid***, ***MidB*** and ***Right***

LenB	Returns the number of bytes used to represent a string.
Syntax	**LenB(string)**
	string is any valid string expression you want the number of bytes for.
Note	Null is returned if *string* contains Null.

Example	``` Dim strLength ```
	 ``` strLength = "123456789" ```
	 ``` MsgBox LenB(strLength) ```

	MsgBox displays **18**.
See Also	***Left***, ***Len***, ***Mid***, ***MidB*** and ***Right***

LTrim	Trims a string of leading spaces; " " or Chr(32).
Syntax	`LTrim(string)`
	string is any valid string expression you want to trim leading (leftmost) spaces from.
Note	`Null` is returned if *string* contains `Null`.
| Example | ```
Dim strSpaces

    strSpaces = " Hello again *"
    MsgBox LTrim(strSpaces)
``` |
| | `MsgBox` displays **Hello again *** |
| See Also | *Left*, *Mid*, *Right*, *RTrim* and *Trim* |

Mid	Returns a specified number of characters from any position in a string.
Syntax	`Mid(string, start[, length])`
	string is any valid string expression you want to extract characters from.
	start is the starting position for extracting the characters. A zero-length string is returned if it is greater than the number of characters in *string*.
	length (Optional) is the number of characters you want to extract. All characters from *start* to the end of the string are returned if this argument is omitted or if *length* is greater than the number of characters counting from *start*.
Note	`Null` is returned if *string* contains `Null`.
| Example | ```
Dim strExtract

    strExtract = "Find ME in here"
    MsgBox Mid(strExtract, 6, 2)
``` |
| | `MsgBox` displays **ME** |
| See Also | *Left*, *Len*, *LenB*, *LTrim*, *MidB*, *Right*, *RTrim* and *Trim* |

MidB	Returns a specified number of bytes from any position in a string containing byte data.
Syntax	`MidB(string, start[, length])`
	string is a string expression containing byte data you want to extract characters from.
	start is the starting position for extracting the bytes. A zero-length string is returned if it is greater than the number of bytes in *string*.
	length (Optional) is the number of bytes you want to extract. All bytes from *start* to the end of the string are returned if this argument is omitted or if *length* is greater than the number of bytes counting from *start*.
Note	`Null` is returned if *string* contains `Null`.
| Example | ```
Dim strExtract

    strExtract = "Find ME in here"
    MsgBox MidB(strExtract, 11, 4)
``` |
| | `MsgBox` displays **ME**, because VBScript uses 2 bytes to represent a character. The first byte contains the ANSI character code when dealing with 'normal' ANSI characters like M, and the next byte is 0. So byte 11 in the string is the first byte for the letter M and then we extract 4 bytes/2 characters. |
| See Also | *Left*, *Len*, *LTrim*, *Mid*, *Right*, *RTrim* and *Trim* |

Replace	Replaces a substring within a string with another substring a specified number of times.
Syntax	`Replace(expression, find, replacewith[, start[, count[, compare]]]))`
	expression is a string expression that contains the substring you want to replace.
	find is the substring you want to replace.
	replacewith is the substring you want to replace with.
	start (Optional) is the starting position within *expression* for replacing the substring. 1 (default), the first position, will be used if this argument is omitted. You must also specify the *count* argument if you want to use *start*.
```

	count (Optional) is the number of times you want to replace *find*. -1 (default) will be used if this argument is omitted, which means all *find* in the expression. You must also specify the *start* argument if you want to use *count*.
	compare (Optional) indicates the comparison method used when evaluating. Use one of the following constants:
	vbBinaryCompare – 0 (Default) Performs a binary comparison, i.e. a case sensitive comparison. **vbTextCompare** – 1 Performs a textual comparison, i.e. a non-case sensitive comparison.
Note	If *start* and *count* are specified, the return value will be the original expression, with *find* replaced *count* times with *replacewith*, from *start* to the end of the expression, and not the complete string. A zero-length string is returned if *start* is greater than the length of *expression* (start > Len(expression)). All occurrences of *find* will be removed if *replacewith* is a zero-length string ("")
	Possible return values for different argument settings:

expression	zero-length	**zero-length**
expression	Null	**Error**
find	zero-length	*expression*
count	0	*expression*

| Example | ```
Dim strReplace

strReplace = Replace( "****I use binary", "I", "You", 5, _
                      1, vbBinaryCompare) ' You use binary
strReplace = Replace( "****I use text", "i", "You", , , _
                      vbTextCompare)      ' ****You use text
``` |
| See Also | *Left*, *Len*, *LTrim*, *Mid*, *Right*, *RTrim* and *Trim* |

Right	Returns *length* number of rightmost characters from *string*
Syntax	`Right(string, length)`
	string is the string you want to extract a number of characters from.
	length is the number of characters you want to extract starting from the right. The entire *string* will be returned if *length* is equal to or greater than the total number of characters in *string*.
Note	Null is returned if *string* contains Null.

Table Continued on Following Page
```

| Example | ```
Dim strExtract

        strExtract = "LeftRight"
        MsgBox Right(strExtract, 5)
``` |
| | MsgBox displays **Right** |
| See Also | *Left*, *Len*, *LenB*, *Mid* and *MidB* |

RTrim	Trims a string of trailing spaces; " " or Chr(32).
Syntax	**RTrim(string)**
	string is any valid string expression you want to trim trailing (rightmost) spaces from.
Note	Null is returned if *string* contains Null.
| Example | ```
Dim strSpaces

        strSpaces = "* Hello again    "
        MsgBox RTrim(strSpaces)
``` |
| | MsgBox displays *** Hello again** |
| See Also | *Left*, *LTrim*, *Mid*, *Right* and *Trim* |

Space	Returns a string made up of a specified number of spaces (" ").
Syntax	**Space(number)**
	number is the number of spaces you want returned.
| Example | ```
Dim strSpaces

        strSpaces = "Hello again"
        MsgBox "*" & Space(5) & strSpaces
``` |
| | MsgBox displays ***   Hello again** |
| See Also | *String* |

Split	Returns a zero-based one-dimensional array "extracted" from the supplied string expression.
```

Syntax	`Split(expression[, delimiter[, count[, compare]]]))`
	expression is the string containing substrings and delimiters that you want to split up and put into a zero-based one-dimensional array.
	delimiter (Optional) is the character that separates the substrings. A space character will be used if this argument is omitted.
	count (Optional) indicates the number of substrings to return. -1 (default) means all substrings will be returned.
	compare (Optional) indicates the comparison method used when evaluating. Use one of the following constants:
	vbBinaryCompare – 0 (Default) Performs a binary comparison, i.e. a case sensitive comparison.
	vbTextCompare – 1 Performs a textual comparison, i.e. a non-case sensitive comparison.
Note	An empty array will be returned if *expression* is a zero-length string. The result of the `Split` function cannot be assigned to a variable of Variant subtype `Array` (8192). A runtime error occurs if you try to do so.
| Example | ```
Dim arrstrSplit
Dim strSplit

        ' Initialize the string
    strSplit = "1,2,3,4,5,6,7,8,9,0"
            ' Split the string using comma as the delimiter
    arrstrSplit = Split(strSplit, ",")
``` |
| | The array `arrstrSplit` now holds 10 elements, 0,1,2...0. |
| See Also | *Join* |

StrComp	Performs a string comparison and returns the result.
Syntax	`StrComp(string1, string2[, compare])`
	string1 is a valid string expression.
	string2 is a valid string expression.
	compare (Optional) indicates the comparison method used when evaluating. Use one of the following constants:
	vbBinaryCompare – 0 (Default) Performs a binary comparison, i.e. a case sensitive comparison.
	vbTextCompare – 1 Performs a textual comparison, i.e. a non-case sensitive comparison.

Table Continued on Following Page
```

Note	Possible return values for different *stringx* settings:

string1 < *string2*   **-1**
string1 = *string2*   **0**
string1 > *string2*   **1**

Null is returned if *string1* or *string2* is Null.

| Example | ```
Dim intResult

        intResult = StrComp("abc", "ABC", vbTextCompare)   ' 0
        intResult = StrComp("ABC", "abc", vbBinaryCompare) ' -1
        intResult = StrComp("abc", "ABC")                  ' 1
``` |
| See Also | ***String*** |

String	Returns a string with a substring repeated a specified number of times.
Syntax	`String(number, character)`

number indicates the length of the returned string.

character is the character code or string expression for the character used to build the returned string. Only the first character of a string expression is used.

Note	Null is returned if *number* or *character* contains Null. The character code will automatically be converted to a valid character code if it is greater than 255. The formula is: *character* Mod 256.
| Example | ```
Dim strChars

        strChars = "Hello again"
        MsgBox String(5, "*") & strChars
``` |

MsgBox displays *****Hello again

See Also	***Space***

StrReverse	Returns a string with the character order reversed.
Syntax	`StrReverse(string)`
Note	*string* is the string expression you want reversed.
	A runtime error occurs if *string* is Null. If *string* is a zero-length string, a zero-length string will be returned.

The case of the characters is not changed.

| Example | ```
        MsgBox StrReverse("Hello again")
``` |

MsgBox displays niaga olleH
```

Trim	Trims a string of leading and trailing spaces; " " or Chr(20).
Syntax	`Trim(string)`
	string is any valid string expression you want to trim leading (leftmost) and trailing (rightmost) spaces from.
Note	`Null` is returned if *string* contains `Null`.
Example	```Dim strSpaces

    strSpaces = " *Hello again* "
    MsgBox Trim(strSpaces)``` |
| | `MsgBox` displays ***Hello again*** |
| See Also | *Left*, *LTrim*, *Mid*, *Right* and *RTrim* |

UCase	Converts all alpha characters in a string to uppercase and returns the result.
Syntax	`UCase(string)`
	string is the string you want converted to uppercase.
Note	`Null` is returned if *string* contains `Null`. Only lowercase letters are converted.
Example	``` MsgBox UCase("ThisIsUpperCase")```
	`MsgBox` displays **THISISUPPERCASE**
See Also	*LCase*

547

Unsupported String Functions, Statements and Constructs

The following VB/VBA string functions/statements and constructs are not supported in VBScript:

Function/ Statement Name	Alternative
Format	*FormatCurrency, FormatDateTime, FormatNumber, FormatPercent*
LSet	*Left, Len* and *Space* functions in conjunction:

```
Dim strTest
Dim strNewText
        ' strTest is now 5 chars wide
    strTest = "01234"
        ' Assign the text to left align
    strNewText = "<-Test"
        ' Use the VB/VBA LSet (Unsupported)
    LSet strTest = strNewText

        ' Check if the New Text is wider than
        ' the variable we will align it in
    If Len(strNewText) <= Len(strTest) Then
            ' Copy the text across and pad the
            ' rest with spaces
        strTest = strNewText & Space(Len(strTest) - Len(strNewText))
    Else
            ' Copy as many chars from the new
            ' text as strTest is wide
        strTest = Left(strNewText, Len(strTest))
    End If
```

In both cases `strTest` will hold the value "<-Tes", because the original string `strTest` is only 5 characters wide and thus cannot hold all of `strNewText`. Had `strTest` been larger, the remaining places would have been filled with spaces.

Mid (statement)	*Left, Mid* and *InStr* functions, or the *Replace* function:

Here is how to replace a substring identified by characters using the *Replace* function:

```
Dim strText
Dim strFind
Dim strSubstitute
    strText = "This is the text I want to replace a substring in"
    strFind = "want to replace"
    strSubstitute = "have replaced"
    strText = Replace(strText, strFind, strSubstitute)
```

`strText` now holds This is the text I have replaced a substring in

Here is how to replace a substring identified by position and length using the *InStr*, *Left* and *Mid* functions:

```
Dim strText
Dim strSubstitute
    strText = "This is the text I want to replace a substring in"
    strSubstitute = "have replaced"
    strText = Left$(strText, 19) & strSubstitute & Mid$(strText, _
              35, Len(strText) - 34)
```

strText now holds This is the text I have replaced a substring in

RSet

Left, *Len* and *Space* functions in conjunction:

```
Dim strTest
Dim strNewText
            ' strTest is now 5 chars wide
    strTest = "01234"
            ' Assign the text to right align
    strNewText = "Test->"
            ' Use the VB/VBA RSet (Unsupported)
    RSet strTest = strNewText

            ' Check if the New Text is wider than
            ' the variable we will asign it in
    If Len(strNewText) <= Len(strTest) Then
            ' Pad with spaces and copy the
            ' text across
        strTest = Space(Len(strTest) - Len(strNewText)) & strNewText
    Else
                ' Copy as many chars from the new
                ' text as strTest is wide
        strTest = Left(strNewText, Len(strTest))
    End If
```

In both cases strTest will hold the value "Test-", because the original string strTest is only 5 characters wide and thus cannot hold all of strNewText. Had strTest been larger, the remaining places would have been filled with spaces.

StrConv

Very unlikely that this will be needed as all variables are Variant and this will be done implicitly.

Fixed length strings (Dim strMessage As String * 50) are not supported.

String Constants

Constant	Value	Description
vbCr	Chr(13)	Carriage Return.
vbCrLf	Chr(13) & Chr(10)	A combination of Carriage Return and linefeed.
vbFormFeed	Chr(12)	Form Feed*
vbLf	Chr(10)	Line Feed
vbNewLine	Chr(13) & Chr(10) *or* Chr(10)	New line character. This is platform-specific, meaning whatever is appropriate for the current platform.
vbNullChar	Chr(0)	Character with the value of 0.
vbNullString	String with the value of 0	This is not the same as a zero-length string (""). Mainly used for calling external procedures.
vbTab	Chr(9)	Tab (horizontal)
vbVerticalTab	Chr(11)	Tab (vertical)*

* = Not useful in Microsoft Windows.

Conversion Functions

Normally you don't need to convert values in VBScript, because there is only one data type, the Variant.

Implicit conversion is generally applied when needed, but when you pass a value to a non-variant procedure in a COM object that needs the value passed ByRef, you will have to pass the value with the precise data subtype. This can be done by placing the argument in it's own set of parentheses, which forces a temporary evaluation of the argument as an expression:

```
Dim objByRefSample
Dim intTest
    ' Initialize the variable
    intTest = "5"
    ' Create the object
    Set objByRefSample = CreateObject("MyObject.ByRefSample")
    ' Call the method
    objByRefSample.PassIntegerByReference (intTest)
    ' Destroy the object
    Set objByRefSample = Nothing
```

The `PassIntegerByReference` method is a VB sub-procedure with just one argument of type integer that is passed `ByRef`.

What happens is that the value 5 stored in the `intTest` variable is actually explicitly coerced into a variable of subtype Integer, so that it conforms to the methods argument type. If you remove the parentheses, you will get a runtime error, because the implicit coercion will treat the string value as a double.

This is just one way of solving the problem. Another way is to use the **CInt** conversion function (listed below) when calling the method.

At some point however, you might need to convert a value of one data subtype to another data subtype. This can be necessary for various reasons:

❑ You need to present a number in hexadecimal notation instead of decimal

❑ You need the corresponding character code for a character or vice versa

❑ You need to pass values to a non-variant property procedure or as a function parameter in a COM object

❑ You need to save data in a database

*See Chapter 2 **Variables and Data Types** for an explanation of the different data types.*

Asc	Returns the ANSI character code for the first character in a string.
Syntax	`Asc(string)`
	string is any valid string expression.
Note	A runtime error occurs if *string* doesn't contain any characters. *string* is converted to a `String` subtype if it's a numeric subtype.

Table Continued on Following Page

Example	`intCharCode = Asc("WROX")`
	`intCharCode` now holds the value 87, which is the ANSI character code for "W".
See Also	*AscB*, *AscW*, *Chr*, *ChrB* and *ChrW*

AscB	Returns the ANSI character code for the first byte in a string containing byte data.
Syntax	**AscB(string)**
	string is any valid string expression.
Note	A runtime error occurs if *string* doesn't contain any characters. For normal ANSI strings this function will return the same as the *Asc* function. Only if the string is in Unicode format will it be different from *Asc*. Unicode characters are represented by two bytes as opposed to ANSI characters that only need one.
Example	`intCharCode = AscB("WROX")`
	`intCharCode` now holds the value 87, which is the ANSI character code for "W".
See Also	*Asc*, *AscW*, *Chr*, *ChrB* and *ChrW*

AscW	Returns the Unicode character code for the first character in a string.
Syntax	**AscW(string)**
	string is any valid string expression.
Note	A runtime error occurs if *string* doesn't contain any characters. *string* is converted to a `String` subtype if it's a numeric subtype. For use on 32-bit Unicode enabled platforms only, to avoid conversion from Unicode to ANSI.
Example	`intCharCode = AscW("WROX")`
	`intCharCode` now holds the value 87, which is the Unicode character code for "W".
See Also	*Asc*, *AscB*, *Chr*, *ChrB* and *ChrW*

CBool	Returns a `Boolean` value (Variant subtype 11) corresponding to the value of an expression.
Syntax	`CBool(expression)`
	expression is any valid expression.
Note	A runtime error occurs if *expression* can't be evaluated to a numeric value.
	If *expression* evaluates to zero then false is returned; otherwise, true is returned.
Example	```Dim intCounter, blnValue
intCounter = 5
blnValue = CBool(intCounter)```
	`blnValue` now holds the value true, because `intCounter` holds a non-zero value.
See Also	*CByte*, *CCur*, *CDbl*, *CInt*, *CLng*, *CSng* and *CStr*

CByte	Returns an expression converted to Variant subtype `Byte` (17).
Syntax	`CByte(expression)`
	expression is any valid numeric expression.
Note	A runtime error occurs if *expression* can't be evaluated to a numeric value or if *expression* evaluates to a value outside the acceptable range for a `Byte` (0-255). Fractional values are rounded.
Example	```Dim dblValue, bytValue
dblValue = 5.456
bytValue = CByte(dblValue)```
	`bytValue` now holds the value 5, because `dblValue` is rounded.
See Also	*CBool*, *CCur*, *CDbl*, *CInt*, *CLng*, *CSng* and *CStr*

CCur	Returns an expression converted to Variant subtype `Currency` (6).
Syntax	`CCur(expression)` *expression* is any valid expression.
Note	`CCur` is internationally aware, which means that the return value is based on the locale settings on the machine. Numbers will be formatted with the appropriate decimal separator and the fourth digit to the right of the separator is rounded up if the fifth digit is 5 or higher.

Example	```Dim dblValue, curValue
	        dblValue = 724.555789
	        curValue = CCur(dblValue)```
	
	`curValue` now holds the value 724.5558 or 724,5558, depending on the separator.

See Also	***CBool, CByte, CDbl, CInt, CLng, CSng*** and ***CStr***

CDate	*See under **Date & Time Functions***

CDbl	Returns an expression converted to Variant subtype `Double` (5).
Syntax	`CDbl(expression)` *expression* is any valid expression.
Note	***CDbl*** is internationally aware, which means that the return value is based on the locale settings on the machine. Numbers will be formatted with the appropriate decimal separator. A runtime error occurs if *expression* lies outside the range (-1.79769313486232E308 to -4.94065645841247E-324 for negative values, and 4.94065645841247E-324 to 1.79769313486232E308 for positive values) applicable to a `Double`.
Example	```Dim dblValue dblValue = CDbl("5,579.56")``` `dblValue` now holds the value 5579.56 or 5,57956, depending on the thousand and decimal separators in use.
See Also	***CBool, CByte, CCur, CInt, CLng, CSng*** and ***CStr***

Chr	Returns the ANSI character corresponding to *charactercode*.
Syntax	`Chr(charactercode)`
	charactercode is a numeric value that indicates the character you want.
Note	Supplying a *charactercode* from 0 to 31 will return a standard non-printable ASCII character.
| Example | ```
Dim strChar
        strChar = Chr(89)
``` |
| | `strChar` now holds the character Y which is number 89 in the ANSI character table. |
| See Also | *Asc, AscB, AscW, ChrB* and *ChrW* |

ChrB	Returns the ANSI character corresponding to *charactercode*.
Syntax	`ChrB(charactercode)`
	charactercode is a numeric value that indicates the character you want.
Note	Supplying a *charactercode* from 0 to 31 will return a standard non-printable ASCII character. This function is used instead of the *Chr* (returns a two-byte character) function when you only want the first byte of the character returned.
| Example | ```
Dim strChar
        strChar = ChrB(89)
``` |
| | `strChar` now holds the character Y which is number 89 in the ANSI character table. |
| See Also | *Asc, AscB, AscW, Chr* and *ChrW* |

ChrW	Returns the Unicode character corresponding to *charactercode*.
Syntax	`ChrW(charactercode)`
	charactercode is a numeric value that indicates the character you want.
Note	Supplying a *charactercode* from 0 to 31 will return a standard non-printable ASCII character. This function is used instead of the **Chr** function when you want to return a double byte character. For use on 32-bit Unicode enabled platforms only, to avoid conversion from Unicode to ANSI.
Example	`Dim strChar` `        strChar = ChrW(89)`
	`strChar` now holds the character Y which is number 89 in the Unicode character table.
See Also	*Asc, AscB, AscW, Chr* and *ChrB*

CInt	Returns an expression converted to Variant subtype `Integer` (2).
Syntax	`CInt(expression)`
	expression is any valid expression.
Note	**CInt** is internationally aware, which means that the return value is based on the locale settings on the machine. Please note that decimal values are rounded, before the fractional part is discarded. A runtime error occurs if *expression* lies outside the range (-32,768 to 32,767) applicable to an `Integer`.
Example	`Dim intValue` `        intValue = CInt("5,579.56")`
	`intValue` now holds the value 5580 or 6, depending on the thousand and decimal separators in use.
See Also	*CBool, CByte, CCur, CDbl, CLng, CSng, CStr* and the *Math Functions Fix* and *Int*

CLng	Returns an expression converted to Variant subtype `Long` (3).
Syntax	`CLng(expression)` *expression* is any valid expression.
Note	***CLng*** is internationally aware, which means that the return value is based on the locale settings on the machine. Please note that decimal values are rounded, before the fractional part is discarded. A runtime error occurs if *expression* lies outside the range (-2,147,483,648 to 2,147,483,647) applicable to a `Long`.

Example	```Dim lngValue```
	 ``` lngValue = CLng("5,579.56")```
	
	 `lngValue` now holds the value 5580 or 6, depending on the thousand and decimal separators in use.

See Also	***CBool, CByte, CCur, CDbl, CInt, CSng, CStr***, and the ***Math Functions Fix*** and ***Int***

CSng	Returns an expression converted to Variant subtype `Single` (4).
Syntax	`CSng(expression)` *expression* is any valid expression.
Note	***CSng*** is internationally aware, which means that the return value is based on the locale settings on the machine. A runtime error occurs if *expression* lies outside the range (-3.402823E38 to -1.401298E-45 for negative values, and 1.401298E-45 to 3.402823E38 for positive values) applicable to a `Single`.

Example	```Dim sngValue```
	 ``` sngValue = CSng("5,579.56")```
	
	 `sngValue` now holds the value 5579.56 or 5,57956, depending on the thousand and decimal separators in use.

See Also	***CBool, CByte, CCur, CDbl, CInt, CLng, CStr*** and the ***Math Functions Fix*** and ***Int***

CStr	Returns an expression converted to Variant subtype `String` (8).
Syntax	`CStr(expression)` *expression* is any valid expression.
Note	***CStr*** is internationally aware, which means that the return value is based on the locale settings on the machine. A runtime error occurs if *expression* is `Null`. `Numeric` and `Err` values are returned as numbers, `Boolean` values as true or false, and `Date` values as a short date.
| Example | ```
Dim strValue
        strValue = CStr("5,579.56")
```<br><br>`strValue` now holds the value 5,579.56. |
| See Also | ***CBool, CByte, CCur, CDbl, CInt, CLng, CSng*** and the ***Math Functions Fix*** and ***Int*** |

Fix	*See under **Math Functions***

Hex	Returns the hexadecimal representation (up to 8 characters) of a number as a Variant subtype `String` (8).
Syntax	`Hex(number)` *number* is any valid expression.
Note	*number* is rounded to nearest even number before it is evaluated. `Null` will be returned if *number* is `Null`.
| Example | ```
Dim strValue
        strValue = Hex(5579.56)
```<br><br>`strValue` now holds the value 15CC. |
| See Also | ***Oct*** |

Int	*See under **Math Functions***

Oct	Returns the octal representation (up to 11 characters) of a number as a Variant subtype `String` (8).
Syntax	`Oct(number)`
	expression is any valid expression.
Note	*number* is rounded to nearest whole number before it is evaluated. `Null` will be returned if *number* is `Null`.
Example	```Dim strValue
strValue = Oct(5579.56)```
	`strValue` now holds the value 12714.
See Also	*Hex*

Unsupported conversion functions

The following VB/VBA conversion functions are not supported in VBScript:

Function Name	Alternative
CVar	Not needed since conversion to a Variant is implicit.
CVDate	*CDate*, *Date*
Str	*CStr*
Val	*CDbl*, *CInt*, *CLng* and *CSng*

Miscellaneous Functions, Statements and Keywords

Some functionality does not fit under any of the other categories, and so they have been gathered here. Below you will find descriptions of various functions for handling objects, user input, variable checks, output on screen, etc.

Create Object	Returns a reference to an Automation/COM/ActiveX object. The object is created using COM object creation services.
Syntax	`CreateObject(servername.typename[, location])`
	servername is the name of the application that provides the object.
	typename is the object's type or class that you want to create.
	location (Optional) is the name of the network server you want the object created on. If missing the object is created on the local machine.
Note	An Automation/COM/ActiveX object always contains at least one type or class, but usually several types or classes are contained within. *servername* and *typename* are often referred to as progid. Please note that a progid is not always a two part one, like servername.typename. It can have several parts, like servername.typename.version.

| Example | ```
Dim objRemote
Dim objLocal

        ' Create an object from class
        ' MyClass contained in the
        ' COM object MyApp on a
        ' remote server named FileSrv
        Set objRemote = CreateObject( "MyApp.MyClass", "FileSrv")

        ' Create an object from class
        ' LocalClass contained in the
        ' COM object LocalApp on the
        ' local macine
        Set objLocal = CreateObject( "LocalApp.LocalClass)
``` |
| See Also | *GetObject* |

Dim	Declares a variable of type Variant and allocates storage space.
Syntax	`Dim varname[([subscripts])][,` `varname[([subscripts])]]...`
	varname is the name of the variable
	subscripts (Optional) indicates the dimensions when you declare an array variable. You can declare up to 60 multiple dimensions using the following syntax:
	upperbound[, *upperbound*]...
	upperbound specifies the upper bounds of the array. Since the lower bound of an array in VBScript is always zero, *upperbound* is one less than the number of elements in the array.
	If you declare an array with empty subscripts, you can later resize it with *ReDim*; this is called a dynamic array.
```

Note	This statement is scope specific, i.e. you need to consider when and where you want to declare your variables. Variables that are only used in a specific procedure should be declared in this procedure. This will make the variable invisible and inaccessible outside the procedure. You can also declare your variables with script scope. This means that the variables will be accessible to all procedures within the script. This is one way of sharing data between different procedures.
	`Dim` statements should be put at the top of a procedure to make the procedure easier to read.
Example	``` ' Declare a dynamic array Dim arrstrDynamic() ' Declare a fixed size array ' with 5 elements Dim arrstrFixed(4) ' Declare a non-array variable Dim vntTest ```
See Also	***ReDim*** and ***Set***

Eval	Evaluates and returns the result of an expression.
Syntax	`result = Eval(expression)`
	result (Optional) is the variable you want to assign the result of the evaluation to. Although *result* is optional, you should consider using the ***Execute*** statement, if you don't want to specify it.
	expression is a string containing a valid VBScript expression.
Note	Because the assignment operator and the comparison operator is the same in VBScript, you need to be careful when using them with ***Eval***. ***Eval*** always uses the equal sign (=) as a comparison operator, so if you need to use it as an assignment operator, you should use the ***Execute*** statement instead.

Example	```
	Dim blnResult
	Dim lngX, lngY
	
	        ' Initialize the variables
	        lngX = 15: lngY = 10
	        ' Evaluate the expression
	        blnResult = Eval("lngX = lngY")
	``

	`blnResult` holds the value false, because 15 is not equal to 10.
See Also	***Execute*** statement

Execute	Executes one or more statements in the local namespace.
Syntax	**Execute statement**

statement is a string containing the statement(s) you want executed. If you include more than one statement, you must separate them using colons or embedded line breaks.

Note

Because the assignment operator and the comparison operator is the same in VBScript, you need to be careful when using them with *Execute*. *Execute* always uses the equal sign (=) as an assignment operator, so if you need to use it as a comparison operator, you should use the *Eval* function instead.

All in-scope variables and objects are available to the statement(s) being executed, but you need to be aware of the special case when your statements create a procedure:

```
Execute "Sub ExecProc: MsgBox ""In here"": End Sub"
```

The `ExecProc`'s scope is global and thus everything from the global scope is inherited. The context of the procedure itself is only available within the scope it is created. This means that if you execute the above shown *Execute* statement in a procedure, the `ExecProc` procedure will only be accessible within the procedure where the *Execute* statement is called. You can get around this by simply moving the *Execute* statement to the script level or using the *ExecuteGlobal* statement.

Example

```
Dim lngResult
Dim lngX, lngY

        ' Initialize the variables
        lngX = 15: lngY = 10
        ' Execute the statement
        Execute( "lngResult = lngX + lngY")
```

`lngResult` holds the value 25.

See Also   *Eval* and *ExecuteGlobal statement*

ExecuteGlobal	Executes one or more statements in the global namespace.
Syntax	**ExecuteGlobal statement**

statement is a string containing the statement(s) you want executed. If you include more than one statement, you must separate them using colons or embedded line breaks.

Note	Because the assignment operator and the comparison operator is the same in VBScript, you need to be careful when using them with *ExecuteGlobal*. *ExecuteGlobal* always uses the equal sign (=) as an assignment operator, so if you need to use it as a comparison operator, you should use the *Eval* function instead.
	All variables and objects are available to the statement(s) being executed.
Example	

```
Dim lngResult
Dim lngX, lngY

        ' Initialize the variables
        lngX = 15: lngY = 10
        ' Execute the statement
        ExecuteGlobal( "lngResult = lngX + lngY"
```

lngResult holds the value 25.

See Also	*Eval* and *Execute*

Filter	Returns an array that contains a subset of an array of strings. The array is zero-based as are all arrays in VBScript and it holds as many elements as are found in the filtering process The subset is determined by specifying a criteria.
Syntax	`Filter(inputstrings, value[, include[, compare]])`

inputstrings is a one dimensional string array that you want to search.

value is the string you want to search for.

include (Optional) is a `Boolean` value indicating if you want to include (true) or exclude (false) elements in *inputstrings* that contains *value*.

compare (Optional) indicates the comparison method used when evaluating. Use one of the following constants:

vbBinaryCompare – 0 (Default) Performs a binary comparison, i.e. a case sensitive comparison.
vbTextCompare – 1 Performs a textual comparison, i.e. a non-case sensitive comparison.

Note	An empty array is returned if no matches are found. A runtime error occurs if *inputstrings* is not a one-dimensional array or if it is `Null`.

Table Continued on Following Page

| Example | ```
Dim arrstrColors(3)
Dim arrstrFilteredColors

      ' Fill the array
      arrstrColors(0) = "Red"
      arrstrColors(1) = "Green"
      arrstrColors(2) = "Blue"

      ' Filter the array
      arrstrFilteredColors = Filter(arrstrColors, "Red")
``` |
|---|---|

arrstrFilteredColors now holds one element (0) which has the value Red.

See Also	*See the **String Function Replace***

GetObject   Returns a reference to an Automation object.

Syntax   `GetObject([pathname] [, class]])`

pathname (Optional) is a string specifying the full path and name of the file that contains the object you want to retrieve. You need to specify *class* if you omit this argument.

class (Optional) is a string that indicates the class of the object. You need to specify *pathname* if you omit this argument. The following syntax is used for *class*:

   appname.objecttype

appname is a string indicating the application that provides the object.

objecttype is a string specifying the object's type or class that you want created.

Note   You can use this function to start the application associated with *pathname* and activate/return the object specified in the ***pathname***. A new object is returned if ***pathname*** is a zero-length string ("") and the currently active object of the specified type is returned if ***pathname*** is omitted. Please note, that if the object you want returned has been compiled with Visual Basic, you cannot obtain a reference to an existing object by omitting the ***pathname*** argument. A new object will be returned instead. The opposite is true for objects that are registered as single-instance objects; the same instance will always be returned. However, you should note the above-mentioned problems with ActiveX DLL's compiled using Visual Basic.

Some applications allow you to activate part of a file and you can do this by suffixing pathname with an exclamation mark (!) and a string that identifies the part of the object you want.

You should only use this function when there is a current instance of the object you want to create, or when you want the object to open up a specific document. Use ***CreateObject*** to create a new instance of an object.
```

| Example | ```
Dim objAutomation

        ' Create a reference to an
        ' existing instance of an
        ' Excel application (this
        ' call will raise an error
        ' if no Excel.Application
        ' objects already exists)
        Set objAutomation = GetObject(, "Excel.Application")

        ' Create a reference to a
        ' specific workbook in a new
        ' instance of an Excel
        ' application
        Set objAutomation = GetObject( "C:\Test.xls ")
``` |
|---|---|
| See Also | ***CreateObject*** |

GetRef	Returns a reference to a procedure. This reference can be bound to an object event. This will let you bind a VBScript procedure to a DHTML event.
Syntax	`Set object.eventname = GetRef(procname)`
	object is the name of the object in which *eventname* is placed.
	eventname is the name of the event to which the procedure is to be bound.
	procname is the name of the procedure you want to bind to *eventname*.
| Example | ```
Sub NewOnFocus()
        ' Do your stuff here
End Sub

        ' Bind the NewOnFocus
        ' procedure to the
        ' Window. OnFocus event
        Set Window.OnFocus = GetRef("NewOnFocus ")
``` |

InputBox	Displays a dialog box with a custom prompt and a text box. The content of the text box is returned when the user clicks OK.
Syntax	`InputBox(prompt[, title][, default][, xpos][, ypos][, helpfile, context])`

prompt is the message you want displayed in the dialog box. The string can contain up to 1024 characters, depending on the width of the characters you use. You can separate the lines using one of these VBScript constants:

   vbCr, vbCrLf, vbLf or vbNewLine

title (Optional) is the text you want displayed in the dialog box title bar. The application name will be displayed, if this argument is omitted.

default is the default text that will be returned, if the user doesn't type in any data. The text box will be empty if you omit this argument.

xpos (Optional) is a numeric expression that indicates the horizontal distance of the left edge of the dialog box measured in twips (1/20 of a printer's point, which is 1/72 of an inch) from the left edge of the screen. The dialog box will be horizontally centered if you omit this argument.

ypos (Optional) is a numeric expression that indicates the vertical distance of the upper edge of the dialog box measured in twips from the upper edge of the screen. The dialog box will be vertically positioned approximately one-third of the way down the screen, if you omit this argument.

helpfile (Optional) is a string expression that indicates the help file to use when providing context-sensitive help for the dialog box. This argument must be used in conjunction with *context*. This is not available on 16-bit platforms.

context (Optional) is a numeric expression that indicates the help context number that makes sure that the right help topic is displayed. This argument must be used in conjunction with *helpfile*. This is not available on 16-bit platforms.

Note	A zero-length string will be returned if the user clicks Cancel or presses *ESC*.
| Example | ```
Dim strInput
    strInput = InputBox( "Enter User Name:", "Test")
    MsgBox strInput
``` |

The MsgBox will display either an empty string or whatever the user entered into the text box.

See Also	***MsgBox***
```

IsEmpty	Returns a `Boolean` value indicating if a variable has been initialized.
Syntax	`IsEmpty(expression)`
	expression is the variable you want to check has been initialized.
Note	You can use more than one variable as *expression*. If for Example, you concatenate two Variants and one of them is empty, the *IsEmpty* function will return false, because the expression is not empty.
| Example | ```
Dim strTest
Dim strInput
    strInput = "Test"
    MsgBox IsEmpty(strTest)              ' true
    MsgBox IsEmpty(strInput & strTest)   ' false
``` |
| See Also | *IsArray, IsDate, IsNull, IsNumeric, IsObject* and *VarType* |

IsNull	Returns a `Boolean` value indicating if a variable contains `Null` or valid data.
	`IsNull(expression)`
	expression is any expression.
Syntax	This function returns true if the whole of *expression* evaluates to `Null`. If you have more than one variable in *expression*, all of them must be `Null` for the function to return true.
	Please be aware that `Null` is not the same as `Empty` (a variable that hasn't been initialized) or a zero-length string (""). `Null` means no valid value!
	You should always use the *IsNull* function when checking for `Null` values, because using the normal operators will return false even if one variable is `Null`.
| Example | ```
Dim strInput
    strInput = "Test"
    MsgBox IsNull( strInput & Null)  ' false
    MsgBox IsNull(Null)              ' true
``` |
| See Also | *IsArray, IsDate, IsEmpty, IsNumeric, IsObject* and *VarType* |

IsNumeric	Returns a `Boolean` value indicating if an expression can be evaluated as a number.
Syntax	`IsNumeric(expression)`
	expression is any expression.
Note	This function returns true if the whole expression evaluates to a number. A `Date` expression is not considered a numeric expression.
Example	

```
MsgBox IsNumeric(55.55)               ' true
MsgBox IsNumeric("55.55")             ' true
MsgBox IsNumeric("55.55aaa")          ' false
MsgBox IsNumeric( "March 1, 1999")    ' false
MsgBox IsNumeric(vbNullChar)          ' false
```

See Also	*IsArray*, *IsDate*, *IsEmpty*, *IsNull*, *IsObject* and *VarType*

IsObject	Returns a `Boolean` value indicating if an expression is a reference to a valid Automation object.
Syntax	`IsObject(expression)`
	expression is any expression.
Note	This function returns true only if *expression* is in fact a variable of Variant subtype `Object` (9) or a user-defined object.
Example	

```
Dim objTest

        MsgBox IsObject(objTest)                                ' false
        Set objTest = CreateObject( "Excel.Application")
        MsgBox IsObject(objTest)                    ' true
```

See Also	*IsArray*, *IsDate*, *IsEmpty*, *IsNull*, *IsNumeric*, *Set* and *VarType*

LoadPicture	Returns a picture object.
Syntax	`LoadPicture(picturename)`
	picturename is a string expression that indicates the file name of the picture you want loaded.

Note	This function is only available on 32-bit platforms. The following graphic formats are supported:

Bitmap	**.bmp**
Icon	**.ico**
Run-length encoded	**.rle**
Windows metafile	**.wmf**
Enhanced metafile	**.emf**
GIF	**.gif**
JPEG	**.jpg**

A runtime error occurs if *picturename* doesn't exist or if it is not a valid picture file. Use *LoadPicture("")* to return an "empty" picture object in order to clear a particular picture.

Example	

```
Dim objPicture

    ' Load a picture into objPicture
    objPicture = LoadPicture( "C:\Test.bmp")
    ' Clear objPicture
    objPicture = LoadPicture( "")
```

MsgBox	Displays a dialog box with a custom message and a custom set of command buttons. The value of the button the user clicks is returned as the result of this function.

Syntax	**MsgBox(prompt [, buttons] [, title [, helpfile, context])**

prompt is the message you want displayed in the dialog box. The string can contain up to 1024 characters, depending on the width of the characters you use. You can separate the lines using one of these VBScript constants:

vbCr, vbCrLf, vbLf or vbNewLine

buttons (Optional) is the sum of values indicating the number and type of button(s) to display, which icon style to use, which button is the default and if the *MsgBox* is modal. The settings for this argument are:

vbOKOnly	**0**	Displays OK button.
vbOKCancel	**1**	Displays OK and Cancel buttons.
vbAbortRetryIgnore	**2**	Displays Abort, Retry, and Ignore buttons.
vbYesNoCancel	**3**	Displays Yes, No, and Cancel buttons.

Table Continued on Following Page

vbYesNo	4	Displays Yes and No buttons.
vbRetryCancel	5	Displays Retry and Cancel buttons.
vbCritical	16	Displays critical icon.
vbQuestion	32	Displays query icon.
vbExclamation	48	Displays warning icon.
vbInformation	64	Displays information icon.
vbDefaultButton1	0	Makes the first button the default one.
vbDefaultButton2	256	Makes the second button the default one.
vbDefaultButton3	512	Makes the third button the default one.
vbDefaultButton4	768	Makes the fourth button the default one
vbApplicationModal	0	When the MsgBox is application modal, the user must respond to the message box, before he/she can continue.
vbSystemModal	4096	The same effect as vbApplicationModal. Presumably this is a "left-over" from the good old 16-bit Windows days. The dialog box will stay on top of other windows though.

Please note how the values are grouped:

Buttons (values 0-5)

Icon (values 16, 32, 48 and 64)

Default button (values 0, 256, 512 and 768)

Modal (values 0 and 4096)

You should only pick one value from each group when creating your *MsgBox*.

title (Optional) is the text you want displayed in the dialog box title bar. The application name will be displayed if this argument is omitted.

helpfile (Optional) is a string expression that indicates the help file to use when providing context-sensitive help for the dialog box. This argument must be used in conjunction with *context*. This is not available on 16-bit platforms.

context (Optional) is a numeric expression that indicates the help context number that makes sure that the right help topic is displayed. This argument must be used in conjunction with *helpfile*.

Note   The following values can be returned:

vbOK (1)
vbCancel(2)
vbAbort (3)
vbRetry (4)
vbIgnore (5)
vbYes (6)
vbNo (7)

The *ESC* key has the same effect as the Cancel button. Clicking the Help or pressing *F1* will not close the *MsgBox*.

Example
```
Dim intReturn

intReturn = MsgBox( "Exit the application?", vbYesNoCancel + _
            vbQuestion)
```

The *MsgBox* will display the message "Exit the application?", the buttons Yes, No and Cancel, and the question mark icon. This *MsgBox* will be application modal.

See Also   *InputBox*

RGB   Returns an integer that represents an *RGB* color value. The *RGB* color value specifies the relative intensity of red, green, and blue to cause a specific color to be displayed.

Syntax   `RGB(red, green, blue)`

red is the red part of the color. Must be in the range 0-255.

green is the green part of the color. Must be in the range 0-255.

blue is the blue part of the color. Must be in the range 0-255.

Table Continued on Following Page

Note	255 will be used, if the value for any of the arguments is larger than 255. A runtime error occurs if any of the arguments cannot be evaluated to a numeric value.
| Example | ```
' Returns the RGB number for white
RGB(255, 255, 255)
``` |

ScriptEngine	Returns a string indicating the scripting language being used.
Syntax	`ScriptEngine`
Note	The following scripting engine values can be returned:
	VBScript MS VBScript
	JScript MS JScript
	VBA MS Visual Basic for Applications
	Other third-party ActiveX Scripting Engines can also be returned, if you have installed one.
See Also	*ScriptEngineBuildVersion*, *ScriptEngineMajorVersion* and *ScriptEngineMinorVersion*

ScriptEngineBuildVersion	Returns the build version of the script engine being used.
Syntax	`ScriptEngineBuildVersion`
Note	This function gets the information from the DLL for the current scripting language.
See Also	*ScriptEngine*, *ScriptEngineMajorVersion* and *ScriptEngineMinorVersion*

ScriptEngineMajorVersion	Returns the major version number of the script engine being used. The major version number is the part before the decimal separator, e.g. 5 if the version is 5.1.
Syntax	`ScriptEngineMajorVersion`
Note	This function gets the information from the DLL for the current scripting language.
See Also	*ScriptEngine*, *ScriptEngineBuildVersion* and *ScriptEngineMinorVersion*

ScriptEngineMinorVersion	Returns the minor version number of the script engine being used. The minor version number is the part after the decimal separator, e.g. 1 if the version is 5.1.
```

Syntax	`ScriptEngineMinorVersion`
Note	This function gets the information from the DLL for the current scripting language.
See Also	*ScriptEngine*, *ScriptEngineBuildVersion* and *ScriptEngineMajorVersion*

Set	Returns an object reference, which must be assigned to a variable or property, or returns a procedure reference that must be associated with an event.
Syntax	`Set objectvar = {objectexpression	New classname	Nothing}`
	objectvar is the name of a variable or property.
	objectexpression (Optional) is the name of an existing object or another variable of the same object type. It can also be a method or function that returns either.
	classname (Optional) is the name of the class you want to create.
	`Set object.eventname = GetRef(procname)`
	object is the name of the object that *eventname* is associated with.
	eventname is the name of the event you want to bind *procname* to.
	procname is the name of the procedure you want to associate with *eventname*.
Note	*objectvar* must be an empty variable or an object type consistent with *objectexpression* being assigned.
	Set is used to create a reference to an object and not a copy of it. This means that if you use the **Set** statement more than once on the same object, you will have more than one reference to the same object. Any changes made to the object will be "visible" to all references.
	New, is only used in conjunction with *classname*, when you want to create a new instance of a class.
	If you use the *Nothing* keyword, you release the reference to an object, but if you have more than one reference to an object, the system resources are only released when all references have been destroyed (by setting them to *Nothing*) or they go out of scope.

| Example | ```
Dim objTest1
Dim objTest2
Dim objNewClass

    ' Create a new dictionary object
    Set objTest1 = CreateObject( "Scripting.Dictionary")
    ' Create a reference to the
    ' newly created dictionary object
    Set objTest2 = objTest1

    ' Destroy the object reference
    Set objTest1 = Nothing
    ' Although objTest2 was set
    ' to refer to objTest1, you can
    ' still refer to objTest2,
    ' because the system resources
    ' will not be released before
    ' all references have been
    ' destroyed. So let's add a key
    ' and an item
    objTest2.Add "TestKey", "Test"
    ' Destroy the object reference
    Set objTest2 = Nothing

    ' Create an instance of the
    ' class clsTest (created with
    ' the Class keyword)
    Set objNewClass = New clsTest
    ' ...
    ' Destroy the class instance
    Set objNewClass = Nothing
``` |
| See Also | **Class** (Chapter 8: Classes in VBScript) and **GetRef** |

TypeName	Returns the Variant subtype information for an expression as a Variant subtype `String` (8).
Syntax	**TypeName(expression)**
	expression is the variable or constant you want subtype information for.
```

Note	This function has the following return values (strings):
	Byte — Byte
	Integer — Integer
	Long — Long integer
	Single — Single-precision floating-point
	Double — Double-precision floating-point
	Currency — Currency
	Decimal — Decimal
	Date — Date and/or time
	String — Character string
	Boolean — true or false
	Empty — Unitialized
	Null — No valid data
	<object type> — Actual type name of an object
	Object — Generic object
	Unknown — Unknown object type
	Nothing — Object variable that doesn't refer to an object instance
	Error — Error

Example	

```
Dim arrstrTest(10)

        MsgBox TypeName(10)          ' Integer
        MsgBox TypeName("Test")      ' String
        MsgBox TypeName(arrstrTest)  ' Variant()
        MsgBox TypeName(Null)        ' Null
```

See Also	*IsArray*, *IsDate*, *IsEmpty*, *IsNull*, *IsNumeric*, *IsObject* and *VarType*

VarType	Returns an integer indicating the subtype of a variable or constant.
Syntax	`VarType(expression)`
	expression is the variable or constant you want subtype information for.

Note	This function has the following return values:		
	vbEmpty	0	uninitialized
	vbNull	1	no valid data
	vbInteger	2	Integer
	vbLong	3	Long integer
	vbSingle	4	Single-precision floating-point number
	vbDouble	5	Double-precision floating-point number
	vbCurrency	6	Currency
	vbDate	7	Date
	vbString	8	String
	vbObject	9	Automation object
	vbError	10	Error
	vbBoolean	11	Boolean
	vbVariant	12	Variant (only used only with arrays of Variants)
	vbDataObject	13	A data-access object
	vbByte	17	Byte
	vbArray	8192	Array

Example

```
Dim arrstrTest(10)

    MsgBox VarType(10)              ' 2
    MsgBox VarType("Test")          ' 8
    MsgBox VarType(arrstrTest)      ' 8204
    MsgBox VarType(Null)            ' 1
```

See Also   *IsArray*, *IsDate*, *IsEmpty*, *IsNull*, *IsNumeric*, *IsObject* and *TypeName*

Differences between VB/VBA and VBScript5

VB/VBA Language Features not in VBScript5

Category	Omitted Feature/Keyword
Array Handling	Option Base
	Declaring arrays with lower bound <> 0
Collection	Add, Count, Item, Remove
	Access to collections using ! character
	(e.g. MyCollection!Foo) [use . instead of !]
Conditional Compilation	#Const
	#If...Then...#Else
Control Flow	DoEvents
	GoSub...Return, GoTo
	On Error GoTo
	On...GoSub, On...GoTo
	Line numbers, Line labels
Conversion	CVar, CVDate
	Str [use CStr instead], Val [use CDbl instead]
Data Types	All intrinsic data types except Variant
	Type...End Type
Date/Time	Date statement, Time statement
	Timer

Category	Omitted Feature/Keyword
Dynamic Data Exchange (DDE)	`LinkExecute, LinkPoke,` `LinkRequest, LinkSend`
Debugging	`Debug.Print` `End`
Declaration	`Declare` (for declaring DLLs) `Optional` `ParamArray` `Static`
Error Handling	`Erl` `Error` `Resume, Resume Next`
File Input/Output	All traditional Basic file I/O [use `Scripting.FileSystemObject`]
Financial	All financial functions
Miscellaneous	`Option Explicit` is checked at runtime instead of compile time.
	Named constants *[either include the* `.inc` *files distributed with the object or create a* `.wsc` *file and a* `<reference>` *element]*
Object Manipulation	`TypeOf`
Objects	`Clipboard`
	`Collection` [use `Scripting.Dictionary Object` instead]
Operators	`Like` [`RegExp` object provides similar functionality]
Options	`Deftype` `Option Base` `Option Compare` `Option Private Module`
Select Case	Expressions containing `Is` keyword or any comparison operators
	Expressions containing a range of values using the `To` keyword

Category	Omitted Feature/Keyword
Strings	Fixed-length strings
	LSet, RSet statements
	Mid statement *[use* Right, *then* Left *statements to pull what you want]*
	StrConv [loop through a string using Asc, adding or subtracting 32 to convert case]
Using Objects	Collection access using ! *[use* . *instead of !]*

VBScript5 Features not in VB/VBA

Category	Feature/Keyword
Declarations	Class [creates a class module]
Miscellaneous	Eval
	Execute
Script Engine Identification	ScriptEngine
	ScriptEngineBuildVersion
	ScriptEngineMajorVersion
	ScriptEngineMinorVersion

Code Conventions

This appendix covers coding conventions that will help us to produce code that is easily readable and understandable, minimize errors, and speed up the inevitable debugging process.

Variable Naming Conventions

To make our variables describe themselves and their purpose, we should choose a name that describes what the variable contains, e.g. dailyincome is better than dollars or x. This can be helped by the use of mixed case, and by the use of **Hungarian Notation** where the variable name is prefixed with a notation based on the data type that that variable is supposed to contain, e.g. dblDailyIncome is much clearer than dailyincome. Consistency is also important, e.g. if you use Cnt as a variable in one part of the script and Count in another, you're likely to introduce runtime errors by confusing the variables.

Hungarian Notation

Data Type	Hungarian Prefix	Example	VarType()
Boolean	bln (or bool)	blnValidated	11
Byte	byt	bytColor	17
Currency	cur	curAmount	6
Date or Time	dtm	dtmBirthday	7
Double	dbl	dblBalance	5
Error	err	errInvalidName	10
Integer	int	intCount	2
Long	lng	lngWidth	3
Object	obj	objRS	9 or 13
Single	sng	sngHeight	4

Data Type	Hungarian Prefix	Example	VarType()
String	str	strName	8
Variant	var	varNumber	12

Control Type	Hungarian Prefix	Example
Animated Button	ani	aniMonkey
Check Box	chk	chkYes
Combo List Box	cbo	cboLanguage
Command Button	cmd	cmdSubmit
Common Dialog	dlg	dlgOpen
Frame	fra	fraOptions
Horizontal Scroll Bar	hsb	hsbBalance
Image Control	img	imgBackground
Label	lbl	lblCaption
Line	lin	linDivider
List Box	lst	lstShipBy
3D Panel	pnl	pnlEffect
Pop-up Menu	mnu	mnuSelection
Radio/Option Button	opt	optIncludeCement
Slider	sld	sldSetLevel
Spin Button	spn	spnCounter
Tab Strip	tab	tabOptionPages
Text Box	txt	txtName
Vertical Scroll Bar	vsb	vsbVolume

Constants

Constants should be clearly identifiable in any code we write by either using capitals or a con prefix, e.g. EXCHANGE_RATE or conExchangeRate.

Arrays

Arrays should be prefixed with the letter a or letters arr, depending on preference, as well as adhering to the conventions already detailed above, e.g. astrName or arrstrName.

Scope

It is also useful to include the scope of a variable by prefixing with g for global, or l for local (to a subprocedure), e.g. gstrCompanyName, lDepartmentRating.

Procedure Naming

Another key to writing easy-to-read code is to descriptively name your procedures. A trick to this is to start your procedure names with a verb, e.g. InitValues, ReadData, CloseWindow, etc. Mixed case and consistency of use between different routines should also be used.

Indentation

The proper indentation of code is probably the greatest way of enhancing its clarity. After a procedure declaration, opening loop statement, or conditional test, we indent by 2 (or 4) spaces, or use tabs; the closing statements follow the reverse indentation. By doing this, you can easily follow the flow of your program, as this example demonstrates:

```
Sub ShowIndentation()
  Dim intCount
  Dim strMessage
  For intCount = 1 to 5
      strMessage = strMessage & " " & intCount
      If strMessage = "1 2" then
        strMessage = strMessage & " -"
      End If
  Next
  MsgBox(strMessage)
End Sub
```

Commenting

Comments are a must, especially when multiple people are in a project and you are writing functions to be used by other team members. Even if you are writing code that only you will ever see, we can guarantee that after a few months of not dealing with it (or even just certain parts of it), you will forget what it does or exactly how it works. This is where commenting comes in handy. By commenting your procedures (describing what they do, pre and post conditions, return values, etc), important variables (ones that are changed in the procedure or passed by reference) and other parts of your code, not only will you then be able to remember what it does six months down the line, but another programmer will be able to easily follow your logic when they take over the maintenance of your code after your promotion!

Visual Basic Constants Supported in VBScript

This appendix covers all of the Visual Basic constants that are supported in VBScript. Constants are useful because they allow us to use a specific value without explicitly writing it. They are divided up into the following sections: **Color**, **Comparison**, **Date and Time**, **Date Format**, **Miscellaneous**, **MsgBox**, **String**, **Tristate**, and **VarType**.

Color Constants

These constants are used within code to specify colors.

Constant	Value	Description
vbBlack	&h00	Black
vbRed	&hFF	Red
vbGreen	&hFF00	Green
vbYellow	&hFFFF	Yellow
vbBlue	&hFF0000	Blue
vbMagenta	&hFF00FF	Magenta
vbCyan	&hFFFF00	Cyan
vbWhite	&hFFFFFF	White

Comparison Constants

These constants are used to switch between binary or textual comparisons *(see also String Functions of Appendix A)*.

Constant	Value	Description
vbBinaryCompare	0	Perform a binary comparison.
vbTextCompare	1	Perform a textual comparison.

Date and Time Constants

These constants are used to format dates (*see also **Date & Time Functions** of **Appendix A**).

Constant	Value	Description
vbSunday	1	Sunday
vbMonday	2	Monday
vbTuesday	3	Tuesday
vbWednesday	4	Wednesday
vbThursday	5	Thursday
vbFriday	6	Friday
vbSaturday	7	Saturday
vbUseSystem	0	Use the date format specified for your computer.
vbUseSystemDayOfWeek	0	Use the day of the week specified for your computer as the first day of the week.
vbFirstJan1	1	Use the week in which January 1 occurs as the first week of the year (default).
vbFirstFourDays	2	Use the week that has at least 4 days in the new year.
vbFirstFullWeek	3	Use the first full week of the year.

Date Format Constants

These constants determine how a date is displayed (*see also **Date & Time Functions** of **Appendix A**).

Constant	Value	Description
vbGeneralDate	0	Displays a date and/or time. The format is determined by your system settings.
vbLongDate	1	Display a date using your system's long date format.
vbShortDate	2	Display a date using your systems short date format.

Constant	Value	Description
vbLongTime	3	Display a time using your system's long time format.
vbShortTime	4	Display a time using your system's short time format.

Miscellaneous Constants

Constant	Value	Description
vbObjectError	-2147221504	Used as the base for user-defined error numbers (see also *Chapter 4* and *Appendix E*).

MsgBox Constants

These constants specify what buttons and icons appear on the message box, and which button is the default. Some of the constants also determine the modality of the MsgBox (see also **MsgBox** under *Miscellaneous Functions, Statements and Keywords of Appendix A*).

Constant	Value	Description
vbOKOnly	0	Display the OK button only.
vbOKCancel	1	Display the OK and Cancel buttons.
vbAbortRetryIgnore	2	Display the Abort, Retry and Ignore buttons.
vbYesNoCancel	3	Display the Yes, No and Cancel buttons.
vbYesNo	4	Display the Yes and No buttons.
vbRetryCancel	5	Display the Retry and Cancel buttons.
vbCritical	16	Display the Critical Message icon.
vbQuestion	32	Display the Warning Query icon.
vbExclamation	48	Display the Warning Message icon.
vbInformation	64	Display the Information Message icon.
vbDefaultButton1	0	The first displayed button is the default.

Constant	Value	Description
vbDefaultButton2	256	The second displayed button is the default.
vbDefaultButton3	512	The third displayed button is the default.
vbDefaultButton4	768	The fourth displayed button is the default.
vbApplicationModal	0	The user must respond to the message box.
vbSystemModal	4096	The user must respond to the message box. The message box is always on top.

The following determine which MsgBox button the user has selected. Note that these constants must be explicitly declared within your code before they can be used *(see also MsgBox under Miscellaneous Functions, Statements and Keywords of Appendix A)*.

Constant	Value	Description
vbOK	1	The OK button was clicked.
vbCancel	2	The Cancel button was clicked.
vbAbort	3	The Abort button was clicked.
vbRetry	4	The Retry button was clicked.
vbIgnore	5	The Ignore button was clicked.
vbYes	6	The Yes button was clicked.
vbNo	7	The No button was clicked.

String Constants

These constants allow non-visible characters to be easily inserted into strings.

Constant	Value	Description
vbCr	Chr(13)	Carriage return.
vbCrLf	Chr(13) & Chr(10)	Carriage return and linefeed combination.
vbFormFeed	Chr(12)	Form feed – not useful in Windows.
vbLf	Chr(10)	Line feed.

Constant	Value	Description
vbNewLine	`Chr(13)` & `Chr(10)` or `Chr(10)`	Platform-specific newline character.
vbNullChar	`Chr(0)`	Character having the value 0.
vbNullString	String having value 0	Not the same as a zero-length string ("") – used for calling external procedures.
vbTab	`Chr(9)`	Horizontal tab.
vbVerticalTab	`Chr(11)`	Vertical tab – not useful in Windows.

Tristate Constants

These constants are used to switch arguments on or off, or to use the default setting (*see also String Functions of Appendix A*).

Constant	Value	Description
vbUseDefault	-2	Use default from computer's regional settings.
vbTrue	-1	True
vbFalse	0	False

VarType Constants

The `VarType` constants determine the subtype of a Variant. Note that these constants must be explicitly declared within your code before they can be used.

Constant	Value	Description
vbEmpty	0	Uninitialized (default)
vbNull	1	Contains no valid data
vbInteger	2	`Integer` subtype
vbLong	3	`Long` subtype
vbSingle	4	`Single` subtype
vbDouble	5	`Double` subtype
vbCurrency	6	`Currency` subtype

Constant	Value	Description
vbDate	7	Date subtype
vbString	8	String subtype
vbObject	9	Object
vbError	10	Error subtype
vbBoolean	11	Boolean subtype
vbVariant	12	Variant (used only for arrays of Variants)
vbDataObject	13	Data access object
vbDecimal	14	Decimal subtype
vbByte	17	Byte subtype
vbArray	8192	Array

VBScript Error Codes and the Err Object

Runtime Errors

Runtime errors occur wherever your script attempts to perform an invalid action. Note that the vast majority of these errors should be caught during the debugging and testing stage. VBScript contains 65 runtime errors, which are listed below with their decimal and hexadecimal representations:

Decimal	Hexadecimal	Description
5	800A0005	Invalid procedure call or argument
6	800A0006	Overflow
7	800A0007	Out of memory
9	800A0009	Subscript out of range
10	800A000A	This array is fixed or temporarily locked
11	800A000B	Division by zero
13	800A000D	Type mismatch
14	800A000E	Out of string space
17	800A0011	Can't perform requested operation

Table Continued on Following Page

Decimal	Hexadecimal	Description
28	800A001C	Out of stack space
35	800A0023	Sub or Function not defined
48	800A0030	Err in loading DLL
51	800A0033	Internal error
52	800A0034	Bad file name or number
53	800A0035	File not found
54	800A0036	Bad file mode
55	800A0037	File already open
57	800A0039	Device I/O error
58	800A003A	File already exists
61	800A003D	Disk full
62	800A003E	Input past end of file
67	800A0043	Too many files
68	800A0044	Device unavailable
70	800A0046	Permission denied
71	800A0047	Disk not ready
74	800A004A	Can't rename with different drive
75	800A004B	Path/File access error
76	800A004C	Path not found
91	800A005B	Object variable not set
92	800A005C	For loop not initialized
94	800A005E	Invalid use of Null
322	800A0142	Can't create necessary temporary file
424	800A01A8	Object required
429	800A01AD	ActiveX component can't create object
430	800A01AE	Class doesn't support Automation
432	800A01B0	File name or class name not found during Automation operation
438	800A01B6	Object doesn't support this property or method
440	800A01B8	Automation error

Decimal	Hexadecimal	Description
445	800A01BD	Object doesn't support this action
446	800A01BE	Object doesn't support named arguments
447	800A01BF	Object doesn't support current locale setting
448	800A01C0	Named argument not found
449	800A01C1	Argument not optional
450	800A01C2	Wrong number of arguments or invalid property assignment
451	800A01C3	Object not a collection
453	800A01C5	Specified DLL function not found
455	800A01C7	Code resource lock error
457	800A01C9	This key is already associated with an element of this collection
458	800A01CA	Variable uses an Automation type not supported in VBScript
462	800A01CE	The remote server machine does not exist or is unavailable
481	800A01E1	Invalid picture
500	800A01F4	Variable is undefined
501	800A01F5	Illegal assignment
502	800A01F6	Object not safe for scripting
503	800A01F7	Object not safe for initializing
504	800A01F8	Object not safe for creating
505	800A01F9	Invalid or unqualified reference
506	800A01FA	Class not defined
5016	800A1398	Regular Expression object expected
5017	800A1399	Syntax error in regular expression
5018	800A139A	Unexpected quantifier
5019	800A139B	Expected ']' in regular expression
5020	800A139C	Expected ')' in regular expression
5021	800A139D	Invalid range in character set
32811	800A802B	Element not found

Syntax Errors

Syntax errors occur where ever your script contains statements that do not follow the pre-defined rules for that language. Note that this type of error should be caught during development. VBScript contains 53 syntax errors, listed below with their decimal and hexadecimal representations:

Decimal	Hexadecimal	Description
1001	800A03E9	Out of memory
1002	800A03EA	Syntax error
1003	800A03EB	Expected ':'
1005	800A03ED	Expected '('
1006	800A03EE	Expected ')'
1007	800A03EF	Expected ']'
1010	800A03F2	Expected identifier
1011	800A03F3	Expected '='
1012	800A03F4	Expected 'If'
1013	800A03F5	Expected 'To'
1014	800A03F6	Expected 'End'
1015	800A03F7	Expected 'Function'
1016	800A03F8	Expected 'Sub'
1017	800A03F9	Expected 'Then'
1018	800A03FA	Expected 'Wend'
1019	800A03FB	Expected 'Loop'
1020	800A03FC	Expected 'Next'
1021	800A03FD	Expected 'Case'
1022	800A03FE	Expected 'Select'
1023	800A03FF	Expected expression
1024	800A0400	Expected statement
1025	800A0401	Expected end of statement
1026	800A0402	Expected integer constant
1027	800A0403	Expected 'While' or 'Until'
1028	800A0404	Expected 'While', 'Until' or end of statement
1029	800A0405	Expected 'With'

Decimal	Hexadecimal	Description
1030	800A0406	Identifier too long
1031	800A0407	Invalid number
1032	800A0408	Invalid character
1033	800A0409	Unterminated string constant
1034	800A040A	Unterminated comment
1037	800A040D	Invalid use of 'Me' keyword
1038	800A040E	'loop' without 'do'
1039	800A040F	Invalid 'exit' statement
1040	800A0410	Invalid 'for' loop control variable
1041	800A0411	Name redefined
1042	800A0412	Must be first statement on the line
1043	800A0413	Cannot assign to non-ByVal argument
1044	800A0414	Cannot use parentheses when calling a Sub
1045	800A0415	Expected literal constant
1046	800A0416	Expected 'In'
1047	800A0417	Expected 'Class'
1048	800A0418	Must be defined inside a Class
1049	800A0419	Expected Let or Set or Get in property declaration
1050	800A041A	Expected 'Property'
1051	800A041B	Number of arguments must be consistent across properties specification
1052	800A041C	Cannot have multiple default property/method in a Class
1053	800A041D	Class initialize or terminate do not have arguments
1054	800A041E	Property Set or Let must have at least one argument
1055	800A041F	Unexpected 'Next'
1056	800A0420	'Default' can be specified only on 'Property' or 'Function' or 'Sub'
1057	800A0421	'Default' specification must also specify 'Public')
1058	800A0422	'Default' specification can only be on Property Get

Err Object and On Err statement

Err Object

The `Err` object is the heart and soul of error handling in VBScript, and exposes information about runtime errors through its properties. Unlike other objects in VBScript, it is an intrinsic object with global scope; hence, there is no need to declare and initialize the `Err` object.

Initially the `Err` properties are either zero-length strings or 0, and when a runtime error occurs the properties of the `Err` object get populated by the generator of the error (e.g. VBScript, an Automation object, or by the programmer). `Err.Number` contains an integer, and `Number` is the default property of the `Err` object. It is easy to test whether the error actually occurred with an `If Err Then` statement because of automatic conversion between integer and Boolean subtypes: the integer 0 (no error) converts to Boolean `False`, and all other numbers evaluate to true.

The following example illustrates a partial IE VBScript (although it could just as easily be from a `.ws(f)`, `.wsc`, or `.hta` file) in which the programmer raises one of the predefined VBScript errors. Note that the `Err` object is not declared, and it cannot be created as a separate object:

```
<SCRIPT LANGUAGE=vbscript>
On Error Resume Next
Err.Raise 11' Division by Zero
MsgBox ("Error # " & CStr(Err.Number) & " " & Err.Description)
</SCRIPT>
```

Err Object Properties

Description

The `Description` property returns or sets a descriptive string associated with an error. By default this is a zero-length string until the property is set by the programmer, or by the generator of an error. The description is useful when displaying or logging errors, and when raising custom errors. If the programmer raises one of the default runtime errors, the `Description` property contains the string associated with the error.

Syntax

`Err.Description [= stringexpression]`

Name	Subtype	Description
Err	Err Object	This is always the `Err` Object
stringexpression	String	A string expression containing a description of the error

Example Usage

```
<SCRIPT LANGUAGE=vbscript>
Option Explicit
On Error Resume Next

IntTest = 5
MsgBox ("Error Description: " & Err.Description)
</SCRIPT>
```

This sample script will produce Variable is undefined inside a message box.

HelpContext

The HelpContext property is used to automatically display the Help topic specified in the HelpFile property. This property either sets or retrieves the value of the help context. If both HelpFile and HelpContext are empty, the value of Number is checked. If Number corresponds to a VBScript runtime error value, then the VBScript help context ID for the error is used.

This property is rarely used, and requires coordination between the person authoring the Help system and the scripter. Finally, use of the HelpFile and of HelpContext only make sense in a non-IE setting with the older .hlp system. Newer HTML help simply uses HTML documents, which may be displayed under most circumstances using techniques discussed in HTML Help manuals. The following sample illustrates the use of the traditional .hlp files with the Windows Script Host.

Syntax

```
Err.HelpContext [= contextID]
```

Name	Subtype	Description
Err	Err Object	This always is the Err Object
contextID	Integer	Optional. A valid identifier for a Help topic within the Help file.

Example Usage

```
On Error Resume Next
Dim Msg
Err.Clear
Err.Raise 6     ' Generate "Overflow" error.
Err.Helpfile = "c:\yourHelp.hlp"
Err.HelpContext = 21
If Err.Number <> 0 Then
   Msg = "Press Help to see " & Err.Helpfile & " topic for" & _
   " the following HelpContext: " & Err.HelpContext
   MsgBox Msg, , "error: " & Err.Description, Err.Helpfile, Err.HelpContext
End If
```

601

HelpFile

The HelpFile property is used to set and retrieve a fully qualified path to a programmer-authored Help File. Often it is used in conjunction with the HelpContext property – see the notes and the example above. The most common way of setting the value is through the Err.Raise method.

Syntax

```
Err.HelpFile [= filepath]
```

Name	Subtype	Description
Err	Err Object	This always is the Err Object
filepath	String	Optional. Fully qualified path to the Help File.

Number

This is the default property of the Err object, and returns or sets a numeric value specifying an error. Custom error handling functions utilize the Number property to diagnose the runtime error. When setting or retrieving a custom error, the vbObjectErr constant is used to ensure custom errors do not conflict with VBScript and common Automation Errs.

Syntax

```
Err.Number [= errornumber]
```

Name	Subtype	Description
Err	Err Object	This is always the Err Object
errornumber	Integer	An integer representing a VBScript error number or an SCODE error value. SCODE is a long integer value that is used to pass detailed information to the caller of an interface member or API function.

Example Usage

```
On Error Resume Next
Err.Raise vbObjectError + 16, ,"CustomObject Error" ' Raise Custom Error #16.
If Err.Number <> 0 Then       ' (If Err Then) can be used too
  MsgBox ("Error # " & CStr(Err.Number) & " " & Err.Description)
End If
```

The sample code above sets a custom error number in Err.Number through the Err.Raise method, and then displays the return value through a Message Box (MsgBox).

Source

The Source property sets or returns the name of the object or application that reported the error. Most commonly the source is the class name or ProgID of the object generating the error. Most of the time the Source property will show 'Microsoft VBScript', but in cases where the error occurs while accessing a property or method of an Automation object, the source property will show the component's class name. This is not only useful because it allows for a greater degree of granularity (or visibility) in error handling, but it also allows for better error display and logging possibilities. This property can be set through the Err.Raise method in both VBScript and in custom COM components.

Syntax

```
Err.Source [= stringexpression]
```

Name	Subtype	Description
Err	Err Object	This always is the Err Object
stringexpression	Integer	A string expression representing the application that generated the error.

Example Usage

```
On Error Resume Next
Err.Raise vbObjectError + 1, "cTestClass", "CustomObject Error"
If Err.Number <> 0 Then            ' (If Err Then) can be used too
  MsgBox ("Error # " & CStr(Err.Number) & " " & Err.Description & " Source: "
& Err.Source)
End If
```

Err Object Methods

Clear

The Clear method resets all of the properties of the Err object to either 0 or a zero-length string. The Err object should ideally be reset after an error has been handled because of the deferred nature of error handling in VBScript, to avoid the potential mistake of handling the same error twice.

The Err object is additionally cleared by any of the following statements:

- ❑   On Error Resume Next
- ❑   On Error Goto 0
- ❑   Exit Sub
- ❑   Exit Function

Therefore, error-handling functions must be called before any of the above statements are executed.

Syntax

```
Err.Clear
```

Name	Subtype	Description
Err	Err Object	This always is the Err Object

Example Usage

```
On Error Resume Next                          ' The Err Object is Reset
Err.Raise 5
Err.Clear
If Err.Number = 0 Then                        ' (If Err Then) can be
used too
  MsgBox ("Error has been reset: Err.Number - " & CStr(Err.Number))
End If
```

Raise

The Raise method generates a runtime error. All of the parameters of the Raise method, except for its number, are optional. When optional parameters are not specified, and the Err object has not been cleared, old values may appear. The best practice is to use Err.Clear after error handling, and to inspect the Err object before using Err.Raise (in case an error has occurred in the meantime). When raising custom error numbers, the vbObjectErr constant should be added.

The HelpFile and HelpContext parameters are used with the traditional .hlp help, and not with the HTML help systems.

Raising errors is a popular technique to stop the execution of a procedure, and handle it via some error handling function. You may raise errors when data is invalid, and when you want to pass an error up the call stack. This is a popular technique when you want to change one error into another, so that it can be handled properly.

Syntax

```
Err.Raise (number, source, description, helpfile, helpcontext)
```

Name	Subtype	Description
Err	Err Object	This is always the Err object
number	Long	This identifies the nature of the error. All VBScript (predefined and user-defined) error numbers are in the range 0–65535.
source	String	This identifies the name of the object or application that generates the error. When setting this property for Windows Script Components, use the ProgID form. If nothing is specified, the current ID of the project is used; often, it just defaults to 'Microsoft VBScript'

Name	Subtype	Description
description	`String`	This is the description of the error. If unspecified, the value in *number* is examined. If it can be mapped to a VBScript runtime error code, a string provided by VBScript is used as the description. If there is no VBScript error corresponding to *number*, a generic error message is used.
helpfile	`String`	This is the fully qualified path to a customized help file in which help on this error can be found. If unspecified, VBScript uses the fully qualified drive, path, and file name of the VBScript help file.
helpcontext	`Integer`	This is the context ID identifying a topic within *helpfile* that provides help for the error. If omitted, the VBScript help file context ID for the error corresponding to the number property is used, if it exists.

Example Usage

```
Dim strMsg
On Error Resume Next
Err.Raise vbObjectError + 1, "prjProject.clsClass", "Custom Error",
"c:\helpfile.hlp", 1
If Err.Number <> 0 Then
   strMsg = "Error Number: " & CStr(Err.Number) & vbCrLf
   strMsg = strMsg & "Description: " & Err.Description & vbCrLf
   strMsg = strMsg & "Source: " & Err.Source
   If Err.HelpFile <> "" Then
      strMsg = strMsg & vbCrLf & "Press Help to see the help file"
      MsgBox strMsg, , "Error: " & Err.Description, Err.Helpfile,
Err.HelpContext
   End If
   MsgBox strMsg     ' No Help file available here
   Err.Clear
End If
```

This example shows a common way of raising an error in Windows Script Host, where the help file is readily available.

vbObjectError Constant

This is a built-in constant that can be used in conjunction with programmer-defined errors and `Err.Raise`. It does not have to be declared or initialized; its decimal value is –2147221504 (or –0x8004000 in hexadecimal). Whereas previous examples have shown how to use the `vbObjectError` constant with the `Err.Raise` method, the example following shows a skeleton of a centralized error handler that combines `Select Case` with custom errors.

Example Usage

```
If Err.Number <> 0 Then              ' this should call separate subs
   Select Case Err.Number
     Case vbObjectError + 1
     ' call sub handling error 1
     Case vbObjectError + 3
     ' call sub handling error 3
     Case Else
     ' call reporting sub to display errors
   End Select
End If
```

On Error Resume Next

Syntax

```
On Error Resume Next
```

This statement enables error handling within the scope of a script or a procedure. Without the On Error Resume Next statement, the default runtime error handler displays the error and stops the execution of the script.

On Error Resume Next continues the execution of the script on the next line following the error. The error handling routine has to exist within the same scope as this statement. The statement becomes inactive with a call to another procedure or when an On Error Goto 0 statement is used. Please see the discussion below regarding the scope of this statement.

> When Internet Explorer's advanced option **Disable Script Debugging** is not selected and the Script Debugger is installed on the same system, On Error Resume Next does not go into effect; instead, the browser automatically goes into the 'debug' mode. Thus, when testing the effectiveness of your error handler through Internet Explorer, make sure that this option is selected.

On Error Goto 0

Syntax

```
On Error Goto 0
```

The On Error Goto 0 statement disables the error handling that was enabled by On Error Resume Next. This statement is especially useful in the testing stage, when there is a need to identify certain errors and yet handle others. On Error Goto 0 can be placed immediately after the error handling procedure is called. Like On Error Resume Next, this statement is also scope dependent.

Scope of On Error Statement and Differences Between VBScript's and VB's (or VBA's) Error Handling

It is important to understand the scope of the On Error statement; otherwise, your error handling procedures may never execute. VBScript – unlike its parent language – does not support labels, and it does not support the VB On Error Goto label. Thus, VBScript provides support only for in-line error handlers that can cause understandable grief. Basically, in order to mimic a block of code in VB that would respond to an On Error Goto label statement you might be inclined to use several If Err Then statements in order to check for an error with each single line of execution. However, with a little bit of programming, this can easily be achieved by enabling an error handler around a given procedure. Should one of the lines in the procedure fail, the error can be thrown up the calling stack. Of course, there is no Resume statement, which complicates some of the scripting. This can only be circumvented by trying to correct the problem that generated the error, and attempting to call the procedure again.

Before we look at some error handling techniques, let's examine the scope of error handling. The script below illustrates an important concept behind the scope of the error-enabling and error-disabling statements, as well as showing the differences in scope, and the importance in clearing of errors:

```
Sub TestError()
  On Error Resume Next
  Err.Raise 6               ' Execution will continue
  MsgBox ("TestError: Error # " & CStr(Err.Number) & " " & Err.Description)
  Err.Clear
End Sub

Sub TestError2()
  Err.Raise 6               ' Execution stops, moves up in scope
  MsgBox ("TestError2: This will never Show Up")
End Sub

' Main body of the script
' TestError() has local Error Handler no need for global Handler
On Error Resume Next
Call TestError()
If Err.Number <> 0 Then
  MsgBox ("Global: Error # " & CStr(Err.Number) & " " & Err.Description)
  Err Clear
Else
  MsgBox ("Global: No Error, It was handled locally and cleared")
End If

' TestError2 has no local error handler
Call TestError2()
If Err.Number <> 0 Then
  MsgBox ("Global: Error # " & CStr(Err.Number) & " " & Err.Description)
  Err.Clear
End If
' Global script Error handling is turned off, cause crash
On Error goto 0
Call TestError2()
```

Upon execution, the error is first handled locally, and after it is cleared, it is ignored. Next, the calls to the `TestError2()` subroutine are first handled by the global error handler and, after it is disabled on the second-last line, a runtime error appears.

Now, to consider the importance of clearing errors and the scope of On Error Resume Next, we make two adjustments, commenting out certain code:

```
Sub TestError()
  On Error Resume Next
  Err.Raise 6                  ' Execution will continue
  MsgBox ("TestError: Error # " & CStr(Err.Number) & " " & Err.Description)
  REM Err.Clear
End Sub

Sub TestError2()
  Err.Raise 6                  ' Execution stops, moves up in scope
  MsgBox ("TestError2: This will never Show Up")
End Sub

' Main body of the script
' TestError() has local Error Handler no need for global Handler
REM On Error Resume Next
```

With these changes, an error message is still displayed after the call to `TestError()`, but the first call to the `TestError2()` subprocedure results in an invocation of the default error handler, and stoppage of the script immediately after the call, i.e. the On Error Resume Next statement was local in scope to the `TestError()` subprocedure.

The code below illustrates the possibility of mimicking the On Error Goto *label* statement by encompassing a block of code in a procedure, rather than trapping errors inline, as in VB. Here the scripter can invoke an error handler at a higher level rather than at the level where the error occurred (in this case, a procedure without a local error handler):

```
Option Explicit
Dim intZero, intNonZero, intResult
intZero = 0
intNonZero = 1

Sub TestError()
  ' Statements that will execute
  MsgBox ("This will always execute")
  ' now cause an error
  intResult = intNonZero / intZero         ' causes error 11
  ' Statements that will not execute if error occurs
  MsgBox ("Finally executed, Result = " & CStr(intResult) )
End Sub

' simulate On Error Goto Label by having a block of code in a sub
On Error Resume Next
Call TestError()
If Err.Number = 11 Then
  MsgBox "Division By Zero - may still continue" & vbCrLf & Err.Description
  Err.Clear
  intZero = 1
  TestError()
End If
On Error Goto 0                              'kill other error handling
```

Error Handling in IE

Besides VBScript itself, some web authors might also turn to DHTML events. IE's DHTML object model supports a variety of events, including events occurring as a result of an error. Essentially, this allows for a different degree of control when authoring scripts for IE. Thanks to the GetRef() function, which returns a pointer to a function, it is now possible to bind VBScript procedures to an event. For instance, the line below will execute the RunMySub procedure in response to the Window.Onload event in IE:

```
Set Window.Onload = GetRef("RunMySub")
```

Similarly, you can write procedures that will execute when the OnError event is fired, either for an element, or for the window object.

There are two additional techniques for error handling in IE:

❑ centralized, through the use of the window.onerror event

❑ decentralized, through the use of the element.onerror event

The following code snippets illustrate the old and the new syntax for handling DHTML errors:

Old Syntax

```
Function element_onerror ( message, url, line)
```

element is the name of the element or window:

```
<SCRIPT language="VBScript">
Function window_onerror ( message, url, line )
    ' handle error here
    window_onerror = true
End Function
</SCRIPT>
```

New syntax

```
Set element.onerror = GetRef("functionName")
```

The new syntax allows us to bind functions to events, just like in JScript. Again, element is the name of the element or window, and functionName is an actual function or a sub:

```
<SCRIPT language=VBScript>
Function onErrorHandler ( message, url, line )
    ' handle error here
    onErrorHandler = True
End Function
set window.onerror = GetRef("onErrorHandler")
</SCRIPT>
```

here are a few important differences between the VBScript's error handling and the use of the `onerror` event in IE. Listed below is a summary of the `onerror` IE handlers:

- ❑ Execution does not resume on the next line. The script may resume with the next user action or handled event – e.g. user 'clicks' on another element. If you want greater error-handling control in individual procedures executed in the browser, the `On Error Resume Next` statement should be used.

- ❑ All errors pertaining to the element (or window) are handled by the event unless handled via VBScript's `On Error Resume Next` technique.

- ❑ Errors can be passed to a higher level element via event bubbling. Please refer to Chapter 12 to learn more about high powered scripting in IE.

- ❑ Custom errors cannot be created; there is no `Err.Raise` counterpart in the DHTML object model.

Considering the broader appeal of JScript (or ECMA Script and JavaScript), the majority of DHTML scripting and error handling is not done in VBScript (VBScript is not supported in Mac and Windows CE versions of IE).

The Scripting Runtime Library Objects Reference

The default scripting languages installed with Windows Office 2000 and ASP 3.0 provide a scripting runtime library in the file `scrrun.dll`, which implements a series of objects that can be used in ASP on the server and in client-side code running on the client:

❑ The **Dictionary** object provides a useful storage object that we can use to store values, accessed and referenced by their name rather than by index as would be the case in a normal array – it's ideal for storing the name/value pairs that we retrieve from the ASP `Request` object, for example.

❑ The **FileSystemObject** object provides us with access to the underlying file system on the server (or on the client in IE5 when used in conjunction with a special type of page named an **HTML Application** or **HTA**) – we can use the **FileSystemObject** object to iterate through the machine's local and networked drives, folders and files.

❑ The **TextStream** object provides access to files stored on disk, and is used in conjunction with the **FileSystemObject** object – it can read from or write to text (sequential) files.

The Scripting.Dictionary Object

The `Dictionary` object provides a useful storage object that we can use to store values, accessed and referenced by their name rather than by index as would be the case in a normal array. The properties and methods exposed by the `Dictionary` object are:

Property	Description
CompareMode	Sets or returns the string comparison mode for the keys. Values are `vbBinaryCompare` (0) to perform a binary comparison and `vbTextCompare` (1) to perform a textual comparison.

Property	Description
Count	Returns the number of key/item pairs in the `Dictionary` (read only).
Item(*key*)	Sets or returns the value of the item for the specified key.
Key(*key*)	Sets or returns the value of a key.

Method	Description
Add(*key*, *item*)	Adds the key/item pair to the `Dictionary`. You can also add items with a simple assignment, and in fact, you must use this syntax in order to store object references in a dictionary: `Set objDict("keyname") = objMyObject`
Exists(*key*)	Returns true if the specified key exists or false if not.
Items()	Returns an array containing all the items in a `Dictionary` object.
Keys()	Returns an array containing all the keys in a `Dictionary` object.
Remove(*key*)	Removes a single key/item pair specified by *key*.
RemoveAll()	Removes all the key/item pairs.

> **An error will occur if we try to add a key/item pair when that key already exists, remove a key/item pair that doesn't exist, or change the `CompareMode` of a `Dictionary` object that already contains data.**

The Scripting.FileSystemObject Object

The `FileSystemObject` object provides us with access to the underlying file system on the server (or on the client in IE5 when used in conjunction with a special type of page named an **HTML Application** or **HTA**). The `FileSystemObject` object exposes a series of properties and methods of its own, some of which return other objects that are specific to objects within the file system. These subsidiary objects are:

❑   the **Drive** object provides access to all the drives available on the machine

❑   the **Folder** object provides access to the folders on a drive

❑   the **File** object provides access to the files within each folder

While these three objects form a neat hierarchy, the FileSystemObject object also provides methods that can bridge the hierarchy by creating instances of the subsidiary objects directly. The diagram opposite shows the way that you can navigate the file system of the machine using the various objects:

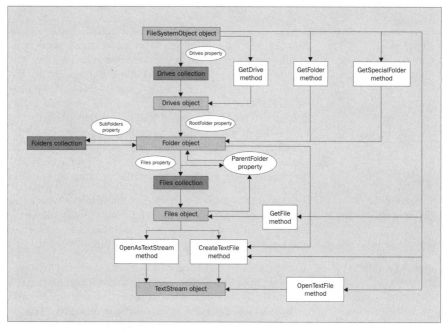

The FileSystemObject Object

The `FileSystemObject` object provides overall access to the underlying file system and is used as a starting point when navigating the file system. The properties and methods exposed by the `FileSystemObject` are:

Property	Description
Drives	Returns a collection of `Drive` objects that are available from the local machine. This includes network drives that are mapped from this machine.

Method	Description
BuildPath (*path*, *name*)	Adds the file or folder specified in *name* to the existing *path*, adding a path separator character ('\') if required. Doesn't check for valid or existing path.
CopyFile (source, destination, overwrite)	Copies the file or files specified in *source* (wildcards can be included) to the folder specified in *destination*. If *source* contains wildcards or *destination* ends with a path separator character ('\') then *destination* is assumed to be a folder; otherwise, it is assumed to be a full path and name for the new file. Note that leaving off the last '\' when the source doesn't contain wildcards throws a "Permission denied" error since the name (assumed to be a filename without an extension) exists as a folder name. An error will occur if the *destination* file already exists and the optional *overwrite* parameter is set to false. The default for *overwrite* is true.

Method	Description
CopyFolder (*source*, *destination* [, *overwrite*])	Copies the folder or folders specified in *source* (wildcards can be included) to the folder specified in *destination*, including all the files contained in the *source* folder(s). If *source* contains wildcards or *destination* ends with a path separator character ('\') then *destination* is assumed to be a folder into which the copied folder(s) will be placed; otherwise, it is assumed to be a full path and name for a new folder to be created. An error will occur if the *destination* folder already exists and the optional *overwrite* parameter is set to false. The default for *overwrite* is true.
CreateFolder (*foldername*)	Creates and returns a reference to a new folder which has the path and name specified in *foldername*. Only the last folder in the path is created – all parent folders must exist. An error occurs if the specified folder already exists.
CreateTextFile (*filename*, *overwrite*, *unicode*)	Creates a new text file on disk with the specified *filename* and returns a `TextStream` object that refers to it. If the optional *overwrite* parameter is set to true any existing file with the same path and name will be overwritten. The default for *overwrite* is false. If the optional *unicode* parameter is set to true, the content of the file will be stored as Unicode text. The default for *unicode* is false for an ASCII file.
DeleteFile (*filespec* [, *force*])	Deletes the file or files specified in *filespec* (wildcards can be included). If the optional *force* parameter is set to true the file(s) will be deleted even if the read-only attribute is set. The default for *force* is false.
DeleteFolder (*folderspec* [, *force*])	Deletes the folder or folders specified in *folderspec* (wildcards can be included in the final component of the path) together with all their contents. If the optional *force* parameter is set to true, the folders will be deleted even if their, or any contained files', read-only attribute is set. The default for *force* is false.
DriveExists (*drivespec*)	Returns true if the drive specified in *drivespec* exists, or false if not. The *drivespec* parameter can be a drive letter as a string or a full absolute path for a folder or file.
FileExists (*filespec*)	Returns true if the file specified in *filespec* exists, or false if not. The *filespec* parameter can contain an absolute or relative path for the file, or just the file name to look in the current folder.

Method	Description
FolderExists (*folderspec*)	Returns true if the folder specified in *folderspec* exists, or false if not. The *folderspec* parameter can contain an absolute or relative path for the folder, or just the folder name to look in the current folder.
GetAbsolutePathName (*pathspec*)	Takes a *path* that unambiguously identifies a folder and, taking into account the current folder's path, returns a full unambigous path specification for the *pathspec* folder. For example, if the current folder is "c:\docs\sales\" and *pathspec* is "jan" the returned value is "c:\docs\sales\jan". Wildcards and the ".", ".." and "\\" path operators are accepted.
GetBaseName (*filespec*)	Returns just the name of a file or folder specified in *filespec*, i.e. with the path and file extension removed.
GetDrive (*drivespec*)	Returns a `Drive` object corresponding to the drive specified in *drivespec*. The format for *drivespec* can include the colon, path separator or be a network share, i.e. "c", "c:", "c:\" or "\\machine\sharename".
GetDriveName (*drivespec*)	Returns the name of the drive specified in *drivespec* as a string. The *drivespec* parameter must be an absolute path to a file or folder, or just the drive letter such as "c:" or just "c".
GetExtensionName (*filespec*)	Returns just the extension of a file or folder specified in *filespec*, i.e. with the path and file name removed.
GetFile (*filespec*)	Returns a `File` object corresponding to the file specified in *filespec*. This can be a relative or absolute path to the required file.
GetFileName (*pathspec*)	Returns the name part (i.e. without the path or file extension) of the path and filename specified in *pathspec*, or the last folder name of there is no file name. Does not check for existence of the file or folder.
GetFileVersion(*filespec*)	Returns the version information from a file in Windows 2000 and Windows Script Host 2.0.
GetFolder (*folderspec*)	Returns a `Folder` object corresponding to the folder specified in *folderspec*. This can be a relative or absolute path to the required folder.
GetParentFolderName (*pathspec*)	Returns the name of the parent folder of the file or folder specified in *pathspec*. Does not check for existence of the folder.

Method	Description
GetSpecialFolder (*folderspec*)	Returns a `Folder` object corresponding to one of the special Windows folders. The permissible values for *folderspec* are `WindowsFolder` (0), `SystemFolder` (1) and `TemporaryFolder` (2).
GetTempName()	Returns a randomly generated file name that can be used for performing operations that require a temporary file or folder.
MoveFile source, destination	Moves the file or files specified in *source* to the folder specified in *destination*. Wildcards can be included in *source* but not in *destination*. If *source* contains wildcards or *destination* ends with a path separator character ('\') then *destination* is assumed to be a folder; otherwise, it is assumed to be a full path and name for the new file. Note that leaving off the last '\' when the source doesn't contain wildcards throws a "Permission denied" error since the name (assumed to be a filename without an extension) exists as a folder name. An error will occur if the *destination* file already exists.
MoveFolder source, destination	Moves the folder or folders specified in *source* to the folder specified in *destination*. Wildcards can be included in *source* but not in *destination*. If *source* contains wildcards or *destination* ends with a path separator character ('\') then *destination* is assumed to be the folder in which to place the moved folders; otherwise, it is assumed to be a full path and name for a new folder. An error will occur if the *destination* folder already exists.
OpenTextFile (filename, iomode, create, format)	Creates a file named *filename*, or opens an existing file named *filename*, and returns a `TextStream` object that refers to it. The *filename* parameter can contain an absolute or relative path. The *iomode* parameter specifies the type of access required. The permissible values are `ForReading` (1), the default), `ForWriting` (2), and `ForAppending` (8). If the *create* parameter is set to true when writing or appending to a file that does not exist, a new file will be created. The default for *create* is false. The *format* parameter specifies the format of the data to be read from or written to the file. Permissible values are `TristateFalse` (0), the default) to open it as ASCII, `TristateTrue` (-1) to open it as Unicode, and `TristateUseDefault` (-2) to open it using the system default format.

The Drive Object

The `Drive` object provides access to all the drives available on the machine. The properties (note that it has no methods) exposed by the `Drive` object are:

Property	Description
AvailableSpace	Returns the amount of space in bytes available to this user on the drive, taking into account quotas and/or other restrictions.
DriveLetter	Returns the drive letter of the drive.
DriveType	Returns the type of the drive. The values are: `Unknown` (0), `Removable` (1), `Fixed` (2), `Network` (3), `CDRom` (4), and `RamDisk` (5). However, note that the current version of `scrrun.dll` does not include the pre-defined constant for `Network`, so you must use the decimal value 3 instead.
FileSystem	Returns the type of file system for the drive. The values include `"FAT"`, `"NTFS"` and `"CDFS"`.
FreeSpace	Returns the actual amount of free space in bytes available on the drive.
IsReady	Returns a `Boolean` value indicating if drive is ready (true) or not (false).
Path	Returns the path for the drive as a drive letter and colon, i.e. `"C:"`.
RootFolder	Returns a `Folder` object representing the root folder of the drive.
SerialNumber	Returns a decimal serial number used to uniquely identify a disk volume.
ShareName	Returns the network share name for the drive if it is a networked drive.
TotalSize	Returns the total size in bytes of the drive.
VolumeName	Sets or returns the volume name of the drive if it is a local drive.

The Folder Object

The `Folder` object provides access to the folders on a drive. The properties and methods exposed by the `Folder` object are:

Property	Description
Attributes	Returns the attributes of the folder. Can be a combination of any of the values: `Normal` (0), `ReadOnly` (1), `Hidden` (2), `System` (4), `Volume` (name) (8), `Directory` (folder) (16), `Archive` (32), `Alias` (64) and `Compressed` (2048). Can also be used to set the ReadOnly, Hidden, System and Archive attributes.

Property	Description
DateCreated	Returns the date and time that the folder was created where available.
DateLastAccessed	Returns the date and time that the folder was last accessed.
DateLastModified	Returns the date and time that the folder was last modified.
Drive	Returns the drive letter of the drive on which the folder resides.
Files	Returns a `Files` collection containing `File` objects representing all the files within this folder.
IsRootFolder	Returns a Boolean value indicating if the folder is the root folder of the current drive.
Name	Sets or returns the name of the folder.
ParentFolder	Returns the `Folder` object for the parent folder of this folder.
Path	Returns the absolute path of the folder using long file names where appropriate.
ShortName	Returns the DOS-style 8.3 version of the folder name.
ShortPath	Returns the DOS-style 8.3 version of the absolute path of this folder.
Size	Returns the total combined size of all files and subfolders contained in the folder.
SubFolders	Returns a `Folders` collection consisting of all folders contained in the folder, including hidden and system folders.
Type	Returns a string that is a description of the folder type (such as `"Recycle Bin"`) if available.

Method	Description
Copy *(destination , overwrite)*	Copies this folder and all its contents to the folder specified in *destination,* including all the files contained in this folder. If *destination* ends with a path separator character ('\') then *destination* is assumed to be a folder into which the copied folder will be placed; otherwise, it is assumed to be a full path and name for a new folder to be created. An error will occur if the *destination* folder already exists and the optional *overwrite* parameter is set to false. The default for *overwrite* is true.

Method	Description
Delete (*force*)	Deletes this folder and all its contents. If the optional *force* parameter is set to true the folder will be deleted even if the read-only attribute is set on it or on any contained files. The default for *force* is false.
Move (*destination*)	Moves this folder and all its contents to the folder specified in *destination*. If *destination* ends with a path separator character ('\') then *destination* is assumed to be the folder in which to place the moved folder; otherwise, it is assumed to be a full path and name for a new folder. An error will occur if the *destination* folder already exists.
CreateTextFile (*filename*, *overwrite*, *unicode*)	Creates a new text file within this folder with the specified *filename* and returns a `TextStream` object that refers to it. If the optional *overwrite* parameter is set to true any existing file with the same name will be overwritten. The default for *overwrite* is false. If the optional *unicode* parameter is set to true, the content of the file will be stored as Unicoded text. The default for *unicode* is false.

The File Object

The `File` object provides access to the files within each folder. The properties and methods exposed by the `File` object are:

Property	Description
Attributes	Sets or returns the attributes of the file. Can be a combination of any of the values: `Normal` (0), `ReadOnly` (1), `Hidden` (2), `System` (4), `Volume` (name) (8), `Directory` (folder) (16), `Archive` (32), `Alias` (64) and `Compressed` (2048). Can also be used to set the `ReadOnly`, `Hidden`, `System` and `Archive` attributes.
DateCreated	Returns the date and time that the file was created where available.
DateLastAccessed	Returns the date and time that the file was last accessed.
DateLastModified	Returns the date and time that the file was last modified.
Drive	Returns the drive letter of the drive on which the file resides.
Name	Sets or returns the name of the file.
ParentFolder	Returns the `Folder` object for the parent folder of this file.
Path	Returns the absolute path of the file using long file names where appropriate.
ShortName	Returns the DOS-style 8.3 version of the file name.

Property	Description
ShortPath	Returns the DOS-style 8.3 version of the absolute path of this file.
Size	Returns the size of the file in bytes
Type	Returns a string that is a description of the file type (such as `"Text Document"` for a `.txt` file) if available.

Method	Description
Copy (destination, overwrite)	Copies this file to the folder specified in *destination*. If *destination* ends with a path separator character ('\') then *destination* is assumed to be a folder into which the copied file will be placed; otherwise, it is assumed to be a full path and name for a new file to be created. Note that leaving off the last '\' when the source doesn't contain wildcards throws a "Permission denied" error since the name (assumed to be a filename without an extension) exists as a folder name. An error will occur if the *destination* file already exists and the optional *overwrite* parameter is set to false. The default for *overwrite* is true.
Delete (*force*)	Deletes this file. If the optional *force* parameter is set to true the file will be deleted even if the read-only attribute is set. The default for *force* is false.
Move (destination)	Moves this file to the folder specified in *destination*. If *destination* ends with a path separator character ('\') then *destination* is assumed to be the folder in which to place the moved file; otherwise, it is assumed to be a full path and name for a new file. An error will occur if the *destination* file already exists.
OpenAsTextStream (*iomode, format*)	Opens a specified file and returns a `TextStream` object that can be used to read from, write to, or append to the file. The *iomode* parameter specifies the type of access required. The permissible values are `ForReading` (1, the default), `ForWriting` (2), and `ForAppending` (8). If the *create* parameter is set to true when writing or appending to a file that does not exist, a new file will be created. The default for *create* is false. The *format* parameter specifies the format of the data to be read from or written to the file. Permissible values are `TristateFalse` (0, the default) to open it as ASCII, `TristateTrue` (-1) to open it as Unicode, and `TristateUseDefault` (-2) to open it using the system default format.

The Scripting.TextStream Object

The `TextStream` object provides access to files stored on disk, and is used in conjunction with the `FileSystemObject` object. The properties and methods exposed by the `TextStream` object are:

Property	Description
AtEndOfLine	Returns true if the file pointer is at the end of a line in the file.
AtEndOfStream	Returns true if the file pointer is at the end of the file.
Column	Returns the column number of the current character in the file starting from 1.
Line	Returns the current line number in the file starting from 1.

Note that the `AtEndOfLine` and `AtEndOfStream` properties are only available for a file that is opened with the *iomode* parameter set with the value `ForReading`. Referring to them otherwise causes an error to occur.

Method	Description
Close()	Closes an open file.
Read(numchars)	Reads *numchars* characters from the file.
ReadAll()	Reads the entire file as a single string.
ReadLine()	Reads a line from the file as a string.
Skip(numchars)	Skips and discards *numchars* characters when reading from the file.
SkipLine()	Skips and discards the next line when reading from the file.
Write(*string*)	Writes *string* to the file.
WriteLine(*string*)	Writes *string* (optional) and a newline character to the file.
WriteBlankLines(*n*)	Writes *n* newline characters to the file.

Windows Script Host 2.0

This appendix contains a summary of the objects that make up the Windows Script Host object model and the XML-based tags used for creating Windows Script (.WSF) files.

Windows Script Host Object Model Reference

The Windows Script Host object model consists of nine objects:

The **WScript** object contains properties and methods that allow developers to access name and path information for the script file being executed, determine which version of the Microsoft Scripting engines is currently installed, work with external objects, provide user interaction and delay or terminate script execution. In addition, this object provides access to the standard input, output and error streams.

The **WshArguments** object provides access to command-line arguments passed to the WSH scripts, and is used to implement drag-and-drop functionality.

The **WshShell** object provides a convenient way to gain access to system environment variables, create shortcuts, access Windows special folders such as the Desktop, and add or remove entries from the registry. In addition, this object offers more customized user interaction – through its Popup method – than offered by the WScript object itself.

The **WshNetwork** object provides connectivity to networked printer and file share resources, as well as information pertaining to the user currently logged on to the computer.

The **WshShortcut** object and **WshUrlShortcut** objects allow for the creation of redirection links to resources on the local file system, network file shares and Web pages on the Internet or local Intranet.

The **WshCollection** object is the base representation for all collections returned by objects, properties or methods internal to Windows Script Host, exposing properties which make enumeration of the collection possible, as well as referencing individual items within the collection.

The **WshEnvironment** object accesses system specifics including execution path and root directory for Windows files. Windows NT and Windows 2000 provide access to far more information from this object, including operating system version, processor type and number of processors. Under Windows NT and Windows 2000, this defaults to returning system variables. With Windows 95/98, only process variables are available.

The **WshSpecialFolders** object provides access to Windows shell folders, including the Start menu, Favorites folder, and the Windows Desktop.

The WScript object

Entry point for accessing the complete WSH object model; all other WSH objects are eventually accessed through this one in some form.

WScript properties

Property	Description
Application	Exposes the WScript object's `IDispatch` interface, which provides programmatic access to an application's internal objects, properties and methods. Read-only. Returns Object.
Arguments	Returns a collection of all arguments passed to the current script either on the command line or in the shortcut used to access the file. Read-only.
BuildVersion	Returns specific build version of Windows Script Host, as Long. Read-only.
FullName	Returns a String containing the complete path to the file being executed. Read-only.
Interactive	Sets or returns a Boolean containing the current interactivity state. False corresponds to the console-mode switch `//B`, and True corresponds to switch `//I`. Read/Write.
Name	Returns a String containing the friendly name of the `WScript` object. Read-only.
Path	Returns a String containing the parent directory of the active WSH environment (`cscript.exe` or `wscript.exe`). Read-only.

Property	Description
ScriptFullName	Returns a String containing the complete path to the script currently executing. Read-only.
ScriptName	Returns a String containing the file name of the script currently executing. Read-only.
StdErr	Provides access to script's error output stream. Only available to scripts being executed from within the command-line host environment. Write-only. Implemented as a TextStream object from the Scripting Runtime library.
StdIn	Provides access to script's input stream. Only available to scripts being executed from within the command-line host environment. Read-only. Implemented as a TextStream object from the Scripting Runtime library.
StdOut	Provides access to script's output stream. Only available to scripts being executed from within the command-line host environment. Write-only. Implemented as a TextStream object from the Scripting Runtime library.
Timeout	Returns a Long containing the current timeout value in seconds. Corresponds to console-mode switch //T: *nn*. Read/Write.
Version	Returns a string containing the version number of Windows Script Host.

WScript methods

Method	Description
Sub **ConnectObject** (objName As Object, strPrefix As String)	Used to hook into the event model of an object previously created via the CreateObject method or <object> tag. objName refers to object to connect, strPrefix is string used for naming event handlers in script.
Function **CreateObject** (strProgID As String, [strPrefix As String]) As Object	Creates an instance of an Automation object from a passed strProgID and provides your script with an optional hook strPrefix which allows you to access properties and call methods of the created object.

Table Continued on Following Page

Method	Description
Sub **DisconnectObject** (objName As Object)	Disconnects event source object objName from your script. Inverse of **ConnectObject**. The object itself is not affected.
Sub **Echo** (arg1 [,…argN] As Variant)	Provides host-dependent user feedback. If cscript.exe is host, arguments are displayed on the command line. If wscript.exe is host, arguments are displayed in a Windows popup dialog. Comma-separated arguments are displayed as a string with spaces separating the arguments.
Function **GetObject** (strPath As String, [strProgID As String], [strPrefix As String]) As Object	Similar to CreateObject. Creates an instance of an Automation object from a file strPath and optional programID strProgID. This gives you access to an object that already exists somewhere on your computer - like an already running instance of a program which has registered in the Running Objects Table, or an application with an unknown automation interface. Can be used with optional strPrefix to sink events from object to script.
Sub **Quit** ([nCode As Long])	Terminates host execution and returns argument as error code. In other words, it kills the cscript or wscript instance. The optional argument nCode allows you to set an error code for the process' exit. If not included, the return value is 0.
Sub **Sleep** (nDelay As Long)	Suspends execution of active script for time specified (in milliseconds). After nDelay has passed, control is returned to the script.

WshArguments object

Provides access to command-line arguments and basic drag-and-drop functionality (files/folders dropped onto the script, or passed to the file from the Send To menu. Advanced drag-and-drop – such as the capability to drop fragments of a Word document onto a WSH script – is not implemented.

Accessing the WshArguments object

Accessed via the Arguments property of the WScript object.

```
Set WshArguments = WScript.CreateObject("WScript.Arguments")
```

WshArguments properties

Exposes the `Count` and `length` properties contained in the `WshCollection` object. See following section on `WshCollection` for details.

WshArguments methods

Exposes the `Item` method of the `WshCollection` object. See following section on `WshCollection` for details. `Item` is the default member of the `WshCollection` interface.

WshShell object

Provides access to shell functionality such as creating shortcuts, interacting with the registry, and executing arbitrary applications.

Accessing the WshShell object

Accessed via the `Shell` property of the `WScript` object.

```
Set WshShell = WScript.CreateObject("WScript.Shell")
```

WshShell Properties

Property	Description
Environment	Returns a `WshEnvironment` Object. Read-only.
SpecialFolders	Returns a `WshSpecialFolders` Object. Read-only.

WshShell Methods

Method	Description
Function **AppActivate** (strTitle) As Boolean	Activates an application window, based on passed `strTitle`, which corresponds to a full or partial window title.
Function **CreateShortcut** (strPath As String) As Object	Returns a `WshShortcut` or `WshUrlShortcut` object at location referred to by String `strPath`, depending on the extension of the created shortcut. Shortcuts created with the extension `.LNK` become `WshShortcut` objects. Those created with the extension `.URL` are `WshUrlShortcut` objects.

Table Continued on Following Page

Method	Description
Function **ExpandEnvironmentStrings** (strSrc As String) As String	Returns a String representing the expanded value of the requested environment string strSrc. Variables passed into the method are surrounded with the '%' character (e.g.: %windir%).
Function **LogEvent** (intType, strMessage As String, [strTarget As String]) As Boolean	Writes an event of type intType, containing text strMessage to the event log. In Windows NT, this is written to the NT Event log, defaulting to local system; strTarget can be used to determine to which system the event should be logged. In Windows 9x, this is written to the file WSH.log in the %windir% directory.
Function **Popup** (strText As String, [nDelay], [strTitle], [nType]) As Long	Shows a modal dialog window containing script-defined settings – message strText, optional title strTitle and display characteristics nType. Optional parameter nDelay sets delay before dialog should self-dismiss (defaults to 0, meaning remain until script times out)The return value from Popup is determined by the button that is clicked in the window.
Sub **RegDelete** (strName As String)	Removes key or value strName from the Windows registry. Note that Windows NT 4.0 and Windows 2000 do not allow the deletion of registry keys which contain subkeys, only keys which contain just values.
Function **RegRead** (strName As String) As Variant	Reads key or value strName from the Windows registry.
Sub **RegWrite** (strName As String, varValue, [varType])	Writes key or value strName to the Windows registry, with value varValue and optional data type varType.
Function **Run** (strCmd As String, [intWindowStyle], [bWait]) As Long	Executes an application or command-line statement strCmd in a new process, with optional window style intWindowStyle and optional Boolean bWait to indicate whether the calling script should wait for the return from execution.
Sub **SendKeys**(strKeys As String)	Programmatically sends keystroke sequences strKeys to an application as if the input were entered from a keyboard.

The WshNetwork Object

Used to connect to resources such as file servers and network printers.

Accessing the Wsh object

Access via the Network property of the WScript object.

```
Set WshNetwork = WScript.CreateObject("Wscript.Network")
```

WshNetwork Properties

Property	Description
ComputerName	Returns a String containing the computer name. Read-only.
UserDomain	Returns a String containing the user domain. Read-only.
UserName	Returns a String containing the username. Read-only.

WshNetwork Methods

Method	Description
Sub **AddPrinterConnection** (strLocalName As String, strRemoteName As String, [bUpdate], [strUserName], [strPassword])	Maps a network printer strRemoteName to a local port strLocalName. Optional bUpdate causes mapping to be stored in user profile; optional strUserName and strPassword allow mapping user network credentials of user other than currently logged on.
Sub AddWindowsPrinterConnection (strPrinterName As String, [strDriver As String], [strPort As String = "LPT1"])	Maps a network printer strPrinterName. Optional strPort defines which local resource should be mapped to network resource (defaults to "LPT1:"). strDriver contains a printer driver name; required for Windows 9x, ignored on Windows NT4/Windows2000.
Function **EnumNetworkDrives()** As IWshCollection_Class	Returns a standard WSH collection containing current network drive mappings.
Function **EnumPrinterConnections()** As IWshCollection_Class	Returns a standard WSH collection containing current network printer mappings.

Table Continued on Following Page

Method	Description
Sub **MapNetworkDrive** (strLocalName As String, strRemoteName As String, [bUpdate], [strUserName], [strPassword])	Maps a shared network resource strRemoteName to a local drive letter strLocalName. Optional bUpdate causes mapping to be stored in user profile; optional strUserName and strPassword allow mapping user network credentials of user other than currently logged on.
Sub **RemoveNetworkDrive** (strName As String, [bForce], [bUpdate])	Removes a network drive strName, whether mapped to a local drive letter or remotely connected. If set to True, optional bForce removes resource whether used or not. Optional bUpdate causes mapping to be stored in user profile.
Sub **RemovePrinterConnection** (strName As String, [bForce], [bUpdate])	Removes a networked printer connection strName, whether mapped to a local port or remotely connected. If set to True, optional bForce removes resource whether used or not. Optional bUpdate causes mapping to be stored in user profile.
Sub **SetDefaultPrinter** (strName As String)	Establishes printer connection strName as default printer.

The WshShortcut Object

The same method of the WshShell object is used for creating both WshShortcut and WshURLShortcut objects (or reading/modifying existing objects) – the primary difference being the file extension given to the actual shortcut file: A WshShortcut object is created when the extension is .lnk, and a WshURLShortcut object is created when the extension is .url.

Accessing the WshShortcut object

Access via the CreateShortcut method of the WshShell object.

```
Set WshShell = WScript.CreateObject("WScript.Shell")
Set WshShortcut = WshShell.CreateShortcut(strPath)
```

WshShortcut Properties

Property	Description
Arguments	Sets or retrieves a String containing the arguments passed to the WshShortcut object. Read/Write.
Description	Sets or retrieves descriptive test representing the WshShortcut object. Read/Write.
FullName	Returns a string containing the complete path to the WshShortcut object. Read-only.
Hotkey	Allows a keyboard shortcut to be created for the WshShortcut object. Hotkeys can only activate shortcuts which exist on the Windows desktop or the Start menu. Read/Write.
IconLocation	Assigns an icon to the WshShortcut object by passing a String containing the path to the icon. Can also be used to retrieve the icon path. Read/Write.
TargetPath	Assigns/retrieves path of executable , or document with a registered file association to which the WshShortcut object.is attached. Read/Write.
WindowStyle	Assigns/retrieves a Long containing window style of the WshShortcut object. Read/Write.
WorkingDirectory	Sets/retrieves a String containing active directory path for the WshShortcut object. Read/Write.

WshShortcut Methods

Method	Description
Sub **Save**()	Saves shortcut object to location specified by argument to CreateShortcut. This method is required to complete creation of a new shortcut.

The WshUrlShortcut Object

This object provides a means to create a special shortcut type: a reference to a Web page on the Internet or a company Intranet.

Accessing the WshUrlShortcut object

Access via the CreateShortcut method of the WshShell object.

```
Set WshShell = WScript.Createobject("WScript.Shell")
Set WshShortcut = WshShell.CreateShortcut(strPath)
```

WshUrlShortcut Properties

Property	Description
FullName	Returns a read-only String containing the complete path to the WshUrlShortcut object.
TargetPath	Assigns/retrieves a String containing path to HTML page (locally or on a corporate Intranet or the Intenet) with which the WshUrlShortcut object is associated.

WshUrlShortcut Methods

Method	Description
Sub **Save()**	Saves shortcut object to location specified by argument to CreateShortcut. This method is required to complete creation of a new shortcut.

The WshCollection Object

This object is the base representation for all collections returned by objects, properties or methods internal to Windows Script Host.

Accessing the WshCollection object

There are five ways to access collections in WSH:

- ❑ the Arguments property of WScript,

  (Note: this is not technically implemented as a WshCollection object – it implements the IArguments_Class interface, whereas WshCollection objects implement the IWshCollection_Class interface. However, it is noted here, as the properties and method of these two interfaces are identical.)

- ❑ the EnumNetworkDrives method of WshNetwork,

- ❑ the EnumPrinterConnections method of WshNetwork,

  (Note: these two collections, while implemented as WshCollection objects, have a different internal structure. See Chapter 10 for more details.)

- ❑ the SpecialFolders property of WshShell,

- ❑ the WshEnvironment object.

```
' Init vars
Set WshShell = WScript.CreateObject("WScript.Shell")
Set WshNetwork = WScript.CreateObject("WScript.Network")
Set collArgs = WScript.Arguments
Set collDrives = WshNetwork.EnumNetworkDrives
Set collPrinters = WshNetwork.EnumPrinterConnections
Set collFolders = WshShell.SpecialFolders
Set collEnvVars = WshShell.Environment
```

WshCollection Properties

Property	Description
Item	Retrieves an item from a collection, by index (as Long). This is the default property for all collections exposed as part of the Windows Script Host object model.
Length	Returns the number of items in the collection as Long. Return value is identical to return value from Count. Implemented for JScript compatibility.
Count	Returns the number of items in the collection as Long.

WshCollection Methods

None.

The WshEnvironment Object

When a developer needs to access system specifics such as the operating system version or information pertaining to processor type, the place to look is within the system's environment variables.

Accessing the WshEnvironment object

Use the Environment property of the WshShell object.

```
Set WshShell = WScript.CreateObject("WScript.Shell")
Set WshEnvironment = WshShell.Environment
```

WshEnvironment Properties

Exposes all properties contained in the WshCollection object.

WshEnvironment Methods

Method	Description
Sub **Remove** (strName As String)	Deletes environment variable strName.

The WshSpecialFolders Object

This object returns strings containing the pathnames to Windows shell folders, including the Start menu, Favorites folder, and the Windows Desktop. The actual file location of Windows special folders is dependent on the operating system and location of the default Windows installation directory, so they may not be in the same place on one computer that they are on another. The WshSpecialFolders collection helps developers get around this, making it very easy to access these folders.

Accessing the WshSpecialFolders object

Use the `SpecialFolders` property of `WshShell`.

```
Set WshShell = WScript.CreateObject("WScript.Shell")
Set WshSpecialFolders = WshShell.SpecialFolders
```

WshSpecialFolders Properties

Exposes all properties contained in the `WshCollection` object.

WshSpecialFolders Methods

None.

Windows Script File Element Reference

There are nine XML-based elements supported by the Windows Script (.WSF) file format, as follows.

`<?xml?>`
Standard XML declaration - forces WSH to parse the file according to XML syntax rules, enforcing case-sensitivity. This is an empty element. This element is optional, and must be the first tag to appear when used. When used, all `<script>` blocks should have their contents wrapped inside a CDATA declaration, as described along with the `<script>` entry.

`<?job?>`
This element is a processing instruction that specifies error-handling attributes. This is an empty element, and should appear prior to the opening `<job>` tag.

`<comment>`
Allows developers to include comment blocks within script file. Container element. Optional. Child of either `<package>` or `<job>`.

`<package>`
Provides a way for developers to include multiple jobs within a single file. Container element. Optional if only one `<job>` is defined; required if multiple `<job>`s are defined.

`<job>`
Allows for definition of multiple jobs within a single file. Container element. Required. If multiple jobs are defined in a single .WSF file, this element must be a child of the `<package>` element.

`<object>`
Used to define scriptable external objects without the use of methods such as `CreateObject` or `GetObject`. Objects defined using the `<object>` tag are available globally. Empty element. Optional. Child of `<job>`.

`<reference>`
Provides an inclusion mechanism to be used as a way to access type library information such as constants defined in the library. Empty element. Optional. Child of `<job>`.

`<resource>`

Allows a developer to declare string or numeric data to be used within a WSH application, while keeping this data separate from the actual script code. Commonly used for strings that require localization. Container element. Optional. Child of `<job>`.

`<script>`

Uses the familiar HTML syntax. Can be used for external script inclusion by setting the `src` attribute to a valid file or UNC path, or for embedding script code directly into your WSH application. Container element. Child of `<job>`. In order to achieve correct interpretation, script code should be enclosed in a CDATA section if the `<?xml?>` processing instruction is declared, as in the following example:

```
<?xml version="1.0"?>
<job>
  <script language="VBScript">
  <![CDATA[
    ' code here
  ]]>
  </script>
</job>
```

Using this syntax forces the XML parser to ignore the content of the script itself, so that no characters in the code itself are interpreted as characters which have special meaning to XML.

`<?xml?>` Element Attributes

Note: all instances where Boolean values are defined using 'True' could also use the values 'yes', 1 or 'on', while all 'False' values could be assigned as 'no', 0 or 'off'.

Attribute	Description
`version="1.0"`	A string in the form *majorver.minorver* specifying the XML level of the file. Use the value 1.0 (the only existing version of XML specification at this time).
`standalone = "yes"`	Denotes whether file includes reference to external Document Type Definition (DTD). WSF files do not use such a reference, so this always has the value "yes." Optional.

<?job?> Element Attributes

Attribute	Description
error="true|false"	Set to 'true' to enable error message reporting. Defaults to 'false'.
debug="true|false"	Set to 'true' to enable debugging. Defaults to 'false'. If this value is not set, or is set to 'False', debugging of .WSF files will not occur even if the console-mode //D and //X switches are set.

<comment> Element Attributes

None.

<package> Element Attributes

None.

<job> Element Attributes

Attribute	Description
id="strID"	Identifier string; must be unique to file.

<object> Element Attributes

Attribute	Description
id="strID"	Identifier string; must be unique to file.
classid="clsid:guid"	Reference to the globally unique class ID registration string (GUID) for the object.
progID="progID"	The program ID of the object.

You must specify either a classid or a progid attribute.

<reference> Element Attributes

Attribute	Description
version="version"	The version number of the type library to use. Should be declared in "*majorVer.minorVer*" format, and is only vald when used with the object attribute.
object="progID"	The program ID of the object.
guid="typelibGUID"	The GUID of the type library to reference.

You must specify either an object or a GUID attribute.

<resource> Element Attributes

Attribute	Description
id	Identifier string; must be unique to file.

To retrieve a stored <resource>, use the getResource method, as in the following example:

```
<?xml version="1.0"?>
<job>
  <resource id="resHello">Hello, World!</resource>
  <script language="VBScript">
    WScript.Echo getResource("resHello")
  </script>
</job>
```

<script> Element Attributes

Attribute	Description
language="strLang"	Name of scripting language used in script block, such as "VBScript" or "JScript". Optional. Defaults to "JScript" Also supports "VBS", "JS", "VBScript.Encode", and "JScript.Encode".
src="strPath"	Path to external script file to include into WSF file.

The Browser Object Model – IE4

The Dynamic HTML Object Model contains 12 **objects** and 15 **collections**. Most of these are organized into a strict hierarchy that allows HTML authors to access all the parts of the browser, and the pages that are loaded, from a scripting language like JavaScript or VBScript.

The Object Model In Outline

The diagram below shows the object hierarchy in graphical form. It is followed by a list of the objects and collection, with a brief description. Then, each object is documented in detail, showing the properties, methods, and events it supports.

Note that not all the objects and collections are included in the diagram. Some are not part of the overall object model, but are used to access other items such as dialogs or HTML elements.

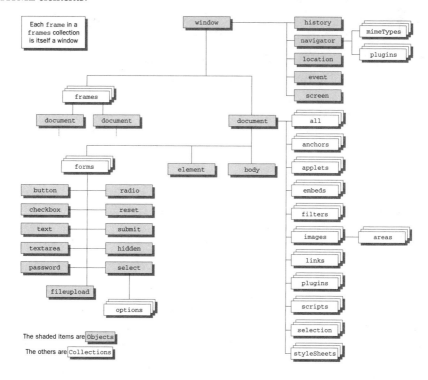

Object Name	Description
Document	An object that exposes the contents of the HTML document through a number of collections and properties.
Event	A global object that exposes properties that represent the parameters of all events as they occur.
History	Exposes information about the URLs that the client has previously visited.
Location	Exposes information about the currently displayed document's URL.
MimeType	An object that provides information about a MIME type.
Navigator	Exposes properties that provide information about the browser, or user agent.
Selection	Represents the currently active selection on the screen in the document.
Style	Represents an individual style element within a style sheet.
TextRange	Represents sections of the text stream making up the HTML document.
Screen	Exposes information about the client's monitor screen and system rendering abilities.
Window	Exposes properties, methods and events connected to the browser window or a frame.
StyleSheet	Exposes all the styles within a single style sheet in the styleSheets collection.

Collection Name	Description
all	Collection of all the tags and elements in the body of the document.
anchors	Collection of all the anchors in the document.
applets	Collection of all the objects in the document, including intrinsic controls, images, applets, embeds, and other objects.
areas	Collection of all the areas that make up the image map.
cells	Collection of all the <TH> and <TD> cells in the row of a table.
elements	Collection of all controls and elements in the form.
embeds	Collection of all the embed tags in the document.
forms	Collection of all the forms in the page.

Collection Name	Description
frames	Collection of all the frames defined within a <FRAMESET> tag.
images	Collection of all the images in the page.
links	Collection of all the links and <AREA> blocks in the page.
options	Collection of all the items in a <SELECT> element.
plugins	An alias for collection of all the embeds in the page.
rows	Collection of all the rows in the table, including <THEAD>, <TBODY>, and <TFOOT>.
scripts	Collection of all the <SCRIPT> sections in the page.
filters	Collection of all the filter objects for an element.
imports	Collection of all the imported style sheets defined for a stylesheet object.
stylesheets	Collection of all the individual style property objects defined for a document.
mimeTypes	Collection of all the document and file types supported by the browser.

The Objects in Detail

This section documents all the properties, methods and events available for each object in the browser hierarchy.

The Document Object

Exposes the entire HTML content through its own collections and properties, and provides a range of events and methods to work with documents.

Property Name	Attribute Name	CSS Name	Description
activeElement			Identifies the element that has the focus.
alinkColor	ALINK		The color for active links in the page - i.e. while the mouse button is held down.
bgColor	BGCOLOR	background -color	Specifies the background color to be used for an element.

Property Name	Attribute Name	CSS Name	Description
body			Read-only reference to the document's implicit body object, as defined by the \<BODY> tag.
cookie			The string value of a cookie stored by the browser.
domain			Sets or returns the domain of the document for use in cookies and security.
fgColor	TEXT		Sets the color of the document foreground text.
lastModified			The date that the source file for the page was last modified, as a string, where available.
linkColor	LINK		The color for unvisited links in the page.
location			The full URL of the document.
parentWindow			Returns the parent window that contains the document.
readyState			Specifies the current state of an object being downloaded.
referrer			The URL of the page that referenced (loaded) the current page.
selection			Read-only reference to the document's selection object.
title	TITLE		Provides advisory information about the element, such as when loading or as a tooltip.

Property Name	Attribute Name	CSS Name	Description
url	URL		Uniform Resource Locator (address) for the current document or in a **\<META\>** tag.
vlinkColor	VLINK		The color for visited links in the page.

Collections	Description
all	Collection of all the tags and elements in the body of the document.
anchors	Collection of all the anchors in the document.
applets	Collection of all the objects in the document, including intrinsic controls, images, applets, embeds, and other objects.
embeds	Collection of all the embed tags in the document.
forms	Collection of all the forms in the page.
frames	Collection of all the frames defined within a \<FRAMESET\> tag.
images	Collection of all the images in the page.
links	Collection of all the links and \<AREA\> blocks in the page.
plugins	An alias for collection of all the embeds in the page.
scripts	Collection of all the \<SCRIPT\> sections in the page.
styleSheets	Collection of all the individual style property objects defined for a document.

Method Name	Description
clear	Clears the contents of a selection or document object.
close	Closes a document forcing written data to be displayed, or closes the browser window.
createElement	Creates an instance of an image or option element object.
elementFromPoint	Returns the element at the specified x and y coordinates with respect to the window.

Method Name	Description
execCommand	Executes a command over the document selection or range.
open	Opens the document as a stream to collect output of write or writeln methods.
queryCommandEnabled	Denotes if the specified command is available for a document or TextRange.
queryCommandIndeterm	Denotes if the specified command is in the indeterminate state.
queryCommandState	Returns the current state of the command for a document or TextRange object.
queryCommandSupported	Denotes if the specified command is supported for a document or TextRange object.
queryCommandText	Returns the string associated with a command for a document or TextRange object.
queryCommandValue	Returns the value of the command specified for a document or TextRange object.
write	Writes text and HTML to a document in the specified window.
writeln	Writes text and HTML to a document in the specified window, followed by a carriage return.

Event Name	Description
onafterupdate	Occurs when transfer of data from the element to the data provider is complete.
onbeforeupdate	Occurs before transfer of changed data to the data provider when an element loses focus or the page is unloaded.
onclick	Occurs when the user clicks the mouse button on an element, or when the value of a control is changed.
ondblclick	Occurs when the user double-clicks on an element.
ondragstart	Occurs when the user first starts to drag an element or selection.
onerror	Occurs when an error loading a document or image arises.
onhelp	Occurs when the user presses the *F1* or *Help* key.

Event Name	Description
onkeydown	Occurs when the user presses a key.
onkeypress	Occurs when the user presses a key and a character is available.
onkeyup	Occurs when the user releases a key.
onload	Occurs when the element has completed loading.
onmousedown	Occurs when the user presses a mouse button.
onmousemove	Occurs when the user moves the mouse.
onmouseout	Occurs when the mouse pointer leaves the element.
onmouseover	Occurs when the mouse pointer first enters the element.
onmouseup	Occurs when the user releases a mouse button.
onreadystatechange	Occurs when the readyState for an object has changed.
onselectstart	Occurs when the user first starts to select contents of an element.

The Event Object

The global object provided to allow the scripting language to access an event's parameters. It provides the following properties:

Property Name	Description
altKey	Returns the state of the *Alt* key when an event occurs.
button	The mouse button, if any, that was pressed to fire the event.
cancelBubble	Set to prevent the current event from bubbling up the hierarchy.
clientX	Returns the x coordinate of the element, excluding borders, margins, padding, scrollbars, etc.
clientY	Returns the y coordinate of the element, excluding borders, margins, padding, scrollbars, etc.
ctrlKey	Returns the state of the *Ctrl* key when an event occurs.
fromElement	Returns the element being moved from for an onmouseover or onmouseout event.
keyCode	ASCII code of the key being pressed. Changing it sends a different character to the object.

Property Name	Description
offsetX	Returns the *x* coordinate of the mouse pointer when an event occurs, relative to the containing element.
offsetY	Returns the *y* coordinate position of the mouse pointer when an event occurs, relative to the containing element.
reason	Indicates whether data transfer to an element was successful, or why it failed.
returnValue	Allows a return value to be specified for the event or a dialog window.
screenX	Returns the *x* coordinate of the mouse pointer when an event occurs, in relation to the screen.
screenY	Returns the *y* coordinate of the mouse pointer when an event occurs, in relation to the screen.
shiftKey	Returns the state of the *Shift* key when an event occurs.
srcElement	Returns the element deepest in the object hierarchy that a specified event occurred over.
srcFilter	Returns the filter that caused the element to produce an onfilterchange event.
toElement	Returns the element being moved to for an onmouseover or onmouseout event.
type	Returns the name of the event as a string, without the 'on' prefix, such as 'click' instead of 'onclick'.
x	Returns the *x* coordinate of the mouse pointer relative to a positioned parent, or otherwise to the window.
y	Returns the *y* coordinate of the mouse pointer relative to a positioned parent, or otherwise to the window.

The History Object

Contains information about the URLs that the client has visited, as stored in the browser's History list, and allows the script to move through the list.

Properties	Description
length	Returns the number of elements in a collection.

Methods	Description
back	Loads the previous URL in the browser's History list.

Methods	Description
forward	Loads the next URL in the browser's History list.
go	Loads a specified URL from the browser's History list.

The Location Object

Contains information on the current URL. It also provides methods that will reload a page.

PropertyName	AttributeName	Description
hash		The string following the # symbol in the URL.
host		The hostname:port part of the location or URL.
hostname		The hostname part of the location or URL.
href	HREF	The entire URL as a string.
pathname		The file or object path name following the third slash in a URL.
port		The port number in a URL.
protocol		The initial substring up to and including the first colon, indicating the URL's access method.
search		The contents of the query string or form data following the ? (question mark) in the complete URL.

MethodName	Description
assign	Loads another page. Equivalent to changing the `window.location.href` property.
reload	Reloads the current page.
replace	Loads a document, replacing the current document's session history entry with its URL.

The MimeType Object

Provides information about the page's MIME data type.

Properties	Attribute	Description
description		Returns a description of the MimeType.
enabledPlugin		Returns the plug-in that can handle the specified MimeType.
name	NAME	Specifies the name of the element, control, bookmark, or applet.
suffixes		A list of filename suffixes suitable for use with the specified MimeType.

The Navigator Object

This object represents the browser application itself, providing information about it's manufacturer, version, and capabilities.

Property Name	Description
appCodeName	The code name of the browser.
appName	The product name of the browser.
appVersion	The version of the browser.
cookieEnabled	Indicates if client-side cookies are enabled in the browser.
userAgent	The user-agent (browser name) header sent in the HTTP protocol from the client to the server.

Collection	Description
mimeTypes	Collection of all the document and file types supported by the browser.
plugins	An alias for collection of all the embeds in the page.

Method Name	Description
javaEnabled	Returns True or False, depending on whether a Java VM is installed and enabled.
taintEnabled	Returns False, included for compatibility with Netscape Navigator

The Screen Object

The screen object provides information to the scripting language about the client's screen resolution and rendering abilities.

Property Name	Description
bufferDepth	Specifies if and how an off-screen bitmap buffer should be used.
colorDepth	Returns the number of bits per pixel of the user's display device or screen buffer.
height	Returns the height of the user's display screen in pixels.
updateInterval	Sets or returns the interval between screen updates on the client.
width	Returns the width of the user's display screen in pixels.

The Selection Object

Returns the active selection on the screen, allowing access to all the selected elements including the plain text in the page.

Properties	Attribute	Description
type	TYPE	The type of the selection, i.e. a control, text, a table, or none.

Methods	Description
clear	Clears the contents of the selection.
createRange	Returns a copy of the currently selected range.
empty	Deselects the current selection and sets selection type to none.

The Style Object

This provides access to the individual style properties for an element. These could have been previously set by a style sheet, or by an inline style tag within the page.

Property Name	Attribute Name	CSS Name	Description
background	BACKGROUND	background	Specifies a background picture that is tiled behind text and graphics.

Property Name	Attribute Name	CSS Name	Description
background Attachment		background-attachment	Defines if a background image should be fixed on the page or scroll with the content.
background Color		background-color	Specifies the background color of the page or element.
background Image		background-image	Specifies a URL for the background image for the page or element.
background Position		background-position	The initial position of a background image on the page.
background PositionX			The x coordinate of the background image in relation to the containing window.
background PositionY			The y coordinate of the background image in relation to the containing window.
Background Repeat		background-repeat	Defines if and how a background image is repeated on the page.
border	BORDER	border	Specifies the border to be drawn around the element.

Property Name	Attribute Name	CSS Name	Description
borderBottom		border-bottom	Used to specify several attributes of the bottom border of an element.
borderBottomColor			The color of the bottom border for an element.
borderBottomStyle			The style of the bottom border for an element.
borderBottomWidth		border-bottom-width	The width of the bottom border for an element.
borderColor	BORDERCOLOR	border-color	The color of all or some of the borders for an element.
borderLeft		border-left	Used to specify several attributes of the left border of an element.
borderLeftColor			The color of the left border for an element.
borderLeftStyle			The style of the left border for an element.
borderLeftWidth		border-left-width	The width of the left border for an element.
borderRight		border-right	Used to specify several attributes of the right border of an element.
BorderRightColor			The color of the right border for an element.

Property Name	Attribute Name	CSS Name	Description
BorderRightStyle			The style of the right border for an element.
BorderRightWidth		border-right-width	The width of the right border for an element.
borderStyle		border-style	Used to specify the style of one or more borders of an element.
borderTop		border-top	Used to specify several attributes of the top border of an element.
borderTopColor			The color of the top border for an element.
borderTopStyle			The style of the top border for an element.
borderTopWidth		border-top-width	The width of the top border for an element.
borderWidth		border-width	Used to specify the width of one or more borders of an element.
clear	CLEAR	clear	Causes the next element or text to be displayed below left-aligned or right-aligned images.
clip		clip	Specifies how an element's contents should be displayed if larger that the available client area.

Property Name	Attribute Name	CSS Name	Description
color	COLOR	color	The text or foreground color of an element.
cssText			The text value of the element's entire STYLE attribute.
cursor		cursor	Specifies the type of cursor to display when the mouse pointer is over the element.
display		display	Specifies if the element will be visible (displayed) in the page.
filter		filter	Sets or returns an array of all the filters specified in the element's style property.
font		font, @font-face	Defines various attributes of the font for an element, or imports a font.
fontFamily		font-family	Specifies the name of the typeface, or 'font family'.
fontSize		font-size	Specifies the font size.
fontStyle		font-style	Specifies the style of the font, i.e. normal or italic.
fontVariant		font-variant	Specifies the use of small capitals for the text.

655

Property Name	Attribute Name	CSS Name	Description
fontWeight		font-weight	Specifies the weight (boldness) of the text.
height	HEIGHT	height	Specifies the height at which the element is to be drawn, and sets the posHeight property.
left		left	Specifies the position of the left of the element, and sets the posLeft property.
letterSpacing		letter-spacing	Indicates the additional space to be placed between characters in the text.
lineHeight		line-height	The distance between the baselines of two adjacent lines of text.
listStyle		list-style	Allows several style properties of a list element to be set in one operation.
listStyleImage		list-style-image	Defines the image used as a background for a list element.
listStylePosition		list-style-position	Defines the position of the bullets used in a list element.

Property Name	Attribute Name	CSS Name	Description
listStyleType		list-style-type	Defines the design of the bullets used in a list element.
margin		margin	Allows all four margins to be specified with a single attribute.
marginBottom		margin-bottom	Specifies the bottom margin for the page or text block.
marginLeft		margin-left	Specifies the left margin for the page or text block.
marginRight		margin-right	Specifies the right margin for the page or text block.
marginTop		margin-top	Specifies the top margin for the page or text block.
overflow		overflow	Defines how text that overflows the element is handled.
paddingBottom		padding-bottom	Sets the amount of space between the bottom border and content of an element.
paddingLeft		padding-left	Sets the amount of space between the left border and content of an element.

Property Name	Attribute Name	CSS Name	Description
paddingRight		padding-right	Sets the amount of space between the right border and content of an element.
paddingTop		padding-top	Sets the amount of space between the top border and content of an element.
pageBreakAfter		page-break-after	Specifies if a page break should occur after the element.
pageBreakBefore		page-break-before	Specifies if a page break should occur after the element.
pixelHeight			Sets or returns the height style property of the element in pixels, as a pure number, rather than a string.
pixelLeft			Sets or returns the left style property of the element in pixels, as a pure number, rather than a string.
pixelTop			Sets or returns the top style property of the element in pixels, as a pure number, rather than a string.

Property Name	Attribute Name	CSS Name	Description
pixelWidth			Sets or returns the width style property of the element in pixels, as a pure number, rather than a string.
posHeight			Returns the value of the height style property in its last specified units, as a pure number rather than a string.
position		position	Returns the value of the position style property, defining whether the element can be positioned.
posLeft			Returns the value of the left style property in its last specified units, as a pure number rather than a string.
posTop			Returns the value of the top style property in its last specified units, as a pure number rather than a string.
posWidth			Returns the value of the width style property in its last specified units, as a pure number rather than a string.
styleFloat		float	Specifies if the element will float above the other elements in the page, or cause them to flow round it.
textAlign		text-align	Indicates how text should be aligned within the element.

Property Name	Attribute Name	CSS Name	Description
textDecoration		text-decoration	Specifies several font decorations (underline, overline, strikethrough) added to the text of an element.
textDecoration Blink			Specifies if the font should blink or flash. Has no effect in IE4.
textDecoration LineThrough			Specifies if the text is displayed as strikethrough, i.e. with a horizontal line through it.
textDecoration None			Specifies if the text is displayed with no additional decoration.
textDecoration Overline			Denotes if the text is displayed as overline, i.e. with a horizontal line above it.
textDecoration Underline			Denotes if the text is displayed as underline, i.e. with a horizontal line below it.
textIndent		text-indent	Specifies the indent for the first line of text in an element, and may be negative.
textTransform		text-transform	Specifies how the text for the element should be capitalized.
top		top	Position of the top of the element, sets the posTop property. Also returns topmost window object.
verticalAlign		vertical-align	Sets or returns the vertical alignment style property for an element.

Property Name	Attribute Name	CSS Name	Description
visibility		visibility	Indicates if the element or contents are visible on the page.
width	WIDTH	width	Specifies the width at which the element is to be drawn, and sets the posWidth property.
zIndex		z-index	Sets or returns the z-index for the element, indicating whether it appears above or below other elements.

MethodName	Description
getAttribute	Returns the value of an attribute defined in an HTML tag.
removeAttribute	Causes the specified attribute to be removed from the HTML element and the current page.
setAttribute	Adds and/or sets the value of an attribute in a HTML tag.

The StyleSheet Object

This object exposes all the styles within a single style sheet in the styleSheets collection

Property Name	Attribute Name	Description
disabled	DISABLED	Sets or returns whether an element is disabled.
href	HREF	The entire URL as a string.
id	ID	Identifier or name for an element in a page or style sheet, or as the target for hypertext links.
owningElement		Returns the style sheet that imported or referenced the current style sheet, usually through a <LINK> tag.

Property Name	Attribute Name	Description
parentStyle Sheet		Returns the style sheet that imported the current style sheet, or null for a non-imported style sheet.
readOnly	READONLY	Indicates that an element's contents are read only, or that a rule in a style sheet cannot be changed.
type	TYPE	Specifies the type of list style, link, selection, control, button, MIME-type, rel, or the CSS language.

Collection	Description
imports	Collection of all the imported style sheets defined for a stylesheet object.

The TextRange Object

This object represents the text stream of the HTML document. It can be used to set and retrieve the text within the page.

Property Name	Description
htmlText	Returns the contents of a TextRange as text and HTML source.
text	The plain text contained within a block element, a TextRange or an <OPTION> tag.

Method Name	Description
collapse	Shrinks a TextRange to either the start or end of the current range.
compareEnd Points	Compares two text ranges and returns a value indicating the result.
duplicate	Returns a duplicate of a TextRange object.
execCommand	Executes a command over the document selection or range.
expand	Expands the range by a character, word, sentence or story so that partial units are completely contained.
findText	Sets the range start and end points to cover the text if found within the current document.

Method Name	Description
getBookmark	Sets String to a unique bookmark value to identify that position in the document.
inRange	Denotes if the specified range is within or equal to the current range.
isEqual	Denotes if the specified range is equal to the current range.
move	Changes the start and end points of a TextRange to cover different text.
moveEnd	Causes the range to grow or shrink from the end of the range.
moveStart	Causes the range to grow or shrink from the beginning of the range.
moveToBookmark	Moves range to encompass the range with a bookmark value previously defined in String.
moveToElementText	Moves range to encompass the text in the element specified.
moveToPoint	Moves and collapses range to the point specified in x and y relative to the document.
parentElement	Returns the parent element that completely encloses the current range.
pasteHTML	Pastes HTML and/or plain text into the current range.
queryCommandEnabled	Denotes if the specified command is available for a document or TextRange.
queryCommandIndeterm	Denotes if the specified command is in the indeterminate state.
queryCommandState	Returns the current state of the command for a document or TextRange object.
queryCommandSupported	Denotes if the specified command is supported for a document or TextRange object.
queryCommandText	Returns the string associated with a command for a document or TextRange object.
queryCommandValue	Returns the value of the command specified for a document or TextRange object.
scrollIntoView	Scrolls the element or TextRange into view in the browser, optionally at the top of the window.

Method Name	Description
select	Makes the active selection equal to the current object, or highlights the input area of a form element.
setEndPoint	Sets the end point of the range based on the end point of another range.

The Window Object

The window object refers to the current window. This can be a top-level window, or a window that is within a frame created by a <FRAMESET> in another document.

Property Name	Attribute Name	CSS Name	Description
client			A reference that returns the navigator object for the browser.
closed			Indicates if a window is closed.
defaultStatus			The default message displayed in the status bar at the bottom of the window.
dialog Arguments			Returns the arguments that were passed into a dialog window, as an array.
dialogHeight			Sets or returns the height of a dialog window.
dialogLeft			Sets or returns the x coordinate of a dialog window.
dialogTop			Sets or returns the y coordinate of a dialog window.
dialogWidth			Sets or returns the width of a dialog window.
document			Read-only reference to the window's document object.

Property Name	Attribute Name	CSS Name	Description
event	EVENT		Read-only reference to the global event object.
history			Read-only reference to the window's history object.
length			Returns the number of elements in a collection.
name	NAME		Specifies the name of the window, frame, element, control, bookmark, or applet.
navigator			Read-only reference to the window's navigator object.
offScreenBuffering			Specifies whether to use off-screen buffering for the document.
opener			Returns a reference to the window that created the current window.
parent			Returns the parent window or frame in the window/frame hierarchy.
returnValue			Allows a return value to be specified for the event or a dialog window.
screen			Read-only reference to the global screen object.
self			Provides a reference to the current window.

Property Name	Attribute Name	CSS Name	Description
status			Text displayed in the window's status bar, or an alias for the value of an option button.
top		top	Position of the top of the element, sets the posTop property. Also returns topmost window object.
window			Read-only reference to the current window object, same as _self.

MethodName	Description
alert	Displays an Alert dialog box with a message and an OK button.
blur	Causes a control to lose focus and fire its onblur event.
clearInterval	Cancels an interval timer that was set with the setInterval method.
clearTimeout	Cancels a timeout that was set with the setTimeout method.
close	Closes a document forcing written data to be displayed, or closes the browser window.
confirm	Displays a Confirm dialog box with a message and OK and Cancel buttons.
execScript	Executes a script. The default language is JScript.
focus	Causes a control to receive the focus and fires its onfocus event.
navigate	Loads another page (VBScript only). Equivalent to changing the window.location.href property.
open	Opens the document as a stream to collect output of write or writeln methods.
prompt	Displays a Prompt dialog box with a message and an input field.

MethodName	Description
`scroll`	Scrolls the window to the specified *x* and *y* offset relative to the entire document.
`setInterval`	Denotes a code routine to execute repeatedly every specified number of milliseconds.
`setTimeout`	Denotes a code routine to execute a specified number of milliseconds after loading the page.
`showHelp`	Opens a window to display a Help file.
`showModalDialog`	Displays a HTML dialog window, and returns the `returnValue` property of its document when closed.

EventName	Description
`onbeforeunload`	Occurs just before the page is unloaded, allowing the unload event to be cancelled.
`onblur`	Occurs when the control loses the input focus.
`onerror`	Occurs when an error loading a document or image arises.
`onfocus`	Occurs when a control receives the input focus.
`onhelp`	Occurs when the user presses the *F1* or *Help* key.
`onload`	Occurs when the element has completed loading.
`onresize`	Occurs when the element or object is resized by the user.
`onscroll`	Occurs when the user scrolls a page or element.
`onunload`	Occurs immediately before the page is unloaded.

Collections	Description
`frames`	Collection of all the frames defined within a `<FRAMESET>` tag.

HTML and Form Controls Cross Reference

Dynamic HTML provides the same integral control types as HTML 3.2. However, there are many more different properties, methods and events available now for all the controls.

The following tables show those that are most relevant to controls

Control Properties	checked	dataFld	dataFormatAs	dataSrc	defaultChecked	defaultValue	maxLength	readOnly	recordNumber	selectedIndex	size	status	type	value
HTML button	N	Y	Y	Y	N	N	N	Y	Y	N	N	N	Y	Y
HTML checkbox	Y	Y	N	Y	Y	N	N	Y	Y	N	Y	Y	Y	Y
HTML file	N	N	N	N	N	Y	N	Y	Y	N	N	N	Y	Y
HTML hidden	N	Y	N	Y	N	N	N	N	N	N	N	N	Y	Y
HTML image	N	N	N	N	N	N	N	N	Y	N	N	N	Y	N
HTML password	N	Y	N	Y	N	Y	Y	Y	N	N	Y	N	Y	Y
HTML radio	Y	Y	N	Y	Y	N	N	Y	Y	N	Y	N	Y	Y
HTML reset	N	N	N	N	N	N	N	N	Y	N	N	N	Y	Y
HTML submit	N	N	N	N	N	N	N	N	Y	N	N	N	Y	Y
HTML text	N	Y	N	Y	N	Y	Y	Y	Y	N	Y	N	Y	Y
BUTTON tag	N	Y	Y	Y	N	N	N	N	N	N	Y	Y	Y	Y
FIELDSET tag	N	N	N	N	N	N	N	N	Y	N	N	N	N	N
LABEL tag	N	N	N	N	N	N	N	N	N	N	N	N	N	N
LEGEND tag	N	N	N	N	N	N	N	N	Y	N	N	N	N	N
SELECT tag	N	Y	N	Y	N	N	N	N	Y	Y	N	N	Y	Y
TEXTAREA tag	N	Y	N	Y	N	N	N	Y	N	N	N	Y	Y	Y

Control Methods

	add	blur	click	createTextRange	focus	item	remove	select
HTML button	N	Y	Y	N	Y	N	N	Y
HTML checkbox	N	Y	Y	N	Y	N	N	Y
HTML file	N	Y	Y	N	Y	N	N	Y
HTML hidden	N	N	N	N	N	N	N	N
HTML image	N	Y	Y	N	Y	N	N	Y
HTML password	N	Y	Y	N	Y	N	N	Y
HTML radio	N	Y	Y	N	Y	N	N	Y
HTML reset	N	Y	Y	N	Y	N	N	Y
HTML submit	N	Y	Y	N	Y	N	N	Y
HTML text	N	Y	Y	Y	Y	N	N	Y
BUTTON tag	N	Y	Y	Y	Y	N	N	N
FIELDSET tag	N	Y	Y	N	Y	N	N	N
LABEL tag	N	N	Y	N	N	N	N	N
LEGEND tag	N	Y	Y	N	Y	N	N	N
SELECT tag	Y	Y	Y	N	Y	Y	Y	N
TEXTAREA tag	N	Y	Y	Y	Y	N	N	Y

Control Events	onafterupdate	onbeforeupdate	onblur	onchange	onclick	ondblclick	onfocus	onrowenter	onrowexit	onselect
HTML button	N	N	Y	N	Y	Y	Y	N	N	Y
HTML checkbox	Y	Y	Y	Y	Y	Y	Y	N	N	Y
HTML file	N	N	Y	Y	Y	Y	Y	N	N	Y
HTML hidden	N	N	N	N	N	N	N	N	N	N
HTML image	N	N	Y	Y	N	Y	Y	N	N	Y
HTML password	N	N	Y	Y	Y	Y	Y	N	N	Y
HTML radio	Y	Y	Y	Y	Y	Y	Y	N	N	Y
HTML reset	N	N	Y	N	Y	Y	Y	N	N	Y
HTML submit	N	N	Y	N	Y	Y	Y	N	N	Y
HTML text	Y	Y	Y	Y	Y	Y	Y	N	N	Y
BUTTON tag	Y	Y	Y	N	Y	Y	Y	Y	Y	N
FIELDSET tag	Y	Y	Y	N	Y	Y	Y	Y	Y	N
LABEL tag	N	N	N	N	Y	Y	N	N	N	N
LEGEND tag	Y	Y	Y	N	Y	Y	Y	Y	Y	N
SELECT tag	Y	Y	Y	Y	Y	Y	Y	Y	Y	N
TEXTAREA tag	Y	Y	Y	Y	Y	Y	Y	Y	Y	Y

The Browser Object Model – IE5

The IE5 Dynamic HTML object model contains 23 **objects** and 29 **collections**. Most of these are organized into a strict hierarchy that allows HTML authors to access all the parts of the browser, and the pages that are loaded, from a scripting language like JavaScript or VBScript.

The Object Model In Outline

The diagram (overleaf) shows the object hierarchy in graphical form. It is followed by a list of the objects and collection, with a brief description. Then, each object is documented in detail, showing the properties, methods, and events it supports.

Note that we haven't included all of the objects and collections in the diagram. Some are not part of the overall object model, but are used to access other items – such as dialogs and HTML elements.

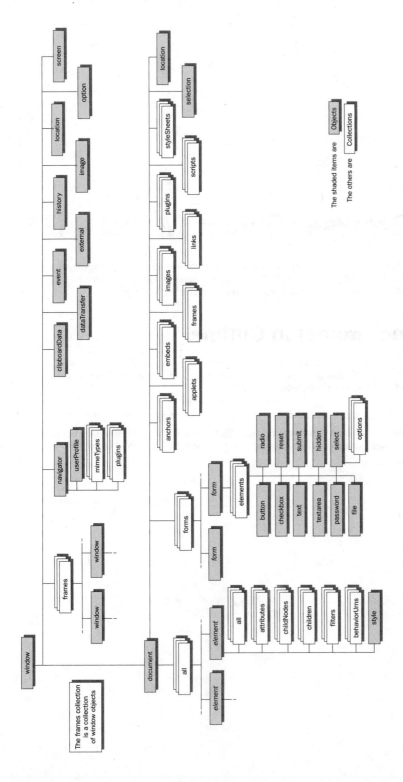

The frames collection
is a collection
of window objects

The shaded items are Objects

The others are Collections

Object Name	Description
Attribute	An object-representation of an attribute or property.
clipboardData	Used with editing operations to provide access to data contained on the clipboard.
currentStyle	Represents the cascaded format and style of its parent object.
custom	A user-defined element.
dataTransfer	Used with drag-and-drop operations to provide access to data contained on the clipboard.
document	An object that exposes the contents of the HTML document through a number of collections and properties.
event	A global object that exposes properties that represent the parameters of all events as they occur.
external	Allows access to the object model of any application hosting Internet Explorer components.
history	Exposes information about the URLs that the client has previously visited.
location	Exposes information about the currently displayed document's URL.
mimeType	An object that provides information about a MIME type.
navigator	Exposes properties that provide information about the browser, or user agent.
rule	A style (i.e. a selector and one or more declarations) within a cascading style sheet (CSS).
runtimeStyle	Represents the cascaded format and style of its parent object, overriding global stylesheets, inline styles and HTML attributes. Overwrites the values of the currentStyle object but not the style object.
screen	Exposes information about the client's monitor screen and system rendering abilities.
selection	Represents the currently active selection on the screen in the document.
style	Represents an individual style element within a style sheet.

Table Continued on Following Page

Object Name	Description
styleSheet	Exposes all the styles within a single style sheet in the styleSheets collection.
textNode	A string of text, represented as a node on the document hierarchy.
textRange	Represents sections of the text stream making up the HTML document.
textRectangle	A set of the four coordinates that represent the rectangle containing a line of text of TextRange object.
userProfile	Allows a script to request read access to and perform read actions on a user's profile.
window	Exposes properties, methods and events connected to the browser window or a frame.

Collection Name	Description
all	Collection of all the tags and elements in the body of the document.
anchors	Collection of all the anchors in the document.
applets	Collection of all the objects in the document, including intrinsic controls, images, applets, embeds, and other objects.
areas	Collection of all the areas that make up the image map.
attributes	Collection of all the attributes of the object.
behaviorUrns	Collection of all the behaviors attached to the element (as a set of URN strings).
bookmarks	Collection of all the ADO bookmarks tied to the rows affected by the current event.
boundElements	Collection of all the elements on the page that are bound to a dataset.
cells	Collection of all the <TH> and <TD> cells in the row of a table.
childNodes	Collection of all the object's children.
children	Collection of all the object's direct descendents.
controlRange	Collection of the BODY's elements.
elements	Collection of all controls and elements in the form.

Collection Name	Description
embeds	Collection of all the embed tags in the document.
filters	Collection of all the filter objects for an element.
forms	Collection of all the forms in the page.
frames	Collection of all the frames defined within a <FRAMESET> tag.
images	Collection of all the images in the page.
imports	Collection of all the imported style sheets defined for a stylesheet object.
links	Collection of all the links and <AREA> blocks in the page.
mimeTypes	Collection of all the document and file types supported by the browser.
options	Collection of all the items in a <SELECT> element.
plugins	An alias for collection of all the embeds in the page.
rows	Collection of all the rows in the table, including <THEAD>, <TBODY>, and <TFOOT>.
rules	Collection of all the rule objects defined in a styleSheet.
scripts	Collection of all the <SCRIPT> sections in the page.
stylesheets	Collection of all the individual style property objects defined for a document.
tBodies	Collection of all TBODY objects in the table.
TextRectangle	Collection of all the TextRectangle objects in the object.

The Objects in Detail

This section lists all the properties, methods and events available for each object in the browser hierarchy.

It's worth noting that there's a set of attributes that are common to almost all of the DHTML elements. These attributes provide properties, methods, and events for manipulating the specific object. This commonality makes it simpler to use the exact same scripting style and techniques to deal with nearly every element in the document object model. Thus, you'll see a certain amount of repetition in these lists.

The Attribute Object

An object-representation of an attribute or property.

Properties	nodeName nodeType nodeValue specified
Methods	None
Events	None
Collections	None

The clipboardData Object

Used with editing operations to provide access to data contained on the clipboard.

Properties	None
Methods	None
Events	None
Collections	None

The currentStyle Object

Represents the cascaded format and style of its parent object.

Properties	backgroundAttachment	layoutGridLine
	backgroundColor	layoutGridMode
	backgroundImage	layoutGridType
	backgroundPositionX	left
	backgroundPositionY	letterSpacing
	backgroundRepeat	lineHeight
	borderBottomColor	listStyleImage
	borderBottomStyle	listStylePosition
	borderBottomWidth	listStyleType
	borderColor	margin
	borderLeftColor	marginBottom
	borderLeftStyle	marginLeft
	borderLeftWidth	marginRight
	borderRightColor	marginTop
	borderRightStyle	overflow
	borderRightWidth	overflowX
	borderStyle	overflowY
	borderTopColor	padding
	borderTopStyle	paddingBottom
	borderTopWidth	paddingLeft
	borderWidth bottom	

Properties	clear	paddingRight
	clipBottom	paddingTop
	clipLeft	pageBreakAfter
	clipRight	pageBreakBefore
	clipTop	position
	color	right
	cursor	styleFloat
	direction	tableLayout
	display	textAlign
	fontFamily	textDecoration
	fontSize	textIndent
	fontStyle	textTransform
	fontVariant	top
	fontWeight	unicodeBidi
	height	verticalAlign
	layoutGrid	visibility
	layoutGridChar	width
	layoutGridCharSpacing	zIndex
Methods	None	
Events	None	
Collections	None	

The custom Object

A user-defined element.

Properties	accessKey	offsetWidth
	canHaveChildren	outerHTML
	className	outerText
	clientHeight	parentElement
	clientLeft	parentTextEdit
	clientTop	readyState
	clientWidth	recordNumber
	currentStyle	runtimeStyle
	dir	scopeName
	document	scrollHeight
	id	scrollLeft
	innerHTML	scrollTop
	innerText	scrollWidth
	isTextEdit	sourceIndex
	lang	style
	language	tabIndex
	offsetHeight	tagName
	offsetLeft	tagUrn
	offsetParent	title
	offsetTop	

Table Continued on Following Page

Methods	addBehavior	getClientRects
	applyElement	getElementsByTagName
	attachEvent	getExpression
	blur	insertAdjacentHTML
	clearAttributes	insertAdjacentText
	click	mergeAttributes
	componentFromPoint	releaseCapture
	contains	removeAttribute
	createControlRange	removeBehavior
	detachEvent	removeExpression
	doScroll	replaceAdjacentText
	focus	scrollIntoView
	getAdjacentText	setAttribute
	getAttribute	setCapture
	getBoundingClientRect	setExpression
Events	onafterupdate	onerrorupdate
	onbeforecopy	onfilterchange
	onbeforecut	onfocus
	onbeforeeditfocus	onhelp
	onbeforepaste	onkeydown
	onbeforeupdate	onkeypress
	onblur	onkeyup
	onclick	onlosecapture
	oncontextmenu	onmousedown
	oncopy	onmousemove
	oncut	onmouseout
	ondblclick	onmouseover
	ondrag	onmouseup
	ondragend	onpaste
	ondragenter	onpropertychange
	ondragleave	onreadystatechange
	ondragover	onresize
	ondragstart	onscroll
	ondrop	onselectstart
Collections	all behaviorUrns children filters	

The dataTransfer Object

Used with drag-and-drop operations to provide access to data contained on the clipboard.

Properties	dropEffect effectAllowed
Methods	clearData getData setData
Events	None
Collections	None

The document Object

An object that exposes the contents of the HTML document through a number of collections and properties.

Properties	activeElement aLinkColor bgColor cookie defaultCharset designMode documentElement domain expando fgColor fileCreatedDate fileModifiedDate	fileSize lastModified linkColor location parentWindow protocol readyState referrer selection uniqueID URL vlinkColor
Methods	attachEvent clear clearAttributes close createElement createStyleSheet createTextNode detachEvent elementFromPoint execCommand getElementById getElementsByName	getElementsByTagName mergeAttributes open queryCommandEnabled queryCommandIndeterm queryCommandState queryCommandSupported queryCommandValue recalc releaseCapture write writeln
Events	onbeforecut onbeforeeditfocus onbeforepaste onclick oncontextmenu oncut ondblclick ondrag ondragend ondragenter ondragleave ondragover ondragstart ondrop	onhelp onkeydown onkeypress onkeyup onmousedown onmousemove onmouseout onmouseover onmouseup onpaste onpropertychange onreadystatechange onstop
Collections	all anchors applets childNodes children embeds	forms frames images links scripts styleSheets

The event Object

A global object that exposes properties that represent the parameters of all events as they occur.

Properties	altKey	reason
	button	recordset
	cancelBubble	repeat
	clientX	returnValue
	clientY	screenX
	ctrlKey	screenY
	dataFld	shiftKey
	dataTransfer	srcElement
	fromElement	srcFilter
	keyCode	srcUrn
	offsetX	toElement
	offsetY	type
	propertyName	x
	qualifier	y
Methods	None	
Events	None	
Collections	bookmarks boundElements	

The external Object

Allows access to the object model of any application hosting Internet Explorer components.

Properties	menuArguments	
Methods	AddChannel	ImportExportFavorites
	AddDesktopComponent	IsSubscribed
	AddFavorite	NavigateAndFind
	AutoCompleteSaveForm	ShowBrowserUI
	AutoScan	
Events	None	
Collections	None	

The history Object

Exposes information about the URLs that the client has previously visited.

Properties	length
Methods	back forward go
Events	None
Collections	None

The location Object

Exposes information about the currently displayed document's URL.

Properties	hash host hostname href pathname port protocol search
Methods	assign reload replace
Events	None
Collections	None

The mimeType

An object that provides information about a MIME type.

Properties	description enabledPlugin name
Methods	None
Events	None
Collections	suffixes

The navigator Object

Exposes properties that provide information about the browser, or user agent.

Properties	appCodeName onLine appMinorVersion platform appName systemLanguage appVersion userAgent browserLanguage userLanguage cookieEnabled userProfile cpuClass
Methods	javaEnabled taintEnabled
Events	None
Collections	plugins

The rule Object

A style (i.e. a selector and one or more declarations) within a cascading style sheet (CSS).

Properties	readOnly runtimeStyle selectorText style
Methods	None
Events	None
Collections	None

The runtimeStyle Object

Represents the cascaded format and style of its parent object, overriding global stylesheets, inline styles and HTML attributes. Overwrites the values of the currentStyle object but not the style object.

Properties		
	background	unicodeBidi
	backgroundAttachment	verticalAlign
	backgroundColor	visibility
	backgroundImage	width
	backgroundPosition	zIndex
	backgroundPositionX	borderTopStyle
	backgroundPositionY	borderTopWidth
	backgroundRepeat	borderWidth
	border	bottom
	borderBottom	clear
	borderBottomColor	clip
	borderBottomStyle	color
	borderBottomWidth	cssText
	borderColor	cursor
	borderLeft	direction
	borderLeftColor	display
	borderLeftStyle	filter
	borderLeftWidth	font
	borderRight	fontFamily
	borderRightColor	fontSize
	borderRightStyle	fontStyle
	borderRightWidth	fontVariant
	borderStyle	fontWeight
	borderTop	height
	borderTopColor	layoutGrid
	pixelBottom	layoutGridChar
	pixelHeight	layoutGridCharSpacing
	pixelLeft	layoutGridLine
	pixelRight	layoutGridMode
	pixelTop	layoutGridType
	pixelWidth	left
	posBottom	letterSpacing
	posHeight	lineHeight
	position	listStyle
	posLeft	listStyleImage
	posRight	listStylePosition
	posTop	listStyleType
	posWidth	margin
	right	marginBottom
	styleFloat	marginLeft
	tableLayout	marginRight
	textAlign	marginTop
	textDecoration	overflow
	textDecorationBlink	overflowX
	textDecorationLineThrough	overflowY
	textDecorationNone	padding
	textDecorationOverline	paddingBottom
	textDecorationUnderline	paddingLeft
	textIndent	paddingRight
	textTransform	paddingTop
	top	pageBreakAfter
		pageBreakBefore

Methods	None
Events	None
Collections	None

The screen Object

Exposes information about the client's monitor screen and system rendering abilities.

Properties	availHeight	fontSmoothingEnabled
	availWidth	height
	bufferDepth	updateInterval
	colorDepth	width
Methods	None	
Events	None	
Collections	None	

The selection Object

Represents the currently active selection on the screen in the document.

Properties	type		
Methods	clear	createRange	empty
Events	None		
Collections	None		

The style Object

Represents an individual style element within a style sheet.

Properties	background	lineHeight
	backgroundAttachment	listStyle
	backgroundColor	listStyleImage
	backgroundImage	listStylePosition
	backgroundPosition	listStyleType
	backgroundPositionX	margin
	backgroundPositionY	marginBottom
	backgroundRepeat	marginLeft
	border	marginRight
	borderBottom	marginTop
	borderBottomColor	overflow
	borderBottomStyle	overflowX
	borderBottomWidth	overflowY
	borderColor	padding
	borderLeft	paddingBottom
	borderLeftColor	paddingLeft
	borderLeftStyle	paddingRight

Table Continued on Following Page

685

Properties	borderLeftWidth	paddingTop
	borderRight	pageBreakAfter
	borderRightColor	pageBreakBefore
	borderRightStyle	pixelBottom
	borderRightWidth	pixelHeight
	borderStyle	pixelLeft
	borderTop	pixelRight
	borderTopColor	pixelTop
	borderTopStyle	pixelWidth
	borderTopWidth	posBottom
	borderWidth	posHeight
	bottom	position
	clear	posLeft
	clip	posRight
	color	posTop
	cssText	posWidth
	cursor	right
	direction	styleFloat
	display	tableLayout
	filter	textAlign
	font	textDecoration
	fontFamily	textDecorationBlink
	fontSize	textDecorationLineThrou
	fontStyle	gh
	fontVariant	textDecorationNone
	fontWeight	textDecorationOverline
	height	textDecorationUnderline
	layoutGrid	textIndent
	layoutGridChar	textTransform
	layoutGridCharSpacing	top
	layoutGridLine	unicodeBidi
	layoutGridMode	verticalAlign
	layoutGridType	visibility
	left	width
	letterSpacing	zIndex
Methods	getExpression removeExpression setExpression	
Events	None	
Collections	None	

The styleSheet Object

Exposes all the styles within a single style sheet in the styleSheets collection.

Properties	disabled id owningElement parentStyleSheet readOnly type
Methods	addImport addRule removeRule
Events	None
Collections	imports rules

The textNode Object

A string of text, represented as a node on the document hierarchy.

Properties	data length nextSibling nodeName nodeType nodeValue previousSibling
Methods	splitText
Events	None
Collections	None

The textRange Object

Represents sections of the text stream making up the HTML document.

Properties	boundingHeight boundingLeft boundingTop boundingWidth	htmlText offsetLeft offsetTop text
Methods	collapse compareEndPoints duplicate execCommand expand findText getBookmark getBoundingClientRect getClientRects inRange isEqual move moveEnd	moveStart moveToBookmark moveToElementText moveToPoint parentElement pasteHTML queryCommandEnabled queryCommandIndeterm queryCommandState queryCommandSupported queryCommandValue scrollIntoView select setEndPoint
Events	None	
Collections	None	

The textRectangle Object

A set of the four coordinates that represent the rectangle containing a line of text of TextRange object.

Properties	bottom left right top
Methods	None
Events	None
Collections	None

The userProfile Object

Allows a script to request read access to and perform read actions on a user's profile.

Properties	None		
Methods	addReadRequest getAttribute	clearRequest	doReadRequest
Events	None		
Collections	None		

The window Object

Exposes properties, methods and events connected to the browser window or a frame.

Properties	clientInformation	location
	clipboardData	name
	closed	navigator
	defaultStatus	offscreenBuffering
	dialogArguments	opener
	dialogHeight	parent
	dialogLeft	returnValue
	dialogTop	screen
	dialogWidth	screenLeft
	document	screenTop
	event	self
	external	status
	history	top
	length	
Methods	alert	open
	attachEvent	print
	blur	prompt
	clearInterval	resizeBy
	clearTimeout	resizeTo
	close	scroll
	confirm	scrollBy
	detachEvent	scrollTo
	execScript	setInterval
	focus	setTimeout
	moveBy	showHelp
	moveTo	showModalDialog
	navigate	showModelessDialog
Events	onafterprint	onfocus
	onbeforeprint	onhelp
	onbeforeunload	onload
	onblur	onresize
	onerror	onunload
Collections	Frames	

HTML and Form Controls Cross Reference

Dynamic HTML provides the same integral control types as HTML 3.2. However, there are many more different properties, methods and events available now for all the controls.

The following tables show those that are most relevant to controls.

Control Properties	checked	dataFld	dataFormatAs	dataSrc	defaultChecked	defaultValue	maxLength	readOnly	recordNumber	selectedIndex	size	status	type	value
HTML button	N	Y	Y	Y	N	Y	N	N	Y	N	Y	N	Y	Y
HTML checkbox	Y	Y	N	Y	Y	Y	N	N	Y	N	Y	Y	Y	Y
HTML file	N	Y	N	Y	N	Y	N	N	Y	N	Y	N	Y	Y
HTML hidden	N	Y	N	Y	N	Y	N	N	Y	N	N	N	Y	Y
HTML image	N	Y	N	Y	N	Y	N	N	Y	N	Y	N	Y	Y
HTML password	N	Y	N	Y	N	Y	Y	Y	Y	N	Y	N	Y	Y
HTML radio	Y	Y	N	Y	Y	Y	N	N	Y	N	Y	Y	Y	Y
HTML reset	N	Y	N	Y	N	Y	N	N	Y	N	Y	N	Y	Y
HTML submit	N	Y	N	Y	N	Y	N	N	Y	N	Y	N	Y	Y
HTML text	N	Y	N	Y	N	Y	Y	Y	Y	N	Y	N	Y	Y
APPLET tag	N	Y	N	Y	N	N	N	N	Y	N	N	N	N	N
BUTTON tag	N	Y	Y	Y	N	N	N	N	Y	N	N	N	Y	Y
FIELDSET tag	N	N	N	N	N	N	N	N	Y	N	N	N	N	N
LABEL tag	N	Y	Y	Y	N	N	N	N	Y	N	N	N	N	N
LEGEND tag	N	N	N	N	N	N	N	N	N	N	N	N	N	N
SELECT tag	N	Y	N	Y	N	N	N	N	Y	Y	Y	N	Y	N
TEXTAREA tag	N	Y	N	Y	N	Y	N	Y	N	N	N	N	Y	Y
XML tag	N	N	N	N	N	N	N	N	N	N	N	N	N	N

Control Methods	add	blur	click	createTex tRange	focus	item	remove	select
HTML button	N	Y	Y	Y	Y	N	N	Y
HTML checkbox	N	Y	Y	N	Y	N	N	Y
HTML file	N	Y	Y	N	Y	N	N	Y
HTML hidden	N	N	N	Y	N	N	N	N
HTML image	N	Y	Y	N	Y	N	N	Y
HTML password	N	Y	Y	Y	Y	N	N	Y
HTML radio	N	Y	Y	N	Y	N	N	Y
HTML reset	N	Y	Y	Y	Y	N	N	Y
HTML submit	N	Y	Y	Y	Y	N	N	Y
HTML text	N	Y	Y	Y	Y	N	N	Y
APPLET tag	N	Y	Y	N	Y	N	N	N
BUTTON tag	N	Y	Y	Y	Y	N	N	N
FIELDSET tag	N	Y	Y	N	Y	N	N	N
LABEL tag	N	Y	Y	N	Y	N	N	N
LEGEND tag	N	Y	Y	N	Y	N	N	N
SELECT tag	N	Y	Y	N	Y	N	N	N
TEXTAREA tag	N	Y	Y	Y	Y	N	N	Y
XML tag	N	N	N	N	N	N	N	N

Control Events	onafterupdate	onbeforeupdate	onblur	onchange	onclick	ondblclick	onfocus	onrowenter	onrowexit	onselect
HTML button	N	N	Y	N	Y	Y	Y	N	N	N
HTML checkbox	Y	Y	Y	N	Y	Y	Y	N	N	N
HTML file	N	N	Y	N	Y	Y	Y	N	N	N
HTML hidden	N	N	N	N	N	N	Y	N	N	N
HTML image	N	N	Y	N	Y	Y	Y	N	N	N
HTML password	N	N	Y	N	Y	Y	Y	N	N	N
HTML radio	N	N	Y	N	Y	Y	Y	N	N	N
HTML reset	N	N	Y	N	Y	Y	Y	N	N	N
HTML submit	N	N	Y	N	Y	Y	Y	N	N	N
HTML text	N	N	Y	Y	Y	Y	Y	N	N	Y
APPLET tag	N	N	Y	N	Y	Y	Y	Y	Y	N
BUTTON tag	N	N	Y	N	Y	Y	Y	N	N	N
FIELDSET tag	N	N	Y	N	Y	Y	Y	N	N	N
LABEL tag	N	N	Y	N	Y	Y	Y	N	N	N
LEGEND tag	N	N	Y	N	Y	Y	Y	N	N	N
SELECT tag	N	N	Y	Y	Y	Y	Y	N	N	N
TEXTAREA tag	Y	Y	Y	Y	Y	Y	Y	N	N	Y
XML tag	N	N	N	N	N	N	N	Y	Y	N

The Integral ASP Objects

This appendix summarizes the objects that make up the ASP object model, listing and describing all the members of each object.

The ASP Object Model

The **ASP** object model is made up of six objects:

- [ ] The **Application** object is created when the ASP DLL is loaded in response to the first request for an ASP page from a virtual application. It provides a repository for storing variables and object references that are available to all the pages that all visitors open.

- [ ] The **ASPError** object is a new object in ASP 3.0, and is available through the GetLastError method of the Server object. It provides a range of detailed information about the last error that occurred in ASP.

- [ ] The **Request** object makes available to the script all the information that the client provides when requesting a page, or submitting a form. This includes the HTTP variables that identify the browser and the user, cookies that are stored on the browser for this domain, and any values appended to the URL as a query string or in HTML controls in a <FORM> section of the page. It also provides access to a range of server environment variables, the contents of any certificate that the client may be using through **Secure Sockets Layer** (SSL) or other encrypted communication protocol, and properties that help to manage the connection.

- [ ] The **Response** object is used to access and generate the response that is being created to send back to the client. It makes available information about the content being sent to the browser, and any new cookies that will be stored on the browser for this domain. It also provides a series of methods that are used to create the returned page.

❑ The **Server** object provides a series of methods and properties that are useful in scripting with ASP. The most obvious is the `Server.CreateObject` method, which properly instantiates other COM objects within the context of the current page or session. There are also methods to translate strings into the correct format for use in URLs and in HTML, by converting non-legal characters to the correct legal equivalent.

❑ The **Session** object is created for each visitor when they first request an ASP page from a virtual application, and remains available until the default timeout period (or the timeout period determined by the script) expires or the session is explicitly ended with the `Abandon` method. It provides a repository for storing variables and object references that are available just to the pages that this visitor opens during the lifetime of this session.

The following diagram shows conceptually how these objects relate to the client and the server, and the requests made by the client and the responses sent back to them from the server:

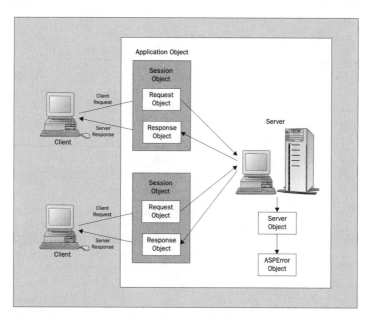

The Application Object

Provides a repository for storing variables and object references that are available to all the pages that all visitors open.

The Application Collections

The `Application` object provides two collections that are used to access the variables and objects that are stored in the global application space:

Collection Name	Description
Contents	A collection of all of the variables and their values that are stored in the `Application` object, and are *not* defined using an <OBJECT> element. This includes `Variant` arrays and `Variant`-type object instance references.
StaticObjects	A collection of all of the variables that are stored in the `Application` object by using an <OBJECT> element.

The Application Methods

The `Application` methods are used to remove values from the global application space, and control concurrent accesses to variables within the space:

Method	Description
Contents.Remove (*variable_name*)	Removes a named variable from the `Application.Contents` collection.
Contents.RemoveAll()	Removes all variables from the `Application.Contents` collection.
Lock()	Locks the `Application` object so that only the current ASP page has access to the contents. Used to ensure that concurrency issues do not corrupt the contents by allowing two users to simultaneously read and update the values.
Unlock()	Releases this ASP page's lock on the `Application` object.

* You *cannot* remove variables from the `Application.StaticObjects` collection at runtime.

The Application Events

The Application object exposes two events that occur when an application starts and ends:

Event	Description
onStart	Occurs when the ASP application starts, before the page that the user requests is executed. Used to initialize variables, create objects, or run other code.
onEnd	Occurs when the ASP application ends. This is after the last user session has ended, and after any code in the onEnd event for that session has executed. All variables existing in the application are destroyed when it ends.

The ASPError Object

Provides a range of detailed information about the last error that occurred in ASP.

The ASPError Properties

The ASPError object provides nine properties that describe the error that occurred, the nature and source of the error, and (where possible) return the actual code that caused it:

Property	Description
ASPCode	*Integer.* The error number generated by IIS.
ASPDescription	*String.* A detailed description of the error if it is ASP-related.
Category	*String.* The source of the error, i.e. internal to ASP, the scripting language, or an object.
Column	*Integer.* The character position within the file that generated the error.
Description	*String.* A short description of the error.
File	*String.* The name of the file that was being processed when the error occurred.
Line	*Integer.* The number of the line within the file that generated the error.
Number	*Integer.* A standard COM error code.
Source	*String.* The actual code, where available, of the line that caused the error.

The Request Object

Makes available all the information that the client provides when requesting a page, or submitting a form.

The Request Collections

The Request object provides five collections that we can use to access all kinds of information about the client's request to the Web server:

Collection Name	Description
ClientCertificate	A collection of the values of all the fields or entries in the client certificate that the user presented to the server when accessing a page or resource. Each member is read-only.
Cookies	A collection of the values of all the cookies sent from the user's system along with their request. Only cookies valid for the domain containing the resource are sent to the server.
Form	A collection of the values of all the HTML control elements in the <FORM> section that was submitted as the request, where the value of the METHOD attribute is "POST". Each member is read-only.
QueryString	A collection of all the name/value pairs appended to the URL in the user's request, or the values of all the HTML control elements in the <FORM> section that was submitted as the request where the value of the METHOD attribute is "GET" or the attribute is omitted. Each member is read-only.
ServerVariables	A collection of all the HTTP header values sent from the client with their request, plus the values of several environment variables for the Web server. Each member is read-only.

The Request Property

The single property of the Request object provides information about the number of bytes in the user's request:

Property	Description
TotalBytes	Read-only. Returns the total number of bytes in the body of the request sent by the client.

The Request Method

The single method of the Request object provides access to the complete content of the part of a user's request that is POSTed to the server from a <FORM> section of a web page:

Method	Description
BinaryRead(*count*)	Retrieves *count* bytes of data from the client's request when the data is sent to the server as part of a POST request. It returns as a Variant array (or SafeArray). This method *cannot* be used successfully if the ASP code has already referenced the Request.Form collection. Likewise, the Request.Form collection *cannot* be successfully accessed if you have used the BinaryRead method.

The Response Object

Used to access the response that is being creating to send back to the client.

The Response Collection

The Response object provides a single collection that is used to set the values of any cookies that will be placed on the client system:

Collection Name	Description
Cookies	A collection containing the values of all the cookies this will be sent back to the client in the current response. Each member is write only.

The Response Properties

The **Response** object provides a range of properties that can be read (in most cases) and modified to tailor the response:

Property	Description
Buffer = true|false	Read/write. *Boolean*. Specifies if the output created by an ASP page will be held in the IIS buffer until all of the server scripts in the current page have been processed, or until the Flush or End method is called. It must be set before any output is sent to IIS, including HTTP header information, so it should be the first line of the .asp file after the <%@LANGUAGE=..%> statement. Buffering is on (true) by default in ASP 3.0, whereas it was off (false) by default in earlier versions.
CacheControl = "*setting*"	Read/write. *String*. Set this property to Public to allow proxy servers to cache the page, or Private to prevent proxy caching taking place.
Charset("*value*")	Read/write. *String*. Appends the name of the character set (for example, ISO-LATIN-7) to the HTTP **Content-Type** header created by the server for each response.
ContentType "*MIME-type*"	Read/write. *String*. Specifies the HTTP content type for the response, as a standard MIME-type (such as "text/xml" or "image/gif"). If omitted the MIME-type "text/html" is used. The content type tells the browser what type of content to expect.
Expires = *minutes*	Read/write. *Number*. Specifies the length of time in minutes that a page is valid for. If the user returns to the same page before it expires, the cached version is displayed. After that period it expires, and should not be held in a private (user) or public (proxy) cache.
ExpiresAbsolute = #*date[time]*#	Read/write. *Date/Time*. Specifies the absolute date and time when a page will expire and no longer be valid. If the user returns to the same page before it expires, the cached version is displayed. After that time it expires, and should not be held in a private (user) or public (proxy) cache.

Table Continued on Following Page

Property	Description
IsClientConnected()	Read-only. *Boolean*. Returns an indication of whether the client is still connected to and loading the page from the server. Can be used to end processing (with the Response.End method) if a client moves to another page before the current one has finished executing.
PICS ("*PICS-label-string*")	Write only. *String*. Create a PICS header and adds it to the HTTP headers in the response. PICS headers define the content of the page in terms of violence, sex, bad language, etc.
Status = "*code message*"	Read/write. *String*. Specifies the status value and message that will be sent to the client in the HTTP headers of the response to indicate an error or successful processing of the page. Examples are "200 OK" and "404 Not Found".

The Response Methods

The **Response** object provides a set of methods that directly manipulate the content of the page being created on the server for return to the client:

Method	Description
AddHeader ("*name*", "*content*")	Creates a custom HTTP header using the *name* and *content* values and adds it to the response. Will *not* replace an existing header of the same name. Once a header has been added, it cannot be removed. Must be used before any page content (i.e. text and HTML) is sent to the client.
AppendToLog ("*string*")	Adds a string to the end of the Web server log entry for this request when **W3C Extended Log File Format** is in use. Requires at least the **URI Stem** value to be selected in the **Extended Properties** page for the site containing the page.
BinaryWrite(*SafeArray*)	Writes the content of a Variant-type SafeArray to the current HTTP output stream without any character conversion. Useful for writing non-string information such as binary data required by a custom application or the bytes to make up an image file.

Method	Description
`Clear()`	Erases any existing buffered page content from the IIS response buffer when `Response.Buffer` is `true`. Does *not* erase HTTP response headers. Can be used to abort a partly completed page.
`End()`	Stops ASP from processing the page script and returns the currently created content, then aborts any further processing of this page.
`Flush()`	Sends all currently buffered page content in the IIS buffer to the client when `Response.Buffer` is `true`. Can be used to send parts of a long page to the client individually.
`Redirect("`*url*`")`	Instructs the browser to load the page in the string *url* parameter by sending a `"302 Object Moved"` HTTP header in the response.
`Write("`*string*`")`	Writes the specified *string* to the current HTTP response stream and IIS buffer so that it becomes part of the returned page.

The Server Object

Provides a series of methods and properties that are useful in scripting with ASP and creating instances of other objects.

The Server Property

The single property of the `Server` object provides access to the script timeout value for an executing ASP page:

Property	Description
`ScriptTimeout`	*Integer. Default* = 90. Sets or returns the number of seconds that script in the page can execute for before the server aborts page execution and reports an error. This automatically halts and removes from memory pages that contain errors that may lock execution into a loop or those that stall while waiting for a resource to become available. This prevents the server becoming overloaded with badly behaved pages. You may need to increase this value if your pages take a long time to run.

The Server Methods

The methods of the **Server** object provide ways to format data, manage page execution, and create instances of other objects:

Method	Description
CreateObject("*identifier*")	Creates an instance of the object (a component, application or scripting object) that is identified by "*identifier*", and returns a reference to it that can be used in our code. Can be used in the global.asa page of a virtual application to create objects with session-level or application-level scope. The object can be identified by its ClassID (i.e. "{CLSID:FDC8-...-37A9}") value or by a ProgID string such as "ADODB.Connection".
Execute("*url*")	Stops execution of the current page and transfers control to the page specified in "*url*". The user's current environment (i.e. session state and any current transaction state) is carried over to the new page. After that page has finished execution, control passes back to the original page and execution resumes at the statement after the Execute method call.
GetLastError()	Returns a reference to an ASPError object that holds details of the last error that occurred within the ASP processing, i.e. within asp.dll. The information exposed by the ASPError object includes the file name, line number, error code, etc.
HTMLEncode("*string*")	Returns a string that is a copy of the input value "*string*" but with all non-legal HTML characters such as '<', '>', '&' and double quotes converted into the equivalent HTML entity—i.e. <, >, &, ", etc.
MapPath("*url*")	Returns the full physical path and filename of the file or resource specified in "*url*".

Method	Description
Transfer("*url*")	Stops execution of the current page and transfers control to the page specified in "*url*". The user's current environment (i.e. session state and any current transaction state) is carried over to the new page. Unlike the Execute method, execution *does not* resume in the original page, but ends when the new page has completed executing.
URLEncode("*string*")	Returns a string that is a copy of the input value "*string*" but with all characters that are not valid in a URL, such as '?', '&' and spaces, converted into the equivalent URL entity—i.e. '%3F', '%26', and '+'.

The Session Object

Provides a repository for storing variables and object references that are available just to the pages that this visitor opens during the lifetime of this session.

The Session Collections

The **Session** object provides two collections that can be used to access the variables and objects that are stored in the user's local session space:

Collection Name	Description
Contents	A collection of all of the variables and their values that are stored in this particular Session object, and are *not* defined using an <OBJECT> element. This includes Variant arrays and Variant-type object instance references.
StaticObjects	A collection of all of the variables that are stored in this particular Session object by using an <OBJECT> element.

The Session Properties

The **Session** object provides four properties that expose details of the session:

Property	Description
CodePage	Read/write. *Integer*. Defines the code page that will be used to display the page content in the browser. The code page is the numeric value of the character set, and different languages and locales may use different code pages. For example, ANSI code page 1252 is used for American English and most European languages. Code page 932 is used for Japanese Kanji.
LCID	Read/write. *Integer*. Defines the locale identifier (LCID) of the page that is sent to the browser. The LCID is a standard international abbreviation that uniquely identifies the locale; for instance 2057 defines a locale where the currency symbol used is '£'. This LCID can also be used in statements such as FormatCurrency, where there is an optional LCID argument. The LCID for a page can also be set in the opening <%@..%> ASP processing directive and overrides the setting in the LCID property of the session.
SessionID	Read only. *Long*. Returns the session identifier for this session, which is generated by the server when the session is created. Unique only for the duration of the parent Application object and so may be re-used when a new application is started.
Timeout	Read/write. *Integer*. Defines the timeout period in minutes for this Session object. If the user does not refresh or request a page within the timeout period, the session ends. Can be changed in individual pages as required.

The Session Methods

The **Session** methods are used to remove values from the user-level session space, and terminate sessions on demand:

Method	Description
Contents.Remove ("*variable_name*")	Removes a named variable from the Session.Contents collection.
Contents.RemoveAll ()	Removes all variables from the Session.Contents collection.

Method	Description
Abandon()	Ends the current user session and destroys the current Session object once execution of this page is complete. You can still access the current session's variables in this page, even after calling the Abandon method. However the next ASP page that is requested by this user will start a new session, and create a new Session object with only the default values defined in global.asa (if any exist).

* You *cannot* remove variables from the Session.StaticObjects collection at runtime.

The Session Events

The **Session** object exposes two events that occur when a user session starts and ends:

Event	Description
onStart	Occurs when an ASP user session starts, before the page that the user requests is executed. Used to initialize variables, create objects, or run other code.
onEnd	Occurs when an ASP user session ends. This is when the predetermined session timeout period has elapsed since that user's last page request from the application. All variables existing in the session are destroyed when it ends. It is also possible to end ASP user sessions explicitly in code using the Session.Abandon method, and this event occurs when that happens.

ADO Object Summary, Constants, and Data Types

Microsoft ActiveX Data Objects 2.5 Library Reference

Properties or methods new to version 2.5 are shown *italicized*.

> **All properties are read/write unless otherwise stated.**

Objects

Name	Description
Command	A Command object is a definition of a specific command that you intend to execute against a data source.
Connection	A Connection object represents an open connection to a data store.
Error	An Error object contains the details about data access errors pertaining to a single operation involving the provider.
Errors	The Errors collection contains all of the Error objects created in response to a single failure involving the provider.
Field	A Field object represents a column of data within a common data type.

Table Continued on Following Page

Name	Description
Fields	A `Fields` collection contains all of the `Field` objects of a `Recordset` object.
Parameter	A `Parameter` object represents a parameter or argument associated with a `Command` object based on a parameterized query or stored procedure.
Parameters	A `Parameters` collection contains all the `Parameter` objects of a `Command` object.
Properties	A `Properties` collection contains all the `Property` objects for a specific instance of an object.
Property	A `Property` object represents a dynamic characteristic of an ADO object that is defined by the provider.
Record	A `Record` object represents a row in a recordset, or a file or directory in a file sytem or Web resource.
Recordset	A `Recordset` object represents the entire set of records from a base table or the results of an executed command. At any time, the `Recordset` object only refers to a single record within the set as the current record.
Stream	A `Stream` object represents a stream of text or binary data.

Command Object

Methods

Name	Returns	Description
Cancel		Cancels execution of a pending `Execute` or `Open` call.
CreateParameter	Parameter	Creates a new `Parameter` object.
Execute	Recordset	Executes the query, SQL statement, or stored procedure specified in the `CommandText` property.

Properties

Name	Returns	Description
ActiveConnection	Variant	Indicates to which `Connection` object the command currently belongs.
CommandText	String	Contains the text of a command to be issued against a data provider.
CommandTimeout	Long	Indicates how long to wait, in seconds, while executing a command before terminating the command and generating an error. Default is 30.

Name	Returns	Description
CommandType	CommandTypeEnum	Indicates the type of Command object.
Name	String	Indicates the name of the Command object.
Parameters	Parameters	Contains all of the Parameter objects for a Command object.
Prepared	Boolean	Indicates whether or not to save a compiled version of a command before execution.
Properties	Properties	Contains all of the Property objects for a Command object.
State	Long	Describes whether the Command object is open or closed. Read only.

Connection Object

Methods

Name	Returns	Description
BeginTrans	Integer	Begins a new transaction.
Cancel		Cancels the execution of a pending, asynchronous Execute or Open operation.
Close		Closes an open connection and any dependant objects.
CommitTrans		Saves any changes and ends the current transaction.
Execute	Recordset	Executes the query, SQL statement, stored procedure, or provider-specific text.
Open		Opens a connection to a data source, so that commands can be executed against it.
OpenSchema	Recordset	Obtains database schema information from the provider.
RollbackTrans		Cancels any changes made during the current transaction and ends the transaction.

Properties

Name	Returns	Description
Attributes	Long	Indicates one or more characteristics of a Connection object. Default is 0.
CommandTimeout	Long	Indicates how long, in seconds, to wait while executing a command before terminating the command and generating an error. The default is 30.
ConnectionString	String	Contains the information used to establish a connection to a data source.
ConnectionTimeout	Long	Indicates how long, in seconds, to wait while establishing a connection before terminating the attempt and generating an error. Default is 15.
CursorLocation	CursorLocationEnum	Sets or returns the location of the cursor engine.
DefaultDatabase	String	Indicates the default database for a Connection object.
Errors	Errors	Contains all of the Error objects created in response to a single failure involving the provider.
IsolationLevel	IsolationLevelEnum	Indicates the level of transaction isolation for a Connection object. Write only.
Mode	ConnectModeEnum	Indicates the available permissions for modifying data in a Connection.
Properties	Properties	Contains all of the Property objects for a Connection object.
Provider	String	Indicates the name of the provider for a Connection object.
State	Long	Describes whether the Connection object is open or closed. Read only.
Version	String	Indicates the ADO version number. Read only.

Events

Name	Description
BeginTransComplete	Fired after a `BeginTrans` operation finishes executing.
CommitTransComplete	Fired after a `CommitTrans` operation finishes executing.
ConnectComplete	Fired after a connection starts.
Disconnect	Fired after a connection ends.
ExecuteComplete	Fired after a command has finished executing.
InfoMessage	Fired whenever a `ConnectionEvent` operation completes successfully and additional information is returned by the provider.
RollbackTransComplete	Fired after a `RollbackTrans` operation has finished executing.
WillConnect	Fired before a connection starts.
WillExecute	Fired before a pending command executes on the connection.

Error Object

Properties

Name	Returns	Description
Description	String	A description string associated with the error. Read only.
HelpContext	Integer	Indicates the `ContextID` in the help file for the associated error. Read only.
HelpFile	String	Indicates the name of the help file. Read only.
NativeError	Long	Indicates the provider-specific error code for the associated error. Read only.
Number	Long	Indicates the number that uniquely identifies an `Error` object. Read only.
Source	String	Indicates the name of the object or application that originally generated the error. Read only.
SQLState	String	Indicates the SQL state for a given `Error` object. It is a five-character string that follows the ANSI SQL standard. Read only.

Errors Collection

Methods

Name	Returns	Description
Clear		Removes all of the Error objects from the Errors collection.
Refresh		Updates the Error objects with information from the provider.

Properties

Name	Returns	Description
Count	Long	Indicates the number of Error objects in the Errors collection. Read only.
Item	Error	Allows indexing into the Errors collection to reference a specific Error object. Read only.

Field Object

Methods

Name	Returns	Description
AppendChunk		Appends data to a large or binary Field object.
GetChunk	Variant	Returns all or a portion of the contents of a large or binary Field object.

Properties

Name	Returns	Description
ActualSize	Long	Indicates the actual length of a field's value. Read only.
Attributes	Long	Indicates one or more characteristics of a Field object.
DataFormat	Variant	Identifies the format that the data should be display in.
DefinedSize	Long	Indicates the defined size of the Field object. Write only.
Name	String	Indicates the name of the Field object.

Name	Returns	Description
NumericScale	Byte	Indicates the scale of numeric values for the `Field` object. Write only.
OriginalValue	Variant	Indicates the value of a `Field` object that existed in the record before any changes were made. Read only.
Precision	Byte	Indicates the degree of precision for numeric values in the `Field` object. Read only.
Properties	Properties	Contains all of the `Property` objects for a `Field` object.
Type	DataTypeEnum	Indicates the data type of the `Field` object.
UnderlyingValue	Variant	Indicates a `Field` object's current value in the database. Read only.
Value	Variant	Indicates the value assigned to the `Field` object.

Fields Collection

Methods

Name	Returns	Description
Append		Appends a `Field` object to the `Fields` collection.
CancelUpdate		Cancels any changes made to the `Fields` collection.
Delete		Deletes a `Field` object from the `Fields` collection.
Refresh		Updates the `Field` objects in the `Fields` collection.
Resync		Resynchronizes the data in the `Field` objects.
Update		Saves any changes made to the `Fields` collection.

Properties

Name	Returns	Description
Count	Long	Indicates the number of Field objects in the Fields collection. Read only.
Item	Field	Allows indexing into the Fields collection to reference a specific Field object. Read only.

Parameter Object

Methods

Name	Returns	Description
AppendChunk		Appends data to a large or binary Parameter object.

Properties

Name	Returns	Description
Attributes	Long	Indicates one or more characteristics of a Parameter object.
Direction	ParameterDirectionEnum	Indicates whether the Parameter object represents an input parameter, an output parameter, or both, or if the parameter is a return value from a stored procedure.
Name	String	Indicates the name of the Parameter object.
NumericScale	Byte	Indicates the scale of numeric values for the Parameter object.
Precision	Byte	Indicates the degree of precision for numeric values in the Parameter object.
Properties	Properties	Contains all of the Property objects for a Parameter object.
Size	Long	Indicates the maximum size, in bytes or characters, of a Parameter object.
Type	DataTypeEnum	Indicates the data type of the Parameter object.
Value	Variant	Indicates the value assigned to the Parameter object.

Parameters Collection

Methods

Name	Returns	Description
Append		Appends a Parameter object to the Parameters collection.
Delete		Deletes a Parameter object from the Parameters collection.
Refresh		Updates the Parameter objects in the Parameters collection.

Properties

Name	Returns	Description
Count	Long	Indicates the number of Parameter objects in the Parameters collection. Read only.
Item	Parameter	Allows indexing into the Parameters collection to reference a specific Parameter object. Read only.

Properties

Methods

Name	Returns	Description
Refresh		Updates the Property objects in the Properties collection with the details from the provider.

Properties

Name	Returns	Description
Count	Long	Indicates the number of Property objects in the Properties collection. Read only.
Item	Property	Allows indexing into the Properties collection to reference a specific Property object. Read only.

Property Object

Properties

Name	Returns	Description
Attributes	Long	Indicates one or more characteristics of a Property object.
Name	String	Indicates the name of the Property object. Read only.
Type	DataTypeEnum	Indicates the data type of the Property object.
Value	Variant	Indicates the value assigned to the Property object.

Record

Methods

Name	Returns	Description
Cancel		Cancels the execution of an asynchronous Execute or Open.
Close		Closes the open record.
CopyRecord	String	Copies the object the Record represents, or a file or directory, from one location to another.
DeleteRecord		Deletes the object the Record represents, or a file or directory.
GetChildren	Recordset	Returns a Recordset containing the files and folders in the directory that the Record represents.
MoveRecord	String	Moves the object the Record represents, or a file or directory, from one location to another.
Open		Opens, or creates a new, existing file or directory.

Properties

Name	Returns	Description
ActiveConnection	Variant	Indicates to which Connection object the specified Recordset object currently belongs.
Fields	Fields	Contains all of the Field objects for the current Recordset object. Read only

Name	Returns	Description
Mode	ConnectModeEnum	Indicates the available permissions for modifying data in a `Connection`.
ParentURL	String	Indicates the absolute URL of the parent `Record` of the current `Record`. Read only
Properties	Properties	Contains all of the `Property` objects for the current `Recordset` object. Read only
RecordType	RecordTypeEnum	Indicates whether the record is a simple record, a structured document, or a collection. Read only
Source	Variant	Indicates what the `Record` represents - a URL or a reference to an open `Recordset`.
State	ObjectStateEnum	Indicates whether the `Record` is open or closed, and if open the state of asynchronous actions. Read only

Recordset Object

Methods

Name	Returns	Description
AddNew		Creates a new record for an updateable `Recordset` object.
Cancel		Cancels execution of a pending asynchronous `Open` operation.
CancelBatch		Cancels a pending batch update.
CancelUpdate		Cancels any changes made to the current record, or to a new record prior to calling the `Update` method.
Clone	Recordset	Creates a duplicate `Recordset` object from and existing `Recordset` object.
Close		Closes the `Recordset` object and any dependent objects.
CompareBookmarks	CompareEnum	Compares two bookmarks and returns an indication of the relative values.
Delete		Deletes the current record or group of records.

Table Continued on Following Page

Name	Returns	Description
Find		Searches the Recordset for a record that matches the specified criteria.
GetRows	Variant	Retrieves multiple records of a Recordset object into an array.
GetString	String	Returns a Recordset as a string.
Move		Moves the position of the current record in a Recordset.
MoveFirst		Moves the position of the current record to the first record in the Recordset.
MoveLast		Moves the position of the current record to the last record in the Recordset.
MoveNext		Moves the position of the current record to the next record in the Recordset.
MovePrevious		Moves the position of the current record to the previous record in the Recordset.
NextRecordset	Recordset	Clears the current Recordset object and returns the next Recordset by advancing through a series of commands.
Open		Opens a Recordset.
Requery		Updates the data in a Recordset object by re-executing the query on which the object is based.
Resync		Refreshes the data in the current Recordset object from the underlying database.
Save		Saves the Recordset to a file.
Seek		Searches the recordset index to locate a value
Supports	Boolean	Determines whether a specified Recordset object supports particular functionality.
Update		Saves any changes made to the current Recordset object.
UpdateBatch		Writes all pending batch updates to disk.

Properties

Name	Returns	Description
AbsolutePage	PositionEnum	Specifies in which page the current record resides.
AbsolutePosition	PositionEnum	Specifies the ordinal position of a Recordset object's current record.
ActiveCommand	Object	Indicates the Command object that created the associated Recordset object. Read only.
ActiveConnection	Variant	Indicates to which Connection object the specified Recordset object currently belongs.
BOF	Boolean	Indicates whether the current record is before the first record in a Recordset object. Read only.
Bookmark	Variant	Returns a bookmark that uniquely identifies the current record in a Recordset object, or sets the current record to the record identified by a valid bookmark.
CacheSize	Long	Indicates the number of records from a Recordset object that are cached locally in memory.
CursorLocation	CursorLocationEnum	Sets or returns the location of the cursor engine.
CursorType	CursorTypeEnum	Indicates the type of cursor used in a Recordset object.
DataMember	String	Specifies the name of the data member to retrieve from the object referenced by the DataSource property. Write only.
DataSource	Object	Specifies an object containing data to be represented as a Recordset object. Write only.
EditMode	EditModeEnum	Indicates the editing status of the current record. Read only.
EOF	Boolean	Indicates whether the current record is after the last record in a Recordset object. Read only.

Table Continued on Following Page

Name	Returns	Description
Fields	Fields	Contains all of the `Field` objects for the current `Recordset` object.
Filter	Variant	Indicates a filter for data in the `Recordset`.
Index	String	Identifies the name of the index currently being used.
LockType	LockTypeEnum	Indicates the type of locks placed on records during editing.
MarshalOptions	MarshalOptionsEnum	Indicates which records are to be marshaled back to the server.
MaxRecords	Long	Indicates the maximum number of records to return to a `Recordset` object from a query. Default is zero (no limit).
PageCount	Long	Indicates how many pages of data the `Recordset` object contains. Read only.
PageSize	Long	Indicates how many records constitute one page in the `Recordset`.
Properties	Properties	Contains all of the `Property` objects for the current `Recordset` object.
RecordCount	Long	Indicates the current number of records in the `Recordset` object. Read only.
Sort	String	Specifies one or more field names the `Recordset` is sorted on, and the direction of the sort.
Source	String	Indicates the source for the data in a `Recordset` object.
State	Long	Indicates whether the recordset is open, closed, or whether it is executing an asynchronous operation. Read only.
Status	Integer	Indicates the status of the current record with respect to match updates or other bulk operations. Read only.
StayInSync	Boolean	Indicates, in a hierarchical `Recordset` object, whether the parent row should change when the set of underlying child records changes. Read only.

Events

Name	Description
EndOfRecordset	Fired when there is an attempt to move to a row past the end of the `Recordset`.
FetchComplete	Fired after all the records in an asynchronous operation have been retrieved into the `Recordset`.
FetchProgress	Fired periodically during a length asynchronous operation, to report how many rows have currently been retrieved.
FieldChangeComplete	Fired after the value of one or more `Field` object has been changed.
MoveComplete	Fired after the current position in the `Recordset` changes.
RecordChangeComplete	Fired after one or more records change.
RecordsetChangeComplete	Fired after the `Recordset` has changed.
WillChangeField	Fired before a pending operation changes the value of one or more `Field` objects.
WillChangeRecord	Fired before one or more rows in the `Recordset` change.
WillChangeRecordset	Fired before a pending operation changes the `Recordset`.
WillMove	Fired before a pending operation changes the current position in the `Recordset`.

Stream

Methods

Name	Returns	Description
Cancel		Cancels execution of a pending asynchronous `Open` operation.
Close		Closes an open `Stream`.
CopyTo		Copies characters or bytes from one Stream to another.
Flush		Flushes the contents of the Stream to the underlying object.
LoadFromFile		Loads a stream from a file.

Table Continued on Following Page

Name	Returns	Description
Open		Opens a Stream object from a URL or an existing Record, or creates a blank Stream.
Read	Variant	Reads a number of bytes from the Stream.
ReadText	String	Reads a number of characters from a text Stream.
SaveToFile		Saves an open Stream to a file.
SetEOS		Sets the current position to be the end of the Stream.
SkipLine		Skips a line when reading from a text Stream.
Write		Writes binary data to a Stream.
WriteText		Writes text data to a Stream.

Properties

Name	Returns	Description
Charset	String	Identifies the character set used by the Stream.
EOS	Boolean	Is set to True if the current position is the end of the Stream. Read only
LineSeparator	LineSeparatorEnum	Indicates the character used to separate lines in a text Stream. The default is vbCrLf.
Mode	ConnectModeEnum	Indicates the available permissions for modifying data in a Connection.
Position	Long	Specifies the current position in the Stream.
Size	Long	Indicates the length, in bytes, of the Stream. Read only
State	ObjectStateEnum	Indicates whether the Stream is open or closed, and if open the state of asynchronous actions. Read only Read only
Type	StreamTypeEnum	Indicates whether the Stream contains text or binary data.

Method Calls

Command

Command.Cancel
Parameter = Command.CreateParameter([*Name As String*], [*Type As DataTypeEnu*]m, _
    [*Direction As ParameterDirectionEnum*], [*Size As Long*], [*Value As Variant*])
Recordset = Command.Execute([*RecordsAffected As Variant*], [*Parameters As Varian*]t, _
    [*Options As Long*])

Connection

Long = Connection.BeginTrans
Connection.Cancel
Connection.Close
Connection.CommitTrans
Recordset = Connection.Execute(*CommandText As String*, [*RecordsAffected As Variant*], _
    [*Options As Long*])
Connection.Open([*ConnectionString As String*], [*UserID As String*], [*Password As String*], _
    [*Options As Long*])
Recordset = Connection.OpenSchema(*Schema As SchemaEnum*, [*Restrictions As Variant*], _
    [*SchemaID As Variant*])
Connection.RollbackTrans

Errors

Errors.Clear
Errors.Refresh

Field

Field.AppendChunk(*Data As Variant*)
Variant = Field.GetChunk(*Length As Long*)

Fields

Fields.Append(*Name As String, Type As DataTypeEnum*, [*DefinedSize As Long*], _
    [*Attrib As FieldAttributeEnum*], [*FieldValue As Variant*])
Fields.CancelUpdate
Fields.Delete(*Index As Variant*)
Fields.Refresh
Fields.Resync(*ResyncValues As ResyncEnum*)
Fields.Update

Parameter

Parameter.AppendChunk(*Val As Variant*)

Parameters

Parameters.Append(*Object As Object*)
Parameters.Delete(*Index As Variant*)
Parameters.Refresh

Properties

Properties.Refresh

Record

Record.Cancel
Record.Close
String = Record.CopyRecord(*[Source As String], Destination As String, [UserName As String], _*
  [Password As String], [Options As CopyRecordOptionsEnum], [Async As Boolean])
Record.DeleteRecord(*Source As String, Async As Boolean*)
Recordset = Record.GetChildren
String = Record.MoveRecord(*[Source As String], Destination As String, [UserName As String], _*
  [Password As String], [Options As MoveRecordOptionsEnum], [Async As Boolean])
Record.Open(*[Source As Variant], [ActiveConnection As Variant], [Mode As ConnectModeEnum], _*
  [CreateOptions As RecordCreateOptionsEnum], [Options As RecordOpenOptionsEnum], _
  [UserName As String], [Password As String])

Recordset

Recordset.AddNew(*[FieldList As Variant], [Values As Variant]*)
Recordset.Cancel
Recordset.CancelBatch(*[AffectRecords As AffectEnum]*)
Recordset.CancelUpdate
Recordset = Recordset.Clone(*[LockType As LockTypeEnum]*)
Recordset.Close
CompareEnum = Recordset.CompareBookmarks(*Bookmark1 As Variant, _*
  Bookmark2 As Variant)
Recordset.Delete(*AffectRecords As AffectEnum*)
Recordset.Find(*Criteria As String, [SkipRecords As Long], _*
  [SearchDirection As SearchDirectionEnum], [Start As Variant])
Variant = Recordset.GetRows(*Rows As Long, [Start As Variant], [Fields As Variant]*)
String = Recordset.GetString(*StringFormat As StringFormatEnum, [NumRows As Long], _*
  [ColumnDelimeter As String], [RowDelimeter As String], [NullExpr As String])
Recordset.Move(*NumRecords As Long, [Start As Variant]*)
Recordset.MoveFirst
Recordset.MoveLast
Recordset.MoveNext
Recordset.MovePrevious

Recordset = Recordset.NextRecordset([RecordsAffected As Variant])
Recordset.Open([Source As Variant], [ActiveConnection As Variant],_
    [CursorType As CursorTypeEnum], [LockType As LockTypeEnum], [Options As Long])
Recordset.Requery([Options As Long])
Recordset.Resync([AffectRecords As AffectEnum], [ResyncValues As ResyncEnum])
Recordset.Save([Destination As Variant], [PersistFormat As PersistFormatEnum])
Recordset.Seek(KeyValues As Variant, SeekOption As SeekEnum)
Boolean = Recordset.Supports(CursorOptions As CursorOptionEnum)
Recordset.Update([Fields As Variant], [Values As Variant])
Recordset.UpdateBatch([AffectRecords As AffectEnum])

Stream

Stream.Cancel
Stream.Close
Stream.CopyTo(DestStream As Stream, [CharNumber As Long])
Stream.Flush
Stream.LoadFromFile(FileName As String)
Stream.Open([Source As Variant], [Mode As ConnectModeEnum],_
    [Options As StreamOpenOptionsEnum], [UserName As String], [Password As String])
Variant = Stream.Read([NumBytes As Long])
String = Stream.ReadText([NumChars As Long])
Stream.SaveToFile(FileName As String, Options As SaveOptionsEnum)
Stream.SetEOS
Stream.SkipLine
Stream.Write(Buffer As Variant)
Stream.WriteText(Data As String, [Options As StreamWriteEnum])

ADO Constants

Standard Constants

The following constants are predefined by ADO. For scripting languages these are included in adovbs.inc or adojava.inc, which can be found in the Program Files\Common Files\System\ado directory. For ASP you can either include the .inc file, or set a reference to the type library with a METADATA tag:

```
<!-- METADATA TYPE="typelib" FILE="C:\Program Files\Common
Files\System\ADO\msado15.dll" -->
```

For Visual Basic these constants are automatically included when you reference the ADO library.

Constants new to ADO 2.5 are shown *italicized*.

AffectEnum

Name	Value	Description
adAffectAll	3	Operation affects all records in the recordset.
adAffectAllChapters	4	Operation affects all child (chapter) records.
adAffectCurrent	1	Operation affects only the current record.
adAffectGroup	2	Operation affects records that satisfy the current Filter property.

BookmarkEnum

Name	Value	Description
adBookmarkCurrent	0	Default. Start at the current record.
adBookmarkFirst	1	Start at the first record.
adBookmarkLast	2	Start at the last record.

CEResyncEnum

Name	Value	Description
adResyncAll	15	Resynchronizes the data for each pending row.
adResyncAutoIncrement	1	Resynchronizes the auto-increment values for all successfully inserted rows. This is the default.
adResyncConflicts	2	Resynchronizes all rows for which an update or delete operation failed due to concurrency conflicts.
adResyncInserts	8	Resynchronizes all successfully inserted rows, including the values of their identity columns.
adResyncNone	0	No resynchronization is performed.
adResyncUpdates	4	Resynchronizes all successfully updated rows.

CommandTypeEnum

Name	Value	Description
adCmdFile	256	Indicates that the provider should evaluate CommandText as a previously persisted file.
adCmdStoredProc	4	Indicates that the provider should evaluate CommandText as a stored procedure.
adCmdTable	2	Indicates that the provider should generate a SQL query to return all rows from the table named in CommandText.
adCmdTableDirect	512	Indicates that the provider should return all rows from the table named in CommandText.
adCmdText	1	Indicates that the provider should evaluate CommandText as a textual definition of a command, such as a SQL statement.
adCmdUnknown	8	Indicates that the type of command in CommandText is unknown.
adCmdUnspecified	-1	The command type is unspecified.

CompareEnum

Name	Value	Description
adCompareEqual	1	The bookmarks are equal.
adCompareGreaterThan	2	The first bookmark is after the second.
adCompareLessThan	0	The first bookmark is before the second.
adCompareNotComparable	4	The bookmarks cannot be compared.
adCompareNotEqual	3	The bookmarks are not equal and not ordered.

ConnectModeEnum

Name	Value	Description
adModeRead	1	Indicates read-only permissions.
adModeReadWrite	3	Indicates read/write permissions.
adModeRecursive	32	Used in conjunction with the ShareDeny values to propogate sharing restrictions.
adModeShareDenyNone	16	Prevents others from opening connection with any permissions.

Table Continued on Following Page

Name	Value	Description
adModeShareDenyRead	4	Prevents others from opening connection with read permissions.
adModeShareDenyWrite	8	Prevents others from opening connection with write permissions.
adModeShareExclusive	12	Prevents others from opening connection.
adModeUnknown	0	Default. Indicates that the permissions have not yet been set or cannot be determined.
adModeWrite	2	Indicates write-only permissions.

ConnectOptionEnum

Name	Value	Description
adAsyncConnect	16	Open the connection asynchronously.
adConnectUnspecified	-1	The connection mode is unspecified.

ConnectPromptEnum

Name	Value	Description
adPromptAlways	1	Always prompt for connection information.
adPromptComplete	2	Only prompt if not enough information was supplied.
adPromptCompleteRequired	3	Only prompt if not enough information was supplied, but disable any options not directly applicable to the connection.
adPromptNever	4	Default. Never prompt for connection information.

CopyRecordOptionsEnum

Name	Value	Description
adCopyAllowEmulation	4	If the `CopyRecord` method fails, simulate it using a file download and upload mechanism.
adCopyNonRecursive	2	Copy the current directory, but not sub-directories.
adCopyOverWrite	1	Overwrite the existing file or directory.
adCopyUnspecified	-1	No copy behavior specified.

CursorLocationEnum

Name	Value	Description
adUseClient	3	Use client-side cursors supplied by the local cursor library.
adUseClientBatch	3	Use client-side cursors supplied by the local cursor library.
adUseNone	1	No cursor services are used.
adUseServer	2	Default. Uses data-provider driver supplied cursors.

CursorOptionEnum

Name	Value	Description
adAddNew	16778240	You can use the AddNew method to add new records.
adApproxPosition	16384	You can read and set the AbsolutePosition and AbsolutePage properties.
adBookmark	8192	You can use the Bookmark property to access specific records.
adDelete	16779264	You can use the Delete method to delete records.
adFind	524288	You can use the Find method to find records.
adHoldRecords	256	You can retrieve more records or change the next retrieve position without committing all pending changes.
adIndex	8388608	You can use the Index property to set the current index.
adMovePrevious	512	You can use the ModeFirst, MovePrevious, Move and GetRows methods.
adNotify	262144	The recordset supports Notifications.
adResync	131072	You can update the cursor with the data visible in the underlying database with the Resync method.
adSeek	4194304	You can use the Seek method to find records by an index.
adUpdate	16809984	You can use the Update method to modify existing records.
adUpdateBatch	65536	You can use the UpdateBatch or CancelBatch methods to transfer changes to the provider in groups.

CursorTypeEnum

Name	Value	Description
adOpenDynamic	2	Opens a dynamic type cursor.
adOpenForwardOnly	0	Default. Opens a forward-only type cursor
adOpenKeyset	1	Opens a keyset type cursor.
adOpenStatic	3	Opens a static type cursor.
adOpenUnspecified	-1	Indicates as unspecified value for cursor type.

DataTypeEnum

Name	Value	Description
adBigInt	20	An 8-byte signed integer.
adBinary	128	A binary value.
adBoolean	11	A `Boolean` value.
adBSTR	8	A null-terminated character string.
adChapter	136	A chapter type, indicating a child recordset.
adChar	129	A `String` value.
adCurrency	6	A currency value. An 8-byte signed integer scaled by 10,000, with 4 digits to the right of the decimal point.
adDate	7	A `Date` value. A `Double` where the whole part is the number of days since December 30 1899, and the fractional part is a fraction of the day.
adDBDate	133	A date value (yyyymmdd).
adDBFileTime	137	A database file time.
adDBTime	134	A time value (hhmmss).
adDBTimeStamp	135	A date-time stamp (yyyymmddhhmmss plus a fraction in billionths).
adDecimal	14	An exact numeric value with fixed precision and scale.
adDouble	5	A double-precision floating point value.
adEmpty	0	No value was specified.
adError	10	A 32-bit error code.

Table Continued on Following Page

Name	Value	Description
adFileTime	64	A DOS/Win32 file time. The number of 100 nanosecond intervals since Jan 1 1601.
adGUID	72	A globally unique identifier.
adIDispatch	9	A pointer to an `IDispatch` interface on an OLE object.
adInteger	3	A 4-byte signed integer.
adIUnknown	13	A pointer to an `IUnknown` interface on an OLE object.
adLongVarBinary	205	A long binary value.
adLongVarChar	201	A long `String` value.
adLongVarWChar	203	A long null-terminated `String` value.
adNumeric	131	An exact numeric value with a fixed precision and scale.
adPropVariant	138	A variant that is not equivalent to an Automation variant.
adSingle	4	A single-precision floating point value.
adSmallInt	2	A 2-byte signed integer.
adTinyInt	16	A 1-byte signed integer.
adUnsignedBigInt	21	An 8-byte unsigned integer.
adUnsignedInt	19	An 4-byte unsigned integer.
adUnsignedSmallInt	18	An 2-byte unsigned integer.
adUnsignedTinyInt	17	An 1-byte unsigned integer.
adUserDefined	132	A user-defined variable.
adVarBinary	204	A binary value.
adVarChar	200	A `String` value.
adVariant	12	An Automation Variant.
adVarNumeric	139	A variable width exact numeric, with a signed scale value.
adVarWChar	202	A null-terminated Unicode character string.
adWChar	130	A null-terminated Unicode character string.

EditModeEnum

Name	Value	Description
adEditAdd	2	Indicates that the AddNew method has been invoked and the current record in the buffer is a new record that hasn't been saved to the database.
adEditDelete	4	Indicates that the Delete method has been invoked.
adEditInProgress	1	Indicates that data in the current record has been modified but not saved.
adEditNone	0	Indicates that no editing is in progress.

ErrorValueEnum

Name	Value	Description
adErrBoundToCommand	3707	The application cannot change the ActiveConnection property of a Recordset object with a Command object as its source.
adErrCannotComplete	3732	The action could not be completed.
adErrCantChangeConnection	3748	The connection cannot be changed.
adErrCantChangeProvider	3220	The provider cannot be changed.
adErrCantConvertvalue	3724	The value cannot be converted .
adErrCantCreate	3725	The resource cannot be created.
adErrCatalogNotSet	3747	The action could not be completed because the catalog is not set.
adErrColumnNotOnThisRow	3726	
adErrDataConversion	3421	The application is using a value of the wrong type for the current application.
adErrDataOverflow	3721	The data was too large for the supplied data type.
adErrDelResOutOfScope	3738	The resource cannot be deleted because it is out of the allowed scope.
adErrDenyNotSupported	3750	
adErrDenyTypeNotSupported	3751	
adErrFeatureNotAvailable	3251	The provider does not support the operation requested by the application.
adErrFieldsUpdateFailed	3749	The Update method of the Fields collection failed.

Name	Value	Description
adErrIllegalOperation	3219	The operation requested by the application is not allowed in this context.
adErrIntegrityViolation	3719	The action failed due to a violation of data integrity.
adErrInTransaction	3246	The application cannot explicitly close a `Connection` object while in the middle of a transaction.
adErrInvalidArgument	3001	The application is using arguments that are the wrong type, are out of the acceptable range, or are in conflict with one another.
adErrInvalidConnection	3709	The application requested an operation on an object with a reference to a closed or invalid `Connection` object.
adErrInvalidParamInfo	3708	The application has improperly defined a `Parameter` object.
adErrInvalidTransaction	3714	Th transaction is invalid.
adErrInvalidURL	3729	The supplied URL is invalid.
adErrItemNotFound	3265	ADO could not find the object in the collection.
adErrNoCurrentRecord	3021	Either `BOF` or `EOF` is `True`, or the current record has been deleted. The operation requested by the application requires a current record.
adErrNotExecuting	3715	The operation is not executing.
adErrNotReentrant	3710	The operation is not reentrant.
adErrObjectClosed	3704	The operation requested by the application is not allowed if the object is closed.
adErrObjectInCollection	3367	Can't append. Object already in collection.
adErrObjectNotSet	3420	The object referenced by the application no longer points to a valid object.
adErrObjectOpen	3705	The operation requested by the application is not allowed if the object is open.
adErrOpeningFile	3002	An error occurred whilst opening the requested file.
adErrOperationCancelled	3712	The operation was cancelled.
adErrOutOfSpace	3734	The operation failed because the server could not obtain enough space to complete the operation.

Name	Value	Description
adErrPermissionDenied	3720	The action failed because you do not have sufficient permission to complete the operation.
adErrPropConflicting	3742	
adErrPropInvalidColumn	3739	
adErrPropInvalidOption	3740	
adErrPropInvalidValue	3741	
adErrPropNotAllSettable	3743	
adErrPropNotSet	3744	
adErrPropNotSettable	3745	
adErrPropNotSupported	3746	
adErrProviderFailed	3000	
adErrProviderNotFound	3706	ADO could not find the specified provider.
adErrReadFile	3003	
adErrResourceExists	3731	The resource already exists.
adErrResourceLocked	3730	The resource is locked.
adErrResourceOutOfScope	3735	The resource is out of scope.
adErrSchemaViolation	3722	The action caused a violation of the schema.
adErrSignMismatch	3723	
adErrStillConnecting	3713	The operation is still connecting.
adErrStillExecuting	3711	The operation is still executing.
adErrTreePermissionDenied	3728	
adErrUnavailable	3736	
adErrUnsafeOperation	3716	The operation is unsafe under these circumstances.
adErrURLDoesNotExist	3727	The URL does not exist.
adErrURLNamedRowDoesNotExist	3737	The URL in the named row does not exist.
adErrVolumeNotFound	3733	The file volume was not found.
adErrWriteFile	3004	
adwrnSecurityDialog	3717	
adwrnSecurityDialogHeader	3718	

EventReasonEnum

Name	Value	Description
adRsnAddNew	1	A new record is to be added.
adRsnClose	9	The object is being closed.
adRsnDelete	2	The record is being deleted.
adRsnFirstChange	11	The record has been changed for the first time.
adRsnMove	10	A Move has been invoked and the current record pointer is being moved.
adRsnMoveFirst	12	A MoveFirst has been invoked and the current record pointer is being moved.
adRsnMoveLast	15	A MoveLast has been invoked and the current record pointer is being moved.
adRsnMoveNext	13	A MoveNext has been invoked and the current record pointer is being moved.
adRsnMovePrevious	14	A MovePrevious has been invoked and the current record pointer is being moved.
adRsnRequery	7	The recordset was requeried.
adRsnResynch	8	The recordset was resynchronized.
adRsnUndoAddNew	5	The addition of a new record has been cancelled.
adRsnUndoDelete	6	The deletion of a record has been cancelled.
adRsnUndoUpdate	4	The update of a record has been cancelled.
adRsnUpdate	3	The record is being updated.

EventStatusEnum

Name	Value	Description
adStatusCancel	4	Request cancellation of the operation that is about to occur.
adStatusCantDeny	3	A Will event cannot request cancellation of the operation about to occur.
adStatusErrorsOccurred	2	The operation completed unsuccessfully, or a Will event cancelled the operation.
adStatusOK	1	The operation completed successfully.
adStatusUnwantedEvent	5	Events for this operation are no longer required.

ExecuteOptionEnum

Name	Value	Description
adAsyncExecute	16	The operation is executed asynchronously.
adAsyncFetch	32	The records are fetched asynchronously.
adAsyncFetchNonBlocking	64	The records are fetched asynchronously without blocking subsequent operations.
adExecuteNoRecords	128	Indicates CommandText is a command or stored procedure that does not return rows. Always combined with adCmdText or adCmdStoreProc.

FieldAttributeEnum

Name	Value	Description
adFldCacheDeferred	4096	Indicates that the provider caches field values and that subsequent reads are done from the cache.
adFldFixed	16	Indicates that the field contains fixed-length data.
adFldIsChapter	8192	The field is a chapter field, and contains a rowset.
adFldIsCollection	262144	The field is a collection.
adFldIsDefaultStream	131072	The fields is the default Stream.
adFldIsNullable	32	Indicates that the field accepts Null values.
adFldIsRowURL	65536	The fields is a URL.
adFldKeyColumn	32768	The field is part of a key column.
adFldLong	128	Indicates that the field is a long binary field, and that the AppendChunk and GetChunk methods can be used.
adFldMayBeNull	64	Indicates that you can read Null values from the field.
adFldMayDefer	2	Indicates that the field is deferred, that is, the field values are not retrieved from the data source with the whole record, but only when you access them.

Name	Value	Description
adFldNegativeScale	16384	The field has a negative scale.
adFldRowID	256	Indicates that the field has a record ID.
adFldRowVersion	512	Indicates that the field time or date stamp used to track updates.
adFldUnknownUpdatable	8	Indicates that the provider cannot determine if you can write to the field.
adFldUnspecified	-1	Attributes of the field are unspecified.
adFldUpdatable	4	Indicates that you can write to the field.

FieldEnum

Name	Value	Description
adDefaultStream	-1	When used as the index into the `Fields` collection of a record, returns the default `Stream` for the `Record`.
adRecordURL	-2	When used as the index into the `Fields` collection of a record, returns the absolute URL for the `Record`.

FieldStatusEnum

Name	Value	Description
adFieldAlreadyExists	26	The field already exists.
adFieldBadStatus	12	The field has a bad `Status` value.
adFieldCannotComplete	20	The action cannot be completed.
adFieldCannotDeleteSource	23	The field cannot delete the source of the field.
adFieldCantConvertValue	2	The field cannot convert the value.
adFieldCantCreate	7	The field cannot be created.
adFieldDataOverflow	6	The data is too long to fit in the field.
adFieldDefault	13	
adFieldDoesNotExist	16	The field does not exist.
adFieldIgnore	15	
adFieldIntegrityViolation	10	The field update failed with a data integrity violation.

Table Continued on Following Page

Name	Value	Description
adFieldInvalidURL	17	The field contains an invalid URL.
adFieldIsNull	3	The field is null.
adFieldOK	0	The field is OK.
adFieldOutOfSpace	22	The field ran out of space for storage.
adFieldPendingChange	262144	The field has been changed, but the provider has not yet been updated.
adFieldPendingDelete	131072	The field has been deleted, but the provider has not yet been updated.
adFieldPendingInsert	65536	The field has been inserted, but the provider has not yet been updated.
adFieldPendingUnknown	524288	
adFieldPendingUnknownDelete	1048576	
adFieldPermissionDenied	9	Permission to modify the field failed due to access permissions.
adFieldReadOnly	24	The field is read only.
adFieldResourceExists	19	The resource specified by the field already exists.
adFieldResourceLocked	18	The resource specified by the field is locked.
adFieldResourceOutOfScope	25	The resource specified by the field is out of scope.
adFieldSchemaViolation	11	The field update failed due to a schema violation.
adFieldSignMismatch	5	
adFieldTruncated	4	The field value was truncated.
adFieldUnavailable	8	The field is unavailable.
adFieldVolumeNotFound	21	The volume specified by the field was not found.

FilterGroupEnum

Name	Value	Description
adFilterAffectedRecords	2	Allows you to view only records affected by the last `Delete`, `Resync`, `UpdateBatch`, or `CancelBatch` method.
adFilterConflictingRecords	5	Allows you to view the records that failed the last batch update attempt.
adFilterFetchedRecords	3	Allows you to view records in the current cache.
adFilterNone	0	Removes the current filter and restores all records to view.
adFilterPendingRecords	1	Allows you to view only the records that have changed but have not been sent to the server. Only applicable for batch update mode.
adFilterPredicate	4	Allows you to view records that failed the last batch update attempt.

GetRowsOptionEnum

Name	Value	Description
adGetRowsRest	-1	Retrieves the remainder of the rows in the recordset.

IsolationLevelEnum

Name	Value	Description
adXactBrowse	256	Indicates that from one transaction you can view uncommitted changes in other transactions.
adXactChaos	16	Default. Indicates that you cannot overwrite pending changes from more highly isolated transactions.
adXactCursorStability	4096	Default. Indicates that from one transaction you can view changes in other transactions only after they have been committed.
adXactIsolated	1048576	Indicates that transactions are conducted in isolation of other transactions.
adXactReadCommitted	4096	Same as `adXactCursorStability`.
adXactReadUncommitted	256	Same as `adXactBrowse`.

Table Continued on Following Page

Name	Value	Description
adXactRepeatableRead	65536	Indicates that from one transaction you cannot see changes made in other transactions, but that requerying can bring new recordsets.
adXactSerializable	1048576	Same as `adXactIsolated`.
adXactUnspecified	-1	Indicates that the provider is using a different `IsolationLevel` than specified, but that the level cannot be identified.

LineSeparatorEnum

Name	Value	Description
adCR	13	The carriage return character.
adCRLF	-1	The carriage return and line feed characters.
adLF	10	The line feed character.

LockTypeEnum

Name	Value	Description
adLockBatchOptimistic	4	Optimistic batch updates.
adLockOptimistic	3	Optimistic locking, record by record. The provider locks records when `Update` is called.
adLockPessimistic	2	Pessimistic locking, record by record. The provider locks the record immediately upon editing.
adLockReadOnly	1	Default. Read only, data cannot be modified.
adLockUnspecified	-1	The clone is created with the same lock type as the original.

MarshalOptionsEnum

Name	Value	Description
adMarshalAll	0	Default. Indicates that all rows are returned to the server.
adMarshalModifiedOnly	1	Indicates that only modified rows are returned to the server.

MoveRecordOptionsEnum

Name	Value	Description
adMoveAllowEmulation	4	If the attempt to move the record fails, allow the move to be performed using a download, upload and delete set of operations.
adMoveDontUpdateLinks	2	Do not update hyperlinks of the source Record.
adMoveOverWrite	1	Overwrite the target if it already exists.

ObjectStateEnum

Name	Value	Description
adStateClosed	0	Default. Indicates that the object is closed.
adStateConnecting	2	Indicates that the object is connecting.
adStateExecuting	4	Indicates that the object is executing a command.
adStateFetching	8	Indicates that the rows of the recordset are being fetched.
adStateOpen	1	Indicates that the object is open.

ParameterAttributesEnum

Name	Value	Description
adParamLong	128	Indicates that the parameter accepts long binary data.
adParamNullable	64	Indicates that the parameter accepts Null values.
adParamSigned	16	Default. Indicates that the parameter accepts signed values.

ParameterDirectionEnum

Name	Value	Description
adParamInput	1	Default. Indicates an input parameter.
adParamInputOutput	3	Indicates both an input and output parameter.
adParamOutput	2	Indicates an output parameter.
adParamReturnValue	4	Indicates a return value.
adParamUnknown	0	Indicates parameter direction is unknown.

PersistFormatEnum

Name	Value	Description
adPersistADTG	0	Default. Persist data in Advanced Data Table Gram format.
adPersistXML	1	Persist data in XML format.

PositionEnum

Name	Value	Description
adPosBOF	-2	The current record pointer is at BOF.
adPosEOF	-3	The current record pointer is at EOF.
adPosUnknown	-1	The Recordset is empty, the current position is unknown, or the provider does not support the AbsolutePage property.

PropertyAttributesEnum

Name	Value	Description
adPropNotSupported	0	Indicates that the property is not supported by the provider.
adPropOptional	2	Indicates that the user does not need to specify a value for this property before the data source is initialized.
adPropRead	512	Indicates that the user can read the property.
adPropRequired	1	Indicates that the user must specify a value for this property before the data source is initialized.
adPropWrite	1024	Indicates that the user can set the property.

RecordCreateOptionsEnum

Name	Value	Description
adCreateCollection	8192	Create a new collection record (directory) at the specified URL.
adCreateNonCollection	0	Create a new record at the specified URL.
adCreateOverwrite	67108864	Overwrite any existing record at the specified URL.
adCreateStructDoc	-2147483648	Create a new structured document record at the specified URL.
adFailIfNotExists	-1	Fail if the URL does not exist.
adOpenIfExists	33554432	Open the record at the specified URL if it exists.

RecordOpenOptionsEnum

Name	Value	Description
adDelayFetchFields	32768	Delay fetching fields until they are requested.
adDelayFetchStream	16384	Delay fetching the `Stream` until it is requested.
adOpenAsync	4096	Open the `Record` asynchronously.
adOpenSource	8388608	Open the source document at the URL, rather than the executed contents.
adOpenURLBind	1024	Indicates the connection string contains a URL.

RecordStatusEnum

Name	Value	Description
adRecCanceled	256	The record was not saved because the operation was cancelled.
adRecCantRelease	1024	The new record was not saved because of existing record locks.
adRecConcurrencyViolation	2048	The record was not saved because optimistic concurrency was in use.
adRecDBDeleted	262144	The record has already been deleted from the data source.
adRecDeleted	4	The record was deleted.
adRecIntegrityViolation	4096	The record was not saved because the user violated integrity constraints.
adRecInvalid	16	The record was not saved because its bookmark is invalid.
adRecMaxChangesExceeded	8192	The record was not saved because there were too many pending changes.
adRecModified	2	The record was modified.
adRecMultipleChanges	64	The record was not saved because it would have affected multiple records.
adRecNew	1	The record is new.
adRecObjectOpen	16384	The record was not saved because of a conflict with an open storage object.
adRecOK	0	The record was successfully updated.

Table Continued on Following Page

Name	Value	Description
adRecOutOfMemory	32768	The record was not saved because the computer has run out of memory.
adRecPendingChanges	128	The record was not saved because it refers to a pending insert.
adRecPermissionDenied	65536	The record was not saved because the user has insufficient permissions.
adRecSchemaViolation	131072	The record was not saved because it violates the structure of the underlying database.
adRecUnmodified	8	The record was not modified.

RecordTypeEnum

Name	Value	Description
adCollectionRecord	1	The record is a collection type (directory)
adSimpleRecord	0	The record is a simple file.
adStructDoc	2	The record is a structured document.

ResyncEnum

Name	Value	Description
adResyncAllValues	2	Default. Data is overwritten and pending updates are cancelled.
adResyncUnderlyingValues	1	Data is not overwritten and pending updates are not cancelled.

SaveOptionsEnum

Name	Value	Description
adSaveCreateNotExist	1	Create a new file if the file does not already exist.
adSaveCreateOverWrite	2	Overwrite any existing file if it exists.

SchemaEnum

Name	Value	Description
adSchemaAsserts	0	Request assert information.
adSchemaCatalogs	1	Request catalog information.
adSchemaCharacterSets	2	Request character set information.
adSchemaCheckConstraints	5	Request check constraint information.
adSchemaCollations	3	Request collation information.
adSchemaColumnPrivileges	13	Request column privilege information.
adSchemaColumns	4	Request column information.
adSchemaColumnsDomain Usage	11	Request column domain usage information.
adSchemaConstraintColumn Usage	6	Request column constraint usage information.
adSchemaConstraintTableUsage	7	Request table constraint usage information.
adSchemaCubes	32	For multi-dimensional data, view the `Cubes` schema.
adSchemaDBInfoKeywords	30	Request the keywords from the provider.
adSchemaDBInfoLiterals	31	Request the literals from the provider.
adSchemaDimensions	33	For multi-dimensional data, view the `Dimensions` schema.
adSchemaForeignKeys	27	Request foreign key information.
adSchemaHierarchies	34	For multi-dimensional data, view the `Hierarchies` schema.
adSchemaIndexes	12	Request index information.
adSchemaKeyColumnUsage	8	Request key column usage information.
adSchemaLevels	35	For multi-dimensional data, view the `Levels` schema.
adSchemaMeasures	36	For multi-dimensional data, view the `Measures` schema.
adSchemaMembers	38	For multi-dimensional data, view the `Members` schema.
adSchemaPrimaryKeys	28	Request primary key information.

Table Continued on Following Page

Name	Value	Description
adSchemaProcedureColumns	29	Request stored procedure column information.
adSchemaProcedureParameters	26	Request stored procedure parameter information.
adSchemaProcedures	16	Request stored procedure information.
adSchemaProperties	37	For multi-dimensional data, view the `Properties` schema.
adSchemaProviderSpecific	-1	Request provider specific information.
adSchemaProviderTypes	22	Request provider type information.
adSchemaReferentialContraints	9	Request referential constraint information.
adSchemaReferentialConstraints	9	Request referential constraint information.
adSchemaSchemata	17	Request schema information.
adSchemaSQLLanguages	18	Request SQL language support information.
adSchemaStatistics	19	Request statistics information.
adSchemaTableConstraints	10	Request table constraint information.
adSchemaTablePrivileges	14	Request table privilege information.
adSchemaTables	20	Request information about the tables.
adSchemaTranslations	21	Request character set translation information.
adSchemaTrustees	39	Request trustee information.
adSchemaUsagePrivileges	15	Request user privilege information.
adSchemaViewColumnUsage	24	Request column usage in views information.
adSchemaViews	23	Request view information.
adSchemaViewTableUsage	25	Request table usage in views information.

Due to a misspelling in the type library, `adSchemaReferentialConstraints` is included twice – once for the original spelling and once for the corrected spelling.

SearchDirectionEnum

Name	Value	Description
adSearchBackward	-1	Search backward from the current record.
adSearchForward	1	Search forward from the current record.

SeekEnum

Name	Value	Description
adSeekAfter	8	Seek the key just after the match.
adSeekAfterEQ	4	Seek the key equal to or just after the match.
adSeekBefore	32	See the key just before the match.
adSeekBeforeEQ	16	Seek the key equal to or just before the match.
adSeekFirstEQ	1	Seek the first key equal to the match.
adSeekLastEQ	2	Seek the last key equal to the match.

StreamOpenOptionsEnum

Name	Value	Description
adOpenStreamAsync	1	Opens the Stream asynchronously.
adOpenStreamFromRecord	4	Opens the Stream using an existing Record as the source.
adOpenStreamFromURL	8	Opens the Stream using a URL as the source.

StreamReadEnum

Name	Value	Description
adReadAll	-1	Reads all bytes from the Stream, from the current position to the end of the stream.
adReadLine	-2	Reads the next line from the Stream. Uses the LineSeparator property to identify the end of the line.

StreamTypeEnum

Name	Value	Description
adTypeBinary	1	The Stream contains binary data.
adTypeText	2	The Stream contains text data.

StreamWriteEnum

Name	Value	Description
adWriteChar	0	Writes the specified string to the `Stream`.
adWriteLine	1	Writes the specified string and a line separator to the `Stream`.
stWriteChar	0	Writes the specified string to the `Stream`.
stWriteLine	1	Writes the specified string and a line separator to the `Stream`.

StringFormatEnum

Name	Value	Description
adClipString	2	Rows are delimited by user defined values.

XactAttributeEnum

Name	Value	Description
adXactAbortRetaining	262144	The provider will automatically start a new transaction after a `RollbackTrans` method call.
adXactAsyncPhaseOne	524288	Perform an asynchronous commit.
adXactCommitRetaining	131072	The provider will automatically start a new transaction after a `CommitTrans` method call.
adXactSyncPhaseOne	1048576	Performs an synchronous commit.

Miscellaneous Constants

These values are not included in the standard `adovbs.inc` include file (and are not automatically supplied when using Visual Basic), but can be found in `adocon.inc` (for ASP) and `adocon.bas` (for Visual Basic) from the supporting web site, http://webdev.wrox.co.uk/books/2750.

Many of these may not be necessary to you as an ADO programmer, but they are included here for completeness, and are only really useful as bitmask values for entries in the `Properties` collection.

DB_COLLATION

Name	Value	Description
DB_COLLATION_ASC	1	The sort sequence for the column is ascending.
DB_COLLATION_DESC	2	The sort sequence for the column is descending.

DB_IMP_LEVEL

Name	Value	Description
DB_IMP_LEVEL_ANONYMOUS	0	The client is anonymous to the server, and the server process cannot obtain identification information about the client and cannot impersonate the client.
DB_IMP_LEVEL_DELEGATE	3	The process can impersonate the client's security context while acting on behalf of the client. The server process can also make outgoing calls to other servers while acting on behalf of the client.
DB_IMP_LEVEL_IDENTIFY	1	The server can obtain the client's identity, and can impersonate the client for ACL checking, but cannot access system objects as the client.
DB_IMP_LEVEL_IMPERSONATE	2	The server process can impersonate the client's security context whilst acting on behalf of the client. This information is obtained upon connection and not on every call.

DB_MODE

Name	Value	Description
DB_MODE_READ	1	Read only.
DB_MODE_READWRITE	3	Read/Write (DB_MODE_READ + DB_MODE_WRITE).
DB_MODE_SHARE_DENY_NONE	16	Neither read nor write access can be denied to others.

Name	Value	Description
DB_MODE_SHARE_DENY_READ	4	Prevents others from opening in read mode.
DB_MODE_SHARE_DENY_WRITE	8	Prevents others from opening in write mode.
DB_MODE_SHARE_EXCLUSIVE	12	Prevents others from opening in read/write mode (DB_MODE_SHARE_DENY_READ + DB_MODE_SHARE_DENY_WRITE).
DB_MODE_WRITE	2	Write only.

DB_PROT_LEVEL

Name	Value	Description
DB_PROT_LEVEL_CALL	2	Authenticates the source of the data at the beginning of each request from the client to the server.
DB_PROT_LEVEL_CONNECT	1	Authenticates only when the client establishes the connection with the server.
DB_PROT_LEVEL_NONE	0	Performs no authentification of data sent to the server.
DB_PROT_LEVEL_PKT	3	Authenticates that all data received is from the client.
DB_PROT_LEVEL_PKT_INTEGRITY	4	Authenticates that all data received is from the client and that it has not been changed in transit.
DB_PROT_LEVEL_PKT_PRIVACY	5	Authenticates that all data received is from the client, that it has not been changed in transit, and protects the privacy of the data by encrypting it.

DB_PT

Name	Value	Description
DB_PT_FUNCTION	3	Function; there is a returned value.
DB_PT_PROCEDURE	2	Procedure; there is no returned value.
DB_PT_UNKNOWN	1	It is not known whether there is a returned value.

DB_SEARCHABLE

Name	Value	Description
DB_ALL_EXCEPT_LIKE	3	The data type can be used in a WHERE clause with all comparison operators except LIKE.
DB_LIKE_ONLY	2	The data type can be used in a WHERE clause only with the LIKE predicate.
DB_SEARCHABLE	4	The data type can be used in a WHERE clause with any comparison operator.
DB_UNSEARCHABLE	1	The data type cannot be used in a WHERE clause.

DBCOLUMNDESCFLAG

Name	Value	Description
DBCOLUMNDESCFLAG_CLSID	8	The CLSID portion of the column description can be changed when altering the column.
DBCOLUMNDESCFLAG_COLSIZE	16	The column size portion of the column description can be changed when altering the column.
DBCOLUMNDESCFLAG_DBCID	32	The DBCID portion of the column description can be changed when altering the column.
DBCOLUMNDESCFLAG_ITYPEINFO	2	The type information portion of the column description can be changed when altering the column.
DBCOLUMNDESCFLAG_PRECISION	128	The precision portion of the column description can be changed when altering the column.
DBCOLUMNDESCFLAG_PROPERTIES	4	The property sets portion of the column description can be changed when altering the column.

Name	Value	Description
DBCOLUMNDESCFLAG_SCALE	256	The numeric scale portion of the column description can be changed when altering the column.
DBCOLUMNDESCFLAG_TYPENAME	1	The type name portion of the column description can be changed when altering the column.
DBCOLUMNDESCFLAG_WTYPE	64	The data type portion of the column description can be changed when altering the column.

DBCOLUMNFLAGS

Name	Value	Description
DBCOLUMNFLAGS_CACHEDEFERRED	4096	Indicates that the value of a deferred column is cached when it is first read.
DBCOLUMNFLAGS_ISCHAPTER	8192	The column contains a Chapter value.
DBCOLUMNFLAGS_ISFIXEDLENGTH	16	All of the data in the column is of a fixed length.
DBCOLUMNFLAGS_ISLONG	128	The column contains a BLOB value that contains long data.
DBCOLUMNFLAGS_ISNULLABLE	32	The column can be set to NULL, or the provider cannot determine whether the column can be set to NULL.
DBCOLUMNFLAGS_ISROWID	256	The column contains a persistent row identifier.
DBCOLUMNFLAGS_ISROWVER	512	The column contains a timestamp or other row versioning data type.
DBCOLUMNFLAGS_MAYBENULL	64	NULLs can be got from the column.

Name	Value	Description
DBCOLUMNFLAGS_MAYDEFER	2	The column is deferred.
DBCOLUMNFLAGS_WRITE	4	The column may be updated.
DBCOLUMNFLAGS_WRITEUNKNOWN	8	It is not know if the column can be updated.

DBCOMPUTEMODE

Name	Value	Description
DBCOMPUTEMODE_COMPUTED	1	The column is a computed column.
DBCOMPUTEMODE_DYNAMIC	2	The column is computed and always returns the value based upon the computation.
DBCOMPUTEMODE_NOTCOMPUTED	3	The column is not a computed column.

DBLITERAL

Name	Value	Description
DBLITERAL_INVALID	0	An invalid value.
DBLITERAL_BINARY_LITERAL	1	A binary literal in a text command.
DBLITERAL_CATALOG_NAME	2	A catalog name in a text command.
DBLITERAL_CATALOG_SEPARATOR	3	The character that separates the catalog name from the rest of the identifier in a text command.
DBLITERAL_CHAR_LITERAL	4	A character literal in a text command.
DBLITERAL_COLUMN_ALIAS	5	A column alias in a text command.
DBLITERAL_COLUMN_NAME	6	A column name used in a text command or in a data-definition interface.
DBLITERAL_CORRELATION_NAME	7	A correlation name (table alias) in a text command.
DBLITERAL_CURSOR_NAME	8	A cursor name in a text command.

Table Continued on Following Page

Name	Value	Description
DBLITERAL_ESCAPE_PERCENT DBLITERAL_ESCAPE_PERCENT_PREFIX	9	The character used in a LIKE clause to escape the character returned for the DBLITERAL_LIKE_PERCENT literal.
DBLITERAL_ESCAPE_PERCENT_SUFFIX	29	The escape character, if any, used to suffix the character returned for the DBLITERAL_LIKE_PERCENT literal.
DBLITERAL_ESCAPE_UNDERSCORE DBLITERAL_ESCAPE_UNDERSCORE_PREFIX	10	The character used in a LIKE clause to escape the character returned for the DBLITERAL_LIKE_UNDERSCORE literal.
DBLITERAL_ESCAPE_UNDERSCORE_SUFFIX	30	The escape character, if any, used to suffix the character returned for the DBLITERAL_LIKE_UNDERSCORE literal.
DBLITERAL_INDEX_NAME	11	An index name used in a text command or in a data-definition interface.
DBLITERAL_LIKE_PERCENT	12	The character used in a LIKE clause to match zero or more characters.
DBLITERAL_LIKE_UNDERSCORE	13	The character used in a LIKE clause to match exactly one character.
DBLITERAL_PROCEDURE_NAME	14	A procedure name in a text command.
DBLITERAL_SCHEMA_NAME	16	A schema name in a text command.
DBLITERAL_SCHEMA_SEPARATOR	27	The character that separates the schema name from the rest of the identifier in a text command.
DBLITERAL_TABLE_NAME	17	A table name used in a text command or in a data-definition interface.
DBLITERAL_TEXT_COMMAND	18	A text command, such as an SQL statement.

Name	Value	Description
DBLITERAL_USER_NAME	19	A user name in a text command.
DBLITERAL_VIEW_NAME	20	A view name in a text command.
DBLITERAL_QUOTE **DBLITERAL_QUOTE_PREFIX**	15	The character used in a text command as the opening quote for quoting identifiers that contain special characters.
DBLITERAL_QUOTE_SUFFIX	28	The character used in a text command as the closing quote for quoting identifiers that contain special characters.

DBPARAMTYPE

Name	Value	Description
DBPARAMTYPE_INPUT	1	The parameter is an input parameter.
DBPARAMTYPE_INPUTOUTPUT	2	The parameter is both an input and an output parameter.
DBPARAMTYPE_OUTPUT	3	The parameter is an output parameter.
DBPARAMTYPE_RETURNVALUE	4	The parameter is a return value.

DBPROMPT

Name	Value	Description
DBPROMPT_COMPLETE	2	Prompt the user only if more information is needed.
DBPROMPT_COMPLETEREQUIRED	3	Prompt the user only if more information is required. Do not allow the user to enter optional information.
DBPROMPT_NOPROMPT	4	Do not prompt the user.
DBPROMPT_PROMPT	1	Always prompt the user for initialization information.

DBPROPVAL_AO

Name	Value	Description
DBPROPVAL_AO_RANDOM	2	Columns can be accessed in any order.
DBPROPVAL_AO_SEQUENTIAL	0	All columns must be accessed in sequential order determined by the column ordinal.
DBPROPVAL_AO_SEQUENTIALSTORAGEOBJECTS	1	Columns bound as storage objects can only be accessed in sequential order as determined by the column ordinal.

DBPROPVAL_ASYNCH

Name	Value	Description
DBPROPVAL_ASYNCH_ BACKGROUNDPOPULATION	8	The rowset is populated asynchronously in the background.
DBPROPVAL_ASYNCH_INITIALIZE	1	Initialization is performed asynchronously.
DBPROPVAL_ASYNCH_ POPULATEONDEMAND	32	The consumer prefers to optimize for getting each individual request for data returned as quickly as possible.
DBPROPVAL_ASYNCH_ PREPOPULATE	16	The consumer prefers to optimize for retrieving all data when the row set is materialized.
DBPROPVAL_ASYNCH_ RANDOMPOPULATION	4	Rowset population is performed asynchronously in a random manner.
DBPROPVAL_ASYNCH_ SEQUENTIALPOPULATION	2	Rowset population is performed asynchronously in a sequential manner.

DBPROPVAL_BG

Name	Value	Description
DBPROPVAL_GB_COLLATE	16	A COLLATE clause can be specified at the end of each grouping column.
DBPROPVAL_GB_ CONTAINS_SELECT	4	The GROUP BY clause must contain all non-aggregated columns in the select list. It can contain columns that are not in the select list.
DBPROPVAL_GB_EQUALS_ SELECT	2	The GROUP BY clause must contain all non-aggregated columns in the select list. It cannot contain any other columns.
DBPROPVAL_GB_NO_ RELATION	8	The columns in the GROUP BY clause and the select list are not related. The meaning on non-grouped, non-aggregated columns in the select list is data source dependent.
DBPROPVAL_GB_NOT_ SUPPORTED	1	GROUP BY clauses are not supported.

DBPROPVAL_BI

Name	Value	Description
DBPROPVAL_BI_ CROSSROWSET	1	Bookmark values are valid across all rowsets generated on this table.

DBPROPVAL_BMK

Name	Value	Description
DBPROPVAL_BMK_KEY	2	The bookmark type is key.
DBPROPVAL_BMK_NUMERIC	1	The bookmark type is numeric.

DBPROPVAL_BO

Name	Value	Description
DBPROPVAL_BO_NOINDEXUPDATE	1	The provider is not required to update indexes based on inserts or changes to the rowset. Any indexes need to be re-created following changes made through the rowset.
DBPROPVAL_BO_NOLOG	0	The provider is not required to log inserts or changes to the rowset.
DBPROPVAL_BO_REFINTEGRITY	2	Referential integrity constraints do not need to be checked or enforced for changes made through the rowset.

DBPROPVAL_BT

Name	Value	Description
DBPROPVAL_BT_DEFAULT	0	Use the value defined in the dynamic property **Jet OLEDB:Global Bulk Transactions**
DBPROPVAL_BT_NOBULKTRANSACTIONS	1	Bulk operations are not transacted.
DBPROPVAL_BT_BULKTRANSACTION	2	Bulk operations are transacted.

DBPROPVAL_CB

Name	Value	Description
DBPROPVAL_CB_NON_NULL	2	The result is the concatenation of the non-NULL valued column or columns.
DBPROPVAL_CB_NULL	1	The result is NULL valued.

DBPROPVAL_CB

Name	Value	Description
DBPROPVAL_CB_DELETE	1	Aborting a transaction deletes prepared commands.
DBPROPVAL_CB_PRESERVE	2	Aborting a transaction preserves prepared commands.

DBPROPVAL_CD

Name	Value	Description
DBPROPVAL_CD_NOTNULL	1	Columns can be created non-nullable.

DBPROPVAL_CL

Name	Value	Description
DBPROPVAL_CL_END	2	The catalog name appears at the end of the fully qualified name.
DBPROPVAL_CL_START	1	The catalog name appears at the start of the fully qualified name.

DBPROPVAL_CO

Name	Value	Description
DBPROPVAL_CO_BEGINSWITH	32	Provider supports the BEGINSWITH and NOTBEGINSWITH operators.
DBPROPVAL_CO_CASEINSENSITIVE	8	Provider supports the CASEINSENSITIVE operator.
DBPROPVAL_CO_CASESENSITIVE	4	Provider supports the CASESENSITIVE operator.
DBPROPVAL_CO_CONTAINS	16	Provider supports the CONTAINS and NOTCONTAINS operators.
DBPROPVAL_CO_EQUALITY	1	Provider supports the following operators: LT, LE, EQ, GE, GT, NE.
DBPROPVAL_CO_STRING	2	Provider supports the BEGINSWITH operator.

DBPROPVAL_CS

Name	Value	Description
DBPROPVAL_CS_COMMUNICATIONFAILURE	2	The DSO is unable to communicate with the data store.
DBPROPVAL_CS_INITIALIZED	1	The DSO is in an initialized state and able to communicate with the data store.
DBPROPVAL_CS_UNINITIALIZED	0	The DSO is in an uninitialized state.

DBPROPVAL_CU

Name	Value	Description
DBPROPVAL_CU_DML_ STATEMENTS	1	Catalog names are supported in all Data Manipulation Language statements.
DBPROPVAL_CU_INDEX_ DEFINITION	4	Catalog names are supported in all index definition statements.
DBPROPVAL_CU_PRIVILEGE_ DEFINITION	8	Catalog names are supported in all privilege definition statements.
DBPROPVAL_CU_TABLE_ DEFINITION	2	Catalog names are supported in all table definition statements.

DBPROPVAL_DF

Name	Value	Description
DBPROPVAL_DF_INITIALLY_ DEFERRED	1	The foreign key is initially deferred.
DBPROPVAL_DF_INITIALLY_ IMMEDIATE	2	The foreign key is initially immediate.
DBPROPVAL_DF_NOT_ DEFERRABLE	3	The foreign key is not deferrable.

DBPROPVAL_DL

Name	Value	Description
DBPROPVAL_DL_OLDMODE	0	Mode used in previous versions of the Jet database.
DBPROPVAL_DL_ALCATRAZ	1	Use new method, allowing row level locking.

DBPROPVAL_DST

Name	Value	Description
DBPROPVAL_DST_MDP	2	The provider is a multidimensional provider (MD).
DBPROPVAL_DST_TDP	1	The provider is a tabular data provider (TDP).
DBPROPVAL_DST_TDPANDMDP	3	The provider is both a TDP and a MD provider.
DBPROPVAL_DST_DOCSOURCE	4	The provider is a document source (Internet Publishing Provider)

DBPROPVAL_GU

Name	Value	Description
DBPROPVAL_GU_ NOTSUPPORTED	1	URL suffixes are not supported. This is the only option supported by the Internet Publishing Provider in this version of ADO.
DBPROPVAL_GU_ SUFFIX	2	URL suffixes are generated by the Internet Publishing Provider.

DBPROPVAL_HT

Name	Value	Description
DBPROPVAL_HT_DIFFERENT_ CATALOGS	1	The provider supports heterogeneous joins between catalogs.
DBPROPVAL_HT_DIFFERE2NT_ PROVIDERS	2	The provider supports heterogeneous joins between providers.

DBPROPVAL_IC

Name	Value	Description
DBPROPVAL_IC_ LOWER	2	Identifiers in SQL are case insensitive and are stored in lower case in system catalog.
DBPROPVAL_IC_ MIXED	8	Identifiers in SQL are case insensitive and are stored in mixed case in system catalog.
DBPROPVAL_IC_ SENSITIVE	4	Identifiers in SQL are case sensitive and are stored in mixed case in system catalog.
DBPROPVAL_IC_ UPPER	1	Identifiers in SQL are case insensitive and are stored in upper case in system catalog.

DBPROPVAL_IN

Name	Value	Description
DBPROPVAL_IN_ ALLOWNULL	0	The index allows NULL values to be inserted.
DBPROPVAL_IN_ DISALLOWNULL	1	The index does not allow entries where the key columns are NULL. An error will be generated if the consumer attempts to insert a NULL value into a key column.
DBPROPVAL_IN_ IGNOREANYNULL	4	The index does not insert entries containing NULL keys.
DBPROPVAL_IN_ IGNORENULL	2	The index does not insert entries where some column key has a NULL value.

DBPROPVAL_IT

Name	Value	Description
DBPROPVAL_IT_BTREE	1	The index is a B+ tree.
DBPROPVAL_IT_CONTENT	3	The index is a content index.
DBPROPVAL_IT_HASH	2	The index is a hash file using linear or extensible hashing.
DBPROPVAL_IT_OTHER	4	The index is some other type of index.

DBPROPVAL_JCC

Name	Value	Description
DBPROPVAL_JCC_ PASSIVESHUTDOWN	1	New connections to the database are disallowed.
DBPROPVAL_JCC_ NORMAL	2	Users are allowed to connect to the database.

DBPROPVAL_LG

Name	Value	Description
DBPROPVAL_LG_PAGE	1	Use page locking.
DBPROPVAL_LG_ALCATRAZ	2	Use row-level locking.

DBPROPVAL_LM

Name	Value	Description
DBPROPVAL_LM_I NTENT	4	The provider uses the maximum level of locking to ensure that changes will not fail due to a concurrency violation.
DBPROPVAL_LM_ NONE	1	The provider is not required to lock rows at any time to ensure successful updates.
DBPROPVAL_LM_READ	2	The provider uses the minimum level of locking to ensure that changes will not fail due to a concurrency violation.
DBPROPVAL_LM_RITE	8	
DBPROPVAL_LM_ SINGLEROW	2	The provider uses the minimum level of locking to ensure that changes will not fail due to a concurrency violation.

DBPROPVAL_MR

Name	Value	Description
DBPROPVAL_MR_CONCURRENT	2	More than one rowset created by the same multiple results object can exist concurrently.
DBPROPVAL_MR_NOTSUPPORTED	0	Multiple results objects are not supported.
DBPROPVAL_MR_SUPPORTED	1	The provider supports multiple results objects.

DBPROPVAL_NC

Name	Value	Description
DBPROPVAL_NC_END	1	NULLs are sorted at the end of the list, regardless of the sort order.
DBPROPVAL_NC_HIGH	2	NULLs are sorted at the high end of the list.
DBPROPVAL_NC_LOW	4	NULLs are sorted at the low end of the list.
DBPROPVAL_NC_START	8	NULLs are sorted at the start of the list, regardless of the sort order.

DBPROPVAL_NP

Name	Value	Description
DBPROPVAL_NP_ABOUTTODO	2	The consumer will be notified before an action (i.e. the Will event).
DBPROPVAL_NP_DIDEVENT	16	The consumer will be notified after an action (i.e. the Complete event).
DBPROPVAL_NP_FAILEDTODO	8	The consumer will be notified if an action failed (i.e. a Will or Complete event).
DBPROPVAL_NP_OKTODO	1	The consumer will be notified of events.
DBPROPVAL_NP_SYNCHAFTER	4	The consumer will be notified when the rowset is resynchronized.

DBPROPVAL_NT

Name	Value	Description
DBPROPVAL_NT_ MULTIPLEROWS	2	For methods that operate on multiple rows, and generate multiphased notifications (events), then the provider calls OnRowChange once for all rows that succeed and once for all rows that fail.
DBPROPVAL_NT_ SINGLEROW	1	For methods that operate on multiple rows, and generate multiphased notifications (events), then the provider calls OnRowChange separately for each phase for each row.

DBPROPVAL_OA

Name	Value	Description
DBPROPVAL_OA_ ATEXECUTE	2	Output parameter data is available immediately after the Command.Execute returns.
DBPROPVAL_OA_ ATROWRELEASE	4	Output parameter data is available when the rowset is release. For a single rowset operation this is when the rowset is completely released (closed) and for a multiple rowset operation this is when the next rowset if fetched. The consumer's bound memory is in an indeterminate state before the parameter data becomes available.
DBPROPVAL_OA_ NOTSUPPORTED	1	Output parameters are not supported.

DBPROPVAL_OO

Name	Value	Description
DBPROPVAL_OO_ BLOB	1	The provider supports access to BLOBs as structured storage objects.
DBPROPVAL_OO_ DIRECTBIND	16	The provider supports direct binding to BLOBs.
DBPROPVAL_OO_ IPERSIST	2	The provider supports access to OLE objects through OLE.
DBPROPVAL_OO_ SCOPED	8	The provider supports objects that have scoped operations.

DBPROPVAL_ORS

Name	Value	Description
DBPROPVAL_ORS_TABLE	1	The provider supports opening tables.
DBPROPVAL_ORS_INDEX	2	The provider supports opening indexes.
DBPROPVAL_ORS_INTEGRATEDINDEX	16	The provider supports both the table and index in the same open method.
DBPROPVAL_ORS_STOREDPROPC	4	The provider supports opening rowsets over stored procedures.

DBPROPVAL_OS

Name	Value	Description
DBPROPVAL_OS_ENABLEALL	-1	All services should be invoked. This is the default.
DBPROPVAL_OS_RESOURCEPOOLING	1	Resources should be pooled.
DBPROPVAL_OS_TXNENLISTMENT	2	Sessions in an MTS environment should automatically be enlisted in a global transaction where required.
DBPROPVAL_OS_CLIENT_CURSOR	4	Disable client cursor.
DBPROPVAL_OS_DISABLEALL	0	All services should be disabled.

DBPROPVAL_PT

Name	Value	Description
DBPROPVAL_PT_GUID	8	The GUID is used as the persistent ID type.
DBPROPVAL_PT_GUID_NAME	1	The GUID NAME is used as the persistent ID type.
DBPROPVAL_PT_GUID_PROPID	2	The GUID Property ID is used as the persistent ID type.
DBPROPVAL_PT_NAME	4	The NAME is used as the persistent ID type.
DBPROPVAL_PT_PGUID_NAME	32	The Property GUID NAME is used as the persistent ID type.
DBPROPVAL_PT_PGUID_PROPID	64	The Property GUID Property ID is used as the persistent ID type.
DBPROPVAL_PT_PROPID	16	The Property ID is used as the persistent ID type.

DBPROPVAL_RD

Name	Value	Description
DBPROPVAL_RD_ RESETALL	-1	The provider should reset all states associated with the data source, with the exception that any open object is not released.

DBPROPVAL_RT

Name	Value	Description
DBPROPVAL_RT_APTMTTHREAD	2	The DSO is apartment threaded.
DBPROPVAL_RT_FREETHREAD	1	The DSO is free threaded.
DBPROPVAL_RT_SINGLETHREAD	4	The DSO is single threaded.

DBPROPVAL_SQ

Name	Value	Description
DBPROPVAL_SQ_ COMPARISON	2	All predicates that support subqueries support comparison subqueries.
DBPROPVAL_SQ_ CORRELATEDSUBQUERIES	1	All predicates that support subqueries support correlated subqueries.
DBPROPVAL_SQ_ EXISTS	4	All predicates that support subqueries support EXISTS subqueries.
DBPROPVAL_SQ_IN	8	All predicates that support subqueries support IN subqueries.
DBPROPVAL_SQ_ QUANTIFIED	16	All predicates that support subqueries support quantified subqueries.

DBPROPVAL_SQL

Name	Value	Description
DBPROPVAL_SQL_ANDI89_IEF	8	The provider supports the ANSI SQL89 IEF level.
DBPROPVAL_SQL_ANSI92_ENTRY	16	The provider supports the ANSI SQL92 ENTRY level.
DBPROPVAL_SQL_ANSI92_FULL	128	The provider supports the ANSI SQL92 FULL level.

Name	Value	Description
DBPROPVAL_SQL_ANSI92_ INTERMEDIATE	64	The provider supports the ANSI SQL92 INTERMEDIATE level.
DBPROPVAL_SQL_CORE	2	The provider supports the ODBC 2.5 CORE SQL level.
DBPROPVAL_SQL_ ESCAPECLAUSES	256	The provider supports the ODBC ESCAPECLAUSES syntax.
DBPROPVAL_SQL_ EXTENDED	4	The provider supports the ODBC 2.5 EXTENDED SQL level.
DBPROPVAL_SQL_FIPS_ TRANSITIONAL	32	The provider supports the ANSI SQL92 TRANSITIONAL level.
DBPROPVAL_SQL_ MINIMUM	1	The provider supports the ODBC 2.5 MINIMUM SQL level.
DBPROPVAL_SQL_NONE	0	SQL is not supported.
DBPROPVAL_SQL_ODBC_ CORE	2	The provider supports the ODBC 2.5 CORE SQL level.
DBPROPVAL_SQL_ODBC_ EXTENDED	4	The provider supports the ODBC 2.5 EXTENDED SQL level.
DBPROPVAL_SQL_ODBC_ MINIMUM	1	The provider supports the ODBC 2.5 MINIMUM SQL level.
DBPROPVAL_SQL_ SUBMINIMUM	512	The provider supports the DBGUID_SQL dialect and parses the command text according to SQL rules, but does not support wither the minimum ODBC level nor the ANSI SQL92 ENTRY level.

DBPROPVAL_SS

Name	Value	Description
DBPROPVAL_SS_ILOCKBYTES	8	The provider supports IlockBytes.
DBPROPVAL_SS_ ISEQUENTIALSTREAM	1	The provider supports IsequentialStream.
DBPROPVAL_SS_ISTORAGE	4	The provider supports Istorage.
DBPROPVAL_SS_ISTREAM	2	The provider supports IStream.

DBPROPVAL_SU

Name	Value	Description
DBPROPVAL_SU_DML_STATEMENTS	1	Schema names are supported in all Data Manipulation Language statements.
DBPROPVAL_SU_INDEX_DEFINITION	4	Schema names are supported in all index definition statements.
DBPROPVAL_SU_PRIIVILEGE_DEFINITION	8	Schema names are supported in all privilege definition statements.
DBPROPVAL_SU_TABLE_DEFINITION	2	Schema names are supported in all table definition statements.

DBPROPVAL_TC

Name	Value	Description
DBPROPVAL_TC_ALL	8	Transactions can contain DDL and DML statements in any order.
DBPROPVAL_TC_DDL_COMMIT	2	Transactions can contain DML statements. DDL statements within a transaction cause the transaction to be committed.
DBPROPVAL_TC_DDL_IGNORE	4	Transactions can only contain DML statements. DDL statements within a transaction are ignored.
DBPROPVAL_TC_DDL_LOCK	16	Transactions can contain both DML and table or index modifications, but the table or index will be locked until the transaction completes.
DBPROPVAL_TC_DML	1	Transactions can only contain Data Manipulation (DML) statements. DDL statements within a transaction cause an error.
DBPROPVAL_TC_NONE	0	Transactions are not supported.

DBPROPVAL_TI

Name	Value	Description
DBPROPVAL_TI_BROWSE	256	Changes made by other transactions are visible before they are committed.
DBPROPVAL_TI_CHAOS	16	Transactions cannot overwrite pending changes from more highly isolated transactions. This is the default.
DBPROPVAL_TI_ CURSORSTABILITY	4096	Changes made by other transactions are not visible until those transactions are committed.
DBPROPVAL_TI_ ISOLATED	1048576	All concurrent transactions will interact only in ways that produce the same effect as if each transaction were entirely executed one after the other.
DBPROPVAL_TI_ READCOMMITTED	4096	Changes made by other transactions are not visible until those transactions are committed.
DBPROPVAL_TI_ READUNCOMMITTED	256	Changes made by other transactions are visible before they are committed.
DBPROPVAL_TI_ REPEATABLEREAD	65536	Changes made by other transactions are not visible.
DBPROPVAL_TI_ SERIALIZABLE	1048576	All concurrent transactions will interact only in ways that produce the same effect as if each transaction were entirely executed one after the other.

DBPROPVAL_TR

Name	Value	Description
DBPROPVAL_TR_ ABORT	16	The transaction preserves its isolation context (i.e., it preserves its locks if that is how isolation is implemented) across the retaining abort.
DBPROPVAL_TR_ ABORT_DC	8	The transaction may either preserve or dispose of isolation context across a retaining abort.
DBPROPVAL_TR_ ABORT_NO	32	The transaction is explicitly not to preserve its isolation across a retaining abort.
DBPROPVAL_TR_ BOTH	128	Isolation is preserved across both a retaining commit and a retaining abort.

Table Continued on Following Page

Name	Value	Description
DBPROPVAL_TR_ COMMIT	2	The transaction preserves its isolation context (i.e., it preserves its locks if that is how isolation is implemented) across the retaining commit.
DBPROPVAL_TR_ COMMIT_DC	1	The transaction may either preserve or dispose of isolation context across a retaining commit.
DBPROPVAL_TR_ COMMIT_NO	4	The transaction is explicitly not to preserve its isolation across a retaining commit.
DBPROPVAL_TR_ DONTCARE	64	The transaction may either preserve or dispose of isolation context across a retaining commit or abort. This is the default.
DBPROPVAL_TR_ NONE	256	Isolation is explicitly not to be retained across either a retaining commit or abort.
DBPROPVAL_TR_ OPTIMISTIC	512	Optimistic concurrency control is to be used.

DBPROPVAL_UP

Name	Value	Description
DBPROPVAL_UP_CHANGE	1	Indicates that SetData is supported.
DBPROPVAL_UP_DELETE	2	Indicates that DeleteRows is supported.
DBPROPVAL_UP_INSERT	4	Indicates that InsertRow is supported.

DBPROPVAL_BP

Name	Value	Description
DBPROPVAL_BP_ NOPARTIAL	2	Fail the bulk operation if there is a single error.
DBPROPVAL_BP_ PARTIAL	1	Allow the bulk operation to partially complete, possibly resulting in inconsistent data.

JET_ENGINETYPE

Name	Value	Description
JET_ENGINETYPE_UNKNOWN	0	The database type is unknown.
JET_ENGINETYPE_JET10	1	Jet 1.0
JET_ENGINETYPE_JET11	2	Jet 1.1

Name	Value	Description
JET_ENGINETYPE_JET2X	3	Jet 2.x
JET_ENGINETYPE_JET3X	4	Jet 3.x
JET_ENGINETYPE_JET4X	5	Jet 4.x
JET_ENGINETYPE_DBASE3	10	DBase III
JET_ENGINETYPE_DBASE4	11	DBase IV
JET_ENGINETYPE_DBASE5	12	DBase V
JET_ENGINETYPE_EXCEL30	20	Excel 3
JET_ENGINETYPE_EXCEL40	21	Excel 4
JET_ENGINETYPE_EXCEL50	22	Excel 5 (Excel 95)
JET_ENGINETYPE_EXCEL80	23	Excel 8 (Excel 97)
JET_ENGINETYPE_EXCEL90	24	Excel 9 (Excel 2000)
JET_ENGINETYPE_EXCHANGE4	30	Exchange Server
JET_ENGINETYPE_LOTUSWK1	40	Lotus 1
JET_ENGINETYPE_LOTUSWK3	41	Lotus 3
JET_ENGINETYPE_LOTUSWK4	42	Lotus 4
JET_ENGINETYPE_PARADOX3X	50	Paradox 3.x
JET_ENGINETYPE_PARADOX4X	51	Paradox 4.5
JET_ENGINETYPE_PARADOX5X	52	Paradox 5.x
JET_ENGINETYPE_PARADOX7X	53	Paradox 7.x
JET_ENGINETYPE_TEXT1X	60	Text
JET_ENGINETYPE_HTML1X	70	HTML

MD_DIMTYPE

Name	Value	Description
MD_DIMTYPE_MEASURE	2	A measure dimension.
MD_DIMTYPE_OTHER	3	The dimension is neither a time nor a measure dimension.
MD_DIMTYPE_TIME	1	A time dimension.
MD_DIMTYPE_UNKNOWN	0	The provider is unable to classify the dimension.

SQL_FN_NUM

Name	Value	Description
SQL_FN_NUM_ABS	1	The ABS function is supported by the data source.
SQL_FN_NUM_ACOS	2	The ACOS function is supported by the data source.
SQL_FN_NUM_ASIN	4	The ASIN function is supported by the data source.
SQL_FN_NUM_ATAN	8	The ATAN function is supported by the data source.
SQL_FN_NUM_ATAN2	16	The ATAN2 function is supported by the data source.
SQL_FN_NUM_CEILING	32	The CEILING function is supported by the data source.
SQL_FN_NUM_COS	64	The COS function is supported by the data source.
SQL_FN_NUM_COT	128	The COT function is supported by the data source.
SQL_FN_NUM_DEGREES	262144	The DEGREES function is supported by the data source.
SQL_FN_NUM_EXP	256	The EXP function is supported by the data source.
SQL_FN_NUM_FLOOR	512	The FLOOR function is supported by the data source.
SQL_FN_NUM_LOG	1024	The LOG function is supported by the data source.
SQL_FN_NUM_LOG10	524288	The LOG10 function is supported by the data source.
SQL_FN_NUM_MOD	2048	The MOD function is supported by the data source.
SQL_FN_NUM_PI	65536	The PI function is supported by the data source.
SQL_FN_NUM_POWER	1048576	The POWER function is supported by the data source.
SQL_FN_NUM_RADIANS	2097152	The RADIANS function is supported by the data source.

Name	Value	Description
SQL_FN_NUM_RAND	131072	The RAND function is supported by the data source.
SQL_FN_NUM_ROUND	4194304	The ROUND function is supported by the data source.
SQL_FN_NUM_SIGN	4096	The SIGN function is supported by the data source.
SQL_FN_NUM_SIN	8192	The SIN function is supported by the data source.
SQL_FN_NUM_SQRT	10384	The SQRT function is supported by the data source.
SQL_FN_NUM_TAN	32768	The TAN function is supported by the data source.
SQL_FN_NUM_TRUNCATE	8388608	The TRUNCATE function is supported by the data source.

SQL_FN_STR

Name	Value	Description
SQL_FN_STR_ASCII	8192	The ASCII function is supported by the data source.
SQL_FN_STR_BIT_LENGTH	524288	The BIT_LENGTH function is supported by the data source.
SQL_FN_STR_CHAR	16384	The CHAR function is supported by the data source.
SQL_FN_STR_CHAR_LENGTH	1048576	The CHAR_LENGTH function is supported by the data source.
SQL_FN_STR_CHARACTER_LENGTH	2097152	The CHARACTER_LENGTH function is supported by the data source.
SQL_FN_STR_CONCAT	1	The CONCAT function is supported by the data source.
SQL_FN_STR_DIFFERENCE	32768	The DIFFERENCE function is supported by the data source.
SQL_FN_STR_INSERT	2	The INSERT function is supported by the data source.

Table Continued on Following Page

Name	Value	Description
SQL_FN_STR_LCASE	64	The LCASE function is supported by the data source.
SQL_FN_STR_LEFT	4	The LEFT function is supported by the data source.
SQL_FN_STR_LENGTH	16	The LENGTH function is supported by the data source.
SQL_FN_STR_LOCATE	32	The LOCATE function is supported by the data source.
SQL_FN_STR_LOCATE_2	65536	The LOCATE_2 function is supported by the data source.
SQL_FN_STR_LTRIM	8	The LTRIM function is supported by the data source.
SQL_FN_STR_OCTET_LENGTH	4194304	The OCTET_LENGTH function is supported by the data source.
SQL_FN_STR_POSITION	8388608	The POSITION function is supported by the data source.
SQL_FN_STR_REPEAT	128	The REPEAT function is supported by the data source.
SQL_FN_STR_REPLACE	256	The REPLACE function is supported by the data source.
SQL_FN_STR_RIGHT	512	The RIGHT function is supported by the data source.
SQL_FN_STR_RTRIM	1024	The RTRIM function is supported by the data source.
SQL_FN_STR_SOUNDEX	131072	The SOUNDEX function is supported by the data source.
SQL_FN_STR_SPACE	262144	The SPACE function is supported by the data source.
SQL_FN_STR_SUBSTRING	2048	The SUBSTRING function is supported by the data source.
SQL_FN_STR_UCASE	4096	The UCASE function is supported by the data source.

SQL_FN_SYS

Name	Value	Description
SQL_FN_SYS_DBNAME	2	The DBNAME system function is supported.
SQL_FN_SYS_IFNULL	4	The IFNULL system function is supported.
SQL_FN_SYS_USERNAME	1	The USERNAME system function is supported.

SQL_OJ

Name	Value	Description
SQL_OJ_ALL_COMPARISON_OPS	64	The comparison operator in the ON clause can be any of the ODBC comparison operators. If this is not set, only the equals (=) comparison operator can be used in an outer join.
SQL_OJ_FULL	4	Full outer joins are supported.
SQL_OJ_INNER	32	The inner table (the right table in a left outer join or the left table in a right outer join) can also be used in an inner join. This does not apply to full outer joins, which do not have an inner table.
SQL_OJ_LEFT	1	Left outer joins are supported.
SQL_OJ_NESTED	8	Nested outer joins are supported.
SQL_OJ_NOT_ORDERED	16	The column names in the ON clause of the outer join do not have to be in the same order as their respective table names in the OUTER JOIN clause.
SQL_OJ_RIGHT	2	Right outer joins are supported.

SQL_SDF_CURRENT

Name	Value	Description
SQL_SDF_CURRENT_DATE	1	The CURRENT_DATE system function is supported.
SQL_SDF_CURRENT_TIME	2	The CURRENT_TIME system function is supported.
SQL_SDF_CURRENT_TIMESTAMP	4	The CURRENT_TIMESTAMP system function is supported.

SSPROP_CONCUR

Name	Value	Description
SSPROP_CONCUR_LOCK	4	Use row locking to prevent concurrent access.
SSPROP_CONCUR_READ_ONLY	8	The rowset is read-only. Full concurrency is supported.
SSPROP_CONCUR_ROWVER	1	Use row versioning to determining concurrent access violations. The SQL Table or tables must contain a `timestamp` column.
SSPROP_CONCUR_VALUES	2	Use the values of the columns in the rowset row.

SSPROPVAL_USEPROCFORPREP

Name	Value	Description
SSPROPVAL_USEPROCFORPREP_OFF	0	A temporary stored procedure is not created when a command is prepared.
SSPROPVAL_USEPROCFORPREP_ON	1	A temporary stored procedure is created when a command is prepared. Temporary stored procedures are dropped when the session is released.
SSPROPVAL_USEPROCFORPREP_ON_DROP	2	A temporary stored procedure is created when a command is prepared. The procedure is dropped when the command is unprepared, or a new command text is set, or when all application references to the command are released.

ADO Data Types

You might find the large array of data types supported by ADO confusing, especially since your language or database might not support them all. This appendix details the DataTypeEnum constants and how they map to SQL and Access data types.

ODBC to Access 97

Database Type	ADO Type
Text	adVarChar
Memo	adLongVarChar
Number (Byte)	adUnsignedTinyInt
Number (Integer)	adSmallInt
Number (Long Integer)	adInteger
Number (Single)	adSingle
Number (Double)	adDouble
Number (Replication ID)	adGUID
Date/Time	adDBTimeStamp
Currency	adCurrency
Long Integer	adInteger
Yes/No	adBoolean
OLE Object	adLongVarBinary
Hyperlink	adLongVarChar

ODBC to Access 2000

Database Type	ADO Type
Text	adVarWChar
Memo	adLongVarWChar
Number (Byte)	adUnsignedTinyInt
Number (Integer)	adSmallInt
Number (Long Integer)	adInteger
Number (Single)	adSingle
Number (Double)	adDouble
Number (Replication ID)	adGUID
Number (Decimal)	adNumeric
Date/Time	adDBTimeStamp
Currency	adCurrency
AutoNumber	adInteger
Yes/No	adBoolean
OLE Object	adLongVarBinary
Hyperlink	adLongVarWChar

ODBC to SQL 6.5

Database Type	ADO Type
binary	adBinary
bit	adBoolean
char	adChar
datetime	adDBTimeStamp
decimal	adNumeric
float	adDouble
image	adLongVarBinary
int	adInteger
money	adCurrency
numeric	adNumeric
real	adSingle
smalldatetime	adDBTimeStamp
smallint	adSmallInt
smallmoney	adCurrency
sysname	adVarChar
text	adLongVarChar
timestamp	adBinary
tinyint	adUnsignedTinyInt
varbinary	adVarBinary
varchar	adVarChar

ODBC to SQL 7.0

Database Type	ADO Type
binary	adBinary
bit	adBoolean
char	adChar
datetime	adDBTimeStamp
decimal	adNumeric
float	adDouble
image	adLongVarBinary

Database Type	ADO Type
int	adInteger
money	adCurrency
nchar	adWChar
ntext	adLongVarWChar
numeric	adNumeric
nvarchar	adVarWChar
real	adSingle
smalldatetime	adDBTimeStamp
smallint	adSmallInt
smallmoney	adCurrency
text	adLongVarChar
timestamp	adBinary
tinyint	adUnsignedTinyInt
uniqueidentifier	adGUID
varbinary	adVarBinary
varchar	adVarChar

Native Jet Provider to Access 97

Database Type	ADO Type
Text	adVarWChar
Memo	adLongVarWChar
Number (Byte)	adUnsignedTinyInt
Number (Integer)	adSmallInt
Number (Long Integer)	adInteger
Number (Single)	adSingle
Number (Double)	adDouble
Number (Replication ID)	adGUID
Date/Time	adDate
Currency	adCurrency
Long Integer	adInteger
Yes/No	adBoolean
OLE Object	adLongVarBinary
Hyperlink	adLongVarWChar

Native Jet Provider to Access 2000

Database Type	ADO Type
Text	adVarWChar
Memo	adLongVarWChar
Number (Byte)	adUnsignedTinyInt
Number (Integer)	adSmallInt
Number (Long Integer)	adInteger
Number (Single)	adSingle
Number (Double)	adDouble
Number (Replication ID)	adGUID
Number (Decimal)	adNumeric
Date/Time	adDate
Currency	adCurrency
AutoNumber	adInteger
Yes/No	adBoolean
OLE Object	adLongVarBinary
Hyperlink	adLongVarWChar

Native SQL Provider to SQL Server 6.5

Database Type	ADO Type
binary	adBinary
bit	adBoolean
char	adChar
datetime	adDBTimeStamp
decimal	adNumeric
float	adDouble
image	adLongVarBinary
int	adInteger
money	adCurrency
numeric	adNumeric

Database Type	ADO Type
real	adSingle
smalldatetime	adDBTimeStamp
smallint	adSmallInt
smallmoney	adCurrency
sysname	adVarChar
text	adLongVarChar
timestamp	adBinary
tinyint	adUnsignedTinyInt
varbinary	adVarBinary
varchar	adVarChar

Native SQL Provider to SQL Server 7.0

Database Type	ADO Type
binary	adBinary
bit	adBoolean
char	adChar
datetime	adDBTimeStamp
decimal	adNumeric
float	adDouble
image	adLongVarBinary
int	adInteger
money	adCurrency
nchar	adWChar
ntext	adLongVarWChar
numeric	adNumeric
nvarchar	adVarWChar
real	adSingle
smalldatetime	adDBTimeStamp
smallint	adSmallInt

Table Continued on Following Page

Database Type	ADO Type
smallmoney	adCurrency
text	adLongVarChar .
timestamp	adBinary
tinyint	adUnsignedTinyInt
uniqueidentifier	adGUID
varbinary	adVarBinary
varchar	adVarChar

Language Types

The following table lists the data types you should use in your programming language.

A blank value indicates that the language does not natively support the data type, although there may be support in other libraries, or other data types might be used instead. For example, the com.ms.wfc.data import library for J++ has support for dates and timestamp types, amongst others, but these are not supported by J++ natively.

Constant	Visual Basic	Visual C++	Visual J++
adBinary	Variant		
adBoolean	Boolean	bool	boolean
adChar	String	char[ ]	String
adCurrency	Currency		
adDate	Date		
adDBTimeStamp	Variant		
adDouble	Double	double	double
adGUID		char[ ]	String, char[ ]
adInteger	Long	int	int
adLongVarBinary	Variant		
adLongVarChar	String		
adNumeric			
adSingle	Single	float	float
adSmallInt	Integer	short	short
adUnsignedTinyInt	Byte	char	byte
adVarBinary		char[ ]	byte[ ]
adVarChar	String	char[ ]	String, byte[ ]
adVarWChar	String	char[ ]	String, byte[ ]

The Microsoft Script Encoder

The Microsoft **Script Encoder** is a simple command-line tool that lets you encode your scripts to deter people from viewing or modifying your source. However, the Script Encoder will not prevent a determined hacker from viewing your code. The Script Encoder can be used to encode the following file types: `asa`, `asp`, `cdx`, `htm`, `html`, `js`, `sct`, and `vbs`. Only the scripting code within those files is encoded – all of the other content is left as plain text. You can use the encoding marker, `'**Start Encode**`, to determine where in the script block encoding starts:

```
<SCRIPT LANGUAGE="VBScript">
'Copyright 1999 by John Doe
'**Start Encode**
...code...
</SCRIPT>
```

Instead of the whole script block being encoded, only the content below the `'**Start Encode**` line is encoded. By using the encoding marker, you can specify a copyright or a description of the script, while protecting the code itself. Once this file has been encoded, the script block would be changed to look like this:

```
<SCRIPT LANGUAGE="VBScript.Encode">
'Copyright 1999 by John Doe
'**Start Encode**
...encoded code...
</SCRIPT>
```

Script Encoder Syntax

This section describes how to use the Script Encoder executable, `screnc.exe`, to encode your scripts.

Syntax

```
SCRENC [/s] [/f] [/xl] [/l defLanguage] [/e defExtension]
inputfile outputfile
```

Parameter	Description
/s	Optional. This switch instructs Script Encoder to not produce any screen output.
/f	Optional. This switch specifies that the input file is to be overwritten by the output file. This option will *destroy your source file*, so be careful when using it.
/xl	Optional. This switch specifies that the @language directive is not to be added at the top of .asp files.
/l defLanguage	Optional. This switch specifies the default scripting language to use during encoding. Any script blocks encountered that do not contain a language attribute are assumed to be of this specified language. If this parameter is omitted, JScript is used as the default language for HTML and scriptlets; VBScript is the default for Active Server Pages. For plain text files, the default language is determined by the file extension (.js or .vbs).
/e defExtension	Optional. This switch associates the input file with a specific file type. Use this switch when the input file's extension is not one of the recognized extensions, or to override the existing extension. If you don't specify this parameter and use an input file with an unrecognized extension, Script Encoder will fail for that file.
inputfile	Required. The name of the file to be encoded.
outputfile	Required. The name of the output file to be produced.

The following table shows what the Script Encoder will encode for the file types:

File Extension	Encodes
.asp, .asa, .cdx	<SCRIPT> . . . </SCRIPT> and/or <% . . . %>
.htm, .html	<SCRIPT> . . . </SCRIPT>
.js, .vbs	The whole file. Extension is changed to .jse or .vbe, respectively
.sct, .wsh	<SCRIPT> . . . </SCRIPT>

Examples

To encode testsrc.asp into test.asp, use:

```
screnc testsrc.asp test.asp
```

To encode testsrc.asp into testsrc.asp, use:

```
screnc /f testscr.asp
```

To encode all of the html files in the `c:\inetpub\test` directory and put them in the `c:\inetpub\wwwroot` directory, use:

```
screnc c:\inetpub\test\*.html c:\inetpub\wwwroot
```

To encode all files in the current directory as `.vbs` files silently and then put the output files in the directory `c:\temp`, use:

```
screnc /s /e vbs *.* c:\temp
```

To encode `testsrc.html` to `test.html` and specifying VBScript as the default language, use:

```
screnc /l vbscript testsrc.html test.html
```

Note: the Script Encoder can't handle empty `<script src="blah.vbs"/>` elements. Even with explicit opening and closing elements (with no content but a src attribute), the external file isn't encoded. This is a known and acknowledged problem and you need to fix these by hand as needed. For file types .ws(f), .wsc, and .hta, you have to use the "/e html" switch and use an explicit encode file name, like:

```
srcenc /e html mytest.hta mytest_encode.hta
```

since the entire file isn't encoded (just the `<script>` elements).

Index

Symbols

' (single quote character), 20
& (concatenation operator), 21, 22
+ operator, 22
= (assignment operator), 32

A

Abandon method (ASP Session object), 426
Active Server Pages
  see ASP
ActiveX Data Objects
  see ADO
Add method (Dictionary object), 214
Add method (Script Control Modules collection), 468, 478
AddCode method (Script Control Module object), 467, 469, 478
AddCode method (ScriptControl object), 478
AddHeader method (ASP Response object), 421
AddObject method (ScriptControl object), 479
  direct sharing of forms, 465
  exposing members of shared classes, 465
  host objects, 474
AddPrinterConnection method (WSH WshNetwork object), 305
AddWindowsPrinterConnection method (WSH WshNetwork object), 305
ADO (ActiveX Data Objects), 439, 441
  commands
    canceling commands, 447
    executing commands, 446
  connections
    canceling connections, 445
    closing connections, 444
    opening connections, 443
  errors, 142
  object model, 442
    Command object, 445
    Connection object, 443
    Error object, 453
    Errors collection, 442, 453
    Recordset object, 447
  origins of ADO, 440
  queries
    executing queries, 444
  recordsets
    canceling recordsets, 451
    disconnected recordsets, 448
    opening recordsets, 448, 452
    saving recordsets, 451
AllowUI property (ScriptControl object), 470
ampersand (&) (concatenation operator), 21, 22
AppActivate method (WSH WshShell object), 298
AppendToLog method (ASP Response object), 421
application level protocols, 404
Application object (ASP), 423, 424
  collections
    Contents collection, 413
    StaticObjects collection, 424
  events, 424
  methods, 424
Application property (WSH WScript object), 290
application scope, 423
Application_OnEnd event (ASP Application object), 424
Application_OnStart event (ASP Application object), 424
applicationName attribute (HTAs), 389

G